DESIGNING FOR THE DIGITAL AGE

DESIGNING FOR THE DIGITAL AGE
How to Create Human-Centered Products and Services

Kim Goodwin

WILEY
Wiley Publishing, Inc.

Designing for the Digital Age: How to Create Human-Centered Products and Services

Published by
Wiley Publishing, Inc.
10475 Crosspoint Boulevard
Indianapolis, IN 46256
www.wiley.com

Published by Wiley Publishing, Inc., Indianapolis, Indiana

Published simultaneously in Canada

ISBN: 978-0-470-22910-1

Manufactured in the United States of America

10 9 8 7 6 5 4 3 2 1

Library of Congress Cataloging-in-Publication Data
Goodwin, Kim, 1971-
  Designing for the digital age : how to create human-centered products and services / Kim Goodwin.
      p. cm.
  Includes index.
  ISBN 978-0-470-22910-1 (paper/website)
1. Design, Industrial. 2. Computer graphics. 3. Human engineering. I. Title.
  TS171.G664 2009
  745.2--dc22
                              2008049813

For general information on our other products and services please contact our Customer Care Department within the United States at (877) 762-2974, outside the United States at (317) 572-3993, or fax (317) 572-4002.

This book is for Bené, my strength and inspiration,

my parents, who taught me I could do anything,

and everyone who believes that design should make the world a better place (today and tomorrow).

About the Author

Kim Goodwin is VP Design and General Manager at Cooper, where she leads both an integrated practice of interaction, visual, and industrial designers and the development of the acclaimed Cooper U design curriculum. Kim knows the design world from multiple angles; she started as an in-house and freelance designer and spent several years as an in-house creative director before joining Cooper 11 years ago. Kim has led projects involving a tremendous range of design problems, including Web sites, complex analytical and enterprise applications, phones, medical devices, services, and even organizations. Her clients and employers have included everything from one-man start-ups to the world's largest companies, as well as universities and government agencies. This range of experience and a passion for teaching have led to Kim's popularity as an author and as a speaker at conferences and companies around the world.

Credits

ACQUISITIONS EDITOR
Katie Mohr

DEVELOPMENT EDITOR
Sara Shlaer

PRODUCTION EDITOR
Liz Britten

COPY EDITOR
C.M. Jones

EDITORIAL MANAGER
Mary Beth Wakefield

PRODUCTION MANAGER
Tim Tate

VICE PRESIDENT AND
EXECUTIVE GROUP PUBLISHER
Richard Swadley

PROJECT COORDINATOR, COVER
Lynsey Stanford

BOOK DESIGNERS
Daniel Kuo, Nick Myers,
Nate Fortin, and Jayson McCauliff

COMPOSITOR
Patrick Cunningham

PROOFREADER
Justin Neely, Word One

INDEXER
Jack Lewis

COVER IMAGE
Emily Nathan and Nick Myers

COVER DESIGNERS
Nick Myers and Nate Fortin

Acknowledgments

This book is in your hands (and is what it is) thanks to the efforts, influence, and support of dozens of people, so please forgive me if I'm long-winded in my thanks.

Some of those people have no idea of their role in the book's creation, starting with my parents, who had me convinced at an early age that I could do anything (except carry a tune). Long-ago art teacher Ron Lupton told me I should find a profession that used both my right and left brain—"Goodwin," he said, "I don't know how you produce such beautiful work, because you never shut up in my class." He's also one of the people who showed me that teaching is a worthwhile endeavor. Many colleagues and clients, at Cooper and elsewhere, have left their mark on my thinking and made me a better designer, and by now thousands of people in classes and workshops have (I hope) helped make me a better teacher.

The book represents my own experience and views; I don't claim to speak for Cooper or anyone who works there. However, many people at Cooper have had a direct impact on the book. A design text needs to be a good example of the craft, and designers Daniel Kuo, Nick Myers, Nate Fortin, and Jayson McCauliff did an admirable job. Nick, Daniel, Rebecca Bortman, Paula Mieselman, Michael Voege, and Emily Nathan all either made my illustrations look better or contributed illustrations or photos of their own. Jayson "pixel stud" McCauliff did that and more: in addition to cranking out or improving on at least a hundred fabulous illustrations, he managed the chaos of assembling the final art and touched every file to make sure it was perfect. Jayson, Daniel, Michael, Nate, and Nick also did some of the great design and research work featured in examples, as did Chris Noessel, Chris Weeldreyer, Dana Smith, Dave Cronin, David Fore, Doug LeMoine, Jonathan Korman, Lane Halley, Noah Guyot, Steve Calde, Suzy Thompson, and Tim McCoy. Many of them also commented on various parts of the book, as did Robert Reimann. I'm especially grateful for the close scrutiny and suggestions from Dave, Nate, Michael, and Steve, who read all or most of the book at least once. Thanks to cover girl Karen Lemen and the many others who agreed to be in photos. Of course, I also owe thanks to Alan and Sue Cooper for introducing me to Chris Webb at Wiley, for donating visual design time to the cause, and above all, for founding a company where great things happen.

Research and design work are generally confidential, so huge thanks to Thorsten Burger of DePuy, Greg Roberts of Accu-Med, V.J. Bonnard and Paul Turner of NetApp, Chris Gielow of Cardinal Health, Chris Dollar of McKesson, Ken Hamma of the J. Paul Getty Museum, and especially John Chaffins of Cross Country Healthcare for being generous enough to share. Thanks also to the friends and colleagues who participated in the example user interviews, and to Rolf Molich for sharing unpublished research.

The Wiley crew has been terrific. Chris Webb not only believed in the book, but said, "Sure, you can design it," which is a privilege I'm sure no editor grants lightly. Katie Mohr generously agreed to make the book bigger so I wouldn't have to cut content. Sara Shlaer offered plenty of helpful comments and knew just when (and how) to nudge me about deadlines. Patrick Cunningham and Liz Britten have been patient with a control-freak-author's comments on layout.

Last, but never least, I must thank family and friends. Eva Emmert provided much of my writing soundtrack. My cats helped tremendously with typing. Everyone in my life offered moral support and didn't complain about not seeing much of me the past 18 months. Finally, I wouldn't have made it through the book without the love and support of Bené Gatzert, whose patience, encouragement, extra chores, and occasional, well-timed doses of chocolate kept me going.

Contents at a Glance

Contents

Foreword

Designing the human-facing behavior of software-powered systems is a relatively new discipline. As any new discipline develops, even its own practitioners are unaware of its ultimate scope, and the breadth of expertise its application requires often comes as a surprise even to its most skilled experts. It certainly surprised me to see just how deep the craft really went as we explored it. The depth of knowledge and the extent of method required is significant, and it truly represents a unique discipline of some magnitude.

This book is the first I've ever read that covers the entire spectrum of interaction design practice as a craft, including visual design and industrial design. While interaction design is a wholly new discipline, visual and industrial design are older, pre-existing fields that have been wholly transformed by digital technology. All three are given full consideration here. Others have written scholarly work on the theoretical underpinnings of software behavior, or described the visually aesthetic component of the field. Some others have attempted to cover the entire ground, but at one point or another, all of them take leaps of faith, exhorting the budding practitioner to "be creative" or "make it easy to use."

But practitioners need to know *how* to make it easy to use, and *how* to be creative. Gaining mastery of these tiny, creative steps is precisely the sticking point that leaves the student of interaction design unable to proceed. Kim's comprehensive book never advocates such leaps without giving the reader detailed instructions on exactly how one goes about making them, and with real world examples. The primary reason why this book will change the way designers learn and practice their craft is because of the thoroughness with which it covers the great span of the field.

Unlike so many of the new disciplines ushered into being by the digital revolution, the design of digital artifacts isn't purely technical. While it is abundantly rationalist and demanding of rigor, it contains generous helpings of cognitive psychology, sociology, and ethnography. One of the reasons why it is a craft distinct from programming is simply because most programmers, who otherwise so value cross-discipline skills, are quite disinclined to include the skills of observation, interviewing, and analysis of the humans who will ultimately use their creations. Interaction designers need to learn the techniques and patterns that empower them to understand humans, as well as software.

The wisdom and methodology set forth in this book is the product of many minds working at my company, Cooper, while operating on many client engagements, over a span of 17 years. Here at Cooper we follow a Socratic method, where, although clever answers are valued, discriminating questions are valued more. The dialogue is what brings forth not just solutions, but also entire frames of reference for how to approach problems in any domain and deconstruct them for solution. And we keep on learning, constantly changing and growing the method and its toolset.

At times, each of us here has played the role of teacher, and each the role of student, and our attention is always on finding the underlying principles. The axiomatic nature of such fundamentals allows the practitioner to build his or her skill over time by seeing the common forces and patterns at work both in the man-machine interface and in the process used to create solutions for that interface. All great craft disciplines share this trait; while their essence can be expressed in a few simple aphorisms, the mastery required to put those aphorisms into practice can take years to learn and decades to master.

The firm foundation of the method doesn't take away from your creativity as a designer.

Kim Goodwin has been a prime participant in the dialogue at Cooper since 1997. She has been one of the major contributors to the development of our design methodology. She is an authority on design, problem scoping, engagement management, and design documentation. Kim has labored in the trenches in a broad variety of design segments, from clinical medicine to conceptual blockbusting. She has led groups of designers, coordinating their work, and synchronizing it with the needs of some very demanding clients.

And she has taught others to design. Many hundreds of people have gotten a taste of Kim's clarity, patience, thoroughness, and rigor by attending her presentations at conferences, her one-day field seminars, or her design courses. In fact, Kim has been the primary creator of training content for our very successful Cooper U classes. Over the years, her particular expertise at observation, synthesis, and communication while in charge of other design teams and honed in the classroom, led her naturally to write this book. Much of the content and wisdom gleaned from those classes is evident here.

Cooper's Goal-Directed Design is a unique and effective method. It is a collection of practices and principles that are used the way any craftsman uses his toolset. On any given project there are tools that are always used. Some tools are used regularly but not always, and some tools are used rarely, but when they are needed they are the only way to get it right. A big part of the skill of the designer is in knowing what tools are available and having the experience to know which one to apply for best effect. Kim provides the strategies for selecting and applying them in professional use.

The firm foundation of the method doesn't take away from your creativity as a designer. There are lots of easy design problems in the world, but there are also lots of very difficult ones. Glib cleverness may work for the former but will leave you afloat in a sea of confusing variables in the latter. The great value of a rigorous methodology is that it gives you a strategy for breaking down the really complex, tough problems into smaller, more familiar, and more manageable tasks that can be readily addressed. While personal creativity helps you create the right answer, mastery of the overarching process helps you address the right problem.

Clients regularly bring to us some of the hairiest, most complex problems set in the most politically demanding situations imaginable. While some agencies shy away from such apparent no-win propositions, we revel in them because of our confidence in our tools. When a software giant, for example, wants us to design a financial application for millions of users, or when a medical services company wants us to design a clinical application for orthopedic surgeons to use during hip replacement operations, our designers put on their green eyeshades or hospital scrubs, and wade in with manic glee, knowing that observation, methodology, experience, and a comprehensive set of effective design principles will reveal the hidden forces at work and allow them to synthesize world-class design. The book you are now holding gives those tools—and that confidence—to you.

If you are just starting out in the world of designing digital products and services, this book will take you step by step through the process of interaction design, from initial ethnographic research, through ideation and design, all the way to final delivery and presentation. Even if you are an experienced designer, this book will help bring a new level of professionalism and efficiency to your practice.

This book is comprehensive in its scope, exhaustive in its depth, authoritative in its practice, and priceless in its wisdom. It will certainly become the anchor document for an entire practice. While I expect to see it on the bookshelves of every practicing designer, I further expect that it will spend the lion's share of its time off the shelf and at the elbow of hard-working designers. I've no doubt that this will become the most dog-eared, annotated, and worn-from-many-readings volume in your library. Most certainly, it will also reshape university curricula and inform the next generation of practitioners.

While my own books have served as either introductory or motivational, Kim's book is nothing less than a complete handbook for an entire profession. Kim's unique background in the practice, pedagogy, and epistemology of the design business has given her the experience needed to write the ultimate "how-to" book of technology design. Every step in this fascinating and multifaceted discipline is described in detail in simple, readable prose, richly illustrated with examples taken from real products, real clients, and real design problems. I know you will come to regard this book as indispensible.

This book is comprehensive in its scope, exhaustive in its depth, authoritative in its practice, and priceless in its wisdom.

Alan Cooper
Founder and Chairman, Cooper
San Francisco, California

Introduction

You've probably picked up this book because you are a designer, whether by profession or by inclination. Design is, arguably, something that every person in the world does—laying out the text in a school report, decorating a living room, and arranging plants in a garden are all acts of creation that can have both utilitarian and aesthetic value. However, most such acts consider a small set of idiosyncratic needs: the habits and preferences of an individual, or perhaps of the handful of individuals who make up a household.

Design *as a profession*—by which I mean everything from product design to architecture—exists to provide both utilitarian and aesthetic value on a large scale. Professional designers must define financially viable products, services, and environments that meet the practical, physical, cognitive, and emotional needs of a wide range of people. Like someone deciding what color to paint the living room, a professional designer can—and, to some extent, does—try something, decide that it doesn't work, and try something else. Yet designers must try, fail, and eventually succeed on a deadline, within a budget, and over and over again. Eventually, all experienced designers develop a set of implicit or explicit techniques to help them do just that, and to do it better and faster over time. This book aims to share a set of explicit process and practices that have worked for many designers over the course of hundreds of diverse projects; in other words, a *method*. An effective method, along with appropriate training and aptitude, is what distinguishes professional designers from anyone else who may perform individual, instinctive acts of design.

Why an Explicit Method?

This book offers an explicit, start-to-finish method for defining and designing the form and behavior of processes, services, and artifacts in our increasingly complex digital age. Some designers are hungry for an explicit method, while others may bristle at the thought, expecting that it will limit their creativity. However, there's nothing inherently good about chaotic or ad hoc approaches. The method described in these pages is not intended as a set of constraints or as a recipe to be unthinkingly followed in every situation; no method should be followed by rote.

Instead, think of the method as something akin to the harness and wire used in martial arts movies: simultaneously providing support, safety, and a powerful boost, but useless without the skill, creativity, and judgment of the practitioner. Or if that analogy doesn't work for

Professional designers must define financially viable products, services, and environments that meet the practical, physical, cognitive, and emotional needs of a wide range of people.

Certainly, good design can happen without an explicit method. However, in the words of Louis Pasteur, "Fortune favors the prepared mind."

you, how about this one: the designer's creative spark is the electricity, and the method is the power grid that channels it where it can do the most good.

Why does a designer's creative spark need to be channeled? Certainly, good design can happen without an explicit method. However, in the words of Louis Pasteur, "Fortune favors the prepared mind." Without the scientific method to structure his thinking, an accident with a spoiled culture would not have led him to the germ theory of disease (and yet the method alone didn't do the trick).

Design and science have something else in common: in each field, ideas are be subject to examination and judgment by others. If you have a method that explains how you got from point A to point B, people are more likely to judge in your favor than if you say, "Trust me—I'm a professional." I expect you'll find the methods in these pages useful if you've ever:

— Had to argue with a powerful CEO about why his personal preferences shouldn't drive the design

— Been uncertain whether design option A or B is better

— Had a group of hard-core engineers smell blood in the water when you used "because it looks cool" as a defense

— Had stakeholders repeatedly change their minds about what the product is

— Needed to convince stakeholders that no, really, people don't use your product that way

— Had a design meeting that resembled a rugby match

— Come up with a cool design concept that turned out to be unworkable a few weeks later

— Wondered how you could possibly learn enough about neurosurgery, stock portfolio management, or chemistry to design a product around it

— Had your design bomb a usability test

— Stared at a blank whiteboard, uncertain where to begin

Both as a consultant and as an in-house creative director, I've been in most of these situations, and I've observed other designers struggle with these and other challenges. An effective method removes much of the worry in these situations so you can instead focus on doing what designers do best: generating usable, desirable solutions.

Of course, no method is perfect, and no method should be engraved in stone. The methods in this book have evolved over the years and will continue to do so as designers try new things and share the successful ones as best practices—one reason I'll be sharing my latest experiences and resources (including materials to use for some of the exercises) at www.designingforthedigitalage.com; I hope you'll share your own experiences, too. However, I'll offer you the same suggestion I share with new hires at Cooper: try the techniques as described over the course of several projects so you can master them before you carve a new trail through the underbrush. You'll probably find that the core methods address a wider variety of situations than you expect and afford all the flexibility you could need.

Why This Book

Every designer has the power to improve or even preserve life for some segment of humanity. Unfortunately, even the best designers can't design everything, and good designers are in limited supply. I also know plenty of potentially great designers who simply don't have the tools they need to make sure their designs see the light of day. This is especially true in our current digital age, when many design problems require the application of multiple disciplines, including interaction design, visual and information design, information architecture, industrial design, and more. Users have only one experience of a product or service, though, so this book attempts to include the perspectives and activities of all of these disciplines. (However, given that industrial design and graphic design make use of long-standing, well-understood methods, I have not attempted to address those disciplines in the broad sense, but only as they relate to interactive products and services.)

Although I love the ability to influence lives through doing meaningful design, I learned long ago that I can influence even more lives by helping other designers be more effective. My aim with this book is to help as many designers as possible make a difference in the world. Because designers cover a wide range of experience and skills, experienced designers may find that some parts of the content (particularly Chapters 15, 17, and 21) are merely useful refreshers. However, each chapter of the book includes content that I hope will:

— Help experienced designers be both rigorous and persuasive in their practice, to ensure not only that they're doing great design, but that their design gets built

— Give designers from different disciplines a shared framework for collaborating on today's increasingly complex products, which often combine software, hardware, services, and environments

— Help design students understand not only a coherent design process, but also the essential practices—from collaboration and project management to leading stakeholder discussions—that make real projects successful

— Show consulting designers how to engage with clients for the long term

— Help in-house designers see how consulting practices can make them more effective

Design is not—and never will be—a science. It will also never be a cookie-cutter process that anyone can do with an appropriate checklist in hand—the method doesn't make the design, the designer does. This book cannot give you the imagination and aptitude for visualization, nor can it give you the judgment and mastery of craft that only come with experience. However, I hope what you'll take from this book will help you more reliably design the right product or service, design it well, and get the design out into the world where it can improve the quality of human lives.

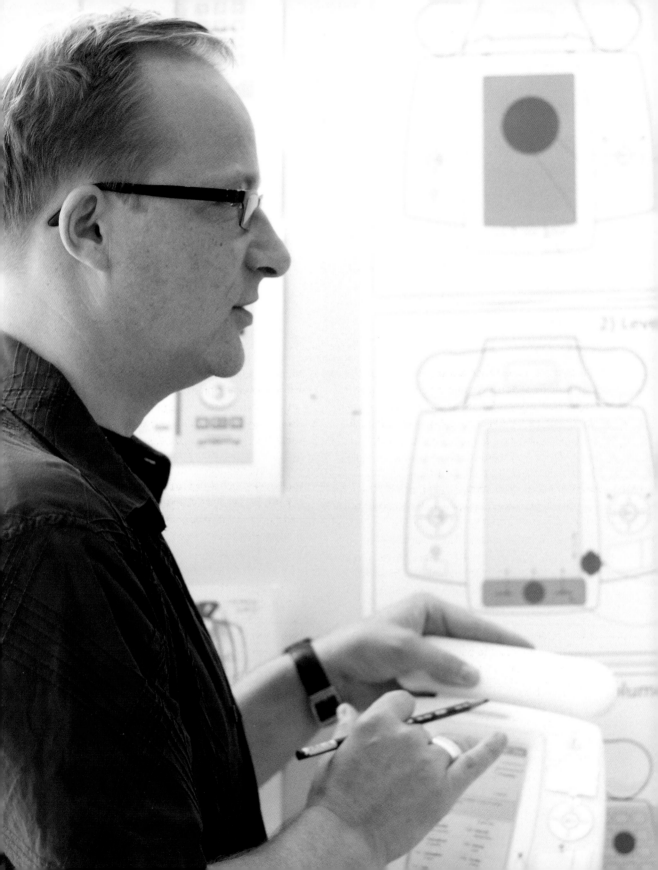

CHAPTER 1

Goal-Directed Product and Service Design

To a greater extent than any other creature, we humans shape the world around us to suit ourselves. Some of that shaping is unintentional, but much of it is deliberate. We create our environments by constructing buildings, roads, furnishings, and landscapes. We make our daily lives easier and more enjoyable by inventing tools, from kitchen utensils and earth-to-orbit spacecraft to social networking and enterprise-spanning IT systems. We communicate with one another in text, imagery, motion, and sound. We even attempt to craft perfect experiences in retail settings and amusement parks. This intentional shaping of the world for mass consumption is often referred to as **design**.

Clearly, "design" is an incredibly broad term. Do choosing what color to paint your bedroom, sculpting the exterior of a car, and planning a complex application's technical architecture all have equal claims to the word? People outside of design professions have difficulty drawing the line, and there are so many philosophies and assumptions attached to it that even designers seldom agree on exactly what "design" is.

All of this explains why most design books begin with some definition of the word. For the purposes of this book, at least, **design is the craft of visualizing concrete solutions that serve human needs and goals within certain constraints.**

Visualizing concrete solutions is the essence of design. These solutions could be tangible products, such as buildings, software, consumer electronics, or advertisements, or they could be services that are intended to provide a specific sort of experience. The inherent aptitude—the drive, even—to imagine the desired end result and express it in a tangible way is what separates designers from non-designers. This doesn't mean that all designers must be good at illustration; I have known many fine designers whose drawing skills were limited. What designers must excel at is looking at a blank surface and filling it with believable representations of an end product so that other people can see, understand, and eventually build it. Building it is a separate task; designers don't build products any more than architects build houses. Instead, they provide precise instructions so that builders can focus on accomplishing the end result.

Design is the craft of visualizing concrete solutions that serve human needs and goals within certain constraints.

Design is a **craft** because it is neither science nor art, but somewhere in between. Science is about understanding how the universe works and why it works that way. Design, while it is informed by scientific learning about human senses, cognition, and ergonomics, focuses on understanding only to the extent that it is necessary to solve the problem at hand. Art is about creating an end product that, above all, expresses the inner vision of the artist. Design is not about expressing the designer's point of view, but it is very much about creation.

In order for design to be design and not art, it must **serve human needs and goals**. All designed artifacts have a purpose. Good design helps humans accomplish something in an efficient, effective, safe, and enjoyable way. Designers draw on fields like ergonomics and HCI (the study of human-computer interaction) to increase efficiency and minimize the potential for injury. At the same time, designers strive to go beyond the simply functional, since pleasure and aesthetic satisfaction are also important human goals.

Finally, design always happens **within certain constraints**. There is no such thing as unconstrained design. Unconstrained classroom exercises may teach imagination, but they do not accurately represent the problem-solving nature of design. Time and cost are always factors on even the most ambitious projects. Designers are also constrained in some way by their materials; physical materials have immutable properties, and even the digital medium introduces limitations due to its very lack of a physical nature. Other common constraints include regulatory requirements, competitive pressures, and the various desires of the people bankrolling the project.

Mind you, this definition of design still encompasses a tremendous range of intentionally created artifacts, environments, and processes—types of things humans have been designing for a hundred years or more. Surely, we ought to have this design thing figured out by now. Perhaps this would be the case if it weren't for an assortment of technologies based on silicon chips. Our increasingly digital age has added a host of new challenges that traditional design, manufacturing, and business mind-sets simply are not equipped to address.

Digital Product and Service Design

This book focuses on the design of the products and services unique to the digital age, including any system or service enabled (at least in part) by a microprocessor. Digital systems include everything from a simple digital alarm clock to complex scientific equipment or supply chain management software. Digitally enabled services might encompass anything from eBay (a service that lets people sell items online) to a comprehensive set of customer touch points for an airline, including its Web site, automated telephone systems, human customer service, and airport check-in.

Although I emphasize the digital realm, the methods described in this book have been applied with equal success to non-digital problems. Over the years, I've even heard from non-designers who have used the basic principles to develop everything from church social events to employee benefits programs.

Some people refer to human-centered product and service design as **experience design**, but I would argue that this term is presumptuous; we can design every aspect of the environment to encourage an optimal experience, but since each person brings her own attitudes, behaviors, and perceptions to any situation, no designer can determine exactly what experience someone has. For this reason, I refer to product and service design—or simply product design, as a service is still the end product of the design effort—throughout the book.

Designing complex products and services requires the talents of several closely related design disciplines, usually some combination of interaction design, graphic and information design, and industrial design. The graphic and industrial design professions are long established, so I won't define them here, but interaction design is still new enough that degrees in the discipline only started becoming available in the 1990s.

Interaction design is a discipline focused on defining the form and behavior of interactive products, services, and systems. Interaction design answers questions such as:

— What activities does the product or service support, and how?

— What workflow provides the best way for users to accomplish their goals?

— What information do users need at each point in that process?

— What information does the system need from users?

— How will users move from one activity to another?

— How is functionality segmented and manifested?

Because interaction design is focused on what people want to do as well as how they can best accomplish it, it's common for interaction design to affect **product definition**, which is about *what functionality a product has* (as opposed to defining how that functionality is manifest, which is what most people see as the role of design).

Interaction design is often confused with related disciplines known as HCI, human factors or, informally, usability. Training in these fields emphasizes evaluative techniques rather than creative problem-solving skills or methods for generating solutions, which are the focus in design. The line between these professions and interaction design is fuzzy because many people have found their way to interaction design from these fields. Although interaction designers must be versed in the principles of HCI, most interaction designers find more in common with graphic designers and industrial designers than with evaluation-focused HCI professionals. The two approaches result in a difference in worldview much like the one between software engineering and quality assurance: complementary, but not at all interchangeable.

Interaction design may also be confused with Web site information architecture (IA). This field is partially rooted in library science, a discipline

Goal-Directed Design assumes the best way to design a successful product is to focus on achieving goals.

that has long focused on how to categorize and organize information for easy retrieval. Some information architects may disagree, but I argue that for all practical purposes, IA is a specialized subset of interaction design. The methods described in this volume work very well for information architecture, though there's no harm in supplementing them with card sorting and other IA techniques.

Goal-Directed Design

Goal-Directed Design[1] is the approach to product and service design developed at Cooper, a leading design consultancy. Its fundamental premise is that the best way to design a successful product is to focus on achieving goals. Although the rhetorical emphasis is on user goals, the method also incorporates the goals of the customers (people who purchase but don't use a system) and of the business creating the product or service. Goal-Directed Design encompasses the design of a product's behavior, visual form, and physical form. Methods for all three are covered throughout the book.

Origins of Goal-Directed Design

The firm's founder, software inventor Alan Cooper, began to develop the kernel of the method when he first started using a sort of proto-persona in 1983. Based on what he learned from informal interviews with seven or eight users, Alan would mentally walk through different interactions he was coding by pretending to be an end user. He would ask himself why he would be performing a certain task in the first place, what he would know at the beginning of the task, and what he was more likely to figure out as he went along. Alan continued to use this mental play-acting approach for more than a decade. Because he was inventing software that he would sell as a finished product, this purely internal approach worked quite well until Alan began consulting with companies about the design of their own products.

In 1995, on a project with Sagent Technologies, Alan and designer Wayne Greenwood found they needed a way to communicate with the client about user behaviors and needs. Alan's experience with his mental constructs based on real users and Wayne's previous experience at T/Maker, where he often invoked the entirely fictitious "Aunt Edna" to encourage engineers to think about less-skilled users, led them to create a small cast of characters to represent various types of people

---

1. Goal-Directed Design® is a registered trademark of Cooper (www.cooper.com), used with permission.

(see Figure 1.1). Thanks to a prior acquaintance with Alan, the client was willing to suspend judgment about this peculiar communication method. It wasn't long before the team at Sagent adopted these new models, making conversations about product design and functionality much easier than they had been. The product was a tremendous success. It became obvious to Alan and Wayne that these *dramatis personae* should play a role on other projects, too, and so personas were born.

Figure 1.1. Rob, Cynthia, and Chuck were the first real personas.

Over the next five years or so, Alan and about a dozen of us working at Cooper took this powerful idea and used it as the basis to develop a rigorous method, which encompasses everything from planning and conducting research to generating, iterating, and communicating detailed design. The advancement of the method was an informal collective effort; we all paid close attention to which approaches were most (and least) successful, then shared those with our colleagues.

The most fundamental aspects of the method were well established by 2000 or so, at which point we began to formalize our techniques in training courses for new hires and for our clients. The cliché about teaching something being the

best way to learn it is true; by articulating the thought processes of our most successful designers and trying to teach them to our newest staff members, we all became even more consistent in our ability to produce great results on a predictable timeline. As our thought processes and rationale became increasingly clear to our clients, it also became easier to persuade them that a particular design direction was the right one. Our clients became more accepting of our designs and more successful in building them.

Of course, any good method is a living thing that continues to evolve and grow. By now, dozens of Cooper designers have left their mark on the method in one way or another, and there's no doubt that dozens more will leave their mark in years to come. We've used these methods to design such a wide array of products and services that we seldom encounter situations the method doesn't have tools for, but that doesn't mean there aren't plenty of them left. When we do see a new problem, we always try new approaches, see what works and doesn't work, and incorporate the successful approaches into the "official" method.

Components of Goal-Directed Design

The Goal-Directed method is a set of tools and best practices developed entirely through practice in the real world. The method is not intended to be a set of rules and constraints; rather, it provides a framework within which skilled designers can do what they do best—generate great solutions—with the confidence that the method will help them get it right. No method can eliminate the need for the knowledge and skill of the designer. At Cooper, we hire skilled, experienced designers and put them through classes and an apprenticeship. On average, it takes them about a year to master the fundamental techniques and two or more years before they can take full advantage of the method's potential.

The method consists of four components: principles, patterns, process, and practices. Successful implementation of the method also requires people with the right skills (see the discussion of team roles in Chapter 2). This book focuses on process and practices, but it's worth briefly discussing principles and patterns to illustrate how these four components fit together.

PRINCIPLES

Principles are guidelines for creating good solutions under specific circumstances. For example, it is generally better for a computer to act immediately on a user's command but provide an option to undo it than it is to require confirmation of every action, but there are exceptions, such as when that action might do truly irreversible damage.

This book does not focus on principles, although Chapters 15, 17, and 21 do include some of the principles that are most useful for certain aspects of design. However, there are plenty of good references available. The canon at Cooper naturally includes the principles articulated in *About Face 3*.[2] I also recommend *Designing Visual Interfaces*.[3] Regardless of where you look for design principles, however, there are two essential things to keep in mind: not all principles apply in all contexts, and not all principles are created equal.

Principles appropriate to one context may not apply to another. A widget that works beautifully with a mouse may get in the way if a user's task is primarily free-form keyboard entry. Approaches to visual design on a monitor differ from those on a television screen or handheld device. However, most desktop interface design principles are equally applicable to Web sites.

When I say that all principles are not created equal, I mean that some supposed principles—including some of those expounded by various design or usability gurus—are simply unfounded opinion. For example, a number of years ago there was a much-touted rule about how many seconds it should take your Web page to load. In 2001, Christine Perfetti and Lori Landesman disproved this assertion when their study[4] showed that perception of page load times has little to do with objective reality and much more to do with whether someone can accomplish her goals on the site.

When evaluating whether a supposed principle is both true and applicable to the problem in front of you, ask yourself whether it passes the following tests:

1. **Does it help your users accomplish their goals?** Not every valid principle is about goals, but any principle that's both true and applicable won't work against them.

2. **Will it help users minimize work?** Work can be cognitive (thinking about whether to press yes, no, or cancel), visual (reading light gray text on a white background), memory (remembering all those complicated passwords), or motor (using an iPod click wheel to traverse from A to Z in a huge music collection). Note that there are rare cases, such as in video games, when introducing a bit of work is good as long as it's done in an engaging way.

2. Cooper, A., Reimann, R., and Cronin, D. *About face 3: The essentials of interaction design*. John Wiley and Sons, 2007.

3. Mullet, K., and Sano, D. *Designing visual interfaces: Communication oriented techniques*. Prentice Hall, 1994.

4. Perfetti, C., and Landesman, L. "The Truth About Download Time," January 31, 2001. www.uie.com/articles/download_time/

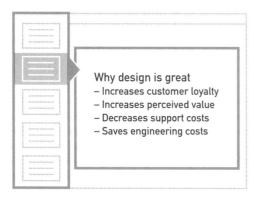
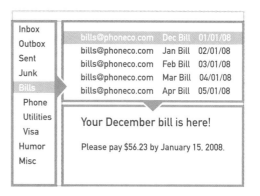

Why design is great
- Increases customer loyalty
- Increases perceived value
- Decreases support costs
- Saves engineering costs

Inbox
Outbox
Sent
Junk
Bills
Phone
Utilities
Visa
Humor
Misc

bills@phoneco.com	Dec Bill	01/01/08
bills@phoneco.com	Jan Bill	02/01/08
bills@phoneco.com	Feb Bill	03/01/08
bills@phoneco.com	Mar Bill	04/01/08
bills@phoneco.com	Apr Bill	05/01/08

Your December bill is here!

Please pay $56.23 by January 15, 2008.

Figure 1.2. Many productivity applications are based on an organizer/workspace pattern.

PATTERNS

Patterns are types of solutions that tend to be useful for certain classes of problems. For example, Figure 1.2 illustrates a common pattern for navigating multi-document interfaces such as e-mail. A pane on the top or left of the screen contains a list of documents or groups of documents, while one or two panes below or to the right allow drilling down into an individual document's contents. This works well for electronic medical records, browser bookmarks, and a host of other design problems that involve looking at each of many documents for a short period of time.

Patterns are essential in design because they are the building blocks of a designer's vocabulary, as principles are the rules of grammar that govern how we use them. Seasoned designers can often work faster and come up with a wider range of ideas because they've had years in which to build up their vocabularies.

I cannot do patterns justice in this book, though Chapters 15, 17, and 21 provide a sampling of some of the most useful. There are a few other references you might find worthwhile. Many designers first became interested in patterns after reading architect Christopher Alexander's seminal book, *A Pattern Language*.[5] For a more specific approach, look at *Universal Principles of Design*.[6] This book muddles principles and patterns together, but is useful in that it straddles multiple design disciplines. Finally, Jenifer Tidwell's *Designing Interfaces*[7] offers a nice collection of interaction and visual interface design patterns.

PROCESS

This book focuses primarily on the **design process**: the steps and techniques involved in planning and conducting design research, using it to develop personas, scenarios, and requirements, then using those to develop and iterate a design solution. This process (outlined in Figure 1.3) can scale up or down depending on the time and budget available as well as the priorities.

5. Alexander, C. *A pattern language: Towns, buildings, construction*. Oxford University Press, 1977.

6. Lidwell, W., Holden, K., and Butler, J. *Universal principles of design: 100 ways to enhance usability, influence perception, increase appeal, make better design decisions, and teach through design*. Rockport Publishers, 2003.

7. Tidwell, J. *Designing interfaces: Patterns for effective interaction design*. O'Reilly, 2005.

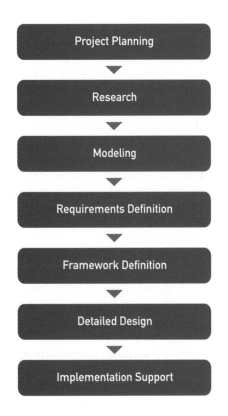

Figure 1.3. An overview of the Goal-Directed process.

Some organizations (such as start-ups in search of additional funding) may believe getting a best-guess product out the door is more important than taking the time to understand their users and customers in any depth, so there are ways to jump to design with little or no time spent on research. Throughout the book, I'll describe each part of the process in its typical form first, then discuss how it can be compressed or expanded.

Project planning

Before dedicating resources to a project, most executives want at least a rough outline of how the project will be structured and what results they can expect. It is essential to identify the key stakeholders, determine from their input what the objectives of the project are, and draft a plan

from there. It is almost never possible to predict exactly how long a completed design will take, since the problem is not yet sufficiently defined and there are likely several possible approaches to solving it. However, it should be possible for an experienced designer to propose an ideal approach and rough schedule, then discuss with stakeholders the trade-offs they could make to reduce the time or cost involved.

Planning is not complete once an initial project plan is done, however. Recruiting research participants and scheduling the interviews is far from trivial. Chapter 6 outlines approaches to this sometimes-daunting task.

Research

To solve a problem, you must first understand it. Good research helps you make the best product definition and design decisions later on. Beyond helping you understand the design problem, research also helps build consensus and move the design process along faster. Once you have objective data, it's no longer necessary to pit one person's opinion against another's.

Interviews with stakeholders, which are the first component of research, provide a clear view of the business objectives and technical parameters, while uncovering risks and assumptions you should examine. This topic is covered in Chapter 5. The next step, ethnographic research with potential users, gives you insight into goals, environments, communication needs, and other important factors. Chapters 7 and 8 tell you how to go about it. Finally, Chapter 9 describes additional methods that can be useful.

Modeling

Although raw research data can be eye-opening, analysis makes that data more useful both to the people who conducted the research and to other members of the product team. This analysis involves identifying trends and developing models that explain what you observed. The most important model is a set of **personas**, which are user archetypes that help you make design decisions and communicate your rationale. Each persona represents a set of behavior patterns and goals. By designing for these archetypal users, you can satisfy the needs of the broader range of people they represent. Every product decision can be tied back to the personas. Other models may include representations of current workflows, the usage environment, or other important aspects of the problem. Chapters 10 and 11 describe how to develop personas and other models.

Requirements definition

The last step in analyzing the data is determining what it implies about the product's functionality and design. The personas' skills, environments, behaviors, and goals help determine their needs. Scenarios, which are stories about the personas using the future product or service, highlight additional needs. In the language of product development, these needs are expressed as requirements. Of course, business objectives and constraints are also incorporated in this list.

Design requirements do not represent a comprehensive list that the engineering team can use to build the product; this would be like handing a building contractor a list that says your house should contain some sort of kitchen and three bedrooms. Rather, these requirements are intended to give business stakeholders a chance to make critical trade-off decisions early in the process. A meeting with the full set of stakeholders at the end of this phase lets you discuss the personas and requirements. The end result should be consensus about the focus and parameters of your design efforts.

Chapters 12 and 13 explain how to develop and communicate requirements.

Framework definition

Once you have agreement on who the users and customers are and what the design must accomplish for them, you can begin laying out the basic framework for the form and behavior of the product. Personas and scenarios are the primary drivers of this process, but a vocabulary of design patterns and a solid grounding in principles are essential, as well. The phase begins with broad exploration of multiple solutions, though whether this exploration takes a few hours or several weeks depends on the project objectives.

As the options are narrowed, the **interaction framework** outlines how functionality is grouped and how the personas will accomplish the most critical tasks. The **visual framework** expresses the brand's qualities in concrete terms, typically using design language studies divorced from the interaction design. The **industrial design framework** consists of an approximate form factor and component architecture, physical expression of the brand developed in conjunction with the visual design language, and a description of any hardware controls that are essential to the interaction. Chapters 14 through 18 describe how to go about framework definition, while Chapter 19 outlines effective ways to communicate about each framework.

In all three cases, the design is articulated at a high level, deliberately omitting details for two reasons. First, stakeholders need something concrete to look at as quickly as possible, which means there simply isn't time to address the finer points. Second, starting design by thinking about the major underlying structures helps ensure that the structure is clear and simple, just as an outline aids clear writing. It also prevents rework later on.

Discussion of the framework with the complete set of stakeholders is another important step in refining the product's focus and parameters. Once people begin to see a solution, they can better assess how critical it is to develop certain aspects now versus later. If the design can be somewhat unconstrained at this stage, stakeholders are more able to see the possibilities and make more informed trade-off decisions.

Detailed design

Once the scope of the product is clearly defined, it is usually possible to develop a detailed project plan for filling out and refining the design. Increasingly detailed scenarios continue to drive the interaction design aspect of the process. However, the role of design principles, design evaluation, and engineering feasibility increases as the level of detail in the design increases. Chapters 20 through 23 describe this process.

This phase ideally involves extensive collaboration with subject matter experts and engineers. Subject matter experts can provide a greater level of detail about best practices and edge cases than you can glean in field research. Engineers can ask questions that will help them build the design and point out aspects of it that may be difficult to implement (though this does not necessarily mean you should use a poor design alternative just because it's easier to build). When the engineers are not certain what it will take to build a specific aspect of the design, they can build some throwaway code or hardware, then feed what they learn back to the design team.

It's best if you can determine how the product looks and works down to the contents of every list box and the colors of the pixels in every icon, then document the results in a detailed specification (see Chapter 24). Arriving at a final specification that is truly ready for construction typically requires two passes through the detailed design; the design team provides as much detail as they can in a first draft, then the engineers and subject matter experts review the design in painstaking detail, looking for areas where they have questions or concerns, and the design team revises things accordingly. The first draft specification

also provides an excellent opportunity for usability testing, though of course you may opt to test earlier if you have concerns about specific issues. To learn more about how testing fits into the design process, see Chapter 23.

Implementation support

Any building architect will tell you that her work is not done until construction is complete. The same can be said for designers of digital products. No matter how good the engineering team or how thorough the specification, unexpected issues or questions inevitably crop up. If the engineers must begin making design decisions in your absence, things may head downhill from there, with some engineers varying from the specification for the sake of easier implementation. Engineers are less likely to take matters into their own hands if they have a good relationship with the design team and know you're available for a day or so each week. Chapter 25 addresses this kind of ongoing support.

PRACTICES

The design process does not stand alone; its effectiveness depends in large part upon the project management practices that support it. The structure of the team, the timing and content of communication, and the way collaboration works within the design team and outside of it all affect the outcome of a project. The Goal-Directed method is optimized to be as efficient as possible without sacrificing effectiveness.

Among other things, this means that the optimal design team is small but has frequent contact with members of a larger product team. Most projects require no more than five people on the design team, two or three of whom are part-time. Some projects require fewer. Of course, such a small team requires rigorous hiring and training practices to ensure that each team member has the required skills. See Chapter 2 for more on the various roles involved and the skills required of each.

Design serves as a process catalyst by making ideas concrete. A handful of formal meetings move the process along either by forcing decisions to happen or by helping people identify what additional information they need. The degree of formality and thoroughness in these discussions varies according to the size and geographical distribution of the product team, the culture of the company, and the need for materials to reference later on. Chapters 13, 19, and 24 describe formal communication at the most critical points in the process.

Not all organizations are able to take full advantage of design's strategic value. Even the best design process carried out by the best designers may not succeed in an environment where the business people are afraid of the engineers, the engineers are not very skilled, or decision-making is dysfunctional in some way, such as when no one has clear responsibility or the commensurate authority to make something happen. Assuming a reasonably healthy organization to start, though, it is entirely possible to introduce design and eventually make it a central part of how products are conceived and developed. Such transformations won't happen overnight, however; they take at least several years, provided you have a coherent plan and executive support. They also rely on designers having fully developed their own skills. Chapter 26 provides some ideas for developing individual and organizational design capabilities.

Summary

An effective design method supports designers in doing what they do best: visualizing concrete solutions to human problems. Goal-Directed Design helps skilled designers ensure thoroughness, timely execution, and consistently high quality of output. It also helps ensure that the design effort is not in vain by making the thought process transparent to the rest of the product team.

The remainder of this book focuses on the process and practices that have helped Cooper teams and other designers we've trained deliver great work on a deadline, from planning the research effort to seeing the product out the door. Of course, these processes and practices are only as good as the people applying them, so Chapter 2 outlines the skills and roles you'll want on your team.

Assembling the Team

Creating a market-leading digital product or service is extraordinarily difficult. You have to get so many things right: a great idea at the right time, desirable design, technically sound and cost-effective implementation, effective sales and marketing, and decent support all come together to determine how well your product will do. A terrific design of a bad idea, a buggy implementation of the world's best design, or poor marketing of even the most outstanding product can result in failure.

This need not mean that every new product is a roll of the dice, because most of the risk factors can be controlled. Certain conditions lead to success more often than others, regardless of whether you're working for a Fortune 100 behemoth or a brand-new start-up. Good process reduces risk and increases the likelihood of coming up with the right answer. A healthy work environment fosters creative thought. The right combination of skilled people can accomplish more in less time and with better quality.

Although a seemingly random collection of smart people can do great things, the most consistently successful teams involve a set of clearly defined roles that complement one another. Effective teams don't bog down the process and compromise the quality of decisions by including everyone in everything. Instead, a small, core group of people involves other team members as needed.

For this reason, it's important to distinguish the **design team** as a subset of the group responsible for delivering and selling the product, which typically includes stakeholders from marketing, sales, and

> The most consistently successful teams involve a set of clearly defined roles that complement one another.

Design team membership should be consistent from research through detailed design.

engineering, plus a subject matter expert or two if the product involves a complex domain. I'll refer to this larger group as the **product team**. Some organizations that establish these groups on a formal basis call them steering committees or governance committees. The design team does much of its work independent of the other product team members but reports to and involves them as needed. Some members of the larger product team collaborate closely with the designers, while others are involved only at critical decision points. Figure 2.1 illustrates these levels of involvement.

The Design Team

The design team conducts design research with potential users and customers, identifies behavior patterns and needs based on that research, and determines the form and behavior of the solution that will address those needs within the constraints. The ideal design team is small enough to keep communication overhead to a minimum but large enough to incorporate the required skills and to ensure that no individual designer's blind spots go unexamined.

This small team is most effective when membership is consistent from the initial research through implementation. It's most efficient when the overlap in skills is limited, though team members must share a common language and overall method. Each team member should understand the key principles and processes specific to the other disciplines but need not be expert in them.

Although each role has specific responsibilities, there is no aspect of the work product that is not influenced by every member of the team. In the most effective teams, there's an ethic of leadership, not ownership;

Design team
- Interaction designer – Generator
- Interaction designer – Synthesizer
- Visual designer
- Industrial designer
- Team lead

Close collaborators
- Project owner
- Design engineers
- Subject matter experts
- Business analysts
- Usability testers

Other stakeholders
- Executives
- Marketing
- Sales
- Other engineers
- Technical writers
- QA

Figure 2.1. Levels of involvement in design.

in other words, each team member is responsible for leading a certain aspect of the work and making sure that it happens, but there should never be a sense that one person owns a specific part and input from others is unwelcome.

There are five roles that cover the needs of nearly every design project:

— Two flavors of interaction designer

— Visual interface designer

— Industrial designer

— Design team lead

One of each role is sufficient for most projects except during activities that involve broad exploration, such as the early ideation for visual and industrial design directions. Each role and the necessary skills associated with it are discussed in the following sections. Figure 2.2 shows which team members typically participate in each phase of the process. It's possible to have a smaller team whose members have multiple skills rather than strictly defined roles, but that team will encounter bottlenecks—when, for example, the same person is trying to work out behavior and visual design—and the overall process will take longer. Also, it's inevitable that one skill suffers at the expense of the others; generalists cannot be the best at everything. If you cannot assemble this kind of team, see the "When You Don't Have the Ideal Team" section at the end of this chapter for ideas about filling the gaps.

Interaction designers

All of the traditional design professions, such as architecture, graphic design, and industrial design, require a similar aptitude: the ability and drive to visualize solutions in concrete (and visual) terms. Interaction design requires the same skill. However, because interaction design includes a unique characteristic not shared by the other design disciplines—i.e., systems that change state over time—interaction design requires an additional aptitude: the ability to think in terms

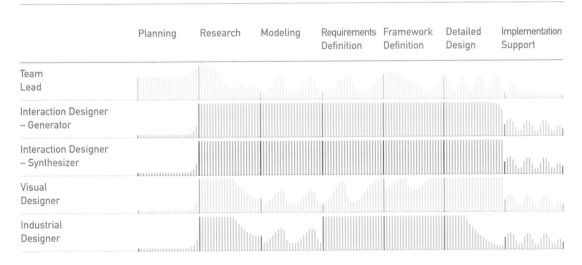

	Planning	Research	Modeling	Requirements Definition	Framework Definition	Detailed Design	Implementation Support

Figure 2.2. An overview of design team member involvement. The team lead may be the only designer involved in project planning. Thereafter, the two interaction designer roles are full-time, and the industrial designer and visual designer are involved at least part-time in every activity, more if budget allows. The team lead maintains some involvement throughout.

of system flow. Since a key part of that system is human, it also requires an understanding of the goals and thought processes of typical humans who will use the system. This combination of human understanding and flow is the story, or narrative, of the design.

At Cooper, we've found that some people excel at the traditional design skill of visualizing but that people whose brains work somewhat differently excel at the narrative aspects of design. For this reason, we use two distinct flavors of interaction designers (IxDs) to ensure that we get both types of skills on each team; people are hired into one role or the other because it suits their aptitudes. We use the terms **generator** (IxDG) and **synthesizer** (IxDS) to distinguish the two. Both roles have a number of skills in common, but each role has a set of very distinct characteristics and responsibilities.

SHARED SKILLS AND RESPONSIBILITIES

During the early stages of a project, any interaction designer (IxD) must be good at understanding complex domains and systems and reducing them to clear models and concepts. Later, interaction designers must contain the entire system design in their heads, thinking about implications for tomorrow's design problem while analyzing today's.

The best interaction designers I know are endlessly curious about how things work and why they work that way; they can't visit someone in the hospital and not itch to ask a nurse how she uses all the knobs and dials on the equipment. A good IxD judges nearly everything by how easy it is for humans to use. (I always drive the sales people in home electronics stores crazy because I'm not just interested in the features or the audio and video quality; I don't want to purchase the television or stereo without trying out the remote.)

It's important for interaction designers to be well versed in the human factors and cognitive

psychology principles that apply to a given problem. This grounding can be acquired in academia or at the local bookstore. Mastery of specific software tools, development platforms, or design problems is not critical for success; tools and technologies are easy to learn. Interaction designers need a general sense of what various technologies are capable of, but should be able to rely on engineers for detailed technical knowledge, just as oncologists and cardiologists are aware of one another's fields but don't attempt to be expert in them. Interaction design skills are independent of the problems they solve; any good designer should be able to grasp the essentials of a new domain within a month or so on the job.

Although it is possible for a junior designer to play a behind-the-scenes role on a large team, most interaction designers cannot avoid presenting their work at some point. This skill, like so many others, takes practice and coaching. Any designer who hasn't done much public speaking should practice presentations within the design team before delivering them to stakeholders.

Collaboration also takes practice. Co-ideation can be a smooth and effective process or a slow and painful one. Most designers go through a phase in which their confidence outpaces their skill, making it difficult for them to see flaws in their thinking. Many eventually recognize they're not infallible.

Both types of interaction designers are usually assigned to a project full-time from research through implementation. Together, and to some extent in conjunction with other team members, the interaction designers conduct stakeholder and user interviews, analyze the results, and use them to generate personas, scenarios, and requirements. Using these tools, they develop an interaction framework, then work with teammates and engineers to expand upon and refine the framework until it is ready for implementation. In the late stages of a project, they support the engineering team in resolving issues that arise during construction.

From the standpoint of developing individual skills and growing a design organization, it's useful to pair a junior designer of one flavor with a senior designer of the other. Early in their careers, IxD generators usually need help developing their narrative sense, while IxD synthesizers tend to need help with their structural thinking. As designers become more seasoned, they start to take on more of the skills of the other role, though they remain strongest at their primary skill.

INTERACTION DESIGNER (GENERATOR)

The IxD generator is the team member responsible for leading the visualization of system behavior, from overall structure and flow to the tiniest details, such as whether an action is initiated at mouse up or mouse down. This includes information architecture for Web sites, as well.

A generator's most critical skill is the one that defines all of the traditional design disciplines: the ability and drive to visualize concrete solutions. If someone isn't facile at generating and sketching ideas with a whiteboard marker in her hand, she's not right for the role. Any team that doesn't include this generative skill will usually struggle to make progress at any speed.

Visualization skill is usually accompanied by a certain amount of confidence; it takes faith in one's own judgment to put rough ideas out in public view for criticism. Although a good generator values user feedback and usability test results, she doesn't hesitate to make decisions without them. Good designers in any discipline "know" they're right, though this confidence can be an Achilles heel if it's not accompanied by a willingness to hear why they might be wrong.

The IxD generator is responsible for articulating the design in visual terms, initially in the form of sketches and eventually in the form of detailed screen shots; this latter responsibility is shared with the visual designer. Of the two interaction design roles, the IxDG works somewhat more closely with the visual and industrial designers on how the visual and physical design communicates the system's behavior, such as the relative importance of information or the behavior of widgets and physical controls. The IxDG also reviews design documentation developed by the IxD synthesizer, helping to ensure that it conveys the behavior clearly and correctly and that it answers the questions engineers will have.

Years ago, many interaction designers of this type came from related disciplines, such as industrial or graphic design, HCI, or engineering, because formal interaction design training was not available. These days, academic programs are starting to turn out more people who are well prepared for this role.

A generative interaction designer's most critical skill is the ability and drive to visualize concrete solutions.

A narrative point of view helps synthesizing interaction designers identify problems that are not evident from looking at the design solely in the structural sense.

INTERACTION DESIGNER (SYNTHESIZER)

The IxD synthesizer is the team member responsible for leading the analysis and communication of the design. There are many people in design jobs today who do much of what an IxDS does, but since it's unusual as an explicit role, perhaps its unique characteristics will make most sense if I start by describing its origins. In the early days at Cooper, the generative interaction designers (just called "interaction designers" at the time) spent a lot of time writing specifications. In 1996, we decided it would be useful to have technical writers or other verbally inclined people take meeting notes and turn them into specifications. We called this role the "design communicator." It soon became evident that the right sort of person not only improved the documentation and allowed more time for design, but also made the design process more efficient and effective. With their narrative point of view, design communicators were able to identify problems not evident from looking at a design solely in the structural sense. They also helped ensure that the design was complete, partly by using documentation as a design aid: When you have to explain the design thoroughly enough for an engineer to build it, you'll naturally ask questions about how it works, what happens when this or that button is pressed, and why a particular solution is good.

It didn't take long before the design communicator role was respected as a full partner in the conception and evolution of the design. For this reason, we've changed the role's name to reflect that it is a flavor of the interaction design discipline, with "synthesizer" representing the activities that are strengths for this role: distilling ideas and using the narrative point of view to analyze design solutions.

Although they are certainly designers in the sense that they are full partners in ideation, IxD synthesizers need not be designers in the more traditional sense; they are either not inclined toward visualization or not so strongly inclined toward it that they feel compelled to fight their design partners for the whiteboard marker. Each IxDS helps his interaction design partner articulate half-formed design ideas, then tests and helps to evolve those ideas by asking questions about the design and its rationale. Although a synthesizer may pick up the whiteboard marker and propose an idea, his primary responsibility in a design meeting is to ensure the clarity and effectiveness of any solution. Ideally the IxDG temporarily picks up this clarifying role if her partner is expressing an idea, but if the whiteboard becomes a competition, then no one is paying attention to this essential function.

Every great synthesizer has a certain discomfort with ambiguity, an ability to identify a fuzzy idea and not let go of it until it becomes clear.

The early stages of design are rife with half-formed ideas, though, so a skilled synthesizer knows the difference between fundamental concepts that must be clarified right away and routine details that can be resolved later.

Communicating about design—which remains a key aspect of the role—requires the ability to organize and prioritize ideas into a coherent, concise, and persuasive narrative that's appropriate to the audience. This includes identifying the key points of what must be communicated, figuring out the best communication medium (whether a photo, a diagram, or a page of prose), and implementing it in a clear, concise manner. IxD synthesizers must be detail-oriented enough to explain everything an engineer needs to build a custom widget, but must also be good at explaining the big picture and the reasons the widget needs to work that way. This quality usually makes synthesizers good at project management, too.

There is no such thing as an academic program in interaction design synthesis, and because visualization is usually not their emphasis, fewer synthesis-inclined people are drawn to academic design programs. Some people with inclinations toward synthesis may have interaction design job titles, but many come from some other field related to product development, such as technical writing, product management, usability testing, or design research.

Visual interface designer

The visual interface and information designer, or visual designer (VisD) for short, ensures that the visual representation of the design effectively communicates the data and hints at the expected behavior of the product. At the same time, the visual designer is responsible for conveying the brand ideals in the product and for creating a positive first impression; this responsibility is shared with the industrial designer if the product involves hardware. In essence, a visual designer must aim for maximum usability combined with maximum desirability.

In an ideal world, the visual designer would be involved full-time from start to finish just as the interaction designers are. In practice, the cost is sometimes difficult to justify. Fortunately, it's possible for visual designers to be very effective as long as they're involved in all of the stakeholder discussions and at least some part of every activity from user research through framework definition. Unless there is a detailed visual system already in place, visual design becomes a full-time role during the creation and refinement of detailed design.

> A visual designer must aim for maximum usability combined with maximum desirability.

The visual designer is usually the person best suited to lead the interviews with brand stakeholders, and may lead other interviews as any other team member would. She is responsible for articulating any visual design requirements, including a list of the product's targeted brand attributes, which are essentially a description of its personality. From those attributes, the visual designer proposes a visual strategy, gets consensus on the direction, and develops and refines a detailed visual system, including color, typography, icons, and visual specifications for each component on the screen. In conjunction with the IxDS, the visual designer also documents this system.

Visual designers also play a less obvious but equally important role in reviewing the interaction design, and may contribute ideas to it as any other team member does. Much as an IxDS can identify flaws in the behavior by thinking through how to explain something, a visual designer can identify flaws by thinking about how things will be represented on the screen. If a particular behavior or set of on-screen relationships is difficult to render in pixels, that's a good sign that it's not as clear and simple as it could be. In addition, visual designers are good at spotting unnecessary inconsistencies because they're trying to develop a visual system that contains as few unique elements as possible. They may also identify issues if they are doing any animation to demonstrate particularly subtle interactions.

Visual designers must, of course, have good visualization and rendering skills. They must also have an excellent understanding of graphic design fundamentals, such as color, type, and layout. Although I know many outstanding interaction designers who have not had formal interaction design training, I have never encountered an excellent visual interface designer who did not have a degree in graphic design or a closely related field.

However, visual interface design is not synonymous with graphic design. Some degree programs offer courses in digital design, but it generally takes a talented graphic designer a few years to master visual design for digital products. Digital media and print involve different constraints. Digital design involves lower resolutions. It requires an understanding of usability principles, such as how to determine type and click target size. It also emphasizes function over form to an extent that much print design does not; brand expression is often secondary in application design. Information design is also a more critical component in application design than in much print design. Visual design considerations differ considerably between Web sites and applications, too; a designer with deep experience in one is not necessarily prepared for the other.

One skill that even some of the best visual interface designers struggle with is icon design. This requires not only a deep understanding of how humans recognize and interpret symbols, but also strong illustration skills. Icon design is relatively easy to separate from the other visual design tasks once you've established an overall style direction, so if your design group is large enough, it's worth having someone who specializes in rendering complex concepts with a minimum number of pixels.

Collaboration skills and empathy are as important in visual design as in the other roles. Communication skills are likewise critical. A visual designer must be able to present work with a convincing rationale. Moreover, the visual designer must be able to steer stakeholders clear of purely subjective preferences, which are even more of an issue for design language than they are for behavior.

Industrial designer

The industrial designer (ID) is responsible for designing hardware that is ergonomically and environmentally appropriate, aesthetically pleasing, and cost-effective to manufacture. The industrial designer also shares the visual designer's responsibility for expressing the brand ideals and creating a distinctive look and feel for the product.

The industrial designer does not need to be full-time during certain parts of the project. However, ID participation in stakeholder discussions and at least some of the user research is essential. An industrial designer may share leadership of the brand stakeholder interviews with the visual designer and should drive any interviews related to the design team's understanding of hardware engineering or manufacturing issues; ideally, the mechanical design engineer is present to assist with extracting the right information and providing any "translation" the design team needs. He is also responsible for articulating hardware-related design requirements and, along with the visual designer, any description of the product's experience attributes.

The ID works closely with the interaction designers on the form factor and interaction framework. Close collaboration with the visual designer is likewise essential to developing a coherent design language. Once the types and approximate locations of hardware controls and displays are determined, refinement of the industrial design often has more to do with engineering considerations than with interaction and visual design, so although collaboration continues to be important, the industrial designer may work more closely with a mechanical engineer in the later project phases than with the rest of the design team.

Industrial designers play a significant role in developing the initial interaction design concepts. While the entire design team shares the same goals, there is a productive tension between interaction designers and industrial designers, especially regarding the number and type of physical controls on a device. Should the team go for a solution that adds physical work or clutter in favor of reducing cognitive work, or vice versa? Each

discipline has an inherent bias, but good collaboration helps make that an advantage rather than a problem.

Industrial designers require the same sort of visualization skill that all the classic design disciplines share, with added emphasis on tactile and three-dimensional thinking. There is really no substitute for formal industrial design training or for experience, which provides an understanding of craft, materials, models, engineering, and manufacturing that even the best schools cannot give their students.

Collaboration and communication skills, as well as empathy, are as essential to industrial designers as to other team members. Like visual designers, industrial designers must be able to help stakeholders avoid decisions based on personal aesthetic preferences.

An ID who is unaccustomed to working with interaction designers may not recognize how cognitive issues should affect the hardware design. (Of course, interaction designers not accustomed to working on hardware have challenges to overcome, too, such as not being accustomed to considering manufacturing cost.) As the collaboration progresses, this consideration comes naturally to most industrial designers, who are inherently focused on problem solving. It's more of a struggle for those who are primarily concerned with aesthetic expression.

I recall one encounter with an ID who insisted that, even though it made the relationship with their on-screen labels hard to understand, a cluster of four buttons needed to look like a paw print, an arbitrary alignment which didn't even have anything to do with the brand aspirations of the client. He would not be persuaded, so all I could do was share my concerns with the client, who decided this person wasn't the right ID for the project. This story highlights a common challenge in the design of interactive devices: many companies treat hardware and software design and engineering as separate efforts. This is a tremendous mistake, because users have only one experience of a product. Any project that doesn't integrate the two efforts will lead to a compromised solution.

Design team lead

The design team lead is a senior designer responsible for ensuring that the organization's needs, as represented by the project owner, are met. At Cooper, we call the team lead the "engagement lead," because he is responsible for the quality of the client's engagement from start to finish. This includes everything from strategic project management (such as how the project will be structured) to design direction and management of relationships with key stakeholders. The way this role is defined should vary based on the structure and culture of your organization, and the extent to which the team lead provides explicit direction versus coaching and support should vary depending on the skill level of the designers on the team. In any situation, though, there are three key characteristics that make the role work:

1. The design team lead is a senior designer who, regardless of her specific discipline background, has had extensive exposure to the other disciplines.

2. The team lead is sufficiently involved to understand exactly what's going on, but sufficiently distant to provide an objective assessment of design solutions.

3. There is no separation of business responsibility (such as scope and business relationship) and design responsibility.

The team lead must be a senior designer because only such a person can assess the quality of work in progress and provide the team with process and skill coaching. The team lead cannot be expert in every role, but needs to understand the

point of view of each discipline on the team in order to help balance their perspectives. In an ideal world, the team lead has easy access to other senior designers who *are* expert in each discipline to provide added support where needed.

The team lead cannot adequately support the rest of the team without a good understanding of the domain, users, customers, and business objectives. This doesn't mean the team lead has to be present in every user interview or design meeting; allocating about a third of the team lead's time over the course of a project should be sufficient if the designers are up to the task and at least one of them is experienced enough to provide leadership in meetings. It's actually best if the team lead's time is not fully allocated to the project, because anyone who works on a solution all day, every day is bound to become a little nearsighted about it. A team lead who isn't personally involved in most of the solution generation can provide a more objective assessment and point out issues the rest of the team may have overlooked.

It's most effective if the person ultimately responsible for the team's delivery of a good solution is also the person responsible for the project's scope and the team's relationship with the key stakeholders. This is consistent with the approach taken by most in-house design teams, but differs from the account manager/creative director separation that exists in most consultancies. Having tried both approaches for a number of years, I can say that the latter approach results in more problems than it solves: The client doesn't benefit from the design team's insights as much as they could, and the person telling the project owner what is or isn't possible cannot really assess what the design team is capable of.

The team lead develops the initial research plan; this is done in consultation with the rest of the team if research is planned after stakeholder interviews, though in our practice at Cooper the plan is drafted as part of the initial sales and scoping process, which means that involving the rest of the design team is often not practical. The team lead typically consults with appropriate leads from other disciplines to ensure that each set of activities is appropriately scoped.

The team lead participates in all stakeholder interviews and some user interviews, but typically does not lead them. Thereafter, the team lead checks in with the stakeholders and design team informally as needed, as well as more formally at certain critical points in the process (which are described throughout the book).

Close Collaborators

Designers are most effective at generating great solutions if they can temporarily set aside concerns with implementation, regulatory issues, and other points of view that tend to hamper initial creativity. However, any design created in a vacuum will be a failure, so it's essential to collaborate closely with people who are not designers but can help ensure that the solution is good, clear enough to build, and practical within

the given time and budget constraints. This set of people always includes design engineers, and may include business or systems analysts, subject matter experts, and usability testers. Ideally, there is also a project owner who works closely with the designers to ensure that the solution will be accepted by other stakeholders and will be viable from a business standpoint. Figure 2.3 provides an overview of how these roles are involved throughout the project.

Project owner

It's not easy to build momentum and convince people to take risks in a committee-driven environment. Every project needs a leader who is responsible for coordinating the involvement of various people and for making the final call if there is not consensus on direction. The project owner is typically a product manager or executive who is held accountable for the success of the product or service, and is the person from whom the design team ultimately takes direction.

Some product managers have considerable authority and are the keepers of the product vision,

Figure 2.3. Close collaborator involvement.

> If your project owner of record is simply passing on direction provided by the executives, you need to identify and get close to the real project owner.

while others are more like project managers: process facilitators with very limited authority. It's important to understand which is the case on any project. If your project owner of record has limited authority and is simply passing on direction provided by the executives, then he or she is not the real project owner. Decisions made by this sort of person are often overturned, so you should strive to identify and get close to the real project owner.

If the project owner of record is an executive or is extremely busy, it's best to have a project manager in addition to the project owner, because otherwise the design team will not get the necessary help with involving stakeholders and removing organizational barriers. A project manager helps identify the right people to help get interviews together, coordinates key meetings, and ensures that you get the necessary support from engineers and subject matter experts. In an in-house design organization, the design team lead might play this role, but in a consulting environment, it must be someone on the client side.

Regardless of other factors, it's critical that the project owner is someone who is receptive to and willing to champion design. It's also best when the project owner is comfortable with the design process, because you'll want someone to review rough work in progress before showing it to the larger group of stakeholders. This helps you refine not only the work, but also the way in which you express it. If the project owner is not the right person to do this, perhaps the project manager is.

Design engineer

Engineers may be focused on software, mechanical, or electrical systems. A design engineer is an engineer from any of these disciplines who is specifically tasked with figuring out how to make the design possible and providing feedback on how difficult various aspects of the design will be to implement.

You'll notice that I don't say the engineers determine what is or is not feasible; though this happens in many organizations, most decisions about feasibility (especially related to software) are really business decisions, since anything that's possible within the laws of physics can be accomplished given enough resources to do it. Many business people don't even realize that an engineer who says something is "not technically feasible" has just taken a business decision out of their hands. What that engineer probably means is that he won't have enough time to do it, he doesn't know how to do it, or, in the case of hardware, the presumed manufacturing cost limits won't accommodate it.

One characteristic that distinguishes a design engineer from other engineers is a willingness to assume that nearly anything is possible. A design engineer responds to a technical challenge by saying, "Let me go try some things and get back to you." A design engineer is perfectly willing to experiment and to throw away code or other technical prototypes; his focus is on determining what it will take to solve the problem, not on solving it completely for a final product.

Once a design direction is proposed, the design team needs regular access to a design engineer from each relevant discipline (software and, if applicable, mechanical and electrical). The design engineers work on difficult problems and work with engineering management to develop estimates for engineering and manufacturing cost; these estimates then inform business trade-off decisions. Of course, the design engineers also need some involvement before the design effort begins to advise the designers about what is and isn't difficult; this early involvement is greater on highly constrained projects.

The design engineers should be at the disposal of the design team for questions and consultation. The relationship is reciprocal, though; as the design process progresses and some engineering starts happening in parallel, the engineers will have questions for the design team, so it's essential to set some time aside for these, as well. Plan on meeting with the engineers at least weekly during detailed design, and ideally more often.

Business or systems analyst

Large IT departments often stitch together systems from a dozen different vendors with little bits of custom code that require serious archaeology to understand. Such organizations usually employ business or systems analysts to help ensure that changes in one place don't wreak havoc in another. Some try to use a business analyst (BA) as a substitute for a generative interaction designer, but most analysts I've encountered don't have the right training or aptitudes for that role. What they generally do have is considerable knowledge of the existing systems and processes, as well as a level of attention to detail that few designers possess. Business analysts can provide a critical translation between a design spec and the current implementation of complex systems, making sure the engineers understand which database tables or other technical structures are affected and in what ways. While analysts are not necessary in many product development initiatives, they can make a big difference in getting changes to large IT systems implemented correctly. (Some organizations that handle few novel design

> A design engineer is perfectly willing to experiment and to throw away code or other technical prototypes.

Getting Started

problems successfully pair business analysts with generative interaction designers; however, the BA must still have the aptitudes of an IxDS.)

Subject matter expert

If you are working on a healthcare application, statistical analysis package, or other complex tool, subject matter experts (SMEs) are indispensable. An SME is essentially a consultant to the design team, answering detailed questions about procedures and regulations, reviewing design work in progress for missing information or incorrect assumptions, and helping to ensure that the design promotes industry best practices. You may have more than one SME if your design overlaps several professional specialties, and it's a good idea to have two even in a single specialty, since even experts can sometimes be wrong. SMEs should be involved as needed from the initial research through implementation. Weekly review meetings during the detailed design phase are a good idea.

Usability tester

Usability testing is to design what QA is to engineering or what editing is to writing: a good way to catch mistakes and refine what's there, but not a substitute for creating good work product in the first place. It's entirely possible to design a great product without usability testing, just as it's possible to write a good document or clean code without editing or QA; for this reason, I encourage most clients with limited budgets to focus their expenditure on design rather than testing. However, if you're not on a shoestring budget or if you're designing for an environment where user mistakes can do real harm, such as an assisted surgery system or automobile dashboard, testing is an important investment. (It's also a great way to convince people there's a problem with an existing design.)

While designers should be versed in testing techniques and capable of conducting a basic test, it's best to have someone who is both expert and objective lead any test sessions. Tests conducted by product managers or anyone else close to the product are a bad idea; they may be done badly, and I've often seen people bring their personal political agendas into tests. This is probably not a conscious thing, but whether it's conscious or not, it's difficult to get valid results when the facilitator is asking things like, "Don't you find this thing over here difficult to use?"

Professional usability testers are generally more inclined toward evaluating design than toward generating it, though they're knowledgeable about design principles. A good tester will work with the design team to understand the design, the users, and the objectives of the evaluation in order to plan an appropriate test. The design team should observe the tests and be involved in interpreting the results, since they have knowledge of the users that the tester probably doesn't.

Other Product Team Members

The success of every product or service depends on more than the people directly responsible for its design and implementation. This group of stakeholders usually includes managers or executives from marketing, engineering, sales, and perhaps other areas. These people need to be informed about the design team's progress and involved in key decisions about direction and trade-offs, but don't need to be (and probably shouldn't be) involved in design meetings and detailed reviews. Some stakeholders are comfortable with the iterative nature of design, but in my experience, half-formed ideas don't sit well with the majority, and their discomfort can derail a project entirely. For this reason, it's a good idea to involve senior stakeholders as early and often as possible, but only at points when you have significant progress to show and can

Figure 2.4. Typical stakeholder involvement.

describe it in a coherent, confident fashion. In other words, they're involved in reviewing work at each major decision point, but not involved in the seemingly messy process of getting to those decision points.

The first critical point for stakeholder involvement is the set of initial interviews you conduct to understand business objectives and project parameters. (See Chapter 5 for information on interviewing specific types of stakeholders.) There are two goals for this interaction: one, to gather the essential information stakeholders can share, and two, to begin establishing your credibility and building a working relationship with each stakeholder.

The next point where every stakeholder should be involved is a meeting to recap your research findings and discuss their implications. This analysis of the users and their domain includes the results of your modeling and requirements definition phases.

A couple of weeks after this meeting, stakeholders are eager to see the design that results from all this effort. The right point for this meeting is the first point at which you're confident in your answers to the big structural questions and can express the concept in clear terms.

The next point at which to involve the larger group of stakeholders varies depending on the scale of the design problem. For a simple problem, the next meeting should occur when you have a detailed first draft of most key functions. For larger, more complex products, it's better to

chunk this delivery and have periodic meetings as you finish a draft of each coherent subset of the functionality.

I'll discuss each of these meetings in detail at the appropriate point in the process. Throughout the process, of course, there is ongoing informal communication about your progress, and there are working meetings with the project owner, engineers, and any subject matter experts. Figure 2.4 indicates the points at which stakeholders typically have explicit input.

When You Don't Have the Ideal Team

Of course, all of this advice about creating the ideal team is great if you're in a position to do it. What if you're not? Many designers are not empowered to create teams with multiple specialties or to determine who is involved in what meeting, and many organizations don't have designated design engineers, subject matter experts, or project owners. Even if you can't set up the right team on a formal basis, you can often find ways to approximate it in an informal way. In one way or another, every designer must find ways to exert influence without authority.

Understaffed design team

If you're a lone designer with no immediate prospects of getting full-time help, there are at least three things you can do. One is to bolster your own skills. Managers who think they can postpone hiring or avoid outsourcing may be willing to send you to a course in whatever aspect of design you're weakest in. Even those without much training budget may be willing to buy a few books. If you're a freelancer or can't get management support, consider making that investment in yourself; it will only make you more marketable.

Another approach is to look for design-inclined people with complementary skills. If you're a visualization-inclined designer, look for someone with IxDS-like qualities, perhaps among the product management or technical writing staff. If you're not strong in visualization, look for someone who is, such as a graphic designer or perhaps an engineer. Solo consultants can look for such individuals on the client team. At a minimum, you may be able to get them to squeeze in an hour or two a week. Better yet, you might be able to get some of their time freed up officially, since managers often don't think of using staff time differently as an added cost (even though they're trading one sort of work for another) because the salary and benefits are already allocated.

A third option is to ask for budget to outsource small parts of the work, such as icon design. This is often as expensive as another hire, but some managers have more flexibility in this kind of spending than they do in adding staff.

No design engineers or subject matter experts

Few organizations have an explicit design engineer role. If your assigned engineering contact isn't skilled enough or is more focused on ease of coding or manufacture than on the best solution, you have a couple of options. One is to see if there's a more helpful engineer whom you can invite to meetings without giving offense. Another is to brief your project owner about the kind of engineering support you're getting, then make sure she attends some meetings to observe the prob-

lem. It might take a while, but either approach may eventually work. You might also appeal to a more sympathetic engineer for help outside of these discussions, but this can backfire.

Although you might also run into less than helpful SMEs, finding subject matter experts is usually less politically fraught than getting the right engineering help. There might be an unacknowledged subject matter expert in product management or marketing. If your company has a professional services group that consults with enterprise clients about making their tools and business processes work together, someone in that group could be a great resource. Another option is to ask a particularly expert and helpful user if he's willing to work with you on an informal basis; some people are thrilled to be involved and will do it for free. If compensation is expected, you can either ask for a small budget or look for other forms of appreciation, such as free attendance at a user conference or free copies of the product. Note that any external expert should probably sign a nondisclosure agreement if you're showing work in progress.

No clear project owner

In risk-averse environments, committees (official or otherwise) are "safe" because no one on the committee is entirely to blame for failures. Committees may also be motivated by a consensus ethic, which is common in academia and healthcare. If a committee has a specified chairperson with authority, then it might make sense to consider that person your project owner.

Your situation is more difficult if there is no clear leadership at all. You can't simply pick someone to be your project owner and take direction from that person in the absence of committee input. However, you can pick someone to lean on for advice and support. Look for a member of the group who seems sympathetic to design; this could be a marketing person who understands the value of achieving user and customer goals or an engineer who's tired of not having clear specs. It's also important that this person have certain leadership qualities, an ability to get things done, and the respect of others in the group.

Ask your chosen champion if she's willing to support you informally. Meet with her from time to time and ask her opinion on how best to convey a conclusion or concept to the group. Ask for a particular type of support you expect to need in an upcoming meeting. Request that she use her influence to nudge someone for help or information.

Don't forget to ask your own manager for help. He may be able to help you identify an informal champion or bring the lack of leadership to someone's attention.

Too many people in working meetings

If your working meetings with engineers or subject matter experts are too large, or if too many stakeholders who aren't good collaborators insist on attending them, your progress can slow to a crawl. It can be even worse if the wrong people insist on attending your design meetings; you may find yourself going in entirely the wrong direction.

There's no simple solution to these challenges. Overcoming them involves educating, building trust, developing processes, and sometimes plain old political maneuvering. Educate stakeholders about the design process and about effective collaboration techniques, as well as the idea of sending, say, an engineering representative instead of the entire engineering team. Build trust by telling stakeholders when they'll have a chance to review what you're working on and then deliver on that promise; if people see that nothing is getting sneaked past them, they may not feel the need to be in every meeting. If an individual's meeting behavior is problematic and direct feedback hasn't helped, discuss it with your project owner.

If you can't escape excessively large meetings, make sure everyone in the meeting has some specific role to play. In Beyer and Holtzblatt's *Contextual Design*,[1] for example, there are a number of techniques designed specifically for corralling big group meetings. I don't recommend these in most design projects, but they're good for companies where everyone is going to be involved no matter what you do. When this is the case, though, be sure to account for the larger group process in your scheduling, since everything will take longer.

> **Build trust by telling stakeholders when they'll have a chance to review what you're working on and then deliver on that promise.**

1. Beyer, H., and Holtzblatt, K. *Contextual design: Defining customer-centered systems*. Morgan Kaufman, 1997.

If you're a consultant, you probably have some contractual room to insist on control of your own process. Clients may say, "But surely you will work faster and do better design with our expertise in the room." Some stakeholder attendance at design meetings is absolutely beneficial because it gives the client organization greater ownership of the outcome. However, a stakeholder who is too uncomfortable with the messy design process may try to take over the meeting, derail the process with details at the wrong time, and squash the design team's ability to be creative. That's a difficult conversation when the person derailing the meeting is the project owner, but it's better to have the conversation than to ignore the problem and have a failed project.

Summary

No matter how good your process is, the skills and working relationships on the design and product teams are critical to the success of the effort. It's not necessary to have every specialized role represented if you're just starting to convince people that design is worthwhile; the important thing is to recognize where you're missing an important skill and look for small, informal ways to help make up for it. The sooner you have the right skills and working relationships, the more effective you will be.

CHAPTER 3

Project Planning

A design project may start at any point in the lifecycle of a product or service, from the first moment a problem or opportunity arises to just a few weeks before the product ships. It's possible for a design team to succeed at any point in that process, so long as everyone understands that design is like a lever: the longer the time between project start and delivery, the greater the effect. Designers provide the most value when they're involved in the early stages—defining the problem and the product or service that will address it—but can still provide some value late in the process by cleaning up screen layouts and making icons more understandable. Your project has a good chance at being considered a success as long as the expectations match the time and budget at your disposal.

One of the keys to setting those expectations for a successful project lies in what *Flawless Consulting*[1] author Peter Block would call the "contracting" phase: getting agreement on what you're expected to accomplish (at least in the first part of your work), how you'll go about it, and how much time and money it will take. Most consultants literally get agreement in the form of a contract; this kind of formality may not be necessary for in-house projects, but it's useful in any case to have some kind of working document that outlines the understanding between the design team and the project owner (see Chapter 2 for more about the project owner role).

> Your project has a good chance at success as long as the expectations match the time and budget.

---

1. Block, P. *Flawless consulting: A guide to getting your experience used.* 2nd edition. Pfeiffer, 1999.

The Ideal Project Starting Point

Ask any designer when is the best time to involve design and she will say, "At the beginning." But what is the beginning? Ideally, it's as soon as the stakeholders identify a problem they want to solve, an idea they'd like to pursue, or a question about user needs or behaviors they'd like to have answered. The designers can be involved either before an initial business case is developed, or immediately thereafter.

Many organizations view "the beginning" as the point at which a **marketing requirements document** (MRD)—sometimes called a product requirements document (PRD)—is written. These documents, which are typically generated either by product marketing or product management, vary widely from company to company, but most are much too long and detailed, take much too long to produce, and even their authors would agree that they're excellent cures for insomnia.

On average, the MRD is perhaps 30 to 100 pages of text statements, both vague ("should be easy to use") and specific ("must allow for 10 simultaneous users"). The MRD shouldn't—but often does—attempt to specify the contents of list boxes and other details. No design has occurred, so how can the document's author even know whether there will *be* a list box? There are much bigger issues to resolve before anyone worries about widgets.

Product managers attempt to be exhaustive because they assume that engineers will use the requirements to build the product. This translation of requirements to code does happen, unfortunately, but it's like telling the construction team for your house that you want it to be airy and filled with light; without an architect, this may be interpreted as a powerful ventilation system and lots of fluorescent fixtures.

Design research and design solutions can provide tremendous insight into the issues product managers struggle with in their MRDs. Given the option, most product managers would prefer to save time and focus on the business aspects of making their products successful, such as identifying the right product positioning and pricing strategy, but right now many of them don't see a better option. Instead of attempting to describe all of the product needs in text, the product manager's initial MRD should function as a brief, preliminary proposal whose audience consists of the stakeholders and design team. The conceptual design and subsequent rough construction estimates serve as the more detailed proposal, which stakeholders can review and request adjustments to. The final design and engineering specifications then function as the blueprint for construction.

The best MRD I've ever seen was two pages long. The target audience for the document was clearly the senior managers who would decide whether to fund the project, followed by the design team who would take it as their marching orders. The MRD stated the product manager's idea in simple terms: a replacement for the current product that would add wireless communication and significantly improve the hardware and software interfaces. The document went on to make the business case for the upgrade, citing the size of the market, projected price range and demand for the improved model, and the costs involved in supporting the current model's problems. Nowhere was there a mention of list boxes or their contents. It was the perfect starting point for scoping a design project.

When you don't have the perfect MRD, you'll have to determine the extent to which the product manager expects it to evolve with the design. I've never yet seen one that didn't change at least a little bit, and I've seen several thrown out the window entirely when design research found flaws in some fundamental assumptions. Most likely, though, much of what's in the MRD will continue to be important.

Determining Your Project's Parameters

Once you're brought into a project, the first part of "contracting" is determining the scale and focus of your project. You might think your stakeholders can provide a simple answer, but the project plan and staffing stakeholders expect may not be the most appropriate for their objectives. To develop the right approach, you first need to understand some fundamental issues:

— Are they focused on increasing revenue or on cutting costs?

— Do they want to innovate or just renovate?

— Is the time horizon short or long?

— How well do they understand the problem, and do they have specific ideas about solving it?

— How much are they willing to invest in a solution?

Each question is a sort of qualitative mental scale you can use to compare each prospective project to others you've done. This helps with anticipating the required effort and skills, as well as potential issues. You can ask some of these questions directly, but you may get misleading answers; it's common for people to claim they want innovation when everything else they say and do shows they're only prepared to make small changes. Note that many of the stakeholder questions in Chapter 5 are helpful in making this assessment.

Revenue or cost focus

If your work is viewed as a minor cost-reduction measure or optional cosmetic effort, you may have a relatively tight timeframe and budget; no design at all may be viewed as better than a design that's too expensive. Sometimes this is an unfortunate perception that you can help change by reaching a bit beyond the project mandate. Don't be disappointed if you can't change it, though, because

some projects really are just about making things marginally better. Stakeholders don't appreciate blue-sky thinking when they're under tight constraints themselves. You'll want to propose a project schedule that's bare bones to begin with, then work with stakeholders to expand it where you feel you can add the most value.

If design is brought in early and is viewed as a differentiator and potential revenue generator, or if there's a very expensive problem to solve, then people are probably thinking of design as an important investment. Stakeholders may be more open to wildly different ideas and could be disappointed if you're too pragmatic early in the project. It's best to start with your ideal project plan, then help stakeholders make trade-offs to get the plan within a target budget or timeline.

Desire to innovate

Are the stakeholders looking for something that's never been seen before, or do they want to do pretty much the same thing, but better? Even with revenue-generating products, many companies need a specific motive (such as moving from second place to first in the market) to do anything other than the same old thing. Don't assume that innovation is necessarily a smarter move than renovation, though. If a product's potential market and margins are very small, the only kind of innovation that makes business sense is the rare kind that's extremely cheap. You may also need to demonstrate what design can do on a renovation project before people look to you for innovation; the key is to do renovation very well but show stakeholders a glimpse of an innovative idea or two.

Length of time horizon

Some organizations are focused on achieving a specific objective, even if it takes a little longer than they'd like. Others are more concerned with hitting a particular deadline, even if what they

Don't shortchange research if you can help it—it's your best hope of building consensus.

finish by that deadline isn't quite right. Designers generally prefer the former, and it's not just to make life easier; there are too many companies that focus on deadlines only because they don't know any other way of defining a target. There are, however, many good reasons that a company might be focused on a deadline, such as the need to ship a consumer product in time for the holiday shopping season. Try to determine what the timeline is and why, so you'll know how ambitious or conservative to be as you estimate the effort to put into each phase. The following sections describe the pros and cons of the most common trade-offs.

Understanding the problem before solving it

Can at least one stakeholder clearly articulate the problem they're trying to solve? It's not unusual to find that no one has a good grasp of the problem or that stakeholders don't really agree on it. Sometimes the project owner recognizes this lack of consensus as an issue. If he doesn't, consider whether he's receptive before pointing it out. Try your best not to shortchange the research in the project plan, since it's your best hope of building consensus.

Stakeholders with very specific solution ideas present a similar challenge if those ideas aren't based on understanding user needs. A technology in search of a problem to solve makes for a particularly difficult project. Thorough research is your best tool in this situation, too, since your opinion won't carry much weight without data to back it up.

Willingness to invest

Don't be afraid to ask what the project owner expects your budget to be. When you're an external consultant, some clients may want to keep it a secret, either thinking they'll get a cheaper bid or more creative approach if they don't share the magic number. This may stem from a general mistrust of consultants. It's also possible they really don't have a budget established. An effective response is to throw out some rough numbers for projects of various scales; this provides a useful starting point for discussion and establishes trust by showing that you have nothing to hide.

The design budget isn't the only aspect of investment that's important, though. What sort of engineering resources do stakeholders expect to allocate? They won't have exact numbers, but should be able to tell you if it's a couple of engineers or dozens. In the case of hardware, ask about any attachment to specific manufacturing processes or existing molds, as well as any rough targets for the per-unit cost ("cost of goods sold," or COGS) and volume. The bill of materials (BOM) for any existing product, which outlines the parts, electrical components, and raw materials, serves as a useful starting point.

Risk factors

Any project may involve various combinations of these characteristics. Problems usually arise when there is a mismatch between the goals and expectations of the stakeholders and the time and resources they expect to invest: Major innovation on a one-week project, a large enterprise system with two programmers allocated to it, and opposition to research on a complex project are all failures in the making. Don't assume that it's a lost cause, though; project owners who are new to design or to their roles may simply need education. If you must do a project with unrealistic parameters that you can't move, it's even more important to be specific about what you can accomplish and to put your agreement in writing.

> If you must do a project with unrealistic parameters, be specific about what you can accomplish and put your agreement in writing.

Developing the Project Plan

Having a detailed project plan will help ensure that you're allowing enough time to succeed on the project, while reassuring stakeholders that you're spending no more time than necessary. It's possible to develop an accurate day-by-day plan for the activities between stakeholder research and the presentation of the design framework. Detailed design is impossible to estimate closely until the design framework exists and there is agreement on the direction; even then, it can vary somewhat due to engineering dependencies. However, you should be able to develop a very rough estimate, such as, "We should be able to do a detailed first draft of the key interactions in six to eight weeks; iteration and additional detail may take another four to eight, depending on the issues we encounter." This kind of estimate is easier for a constrained renovation than for a brand new product or extensive redesign.

It's not possible to provide a specific formula for scoping a project because this depends on your experience with similar projects, the skill level of your team, the amount of support they'll have, and the amount of time they can dedicate to the project. Any time estimates provided in this book are based on typical timeframes for teams who are trained and experienced in a shared method, dedicated to just one project on any given day, and well supported by senior designers—the ideal scenario. Most people should adjust these numbers upward.

You'll be much better at estimating projects after you've done a number of them using a consistent method; if you're trying to estimate your first project, get help doing so if you can and pad your estimates if you can't. Even a seasoned project lead can seldom develop an accurate multidisciplinary project plan without help.

Project plan development is usually an iterative process. Propose what you believe will best accomplish the project's goals, explicitly define what the design team can and cannot accomplish during that timeframe, and articulate any assumptions about the frequency of collaboration meetings, support you need from outside the design team, turnaround time for feedback, or other aspects of the project that may affect how quickly you work. Help stakeholders understand where they are giving up certainty or thoroughness for speed, since this introduces some risk of rework later. Rough out two different plans in detail if the stakeholders need that to understand their choices.

Communicate assumptions, priorities, and any specifics about what's in or out of scope at the same time that you share the project plan. Distinguish informal check-ins and small group working meetings from major meetings requiring all stakeholders. Be specific about what you'll need from various stakeholders at different points in the project.

For each phase outlined below, there is an example project plan for a large communications system project. The example assumes a reasonable but not quite ideal budget. You'll find more detail on the specific activities in each phase, along with advice for scoping the effort required, in the relevant chapters.

Note that the following outline of project planning is an overview; you'll find more detailed discussions of scheduling and other project management considerations alongside the detailed discussions of process throughout the book.

Research

The two biggest factors in determining how much time research takes are how many people you need to interview and how much travel will be required. Plan on a day for the project lead to brief the rest of the team if they haven't been involved to date, a day for a group meeting with the stakeholders and a few stakeholder interviews, and an additional day for every half-dozen stakeholders. (See Chapter 5 for more on identifying stakeholders.) In most cases, allow a day for every six user interviews if they're in one location, plus travel time to move between locations. Don't plan on doing your flying in the evenings because interviewing is very tiring; you'll become ineffective if you don't get enough rest. (See Chapter 6 for more detail on determining how many interviews you need.) Consider adding a couple of days for reviewing an existing product, looking at competitors, or doing more general industry research. Whether it's before the stakeholder interviews or after, allow anywhere from two to four weeks of lead time for getting user interviews scheduled in an efficient way; the design team need not be involved in this activity other than to guide it.

Trade-offs in research usually involve the number and variety of people and their locations. More interviewees can provide more certainty in the results, but more data will require more time to gather and analyze. I often give stakeholders two numbers: the number of people I'd like to interview and the number I believe is a bare minimum to get useful data. In some cases, the project owner may choose not to do research at all, other than what you can extract in an afternoon with the stakeholders. Most projects benefit from research, but it may be reasonable to skip it if the budget is tight and the design problem is constrained, familiar to the design team, and low risk for the company and its customers. The other big cost in research is usually travel; doing only local research can save considerable time and money, but may lead to critical holes in the data on some projects. See Chapter 6 for more on when a geographically diverse sample is important.

In the example plan for this phase, outlined in Table 3.1, there are 15 stakeholders to interview. The team is conducting a hefty 40 user interviews in four geographic regions. A few interviews are

Table 3.1. **Example project plan for research**

Day	Interaction designers (IxDs)	Visual designer (VisD)	Industrial designer (ID)
1	Design team briefing	Design team briefing	Design team briefing
2	Travel to client	Travel to client	Travel to client
3	Stakeholder kickoff	Stakeholder kickoff	Stakeholder kickoff
4	Stakeholder interviews	Stakeholder interviews	Stakeholder interviews
5	Stakeholder interviews, travel home for weekend	Stakeholder interviews, travel home for weekend	Stakeholder interviews, travel home for weekend
6	Travel to location #1	Travel to location #1	Technology and trend research
7	User interviews	User interviews	
8	User interviews	User interviews	
9	Travel home	Travel home	
10	Local interviews (location #2)	Local interviews (location #2)	
11	Travel to location #3		Travel to location #3
12	User interviews		User interviews
13	User interviews		User interviews
14	AM: user interviews PM: travel home		AM: user interviews PM: travel home
15	Local interviews		
16	Competitive system review	Competitive system review	Competitive system review

close to home. The visual designer and industrial designer each attend different user interviews to keep the interviewing team size and travel costs manageable. The team lead has been working interview planning and logistics for several weeks, so the team is ready to move from stakeholder interviews directly into user interviews.

Modeling and requirements definition

The amount of time necessary for modeling and requirements definition depends primarily on how much data there is to analyze. It won't take long to synthesize what you learned by grilling stakeholders for an afternoon, but any time you conduct a week or more of research with users, it typically takes a week or more to summarize your findings and develop personas, scenarios, and requirements. A large data set might require three weeks or more to analyze if you plan to be thorough. You can, of course, spend less time, but the amount of analysis time should always be scaled to the amount of research time; it doesn't make sense to have two days of analysis for three weeks of research or two weeks of analysis for just a handful of interviews.

The most common trade-off decision for these phases regards documentation. If you're doing a small amount of research or if the product team is small and not widely distributed, it often makes sense to summarize your findings, personas, and scenarios in slides and discuss any details verbally. When research is extensive or the product team is large, growing, or geographically widespread, a more detailed prose document ensures that the organization retains the maximum value from the research effort. It also provides a tool for educating new hires. The time difference is usually just three or four days, so the benefits of skimping on documentation are minimal.

In the example plan shown in Table 3.2, the budget is reasonable but not quite sufficient to have every team member be full-time.

Table 3.2. **Example project plan for modeling and requirements definition**

Day	IxDs	VisD	ID
17	Synthesis: stakeholder	Synthesis: stakeholder	Synthesis: stakeholder
18	Synthesis: user findings	Synthesis: user findings	Synthesis: user findings
19	Document findings; internal check-in	Document findings; internal check-in	Document findings; internal check-in
20	Begin personas		
21	Continue personas		
22	Finish persona characteristics and goals; internal check-in	Finish persona characteristics and goals; internal check-in	Finish persona characteristics and goals; internal check-in

Day	IxDs	VisD	ID
23	Refine and document personas; findings and personas check-in with project owner	Experience attributes; findings and personas check-in with project owner	Experience attributes; findings and personas check-in with project owner
24	Model development and internal check-in	Model development and internal check-in	Model development and internal check-in
25	Context scenarios and requirements	Context scenarios and requirements	Context scenarios and requirements
26	Context scenarios and requirements	Context scenarios and requirements	Context scenarios and requirements
27	Wrap up context scenarios and requirements, revise/add to findings	Wrap up context scenarios and requirements, revise/add to findings	Wrap up context scenarios and requirements, revise/add to findings
28	Refine scenarios and interaction design requirements, internal check-in, document outline	Refine experience attributes and visual design requirements, internal check-in, document outline	Refine experience attributes and hardware requirements, internal check-in, document outline
29	Scenarios and requirements check-in with project owner, begin first draft of document, presentation	Scenarios and requirements check-in with project owner, begin first draft of document, presentation	Scenarios and requirements check-in with project owner, begin first draft of document, presentation
30	Document and presentation first draft	Illustration of models, other illustrations	Illustrations, especially related to hardware
31	First drafts for internal review by end of day		
32	Document and presentation refinement	Document and presentation refinement	Document and presentation refinement
33	Finalize document and presentation, document to production by noon, practice presentation	Finalize document and presentation, document to production by noon, practice presentation	Finalize document and presentation, document to production by noon, practice presentation
34	Deliver to stakeholders and plan next steps	Deliver to stakeholders and plan next steps	Deliver to stakeholders and plan next steps

Framework definition

The big trade-off decision in framework definition is whether you're doing broad concept exploration (especially across multiple hardware platforms) or simply aiming for the first good solution you find. Developing a range of concepts is ideal with an ambitious design mandate, but not always feasible when deadlines and budgets are tight. In that case, the next best option is usually to focus on a single interaction framework and hardware architecture fairly quickly (since these are the most time-consuming aspects of broad exploration) but leave yourself some room to develop multiple design language options.

The tricky thing about planning the framework definition phase is estimating how quickly you can get to a coherent concept. This varies based on how complex the design problem is and how many unique software interfaces you think will exist. It's possible to develop a solid concept for a relatively simple, single-interface problem in just over a week, but this takes closer to two weeks when you consider assembling a presentation that will show exactly what is compelling about that concept; even the best design concepts seldom speak for themselves. A more complex or multi-interface product may take three to four weeks, occasionally even more,

especially if you're doing much exploration. Of course, any estimate of the number of unique interfaces and hardware platforms is only a hypothesis at this point unless the scope is very constrained, so be sure to state your assumptions when sharing the project plan.

Because this phase is intended to show work as soon as there's anything to show, it's nearly impossible to offer stakeholders trade-offs that will let them trim the amount of effort if you've already cut the exploration time. Multi-interface applications are the exception; you can choose to focus on a single interface in the interest of shipping it first, but this is very short-term thinking, because another week or two of effort will almost always save considerable rework later on.

Design language exploration for a single product nearly always fits within the same timeframe as the more structural design work, though it does take longer to define a design language that will span multiple products.

In the example framework definition plan shown in Table 3.3, the team's goal is to present a somewhat ambitious design approach based on novel hardware and a more conservative one based on readily available parts. For budget reasons, the exploration period is somewhat limited; it could be far more extensive.

Table 3.3. **Example project plan for framework definition**

Day	IxDs	VisD	ID
35	Exploration of form factor and rough interactions	Exploration of form factor and rough interactions	Exploration of form factor and rough interactions
36	Further exploration of on-screen interaction		Further exploration of form factors, begin hardware style studies

Day	IxDs	VisD	ID
37	Internal review of platform explorations, focus on two most promising directions	Internal review of platform explorations, focus on two most promising directions	Internal review of platform explorations, focus on two most promising directions
38	Refine interaction for platform #1	Begin visual language studies	Sketch 3-5 concepts for platform #1, work on design language, rough foam sketching
39	Refine interaction for platform #2	Refine visual language studies	Sketch 3-5 concepts for platform #2, work on design language, rough foam sketching
40	Refine interaction for both platforms	Refine visual language studies	Narrow concepts for platforms 1 and 2, work on design language, rough foam sketching
41	Internal review, refinement, planning for check-in with project owner and design engineers	Internal review, refinement, planning for check-in with project owner and design engineers	Internal review, refinement, planning for check-in with project owner and design engineers
42	Check-in with project owner and design engineers, refine	Check-in with project owner and design engineers, refine	Check-in with project owner and design engineers, narrow to 1-2 concepts for each platform to develop foam models
43	Refine #1		Refine concepts for platform #1, CAD modeling
44	Refine #2		Refine concepts for platform #2, CAD modeling
45	Refine #3		Give CAD files to model shop for quick foam models, work on rough surfacing
46	Internal review, identify areas to refine, plan presentation	Internal review, identify areas to refine, plan presentation	Internal review, identify areas to refine, plan presentation
47	IxDS drafts slides, IxDG draws screens	Slides for style studies	3D renderings, slides

Continued

Day	IxDs	VisD	ID
48	IxDS drafts slides, IxDG draws screens		Renderings, slides
49	Presentation review, refinement, practice	Presentation review, refinement, practice	Presentation review, refinement, practice
50	Deliver presentation to stakeholders and agree on next steps	Deliver presentation to stakeholders and agree on next steps	Deliver presentation to stakeholders and agree on next steps

Detailed design

There's no way to know exactly how long this will take even after the framework is defined, though estimates at that point should be reasonably close. Working out and documenting a detailed first-draft design for the key path scenarios (see Chapter 16) and visual system generally takes three to six weeks per distinct interface, depending on the complexity of the product; some very complex systems take months. Detailed industrial design usually takes at least two to three weeks for a single hardware architecture. For both hardware and software, iterating that first draft with the design engineers and working out every possible design detail could easily take twice that. Ideally, each interface evolves in parallel to some extent, but this is seldom the case due to time pressure on the development effort.

Delivering software design in chunks allows for significant amounts of construction to happen in parallel, which means the product is delivered sooner. There may be a small inefficiency when something has to change in part of the design that was already delivered, but if the design team does a good job of thinking through the whole system, these adjustments are fairly minor. Most stakeholders prefer the chunked approach to a monolithic deliverable, and it's generally more successful for all but the simplest designs that can't be carved up into distinct screens or tasks.

Delivering hardware design in chunks can be difficult, but the ID and mechanical engineer may be able to send out specs for prototyping certain parts while other parts are not quite finished.

While you can't plan each day in detail more than a few weeks out, you may be able to take an educated guess at what some of the functional chunks might be and how long it will take to get to a draft design. Be sure to allow time each week for collaboration with design engineers and subject matter experts, as well as collaboration among design disciplines. Build in time for internal design team reviews and stakeholder check-ins. Plan on drawing and documenting solutions taking about a quarter of the available time.

The software "cost-cutting" decision that many stakeholders are tempted to make, especially when hiring a consultancy, is to have the design team deliver the specification for design to cover the key path scenarios plus a bit more, leaving the product managers or engineers to fill in the gaps left by an incomplete specification. This is a false economy because a good design team can always do such detailed design work more effectively and efficiently than non-designers can. Stakeholders may also be tempted to get more design faster by trimming the collaboration time; this works in the short term, but often results in design that's harder to implement and needs more revision.

The example in Table 3.4 is not a complete detailed design project plan, but is simply an example of how to coordinate chunked delivery, starting with the first couple of segments. It's important to leave some time at the end of the schedule to clean up any inconsistencies that have crept into the design as a result of piecemeal design and documentation.

Don't forget to leave a few days at the end to ensure that all previously delivered chunks are consistent.

Table 3.4. **Example project plan for chunked delivery of detailed design for one interface**

Day	IxDs	VisD	ID
51	Detailed phase planning	Detailed phase planning	Detailed phase planning
52	Chunk 1 topic A scenario 1		Working meeting with design engineers to discuss latest manufacturing requirements, part count, material choice, and assembly methods.
53	Chunk 1 topic A scenario 2	Apply style to archetype #1	Refine form and design language
54	Internal review, refinement	Internal review, refinement	Internal review, refinement
55	Check-in with project owner, design engineers, SMEs, refine	Check-in with project owner, design engineers, SMEs, refine	Check-in with project owner, design engineers, SMEs; review mechanical engineer's work on final 3D database
56	Chunk 1 topic B	Apply style to archetype #2 and refine	Continue refining and reviewing ME's database, do foam models as needed for ergonomic adjustments, etc.
57	Chunk 1 topic C	Set up assets in shared file, begin draft of visual system	Continue refining
58	Chunk 1 topic D	Refine	Create color, material, and finish (CMF) specs, do photorealistic renderings from ME database
59	Internal review, refinement	Internal review, refinement	Internal review, refinement

Continued

Day	IxDs	VisD	ID
60	Check-in with project owner, design engineers, SMEs, refine	Check-in with project owner, design engineers, SMEs, refine	Check-in with project owner, design engineers, SMEs, refine
61	Draw and document chunk 1	Collaborate closely with IxD on screens, and with ID on surface graphics for appearance model(s)	Finalize 3D database and CMF specs for appearance model(s)
62	Draw and document chunk 1	Collaborate closely with IxD on screens	Finalize 3D database and CMF specs for appearance model(s) and prototypes
63	Draw and document chunk 1	Collaborate closely with IxD on screens	
64	Review and refine documentation	Review and refine documentation	
65	Deliver draft document for chunk 1	Deliver draft document for chunk 1	
66	Chunk 2 topic A	Refine system	Work with model vendor to fine-tune appearance model colors, finishes, etc. as needed
67	Chunk 2 topic A	Refine system	
68	Chunk 2 topic B	Archetype #3	
69	Internal review, refine	Internal review, refine	
70	Check-in with project owner, design engineers, SMEs, get feedback on chunk 1	Check-in with project owner, design engineers, SMEs, get feedback on chunk 1	Check-in with project owner, design engineers, SMEs, get feedback on appearance model
71	Refine chunk 1	Refine system, begin draft styleguide	Working meeting with design engineers, assembly, parts issues
72	Draw and document changes to chunk 1	Draw and document changes to chunk 1	Refine CAD specs as needed

Day	IxDs	VisD	ID
73	Chunk 2 topic C	Refine system	Refine CAD specs as needed
74	Etc.	Etc.	Etc.

Ongoing support

Even when the design is considered both complete and final, some problems or questions inevitably arise. Many software issues focus on implementation difficulty, performance, or minor issues that were missed (or could not have been predicted) in engineering reviews during detailed design. Hardware issues tend to be related to manufacturing problems; ongoing involvement also gives the industrial designer a chance to control the quality of the end product.

In an ideal world, the design team continues to be available to the engineers on a regular basis. Specific office hours at least once a week are the best way to assure the engineers that there is a time to bring up their concerns, which tends to keep them from winging it. Office hours are useful even if the engineers have no specific concerns because they give the designers a chance to make sure that the implementation is true to the design intent.

Summary

Whatever your starting point in a project, it's possible to make it a success as long as you understand the stakeholders' expectations regarding the solution, as well as the timeline and investment required to achieve it. Work with stakeholders to make trade-off decisions that affect your thoroughness, speed, and budget and to develop realistic expectations for what you can accomplish within the given parameters; use this as the basis for a detailed plan from research through framework. Provide the best estimate you can for detailed design, while being clear that it's only a rough estimate. Be very specific about your assumptions, the support you need, and what your team will and won't do during the time you have. Even if you don't need a legal contract, the process of writing down your shared understanding of all these issues will lay the foundation for a better project.

CHAPTER 4

Research Fundamentals

To solve a problem, you must first understand it. Designers helping users solve complicated problems—flying an airplane, replacing a human knee, streamlining a supply chain, or modeling the potential damage from a hurricane—must understand an incredible range of things, from new vocabulary to intricate procedures that require a specialized license or degree to perform. Regardless of the degree of technical difficulty, all design problems involve at least one complex variable: human behavior. Even something as simple as organizing a digital music collection requires knowing how much music someone has, how she mentally categorizes it, and how her listening behavior differs in various circumstances.

Research is a systematic study to establish facts. Designers do research not only to grasp new vocabulary and understand unfamiliar processes, but also to fathom the needs, views, and goals of the people building, selling, buying, using, and maintaining a product or service. The right kind of research will give you the information you need to make good decisions from the highest level (who is your audience and what should you build for them?) to the lowest (how many characters should you allow in a medication name field?). Figure 4.1 provides an overview of the research process.

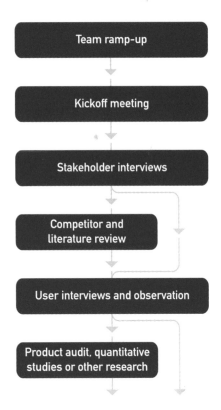

Figure 4.1. Research process overview.

Research

Benefits of Doing Research

Is it possible to design a great product or service without research? Absolutely. Any good designer can improve on something like online ordering or desktop file retrieval without doing much research. However, unless the problem is straightforward and very familiar, research is likely to reveal plenty of things you would not have considered.

Even if you feel confident that you understand what it will take to improve the user experience, it's worth considering the less obvious benefits of research. Solid research speeds up the decision-making process because it prevents much of the opinion-based wrangling that goes on among members of a product team; companies that don't start with good information about customers and users may waste months or even years getting a product out the door, only to find that the product doesn't meet the market need. Research is also a product designer's best persuasion tool; it's much easier to convince people you have a good design when you can back up your reasoning with data and not just your professional expertise. It's incredibly powerful to be able to say, "Yes, I understand why you'd think that, but let's compare that to what our research showed." When it's just your judgment versus the CEO's, you can guess who will win the argument.

Barriers to Doing Design Research

Considering that an organization is going to spend large amounts of time and money building and marketing a product or service, it seems like a good idea to understand the problems that product or service needs to solve, right? Unfortunately, you may have to persuade others that research is a good idea, and then persuade them to go about it in ways they may not be accustomed to. There are a number of reasons why organizations avoid research.

"It will cost too much and take too long."

Many executives are frightened off by the idea of research because they envision a university-scale effort that will take forever and cost a fortune. This need not be the case. Certainly, research in both corporate and academic contexts should be as objective as possible and should avoid shoddy technique. However, even if design research is more abbreviated than is ideal, a small amount of good data can still provide a greater level of confidence and a better-targeted product than most product development processes yield today. Also, you don't need to do research for every incremental revision to a product; although you will certainly tweak any product over time, you can typically rely on the results of good research for many years.

"We already did market research."

At Cooper, we often get calls from marketing people frustrated because they've spent piles of money on market research that doesn't help them make decisions. In other companies, you may hear the marketing department assert that they already know everything about customers because they've done extensive market research. From a design point of view, there are a couple of flaws in this assumption.

First, many companies conduct market research with the customers who buy the product, but ignore the people who use it. This is common in enterprise software, where marketing is often focused on the managers or IT people who buy the system, rather than on the people who will use it to do their jobs every day. Although pleasing the customer is absolutely essential, it's not enough to ensure long-term loyalty.

Second, even if the customer and user are the same person, typical market research provides insight into how to sell the product, but not how people will use it. For example, demographic data may tell you that N% of people who buy sport-utility vehicles have two children under the age of 10, an average income of $X, a mortgage of $Y, and a dog. Psychographic market research might tell you that safety and practicality are important to them. Both types of data are useful starting points, but neither will tell you what the average family uses their vehicle for, what knobs they're most likely to fiddle with when driving, or what things they bring along to keep the kids entertained in the back seat. Much of what is annoying about a product is the sort of thing you don't notice until after you've bought it—like the fact that a piece of software takes a dozen steps to do something that should take two. This is where design research helps, because it focuses on the context where the product will be used and the behavior of people in that context. Marketers generally understand what you mean if you tell them good marketing pulls the customers in, but good design makes them loyal.

When the marketing team says they have all the research you need, ask them to describe a typical user's desk, what information users employ in a typical day and for what reasons, or other specific behavioral questions. When they can't answer, you will have made the case for why a different type of research is necessary. Market research and design research are not the same things; Table 4.1 summarizes the key differences.

Many companies conduct market research with the customers who buy the product, but ignore the people who use it.

Table 4.1. **Market research versus design research.**

	Market research	Design research
Focus	Market size, initial sale	Satisfaction over time, initial sale
People involved	Customers	Customers and end users
Methods	Quantitative (usually surveys) or qualitative (usually focus groups)	Primarily qualitative (individual interviews and observation)
Good for learning about	— Market size and demographics — What makes people buy — What messaging will be appealing	— What to build and how it should behave — What makes people buy — What makes people loyal customers — What messaging and style will be appealing

"Our subject matter experts know the users."

If your product is in a complicated domain, your product team may include subject matter experts, who are often assumed to be experts on users, as well. If you have these people, do you really need to conduct user research? Absolutely! Subject matter experts usually have more industry knowledge than typical users do, so some will focus on best practices rather than the reality of user behavior. Some have narrow expertise that doesn't cover all the types of potential usage. In many cases, it's been a while since they've been in a user's shoes, or their perspective has shifted now that they're part of the product team. For example, on a project to design a medical device used by nurses in a hospital setting, I heard a nurse-turned-product-marketer suggest that we give nurses printers to belt around their waists, similar to the ones rental-car agents carry. This would be impractical because nurses in action are constantly bending, moving, lifting things, and squeezing in between beds and equipment. This particular marketer recognized the problem when it was pointed out, and this is probably an extreme example, but this unconscious shift in perspective is common.

Components of Design Research

Design research consists of multiple activities aimed at understanding the organization that will develop and sell the product or service, the people who will buy and use it, and the competitive marketplace.

The first part of your research should focus on understanding the business or organization creating the product or service. After a project kickoff meeting, the research starts with stakeholder and subject matter expert interviews, which inform the design team about the business and the domain

of the problem, while also allowing stakeholders to get familiar with the design team and project plan. This may include two or three days to review any marketing requirements documents, white papers, and previous versions of the product. The "business" component of design research might also include a brief review of competitive products, but it's seldom worth dwelling on this aspect for more than a day or two—you will leapfrog the competition by understanding users better than they do, not by studying what they've already done.

The remainder of the research focuses on understanding who the potential customers and users are, how they think and act, and what they need. In our consulting practice at Cooper, the design team lead does a limited amount of stakeholder research prior to the official kickoff meeting and lays out the user research plan ahead of time, since it can take a couple of weeks to schedule interviews. The whole team then does an official kickoff meeting and a more thorough round of stakeholder discussions. This is more efficient than having the whole team sit around for a couple of weeks while user interviews are being scheduled. If your team is in-house, you may find that it makes sense to do stakeholder interviews while you're wrapping up another project to allow time for recruiting users.

User Research Methods

There are numerous ways to collect data about prospective users and customers. The largest distinction is between **quantitative** methods, such as surveys, and **qualitative** ones, including focus groups and interviews.

Quantitative research about human behavior is useful if you're studying how long it takes people to scan text at various sizes or what size target provides the greatest accuracy on a touch screen. Such detailed ergonomic and cognitive studies are seldom practical or necessary for designing a specific product; thankfully, most of these fundamentals are easy enough to look up in the literature. Quantitative market studies are also useful when you're trying to identify how large a potential market is, what the typical demographics are, or whether enough people are using outdated technology to make backward compatibility worthwhile.

When it comes to understanding user behavior to inform design, though, qualitative methods are far more effective. You can conduct qualitative research with a small sample and a small amount of time (though some quantitative studies can be done quickly, too). Most important, qualitative techniques are better at revealing the information you need—how people behave, how they think about certain activities, and what factors affect their behavior and thought patterns. With qualitative techniques, it's also easier to change your approach midway through the research because you can very quickly see whether you are getting the necessary information.

Although qualitative techniques can be applied with considerable rigor, some people shy away from them because they feel less "scientific" or objective. This wariness about qualitative data tempts many people to give essentially qualitative information a quantitative veneer. For example, you might conduct a survey showing that 25% of people rate your product's usability a 3 out of 5 on a Likert scale, or note that 80% of people in a focus group prefer direction A to direction B. Such results can be difficult to translate into action; how does knowing that your usability rates a 3 out of 5 help you improve it? Even quantitative information about how long it takes test participants to complete certain tasks is more useful in identifying problems and supporting the argument for redesign than in actually solving the problems.

One of the greatest challenges in qualitative research is **self-reporting error**, in which people provide incorrect information not out of dishonesty, but because their memories or self-perception differ from their actual behavior. When I teach, I often illustrate this point by asking someone what he did before class that day. Most will say something like, "I got up, took a shower, ate breakfast, and got on the bus," to which my response is "So, you got on the bus naked?" Because getting ready in the morning is mostly habit, my victim is not very conscious of his own behavior, so he forgets to mention that he also brushed his teeth, fed the dog, checked the weather or traffic report, and oh, yes … got dressed. It's an absurd example, but just imagine if you designed someone's house and its contents around such a description—there would be no closet for clothes, no toothbrush … you get the idea. Some self-reporting error in qualitative data is inevitable,

When it comes to understanding user behavior to inform design, qualitative methods are generally far more effective than quantitative techniques.

Research

but when you're trying to understand what's going on inside a user's head, it's pretty much the only way to get information. It takes good technique to minimize this kind of error.

The qualitative approaches most commonly applied to product design are focus groups, individual interviews, direct observation of users, and a combination of interview and observation. Some people describe usability testing as a qualitative research technique, as well, though this is not entirely accurate. Table 4.2 summarizes the common methods and their uses.

Usability testing

There are several different usability testing techniques, but fundamentally, they all involve sitting prospective users down in front of either an existing product or some sort of prototype one at a time, and then asking them to perform specific tasks. This can be very useful in evaluating a design (more on this in Chapter 23) or in persuading people that there are problems; nothing beats watching user after frustrated user struggling with a simple task. However, unless you're expecting your redesign to be fairly limited, testing isn't that worthwhile as an up-front research technique, because, in many cases, the design will change so significantly that the results of testing the prior design are of little value.

Focus groups

Focus groups can be informative if you are just starting out and want to get quick feedback about whether a product idea is even viable. They can also be useful (with appropriate caution) in later stages, when you want a response to the aesthetic aspects of a design solution.

However, focus groups are not particularly helpful for understanding how people will use a product or service—you may get some initial ideas, but

they will be insufficient for design purposes. This is due to several factors. First, what you hear is affected by the group dynamic; things may tend toward consensus, when you actually want to see what the differences are, too. People may also be less forthcoming in a crowd, since they don't want to feel stupid or different. As an artificial environment, a focus group won't tell you anything about how lighting, sound, interruptions, or other aspects of the physical setting affect things. Finally, it's difficult to account for self-reporting error in a focus group, so you might just wind up building that house with no plumbing.

Individual interviews

Many product teams conduct individual user interviews to avoid the problems with group dynamics and allow for greater detail about individual behavior. However, an interview conducted in a conference room somewhere is subject to the same kind of self-reporting error found in focus groups, though there are types of questions that can help minimize this. Even though they are suboptimal for *users*, simple interviews will generally be the best option for *customers* who are not also users, since you don't need behavioral detail from them. Of course, if all you can get is conference-room interviews with users, that's still far better than no data at all.

Direct observation

Observing people as they go about their tasks is perhaps the best way to minimize self-reporting error (though of course there is the possibility of the observer's presence affecting behavior). Watching people interact with their usage environment reveals physical clues about the tasks they perform and the problems they may be having. There are challenges with direct observation, though. In order to see *all* of the behaviors related to your product, you might need to spend anywhere from one to several days observing each user, which is unlikely to be practical for you or for your participants. In addition, you may still be missing important tasks; for example, if you watched an accountant for several days but did not observe what happens at month-end close, you would miss critical parts of the job. Finally, observation alone won't help you understand and interpret what you're seeing, and you could come away with incorrect impressions.

Combining observation and interviews

No research approach is perfect, but combining observation with interviews will allow you to gather rich, useful information very quickly while minimizing self-reporting error. By spending time with individual users in their own environments, you can ask them to demonstrate their typical activities, while also getting their help in interpreting what you observe, since *why* people do something is often just as important as what they do or how they do it. The description of conducting user research in Chapter 7 will focus on this set of techniques.

Table 4.2. **Comparison of research methods.**

	Good for	Not good for
Quantitative measurement of detailed tasks	Deriving detailed design principles, such as how big a touch target should be in certain circumstances	Understanding what to design or how it should behave
Surveys	Understanding market demographics	Understanding what to design or how it should behave
Focus groups	Quick feedback on viability of a product idea Reactions to aesthetics	Understanding behavior, understanding differences between individuals
Usability testing	Demonstrating that a problem exists	Understanding what to design or how it should behave
Individual interviews	Understanding how individuals think	Minimizing self-reporting error, getting behavioral detail
Direct observation	Understanding how people behave in their actual contexts of use	Interpreting behavior, understanding how people think
Interview plus observation	Understanding how people behave in their actual contexts of use and why they behave as they do. Best for most circumstances.	Understanding market demographics

The Research Team

It is essential for several reasons that the people doing the design also conduct all of the interviews. They will be more effective at getting the data they need than anyone else will. While it's possible for a professional researcher who does not do design (such as an anthropologist or ethnographer) to capture good behavioral information, experienced designers are most able to distinguish potentially sticky design problems that require deep exploration from those that are fairly simple to solve and don't require a lot of detail. Although people who are experts in the project's domain may be better equipped to understand the detail of what they are seeing, designers who are not domain experts are more likely to ask the naive questions that illustrate how users think differently from the product team. (If one member of the product design team has been around the domain for a long time, it's a good idea to include a team member who is not so well versed.) In-person research is also important in keeping designers focused on reality; when you have seen multiple users struggle with the same things, that image will be impressed upon your brain in a way no one else's interview notes (or even photos and videos) can achieve.

Figure 4.2 shows typical team member participation in research. The two interaction designers should attend every interview, since identifying and addressing behavior patterns is primarily their responsibility. The other design team members—the design team lead

It is essential that the people doing the design also conduct all of the interviews.

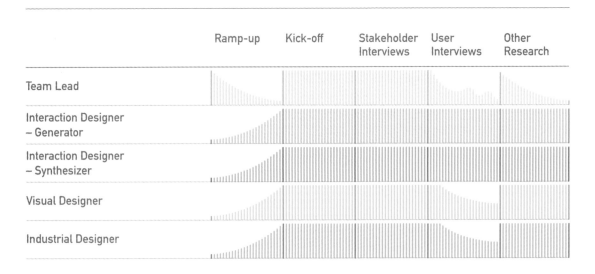

Figure 4.2. Team member participation in research.

(design director or similar role), visual designer and, if appropriate, an industrial designer—should attend at least a few interviews, but they need not attend all. Having four or five people in every interview can be expensive, intimidating for the participants, and impractical in most environments. Try to send only one of the part-time team members along on each interview.

Some methods advocate sending each member of the larger product development team out on a couple of interviews, then synthesizing the findings as a group. There are obvious benefits to this approach—every team member has an opportunity to see real users and (hopefully) empathize with them, and everyone presumably feels greater ownership because of this.

However, the disadvantages are numerous. It takes a considerable amount of time and expense to train people in research techniques; such training is important, since poor technique reduces the value and accuracy of qualitative data. Having too many interviewers also makes synthesis more difficult and time-consuming. Rather than being able to spot a behavior pattern quickly because you did a dozen interviews, you have to debrief from all those interviews as a group (which takes as long as doing the interviews themselves) and fill the walls with diagrams and sticky notes because no one's brain holds more than a couple of interviews. As an outsider, I consistently see that people who are close to the product—even if they have excellent interview skills—allow their own agendas to influence the interviews. Finally, each interviewer tends to cling to what she saw in the one or two interviews she did, which may be idiosyncratic, rather than being able to focus on the pattern that emerged from *all* of the interviews. Having two or three skilled people conduct the interviews avoids these problems, and there are other ways—including personas, scenarios, and good collaboration—to help the larger product team develop a sense of empathy and shared ownership.

Essential Research Skills

I discuss the issues particular to ethnography-based user research in Chapter 7, but a couple of skills—listening and capturing data—are essential to all research, whether it is with stakeholders, customers, or end users.

Active listening

One of the most important skills in design research is active listening. It sounds like a strange concept, since most of us listen to other people every day. However, most of that unconscious listening is half-hearted; we're thinking about what to have for lunch, or we're as interested in sharing our own stories and opinions as we are in listening to those of others.

To demonstrate this in classes, I sometimes give participants an exercise in which they have to listen to another person tell a story for three minutes without saying anything. The listeners are usually squirming in their seats by the end of the first minute, which makes them conscious of how much they really do talk during ordinary "listening." It's interesting to note, though, that the people speaking are usually a little bit uncomfortable after a couple of minutes, too, because they're not getting *any* reinforcement or encouragement from the listeners, which makes the speakers wonder if they're saying ridiculous or offensive things.

In research, it helps to focus not only on absorbing what the other person is saying, but also on encouraging them to say more and making sure you truly understand what you're hearing and observing. Doing that without injecting your own stories and thoughts into the interview takes conscious effort.

Research

Open-ended questions help prevent "leading the witness," which is one of the biggest potential problems in interviewing.

LISTEN WITHOUT THE MOTOR RUNNING

We all know that when we're listening to someone else, we shouldn't be thinking about our love lives or home-improvement projects, because if we are, we're going to miss some of what the other person is saying. In an interview, though, it's hard not to think about what question you want to ask next or what the design implications of the speaker's comments are. Instead, just accept that, once the interviewee finishes, you may have a brief pause in conversation while you take a moment to frame your next question. Once you have a bit of practice at it, this doesn't end up feeling odd to the interviewee; rather, it feels as if you're taking the time to absorb what they're saying instead of interrogating them with rapid-fire questions.

USE PRIMARILY OPEN-ENDED QUESTIONS

Whether they're stakeholders or end users, most people are eager to talk with you and willing to share detailed information. However, some questions elicit more and better information than others. A closed-ended question tells the person you're asking that a limited answer is all you're looking for. If you ask, "Do you like cheesecake?" for example, you're likely to get a yes or no response. If, instead, you ask, "What are some of your favorite desserts?" you'll get a much more extensive and useful answer.

Closed-ended questions usually start with phrases like "Do you" or "would you":

— Do you like your job?

— Would you use this feature?

— Do you think the product should be aimed at novices or intermediates?

Open-ended questions use the "five Ws and an H" questions taught to journalism students—who, what, where, when, why, and how:

— Who else relies on this information?

— What happens next?

— Where do you keep that information?

— When do you do that?

— Why is that particular ship date important?

— How do you go about changing that setting?

The structure of open-ended questions also helps prevent "leading the witness," which is one of the biggest potential problems in interviewing. Most of your interview questions should be open-ended.

However, closed-ended questions are useful for getting clarification or for redirecting an interview. Once in a while, you'll find an interviewee who rambles on, either getting sidetracked or providing far more detail than you need. It's off-putting to tell someone they're giving you too much detail or the topic isn't useful. Instead, when the speaker pauses, you can ask a closed-ended clarifying question to which you already know the answer, such as, "Do you do this every morning when you come into the office?" The interviewee will say, "Yes," thereby creating a natural pause that lets you ask a new question.

USE MINIMAL ENCOURAGERS

When I ask students in a class to listen without speaking at all for three minutes, there's a reason the speakers become uncomfortable, too: Most people with reasonable social skills seek some kind of affirmation that they're being heard and understood. What this affirmation looks like seems to vary slightly by culture; some view attentive silence with an occasional head nod as polite and appropriate, while others feel the listener is not engaged unless there are occasional questions or brief comments. When in doubt, assess how the speaker is responding to your approach and vary it accordingly.

Minimal encouragers are compact bits of verbal feedback that tell the speaker you're listening, understanding, and interested in what's being said. Many people use "Uh-huh" and "Mmm-hmm" noises in this fashion. Such little noises at the right moments tell the speaker that he's been understood, or that you see the importance of his point, though overusing these can leave the impression that you're *not* listening. "Could you say more about that?" is often a better option for encouraging detail while demonstrating that you're paying attention.

LOOK LIKE YOU'RE INTERESTED

Humans read a great deal into one another's facial expressions and body language. This may be one reason why telephone and video conferencing have not replaced in-person business meetings; when we are making major decisions, most of us want all of those little cues that tell us whether someone is credible, receptive, or skeptical. Pay attention to the signals you're sending with your body language. Slouching back in your chair says you're not engaged. Crossing your arms across your chest may imply that you're not receptive. Fidgeting says you're bored. Don't focus on your body language to the exclusion of the interview content, but if you tend to slouch, fidget, or frown, a little practice can't hurt.

PARAPHRASE WHAT YOU'RE HEARING

Sometimes what you think you hear isn't the same as what the speaker is trying to say, so it's a good idea to check in periodically and make sure you understand. One way to do this is to paraphrase your understanding of the key points. For example, "Do I understand correctly that you only generate this kind of document after creating that one?" This can also be an opportunity to elicit further information, such as, "It sounds like your biggest concerns are A, B, and C. Is that right, and do you have any others?" Of course, it would be both inefficient and annoying to do this sort of thing after every other sentence, so use it for the key points in the interview or when you really do need clarification.

PRACTICE

Active listening is a skill like any other, which means it takes practice. Try doing it in everyday interactions at the office or at home. The more you can practice outside of interviews, the more naturally it will come. After all, if you're focusing too much on how well you're using your active listening skills during a real interview, you're probably not listening very well.

Capturing the data

Whether you're interviewing a stakeholder or a prospective user, capturing the information is critical because, after an intense round of research, it's difficult to remember how many people you've interviewed, much less what they've all said and done.

TAKING NOTES

If you haven't done much note taking since your last college lecture class, it's time to dust off those skills. A typical interview contains even more content than the average lecture, and since you're conducting the interview at the same time, it's even harder to capture. Having one person lead the interview while another is the primary note taker helps, but everyone should take at least some notes because you'll each capture slightly different things.

A notebook or sketchbook with a hard cover is ideal, since in user interviews you may not have a writing surface. A laptop has the advantage of creating digital notes that are easy to share with your teammates, but it has two disadvantages: one, you may not have a good surface to set it on, and two, it can be off-putting for the interviewee to hear you typing and to have the laptop screen as a "wall" between you. A tablet PC (shown in Figure 4.3) may be a good compromise for some people, though most people find they write more slowly with a tablet than with paper.

AUDIO AND VIDEO RECORDING

Audio or video recording may seem like the obvious answer to capturing large amounts of data. The advantages are self-evident: You can focus on the interview rather than on taking notes, and you have an accurate and detailed record. There are significant disadvantages, however. Whether in stakeholder or user interviews, many people will be less forthcoming if they know they're being recorded, even if you assure them of confidentiality

Figure 4.3. A tablet PC allows electronic notes and audio recording without the awkwardness of a laptop.

(and if your boss or client demands to see the tape, are you really going to be able to refuse?). The things people don't want to say "on the record" are often the most valuable. Also, you'll either need to use a transcription service or spend your own time turning the recordings into notes you can use for easy reference.

Some interviewers like using Microsoft OneNote on a tablet PC, which records audio as you take notes, allowing you to tap on a phrase later and hear what was being said as you wrote it. This is a nice compromise between a thorough record and easily accessible notes. People may be a little less distressed because the tablet's microphone is unobtrusive; however, this doesn't mean you should record them without their consent.

If you do feel it's critical to record the interviews, consider video. Audio recording is fine for stakeholder discussions, but of limited use with user interviews since much of the data is visual. Introduce the camera or audio recorder in a casual way, such as, "Do you mind if we record the interview just to supplement our notes? It's hard to write everything down without missing something." Ideally, prepare the interviewee beforehand so the recording isn't a surprise. Make it clear that your recording is only for internal use. If the interviewee seems uncomfortable, don't push the issue. Use the smallest camcorder you can find so it's unobtrusive; hold it in front of your chest, rather than in front of your face, so the interviewee can look at you and be less conscious of the camera (see Figure 4.4).

PHOTOS

Bringing a little snapshot camera to an interview can help you attach faces to names and, in the case of user interviews, capture details about the usage environment. More people are comfortable being photographed than videotaped, since a photo doesn't create a record of what they're saying. Using a small camera and being very casual about it, as with audio or video recording, will make people more receptive. Using the camera built into your cell phone may make

Figure 4.4. Keep the camera unobtrusive to avoid making the interviewee self-conscious.

it even less of a big deal. When combined with good notes, a camera will usually be enough to capture what you need.

Summary

While you may have to persuade stakeholders to build in a little bit of time for design research, easier decisions and a better chance of meeting user needs are compelling reasons for making the investment. There are benefits to using multiple methods if you can afford it, but you'll get by far the most value from sending the design team to interview and observe people in their contexts of use. Chapters 6, 7, and 8 will help you plan and conduct this sort of research, while Chapter 9 describes other approaches.

CHAPTER 5

Understanding the Business

While we designers like to think of ourselves as advocating for end users, we're ultimately responsible for helping *our* customers: the employers or clients who hire us to help achieve certain organizational goals. This means every project should begin with understanding what the product or service is meant to accomplish. Is it primarily intended to build brand equity, reduce operational costs, or generate revenue? Blue-sky design won't be helpful if the tool is only meant to save the company $100,000 a year, but may be just the thing if it has the potential to bring in tens of millions. Why is the project important? What's driving the launch timeline? How ambitious a design is the organization capable of digesting? If you'd like to see your design make it out into the world instead of gathering dust on your shelf, these questions and many others about the business should be your point of departure.

Understanding the business starts with stakeholder interviews. As discussed in Chapter 2, stakeholders are the people in your organization (or your client's organization, if you're an outside consultant) who fund, build, test, market, sell, and support the product, plus anyone else who will influence the product's direction. Who these people are varies from company to company, but the most influential are usually a product marketing or product management executive, the technical lead, and—in an ideal world—an executive to whom both of those people report. Sales people are as influential as marketing in some cases, less so in others. Enterprise software companies often have influential professional services organizations (people responsible for customization and implementation at customer sites). You may also need to include someone from corporate marketing to discuss brand ideals and interpretation of the identity in the product. Subject matter experts may be stakeholders, also. In most companies, QA and support have very little authority or influence, but they often have useful information (and it's always helpful to be on their good side, anyway). Don't forget to account for other influencers, such as a consultant who has the CEO's ear or a long-time employee who is not in a management role, but is an opinion leader. Table 5.1 lists these stakeholders and the information they can offer.

Table 5.1. **Typical stakeholders to interview.**

Role	Typical titles	What they know about
Product marketing lead	Product manager, product marketing manager, program manager, director or manager of online marketing (for Web sites)	Business case, mandate for the product or service, customer characteristics
Technical lead	Director of engineering or R&D, architect	Existing technical parameters, capabilities of the engineering team
Executive	In large companies, a director or VP of products or marketing (for Web sites) In small or single-product companies, a CEO	Any of the above, plus a perspective that hopefully balances objectives (marketing) and capabilities (engineering)
Sales	VP or director of sales	Customers
Brand steward	Founder or CEO in small companies, director or VP of corporate marketing or brand strategy in larger ones	What the brand means and how it's evolving, where brand guidelines can be bent
Subject matter expert	Usually found in the product marketing or product management group	Domain, users (to some extent)
QA	Manager or director of QA	Another perspective on engineering skill level
Support	Technical support or customer service manager	Most common problems people have with the product
Professional services	Manager or director of professional services or consulting	Domain, customers, users (to some extent)
Other influencers	Variable; typically consultants or long-time employees	Variable

It's crucial for the design team to establish relationships with these stakeholders as early as possible. Some of these are the people with the initial vision for the product, which will obviously drive what you do. Others may not be decision-makers, but can get you off on the right foot when it comes to the business issues, the domain, and sometimes even the political landscape ("You should probably know that Jim's hot button is ..."). Early interviews are also an opportunity—sometimes your *only* opportunity—to build credibility and establish a line of communication with the stakeholders. It's possible they're still thinking of the design team as the people who will make the product pretty or fill the "easy to use" checkbox on the requirements list. By engaging the stakeholders at the right level, you can demonstrate that your work will be of far more than cosmetic value.

Identifying Stakeholders and Scheduling Interviews

If you're an insider, you may already have a good idea who the influential stakeholders are. You may also think interviewing them is not necessary, but avoid this trap; hearing that executive's point of view filtered through middle management isn't the same as hearing her thoughts in her own words. If you're a consultant, ask for your designated project owner's help in identifying stakeholders. Give that person the list of roles that are usually important to involve; advise him to include anyone else who has information you might need or whose opinion has the potential to derail the project later.

The number of stakeholder interviews varies quite a bit from company to company; a small startup may only have two or three, whereas a large corporation might have 50 stakeholders for a highly visible, political project, such as an intranet or corporate Web site. In reality, you're not likely to have 50 people who have significant influence on the direction of the project, but some organizations don't do a good job of distinguishing between interest in the project and influence over its direction. If you don't have time to interview them all, prioritize individual meetings with the decision-makers, top influencers, and people who have vital information, then conduct a brief group session with the rest.

Conduct stakeholder interviews in person when possible; it's easier to develop a rapport when you're face-to-face. Also, it gives stakeholders a chance to assess your credibility and goodwill, which are important to establish early on.

Try to speak with stakeholders individually. When it's necessary to group a few stakeholders together, keep them grouped by role (e.g., talk with several engineers and then several sales people, but don't mix the engineers and sales people). You need to hear about who is frustrated with whom and what the range of viewpoints is.

When scheduling stakeholder interviews, plan on having the whole design team attend, since every one of these discussions is likely to contain vital information. Allow for about an hour with most stakeholders,

Prioritize individual meetings with decision-makers, top influencers, and people who have vital information.

Research

Beware "torpedoes"— previously unseen stakeholders who can sneak up at high speed and blow the project out of the water.

sometimes two hours with a technical lead or subject matter expert. Also plan on longer interviews if you and the stakeholder are not fluent in the same language; you will at least experience some long pauses as you both think through your communication, even if you don't require a translator. Ask the stakeholders ahead of time to gather any white papers, specifications, or other information you think might be useful. The following sample invitation provides an example request for stakeholder participation.

Example of an invitation to stakeholders

As you may know, my colleagues and I are responsible for the product's design. We understand that you are ultimately responsible for marketing Product X. We'd like to schedule a one-hour meeting with you next week to discuss the project. We'll ask questions about your vision, goals, and concerns, as well as the role you expect to play in the project. We'd like to take advantage of your expertise, too, so we'll have plenty of questions about XCorp and the industry. We would also appreciate it if you could share any useful documents, such as MRDs, white papers, or competitive product information.

Within your team, outline the key topics you want to cover with each stakeholder. After each team member has done several projects, you'll find that preparation is minimal, since the information you need from each sort of stakeholder is fairly consistent from one project to another.

Beware invisible executives. A friend of mine calls them "torpedoes"— previously unseen stakeholders who can sneak up at high speed and blow the project out of the water. The product manager may seem to have total authority, but that's only true as long as the CEO or other senior manager agrees with the project's direction. If an executive sees something he doesn't like or understand, the project could experience a 180° turn at any point. Identifying the final authority can be difficult; the project owner is often oblivious to the potential for executive intervention. Listen closely in stakeholder interviews to identify likely issues. For example, "We tried to go that direction, but Dan hated it," should prompt you to ask, "Who's Dan? I haven't heard his name before..." Another option is to ask each stakeholder you interview if there are any key influencers not already on your list.

Once you have identified these people, it can still be tricky to get the project owner to let you talk with them. I use examples from past projects to make my case. On the negative side, I describe a couple of projects in which senior executives who were excluded for months disliked the final design because they hadn't been part of the thought process that got us there. In one case, we smoothed things out within a few days, but the other took several months of comparative usability testing before we could move on. On the positive side, I describe another project in which the client's internal project team had shown idea after idea to an executive, only to have him reject every one of them. As a result, they tried to "protect" our design team by excluding that executive from our interview list. We insisted on doing something the internal team hadn't done: We spent an hour asking him about his concerns, objectives, and ideas. It didn't take long to understand why he had rejected the earlier designs. When we later presented our initial concept, he said, "That's what I was looking for!" If we had not understood his concern, we might have gone down exactly the path he didn't want to see.

Officially "Kicking Off" the Project

For some reason, the business world is rife with military and sports-related language: deploy a product, kick off a project, employ tactics … perhaps it's because in business, just as in sports and the military, we have to rally the troops and get everyone on the same page of the playbook? Regardless of what we call it or why, an official project kick-off meeting is useful for several reasons. It:

— Draws everyone's attention to what may be a major effort.

— Sets expectations about how much of their time will be required and when.

— Gets all of the key stakeholders in the same room at the same time to discuss goals, deliverables, assumptions, and timelines.

— Exposes the whole team directly to the executives' vision, often for the first time.

Depending on how familiar the project is and how large the team is, a kickoff meeting will take anywhere from one to two-and-a-half hours. After introductions, start by recapping your understanding of the project's goals and parameters and then walk everyone through the project plan and a high-level overview of the method. Often, there are multiple people in the room who weren't involved with defining the project's parameters (or the decision to hire a consultant, if you are one), so chances are this is information they need. Highlight the dates of critical meetings (such as the presentation of findings, personas, and requirements, as well as the design framework discussion) and ask everyone to reserve them, since you'll need a full complement of stakeholders involved at each key decision point. See Figure 5.1.

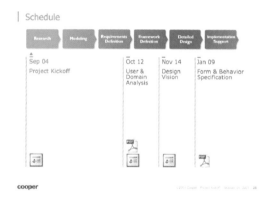

Figure 5.1. Example of a project schedule overview from a kick-off meeting.

The research plan might engender controversy if it's already been determined. Hopefully, the most knowledgeable stakeholders have had a hand in its creation, but in most organizations, everyone has an opinion. Make a note of any suggested additions or changes to the plan, and then check in later with your project owner to determine what, if anything, you should do about them.

Whenever possible, have a group discussion centered on a few basic stakeholder questions. This is easier with some groups than with others. In a small group of stakeholders who are comfortable with one another, a simple, facilitated discussion can be very effective. A group that's large or very conscious of what the most senior person in the room thinks may call for more elaborate facilitation tools. Write several essential questions on large sheets of paper and tape them to the walls, then give everyone a pen and some sticky notes to use in responding to the questions. Any of the questions from later in this chapter might be useful, but good starting points include:

— What is the product?
— Who will use it?
— What do users need?
— What customers and users are most important?
— What challenges do we face?

You can get creative with this and use different colors to distinguish hopes from concerns or facts from hypotheses, but don't make the color coding so elaborate that people have to think much about it. Once you've gathered everyone's thoughts, walk through them with the group, pointing out where there seems to be consensus. Use contrasting points of view as a basis for discussion with the large group, then pursue those topics further during the individual discussions.

Once the kick-off meeting is done, you'll proceed into stakeholder discussions. It's ideal to start with one or more of the executives primarily responsible for the vision, followed by several other stakeholders. Consider saving your project owner or one of the primary vision-keepers until the end, since that provides a good opportunity for clarification if you've heard a wide range of responses.

Conducting Stakeholder Interviews

Have one team member lead the discussion so the stakeholder doesn't feel overwhelmed. All design team members should take notes, though one person should be designated as the primary note taker. This is usually one of the interaction designers, since these two people attend all of the interviews. When the stakeholder is primarily concerned with brand or physical hardware, as opposed to product definition or software, the visual designer or industrial designer should lead the discussion. Team members who aren't driving the interview should, at a minimum, have a chance to ask a few questions before the primary interviewer changes topics, as well as at the end of the interview.

Getting started

Hopefully, each stakeholder has attended the project kick-off meeting and is already acquainted with the basic goals and timeline of the project; if not, that's a good place to start the discussion after everyone has been introduced. Before you start asking questions, talk about the way you'll be approaching the interview. One essential disclaimer is something like, "We're going to ask some deliberately naive questions. That doesn't mean we haven't done our homework—just that we want to hear *your* point of view." Without this disclaimer, I've seen stakeholders go back to the project owner and ask why they hired such dumb designers who clearly know nothing about the business. You might also reassure interviewees that you won't quote them to anyone else, although you are obliged to tell the project owner in general terms when you hear significant disagreements. This kind of anonymity is something an outside consultant can insist upon, but is harder to manage if you're an insider.

Things to watch out for

When it comes to design, everyone has opinions. You absolutely need to hear these ideas from stakeholders for a couple of reasons; first, there may be value in them, and second, telling the CEO you don't want to hear her design ideas is unlikely to help your career. Of course, you also need to know what everyone's pet ideas are so you can explain later why you didn't take that direction with the design.

However, don't take these assertions at face value—if the stakeholders had the design problem solved, you wouldn't be there. Keep in mind that some people—especially busy executives—communicate by proposing solutions when what they really mean is, "I see a problem and I want you to fix it." One of my clients had a running joke about how an executive would see an idea for the hardware design, sigh, flip open his cell phone, and tell them to make the large, complex device more like the phone. The whole team was frustrated because their complex medical device didn't have much in common with a cell phone, and the executive was frustrated because his team wasn't getting it. What he really meant was that they weren't exploring any ideas with hinges or moving parts, which would allow the bulky device to take up less space when not in use (resolving a common customer complaint with the existing device). The moral of the story is this: When you hear someone propose a specific solution, listen to the proposal, then ask what problem that solution is meant to solve.

You may also hear long lists of constraints, musts, and deadlines, not all of which are as real as people believe them to be. Always ask why the stakeholder believes an assumption to be true. One of the more common assertions is that the product has to be browser-based—in 2001, I think I heard that on every project I did; today,

people seem to be a little less thrilled with the idea, but it still comes up. This belief exists either because the customers are asking for it (and no one has asked the customers why they want it) or to avoid the need for individual workstation installation, which can be addressed in other ways. Deadlines are another good example. Although some deadlines are driven by external forces, such as the need to show something new at a critical industry event, others are arbitrary targets the management team sets because they're afraid of the product that never ships. If you know what's driving a deadline, you'll know whether it might be flexible.

The other thing to look for in stakeholder interviews is points of difference. In a perfect organization (if there is such a thing), all the stakeholders will say much the same things about the product, the customers, and the timeline, but some variation in views is normal. Pay attention to any extreme differences, as these represent both risks and opportunities. The risk is that such divergent perspectives could cause headaches in your future or derail the project entirely. The opportunity lies in using your later research data to help resolve those issues.

Topics applicable to most stakeholders

Try to keep the interview conversational rather than reading from a list of questions, but consider writing a list of topics on the inside cover of your notebook where you can glance at them when you get stuck. These are some questions applicable to most stakeholders; topics specific to particular stakeholder roles follow. Note that it's as important for in-house teams to ask most of these questions as it is for consultants; you may know *one* answer, but do you know this particular stakeholder's answer?

Research

What's your role with respect to this product?

If you're a consultant, the reason for this question is obvious, but even if you're an insider, you or one of your teammates may not understand someone's role as well as you think you do. It's also an easy, nonthreatening way to get the conversation started.

What did you do before this?

Answers to this question will tell you whether this person has some unexpected expertise to share and will give you some clues about how this person might view the world; a product manager who has a background in the domain but not in product management won't have the same concerns as an experienced product manager who doesn't know the industry.

What is this product or service supposed to be?

It's interesting to see what aspects of the product or service each person emphasizes. One of the key things to look for in the response is any hint of functionality no one has mentioned before, since this is important not only in helping the product team achieve consensus, but also in keeping the project timeline within bounds. Some stakeholders will answer you with an impenetrable wall of buzzwords: "It's a distributed, service-model three-tier architecture that will leverage existing technology," and so forth. In such cases, ask them to break down what that means by asking how they would explain what it does for the average user.

You'll also want to ask the reverse of this question: What is the product *not* meant to be? Some stakeholders have difficulty being realistic about what they can accomplish, so it's important to build consensus about boundaries as well as goals.

Expect a wide range of answers. With respect to software, this diversity is usually due to what

people think will be in the first (or next) version versus what will be in later versions. You may be able to clear things up by asking each interviewee to compare the immediate release to what the product will eventually become.

Who is this product for?

Although the marketing or product management people have the most informative answers to this question, the range of answers from other stakeholders can highlight issues your research will need to address. It's also important to know what assumptions there are about users so you can test them and see if they're true.

There may be variation due to a poor understanding of who the users are. On a recent project, for example, one stakeholder told us the product was going to be so indispensable that executive users would want to log in remotely from the airport, while another told us executives would only consume monthly reports generated by subordinates. Both agreed that executives were the targets for the information, but they had differing opinions about whether executives would see the information as so mission-critical that it had to be accessible at all times. This sort of variation doesn't mean the organization is dysfunctional; it just means people need better user data to clarify things.

When is the version we're designing going to be released?

It's normal to hear optimism from the marketing and sales people and pessimism from the engineers, but if the answers to this question differ by more than a month or so, mention it to your project owner. Also, don't forget to ask why the timeline is what it is. Sometimes there's a serious mismatch between goals and timeline—stakeholders may say this project is going to be the basis for all of their products in the next ten years, but they want to launch it in just a couple of months. Don't just let this slide; it will bite you later. Instead, point out the apparent contradiction and ask about it. "You've said the product has to be all things to all people. You've also said it has to ship by the end of this year. Those two things are potentially conflicting. Which is more important and why?" A reasonable executive stakeholder will clarify what the priorities are.

What worries you about this project? What's the worst thing that could happen?

This is a good topic for the later part of the interview, after the stakeholder has relaxed a bit. Sometimes the anxieties will be things you can help with, such as worries that the product won't have the right functionality. In other cases, the worries may point out organizational weaknesses you need to be aware of. While engineers always worry that there won't be enough time to build the product the way they'd like to (and they're always right), listen for truly unrealistic expectations. You may hear concerns beyond the usual level of grumbling that one part of the company is not up to doing what it needs to. If you hear that the marketing team is largely inexperienced in the product development world, you may be able to help by educating as you go. If it appears the engineering team is less capable than most, you'll either need to suggest some additional engineering resources if you're in a position to do so, or you'll need to be fairly conservative in your design.

What should this project accomplish for the business?

In a highly functional company, most stakeholders can answer this question to some extent, but it's amazing how often a senior executive is the only one who can do so. When this happens, you can help the organization by disseminating the business goals during the design process.

If stakeholders struggle with articulating this, try asking more specific questions: How will this product generate revenue? How will this product save money? How should this product affect the company's brand and position in the marketplace? What should the company be able to accomplish with the product that it hasn't before?

How will you, personally, define success for this project?

Many stakeholders will simply reiterate the business goal, or they'll say the thing they're most worried about won't happen. Some will give you insight into other things that worry them or what will get them excited about the design. You might hear things like, "If we just avoid this problem we've had before, I'll be happy," or "Other people in the company will finally see the value my team can offer." Understanding these issues is essential in building support for the design.

Is there anyone you think we need to speak with who isn't on our list? Who are those people?

Ask this one toward the end of the interview. Check in with the project owner later to see if discussion with any of the people mentioned is really a good idea.

How would you like to be involved in the rest of the project, and what's the best way to reach you?

This is a good one to save for last. It's an especially good opportunity to make sure the senior people stay involved at key decision points. If you have a middle manager who's reluctant to involve senior management, this gives you room to say, "The CEO specifically said she wanted to be involved in that meeting."

Marketing stakeholders

Marketing stakeholders (such as marketing executives and most product managers) are usually responsible for promoting the company's brand, identifying new market opportunities and products that could address them, or both. Most marketing people will immediately view designers as allies who will promote a customer-centric point of view. Some view designers as threatening rather than helpful, though; when you talk about doing research and driving some of the requirements, you may be treading on territory they view as theirs. If they've just spent hundreds of thousands of dollars on market research that doesn't provide the answers you need, you also have the potential to make them look bad. Talk about how the design team's work is *in addition to* theirs, not *instead of* it, and describe how you can help communicate their vision to the engineering team (which is often a point of frustration).

There are a number of questions the marketing people are best equipped to answer; some examples follow. The more brand-focused questions are things a visual or industrial designer will particularly want to know, though the answers can prove useful to the whole team. These questions are in no particular order; they generally fall somewhere in the middle of the questions for all stakeholders listed above.

Who are your customers and users today, and how do you want that to be different in five years?

It's essential to see where the marketing team wants to take the product or the brand, especially if it involves a change in direction. This will affect how you plan your user and customer interviews, since you won't want to limit your research to existing customers if the idea is to break into a new industry vertical. (Note that a consultant planning the research before the project kick-off should have asked this question at that time.)

Sometimes the vision is so ambitious that it sounds impossible. For example, the interviewee might paint a very broad picture about handling all types of business communication. This could turn into a monstrous product that attempts to replace phones, e-mail, instant messaging,

online conferencing, and more. Try asking what business they definitely *don't* want to be in.

Ask for clear timelines. Sometimes, the engineers think the marketers are unrealistic because they talk in very grandiose terms, but don't always clarify *when* they want the vision to be fully realized. Often, the marketing folks are talking about a five-year vision and don't expect the whole thing to be accomplished in the first release a year from now. This is one of many opportunities to help improve communication between groups.

How does this product fit into the overall product strategy?

If the product is part of a bigger suite of related offerings, you need to know what role it plays in that greater plan. For example, if you're designing the entry-level product in a set and the marketing team envisions getting people to upgrade as their needs change, you know you'll need to focus on giving that product limited-but-excellent capabilities and a design that can scale up. If they're envisioning the product as some sort of platform for future growth, you'll need some idea what those possible directions are if you're going to have any chance of anticipating them in the design.

Who are the biggest competitors and what worries you about them? How do you expect to differentiate this product?

While it's seldom helpful to spend a lot of time on competitive research unless you want to build a "me too" product, you at least need to know what else is out there. Ideally, you will get to interview and observe people using these competitive systems, too. Some people see the competition as the other companies trying to sell similar products, but be sure to discuss the hidden competition, which might even be some combination of paper, telephones, and face-to-face communication.

What three or four qualities do you want people to attribute to your company and your product?

In an established company, good marketing people have a clear answer to this sort of question, and that answer guides everything they do. This answer is essential when your mandate includes developing a unique design language for hardware or software. It can be useful for interaction design, as well; when you are presenting a particular bit of functionality or behavior, describing how it supports the brand values can be a powerful argument. Mind you, this argument works best with very brand-driven organizations, such as consumer product and service companies—in a company that thinks the brand is just the logo, you won't have much luck with this approach.

In organizations that are less sophisticated about brand, people may struggle with this question. This is where analogies can come in handy. Some people try to get at this information by asking, "If your company were a car, what kind of car would it be?" It can sound less silly and be more productive to frame the question in human terms, such as, "If your product were a person, how would you describe its qualities?" You might also ask for examples of other brands or products they think embody each attribute, and why.

Note that most larger companies separate product marketing and corporate marketing; the product marketing people may be focused more on understanding their particular segments, leaving the brand issues to the corporate people. If that's the case, ask this question of the corporate team.

What is the current state of the identity, and could we have a copy of the style guide (if there is one) and examples of it applied to materials?

This question is essential for consultants, but in-house teams probably have this information already. Like the previous question, this is more geared toward corporate marketing than product

marketing. In a company that's sophisticated about marketing, you'll see consistent visual themes across print and online collateral, as well as the visual and industrial design of products; you can look at any Apple product or marketing piece from ten feet away and immediately see that it's from Apple, for example.

In less sophisticated companies, you may see one style applied to print, another to the Web site, and still another applied to the products (or even worse, no consistent style across any of them). You might also find that the company has a style guide geared almost entirely toward print rather than pixels or hardware. If you're lucky, the style guide will at least take into account the visual design differences between print and Web design. It's a rare company, though, that has much of a style guide suited to digital product design, so visual and industrial designers must often interpret the spirit of those guidelines across platforms.

When the style guide doesn't seem appropriate to what you're designing, it's critical to get access to a senior brand stakeholder; a less-senior marketing person dedicated to a product or group often enforces the guidelines without seeing where they should be bent. For example, when my team was designing a phone for one company, the relatively junior marketing person assigned to the product told us it absolutely had to be a certain color and had to contain certain style elements common to the company's other phones, even though our mandate was total reinvention of the product family. When we were eventually able to get a senior marketing executive involved, he immediately understood why the parameters needed to be varied, so long as the design still conveyed the brand attributes in other ways. This is certainly a tricky situation when you're an in-house designer; your best option might be to let it go for now, but later try a style treatment that follows the guidelines and one that captures the spirit of the brand even if it breaks the guidelines.

Engineering stakeholders

Try to speak with engineering management as well as the design engineer(s), if such a role exists; it's seldom a good idea to involve the *entire* engineering team at this point. If there are no design engineers, a system architect and GUI lead may be the best option for software expertise. When hardware is required, be sure to involve the electrical and mechanical engineering leads, as well as anyone responsible for manufacturing.

Programmers and engineers may initially be wary of designers. They may have worked with people who called themselves designers, but who proposed horrendously difficult solutions that seemed "cool." Programmers may feel that designers are stepping on their toes, since some currently design screens themselves. You might also encounter mechanical engineers who view industrial designers as stylists rather than problem-solvers. However, any technical group's reluctance to give up control over design is usually due to the fact that so far, they've been the most competent to do it. It sometimes takes a while, but once they see that good designers can actually do a better job than they can, most engineers are delighted to let go of the design.

The focus and length of engineering interviews differs quite a bit between a new product and a revision of an existing one; in the first case, there is more room for the design to drive the technology, while in the second, the capabilities of the existing technology, when combined with the project budget and timeline, may introduce significant design limitations.

However, don't ask what you "can" and "can't" do, because in a healthy organization, that will be a business decision and not a technical one—although physics really does limit what you can do with hardware, there's very little you can't do with software given sufficient time and budget. Instead, ask what kinds of things would be hard to do and why. Engineers also tend to relax more when you say you're not trying to get them to commit to anything at this point, but simply to get a sense of what they already expect may be challenging. The following questions are helpful on most projects, though most projects call for additional, unique questions, too.

What technology decisions have already been made? What's driving them?

In the case of a new product, the technology decisions would ideally happen once the design started to take shape, but this is not always the case. When an existing product is being re-worked, the technology train may have left the station a long time ago; the software development platform or perhaps several of the electrical components may already have been identified. Even decisions that have already been made are sometimes unmade later, though, if the reasons are compelling enough. For example, one client told us they had already sunk millions of dollars into a particular system as the basis of their development. However, our later research showed that users had needs this system simply couldn't address. The company's executives weren't excited to see those millions go down the drain, but they were glad they'd learned about the issues before throwing away the additional millions they'd planned to spend.

How large is the engineering team assigned to the project, and what are their skills?

This is ideally determined by what the design requires, but in practice there may be a fixed number of people and days allotted to the work. As with technology decisions, though, designers often better serve the business by questioning such parameters than by accepting them. The most important thing to look for is a mismatch between the expectations for the product and the number and skills of the engineers. If you're designing a big enterprise product and there are only two developers assigned, you're going to run into trouble. Likewise, if the software or hardware team has very limited skills, you may need to scale back your design ambitions, though it's better to find a tactful way to encourage stakeholders to bring in the appropriate expertise if you can. Lack of skilled programmers was an enormous problem at the height of the dot-com boom, when companies hired anyone who'd taken an HTML class and called them software developers; this seems to be less of a problem during "bust" cycles, but is likely to crop up any time there is a shortage of talent. I've seen similar issues in organizations where mechanical engineers are only accustomed to doing plastic casings and not designing moving parts.

You may wonder how a designer can assess the skills of an engineer. In truth, most designers can't. However, if you have enough experience working with skilled people and less-skilled people, you'll learn that certain attitudes and behaviors tend to indicate skill level. If you hear engineers saying that something is impossibly hard when half of your last ten project teams were able to build it, you might start to wonder. It's also a bad sign when programmers are anxious about designs they can't assemble from off-the-shelf libraries; it could mean the timelines are ridiculously short or they've seen truly absurd solutions proposed, but sometimes it means they simply don't know how to build it. The most skilled programmers and engineers get excited about technical challenges, as long as the challenge is there for a good reason and the timeline is reasonably sane.

Could you draw a diagram and tell me in lay terms how the existing system works?

Sometimes this is important information; sometimes it isn't. You probably won't know until later whether you need it. Certain system limitations,

such as client-side data that's not always synchronized or response times that are very slow, can make interaction design more challenging. The same is true of hardware systems; if it won't be possible to change certain kinds of boards or other components, you may not have much room to change the form factor. Just be sure to take this information as food for thought, rather than as something carved in stone.

Note that there's a reason to ask for an explanation in both visual and lay terms, as shown in Figure 5.2, even if you think you're well versed in techno-speak—it encourages clarity and can be another indication of an engineer's skill level.

Figure 5.2. Example of an engineer's system diagram.

Sales stakeholders

Sometimes sales and marketing are lumped together in an organization, but most large companies split the two functions. In either case, sales and marketing people tend to have different concerns, so it's important to include one or more senior members of the sales group as part of the product team. This is true even in companies that ship consumer products, since the distributors or stores to which they sell have their own concerns about things like shelf space.

An enterprise system sales team is often closer to the customers than the marketing team is. In most cases, though, that doesn't mean they're closer to end users—IT tools and systems used by small groups of experts are the likeliest exceptions. They may also be more focused on the here and now, since they're getting evaluated and compensated based on today's sales, while the marketing group is more focused on the future. Sales people may be among the voices pushing to ship the product right away. However, this is tempered by the fact that sales people get an earful when the customers are unhappy, so it's not in their best interest to push for shipment of a product that isn't ready.

A sales person's biggest worry during design research is that there will be other people spending time with *his* customers, possibly making a bad impression, promising things he can't deliver, or saying something that will cause the customer to wait and buy next year's version instead of next month's incremental upgrade. It's important to acknowledge these concerns and to promise that you won't do any of these things.

Good questions for sales people often focus on what they hear from customers or see at customer sites.

Who is typically involved in the purchase decision?

This question will help you identify all of the right people for design research. For example, a hospital IT department may be the apparent customer for an information system, but you may not realize that the heads of medicine, nursing, the lab, and other departments are very influential.

Why do customers buy a product like this one, and why this one over a competitor's?

This is good preparation for later interviews with customers. A related but sometimes useful question is, "What one thing could we do to this product that would make sales easier?"

When you lose sales, what are the most common reasons?

People are sometimes puzzled at having a designer ask this kind of question, but it's helpful in identifying potential product weaknesses. In some cases, though, what customers say is not really what they mean. For example, when people cite a competitor's user interface as better, sometimes it's not that the behavior is better, but that the visual design is more attractive. In other cases, the deal is lost because the product lacks important functionality or the workflow is inferior. Naturally, there are also reasons that designers are less able to address, such as poor customer service or shoddy manufacturing, though these are worth pointing out to stakeholders.

What things do customers complain about or ask for most often, and why?

Customers, like stakeholders, may ask for certain solutions without identifying the problem they hope to solve; be sure to ask the sales person *why* customers are asking for particular things. Sales people often don't take the time to probe and learn the need behind the feature request, but the answer to this question may hint at some things to look for in customer and user interviews.

Senior executives

Ideally, there is at least one executive involved who has cross-functional authority and can balance the perspectives of both marketing and engineering; you need this person to make critical decisions, such as what's worth waiting a little longer for. These are usually the most critical stakeholder interviews because the way other team members approach product development depends on the views of the people at the top.

It can be difficult to get on a senior executive's schedule, particularly if the executives regard the product's design as a secondary concern. If they seem reluctant to spend the time, point out the kinds of strategic decisions that will be made in the course of the design work. However, most executives are more willing to spend this kind of time than people expect.

The concerns of senior executives may include any of the concerns mentioned above for marketing, sales, or engineering, as well as a common concern that they can't get their subordinates to "see the big picture."

What do we need to know that you don't think other members of your team have said?

Senior executives often have a vision or perspective that others in the organization don't. If they've shared that vision much at all, you will have heard it already from multiple people, but some executives communicate about their vision less than they think they do.

We know that both timeline and functionality are important, but if you had to choose one, which would it be?

When there seems to be some controversy about schedule, it's usually because senior executives are asking their teams to make omelettes without breaking any eggs. Mention the controversy; ask what timeline they want you to design for, and whether they would rather go to market with an incomplete product or delay shipment to get a product that meets more user needs. (Some designers frame this as "do it fast or do it right," but it's best to suspend this kind of judgment; sometimes, doing it "right" means shipping at a certain time to get critical revenue in the door, so trade-offs have to be made.)

Subject matter experts

If you are working on a consumer product or a business product that involves common work or life activities, you probably won't need domain

experts to help you understand what you see in your research. For products in complex industries, though, **subject matter experts** (SMEs) are incredibly helpful to have around—so helpful that you might want to hire a consultant to spend a few hours here and there, if there is no expert already on the product team. Even in-house designers with a lot of experience working on certain products can benefit from the perspective of people with deep industry expertise, though they may be able to skip some of the following questions. In-house SMEs are usually part of a product management or professional services group.

A subject matter expert isn't just someone who was a user (or did a similar job) once upon a time—it's someone who has broad and deep industry experience and who understands industry best (and worst) practices. If your product overlaps a couple of disciplines, it's best to have a SME in each; for example, when designing a device that delivers intravenous medication to patients in a hospital, we found it helpful to have the perspectives of both a pharmacy expert, who had a thorough understanding of the drugs, and a nursing expert, who had a thorough understanding of clinical practice. Beware of getting presumed SMEs who are a little outside their expertise, though—for example, a surgeon who spends his time in the operating room is not an expert in how nurses do their jobs on the hospital ward.

Unless they've worked with you before, SMEs will be more concerned than anyone else that you won't be able to understand their incredibly complex world, since it took them many years to get where they are. They usually wind up surprised at how quickly immersion in the usage environment can educate the design team. However, it's important to be clear that good research techniques will let you develop a working vocabulary and high-level understanding very quickly, but you will be absolutely reliant on the SMEs for their detailed knowledge.

Spend a couple of hours with SMEs before the user interviews to get some background. Get definitions of terms and ask about best and worst practices, common processes, and regulations. If you're talking about processes, ask the SME to diagram them on the whiteboard or do this yourself, using your sketches as a discussion tool.

Specific topics will vary by domain, but here are some typical topics to cover with SMEs.

What are the typical demographics and skills of potential users, and how much do these vary?

This information is handy for planning your interview sample, as well as for assessing how typical your actual interviewees seem to be in these respects.

What distinctions in user roles and tasks would you expect us to see?

A SME may be able to tell you about likely differences, such as tasks that vary based on seniority or skill levels that differ with geography. They probably won't be able to point out all of those factors that make people behave differently, but they should at least be able to give you enough background to help determine how large an interview sample you need.

What sorts of workflows or practices do you think we'll be seeing in the field?

Some SMEs will describe only the best practices in their industry, while others are very good at pointing out where reality tends to deviate from what people are supposed to do. This kind of discussion is a great way to think about topics you'll want to explore in user interviews. However, avoid getting into tremendous detail or spending more than an hour or so on this, because you will still want to look at user behavior from a fresh point of view. A certain amount of ignorance helps you ask the naive questions that can lead to important insights.

Other product team members

In theory, some organizations place QA and support on a par with marketing, sales, and development, but in practice, these organizations seldom have much influence over product direction. However, they may have a variety of useful insights; at a minimum, they will be able to answer two important questions. An experienced QA manager can often tell you how solid the engineering team is and can point out process holes that are currently leading to problems. The support or customer service team can tell you where users are most often encountering problems today, whether this is based on tech support calls for software or common failures for hardware—either could mean a flaw in the current design. In some companies, there are other groups that can provide useful information, as well, such as the training staff or technical writers, who may be able to identify where users most often get confused with the current products. Regulatory experts are also indispensable for medical products.

CHEAT SHEET

If you need a little help in your stakeholder interviews, tape a copy of this summary inside the front cover of your notebook.

Things to watch out for

— Presumed constraints—ask why they are constraints

— Jumping to solutions—ask what problem the solution would solve

All stakeholders

— What is your role in this project?

— What did you do before this?

— What is this product going to be?

— Who is this product for?

— When is the version we're designing going to be released?

— What worries you about this project? What's the worst thing that could happen?

— What should this project accomplish for the business?

— How will you, personally, define success for this project?

— Is there anyone you think we need to speak with who isn't on our list? Who?

— How would you like to be involved in the rest of the project, and what's the best way to reach you?

Marketing stakeholders

— Who are your customers and users today, and how do you want that to be different in five years?

— How does this product fit into the overall product strategy?

— Who are the biggest competitors and what worries you about them?

— How do you expect to differentiate this product?

— Using a few key words, how do you want people to see your brand (both the company brand and the product brand)?

— What is the current state of the identity, and can we see a style guide (if there is one) and examples of it applied to materials?

Engineering stakeholders

— What technology decisions have already been made, and how firm are they?

— How large is the development team assigned to the project, and what are their skills?

— Would you draw a diagram and tell me in lay terms how the system works? (existing products only)

Sales stakeholders

— Who is typically involved in the purchase decision?

— Why do customers buy a product like this one, and why this one over a competitor's?

— When you lose sales, what are the most common reasons?

— What things do customers complain about or ask for most often, and why?

Senior executives

Questions similar to those for marketing stakeholders, plus:

— What do I need to know that you don't think other members of your team have said?

— If you had to choose between going to market on schedule with a flawed product, or going to market late with a solid product, which would you choose? (if there seems to be some conflict on this point)

Subject matter experts

— What are the typical demographics and skills of potential users, and how much variation in these is typical?

— What distinctions in user roles and tasks would you expect us to see?

— What sorts of workflows or practices do you think we'll be seeing in the field?

Other product team members

— QA: What problems do you currently see in development?

— Support or customer service: What problems do you see most often?

— Training or technical documentation: Where do users most often get confused today?

Research

Project Management for Stakeholder Interviews

With good planning, most of your stakeholder interviews should fit within three or four days. Don't plan on more than six interviews in a day, since they require a lot more energy than most people expect—you have to absorb what people are saying, figure out what the implications are, lead an effective interview, and take thorough notes, all at the same time. A quick lunch and the occasional restroom break are essential. Plan on a short break after every couple of interviews to chat with your teammates, if possible. Table 5.2 shows an example schedule.

Try for at least a couple of the most critical stakeholders near the beginning of your schedule. If a few of the others need to be worked in between user interviews, that may not be a problem, but it's preferable to finish stakeholder discussions first. That way, you'll be aware of all the assumptions, opinions, and open issues you need to address in the user research.

Table 5.2. **Example stakeholder interview schedule.**

	Monday	**Tuesday**	**Wednesday**
8:00	Kickoff meeting		Simon Parker (European sales)
8:30			
9:00		Cristina Walker (clinical SME)	Nothing scheduled—debrief, review materials
9:30			
10:00			
10:30	Ellen Kent and Ed Lieberman (product managers), walk through existing system	Maria Torres (QA manager)	Marty Long (mechanical engineer) and Jay Adachi (electrical engineer)
11:00			
11:30		Lunch and debrief	
Noon	Lunch and debrief		Lunch and debrief
12:30		Vijay Gupta (GUI lead) and Adam Matievich (lead architect)	
1:00	Anders Haglund (sales VP)		Collin Smith (CEO)
1:30			
2:00	Ron LaFleur (products VP)	Cynthia Woo (corporate marketing)	Debrief, review schedule with Kate Riley (project owner)
2:30			

	Monday	Tuesday	Wednesday
3:00	Debrief	Debrief	Gunter Vering (professional services)
3:30	Tim Walsh (director of product management)	John McIntyre (support manager)	
4:00			Robin Sachs (regulatory issues)
4:30	Debrief, review schedule	Debrief, review schedule	

When You Can't Interview Stakeholders

The approach outlined above works well when you have an officially sanctioned project with support from the management team. If you don't, how can you get some of this information? First, consider trying to get some of these meetings anyway; you may be surprised at how willing some executives are to spend time with you if you ask for help. Send them a persuasive, thoughtful e-mail about how what they know could influence the design and how design decisions can affect business issues. Consider giving them a compelling article or short, interesting book on the subject. Seriously, try anything that won't get you fired, because their involvement is ultimately necessary for the project to succeed. The one thing that won't work is whining that you're being excluded—instead, show them something so impressive they'll see the value of including you for themselves.

If you simply cannot get access to the right people, see if you can get access to relevant documents they've created—white papers, memos, presentations, or whatever you can find. Build relationships with people in their departments so you can at least get indirect information. Above all, don't give up—keep looking for opportunities to get them involved. Otherwise, they may very well involve themselves later, often with unfortunate results.

Summary

Goal-Directed Design isn't just about accomplishing user goals; a product or service that doesn't also accomplish a business goal is a failure. Never shortchange your stakeholder research, even if it means compressing your time with potential users. Always:

— Identify the full range of stakeholders and meet with each

— Take advantage of the expertise that's available

— Learn about hopes, fears, beliefs, and goals

— Avoid taking assumptions at face value

— Remember that you're not just asking questions—you're also building essential relationships

Once you have a solid understanding of the business, you're ready to move on to research with potential customers and users.

CHAPTER 6

Planning User Research

Once you understand the basics of the business, it's time to move on to understanding the people who will buy and use the product. These may include the customers who make the purchase decision (as well as those who influence the decision), current users of the product or service, and potential users. Once in a while, there are also people who are affected by the product but never encounter it directly, such as hospital patients who are indirectly served by hospital information systems.

The object of planning is to ensure that your sample is broad enough to cover likely variations in behavior, but not so large that your time will be wasted. Hopefully, you will have at least a little bit of market data to use as a starting point. The marketing team and subject matter experts are the most helpful in planning, but other stakeholders may also have useful information. The stakeholder questions about customers and users (see Chapter 5) should yield the answers you need to get started.

In the rare case that your stakeholders can't at least give you educated guesses—such as in a brand-new startup—start with a focus group.

Cast a broad recruiting net and ask the participants about demographics, skills, roles, tasks, and issues. (See Chapter 9 for more on focus groups.) The following sections explain the planning steps in detail; there is also a summary chart for future reference.

Identifying the Number and Type of Interviewees

Your interview plan is a persona hypothesis of sorts, since you need to figure out what kinds of people you think will have different needs, goals, and ways of thinking. The planning process generally looks something like this:

— Identify likely user roles.

— Start with a minimum number based on how narrow the roles are.

— Multiply for the factors most likely to affect behavior.

— Look for ways to condense your schedule and incorporate other factors.

— Adjust for possible no-shows and poor interviews.

> **A role is defined largely by tasks; if you have types of users whose tasks will differ widely, you probably have distinct roles.**

Note that determining whom to interview is not an exact science; the numbers suggested here are simply based on patterns observed over hundreds of projects. If your instincts on a particular project tell you these numbers are insufficient, listen to them. If you think you can get away with fewer interviews, go ahead and try it—just be prepared to adjust your schedule later if you need to.

Step 1: Identify likely roles

From your stakeholder discussions, you should be able to develop an educated guess about the **roles** of the people who will buy, maintain, and use the product. A role is defined largely by tasks; if you have types of users whose tasks will differ widely, you probably have distinct roles.

In a business setting, user roles tend to align with job descriptions when the product's function is highly specialized, but may not always do so. With more generalized tools, such as operating systems and word-processing software, there will be a broad range of job titles that all fall into the same role. Consider the people who are likely to buy and maintain the product, as well. With consumer products, there is often just one role (a purchaser/user), but sometimes there are role distinctions that aren't obvious at first glance. Table 6.1 offers some examples.

Table 6.1. **Examples of likely roles for various design problems.**

Product	Expected roles	Relationship to job titles
E-mail system	— System administrator — E-mail account holder — External e-mail recipient — Purchase decision-maker	E-mail account holders have a variety of job titles.
Consumer digital camera	— Photographer — Buyer (usually the photographer)	Not applicable
Camera company Web site	— Potential buyer — Current camera owner — Camera dealer — Investor — Press — Job seeker	Not applicable

Product	Expected roles	Relationship to job titles
Inbound call center software	— Call center agent — Escalation agent — Call center supervisor — System administrator — Customer on the phone — Purchase decision-maker	Seem likely to map to job titles. Distinctions between agents and escalation agents may be blurry.
Complex purchasing application	— Person who requests things — Person who processes requests — Person who authorizes purchases — Person who receives shipments — Person who pays bills — System administrator — Purchase decision-maker	Most seem likely to map to job titles. People requesting things might have any job title.
Family calendaring system	— Family member — Perhaps one adult manages calendar	Not applicable
Device used to deliver intravenous medications in a hospital	— Person who administers medication — Person who prescribes medication — Person who dispenses medication — Person who monitors patients — Patient — Purchase decision maker	These seem likely to map to job titles (nurses, doctors, pharmacists, nursing aides).
Clothing store targeting women aged 25 to 40	— Woman shopping for her own clothing — Someone buying a gift	Not applicable

When estimating how many roles exist and what they are, consider the *entire* system, including any parts of it that may not be digital, such as a manager who consumes paper reports or a pharmacy assistant who gets computer-generated orders on a fax machine. Many business processes couldn't function without "sneaker-net"—people getting out of their chairs and walking down the hall to chat with colleagues.

Step 2: Determine the base number of interviewees per role

Next, you will need to determine the minimum number of people to interview from each role. The idea is to get an estimate of how much research you need to do, though you can expand or reduce that research plan if you find your estimates are off.

If the product or service is in a highly specialized industry with narrowly defined roles, such as stockbrokers or nurses, assume that you will need a minimum of about four interviewees per role; this is usually the minimum number required to see a behavior pattern. While this number may sound small, it's just a starting point; there are usually other factors that call for an increased sample size.

If you're designing for a broad consumer audience or widely used business product, such as a word processing tool, the minimum interview set needs to be larger because there is inevitably more variation in behavior. The factors that lead to those variations may be harder to predict, as well. The bare minimum is eight to 12; try for 20 when the range of behavior may be especially broad (such as with mobile phones).

Table 6.2 revisits our examples, adding in the estimated number of interviews for each role.

Table 6.2. **Potential number of interviewees per role.**

Product	Expected roles	Minimum number to interview
E-mail system	— System administrator	This is fairly specialized, so start with 4.
	— E-mail account holder	As long as the product is strictly e-mail, 12 would be a good starting point.
	— E-mail recipient	People who send e-mail also receive it, so you don't need to interview separately for this role.
	— Purchase decision-maker	These people seem unlikely to vary much, so start with 4 CTOs or other customers.
Consumer digital camera	— Photographer — Potential buyer	Emphasis is on use rather than purchase, so start with 12 photographers and 4 buyers (these roles may overlap).
Camera company Web site	— Potential buyer	Needs are probably varied, so start with 12.
	— Current owner of a camera made by that company	There is some overlap between these and buyers, so 4 current owners in addition to the 12 above should do.
	— Camera dealer	Dealers are fairly specialized, so start with 4.
	— Investor — Press — Job seeker	Timeline or budget may force you to skip such people. If so, you can represent them as provisional personas (see Chapter 11).

Product	Expected roles	Minimum number to interview
Inbound call center software	— Call center agent	Start with 4.
	— Escalation agent	Start with 4.
	— Call center supervisor	Start with 4.
	— System administrator	Start with 4.
	— Agent's customer	You could skip these interviews if you've been through similar pain. Otherwise, 4 will do for purely human support, but speak with 8 if they'll be using a phone tree.
	— Purchase decision-maker	Start with 4.
Purchasing application	— Requester	Start with 4.
	— Purchasing agent	Start with 4.
	— Authorizer	Start with 4.
	— Receiving	Start with 4.
	— Accounting	Start with 4.
	— System administrator	Start with 4.
	— Purchase decision-maker	Start with 4.
Family calendaring system	— Family member — Calendar manager	This one is potentially very broad, so aim for 20 and include a good number of parents (at least 8).
Device used to deliver IV medications	— Nurse	Start with 4.
	— Doctor	Start with 4.
	— Pharmacist	Start with 4.
	— Nursing aide	Start with 4.
	— Patient	Start with 4.
	— Purchase decision-maker	Start with 4.

Continued

Research

Product	Expected roles	Minimum number to interview
Clothing store	— Woman shopping for herself	12, perhaps 20 if the store sells everything from T-shirts to business suits.
	— Gift shopper	This is a less important target, so start with 4.

Step 3: Multiply for important factors

Next, you may need to increase the sample size based on other factors you expect to cause behavioral differences. What those are depends on whether you are looking at enterprise and productivity applications or at products and Web sites geared toward general consumers.

ENTERPRISE SETTINGS

With enterprise applications, the most common predictors of behavioral difference are company size and employee skill level; geography and industry may also have an effect, but typically to a lesser degree.

Company size usually affects the degree of specialization in a role; for example, a large company has one or more IT people focused on each system (such as the e-mail server, various applications, and the telephone system). In a small company, one or two less specialized (and therefore less expert) people must handle all of these systems. Company size also affects concerns with the scalability of a system and the cost of deploying it to each employee.

Varying **skill levels** are a factor in many industries, either because there are lengthy learning curves (such as in medicine or programming) or because there is high turnover (such as in call centers or retail).

Geography sometimes influences business processes; for example, practices in one country may be less flexible than those in another due to how much freedom employees have or how an industry is regulated. Whether you need to expand the set for local regulatory differences or cost structures depends on whether they are likely to affect behavior. Major distinctions, such as the difference between single-payer health care versus the system in the U.S., can have a significant effect on processes and decision-making, but minor differences in the forms people fill out can be accounted for later.

Industry is the last factor that often leads to behavioral variation. This is sometimes more of a work environment difference than a true industry distinction; for example, people in offices versus retail stores use telephones differently, but people in offices use them much the same way whether their company sells financial services or airplane parts. For industry-specific applications, there may also be important distinctions *within* that industry, such as insurance versus reinsurance, brokerages versus banks, or hospitals versus long-term care facilities.

CONSUMER ENVIRONMENTS

With consumer-focused or broadly targeted products, services, and Web sites, it's more difficult to generalize about factors that are likely to affect behavior.

One place to look for potential differences is across **demographics,** such as age, ethnicity, and gender. Gender and ethnicity make little difference in most cases, but can have a substantial impact on some behaviors and attitudes, such as willingness to seek health care. It's especially important to address gender differences in ergonomics; a device should fit comfortably in a woman's hand as well as a man's, and touch screens should account for men's larger fingers and women's often-longer fingernails. Age tends to have limited effects among working-age adults, but seniors and children often have specific concerns or physical needs. Children cover such a wide range of cognitive and physical development from infant to teenager that you may need to include several age ranges, depending on your target audience.

Differences in **family structure** (single adults, couples, people with or without children) can create important behavioral differences related to communication, time planning, and certain aspects of lifestyle. Having children may affect an adult's attitudes and priorities, as well.

Geography can sometimes make a difference in culture or economics, though globalization seems to be eroding some of those differences over time. Often the differences between urban and rural areas are as important as those between countries.

Enthusiasm can affect behavior in a couple of ways. Enthusiasts may demand more of a product, but they may also be willing to expend more effort to get it. For example, someone very serious about model trains may want to make the trains run on precise, realistic schedules, whereas a more casual user may just be thrilled that it's easy to make the trains run.

ACCOUNTING FOR OTHER FACTORS

The simple categories discussed so far account for a surprising amount of the variation within any user population, but on occasion, you may suspect from your own experience that other factors specific to the design problem will affect behavior. Just make sure your recruiting is based on factors you think will be **predictors** of different behavior, rather than on the behavior itself. In other words, if you specifically look for people who organize their photos into albums and for people who tag each individual photo with attributes, you're not only relying entirely on self reporting: you're also biasing your sample toward a behavior that may not be very common. If you believe that pros and serious amateur photographers are more likely to tag photos, recruit both serious and casual photographers to see if you're right. However, it's usually safe to use very distinct quantitative factors in your recruiting, such as looking for people who use the Web at least four times a month, in order to filter out people who aren't likely to use your product or service, or to ensure that you're getting frequent and infrequent users.

> Make sure your recruiting is based on factors you think will be *predictors* of different behavior, rather than on the behavior itself.

Marketing or sales people focused on a particular segment or region may assert that their customers are unique in some way. They may be right. They may also be playing company politics, but it's worthwhile to conduct the additional research anyway; if you don't, the sales team for that region may bog down the entire process by continuing to insist that the design doesn't suit their customers.

HOW ALL THIS TRANSLATES INTO NUMBERS

The ideal is to multiply the minimum numbers of users for each role by the number of different environments, age groups, or other factors you expect to affect behavior. For the moment, ignore factors that don't seem likely to affect behavior. Table 6.3 shows what this step might look like for our example projects.

Table 6.3. **Examples of increased sample sizes for key factors.**

Product	Expected roles	Minimum number to interview
E-mail system	— System administrator	Company size may affect specialization and skill, so double to 4 in small companies, 4 in big companies.
	— E-mail account holder	Size doesn't seem like a factor; stick with 12.
	— Purchase decision-maker	Company size may raise issues about scalability, so double to 4 in small companies, 4 in big ones.
Consumer digital camera	— Photographer — Potential buyer	Add 4 teens and/or 4 enthusiasts if this is the sort of camera they're likely to use.
Camera company Web site	— Potential buyer	Aim for 20 if the company makes cameras for both enthusiasts and average consumers.
	— Current owner	Increase your sample to 4 enthusiasts and 4 average consumers.
	— Camera dealer	Small and large stores and Web-only retailers may have different concerns; start with 4 of each.
Inbound call center software	— Call center agent	There are a lot of experienced agents, but there's high turnover, so expand to 4 experienced and 4 new.
	— Escalation agent	Low turnover means 4 should be fine.
	— Call center supervisor	4 should be fine.

Product	Expected roles	Minimum number to interview
	— System administrator	Double to 8 if targeting a range of company sizes.
	— Agent's customer	4 should be fine.
	— Purchase decision-maker	4 in small companies, 4 in big companies.
Complex purchasing application	— Requester	4 in small, four in big.
	— Purchasing agent	4 in big companies and 4 administrative assistants who handle purchasing in small companies. Purchasing for manufacturing is complicated and critical, so add 4 more.
	— Authorizer	4 in small, 4 in big.
	— Receiving	4 mailroom staff in big companies, 4 receptionists in small companies.
	— Accounting	4 accounts payable staff in big companies, 4 accountants or office managers in small ones.
	— System administrator	4 in small, 4 in big.
	— Purchase decision-maker	4 in small, 4 in big.
Family calendaring system	— Family member — Calendar manager	8 to 12 from each group: couples with children, couples without, single parents, children of various ages.
Device used to deliver IV medications	— Nurse	Oncology, intensive care, pediatric, and neonatal units differ from medical/surgical wards, so get 4 nurses per area. Should you double to account for the U.S. and Canada? See the next section.
	— Doctor	4 anesthesiologists, 4 physicians who prescribe but don't administer medication.
	— Pharmacist	4 should be fine.
	— Nursing aide	If nurses in various units have unique needs, do aides? SMEs say no, 4 will be fine.

Continued

Research

Product	Expected roles	Minimum number to interview
	— Patient	4 should be fine.
	— Purchaser	4 should be fine.
Clothing store	— Woman shopping for herself	You already have 20, but what about women with or without children to entertain as they shop? See the next section.
	— Gift shopper	4 should be enough.

Step 4: Trim the sample and incorporate other factors

Time and cost may become prohibitive when the numbers get large. Also, there comes a point when there's simply too much data to analyze in a reasonable timeframe. For most projects, the optimal sample size turns out to be the base number of people per role (usually four or eight) multiplied for your top one or two factors, such as three industries and two countries, or four age groups. For an enterprise product involving three to five roles, try not to have the total sample for all roles exceed 50 or so, because more interviews in one time period simply won't be manageable. For single-role products, a sample size of more than 20 is seldom necessary.

No doubt a quantitative researcher would argue that a sample size of 20 is hardly sufficient, but few companies are willing to expend the time and money on qualitative methods with a larger sample. It's not the best use of your budget, anyway. The idea is not to uncover every possible variation in human behavior (if that's even possible), but to see the range of normal behavior among different sorts of people, so you can reduce risk by accounting for most of it. If you want to verify certain things with quantitative data—and have the time and funds to do so—you can use the results of the qualitative research to help construct those studies.

DIVIDING YOUR SAMPLE

Once your sample shouldn't (or can't) get any larger, list any important factors you haven't accounted for; then divide your sample into groups that account for those factors. So, if multiplying four people × three roles × three industries × two countries gives you too many interviews—and after 72 interviews, your brain is guaranteed to be full!—you might instead divide by industry rather than multiplying by it, so you get a total of 24 interviews, with eight of them in each industry.

When possible, the demographics of your set should reflect those of your target market (e.g., 40% men and 60% women). However, you will seldom be able to do this when setting up enterprise interviews. Other than age, demographic factors seldom have enough impact to be multipliers, so divide your sample demographically unless you expect culture or gender to be a major factor. Most interface localization issues (such as language, currency, colors, and symbols) are easy to deal with later.

For revisions to existing products, ask the technical support or sales staff for a few unhappy customers and users; that unhappiness may point to design flaws. It may also highlight problems with reliability or customer service, which are outside your purview, but still helpful to pass along to the right people. If enterprise sales people are concerned about you damaging already fragile relationships, point out that—short of an immediate solution—nothing could be better than having someone go listen closely to the customer's concerns.

If your product already has competitors, including non-electronic or homegrown systems, interview a few people who are using them. The products themselves can skew the way people behave, so having a broader view will help you distinguish the behaviors inherent in the activity from the behaviors imposed by a particular product.

ACCOUNTING FOR ACCESSIBILITY

As designers, our ideal is to make products accessible to people with a wide range of abilities. However, the range of needs is vast; considerations for someone with impaired vision aren't necessarily the same as for someone with impaired fine-motor skills, for example. You would have to conduct a tremendous number of interviews to observe people with all of the possible challenges. Unless required by regulation, most businesses are unwilling to consider such an investment because, compared to the overall user population, the number of people with any specific challenge is relatively small. Your best option in these cases is often to rely on existing guidelines and any other insights you can find in the literature. Recent lawsuits regarding accessibility on major e-commerce sites may encourage more companies to invest in this area.

TRIMMING YOUR SAMPLE

If you still have too many interviews and you can't expand your timeline or budget, trim the interviews that seem less important or that you know the most about. For example, enterprise sales people probably understand the customer point of view reasonably well, so if you only talk with a couple of customers, that's better than reducing the number of end-user interviews.

If you have more than four interviewees in a narrowly defined role because you multiplied for other factors such as company size, you can use three instead of four as your base number of interviews (e.g., three people in big companies and three in small ones instead of four in each), because you'll still see enough overlap to identify patterns.

Where you expect considerable overlap between fuzzy roles, which is common in consumer domains, you may be able to trim by as much as 30 to 40 percent. For example, if your interview set for a camera maker's Web site includes 12 potential buyers and 12 current owners, you could

> For most projects, the optimal sample size turns out to be the base number of people per role (usually four) multiplied for your top one or two factors.

Research

trim six or eight of those people, since you can also talk with current owners about their buying behavior if their purchases were relatively recent.

When asked to reduce the number of interviews to the point where you won't be confident in the data, be sure the stakeholders understand that you'll also be less confident in your design solutions. The difference between a solid interview set and a weak one is often a matter of a few days, so many stakeholders can be persuaded to give you more

time or budget. If, on the other hand, your stakeholders are attached to larger quantities of interviews, be sure they understand that it may not be necessary and will also take longer to digest what you learn. Stakeholders generally appreciate knowing when they can spend less time and money, and pointing this out adds to your credibility if you need to ask for more time or budget later.

Table 6.4 shows how our varied interview sets might look after division and subtraction.

Table 6.4. **Examples of reduced interview samples.**

Product	Expected roles	Minimum number to interview
E-mail system	— System administrator	3 in small companies, 3 in big, including 1 to 2 unhappy users and 1 to 2 using a competitive product.
	— E-mail account holder	12 users (1 or 2 unhappy, 1 or 2 using a competitive product). Trim to 8 if necessary.
	— Purchase decision-maker	6 to 8, including 1 or 2 unhappy decision-makers and 1 to 2 who bought a competitor.
Consumer digital camera	— Photographer — Buyer	4 teens and 12 adults, half male and half female, 4 without children, 4 with young children, and 4 with older children.
Camera company Web site	— Potential buyer	20, including 10 enthusiasts and 10 non-enthusiasts. Divide the non-enthusiasts as you would the camera buyers above. Enthusiasts are better divided by the sort of photography they do (macro, wildlife, landscape, portraits and weddings, etc.).
	— Current owner	4 enthusiasts and 4 non-enthusiasts, divided as above. Half might overlap with the above, reducing total interviews by 4.
	— Camera dealer	12 dealers, including 1 to 2 unhappy ones and an equal mix of high volume and low volume.

Product	Expected roles	Minimum number to interview
Inbound call center software	— Call center agent	4 experienced agents, including 1 who takes some escalation calls, plus 4 newer agents.
	— Escalation agent	4 including 1 who takes some front-line calls.
	— Call center supervisor	Getting unhappy users and competitors into a group of just 4 supervisors might be hard, so increase to 6.
	— System administrator	4 at small companies and 4 at big ones, including 1 to 2 unhappy and 1 to 2 using competitive systems.
	— Agent's customer	4 should be fine.
	— Purchase decision-maker	4 at small companies and 4 at big ones, including 1 to 2 unhappy and 1 to 2 who bought competitive systems.
Purchasing application	— Requester	Ideally, 4 in small companies and 4 in big companies, but you could trim to 3 of each because it's a very small part of the system.
	— Purchasing agent	8 dedicated (including 4 in manufacturing) and 4 part-time.
	— Authorizer	2 to 3 in small companies and 2 to 3 in big ones should be fine, since it's a small part of the process.
	— Receiving	Ideally, 4 in small companies and 4 in big companies, but you could trim to 3 of each.
	— Accounting	4 dedicated and 4 part-time are still ideal, but you could trim to 3 of each.
	— System administrator	4 in large companies and 4 in small ones are still ideal, but you could trim to 3 of each.
	— Purchase decision-maker	3 in large companies and 3 in small ones.
Family calendaring system	— Family member — Calendar manager	Because you have such a large sample, you could trim to 8 from each group.

Continued

Product	Expected roles	Minimum number to interview
Device used to deliver IV medications	— Nurse	40 nurses (4 × 5 units × 2 countries) is excessive; trim to 3 × 5 units × 2 countries, or even 15 in one country and 10 in the other.
	— Doctor	4 prescribing doctors and 4 anesthesiologists are a small group; avoid trimming if possible.
	— Pharmacist	4 should be fine.
	— Nursing aide	4 should be fine.
	— Patient	4 should be fine.
	— Purchase decision maker	4 should be fine.
Clothing store	— Woman shopping for herself	20 women, including 4 with children.
	— Gift shopper	4 should be enough.

Step 5: Adjust for no-shows and poor interviews

Well-planned interviews usually go just fine, but once in a while you will have no-shows or site visits that simply don't go well. When you use a market research firm to recruit consumers, they will suggest how much to over-recruit in case of no-shows. Ten percent is a typical number but may vary a bit depending on where you are recruiting, what sort of people you are recruiting, and how much incentive you are offering. No-shows are rare in business settings, but consider planning for one site visit that goes poorly in some way. In a fast-paced environment such as a hospital, where you may be the last thing on the interviewee's mind, allow for two poor visits if possible.

Less-experienced interviewers should consider scheduling a few extra interviews for practice. If user interviews are so hard to schedule that you don't want to "waste" any of them by trying out

your skills, try doing a few practice interviews with friends or colleagues for one of the following exercises. If possible, get an experienced interviewer to observe you and offer some coaching.

Introducing the Practice Design Problems

Throughout the rest of the book, there will be a variety of exercises to help you apply what you've just read. To illustrate how one step follows from the last, many of those exercises will draw on one or both of the following fictional (but realistic) design problems. One is a business tool, while the other is directed at consumers.

Consumer device and service: LocalGuide

LocalGuide Systems (LGS) is a startup founded by two entrepreneurs: an expert in GPS technology and an expert in helping local governments promote tourism. Their vision is to launch a product and service (also called LocalGuide, of course) that uses GPS and wireless networking capabilities to provide rich information and advertisements appropriate to a user's location. LGS will initially contract with chambers of commerce or other local business associations to make the devices available at airport and hotel kiosks and other popular tourist spots. Visitors will rent the devices for a small fee or simply provide a security deposit, then return them to any LocalGuide kiosk.

The founders envision that the LocalGuide will give tourists (like the one in Figure 6.1) maps, directions, information about local history and landmarks, and a directory of services such as restaurants, shops, and transportation near each user's location. The LocalGuide will generate revenue through some combination of setup and licensing fees paid by the local organization, rental fees (if any) paid by end users, and advertising fees paid by local businesses (which could be higher when users act on ads by patronizing attractions or stores).

As is always the case with hardware, unit production cost will be a concern. The LCD is an expensive component, as is a touch screen if you opt for one. Using a commonly available LCD screen size and resolution would help with costs. Be prepared to justify the need for color if you use it. The engineers also need to know what kind of battery life is expected (standby time and in-use time).

Your mission is to define what the device and service do, then design how they work together in a seamless experience that will make a profit for LGS. Eventually, LGS wants to license the LocalGuide for other uses, such as educational and visitor information at museums and zoos or new student orientation on college campuses, so feel free to focus on one of these contexts if you prefer.

Figure 6.1. A tourist looks at a map at Fisherman's Wharf in San Francisco. The LocalGuide could provide far more useful information than a static map.

Business application: Room Finder

Finding and reserving meeting space at BigBizCo is a nightmare. Employees have difficulty finding rooms that are available at the desired meeting time, are the right size for the number of people meeting, and have the right equipment (such as projectors or videoconferencing equipment). They have to invite each room to the meeting to see if it's available; even this only works if they know the room's name in Microsoft Outlook, which doesn't tell them whether the space is suitable.

What makes this problem even worse is that many BigBizCo employees travel among offices, so they're often not familiar with the buildings in which they're trying to reserve rooms.

Employees have started to circumvent the problem by "squatting" in empty conference rooms, creating hassles later for the people who have reserved them. Some departments have begun staking claims to half a dozen specific conference rooms in their locations, refusing to let other teams use them even if the rooms are sitting empty, like the one in Figure 6.2. The department administrative assistants responsible for managing the rooms either have to force all scheduling to go through them, which creates a lot of work, or let anyone schedule the rooms, which can cause a different kind of work when the department's rooms are all booked and no one can find space.

Figure 6.2. Why is it so hard to find a conference room at BigBizCo?

The executive team has asked BigBizCo's IT department to solve the problem through technology. However, the budget is limited—the IT team can write code that connects to any of the existing systems, but cannot buy new hardware for more than 500 conference rooms. Currently, every room has an IP telephone (which has a speakerphone, six programmable function buttons with LCD text labels, and a two-line, monochrome text display). About two thirds of the rooms have a Windows PC with a wireless keyboard, mouse, network connection, and projector. About five percent of the rooms have videoconferencing equipment.

Exercise

Create a recruiting plan for the LocalGuide or BigBizCo. Use the following questions as a guide to get started:

— What kinds of customers would you interview?

— What user roles would you expect to see?

— What factors do you expect would affect behavior within each role?

— How many people with what characteristics would you interview for each role?

— If you only had the time and budget to interview a dozen users, how would you adjust your interview plan?

Recruiting and Scheduling

Determining what your interview set should be is the easy part; acquiring interviewees is more challenging. Difficulty with recruiting and scheduling is the most likely cause of project slippage. Allow yourself at least a couple of weeks to recruit, and preferably a month when planning enterprise site visits—willing participants are harder to find and less likely to fit your scheduling needs. This is especially true of fast-paced environments (such as hospitals) and for businesses under tight deadlines (such as accountants during tax season).

There are multiple ways to recruit interviewees. If you're designing enterprise software, the best option is to arrange site visits where you can interview people in multiple roles. If you're recruiting individuals—or if site visits are proving impossible to get—the options include market research firms, advertising, and recruiting at conferences. When you're truly desperate for interviewees, canvassing friends, family, and coworkers for contacts can yield results when other measures fail. Most of the following considerations apply whether you are able to visit interviewees in person or not; special considerations for remote interviews are addressed in Chapter 7.

Enterprise site visits

When designing any tool that will be used in a work setting, the ideal is to visit people in their work environments. This means arranging site visits with current and prospective customers. Try to get one person in each role in each company, though not all companies may have every role. Visiting multiple companies lets you see a wider range of behavior and business practices. Seeing how multiple roles work together within a single company will give you a good sense of overall workflow, which is critical for multi-role systems; seeing roles scattered piecemeal across multiple companies makes it hard to assemble a coherent mental picture of processes and relationships.

SITE VISITS WITH EXISTING CUSTOMERS

If you're revising an existing product or developing a new but related product, start by recruiting from the existing customer base. The sales staff can usually help you identify good companies to visit, once you've established a bit of trust (see Chapter 5). If a sales person still won't trust you alone with "his" customers, suggest that he come along as an observer.

Keep in mind that your needs are probably near the bottom of the sales person's priority list; she's evaluated and compensated on the sales she makes this quarter, so longer-term projects are not her focus. Help her help you by providing clear guidance about the kind of customers you want to visit. Tell her you don't want to visit only her most vocal or demanding clients, who are often demanding because their needs are atypical. Also watch out for "site-visit fatigue" if you're working for a large company that makes multiple products—it's entirely possible that some customers get asked for visits much too often.

Keep your requests simple. Rather than asking a sales person to arrange every detail of a visit, ask him to introduce you to a contact at the customer site; work with that person to schedule the specific interviews. An e-mail like this one usually helps:

Example sales team e-mail

As you may have heard, my colleagues and I are working on the design for version 3 of PurchasePro. To make sure the new version delights our customers (and hopefully makes your job easier), we're trying to get interviews with a variety of people involved in the purchasing process today. We're working with Terry to get U.S. visits, but could really use your help with Europe. Here's what we're looking for:

— 3 large companies who do purchasing for a manufacturing supply chain. We hear there are some companies who maintain inventory and others who do just-in-time purchasing, so it would be great if we got at least one of each.

— 3 smaller companies (about 100 people or less) that don't have dedicated purchasing agents.

We'd like to schedule a day with each company so we can interview purchasing agents, people who request and approve purchases, and people who handle receiving and accounting. (We know only the purchasing agents touch PurchasePro today, but we're hoping there are other opportunities to streamline the process.)

We would prefer to visit not just the most vocal customers or those who get visited frequently. If possible, we'd love to see an unhappy customer or two. Better yet, if you have any brand new customers who have just implemented PurchasePro or haven't installed it yet, it would be helpful if we could talk to them about the systems they've been using.

We're hoping to get all of our European visits done in the first two weeks of April so we can keep travel costs under control. We know you're busy, so if you could just introduce us to someone on-site and get them to agree to a visit, we can handle the details from there. We need to get our scheduling wrapped up in the next two weeks.

If your contacts need more detail before they can agree, here's the letter we'd be sending them: [attach a letter like the one below]

Of course, we'll copy you on our correspondence with each client. I'm happy to answer any questions or talk about any concerns you might have.

Provide your on-site contact with specifics about the types of people you want to observe and interview, how long you will need to spend, and what the interview will be like (i.e., observing people individually and discussing their work in their actual workspaces). Ask that supervisors not be present if possible—you need to see how people really work, not what they do when the boss is around.

The exception is when employees in a very secretive company are discussing a process they see as proprietary; interviewees may need a manager in the room to tell them what they can and can't discuss. Customer contacts usually want to steer you toward their best employees; ask specifically for some average employees, since you don't want to design the system for superstars. Some customer contacts may ask you to sign a nondisclosure agreement or refrain from taking photos on their premises, but this is more rare than you might expect. If you do want to take photos or videotape, it's a good idea to mention this beforehand so no one is surprised. Also consider carefully whether you want to be specific about what you're working on; sometimes being too specific can set customer expectations for a new product release in the near term. Here's an example of an e-mail to a site contact:

Example site contact e-mail

[Sales person name] gave me your contact information. As I'm sure he told you, my colleagues and I are working on the design for future products. We want to make sure we have an in-depth understanding of how customers like Acme Widgets handle purchasing and where we could better meet your needs in the future. Thanks very much for agreeing to help with our research!

We would like to speak with a variety of people involved in the purchasing process at Acme, preferably in each of the following roles:

— Someone who frequently requests purchases for manufacturing

— A purchasing agent who handles manufacturing requests

— A purchasing agent who handles non-manufacturing requests

— A manager who approves purchasing requests

— Someone in receiving who checks shipments against purchase orders

— Someone in accounts payable who handles purchasing-related invoices

— A system administrator responsible for configuration and maintenance

— A purchase decision maker. (I understand from [sales person] that you are this person.)

Would you be willing to schedule some time for us with typical people in each of these roles? If possible, we would like to have a private interview with each person in his or her work space for about an hour. There will be three of us, so we can crowd into a cubicle or small space to observe the process. We will be asking questions about how people use PurchasePro (if they use it today) and about purchasing-related activities that don't currently involve PurchasePro. We'll ask about each person's tasks, frustrations, objectives, and background, as well as how they share information with other people in the process. We may ask to take a few photos of various things in each person's work space; these will be used only for our own reference.

We will be in your area in early April. Would the 4th, 5th, or 6th work for you? We will only be able to spend one day at your site. We would be delighted if you could join us for lunch on whatever day we're able to visit.

Thanks again for your help. Please let me know if there are any questions or concerns I can address. You can reach me at...

Current customers are usually delighted that you are seeking their input to make their tools more effective, so other incentives are seldom required. However, most people will appreciate a small thank-you gift, even if it is just a nice little corporate giveaway for the interviewees or a box of chocolates for the person who arranged the interviews. In rare cases, you might need to offer a cash incentive if you can only speak with employees during their own time, such as at lunch or on a break.

SITE VISITS WITH SOMEONE ELSE'S CUSTOMERS

The biggest challenge in scheduling customer interviews is often in finding customers who don't currently use your product, whether that is because your product doesn't exist yet or because they work with a competitor. When you have no client base, you will need to visit prospective partners or customers if you have them. Otherwise, you may have to try recruiting through less conventional means. Advertising is seldom an option because you don't want to give away what you're doing, so using the personal contacts of subject matter experts or friends of friends is sometimes the only option.

"UNOFFICIAL" SITE VISITS

If your company or client does not support having you do site visits specifically for design research, the chances of getting the sales team to help you schedule them are pretty slim. Instead, you may have to try to get yourself invited on a visit being conducted for some other purpose. Build relationships with individual sales people or other staff who visit customers so you can ask to tag along on their next outing to get at least some contextual information.

ALTERNATIVES TO SITE VISITS

Unfortunately, there do not seem to be simple solutions to finding customer sites to visit; the typical market research firm does not offer any such service. If you simply cannot obtain site visits, consider some of the methods for recruiting individual users discussed in the next section. You will miss contextual data that would be available in the workplace; extra interviews can't entirely make up for this, but may help a little.

Recruiting individuals

Happily, there are more options for recruiting consumers than for arranging enterprise site visits. In-house research groups in some large companies can set up interviews with existing customers, though they may be less able to recruit prospective customers. More common options include market research firms, advertising, or—if you're desperate—the friends-and-family approach.

MARKET RESEARCH FIRMS

Market research firms are usually the best choice for recruiting consumers. Note that the common name for these firms is misleading; most specialize in recruiting participants rather than actually conducting the research, which is fine, since it's better for the design team to do this work.

Once you have identified the cities where you want to conduct research, look for firms with offices in those areas. Firms and individuals vary widely in their effectiveness; companies with good national reputations may have local offices that aren't up to snuff, and local independent operators may provide great results. Ask for recommendations from the marketing team or anyone else you know who has used recruiting services in that region. If there's no one you can ask, you may be able to get recommendations from other members of professional organizations, such as the Usability Professionals Association (www.upassoc.org).

The best firms can provide advice to maximize your recruiting effectiveness. At a minimum, you should expect that a good recruiter is organized,

communicative, and has a substantial database of possible interviewees. Avoid firms that suggest over-recruiting by a large percentage or that expect to be paid for no-shows. Most good firms work on a pay-for-performance basis, so avoid paying up-front "setup" fees.

When you've found several possible recruiters, get competitive quotes for the number and types of participants you need, as well as recommended participant incentives and a projected timeline for recruiting. The quotes you get will usually be very similar, but both recruiting costs and incentive costs vary by geography (big cities are more expensive) and type of recruit (busy professionals are more expensive). Don't be surprised by recruiting costs of $100 to $200 per participant and incentives of anywhere from $50 to $200 in most locations, or perhaps $300 for physicians, attorneys, or other highly compensated professionals. These quotes will be most accurate if you provide detailed information about your needs; any quote provided without some detailed parameters is suspect. You may get a small discount on recruiting if you also rent interview space.

When in-context interviews are not practical, you will need to use a market research facility or conference room. Avoid very large rooms and those with two-way mirrors; a small, private room with comfortable furnishings is usually better. Be sure to specify the physical setup of furniture and any equipment you will need (though it is usually cheaper to bring your own laptop or camcorder than to rent what the facility has). Most recruiters are willing to schedule interviewees for other locations, such as your office or the interviewee's home.

Using a screener

The most critical tool in working with a market research firm is a screener. This is a combination script and decision tree for the people calling prospective participants. A good recruiter will critique your screener and help you refine the questions at each step to encourage participation, but you'll probably want to create the first draft yourself. Be sure to review the screener with stakeholders before starting to recruit.

The ideal screener is relatively short and quickly eliminates ineligible people. Construct questions so they are black-and-white and don't require interpretation by the person doing the screening. Avoid any phrasing that tells the prospective participant what answer you're looking for, since some people may give desirable answers in order to participate. Also consider whether you want to reveal the product or company name to participants; most screeners avoid this to prevent potential bias. Along with each question, provide options such as "continue to next question," "stop," or "recruit up to N participants." It's a bit like writing simple code: if X, then go to line Y.

Table 6.5 is an example of what you might hand to the recruiter for the Acme camera Web site, if your target sample is a total of 20 people— ten enthusiasts (at least two of whom own Acme cameras, all of whom have a variety of photographic interests) and ten casual photographers (at least two of whom own Acme cameras, evenly distributed among people with young children, older children, and no children).

> The ideal screener is short, quickly eliminates ineligible people, and doesn't require interpretation by the person doing the screening.

Table 6.5. **Example screener for Acme Camera Web site research.**

	Question	Actions	Comments
1	Hello, this is _____ calling from Sprocket Research. Is _____ available?	Yes → Continue No → Ask when you can reach the participant. Thank the speaker for his or her help.	*Some firms have a standard greeting they prefer to use.*
	Once possible participant is on the phone:		
2	Hi, I'm _____ from Sprocket Research. If you have just a moment, could I ask you a few questions to see if you're eligible to participate in a study we'd be conducting next week? We're offering a $50 honorarium for an hour of your time.	Yes → Continue No → Okay, thanks for your time.	*Be vague about what the research is. Some firms prefer to discuss the incentive at the end.*

Continued

	Question	Actions	Comments
3	Great. First, would you be available to join us in San Francisco for about an hour on April 4th or 5th?	Yes → Continue No → End	*If they're not available, don't waste anyone's time.*
4	OK. Are you or any member of your immediate family employed by a camera manufacturer or anyone else in the photography industry?	Yes → End No → Continue	*This helps avoid anyone who works for a competitor or who knows more about the industry than the average consumer.*
5	OK. When are you considering buying a new camera or lenses—in the next six months, next year, more than a year, not considering, or don't know?	Next six months → Continue Other → End	*Multiple choice is better than yes or no, since it does not imply the desired answer.*
6	All right. Where do you intend to find information about a possible purchase: in magazines, from friends and family, at a store, or online? *(Circle responses)*	Online is one of the responses → Continue Online not mentioned → End	
7	Terrific. What brand of camera do you currently own? Acme, Canon, Fuji, Nikon, Olympus, Pentax, another brand, or no camera? *Brand:_____*	Acme → Continue unless 16 recruited Other brand or no camera → Continue unless 16 recruited	*Many people need a bit of prompting, but listing a number of brands conceals which brand you're interested in.*
8	OK. Would you consider yourself a professional photographer, photography enthusiast, casual photographer, or someone who almost never takes photos? *(Circle answer)*	Professional or enthusiast → Continue unless 14 recruited Casual → Skip to 11 unless 14 recruited Almost never → End	*Asking people to self-identify is a little risky, although these categories will be clear to many people.*
9	Great. Is your current camera an SLR or point-and-shoot?	SLR or both → Continue Point-and-shoot or don't know → End	*This will help eliminate anyone who doesn't fit your definition of enthusiast.*

	Question	Actions	Comments
10	OK, thanks. If you had to choose one category that best describes most of your photography, what would it be: in-studio, people and places, sports or action, wildlife, landscape, or macro? *(Circle answer)*	All answers → Recruit up to 2 for each answer Doesn't understand categories → End	*More risky self-reporting. However, someone who doesn't understand these categories is probably not an enthusiast.*
11	Many people who take photos of their children have specific photography needs. Do you have young children, school-age children, or no children?	Young or young and school-age → Recruit up to 4 School-age → Recruit up to 3 No children → Recruit up to 3	*If you must ask a question that may seem overly personal, a brief explanation of why you're asking it can help.*

Recruit

It sounds like you're a great fit for our study. Which of these times would work best for you? *(see schedule)*

Great, you're confirmed for [date and time]. You'll be coming to 100 First Street in San Francisco, on the corner of First and Mission. It's close to Montgomery station and the bus terminal. If you drive, you'll want to allow 15 minutes or so to park.

Please plan to arrive ten to 15 minutes early so we can get you signed in. If possible, please bring any information you've been using as you consider camera purchases, including a list of any Web sites you've looked at. A few samples of your photographs would be great, too.

If you're running late or need to reschedule, just give us a call at 555.123.4567. Any questions?

Excellent. Thanks for your time, and we'll see you on [date] at [time].

Include any information you want the recruiter to pass along to participants, such as items they should bring along.

End

Okay, it sounds like you don't quite fit the criteria for our study. Thanks very much for your time, and have a nice day.

Market research firms will often require a couple of weeks to complete the recruiting, so set a check-in point with the recruiter after two or three days. If recruiting is proving difficult, a good recruiter will suggest changes, such as alterations to the screener or incentive. Be sure to request copies of the screener worksheets so you know how participants responded.

Exercise

Develop a screener for one of the following:

— An online pharmacy

— A "smart" mobile phone that includes e-mail, calendaring, and basic office applications

— The LocalGuide (see the "Consumer device and service: LocalGuide" section earlier in this chapter for a description)

ADVERTISING

If you can't afford a market research firm, you can advertise online or in a targeted print publication to recruit. Online options include your own Web site, targeted discussion groups, or community sites such as craigslist.org. This approach means you will need to do your own screening and scheduling, so when you think about what your time is worth, it may be even more expensive than using a recruiter. However, internal teams often have more ability to spend time than money.

Because you generally have to advertise the incentive and at least a couple of your screening criteria, you may get a larger percentage of people responding just because they want the extra cash or think the study sounds like fun. Write a screener as you would for a market research firm; use it when someone responds to your ad. You will also get a larger percentage of no-shows, so over-recruit a little bit.

CONFERENCES AND EVENTS

If you're designing a professional tool, you may be able to take advantage of conferences or trade shows coming up. Put an ad in the conference program or recruit at your company's booth, then reserve a room at the conference venue to conduct interviews. You can still screen people

to make sure they meet the right criteria. The advantage of this approach is that you have easy access to a lot of people in one place and in a short timeframe. The disadvantage, of course, is that you won't get to see people in the context of use. You may be able to simulate a typical environment by, for example, setting up a PC with your application running. Without their own artifacts and tweaks to the system's configuration, though, most people can't provide entirely realistic data.

DESPERATE MEASURES

The friends-and-family plan is the recruiting mechanism of last resort. Obviously, it can be difficult to find the right sorts of people just through your own acquaintances or colleagues, and there's a good chance your sample will be skewed somehow. Still, when you're on a tight deadline and an even tighter budget, sometimes it's the only way to get user data.

As with other methods, be specific about what kinds of people you're looking for, the timeframe in which you need those people, and any incentive you can offer (even if it's just a cup of coffee when they meet you at the café).

PREPARING PARTICIPANTS

Once you've recruited your participants, you'll need to prepare them for their interviews. Send a note or verbally describe the interview process—how many people there will be, where you'd like to conduct the discussion, activities you'd like to observe, and the types of questions you'll ask (though not a detailed list of questions, as you'll see in Chapter 7). Be sure to indicate that you want to see their environment as it normally is, not cleaned up or prepared in any particular way.

If you must have interviewees come to a conference room or market research facility, ask them to bring along some relevant artifacts. For office workers, these might be forms, reports, or to-do lists. For consumer products, what you ask people to bring might be as varied as their current mobile phone or mp3 player, photos of their home environment, or the notes, Web sites, and articles they've been using to research new cars. If you're asked to conduct interviews in a conference room because conversation might be disruptive to the work environment, ask if you can get a five-minute tour of the interviewee's desk at the end of the hour.

Exercise

For the LocalGuide (described earlier in this chapter), draft an e-mail you would send to potential interviewees. Where would you like to conduct your research? If you were interviewing people outside the context of use, what artifacts, if any, would you ask them to bring?

The interview schedule

It's ideal to schedule the interviews for an hour and 15 minutes each if they are all in the same location; this allows for short breaks. Interviews will last 45 to 60 minutes for simple or consumer products, closer to 60 for more complex activities. The little bit of extra time between interviews will give you a minute to breathe, collect your thoughts, and strategize about the next interview. Scheduling is often easiest with teens, retirees, or people who work at home. If your interviewees are at work all day, your interviews will be easiest to schedule in the early morning and evening, which also means your interviews may be spread over more calendar days than they would take if scheduled back-to-back.

Try to avoid doing more than six interviews in a day—your brain will be so full that you will be less effective in the later interviews. You may also be surprised at how much energy it takes to keep the interview moving, be a great listener, and take useful notes all at the same time. Of course, if you only have a day at a particular site and you need to interview eight people, you will need to lengthen your interview day or minimize breaks between interviews. However, especially if you're traveling, resist the temptation to put in multiple long days and fly in the evenings. You may save calendar time, but you'll be so much less effective that you won't get the kind of value from the interviews that you would if you were rested.

Although consultants are often pressured to fit large numbers of interviews into very small timeframes, you might have a different problem if

A few minutes between interviews will give you time to breathe, collect your thoughts, and strategize.

If you aren't getting enough interviews to meet your original schedule, discuss the options with your stakeholders.

you're an in-house designer; pressures from other projects might make you inclined to spread out your interviews if the schedule allows for it. Consider spending at least half your time interviewing, though—the valuable thing about absorbing a lot of facts in a short period is that some of them are bound to stick together in your brain and form patterns more easily.

A typical project involves anywhere from a dozen to fifty interviews, so in theory, conducting the user research takes anywhere from two days to about nine days. In reality, there's usually some travel and project management time interspersed with the interviewing, so plan on a few days at the low end to a month on the high end if you have a lot of interviews that are scattered around the world. Of course, you can get very specific in your planning once you know where all of your interviews will be. Even so, many people underestimate travel time, especially when traveling to locations that aren't major airline hubs. Travel Web sites such as Expedia are great tools for estimating how long it takes to get from point A to point B.

Dealing with Challenges

If a design project schedule is going to slip at any point, the initial research is where it's most likely to happen, particularly when enterprise site visits are involved. Slippage seldom happens with consumer interviews provided you've allowed enough time for recruiting. If you aren't getting enough interviews to meet your original schedule, discuss the options with your stakeholders. Is it more important to hit the schedule knowing less than you'd like to, or is it better to add a week or two so you're more confident in your findings? It's usually worth another week or two to get the most out of the time you're already spending.

When time or cost constraints make it impossible to stretch the schedule, look for ways to minimize the impact of not having all the interviews you'd like. The best option is usually to spend your time between interviews talking with subject matter experts or hunting for information in other ways. See Chapter 9 for more on alternate research methods.

Summary

User research planning requires you to make an educated guess about what kind of sample will give you the best data in the shortest time, then use every resource at your disposal to find and schedule interviewees. It takes experience to make accurate guesstimates, but following the guidelines in this chapter should get you off to a good start:

— Identify likely roles.

— Begin with four users for narrowly defined roles, eight or 12 for broader ones.

— Multiply by the number of factors you think will be most critical.

— Divide by less critical factors.

— Trim if necessary, but allow for a couple of no-shows or poor interviews.

Don't underestimate the difficulty of scheduling interviews. Also be sure to plan a sane schedule; as you'll see in the next chapter, conducting effective interviews is harder than it looks.

Research

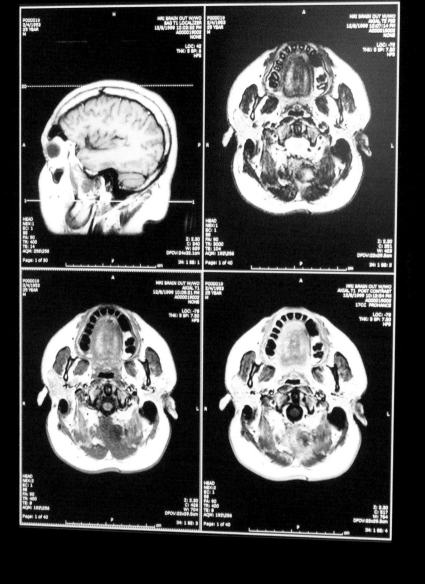

CHAPTER 7

Understanding Potential Users and Customers

There's a Dilbert comic strip in which the character says, "None of us has designed a nuclear power plant. In phase one we will gather customer requirements." In the next frame, one of Dilbert's colleagues sits with a wide-eyed energy consumer, saying, "So...you want free electricity, without mutating, unless the mutation gives you X-ray vision." Clearly, Scott Adams, Dilbert's creator, has encountered the most common way companies conduct research: by asking their customers what they want.

The problem with this approach is that customers and users are not experts in product design. There is a deeply held belief among some usability and design professionals that users are the *only* experts. I would argue that users are the only experts in what their problems are, but that they are seldom equipped with the expertise to solve those problems. It's a bit like the doctor-patient relationship: Patients have the best information about their symptoms and can assess whether particular treatment plans fit their lifestyles, but physicians are experts in diagnosing and treating. The right solution involves the knowledge and co-operation of both parties.

When people ask for feature X, it's often their way of identifying that they have a problem with how things work now; the suggested solution is sometimes workable, but a skilled designer can usually come up with a solution that's not only better, but that also suits the needs of a wide range of users. The techniques in this chapter will help you get beyond what customers and users say they want to what they really need. Chapter 8 is a dissection of an actual interview, which shows you how to put these techniques into practice.

Interviewing Customers in a Business Environment

Customers are the people who buy the product or service. The customer and user of most consumer products are one and the same. In a business environment, chances are the user and buyer are different people with different—even conflicting—needs. In some cases, there are a few customers who share the purchasing decision, such as the heads of IT, clinical operations, and business operations in a hospital. If you're designing an internal tool, your "customers" are probably one

In a business environment, chances are the user and buyer are different people with different—even conflicting—needs.

or two of your stakeholders, most likely the heads of whatever business functions the tool supports. Most of these customers never touch the product, or only do so to install and configure it, so interviews with them focus on goals and concerns rather than behavior. This makes stakeholder interviews somewhat simpler than user interviews.

When possible, interview the customer(s) at any site before meeting with the potential users. This will give you more context for how the various roles work together, so you can spend more of your precious time with users focused on their individual roles and less on how the company functions. Also, setting the stage with the customer will typically ease your entry into the user interviews. Once you establish a rapport with the customer, she is reassured that it will be worthwhile for other employees to spend time with you.

In many cases, the sales person for a particular customer account will want to accompany you to the interview. This can be helpful provided there's a good rapport between sales person and customer. However, some sales people can impede the interview by taking over, interjecting leading or otherwise unhelpful questions, or preventing you from asking questions to which they feel you should know the answers. Even if you've prepared the sales team with a note or phone conversation, a five-minute discussion of interview etiquette right before the meeting is a good idea. Ask the sales person to hang back during the interview, but say you'll be sure to defer to him for any customer questions. Also, plan on giving him a couple of minutes at the end for any questions of his own.

Customers are useful sources of two types of information: how the organization works and what their goals and concerns are related to purchasing and maintaining a product or service. If you're improving or adding well-understood functionality to an existing product, your interview focus can be fairly narrow. If you plan to launch a product unlike anything they've ever seen, your inquiry will of course be broader.

Begin the interview by thanking the customer for agreeing to meet with you. Introduce the members of your team and briefly state why you're there. You might be specific if this is a customer with whom your company has a close relationship. It's usually best, though, to be a little vague about what you'll be designing, just as in the introductory note described in the previous chapter.

Long-time customers occasionally have an expectation that everyone from your (or your client's) company should already understand their business. If you think this might be the case, consider explaining that because you're starting from scratch or doing significant rework, you're asking some deliberately naïve questions to make sure you don't make any bad assumptions.

Useful questions for customers

The following useful questions are applicable to most customer interviews, though they certainly don't cover everything you'll need to know from every customer. Don't take this for a script, however—keep the interview loose and conversational.

Could you please tell us a little bit about your background and your role here at (company)?

You may not always know going into an interview exactly what role this person plays. Is she the only decision-maker or one of several? Does his job title mean the same thing at this company as at other companies? Does he have an IT background or a business background? This information helps put the subsequent answers in context. This is also a good starting point for an interview because it's a simple, comfortable question this person has probably answered before.

How does (the function or process to be addressed by the product) work here at (company)?

This may seem like a vague question. It is. Some loquacious customers may respond by drawing you a process diagram or organizational chart, which is an excellent starting point. Others will give you a quick verbal summary, such as, "Someone initiates a purchase request in e-mail or in the purchasing system. It goes to one of our purchasing agents who gets quotes, bounces the best one to the right manager for approval, then places the order." Even this kind of brief answer will give you entry points to any number of additional questions. Still other customers, if they're especially frustrated, might jump right to: "How does it work?

Not very well!" This is your cue to ask about the problems, though that's usually a topic covered a bit later. The next question digs a bit deeper if the customer doesn't provide all the detail you need.

What are the different groups or roles involved in (whatever function or process the product will address) today? How do the various roles work together?

The customer will mention one or more job titles and hopefully elaborate on what they all do. Ideally, you will get some sense of sequence from this, as well. Don't hesitate to ask for it if you don't get it. If the process is complicated, consider asking the customer to draw a diagram of the workflow. Ask follow-up questions to get clarification or additional detail. Be sure to summarize your understanding and ask the interviewee if it's correct.

How does this compare to your previous companies?

If an interviewee has considerable industry experience, it's worth spending a couple of minutes to compare her current company to others. Although this information won't be terribly detailed, it's a good sanity check. You can skip this topic if you're short on time.

What are the biggest problems or inefficiencies in this process/function today?

Notice that this question still isn't asking about the product, but is looking at the business process or function. If the customer wants to zero in on the product, see if you can get him to broaden his focus a bit. This will allow you to see where there might be opportunities to address needs beyond what the customer or product team might be considering. The customer may not be able to diagnose why these problems occur, but between the customer and user interviews, the design team often can. The customer's perspective on this question likely differs from what users will tell you.

Note that a number of the issues raised may not be anything you can address with design, but may point out where business-process consulting, better support at installation, or better training and customer support could help.

What are the biggest problems with the product/system today?

This question is critical when the customer already has your system or a similar one, but not terribly useful if you're creating a new product category. Note that this question should come after the broader one—once you've focused the interviewee on a single product or system, it's more difficult to broaden the discussion again. If the customer is in IT, chances are these concerns will focus on things like installation and maintenance in addition to some common user complaints.

What are the best things about the product/system? Why did you choose it over other options?

While you don't want to sound like you're fishing for marketing quotes, it's important to understand what the most valuable aspects of the system are so you don't change those. Also, since you're asking for complaints—and you might get a lot of them—it's a good idea to have customers remind themselves of what they like about your product, if that's what they're using today.

Could you tell us more about the other systems that work with this one?

Few enterprise tools exist in isolation. Most are connected to other products or homegrown systems, often including antiquated legacy systems with severe limitations. This creates a fragile patchwork that's held together only by the constant attention of the IT staff. A seemingly minor change in one of those systems can cause tremendous amounts of rework, especially when it affects data structures. This is important to understand, since it may make

customers reluctant to adopt changes that don't provide significant benefit.

What issues have you been addressing with homegrown solutions?

When various systems don't play nicely together, IT groups often develop their own systems to mediate. The other reason for homegrown systems is usually that some otherwise-valuable tool doesn't do everything the users need. If the vendor isn't responsive or the cost structure seems prohibitive, something gets cobbled together. Either situation represents an opportunity for your product. If these internal tools don't work well, customers may be perfectly willing to throw them out for something better. A customer who has invested considerable resources on internal tools that work just fine may not care to adopt your solution, but chances are that another customer will.

What do you expect a system for (process/function) should do for (company)?

This question should begin to uncover some goals. Common responses include making people or business processes more efficient, cutting business operations or IT costs, or providing some capability that didn't exist before. You might hear about a desire to enforce certain business practices or regulatory compliance through rules or workflow in the software; this is an indicator that you should look for why users don't comply with the rules now.

What other factors are/were most important to you in selecting a product for (process/function)?

You'll often hear about things like total cost of ownership, ease of installation and updates, security, reliability, and other issues users may not mention unless they work in IT. Other responses probably overlap with the answer to the previous question.

Other questions and wrap-up

No doubt other questions will come to mind. Responses to each of these questions will provide opportunities for further exploration and will sometimes require clarification. Once your time is nearly up or you have all the information you need, offer to answer any questions the customer has. Establish a means to get in touch with one another later if necessary. Be sure to thank the customer again for her time.

What not to do when interviewing customers

When interviewing customers, it's important not to turn into the complaint department or the product expert. It's fine to make a note of a few concerns and let the customer know you'll pass them along to the customer service or sales team (if the sales person is not in the room with you). If you suspect those concerns are extensive, bring someone from support or sales along to have a separate discussion about anything that needs to be solved right away.

Never step on the toes of the sales person who got you the interview. It could damage the company's relationship with the customer and will definitely erode the sales team's trust in you. Don't make any promises to the customer other than, "We'll pass that along to the appropriate people," since the design team is almost never in a position to fix a customer's problem. Avoid specifics about what the new or updated product will do and when it will ship, since you may set expectations the company won't be able to live up to. If the sales person has set any rules about things you can't say or discuss, you can try to educate her if those rules will cause you problems, but in the end you need to follow those guidelines. The sales person knows things about that relationship that you don't.

If you work in a large company with many product groups, some favored customers may suffer from a sort of interview fatigue if they've been visited too often. This can make your interview feel like an imposition and can make customers cranky about answering questions they've already been asked. In your planning, try to find customers who haven't been interviewed in the last couple of years. If you can't find any, ask the sales person or previous interview teams for answers to some of the basic organizational questions each interviewer is likely to repeat.

Exercise

What specific questions would you ask customers if you were designing the Room Finder or LocalGuide? (See Chapter 6 for a description of each.)

When interviewing customers, it's important not to turn into the complaint department or the product expert.

Interviewing and Observing Prospective Users

Every good interaction designer I know is a keen observer of people, insatiably curious about how people think and what tools they use: Why does the ticket barcode scanner at an airport boarding gate sometimes beep and sometimes not? How does that ultrasound machine work? I know I'm supposed to be applying for a mortgage, but what's that software that has you so frustrated? User interviews are more than the world's best excuse for indulging your curiosity, though—they'll help you see the world through the eyes of other people. This is immensely valuable even when you have a good understanding of the design problem.

The interview setting

The best data comes from individual interviews conducted in the context where the product is (or will be) used. Interviewing people in context yields greater specificity and decreases self-reporting error. When people have artifacts around to prompt their memories, they're less likely to gloss over the details they don't usually think about. Looking around the home or work environment can give you clues to other good questions or issues, as well. For instance, if someone has instructions for using their voicemail taped to the telephone, as in Figure 7.1, it's probably an indicator that the current system does a poor job of supporting those tasks.

Try to avoid having the interviewee's supervisor or other third parties involved in the interview. It's essential that you understand the things people do to circumvent cumbersome systems or policies, but few people will confess to breaking the rules with the boss in the room. You might occasionally need to do a group interview but, as with focus groups, it can be difficult to get accurate detail on individual behavior. However, small group interviews can be appropriate for products normally used by groups, such as interactive museum exhibits.

Figure 7.1. This telephone has a small cheat sheet of common voicemail commands taped to it. It probably represents an opportunity for improving the design of the system.

Check in about appropriate dress before going to an interview. Some industries and regions are more formal than others—slacks and a sweater are fine at a California software company but unacceptable at a London insurance company. Avoid dressing too much better than your interviewees, though; wearing a suit on a factory floor will instantly mark you as an alien who's not to be trusted.

Essential techniques

An effective interview doesn't just provide useful facts; it also helps the interviewer understand how the interviewee sees the world. This is a good reason to use techniques borrowed from ethnography.

We designers often describe what we do as "ethnographic research." No doubt the average ethnographer would disagree with that assertion, but the parallels between ethnography and the most effective design research are striking. In his classic work[1] on the subject, James Spradley defines ethnography as the work of describing a culture from the native point of view. We're examining the native point of view, certainly, but are we really studying cultures?

In *The Rise of Anthropological Theory,*[2] Marvin Harris defines culture as "the behavior patterns associated with particular groups of people." Perhaps teenagers who text, golf course superintendents, or orthopedic surgeons don't really comprise their own "cultures" in the usual sense, but in each case, designers are outsiders who don't share the experience, vocabulary, or perspective of the interviewees (called **informants** in ethnography). Like ethnographers, we must strive to put aside our own assumptions and see the world through someone else's eyes. For example, most of us see a brown spot on the lawn as a minor annoyance, so we don't exactly stay awake at night wondering if the sprinkler system is properly adjusted. To the superintendent at an exclusive golf course, though, a brown spot on the fairway is a catastrophe that could lead to the unemployment line. If we assume a little dead grass means the same thing to the superintendent that it does to us, we won't be able to design an irrigation control system that meets his needs.

Conducting a great interview isn't only about asking the right kinds of questions; it's also about the attitude with which you approach the conversation. The following sections offer some principles to keep in mind.

MAKE IT A CONVERSATION, NOT AN INTERROGATION

A loose, conversational structure lends itself to open, revealing discussion. When you start interviewing, you won't yet know what you don't know, so any fixed set of questions you prepare beforehand is likely to be inadequate. Barreling through a detailed question list may mean you miss the opportunity to pursue unexpected (but potentially fruitful) lines of inquiry. It also tends to make interviewees feel like they're being interrogated. However, having a list of half a dozen topics taped inside the cover of your notebook can help if you draw a blank during the discussion.

> When people have artifacts to prompt their memories, they're less likely to gloss over details they don't usually think about.

Research

1. Spradley, J. *The ethnographic interview.* Wadsworth, 1979.

2. Harris, M. *The rise of anthropological theory: A history of theories of culture.* Routledge, 1969.

Establish a rapport before bringing up potentially touchy questions.

No matter how relaxed the discussion, though, don't forget this is an interview. Stick to the active listening techniques covered in Chapter 4. Keep the focus on the informant's experience rather than your own. The one exception to this rule is when you have a particularly shy interviewee (which is surprisingly rare); telling a brief story of your own early in the conversation can coax a reluctant participant to open up.

BE SYMPATHETIC AND NON-JUDGMENTAL

We all have unique challenges and points of view. Assume that your interviewee is a good and capable person. If he has a negative attitude about work, perhaps there's a reason; perhaps it's even due to a problem you could help solve. If she doesn't take her medication or follow her treatment plan, there's probably a reason for that, too.

Most people can tell if they're being judged, and it tends to make them reticent. If you can be a good, receptive listener, though, you may be surprised by the extent to which people share very personal information. When my team was designing the software for an early consumer Web cam, we naïvely expected to see grandparents chatting with little Tommy or watching bad video of a birthday party. Instead, we heard more about birthday suits than birthday parties—our random sample of adults mostly used their cameras for very adult activities. The first interview didn't go especially well; the interviewee could tell we were surprised by his story about making his own pay-per-view movies. Once we were prepared for this kind of thing to come up, we weren't surprised in subsequent interviews, so the other interviewees all felt comfortable enough to share the necessary details (and a few unnecessary ones). Being a sympathetic listener can get people to talk about almost anything!

BE THE LEARNER, NOT THE EXPERT

Try to establish a rapport with the interviewee before bringing up potentially touchy questions, such as frustrations, relationships with others, and so on. Think of yourself as a student learning how the informant does her job or lives a certain aspect of her life. Particularly in business settings, having someone look over one's shoulder can feel threatening, so adopting this mind-set will help you send those reassuring signals that the interviewee is the respected expert. Spradley describes this as encouraging elaboration by "expressing ignorance and interest" more often than you would in a typical conversation.

ASK NAÏVE QUESTIONS

As a consultant working in complex domains, such as healthcare and financial modeling, I've often been asked how the design team can possibly be effective in a field they don't know. I always respond that ignorance is actually a blessing; interviewers who believe they know the industry or topic very well tend to make assumptions about processes, mind-sets, and terminology. Because the design team doesn't know what terms mean or how particular processes are supposed to work, they ask the "dumb" questions that often reveal critical design insights. In a business domain, of course, you never want to leave the customers with the impression that the product designers aren't very bright, so as with stakeholders, be sure to mention at the beginning of the interview that you're being *deliberately* naïve.

ASK PEOPLE TO SHOW YOU

People self-reporting about their own behavior tend to generalize, which can cause them to obscure or omit important details. If you can see people in action, you'll be able to observe numerous things they're unlikely to mention. The ideal is to see a task through from start to finish. When time is too short because processes are complex, think about your interview as a cooking show in which you want to see the important things happen, but don't necessarily have to watch the chef dice every onion. Ask the participant to walk you through each step in the process without completing it. For example, a statistician running a complex analysis may take a day or more to clean the data before setting up the analysis parameters and running the job. You need to watch enough data cleaning to get a sense of the flow and to identify problems, but more than a few minutes of observing that particular task isn't worthwhile. The exception to this last point is most likely to crop up in critical situations that are hard to replicate through show-and-tell, such as surgery or air traffic control; in these cases,

you need time and patience because you never know when an emergency will arise and provide you with critical insight.

ASK FOR SPECIFIC STORIES, ESPECIALLY ABOUT ANYTHING YOU CAN'T OBSERVE

Asking participants to tell you specific stories—what ethnographers call being "case-specific"—is another good strategy for avoiding the self-reporting problem. Rather than asking how someone shops for home entertainment, ask, "What was the last home entertainment product you bought? Could you tell us about your decision-making process and your shopping experience?" In many ways, stories are the foundation of any interview; they encapsulate tasks and sequence, problems, thought processes, and even emotional responses to situations. Even if all you know about interviewing technique is "tell me stories" and "show me how you did that," you'll get at least some useful information for doing design.

TAKE OPPORTUNITIES WHEN THEY'RE OFFERED

When an interviewee provides an opportunity by referring to a particular person, process, or thing that may be relevant to the design problem, follow up on it by asking for more detail. If that would interrupt the flow, make a note (mentally or perhaps in the margin of your notebook) and then bring it up once the current train of thought is complete: "You mentioned a few minutes ago that you prepare a weekly report. Could you show us an example of that?"

WATCH FOR INCONSISTENCIES

Participants may also have inaccurate perceptions of their own behavior. This kind of inconsistency can help uncover self-reporting error. I recall one interviewee who saw herself as a very decisive shopper. She insisted she never, ever returned things to stores, because she was always confident in her purchases, but later described the Amazon return process with considerable familiarity. Sometimes, apparent inconsistencies are about differing worldviews between interviewer and interviewee. When I asked her about the inconsistency, she said, "Oh, you're right. I really never return clothes, but I guess I just don't think of buying books as shopping." Her view of "shopping" was that it was a recreational activity, typically involving clothing, shoes, or housewares. Finding and purchasing books had no entertainment value for her, so she didn't equate it with other shopping activities.

GO BEYOND THE PRODUCT, BUT NOT BEYOND THE DESIGN PROBLEM

If you're designing the ultimate e-mail system, do you really just want to see how people create, view, and organize their messages today? Chances are, some of the communication that happens outside of e-mail now would be more effective if it were integrated into that application. This is where the design team can identify compelling opportunities that affect the product's definition as well as its design.

Think about what major problem the product or service is supposed to address, then focus on that problem rather than on the current instantiation of your product. If you're designing a mobile phone, you're addressing the communication and information needs people have when they're not sitting at a desk. If you're designing an electronic medical record, you're looking for opportunities to make clinicians' use of information more effective and efficient.

Your interview time on any project is necessarily limited, so it's equally important to be clear about what problems you're not solving. For the electronic medical record example, you need to understand what electronic devices (such as vital-signs monitors or glucose meters) could automatically feed

data to the system, but you don't need to understand those devices well enough to redesign them.

PAY ATTENTION TO NONVERBAL CUES

If you've ever had the tone of an e-mail misinterpreted, you know that even seemingly straightforward communication often relies on nonverbal cues for accurate interpretation. UCLA psychology professor Albert Mehrabian[3] posited that communication about feelings and attitudes is only seven percent verbal; tone of voice and body language account for the remainder of the meaning.

While I question the utility and accuracy of such detailed percentages, the basic concept rings true: If someone's response to "How are you doing today?" is "Fine," pronounced with a sigh and accompanied by a slumping posture, which part of the communication will you believe? It would be mistaken to apply these ratios to more factual information—the answer to "What's the square root of 25?" is unlikely to carry much emotional content; at most, body language might tell you whether the person you're asking finds the question difficult. Nevertheless, product design usually touches on multiple topics that can carry emotional weight, ranging from enjoyment to frustration. This is one reason that transcripts, audio recordings, and telephone interviews are not the most effective tools for understanding how people think and feel, though they're fine for simple facts.

If someone seems to exhibit discomfort, or if the verbal and nonverbal content don't agree, gently remark on it and ask why. In an interview related to managing digital photos, for example, an interviewee said he disliked the time he spent organizing photos. However, when he showed us how he laid out the photos of his child on a Web site, he seemed much more animated than he did earlier in the interview. When one interviewer said, "I know you mentioned that you didn't enjoy organizing

---

3. Mehrabian, A. *Silent messages.* Wadsworth, 1971.

photos, but you seem enthusiastic about this part," he responded, "Oh, well, I don't like having to rename all the files and rotate them and so on, but laying them out and sharing them with family is actually kind of fun. It gives me a chance to enjoy the photos and the memories of time with my son." This is important information for guiding the design later on. Observe the interviewee's communication style for a little while before doing this, though, since you might be misreading the cues; some people simply fidget or make faces when they're thinking. Also consider whether this will be seen as invasive; it's usually fine in the United States or other countries where people are very expressive, but may be rude elsewhere.

THINK AHEAD A LITTLE (BUT NOT TOO MUCH)

If you're the inquisitive sort, as most good designers are, it's easy to get immersed in learning about the informant's world. However, it's important to focus on the information you'll most need for design later. It will be essential that you understand process, priorities, what types of information are used when, and so forth. Be careful about jumping too far ahead, though; if you find yourself thinking about solutions during the interview, you're no longer giving your full attention to listening and observing, and you may be pulling the interview off course.

RELY ON YOUR TEAMMATE(S)

Interviewing is hard work. Simultaneously listening, taking notes, providing the right kind of feedback to the interviewee, thinking up the next question, and making sure you're covering the right topics without jumping too far ahead is pretty much impossible to do without help—especially for six or eight hours a day while you're also jet-lagged. Alternate which team member is driving the discussion and which one is mostly taking notes.

Even when you're in the pilot's seat, make use of your teammate as a copilot when you can't

think of where to take the interview next. A small amount of intra-team communication during an interview is never problematic if handled well. Work out a code beforehand; for example, turning to your teammate and asking, "What topic would you like to cover next?" means "Help! I'm not sure what direction to go." Also, be sure to ask your teammates if they have follow-up questions on any topic before you move on to the next.

What not to do in user interviews

Your interviews don't need to be perfect; you can make a mistake or have an off day and still get plenty of useful data. However, there are a few things that tend to make interviews less productive.

DON'T ASK LEADING QUESTIONS

One of the worst things you can do in an interview is ask leading questions that imply the answer you're looking for. Even experienced interviewers can find themselves "validating" their preconceived notions about new features or design changes. If you're convinced you're right and you just can't wait to get confirmation from users, it's hard to resist asking, "Would you like to be able to access your calendar on the Web?" A typical interviewee who is trying to be polite and cooperative might say, "Sure, that could be useful."

What's the problem with this? Even if this is a truthful answer, you have no idea where it really falls in the participant's list of priorities—maybe she said yes, but maybe there are 27 other things that are more important. Instead, wait to see what points of pain people bring up on their own; these are almost certainly at the top of the priority list.

Using open-ended questions will help you avoid leading; it's very difficult to ask whether feature X would be helpful without anticipating a yes or no answer. If you really must ask your leading question, at least save it until the very end of the interview, so you'll have a chance to see if it comes up at all before that. If it doesn't, you'll be more able to put the answer in context.

AVOID ASKING THE INTERVIEWEE FOR SOLUTIONS

Solving the problem is your job, not the informant's. If you start asking for solutions or running with solution ideas the interviewee proposes, you're most likely missing some important information about the problem. If you feel compelled to ask interviewees what they want, there's a constructive way to do it: "If you had a magic tool, what would it help you *accomplish*?" Note that this question doesn't ask what the tool is or how it works; rather, it's focused on goals. When an interviewee suggests a solution, don't take it at face value. Instead, ask, "What problem would that solve for you?"

DON'T SOLVE PROBLEMS DURING THE INTERVIEW

Designers are solution-minded people, so it can be difficult to see problems in an interview and not try to solve them right then. It's painful to watch an interviewee struggling with the product in some way. Unless it's completely impossible for him to accomplish a task you need to see, though, pay attention to what he's struggling with and why, rather than helping him out. There are at least three good reasons for not helping: You'll miss important data, you'll eat up precious interview time, and you'll turn the interview dynamic on its head, since the interviewee is supposed to be the expert while you're the learner. If you feel you really must offer a helpful hint, try to save it for the end of the interview.

The other kind of problem solving that can be tempting is, "So, what if we put another button over here to help you add a new item to the list?" Again, this consumes time and energy you could be using to learn. Even if it's a spontaneous idea born from a genuine wish to be helpful, this is really just another type of leading question. Participatory design may have its place, but this isn't it.

Structuring the user interview

A conversational interview is somewhat loose and free-flowing, but there is an inherent structure: introduction, overview, details, more challenging topics, and wrap-up. There are surprisingly few structural differences between user interviews for consumer and business products. This is a typical structure; details on each topic follow.

— **Introductions:** who we are, why we're here, what the next hour will be like

— **Chitchat:** a get-to-know-you question or two (most important with consumer products)

— **Overview question:** a broad topic meant to elicit information about major activities and flow

— **Demonstration of activities**: user walks through key tasks usually based on response to the overview question

— **Looking for gaps:** a recap of activities covered so far and a request to fill in anything not mentioned so far

— **Details as needed:** other topics you need to cover that haven't come up yet, typically involving information and objects, actions, relationships, frustrations, background, and goals

— **Grand tour:** a guided walk-through of the usage environment and relevant artifacts, if it hasn't already happened naturally

— **Remaining follow-up questions**

— **Any leading questions:** only if you really must ask them (the "magic solution" question is better)

— **Establish means for future contact** if necessary

Getting started: introductions

You may or may not have spoken with the interviewee before this. If this is a business setting, you most likely worked with someone else at this company who scheduled time with several people on her team. With consumer interviews, the market research firm may have passed on only the basic information you provided about what to expect from the interview. Your information may not have been transmitted clearly or completely. This means the first thing you have to do is establish who you are and why you're here. As with the recruiting screener or the e-mail you may have sent to the site contact, avoid being overly specific about what you'll use the information for; otherwise, the interview focus might get too narrow right away.

If you are offering an honorarium or other incentive, it's nice to get this out of the way up front, so interviewees can simply relax and not worry about when they're getting paid. Take care of any forms you need them to sign now if you haven't been able to do so beforehand.

Briefly describe how the interview will go and the sorts of things you'll ask. Mention that you'll be taking notes. Ask permission in a casual way for any recording but—if you can do so—reassure the interviewee that you won't be sharing the notes or recording with anyone else outside your team. You'll probably want to take photos, but people are usually more receptive if you bring this up later in the interview. Finally, give the interviewee the chance to ask any questions before you get started.

OVERVIEW QUESTIONS AND FOLLOW-UP

Start the interview with a broad, descriptive question. Although a detailed question list is often counterproductive—turning the interview into an interrogation rather than a conversation—the phrasing of the opening question is worth crafting ahead of time, because the answer sets the context for the rest of the interview. The idea is to get an overview of the relevant activities so you have a rich list of topics to pursue in greater detail. If you don't get this kind of overview early in the discussion, you may find yourself struggling to find the next question and introducing more

leading questions just to keep the conversation going. The right overview question will make it seem like the interview structures itself.

BUSINESS SETTINGS

In most business contexts, asking someone to walk you through a typical workday is a great way to start. The response to this will give you a sense of overall process as well as a list of specific activities. For example:

INTERVIEWER: I'd like to hear about what your typical workday is like. Could you walk me through what you did yesterday, from the time you started work until you were done for the day?

PURCHASING AGENT: Yesterday was pretty typical. The first thing I did was check my e-mail and voicemail to see if there was anything urgent. I do that every day. There were a couple of urgent things I dealt with first. After that, I did some follow-up with the vendors who needed something before they could get things shipped, then got through as many new purchase requests as I could. That's a challenge sometimes, between phone calls from vendors and people wanting to know where their stuff is. At the end of the day, I put the most urgent stuff at the top of the pile for the next day.

Even this brief response provides the basis for a whole series of follow-up questions, such as:

— What things were urgent enough to deal with first?

— How many purchasing-related messages were there to deal with?

— What were those messages about?

— How many were new requests and how many were follow-up?

- What kind of vendor follow-up is usually needed and why?
- Where do you find the information you need for that follow-up?
- Could you walk me through an example of how you create a new purchase order from a requisition?
- What are the phone calls or other interruptions usually about?
- Which of those interruptions are a waste of your time?
- What else happens in a typical day that didn't happen yesterday?

CONSUMER OR OTHER BROAD DOMAINS

The right overview question is usually a bit more challenging to find in consumer domains (or any other time that a typical workday isn't a useful starting point). A good overview question in these cases is usually a matter of focusing on the larger design problem, rather than an existing product.

For example, "How do you use your television today?" may not be a great starting point if you hope to turn the TV into a home media hub. Instead, you're probably better off starting with, "What kinds of things do you do for entertainment at home?"

A good overview question elicits a lot of information about typical activities and how they fit together; the topics raised by the interviewee's response can often fill a large part of your interview time. Sometimes it's useful to be a bit vague, allowing interviewees to make what they will of the question, but if the question is too vague, the interviewees won't know where to start. A short series of two or three questions will usually cover the ground you need if one question isn't enough to give you a good overview. If an interview covers disparate activities, such as shopping for a product and getting support for it, you'll want to ask about shopping behavior, discuss that for a while, and then ask your second overview question about getting support after the purchase. Table 7.1 provides some examples; these are by no means the only possible overview questions for these situations.

Table 7.1. **Good and bad overview question examples.**

Product	Poor overview questions	Good overview questions
Business e-mail system	What kind of e-mail do you use?	We're interested in the various kinds of communication you have with other people during a typical workday. Could you start by walking us through what you did yesterday?
Consumer digital camera	What kind of camera do you have?	What role does photography play in your life? What do you take photos of and how often?
Camera company Web site	How do you use our Web site?	*First overview question:* Please tell us about the last time you shopped for a camera. *Second overview question:* Could you tell us about any occasions since you bought your camera when you've wanted additional information or support?

Although asking specifically about yesterday usually works in business settings with fairly narrow activities, be wary of getting too specific in broader domains. For example, asking someone about the last time she took photos might not be the most useful starting point, since it might be an example of her least typical photography situation. Instead, get a sense for what kinds of situations exist before you focus on one type of situation in more detail (followed by the others).

Unfortunately, the best overview questions are often socially awkward starting points, so you'll want to ask them after a few getting-to-know-you questions like those you might use at a company party, such as, "Tell me a little bit about yourself," or "How did you come to work here?" Once the conversation has started, take the next opportunity to pose your overview question.

Also note that the same overview question may not work for each role. If you're designing the end-user interface as well as the system administrator's tool for an e-mail application, you probably won't want to start the conversations with each type of interviewee in the same place.

A good overview question elicits a lot of information about typical activities and how they fit together.

Exercises

1. What overview question(s) would you ask potential users of the LocalGuide or Room Finder (see Chapter 6)? Don't forget to account for any different roles.

2. Imagine that you're trying to design a better grocery store. You've asked an interview participant to tell you about the last time she went grocery shopping, and she's given you the answer below. What follow-up questions would you ask based on the information provided in her answer?

   "It was Saturday morning. There wasn't much in the house, so I went shopping to get food for the rest of the weekend. I went to a store I don't usually go to. I started in the produce section because I knew one thing I wanted to cook, and I was planning to see what was fresh to get inspiration for some other meals. They didn't have some of what I wanted, and some of the produce didn't look very good. I thought of a couple of other ideas, but had to wander around the store to see if they had the other ingredients. It took forever. I had to look in three different parts of the store to get milk, cheese, and cream cheese. I had to ask a stock person where to get the cream cheese. Once I figured out what other ingredients they had, I went back to the produce section to get the rest of what I needed. Of course, after I stood in line and eventually got everything home, I realized I'd forgotten one of the things I needed."

Essential interview topics

To do design later on, you'll need to understand the objects users work with, the things they do with those objects, and what skills they bring to bear on their tasks. You'll also need to understand their goals—their reasons for doing those tasks in the first place—and the frustrations that keep them from achieving those goals today.

An ethnographer such as Spradley would say most of the interview questions on these topics are either **descriptive**—focused on identifying and understanding the important things, concepts, and activities that exist in the domain—or **structural**, focused on how those things, concepts, and activities are related. **Contrast** questions help clarify descriptions and relationships by asking how things are different.

INFORMATION AND OBJECTS

To design an effective kitchen, you'd need to know what kinds of things get stored and used there; storage for cookie sheets is very different from storage for ice cream. If you knew roughly how many of each thing there were, you could be sure to get the right ratio of cabinets to drawers to refrigerator space. You could do an even better job if you knew how frequently things were used, so you could make the everyday dishes easier to reach than the best china that only comes out for big holiday dinners. This same understanding is required for good product design.

Note that the following discussion is an example of "thinking ahead to the design," in that it covers what you will need to understand later. Don't try to create a definitive catalog of objects and relationships during the interview, since in a complex domain this could easily consume an hour or more. Instead, seek out the information that will help you synthesize such a catalog later on. Don't be too dismayed if you miss a few things in any given interview, since the gestalt of all the interviews will help you fill in gaps.

Mental model objects

In 1943, Kenneth Craik posited in *The Nature of Explanation* that humans use internal representations (which may be based on imagination as well as experience and perception) to understand and predict events in the world. People act and react based on these **mental models**. When the conceptual structure and behavior of a system match a user's mental model, the system is generally easier to learn and use. While it is possible for mental models to evolve over time, system behavior that conflicts with user mental models tends to cause problems.

To create an effective system, designers must understand a user's mental model of the data: What are the meaningful **object types** and how are they **related** in her mind? Folders, documents, and other discrete collections of information are all types of objects; "chapter 8.doc" is an object of the "document" type and "chapters in progress" is an object of the "folder" type. In most enterprise settings, there are multiple object types. In an e-mail and calendaring application, for example, there are messages, groups of messages, appointments, and probably contacts. If it's something with multiple instances a user creates, it probably fits the definition of an object in your user's mind. There may be other things, such as user preference files, that are objects in the programming sense but that users don't think of as objects, which means they're not part of the mental model. Table 7.2 shows some examples of mental model objects.

The mental model objects aren't necessarily the same as the ones shown in an existing product's interface, though; these sometimes reflect what software engineers call the **implementation model**. For example, a clothing store database might note three separate product numbers for a navy blue sweater, a black sweater, and a red sweater of the same style. This structure is useful from the standpoint of inventory management, but it shouldn't be surfaced to shoppers, who will be

Table 7.2. **Example mental model objects.**

Design problem	Likely mental model objects
E-mail system	— Messages — Conversations consisting of related messages — People — Collections of messages that are related in some way other than as part of a conversation
Organizing photos	— Photos — Collections of related photos (represented by an envelope or box in the physical world, or by a folder in the digital one) — Collections of related photos that have been arranged in some way (a photo album in the real world, a Web page or other layout in the digital realm)
Camera company Web site	— Products — Orders
Purchasing agent's tools	— Requisitions — Purchase orders — Invoices — Vendors
Family calendaring system	— Family members — Events

frustrated if your site has three separate listings for what they think of as a single sweater available in three colors. In other words, in a shopper's mental model, each clothing *style* exists as an object; things like color and size are variable attributes. People who have used a system for a long time may eventually become accustomed to the fact that it represents the back-end implementation in the interface, but this doesn't mean it's a natural structure that was easy for them to learn.

Try to understand whether it's the implementation itself that has meaning for the interviewee, or whether the implementation just happens to

approximate a mental model object that's slightly different. For example, people accustomed to film photography may refer to a "roll" of film as a meaningful collection. However, people who have used only digital cameras have never encountered the concept of a "roll" and don't seem to miss it. It's not that they substitute the "memory card" for the word "roll"—they're also unlikely to say "Oh, that was on the same card as this," because they can process images at any time; they're not limited to either waiting for the roll to fill up or wasting film by processing half a roll. So what's useful about the roll concept? It often represents a group of pictures taken *at the same time*, such

Don't be shy about asking for definitions or distinctions even if you think you know the answer.

as at an event or on a particular vacation. That time-related grouping, not the roll, is the mental model object. Seeing people use different systems will help you uncover such distinctions.

Of course, if you ask someone directly to describe his mental model of the data, you'll get a blank stare. Listen and observe for a while to see if you can identify some of the objects, then use them as examples to elicit others. Try asking something like this: "I've seen you work with three types of documents so far: purchase orders, service orders, and requisitions. What other types of documents do you use, and why?" Given that small amount of structure as a starting point, most interviewees can help you fill in the rest, though they're still likely to leave some out unless they're telling specific stories, demonstrating processes, or looking at actual artifacts.

Don't be shy about asking for definitions or distinctions, such as the difference between a requisition and a purchase order, even if you think you know the answer. This is one place where the interviewer who is ignorant of the domain has an advantage, because people who think they know what the terms mean may miss the fact that the word "report" means three different things in three different companies. Asking about distinctions can help clarify which ones are truly meaningful to the interviewee. For example, a purchasing system we were redesigning made a distinction between purchase orders (for goods) and service orders (for everything from consulting to light bulb installation). When we asked about the distinction, a number of the purchasing agents told us they were "really the same thing" even though the system didn't seem to think so. If they started creating a purchase order and later realized they needed a service order because something like installation was included, they had to start over because it required a couple of different fields.

Details (attributes of the objects)

Many people confuse mental model objects with database fields. An insurance underwriter, for instance, cares about how many properties are covered by a policy, what their total insured value is, and what deductibles, premiums, and limits are applied. However, all of those bits of information, which exist as fields in a database, are attached to policies. They're meaningless without that attachment, which means they're not objects, but are important **attributes** of objects. Table 7.3 provides some examples of meaningful attributes for various mental model objects.

Table 7.3. **Examples of meaningful attributes for mental model objects.**

Objects	**Example attributes users care about**
E-mail message	— Who sent it — Who else received it — When it was sent — What it's about — What's attached to it — What action was taken on it (forward, reply, etc.) — How urgent it is
People (business contacts)	— How to reach them — Where they work — What their titles are — Important personal details (birthdays, etc.)

As you identify meaningful types of objects, you should also be asking for details about the properties of those objects, such as:

- What information goes into a purchase order?
- How many items are in a typical PO?
- What's the biggest number of items you've ever put on a single PO?
- Is the format always the same? Why does it vary?

Try to get what detail you can about the typical contents and attributes of reports, forms, or other objects, but recognize that you won't be able to cover all of this in an hour unless the domain is very simple. Whenever possible, ask if you can take photos of typical examples like the one shown in Figure 7.2. Better yet, get copies of a few. When dealing with sensitive data, such as medical or financial records, you may not be able to do so; ask if you can at least have a blank form. In some cases, it's acceptable to copy such a record if any identifying information is covered up. Failing these options, try to take a moment to sketch the approximate contents and format (minus the confidential information) in your notebook.

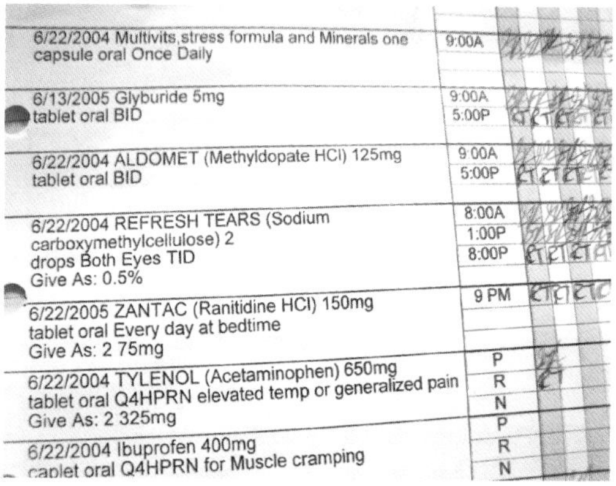

6/22/2004 Multivits,stress formula and Minerals one capsule oral Once Daily	9:00A
6/13/2005 Glyburide 5mg tablet oral BID	9:00A 5:00P
6/22/2004 ALDOMET (Methyldopate HCl) 125mg tablet oral BID	9:00A 5:00P
6/22/2004 REFRESH TEARS (Sodium carboxymethylcellulose) 2 drops Both Eyes TID Give As: 0.5%	8:00A 1:00P 8:00P
6/22/2005 ZANTAC (Ranitidine HCl) 150mg tablet oral Every day at bedtime Give As: 2 75mg	9 PM
6/22/2004 TYLENOL (Acetaminophen) 650mg tablet oral Q4HPRN elevated temp or generalized pain Give As: 2 325mg	P R N
6/22/2004 Ibuprofen 400mg caplet oral Q4HPRN for Muscle cramping	P R N

Figure 7.2. This is a good example of a form to get a copy or photo of in an interview. Take note of the form content and design as well as the extent to which it appears to work. What scribbles have people made? Does the format appear to break down in any way, or is it working well?

Also, try to identify which of these attributes or details users actually care about. Chances are that no one will mention file size as an interesting attribute of an e-mail message; what people truly care about is whether an attachment will make it through the recipient's email system. Similarly, you need to know roughly how many items a purchase order might contain so you can design appropriately, but this doesn't mean purchasing agents want to see a running total of how many lines there are in the document. Note what information your interviewee has emphasized, such as that shown in Figure 7.3.

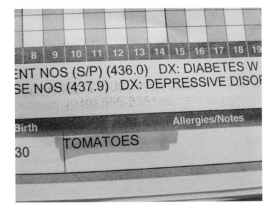

Figure 7.3. Note how a nurse has manually highlighted the allergy information on this medical record to make it stand out. This is the patient attribute she most needs to see at a glance.

Though it's best to get as much information as you can, missing some details won't be a problem as long as you have access to the same users or a subject matter expert later in the project.

Relationships

You also need to see how each type of file or information is related to the others.

"Any-to-any" relationships are common in most applications. These may be:

Many-to-many	Many people may send many messages
Many-to-one	Many people may live in one city
One-to-many (many-to-one from a different perspective)	One city may contain many people
One-to-one	One person has one legal spouse

However, these descriptions are only the starting point. Object types often have various hierarchical and dependent relationships, as well. Table 7.4 shows examples of each type.

In a **hierarchical** relationship, one type of object contains another. If two object types have a **dependent** hierarchical relationship, one type of object cannot exist independent of the other. This dependency can go either up or down the hierarchy. For example, a suit consists of a matching jacket and pants. Someone getting dressed in the morning might look for her black suit, or may just want the pants that are part of the suit. The jacket and pants exist independent of the suit, but the superior object type, the suit, does not exist without both inferior objects, the jacket and pants. A bank transaction is an example of an inferior object that cannot exist without a superior object, which is an account. Albums and photos, on the other hand, have an **independent** hierarchical relationship: Photos can exist without albums and albums without photos, though empty albums are uncommon.

Another type of dependent relationship is **temporal**: One type of object is created using another object as its basis, and largely removes the need for the original object. In corporate purchasing, for example, someone creates a requisition that asks a purchasing agent to acquire some product or service. The agent then creates a purchase order that serves as an agreement between the

Table 7.4. **Examples of object relationships.**

Objects	Examples of relationships
E-mail messages	— One sender (person or company) to one or many recipients
	— May or may not be part of a longer conversation
	— May or may not exist in some other collection of messages with a shared topic (such as a project folder) or other properties (such as a folder of new or deleted messages)
	— Dependent on the existence of a sender and (usually) one or more recipients (Whether a message is dependent may seem ambiguous if contacts don't exist as remembered objects in the system, but in the average human's brain, there's no such thing as a message not created by a person or company.)
Conversations of related messages	— A superior object that's dependent on the existence of two or more inferior message objects (an initial message and at least one reply)
Contacts (people or companies)	— Independent objects that may get messages from one or many people, send messages to one or many people, and participate in multiple conversations
Inbox	— An independent object superior to messages

company and the vendor. The requisition must exist before the PO is initiated, but the requisition has largely served its purpose once the PO is created; the only reason for its continued existence is to provide an audit trail.

Just as you can't ask users what data objects exist in their heads, you'd get a blank stare if you asked about hierarchical and temporal relationships in an interview. Instead, look for clues that a certain type of object may exist, then learn about it using structural and contrast questions, such as, "What does a photo album contain?" or "How is a requisition different from a PO?" Follow these with the sort of clarifying questions Spradley describes as **semantic relationship verification questions**, such as, "I understand that a portfolio can contain accounts. Does it ever contain other portfolios?" or "Would you ever have an empty portfolio?"

Don't try to draw a mental map of relationships in your head during the interview; this discussion of object types and their relationships is merely intended to illustrate the kind of information you need to get from the interview. However, do take a few minutes afterward to think through the object types and relationships with your teammates to see if you understand them. If not, you'll know what you need to get clarified in the next interview. By the time you're done with your research, you should be able to describe these relationships with no trouble at all.

Quantity

You also need to understand how many of each object type there are overall and how many are accessed in a typical session or day. Exact quantities aren't necessary; you just need to know whether people have dozens, hundreds, thousands, or many thousands of files, since this will affect how you design the file-management behavior. This information may reveal itself in the interview without you having to ask. If the informant indicates a quantity, see if your observations match her numbers and ask about any disparity. It's usually just self-reporting error, but sometimes those differences can be due to some behavior you haven't heard about so far. An interview with a professional photographer is a good example:

> INTERVIEWER: You mentioned that you typically take 400 pictures in a day of shooting, but each day's folder seems to contain a lot less than that. Are the folders I'm seeing not typical, or is there some other reason for that difference?

> PHOTOGRAPHER: Hmmm. No, these are about the usual size. I do take upward of 400 shots at a time, but that's just what I start off with. Well no, actually, I probably take closer to 500, since I delete some from the camera as I go, then wind up with maybe 400 to load onto the laptop. But then I trash at least a quarter of them when I first import from the camera, if I can see from the thumbnail that the exposure was off or the frame didn't capture quite what I wanted. I usually get rid of a lot more as I look closely at each one, so I'd guess in the end I have 200, maybe less.

Does every product involve "objects?"

In consumer applications with very simple data structures, people don't see themselves as working with files, but they're still looking for certain things or pieces of information. Imagine for a moment that you're designing a touch-screen information kiosk at a shopping mall. The mall management might think of the various things people need as merchants and services, but you

need to understand whether this makes sense to the people who will use the directory. You might find, instead, that people think of stores, food, and restrooms. Knowing how people think about that information is still important, even if the data is very simple.

ACTIONS

Of course, nouns aren't much use without verbs. To belabor the kitchen analogy I used earlier: Peeling vegetables, cooking them, and cleaning up afterward are all activities that require different tools and workspaces. Similarly, the things people do with information and objects will require different tools and possibly different workspaces in your product.

As with objects, you first need to understand what types of activities there are and what's involved in each. The overview question is a great starting point. Once you've covered what's involved in a typical day, recap the activities you've seen and heard about, then ask what others happen less frequently. Continue doing this until the interviewee doesn't have any more tasks to discuss.

Reasons for each activity

Understanding the tasks is important, but it's equally critical to understand why the tasks even exist. What goal is the task supposed to help achieve? Is the task something people believe is necessary, or do they do it because a bad system forces them to? In redesigning an online pharmacy, for example, we learned that most people just wanted to get their prescriptions filled online because it was cheaper and potentially more convenient. They were all happy to provide their names, addresses, and insurance information at registration because they saw how this information would help accomplish the goal. However, they were frustrated by any question that didn't seem to serve that goal, such as what health topics they wanted more information about.

If some activity doesn't seem to make sense, that's a good indication that you should be asking, "Why is this important?" You'll either find that the participant says, "It's not important, but my company/boss/ software makes me do it," or you'll learn something very useful. I once encountered a nurse manager who spent considerable time copying patient problems from the paper medical records into her own spread-sheets. When asked why she did this, she explained that any increase in certain conditions or types of incidents would help her see potential problems with the quality of patient care. This pointed to a tremendous opportunity for using an electronic medical record not just to replace paper entry, but also to make clinical managers more effective by help-ing them identify and analyze problematic trends.

How tasks are performed and described

The way tasks are performed is also useful to observe. What informa-tion does the informant have when she begins a task? What steps fol-low from that? Where does she expect to find certain things? See if you can determine whether what you're seeing is the mental model at work or the result of poor implementation.

Listening to interviewees describe their tasks (using what words and in what sequence) can be informative. For example, most of us who con-vert documents to PDF eventually learn that we need to go to the print dialog and pick PDF from the list of printers on a Windows PC. However, most users will say, "And then I *save* the file as a PDF." This function may reside in the print dialog because of the format's desktop publishing origins, but novice users are inevitably flummoxed because they view the action as exporting or saving in a different format rather than as printing.

In another example, some colleagues who were designing a PDA specif-ically for teenagers heard their interviewees describe their next classes or other time commitments in terms of a countdown. Whereas most adults say, "I have a meeting at 3:00," teens would say, "I have 40 minutes until I have to be in class." Their focus was not on what they needed to do, but was instead on how much time they had free before they had to do something.

If you're not sure why someone is doing things in a certain sequence or manner, ask. Sometimes it's because people just think that way, but it could also be because the tool forces them to do so, or because system performance is better one way than another. This is one of the reasons it's so helpful to see people who use your current product (if there is one) as well as people who don't: It highlights where your sys-tem might be doing things in an awkward way.

Understanding the tasks is important, but it's equally critical to understand why the tasks even exist.

Research

135

You'll probably have to rely on self-reporting to understand task frequency and priority, so look for clues to validate this information.

Task frequency and priority

It's easy to assume that frequency and time spent imply importance. A task may be necessary, but the amount of time spent on the task might just indicate that the existing tools are inadequate. The purchasing process is a good example. Many people view purchasing agents as human automatons who exist to type things into purchase order forms. Although agents do spend most of their time doing this, the important parts of the job are actually sourcing and negotiating: finding the vendor who will provide the best quality and customer service in the right timeframe, then getting the best price (or vice versa). Your job as a designer is to maximize the time users can spend on important things and see how much you can automate the rest. Of course, time spent on a task can also indicate enjoyment; a teenager who spends an inordinate amount of time playing video games isn't doing it because he has to.

Unless you can afford to do an extended field study with each participant, you'll have to rely primarily on self-reporting to understand task frequency and priority, especially for tasks that don't take place on a daily basis. Ask how often people perform each task, but look for clues to validate this information. If an interviewee tells you he transfers photos from his camera every couple of weeks, see how accurate this is by looking at the date stamps on the files.

To understand priority, ask questions like these:

— What things do you usually do first, and why?
— What do you put off as long as you can, and why?
— What things waste your time?
— If you had more time to spend on just one or two things, what would they be?
— What keeps you from spending more time on those things now?

Of course, the answers to these questions might illustrate other issues; if someone puts off a task, it might be unpleasant but still important. Asking why someone procrastinates will help you assess whether the behavior reflects priorities or is a symptom of inadequate tools or processes.

The role of the current product

If you're redesigning an existing tool or developing a competitive product, observe what parts of each task take place in that product and what parts take place outside of it. Are there opportunities for streamlining by integrating certain tasks currently performed elsewhere? For example, some of my colleagues working on a computer-assisted surgery system saw assistants holding up pieces of paper outside the clean zone, but where the surgeons could see them if they leaned over and squinted (see Figure 7.4). It turned out that most of these were handwritten pre-op notes the surgeons had taken but couldn't access via the surgery system. The team couldn't determine at that point whether such notes should be available in the system, but it was the sort of workaround that merited close attention.

Also be honest with yourself about how large a role your product really plays in the interviewee's day; will someone who refills a prescription once

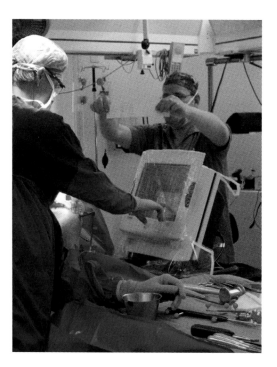

Figure 7.4. This surgeon performing a knee replacement had someone bring him a printout with data not available in his assisted surgery system. The design team knew this must be important information, so they asked what it was and why it was on a sheet of paper.

a month be frustrated by going to her "inbox" on your Web site to see if her order is delayed, rather than seeing that information in her own e-mail inbox? Many of these things should come up naturally as users demonstrate their activities for you.

Good questions about current products might include:

— How often do you use the product?
— What do you most often use the current product for?
— Could you show me how you do that?
— What other tools do you use before turning to this product?
— What tools do you use alongside it?
— What tools do you use after this product?
— How would you compare this product to others you've used for the same tasks?

When there's no single product currently filling the niche you're aiming for, these questions may seem less useful. However, you can often ask similar questions about other products that do parts of the task, or even about existing paper or informal systems (such as hallway conversations).

Relationships with other people

Surprisingly few activities involve only one person, so it's usually necessary to understand what roles other people play in any process. With enterprise tools in particular, there are often opportunities to improve the information flow upstream, downstream, or both. Even in a consumer environment such as a family, you might need to understand such things as how parents want to control what children can see online, or how various family members annoy one another by changing the television settings. Of course, you're not trying to identify the solutions during the course of the interview; you're simply trying to see where the opportunities for improvement might exist.

Research

Collaborative activity is messier and less predictable than a more linear process, so observation of the behavior is even more critical.

Relationships with other people can be a sensitive subject, so it can work better to bring this up somewhat later in an interview, except where the interviewee touches on relationships with respect to a particular task. Effective questions about relationships will vary, but in a sequential work-flow (such as a purchasing process or call center), they might include:

— Who provides the information you use in this process?
  — How do you get that information?
  — What's inefficient or ineffective about that process?
— Who reviews or consumes the results of your work?
  — What do you provide to them?
  — How well do you think that meets their needs?
  — What kind of extra effort is required on your part?
— Who else is likely to touch this file?
  — Why might multiple people work on it?
  — What do they do with it?
  — When you get the file, what do you need to know about what they've done?
  — What problems arise from having multiple people work on it?

Questions about real-time collaboration differ somewhat. If you were to design a remote meeting tool, for example, you might ask:

— What kinds of information do you need to share during the course of a meeting?
— How often do you use information you already had prepared, and how often are you looking for other information?
— How does each participant need to interact with that information?
— What do you find yourself doing in remote collaboration that you don't do in person?
— What do you miss about in-person meetings when collaborating remotely?

Collaborative activity is messier and less predictable than a more linear process, so observation of the behavior is even more critical.

Workarounds

You may observe people apparently circumventing a procedure. Ask whether they're doing so and why, perhaps with a reassurance of confidentiality. For example, when designing a hospital glucose meter for bedside testing, my team saw nurses asking other nurses for their operator IDs. From a regulatory standpoint, a glucose reading is a laboratory test, and any operator performing a lab test must be periodically recertified on the instrument she's using. This recertification is so low on the average nurse's priority list that it's common for certifications to expire. Unfortunately, the patient's test had to be performed regardless of the nurse's certification status, so having the instrument block nurses with expired certifications actually introduced a worse regulatory problem: inaccurate records of who administered the test.

If you haven't seen anyone circumvent a procedure, it doesn't mean they don't; they may just be on their best behavior for you. Once you've established a good rapport with your interviewee, try asking about any procedures that don't work for them. "I know that in a lot of places, there are procedures or rules that seem like a good idea, but that end up getting in the way. Are there any of those you find yourself working around?"

FRUSTRATIONS

Listening to user frustrations is the product designer's equivalent of asking a patient where it hurts. As your informant relaxes during the course of the interview, he will probably raise a number of frustrations on his own. He may not explicitly say, "This frustrates me," but it will be obvious from his tone that it does. When describing the process to confirm that a shipment had arrived and was correct, an interviewee once said to me—in a thoroughly disgusted tone—"It takes me 23 clicks just to say that the box is here!" His number may or may not have been accurate, but the fact that he took the time to count clicks spoke volumes about how cumbersome the process was.

Once you've covered the range of activities and heard some of the related frustrations, it's still useful to ask more explicit questions about what makes people cranky. If the interviewee has been forthcoming about pet peeves, one good approach is to recap some of them, then ask what else seems more difficult than it ought to be. If your participant has been too polite to complain, try asking what handful of things about the product could most use improvement.

Though it can be a less informative line of inquiry, also consider asking what works well about the product or process today. People usually struggle with the answers if the question is too broad, since it's easier to point at problems. Try asking what the best thing about the product is or what useful thing it lets the interviewee accomplish that she couldn't do before. If you're introducing an electronic system that substitutes for paper or for conversation, ask, "What about how you do

> Listening to user frustrations is the product designer's equivalent of asking a patient where it hurts.

things today would you not want to lose in an electronic system?" Ideally, asking about what's good will point to some areas that don't need as much of your attention. If you have an existing product, it may also help remind participants that even though they've just given you a long list of gripes, there are good things about your product, too.

SKILL

By the time you wrap up your interview, you should have a good idea of how skilled and experienced a particular interviewee is relative to others, provided you've already done more than a couple of interviews. This will give some context to each person's behaviors and frustrations, while also helping you assess what amount and type of support you need to provide.

Assess both skill and experience with respect to three things: technology in general, the existing tool in particular (if there is one), and the domain. This will help you determine how much support to provide in the design, and of what kind. People who are comfortable with technology in general may be more likely to poke around in a new tool to figure it out. Knowing whether people are comfortable with your existing product will help you assess what kind of learning curve really exists today.

Perhaps the most important aspect of skill and experience is how much people know about the domain of the problem. Sometimes a role implies a certain level of skill. A nurse, for example, knows how to be a nurse; she will likely be offended if a product attempts to tell her how to do her job. A call center agent, on the other hand, typically has little training or experience, and may need help with determining how to handle a call. With some design problems, though, you'll see a variety of skill levels; a tool for organizing photos might have to address the needs of both professional photographers and people who simply take family snapshots.

To assess experience with the tool or domain, you don't have much choice but to trust the interviewee's assessment. You can often get a sense for experience by casually asking about it prior to your overview question. "How did you come to be in this job?" and "How long have you been using this product?" are good openers in a work environment. Don't delve too deeply into experience at first, or it will start to feel like a job interview and upset the "user-as-expert" dynamic you're trying to establish in the conversation. Later on, as the discussion starts to wind down, you might say, "You certainly seem to know your way around an emergency room. How long have you been doing this?" or "You seem to know a lot about the technology. What did you do before this?"

Assessing skill can be difficult. It's not a good idea to ask the participant to assess his own skill because he may not be comparing himself to the same measures you are. It may seem presumptuous or even absurd for a designer to assess the skill of a professional in a field other than her own, but, thankfully, you're not deciding whether to hire someone; you're simply trying to assess how skill level affects behavior. It's possible to develop a sense for skill level just from how people use language. Compare how these two photographers talk:

> PHOTOGRAPHER A: If the lighting doesn't seem very good, sometimes I turn the dial to the low-light setting.

> PHOTOGRAPHER B: If I'm not sure about the lighting in an action shot, I'll set my shutter speed first, then bracket the exposure. I pick the aperture I think is right based on the metering, then take a shot at one f-stop on either side of it.

It seems pretty obvious just from the photographic vocabulary that Photographer B is more sophisticated. Of course, it's possible that Photographer B still doesn't take very good photos, so it's probably more accurate to say we're really assessing knowledge or comfort with the domain rather than actual skill. The only way to get a better appraisal of skill is to have a subject matter expert accompany you and make the same assessment.

GOALS

Truly great products and services help people accomplish not only their tasks, but also their goals. Searching for restaurants, reading reviews, getting directions, and making reservations are all tasks; enjoying a terrific dinner is a goal. Later in the process, goals will help you identify and prioritize features and design product behavior.

Goals may come up at any time in the course of the interview, but they're hidden among other bits of information. Some goals are expressed in the context of frustrations. For example, a manager might say, "I spend so much time responding to little crises that I have no time to plan ahead. That's a big problem." Being able to plan ahead certainly sounds like a goal.

People describing their behavior can provide clues about goals, too, as illustrated in this comment by an elderly woman who lives alone and seldom sees friends or family: "I have my programs that I like to watch. In the afternoon, I'll sit and have a cup of coffee with Ellen. Mostly I just leave the TV on for noise." If you realize that Ellen is the host of a favorite talk show, you might also notice that the interviewee describes watching the show as if it were a social engagement with a friend. Between that and the fact that she describes leaving the television on "for noise," her behavior seems to point to alleviating loneliness. Rather than assuming this, though, the interviewer follows up with a comment to see if her interpretation is accurate:

> INTERVIEWER: It sounds like you use the television as a way to have people around during the day.

> INTERVIEWEE: Why, yes, I suppose you could put it that way. Since my husband passed last year, it gets so quiet. It's a little lonely sometimes.

Observed behavior can also point to possible goals. After watching an interviewee create a task and then cross it off his to-do list with a flourish, you might observe, "You really seem to enjoy crossing things off your to-do list." The participant will probably confirm your interpretation with something like, "Yeah, it always feels good if the list is shorter when I leave than it was when I came in. This job is kind of like doing laundry: There's always a pile of stuff to do, so you have find ways to feel like you accomplished something."

Goals may come up at any time in the course of the interview, but they're hidden among other bits of information.

Research

As with most aspects of interviewing, you probably won't get a useful answer if you ask someone directly about goals. However, there are a couple of questions that tend to elicit information about goals. The one that's usually most effective is some variant of "What makes a good experience?" Phrase this in terms more specific to your design problem:

— What makes a good shopping experience?

— What makes a good workday?

— What makes a good travel experience?

It's also helpful to use this as a follow-up question when someone describes an experience and seems pleased about it. "It sounds like you enjoyed your experience. What made it good?" In the rare instance that the good experience question doesn't seem to work, you can try its opposite: "What makes a bad experience?" The answers to this are probably the opposite of goals, so the goal might be for those bad things not to happen.

Understanding why someone undertakes a particular activity in the first place can also reveal goals. Consider these reasons cited for taking photos:

— I take pictures because she's growing up so fast. Now that she's two, I can barely recall what she was like at one.

— When I see a gorgeous bird, or an unspoiled landscape, or some other amazing thing, I want to make an image that will convey how incredible that is.

— When I'm designing a garden, I take pictures of what's there now to use as a reference while I'm designing. After the landscape is done, of course, I take pictures of it for my portfolio to show people I can do great work.

These statements indicate that these people all have different goals: remembering an evolution over time, capturing an impression of something, and facilitating work and sales. All imply slightly different things about what the product design must accomplish.

Observation and the guided tour

Throughout your discussion, you will hopefully observe people using their tools and interacting with their environments as they demonstrate typical activities. If these activities have not led to explanations of various things in the work setting, at some point you will need to ask for a sort of guided tour of the environment and artifacts. This is also a good technique to fall back on if you're only partway through an interview and have no idea what to ask next.

The observational aspect of an interview involves developing an eye for anomalies and details. What in the environment looks like it might be related to the problems you're trying to solve? What seems out of place or unexpected? What things are placed close at hand, and which are tucked away in inaccessible spots? How have people added to or altered their tools? Which other conditions—distance from the screen, distractions, lighting, and so on—will dictate aspects of your design?

ERGONOMICS

In solving any design problem, it's important to look for ways to decrease fatigue and stress on the body. For desktop-based systems this means reducing eyestrain as well as unnecessary mouse clicking and typing.

Varied lighting conditions are a common challenge in designing anything with a digital display. The radiologist reading digital films in Figure 7.5, for example, is doing so in a dark room to enhance

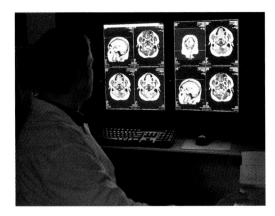

Figure 7.5. A radiologist reads digital films in a dark room.

the contrast and detail he can see on the screen. This means your interface will need to be optimized for that dark room, with no high-contrast screen elements that compete with the images. A surveyor using a GPS device outdoors, on the other hand, may struggle with screen contrast not being great enough to be readable in full sunlight. This has important implications for your hardware (if it's custom) and visual design.

Device design offers a whole host of other possible ergonomic problems. These are largely the province of the industrial designers on the team, but interaction designers should be aware of these issues if an industrial designer isn't along for the research. When redesigning a pole-mounted medical device with a screen that was meant to be read at eye level, for example, we found that nurses were mostly mounting the device at waist height, then crouching to read the screen. At about 30 pounds with all of its attachments, the device was difficult for nurses to lift above waist height while also tightening a large screw clamp on the IV pole (see Figure 7.6).

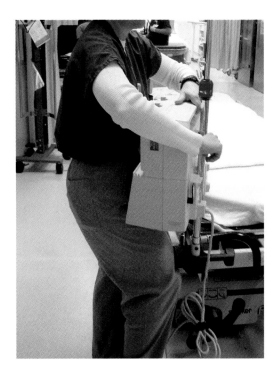

Figure 7.6. This heavy device has an awkward screw clamp, so this nurse is trying to support its weight with her leg while she gets the device fastened to the pole.

CONTENTS OF THE ENVIRONMENT

In a work environment, consider what things are available and where. Why are certain things close at hand and others not? Also look for anything that seems unusual. If an office worker has a printer at her desk, why is it there? These things are sometimes clues to inadequate systems. I once interviewed a purchasing agent using a supposedly paperless system who had crammed two large file cabinets into his cubicle. When I asked him why they were there, he said, "Just because I can get a PO into the system doesn't mean I can get it out again." Someone either hadn't anticipated the need for him to review older purchase orders once they were created, or that functionality was difficult to find or use.

Also look at things like to-do lists, whiteboards full of work in progress, or other textual artifacts that might provide clues to activities or objects that haven't been mentioned. You might be able to tell at a glance that some things are entirely unrelated to what you're working on, while others might take more scrutiny.

Don't feel like you have to sneak peeks at things; this likely won't give you good information and might just make you seem nosy. Instead, say something like, "Just to make sure we're not missing anything important, it would be very helpful if you could you give us the grand tour of your workspace and tell us what everything is and how you use it. Could we start with these different piles of paper on your desk? What's in them, and why are they in different piles?" Follow up with specific questions about each artifact, such as why things are done or represented in certain ways, or how typical these examples are (see Figure 7.7).

UNUSUALLY HARSH CONDITIONS

In the electronic world, desktop computers have it easy: They sit in one place where they're protected from the elements. Everything else, from laptops to mobile phones to military devices, has to put up with more: extreme temperatures, dirt and dust, shocks, moisture, even submersion. Understanding where and how people will use a device is essential. Even if you're not tasked with the industrial design of a product, take note of these difficult conditions and pass them on to the appropriate people. On one project, for example, we saw a medical device that suffered from serious deterioration of its screen in some hospitals, while the same device looked fine in other facilities. It turned out that California regulations required the device to be cleaned with bleach between uses, which the original materials specification had not accounted for.

SIGNS OF DESIGN FAILURE OR UNMET NEEDS

Where there are cheat sheets, notes, or passwords taped to a monitor or tacked to a cubicle wall (such as in Figure 7.8), this could be a sign of infrequent use, but is more often an indication of a design failure or unmet information need.

Figure 7.7. The interview team asked this nurse multiple questions about the sticky notes on her clipboard. What are they for? What do the notations mean? Is there anything significant about the arrangement? Why sticky notes?

Figure 7.8. When we were doing research to design an IV medication pump, we often saw unit conversion and dosage information for the most common medications taped up on the wall of the nursing station. This was a clear indicator of an unmet need.

If the product involves hardware, how have people altered it? It's common to see voicemail passwords or forwarding instructions taped to telephones, or signs on checkout-counter card readers that say, "Press THIS button ➜." We once had a phone system at Cooper that displayed a blinking red light to show that the system was on. It drove most of us crazy because when we saw the red light, it seemed like we either had new voicemail or had someone waiting on hold. Within a fairly short time, pretty much all of the designers had covered the red light in some way, either with black permanent marker or with electrical tape. (Non-designers were less inclined to take matters into their own hands.) Figure 7.9 shows another example.

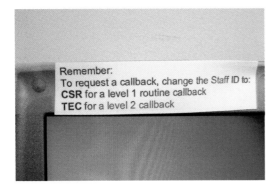

Figure 7.9. This note, which is attached to a shared computer running a customer relationship management system, shows that this company has created an official workaround for a system shortcoming.

Physical damage can be another sign of either an engineering or design failure. In many cases, a design change can eliminate the need to spend a small fortune on stronger plastics or shock-absorbent materials. On one project to redesign a complex device, we saw numerous instances of cracks in a plastic access panel that users often had to open. It would be easy to assume the plastic just wasn't sturdy enough, but we were able to identify a design cause for the problem: The latch

for the access panel was on the side of the device, but users kept tugging at the bottom of the panel, where the affordance of a curved indentation in the plastic all but yelled, "Pull me!"

Another way to spot possible hardware design failures is to look for protective covers or other adaptations that shouldn't be needed for ordinary use, such as the case I bought to keep my exceptionally slippery cell phone from leaping out of my hands like a wet bar of soap, or the protective sheet I use to keep my laptop keyboard from making a permanent imprint on the screen when it's closed.

GETTING PHOTOS

Unless you are in an especially security-conscious environment, most people don't object to photos of their workspaces, whiteboards, or even their to-do lists. Ask in a casual way before taking any photos, and reassure people that those photos are only for reference within your product team. If you plan to make broader use of the images, you will usually need permission in the form of a signed model release for anyone who is identifiable in the photo. Also, be aware that photos you take will probably be covered by any nondisclosure agreements your company has signed.

Exercise

These activities are not quite the same as what you'll do in an interview, but they're good practice for noticing details and considering what they might mean.

— Spend time in another person's work or study space. How is their space arranged differently from yours? What kinds of things are on the desk? What seemingly unusual things might you ask questions about?

Continued

— Spend a half hour or so in a busy public place such as an airport or shopping mall. What things are people carrying with them? How are they dressed? What are they doing as they sit or walk? Hypothesize about their backgrounds and why they're here; consider what kinds of questions you would ask to test your hypotheses without leading your interviewee.

— In the ordinary course of your day, observe someone doing some kind of work you're unfamiliar with: a travel agent making a reservation, a store clerk using a computer to see whether something is in stock, or a barista at the coffee shop using a touch-screen order system. What strikes you as an interesting design issue?

Wrapping up the interview

You can finish most interviews in 45 minutes to an hour. Unless the domain or design problem is exceptionally simple, you're probably missing something if you do a 20-minute interview. As things begin to wind down, check the margins of your notebook (or wherever you've made notes about things to follow up on) to make sure you've got everything covered. Turn to your teammates and ask if they have any additional follow-up questions. If you have any leading questions you really feel you must ask, now is the time to do so.

When you're done with your questions, tell the interviewee how much you appreciate his time and help. If offering an honorarium that you can't pay up front, let him know when to expect a check in the mail. Finally, establish some means for contacting him again if you have follow-up questions (and whether he's willing to answer); also make sure he knows how to contact you.

Dealing with challenging interview circumstances

Not every project involves ideal interview circumstances. Whether due to the nature of the design problem or to some constraint of time and budget, you will sometimes find that the techniques described here need to be adapted in some way. Some of the common challenges and adaptations follow; no doubt there are other circumstances not covered here.

LANGUAGE AND CULTURAL DIFFERENCES

If your product or service has an international audience, it's a good idea to conduct research internationally if the budget will allow it. This may mean you're speaking something other than your native language, or that the interviewee is doing so.

If you're both reasonably fluent in a common language, you can probably do without a translator, but you should allow some extra time for finding vocabulary words or explaining difficult concepts. Scheduling an hour and a half should be sufficient. If the language barrier is such that you need a translator, plan on two hours, since everything you'd ordinarily say in an hour has to be said twice. If the translator is a colleague or member of the sales team rather than a professional interpreter, be sure they understand that you need the most precise translation they can manage, since *how* interviewees say things can be as important as *what* they say. Even a professional translator will be most effective at helping you if you meet beforehand to discuss your interviewing goals and techniques.

Interviewees may already feel like they're going to be judged, so speaking in a language other than their own can increase their anxiety. Some will apologize for not speaking as well as they'd like. It can help to find some self-deprecating way to thank them for the courtesy of speaking in your language: "Thank you so much for agreeing to speak with us in English. I wish I spoke German half so well. I'm afraid I'm limited to asking for directions!"

Cultural differences are usually not a tremendous barrier. If your company or client has a local sales office where you're interviewing, the staff there can usually help with a cultural "dos and don'ts" list. Failing that, a local market research firm that's helping with recruiting should be able to offer some tips, such as whether it's considered rude to take notes without asking.

CHILDREN AND TEENAGERS

Speaking of cultural differences, the gap between teens and older adult interviewers can pose similar problems. My colleague Ernest Kinsolving shared this bit of excellent advice about interviewing them:

"Take them seriously. This may sound trivial and obvious, but it's essential to treat their observations, concerns, and lives as truly significant and worthy of serious attention. It can be easy for an adult interviewer to trivialize the issues that are of significance to a teen subject, since most of us have moved on to other concerns and don't necessarily remember what it was like to be 14 or 16 and know absolutely that life and death hinged on your standing on the crew team or whether you were wearing the right pants."

Teens may be more reticent about sharing with adults, whether it's because they think you don't care about the details, or because they're concerned about getting in trouble. You may need to reassure them more than once that what they say won't be passed on to their parents, teachers, or peers. In general, though, they'll appreciate being treated as adults. The same techniques that work with adult interviewees, such as looking at artifacts and asking for detailed stories, can help get a teen who responds with, "You know…stuff," to open up. Starting off with a group interview can help break down barriers, as well.

The unique cognitive, developmental, and ethical aspects of conducting research with children are worth an entire book. Thankfully, there are plenty of good resources available for responsible researchers, so I won't address this complex topic here.

In either case, it's a good idea for at least one of the interviewers to be comfortable conversing with teens or children in the target age group. If you're not comfortable, it will show, and it will take longer to establish a rapport.

REMOTE INTERVIEWS

Design research often has tight time or budget constraints, so international or even domestic travel may be out of the question. Remote interviews are generally the best compromise in this situation, if you need cultural diversity in your sample or if you're designing a business tool without many users in your area.

If possible, use remote interviews as a supplemental technique rather than as the bulk of your research. Remote research, even with the best videoconferencing tools, is missing the nuance and detail you can get from in-person discussion and observation. For this reason, start with as much local research as you can manage, then use remote research primarily as a way to see if there are any significant differences. If what you're hearing sounds very similar, that's good news. If not, it might give you enough evidence to argue for some in-person research.

Videoconferencing can be somewhat helpful for remote interviews, but it's less useful than you might think. Transmissions are often low resolution with low refresh rates, so the nuances of body language and facial expression may be lost. It's also a rare interviewee who has videoconferencing capability in the actual context of use. If you're working on a Web site or an application, a telephone conversation plus a desktop-sharing tool (such as WebEx) may be the best option.

To get some rich information in a sterile conference-room setting, ask the interviewees ahead of time to bring some artifacts with them.

Often, you'll find you're limited to a simple phone call. Try to prepare interviewees ahead of time by specifying the kinds of tools or documents you may be interested in. If possible, get your interviewees to send photos or copies of examples so you can talk through them in the interview. When someone mentions an interesting artifact that you haven't seen, ask if you can get a copy later.

Remote interviews will also require the best active-listening skills you can muster. It's even more important that you summarize back what you're hearing to confirm that you're interpreting correctly. Also allow for longer pauses than you would in face-to-face conversation, since you don't have body language cues to tell you when someone is finished speaking. Be sure to use a full-duplex conference phone, as well; some ordinary office phones don't transmit signals both ways at the same time, so you may not be aware when you're speaking over the person on the other end.

LITTLE OR NO ACCESS TO THE CONTEXT OF USE

You may be too pressed for time to visit people's homes or offices, or an interview might be too disruptive in an open-plan workspace. Whatever the reason, it's not unusual to have limited or no access to the actual context of use. A few design problems, such as consumer Web sites, lend themselves to out-of-context interviews more than others, though you'll always lose some information by not conducting them in context.

Consider how you can still get some rich information in a sterile conference-room setting. Ask the interviewees ahead of time to bring some artifacts with them, and offer examples of the kinds of things you're looking for. If designing a car maker's Web site, for example, ask people to bring in any magazines or articles that have influenced their thinking, any notes they have, and a list of any Web sites they've been looking at.

Set up a computer with the existing version of the software or Web site; approximate the most common user hardware and software setup. Of course, users may struggle due to different settings or lack of familiar files, so your data won't be entirely accurate; this is particularly problematic with enterprise or productivity software that may be highly configurable.

In the event that a full-length interview is disruptive in a work setting, see if just a five- or ten-minute tour in the work area would be acceptable. At some point during the interview, use this as your opportunity for a condensed version of the "grand tour." Try not to do it at the very end of your time, since what you see might raise useful questions you'll want to discuss back in the conference room. Snap a few digital photos or use a video camera so you can point to workspace artifacts during the remainder of the interview.

PERIPATETIC OR HARD-TO-INTERRUPT ACTIVITIES

Not all activities are conducive to having the interviewer ask to see a demonstration of this or that behavior. If the users are peripatetic—such as nurses who make notes while walking around a medical ward, or golf-course superintendents who look at their greens and want to adjust their watering parameters on the spot—try to follow along and observe this behavior, asking questions about what you're seeing when it's feasible or polite to do so. Plan on a long interview in such settings, if possible, so you can start with an introduction to what you're about to see, then wrap up with a more thorough debrief of what you observed. With very busy users, you may need to work in this discussion over a cup of coffee or during lunch.

There are also some behaviors that would be unwise to interrupt, such as driving a car or doing knee surgery. The interviewee may have some limited ability to comment as she goes about her activity, but can't stop or take detours to answer your questions. An ideal approach in these situations is to videotape the action, then watch it with the interviewee as you ask questions in a more typical interview style.

ACCESS TO SENSITIVE DATA

Interviewees dealing with medical, financial, or other sensitive data may be reluctant to show you actual documents or records. You can often address this concern by signing a nondisclosure agreement, which is best to take care of in advance. If this doesn't do the trick, you may need to ask the informant to work with a blank record or to create some fake data; neither is optimal. In most cases, it's acceptable for you to look at the real data as long as you don't capture it in any way.

An interviewee might mention a document that sounds particularly useful, but then be uncertain whether he can share it with you. Ask for the name of the document and see if the interviewee would mind you requesting it through his or her manager; most people are relieved to pass such decisions along.

In particularly secretive environments where, for example, a business process is seen as proprietary, it's occasionally useful to make an exception to the "no manager in the room" rule. Otherwise, interviewees may be so uncertain whether they can answer your questions that you get nothing from the interview; if they can look to a manager for permission, you will at least get something, even if you don't get the workarounds. Hopefully, not all the companies you visit during your research will be so reticent.

GROUP INTERVIEWS

Individual interviews are almost always better, though group interviews can be ideal either as a warm-up for individual discussions or when you know almost nothing about a domain. They can also be useful as a follow-up later on, since they offer an opportunity for people to compare and contrast their approaches and processes; after people have participated in individual interviews, they're a bit more self-aware about how they do things.

In rare cases, you may work on a product that's likely to be used by two or more people together, in which case a group interview makes sense. Informational kiosks in a museum or home entertainment systems are good examples of this. It's important to see how users behave together—do they all engage directly, or does one person drive the interaction while others watch?

You might also encounter group interviews when you don't particularly want them. A colleague who had to recruit interviewees at the local mall lamented that teenage girls always seemed to "travel in packs" and were reluctant to participate in interviews without their friends. If the manager at a customer site schedules things in the easiest way, you might find yourself unexpectedly facing a roomful of users for an hour or two, instead of the two or three users you hoped to see individually. In essence, your interview has just turned into a focus group, which can't accomplish what an individual interview can.

If you must do group interviews, plan for 90 minutes rather than an hour. In most cases, you'll want people in the group to have some key characteristic (such as role or age) in common, so you can compare apples to apples. People are also more likely to speak openly with their peers in the room than if some authority figure is present. Seat the participants so they can see one another.

The biggest challenge with groups is getting everyone's thoughts rather than letting one or two people drive the conversation. One way to minimize this is to ask for individual responses from each participant, then discuss what's been said. This can feel very stilted, though. You can accomplish something similar by asking a question of someone in particular, then asking other members of the group how their own thoughts or behaviors differ.

If the group consists of more than two or three interviewees, it can be difficult to conduct the interview as a team, since group facilitation requires more attention as the group size increases. Consider a more explicit division of labor, with one person focused entirely on taking notes while the other just facilitates.

INTERVIEWS IN THE HOME

When visiting someone's home for research, you may be imposing on their hospitality as well as their time. Depending on the time of day, you might offer to bring food, such as bagels for breakfast or pizza for dinner. This is a good way to break the ice and meet the family. In any case, interviews in this environment feel more like a social call than they do in other settings, so plan to start off with small talk about the interviewee's lovely house, evident hobbies, or adorable children.

The home environment is often more filled with interruptions and distractions than an office setting, whether it's the telephone ringing, the pets grabbing for the snacks, or the kids needing something. Consider whether this is part of what you need to observe in your interview or whether it's likely to present a problem, then let the interviewee know in advance if you need them to plan on not taking phone calls or dealing with the home's other residents.

Also be aware that many people feel compelled to neaten up their homes before someone visits. This is likely to gloss over things you need to see, so it's worth asking people explicitly not to do so (and mentioning that your place has a pile of laundry in the hall and dust bunnies on the stairs).

NO RAPPORT WITH THE INTERVIEWEE

Every now and then, you might see that you're just not developing a good rapport with an interviewee. This could be a matter of personality or style. My female colleagues and I have sometimes seen male interviewees more inclined to converse with our male teammates, even if the female team member is clearly leading the interview; I've encountered this more often outside the U.S. I've also seen female interviewees more inclined to converse with me than with a male colleague. Whatever the reason, if you don't see a rapport developing, try switching interview roles with a teammate. You certainly don't want to give offense by saying, "I'm not connecting with this person, so you try," but you can pull it off if you say something that sounds like you planned it ahead of time, such as, "Great, that's all I had. Steve, I know you had some other questions..." Discuss this sort of signal with your partner ahead of time so he's not taken by surprise.

UPSET INTERVIEWEES

Most design research won't dig into anything more sensitive than collaboration with difficult coworkers, but some topics, such as dealing with medical conditions or personal finances, can be difficult to discuss. It's obviously important to be sensitive to this, but you may still hit a nerve without intending to. If someone becomes very upset, acknowledge his distress: "That seems like it must be very difficult for you." After that, you might sit quietly while the interviewee collects himself or perhaps excuse yourselves for a glass of water to give him a bit of space. Ask if he would prefer to continue the interview or end it.

"BAD" INTERVIEWS

Happily, truly unpleasant interviews are very rare; in hundreds of interviews, I can only think of one or two interviewees who were downright uncooperative or rude. More often, a "bad" interview is the result of someone not fitting the right profile, such as someone whose job doesn't really involve the activities you need to learn about. There's often one person in a set of consumer interviewees who doesn't fit the parameters, but this is more rare in enterprise projects. If you find there are several participants who don't meet your criteria, review your screening questions to see if any of them hint at the answer you're looking for—unfortunately, there are people who will answer screening questions incorrectly because they want to participate in the research or get the honorarium. If the problem isn't with your

questions, then complain to your recruiter; you shouldn't have to pay them for sloppy work.

Of course, there's the problem of what to do with the informant who's sitting there in front of you. Unless you did the screening yourself, you have to assume this person is there with good intent. It might be fine in a consumer study to say, "I'm sorry, it seems like we made an error; you don't quite fit the parameters of our study. Of course we will pay you for your time." However, if this is someone recruited by your sales team or for whom helping out is the incentive, then it would be rude to send her away unheard. Your time is scheduled anyway, so the best approach is often to interview this person even if it's not going to be helpful. You will need to adapt your questions to what the interviewee has to offer. A half hour is usually enough to make someone feel like she's provided valuable information.

Project Management for Interviews

Research with customers and users is a significant investment, so you'll want to make the most of it. This usually means packing a lot of research into a short period. However, it's important to make sure you aren't moving so quickly that you start to miss details.

Between interviews

If possible, spend a few minutes after each session clarifying your notes and debriefing with your teammate(s). If that's not possible, do so at the end of each day. This helps you get the most out of each precious interview.

Discuss what you saw that was interesting, consistent with other interviews, or surprising. This helps solidify the data in your mind. It also shows whether you're interpreting the information the same way as your teammates. Consider whether you have enough depth on particular topics; this affects whether you try to spend more or less time on them in subsequent interviews.

Also bring up any interview techniques or interactions that worked well or not so well. Was there a point when you were stuck and didn't know how to get help from your partner? Did you have follow-up questions but not enough opportunity to ask them? This should become less necessary after you've conducted a number of interviews with someone.

You should be starting to see behavior patterns emerge as you do more interviews. If you find yourself able to predict what an interviewee will say, you probably don't need to continue interviewing. Don't worry if you're not seeing sharp distinctions, though, especially in cases where the boundaries between roles are blurry. Provided you've gotten the necessary information, later analysis will find the patterns where intuition doesn't see them.

Staying sane

It's entirely possible to do 20 or more interviews in a week if they're all in the same region and can be scheduled tightly. However, it's essential in laying out your research plan to allow for travel time, as well as the reality that interviewees won't always be available when you'd like. If your manager or client asks that you interview during the day and hop on a plane for the next city in the evening, point out that interviewing takes a great deal of focus, so it won't be long before this kind of schedule makes you less effective at getting value out of the research. There's not much point in spending money on your time and travel if you're going to be half asleep during the interviews.

If at all possible, plan out your whole interview schedule before you hit the road. It's extremely difficult to manage logistics and focus on interviewing

at the same time, so ask for project-management help from someone not traveling if your schedule isn't finalized by the time you start.

Team roles and responsibilities

If you can afford to have every member of the team do most of the interviews, that's great, though you'll want to avoid having a big crowd overwhelm the participants. If your budget is as constrained as most, send the two flavors of interaction designers to every interview, since they are the team members who most need to understand the behavioral details, then send the project lead, visual designer, and industrial designer (if there is one) on just enough interviews to get a sense of the users and domain. However, the team members doing the interviewing should stay in touch with the rest of the team and share what they're learning, since it gives the other team members a chance to suggest other lines of inquiry as the research progresses.

If two interviewing partners have different levels of skill and experience, it's common for the senior team member to drive most of the interviews while the other is primarily focused on capturing information and asking clarifying questions. However, it's a good idea for both team members to lead at some of the discussions; switching roles can help a team survive a long interview day.

Communicating outside the team

Project owners or stakeholders outside the design team may get a bit nervous during research, since the project's success may depend on how well it goes, and the design team is likely out of sight for several weeks. Be sure to reach out at least every few days to let the project owner know how it's going. Don't feel that you need to synthesize on the go, but do provide general feedback about how things are going and perhaps share an interesting observation or two: "The group manager at site

Research

X was exceptionally helpful. We got several excellent interviews there, plus a couple of good ones at site Y. We're getting what we need so far. One technician at site Y showed us something we've never seen before…"

Of course, you should alert your project owner as soon as possible if things aren't going as expected. If you're not getting enough interviews or you're getting the wrong interviews, you need to discuss whether to extend the schedule or work with what you're getting. If you're finding that the research contradicts important assumptions the product team is making, it's best to alert the project owner to this early on, so stakeholders can assess whether you're getting the wrong interviews or whether their assumptions are off base.

Not all unexpected news is bad. The interview team may discover a new role or other unanticipated factor that provides important insight. I remember the first time my teammates and I encountered a case manager in healthcare, while doing research for a comprehensive facility information system that combined financial and clinical data. This new role straddled the clinical and financial worlds, looking at which medical approach to a problem was the least expensive. With the growth of managed care in the United States, it seemed clear to us that this role would become increasingly common, so we called up the client project owner that evening, told him what we'd found and why it seemed important, and asked if we could find any more such people to interview.

Summary

The quality of your interviews will determine whether you're designing on a foundation made of bedrock or one made of sand. A good set of interviews need not anticipate every tiny question you might have during detailed design, but should equip you with a good understanding of goals, major tasks, mental models, and opportunities for design to improve the effectiveness of a business or the quality of someone's life.

Just remember that if you understand how people think and behave, the design will follow. You won't do perfect interviews, especially at first, but if you avoid the worst mistakes—asking users what they want you to design or whether they agree with your preconceived notions—keep things conversational, use your active-listening skills, and refer to a cheat sheet of topics and question types inside the cover of your notebook, you'll probably do just fine.

CHAPTER 8

Example Interview

Now that we've covered the interview techniques in theory, let's see how they work in practice by dissecting an actual interview for the LocalGuide. This interview includes some good examples of effective technique, and the interviewee is very reflective about her own behavior. However, there's also plenty of room for improvement; in particular, you'll see there are a number of missed opportunities for follow-up.

The interviewers introduce themselves and everyone gets seated. The interview takes place in a very informal meeting room at the interviewee's place of business. It has pillows on the floor and some books scattered around. After a little bit of social chat, the primary interviewer introduces the design problem.

Interview transcript	Comments
PRIMARY INTERVIEWER: We're designing a product called the LocalGuide. It's a device with a screen and GPS capability for people going new places. Something they will be able to pick up there. So, we're doing research into the way people travel, both the planning for the trip, activities during the trip, and activities once you actually get to your destination and how you decide what you're going to do. To start off, how often do you travel during the year, and what proportion is business versus pleasure?	The interviewer could skip the first three sentences, which would distract most interviewees, and focus on what he's trying to learn rather than on describing the product.
	The overview question is pretty good, in that it's broad and designed to uncover different types of travel. Unfortunately, it assumes that the interviewee categorizes travel in two ways; some people may see travel related to family obligations, for example, as neither business nor pleasure. This phrasing also implies that the interviewers are only interested in two categories, which may prevent the interviewee from mentioning others. Better would be, "How often do you travel, and for what reasons?"

Interview transcript	Comments
	It would also be good to ask for a brief description of the interviewee's family and occupation, since these might shed light later on.
PARTICIPANT: Business tends to just be once or twice a year. Mind you I'm new to business. But personal is more like once every other month or so. Short trips, long trips.	
PRIMARY INTERVIEWER: Can you talk to us about one of your recent long trips?	This is a nice case-specific question. Before diving in to a specific trip, though, it would be worth asking for examples of those short and long trips so the interviewers could decide which is more interesting.
PARTICIPANT: A recent long trip? Let's see… Now, does a new destination count? Because there's… So the longest trip I've taken recently was a trip to Colorado on the way home for winter break.	Interviewees often pause to think. The interviewers are just listening, as they should.
PRIMARY INTERVIEWER: Where's home?	
PARTICIPANT: Kansas. So, I had driven with some friends to Colorado, and they were from Colorado, so I dropped them off there and stayed with them for a few days, and then went on to Kansas, and then flew back, because I was basically getting rid of my car because I was tired of having it in the city.	
PRIMARY INTERVIEWER: Tell us about that trip.	This kind of vague encouragement can work well if you're not sure yet what to ask next.
PARTICIPANT: So it was kind of one of those trips that takes two weeks, but I get three or four big things done. Like, holiday with the family, dropping the car off, taking some friends home and celebrating Hanukkah with them, and then Christmas with my family. And I have never driven this direction, from California back that way, so that's part of the reason I was looking forward to having friends with me so that we could figure out … they could all navigate.	There's an implied sense of safety in numbers or discomfort with navigation that's probably worth exploring. It might be too personal for this early in the interview, but it's the sort of topic to make a note about and return to later.

Interview transcript	Comments
PRIMARY INTERVIEWER: Talk to us a little about the planning for that trip. How many friends were you traveling with?	These are fairly distinct questions, so it would be best to ask them one at a time. Otherwise, interviewees (and interviewers) can forget what was asked.
PARTICIPANT: It was two guys and so there were three of us. That was nice actually because I sort of took charge of the date and just making sure that we were all planning on leaving Friday evening and that type of thing; that everyone was sort of packed. And the two guys actually looked stuff up on maps and were checking the weather because we were driving and this was December so there were all those snow storms. And we actually made it to Colorado right as they had cleared the roads after that really bad storm in Denver so that was amusing. We were driving through Denver and there were all these cars out on the side of the road, like they had just spun off the road and had just crashed.	There are a couple of things worth following up on here. What else does she mean by "...that type of thing?" What kinds of information did the guys look up on maps? (Note that third-party behavior is sometimes worth asking about as long as you take the answer with a grain of salt). Also notice that although the storm was a memorable part of her trip, it has little to do with the future product. It's best to acknowledge that this must have been scary, then ask a closed question to redirect the conversation in an unobtrusive way. Ideally, the interviewer should ask for the sequence of events from the point of deciding to go on the trip through arriving in Colorado.
SECOND INTERVIEWER: You really did just miss the danger.	This statement without any question following it elicits more on the same topic.
PARTICIPANT: Oh yeah. And it was a fun trip, too, because one of the guys had just gotten a GPS in-car device, so we probably shouldn't have done this, but we drove through snow storms that we probably shouldn't have because the two guys were assuming that it probably maps to the road pretty well, so we can drive faster than normal because we can tell what's coming up.	Not entirely relevant to the research, though it's worth noting what they expected the GPS device to be capable of.
PRIMARY INTERVIEWER: So the visibility was bad enough you couldn't quite see the road?	Now the car isn't the only thing at risk of going off the road; so is the interview. There's no harm in this kind of digression if you have lots of time, but that's not the case in most sessions.
PARTICIPANT: There were times when I would have driven really, really slowly and when the guys got behind the wheel, the two of them were in charge and they, despite the fact that that's not what I wanted, drove much faster than I would have liked. I was scared.	

Interview transcript	Comments
PRIMARY INTERVIEWER: So you were awake during this, you weren't sleeping.	The digression continues.
PARTICIPANT: Well, I was trying to sleep. Because we were heading up through Tahoe, for example, the visibility was really bad and the roads were pretty nasty, and I would have gone 20 (mph) or 30, but they were going 50, 60.	
PRIMARY INTERVIEWER: What kind of car?	More digression.
PARTICIPANT: RAV 4.	
PRIMARY INTERVIEWER: A bit of false confidence there, too.	More digression, as well as a big assumption about what's driving the behavior.
PARTICIPANT: Yeah. Handles pretty well, but not that well. Let's see… they were fun to travel with too, because they're pretty laid back so as far as getting food and stuff, we kind of had some ideas. They knew some destinations in Colorado to check out along the way and just things like, "Let's hit In-N-Out Burger before we leave," so we used the GPS device to find out where the nearest In-N-Out Burger was as we were moving along. Because our trip was being planned along with the weather. When the weather would get really bad, we'd have to stop, and so we'd use the GPS device then to find out what was nearby.	It's actually the interviewee who pulls the discussion back onto the road. She also presents several opportunities for follow-up questions: — How did finding things work? — What kinds of things did you look for besides food? — When did you look for specific names, and when not? This would be a good time to see how the GPS device worked if it were available, find an image of it online so the interviewee could have a visual prompt, or at least ask about its name to look up later.
PRIMARY INTERVIEWER: How did you check the weather?	The interviewee didn't mention checking the weather, so this is another assumption.
PARTICIPANT: Well, if we were in it, and it didn't seem to be clearing and the radio said that it would only get worse…	
PRIMARY INTERVIEWER: Okay, so, through the radio and reality. So, when the weather was particularly bad, you'd use the GPS to find… what?	This question is headed in the right direction.

Interview transcript	Comments
PARTICIPANT: It actually lets you search for nearby restaurants, and you could search restaurant genres, so, "Does everyone feel like Mexican? Yeah? There's something nearby."	So what came first? Was it the kind of food people want to eat, or what's close by? It's important to understand the starting point.
PRIMARY INTERVIEWER: Did you have lodging planned? How many days did you take from San Francisco to Colorado?	This question is somewhat leading, since the interviewee hasn't mentioned lodging yet. It may be necessary to bring up later, but there are plenty of other questions the interviewers could have asked.
PARTICIPANT: We had planned not to stop.	The reason she didn't mention it.
PRIMARY INTERVIEWER: Well, with three people…	
PARTICIPANT: I'm trying to remember if we ended up actually stopping or not. I can't quite remember if we did. No, I don't think we stopped. I think we just went straight through. I've done that a couple times.	Memories can be fuzzy, even with fairly recent events. This is one reason trip artifacts (even receipts) could be helpful.
PRIMARY INTERVIEWER: So how long did it actually end up taking you, with the weather?	
PARTICIPANT: With the weather, to Denver, I think it took about 19 hours or so.	
PRIMARY INTERVIEWER: Okay, once you were in Colorado, what did you do?	This is a reasonable second overview question for this segment of the interview. However, it's a bit early to move on from the previous topic. How often did they stop on the way? Where did they stop? What difficulties did they encounter in finding things? While road trips are not strictly part of the LocalGuide plan, there's still useful information to be had.
PARTICIPANT: Okay, so we get there, and we stay at…	
PRIMARY INTERVIEWER: This is in Boulder?	It's best not to interrupt.

Interview transcript	Comments
PARTICIPANT: Uh-huh. Yeah, we stayed with one of the guys, his family, and we sort of took it easy because of the storm, and I actually had to go get my car checked for... the lights had turned off on the inside of the car and were not turning back on, even though the car was running, for the last... This is funny, we were driving with a flashlight in the morning as we were coming into... because there were no lights. Just a fuse had burned out. So we had asked my friend's parents where to go, and they suggested a Sam's Club or a Wal-Mart or one of those attached car stations.	Unexpected car repairs are an interesting need to note for the LocalGuide. Follow-up opportunities: — Where did you go? — How did you decide? — How did you find it?
PRIMARY INTERVIEWER: So otherwise you just hung out with them?	Reflecting back what you hear is good, but don't assume there's no interesting behavior in "hanging out."
PARTICIPANT: Yeah.	
PRIMARY INTERVIEWER: How many days were you in Boulder?	
PARTICIPANT: Let's see, I was there for... I think it was just two days. There was a little bit of shopping and a little bit of visiting with friends at a coffee shop or planning for the dinner and going out and getting supplies for the dinner, the Hanukkah dinner. And most of that was word of mouth, as far as knowing where to go. "Where should we go buy some wine?"	Again, the interviewee helps out by volunteering more. This is one reason to make interviews very conversational; once people get going, the interview flow is less reliant on the interviewers asking just the right questions. Several follow-up opportunities here: — What did you shop for and where? — How did you decide where to go? — How did you find the coffee shop?
PRIMARY INTERVIEWER: From whom?	
PARTICIPANT: From my friend's parents. Both of those guys had lived in that area just a while ago, so they would call someone and confirm that a restaurant they used to go to was still there. So, pretty much all friends. I tend to like to travel to places where I know somebody there already. It just makes it a little bit easier, right?	An affirmation of the basic product concept, plus an interesting point about the importance of having current information. Follow-up opportunity: What's easier about knowing someone who lives there?

Interview transcript	Comments
PRIMARY INTERVIEWER: Yeah.	
PARTICIPANT: Or I end up traveling somewhere that someone else I know has traveled recently.	
SECOND INTERVIEWER: Why is that better?	This is exactly the kind of follow-up opportunity the second interviewer should be looking for, in case the primary interviewer doesn't catch it.
PARTICIPANT: It's just so much easier when somebody can give you a few pointers to get started. I tend to travel in such a way that I have a couple destinations that I'd like to go to and maybe they helped me figure out, oh, you should go to this landmark because there's that, plus there's other stuff around it if you don't like that. And then I tend to… "Okay, we're going to go somewhere." But I never really stick to going there, so if something else more interesting shows up or whatever, I like to be very flexible, but still a destination to at least get started towards.	This would be a good point to paraphrase: "So, it sounds like you start out with a loose plan, but you often change it if something else seems more interesting."
PRIMARY INTERVIEWER: When you're traveling like that, how do you decide what other things to do? So if you planned to go one place, how do you find other things to do?	Don't worry if your first attempt at a question is a bit unclear; you're trying to track too many things in the interview to be perfectly articulate at all times. If you realize it's unclear, immediately try a different rendition. The interview is dealing in generalizations at this point, so it would be good to get case-specific again soon.
PARTICIPANT: Yeah, I guess it depends on how you're moving about. So I had gone to Venice last November, and my friend and I had both looked in some tour books. So we went to Venice, which is a pretty small place, and so we had picked out a couple of things like, "Oh, we really need to go see this, and this." And we were there for an event. Again, this is like, I like going somewhere where there are people involved.	Once again, the interviewee volunteers just the right sort of thing.
PRIMARY INTERVIEWER: What was the event?	

Interview transcript	Comments
PARTICIPANT: Architectural Biennial show that was put on by one of the universities there. So, we knew that that event was going to take most of the time, and so we had a little standing list of things that when we had free time, we should do. Check out the major square there. Go to the major shopping street. There was a glass blowing... island actually. An island with glass blowing workshops, which we did not make it to.	Opportunities for follow-up: — Was this just a loose list of possibilities in your head, or did you have them laid out more specifically as an itinerary? — What information did you note before you left on your trip, and what did you find while you were there? — What other preplanning did you do?
SECOND INTERVIEWER: But you wanted to?	
PARTICIPANT: Yeah, it was definitely on the list. But I guess that's the thing. I don't like making the list solid because then I regret if we didn't get somewhere. But maybe there's something more interesting.	This sounds like a goal: Have a plan to use as a starting point, but maintain flexibility. This would be a good thing to paraphrase back for confirmation. Follow-up opportunities: — Can you give us an example of a time when you dropped your plans because something else seemed more interesting? What made you decide that? — How did you come across these opportunities?
PRIMARY INTERVIEWER: So once you had some free time, and you wanted to get to one of these places, how did you find it?	This question should yield some good information. It's still a little general, though. The interviewers would get more detail and ensure better coverage by asking for an overview of each day's itinerary, then focusing on a few different examples of behavior.
PARTICIPANT: We were looking at tourist maps in tourist books for the most part.	
PRIMARY INTERVIEWER: Guidebooks that you brought with you?	Good clarification. It would also be useful to take a look at the guidebooks if they were nearby, or at least ask for their titles and look at them later.
PARTICIPANT: Yeah, guidebooks. And attempting to ask directions.	

Interview transcript	Comments
PRIMARY INTERVIEWER: Neither of you spoke the language?	Good clarification. This highlights an interesting design issue: How will the device account for people who don't speak the language very well, or at all?
PARTICIPANT: No, not really.	
PRIMARY INTERVIEWER: How did that work out?	Good follow-up.
PARTICIPANT: We'd usually figure out where we were going eventually. One of the people who had... so I went with a friend and there was another group of people who met us there. And when we finally connected with them, one of them spoke better Italian and had been to Venice before. Again, using people is the easiest way. So he would direct us. I think the hardest part became that you'd get somewhere, and then getting back was usually the hardest part.	Follow-up opportunity: Why, exactly, is it easiest to ask a person? It might sound like a question with an obvious answer, but the interviewee's reasons might be different from yours: Local people have more recent information, the guidebooks lack detail, she doesn't want to carry a map...there are many possibilities.
PRIMARY INTERVIEWER: Why?	
PARTICIPANT: Because I felt like I should know how to get back, and so it's really frustrating when you can't retrace your steps. I *should* know how to get back to the apartment that we're staying at but everything's in reverse and I can't quite keep it in my head straight. I think the hardest part usually of traveling is dealing with the mass transit. I don't usually get to rent a car when I go somewhere, but I always kind of like that because you can just sort of head out in the right direction and hopefully you'll end up there. If you're stuck with mass transit, you have to know how to do it.	Be sure to note her mental model regarding navigation: The place she's staying is the center of her universe and the ultimate point of reference. This will have design implications later on.

Opportunity for follow-up: What in particular is hard about dealing with mass transit? |
| **PRIMARY INTERVIEWER:** Can you give us an example of when you ran into that? | Good, case-specific follow-up. |

Interview transcript

Comments

PARTICIPANT: So in Venice, for example, we were trying to get to the airport to leave. And my friend was sort of in charge of navigating that day. And we took the wrong boat but we didn't know it, and we didn't know it for a very long time, because it was supposed to be a very long boat ride. And ended up on some other island, not the mainland, and missed our flight back to the states. So, that's pretty scary.

It sounds like there might be another goal here: Avoid the negative consequences of navigational error.

Opportunity for follow-up: What resources did you use to figure out how to get where you were going?

I lived in Japan for a while, and we would travel to other cities. Their mass transit's pretty easy to use, but when you'd end up on one of the older systems that didn't announce very well which stop was coming up or that sort of thing... I was with a friend and we were headed to Kyoto and the station that we were supposed to get off on never got announced and then there was a 20 minute ride to the next station. And it was very late at night and so we were very disappointed in having to turn around and come back. And we were nervous that there wouldn't be any trains going back. None of that stuff was very obvious because of the language issue.

PRIMARY INTERVIEWER: How long were you in Japan?

This is tempting to ask, since it sounds like travel, though living somewhere long-term is not the situation for the LocalGuide.

PARTICIPANT: I lived there for a year and did a lot of traveling while I was in the country.

PRIMARY INTERVIEWER: What took you there?

This is a bit off the track, but okay if you have time.

PARTICIPANT: I taught English in the JET program. Japanese Exchange and Teaching program, I think, because it's not just English. Yeah, it's run by the government and it's a very sweet deal if you can run off for a year. If you're a college graduate, they pay you well and give you lots of vacation and send you out to the boonies, that's the catch.

PRIMARY INTERVIEWER: Oh, how far out were you?

Still wandering a bit.

Interview transcript	Comments

PARTICIPANT: Nobody ends up in Tokyo. They only have one placement in Tokyo, they had four placements in Osaka, and the other two thousand people end up just… everywhere. So I was on an island called Shikoku, well, okay, everything in Japan's an island, but in a very small farming town. In my town, taking the buses, and even using a taxi was incredibly difficult. So, navigating in Japan is incredibly difficult because they don't have street numbers and they don't have ordered building addresses. So, your apartment could be 225 apartment on something street, and the building next to you could be 5 apartment building, same street. Because the numbers don't go in order, they go in order of when the building was built. So it's a little different. But one thing that is nice is the way they organize the… the cities, the way that you organize the mailing addresses and stuff like that… it's about chunking. So you start with… they even write their postal address flipped from us. So their first line is Japan, and the very second line is the county or the zip code. I think it's the… no you probably write the zip code first, now I can't even remember. Anyway, so it's sort of like, the county, the city, the street, and the address number. And in some bigger cities there's a… trying to remember the equivalents, there's like the…

> The helpful interviewee eventually brings it back to navigation, though some of the mailing address information is less relevant.

PRIMARY INTERVIEWER: Neighborhood?

PARTICIPANT: Yeah, the borough, you'd enter that as well.

SECOND INTERVIEWER: So how did you get around?

> The second interviewer realizes they've digressed a bit and gives the conversation an appropriate nudge.

PARTICIPANT: You can see why GPS has taken off there, way more than in other places. 'Cause that was great. We'd be walking somewhere, and you could pretty much ask people on the street, "I need to get to this restaurant or this place," and they would almost always pull out a cell phone and look it up on a map. And show you, "My cell phone says, we are here, and you have to go this way, this way, this way."

> This functionality was not yet common in the U.S. at the time of the interview. The LocalGuide stakeholders will want to know they should consider cell phones as competition or as a possible channel for the service.

Research

Interview transcript	Comments
PRIMARY INTERVIEWER: So is that what you did, you would mostly ask people? Or did you have any other methods?	Better phrasing would be, "So, did you mostly ask people versus using other methods? How else did you find your way round?" Still, this does the trick.
PARTICIPANT: In the cities I'd mostly ask people. There's also… they have police boxes in all cities. In my little city it wasn't really that useful, but, so if you were super lost or just had questions, you could go to the police box and they had huge drawers full of maps and they would point you in the right direction.	Follow-up opportunities: — Besides getting directions, what kinds of questions did you ask? — Do you happen to have any photos of one of these boxes?
PRIMARY INTERVIEWER: So like an information kiosk?	Good clarification.
PARTICIPANT: Yeah, they're the police, but it's like… maybe they don't have that much to do in Japan 'cause it's safe. They're much more like a civil servant than they are an enforcement agency. Yeah, I very specifically remember being in Tokyo and looking for an art gallery and seeing one of the police boxes, when I was with a friend. Mind you, I don't really travel alone very much. Well, if I do travel alone it's usually out to the woods or something, so there's no need for directions. So the two of us went to the police box, had the address of the place. I don't think they like dealing with foreigners very much, so if your Japanese isn't that great—my Japanese was pretty bad at this point—you could tell he was frustrated. Like, oh, no, I have to help this person. And he gave us bad directions, and we ended up walking in a spiral after a while and realized this was completely not the right place, and asking someone on the street who pulls out a cell phone and then actually walks with us to the gallery.	Here's a good opening to follow up on that desire for help with navigating, which came up earlier in the discussion.

Interview transcript	Comments

But for the most part, mass transit, the sub-ways were so easy to use. So, so, easy to use because you could see that big map up front and you could say I'm going from "here" to "here" [points], and there were very few time schedules to deal with because they ran pretty regularly. And so you had very few factors to handle at once, especially with language issues.

SECOND INTERVIEWER: So what about the first time you used one of those maps. What was it like for you?

Good case-specific follow-up.

PARTICIPANT: Oh, yeah, it was in Tokyo, and it was like, oh my God, the subway map is this big? What?!? So the hardest part was actually finding the right destination on the huge map, because it just took so long. You had to wander around with your eyes and try to find the right spot. And I think later on I realized there was a listing in alphabetical order, in English, in a corner somewhere.

Follow-up opportunity: Do you happen to have a photo or a copy of the subway map?

It may be possible to find one online later.

PRIMARY INTERVIEWER: In a corner of the map or a corner of the train hall?

PARTICIPANT: Oh, up on this big board, over in a corner somewhere so you had to get up closer to so you could actually read it type of thing. But the color coding was always really great, especially in the newer systems they'd even color-coded the trains themselves, so you could really understand what was going on. Boston's like that too. The different lines, like the Red Line and the Blue Line, the stations are actually red and blue.

This shouldn't surprise a designer, but it's a good indication of the clues people use to associate things, such as a red train with a red line on the map.

SECOND INTERVIEWER: And that helped?

PARTICIPANT: Oh yeah. And it was beautiful too. Like the stations near Harvard are these beautiful, ruby red tiles everywhere. And if you're more downtown, it's shimmery blue everywhere.

Interview transcript	Comments
PRIMARY INTERVIEWER: When were you in Boston?	This isn't particularly relevant, but it expresses interest in what's being said, and may elicit whether she was a tourist or a resident.
PARTICIPANT: I lived there for a little while, actually when I got back from Japan, so I guess that was two years ago.	Since she was a resident, Boston probably isn't worth pursuing in detail.
PRIMARY INTERVIEWER: So, in Japan, with all this free time they gave you, how did you decide what things you wanted to see?	Good redirection.
PARTICIPANT: Interesting. It's always kind of a mix of things, right, because there's people's recommendations, but a lot of it is based on… I've got this hobby, I've got this interest, so what's unique to this place that sort of caters to that. So if I went to Osaka or I went to Tokyo or I took the time to go that direction, I would make sure I was going to see some art or some design.	
PRIMARY INTERVIEWER: How would you find out what's there?	Nice follow-up.
PARTICIPANT: So, the Internet. A lot of the Internet. I kept running into About.com, which is not one of my favorite Web sites, so that was always kind of frustrating.	
PRIMARY INTERVIEWER: It would just turn up a lot in the search results?	Fine clarification. The question is leading, though relatively harmless. It would be better to ask how she kept "running into About.com" and why it isn't one of her favorites.
PARTICIPANT: Yeah. Exactly. Occasionally you'd read cool things in a blog; someone had visited somewhere and made good notes of it.	Opportunities for follow-up: — How did you know what blogs to read? — What in those blogs would catch your eye?

Interview transcript	Comments

PRIMARY INTERVIEWER: What don't you like about About.com?

Good follow-up, since it could help point to things to avoid in the LocalGuide design.

PARTICIPANT: The information is really weird. Sometimes it's too vague, and sometimes it's too in-depth. And it's rarely what I actually need. Because it's not catering to any one use, it's just if you were curious about the subject and wanted to read up on it. But that's not what I'm doing. That's what bugs me about tour books a lot too. Like, I don't actually want to read about this city, that's why I'm going there. And if I'm going to read about a city, I'd prefer it actually be in story format. So I actually did that a lot. When I was in Japan I bought books that were... *Wind-Up Bird Chronicles* or people's stories of their visits to the city of Tokyo, Osaka, wherever. 'Cause if I'm going to read about the city, I find just reading about the location really bland. Like, it doesn't have any context, it's not associated with people in any way. It's usually about buildings and purchases and stuff that's just really not that interesting. So, for example, in Venice I bought a few books while I was there, like a murder mystery that happened in Venice and that was supposed to be based on some true stories. Like, the stories themselves were not, but some of the characters in the book were real people. It was trying to be historically accurate and it was trying to be very truthful to the feeling of the city. That kind of thing I'll learn about a city from.

If only they had a computer and Internet connection nearby, they could look at an example.

Interesting data about what kind of information appeals to her: stories involving people. Given how often she's spoken about involving people, as well as the enthusiasm she shows here, it seems there's some goal waiting to be discovered. A good follow-up to uncover it might be: "It sounds like you really enjoy getting to know a place through stories about people who live there, even fictional ones. Why do you think that's so appealing to you?"

SECOND INTERVIEWER: You mentioned that you... what do you find valuable in these books or why do you have them?

A good follow-up from the second interviewer; it does the job, even if awkwardly phrased.

Interview transcript	Comments
PARTICIPANT: I like that a lot of those books give you a sense of scale. Like, I love that San Francisco Moleskine book because it gives you so many pieces of the scale of the city. So, you can see the full city, you can see the chunks of the city. I guess it goes back to the way they do things in Japan, with the chunking. I guess that is a very easy way to get around, as it turns out, because you just head in the right direction, and then you get there. And from there you chunk down. And you head in the right direction and chunk down. And you head in the direction… so as long as you're traveling and you don't have to be there at a specific time, that's actually a really great way to move about. So, a lot of tour books are good about … I'm trying to remember the one I always look for. It has a lot of pictures and their logo is a little open book. And they also do a series of… *[Looks around the room, spots a book by the same publisher next to her on the floor. Pulls out the book so interviewers can see the logo.]* Oh, DK. You know, they do all these look-books and then they also started doing tour books.	More openings to look at artifacts (the Moleskine book and DK tour book) if such things were nearby. If not, the team can look them up later. This is a good example of how artifacts can prompt memory; there happens to be a book by the same publisher in the room. You can see where the interview suffers a bit from not being done in context. It's clearly not possible to follow the interviewee on all of the trips she discusses, but asking her to bring her guidebooks and other artifacts would have helped. The explicit discussion of information chunking is an unusual level of analysis to get from an interviewee.
SECOND INTERVIEWER: And you were saying that's one that you like?	
PARTICIPANT: Yeah, lots of pictures. I think that's part of the fun before you go somewhere, is looking at the pictures and getting excited about it. But I try not to put too much pressure on actually deciding. It's more like it's just a fun part of the process, but actually trying to make a decision before I get there is stressful.	More useful data about the kind of information that appeals to her.
PRIMARY INTERVIEWER: So let's shift a little bit to business travel, unless you've got any questions? *[Turns to second interviewer.]*	This is exactly the kind of team communication that should be happening when the primary interviewer goes in a new direction. It's best not to mention the new topic before checking in with your partner, though.

Interview transcript	Comments
SECOND INTERVIEWER: Sure, let me take a look here, just a second. [Flips through her notebook.] Let's just talk about Venice for one more minute. You were talking about…	The second interviewer is looking for things she's marked for later follow-up, which is a good thing to do in your notes.
PARTICIPANT: And I don't have that much business travel experience. I went to South by Southwest *[a conference]*. Does that even count as business travel? We were actually there doing work, but it was kind of… I work at a start-up. There's no suits, there's no briefcases.	The interviewee is distracted by the new topic.
SECOND INTERVIEWER: It's still business travel. So… you knew about the architectural show before you went over there. How did you find out about that?	The interviewer has to wrest the focus back to the earlier topic.
PARTICIPANT: That was, again, through a person.	
SECOND INTERVIEWER: So, can you tell me how that happened?	Note that the second interviewer is temporarily taking the primary interviewer role. This is typical at the end of an interview segment. The primary interviewer should pick up the second interviewer's role for a few minutes.
PARTICIPANT: Yeah, it was a friend. He knew about it through a friend, and that friend knew about it because he was friends with a few of the designers who were in the show, and actually worked on one of the projects that was being showcased.	
SECOND INTERVIEWER: Did you take any actions to find out any information about it for yourself?	Open-ended phrasing would be better, but the interviewee is speaking freely enough that it's not a problem.

Research

Interview transcript	Comments
PARTICIPANT: I had looked at the Web site before we went, and found that to be kind of... It's hard because a lot of times I want to go see art and design, and Web sites are never very good representations of what you're about to go see. If I'm visiting a historic location, a lot of times the Web sites are a little more interesting because they'll have some of that history up there. If it's a current event type thing that you're going to, it seems like there's not that much you can do beforehand to prepare for it. It's interesting, too, because I think that as I travel more in the states and start to see certain things over and over again, then I'll start to see maybe less current event stuff and start to see more normal destinations I guess. But it's the current event that was... it's the neat thing happening right now is enough motivation to get me to go, whereas going to a park or going to go see a monument is necessarily motivating enough.	The interviewee starts to answer the questions, then takes a detour to some general statements. The interviewer must decide whether to ask again for the answer to her original question or follow up on this new direction. It's possible to do both if you make a note to return to a topic later.
SECOND INTERVIEWER: Are those the "normal" destinations?	She chooses the new direction.
PARTICIPANT: That's what it seems like.	
SECOND INTERVIEWER: Okay.	This response is too minimal. The interviewer should be giving an indication of where she wants the interviewee to go next.
PARTICIPANT: Travel is a little stressful, so those don't make it worth it, but if I've been there already or know someone now in that city that stuff seems more worth it.	Follow-up opportunity: What's stressful about travel?
SECOND INTERVIEWER: Oh, interesting.	Still not giving any direction.
PRIMARY INTERVIEWER: What do you find stressful about travel?	The primary interviewer (who has briefly played the second interviewer role) steps in to pick up the follow-up opportunity and resume the primary role.

Interview transcript	Comments
PARTICIPANT: Mostly making decisions. Knowing that you have a certain amount of time there and you're with other people, and they have certain things that they want to do. And so when you're making decisions, you're making compromises. You're deciding not to go somewhere else, you know that you're possibly not making the right decision.	There seems to be another goal here: Don't miss the good stuff by making a bad choice. Other follow-up opportunities: — Could you give us an example of how one of the compromises was negotiated? — What information did you use to make the decision?
PRIMARY INTERVIEWER: In Japan, were you traveling on your own most of the time?	
PARTICIPANT: Not really, it was actually a lot of times with other people. If I traveled alone it would be to go visit a temple in another city or a hiking destination.	Follow-up opportunity: How was that different from when you traveled with someone? Could you give us an example?
PRIMARY INTERVIEWER: Did you find that less stressful?	This is leading, but she's already indicated that group decision-making is stressful, so it's not likely to cause a problem.
PARTICIPANT: Yeah, yeah, because if you make a mistake nobody knows, nobody's affected except for you. It's also really just sort of empowering when you can just walk about on your own in a foreign country. You connect with more interesting people along the way, for example.	The comment about a sense of empowerment is interesting. It sounds like achieving some sense of freedom or mastery might be a goal, so this is worth a follow-up: What exactly is empowering about it?
PRIMARY INTERVIEWER: It sounds like a lot of your trips involve other people. What is it about that that you enjoy, that's worth putting up with the stress?	This is a good question with the potential to uncover a goal.

Interview transcript	Comments
Participant: Yeah, I think in some ways it de-stresses a little bit, too. You get to share the responsibilities of the travel with other people. It's not that I can't figure out the map on my own or that I don't have ideas about where to go, but it's nice when you're with someone because you can double check your own thinking on the directions, you can toss it off to them when you're tired or you just want to be enjoying the scenery. So, my little brother had come to visit, and I had taken him around to many different places and ended up in Tokyo, and that was more stressful than normal because he's very bad with directions and so it was not only trying to appease him, but also having to do all of that stuff. Figuring out where to go, and how to get there, and paying for all of it... But it was nice because there was also a lot of shared experiences and so later on when you come back you get to talk to someone about it. Like, I have beautiful memories of hiking and of seeing these temples and things, but I always feel funny trying to tell people about it. It's just... you weren't there, especially nature type of settings and things like temples, where the beauty was what it made you think or feel, not itself.	There are a couple of goals implicit here: — Don't stress about navigating and planning. — Share the wonder of new experiences with someone. Both should be paraphrased back to the interviewee for confirmation. The second goal seems to answer the question of why she travels with people, but so far the interviewers have not asked a fundamental question: Why does she travel? What does she want to get out of a trip? Note that these goals are coming up fairly late in the interview; this is common, and is one reason not to cut your interviews too short.
Primary interviewer: Okay, so, the trip to South by Southwest. Business travel.	There are only about 20 minutes left to the interview, so it's entirely reasonable that the interviewer shift gears around this time. The transition could be smoother, though.
Participant: It was business travel.	
Primary interviewer: What was business about it? Was it the conference, or...?	

Interview transcript	Comments
PARTICIPANT: We had gone as a company. We were still pretty early in the stages of the production of our product. But at that point we had wanted to show the concept to some different people and get their feedback on it and just see what else was out there right now. It was an information-gathering trip, which is why the company paid for it. I think most of us would have gone anyways, because for a lot of us it's just a really fun conference and event. But it was really nice having the company because they actually paid for a house rental, and we all stayed at the house. And we had a few planned company things. Like, "You need to be here at this time because we need to go over... we need to do some work." That was one of the days, and then we were going to have this big company dinner at this point, and all of us had various people that we wanted to meet with and show the project to. See, we each had our own schedules around that. And of course the conference. Trying to go to the panels that mattered, and also I think all of our founders were speaking at various panels, so making sure that we got to those.	Knowing what she did for a living would help give this response a bit more context.
PRIMARY INTERVIEWER: How did you decide which panels mattered?	This may be another detour, but it's probably just occurred to the interviewer that the LocalGuide might be of use at large conferences. Design research often provides insight into new opportunities, so it's worth pursuing such possibilities for a few minutes.
PARTICIPANT: We were sort of allowed to do just what interests us, which is part of the reason that I work for a start-up. You do a job that interests you, or else you wouldn't be here. So, I do game design, so I went to a lot of game design panels, and talked to a lot of game designers. And it was the same pretty much for everyone else. They would go to the panels that were both interesting and relate to their jobs, but it's practically the same thing.	
PRIMARY INTERVIEWER: So, did you have any free time?	This is not open-ended, but it doesn't matter much since the interviewee doesn't need encouragement at this point.

Interview transcript	Comments
PARTICIPANT: Yeah, there was actually a fair amount of free time, because the conference panels are over around 6:00 or so, and then that whole week is just jam-packed full of parties and events. And we had a party as well. I forgot about that. I can't believe I forgot, it was a big party. So this is kind of interesting because it's business, but it's… especially in the small start-ups you have to be… it's about having a lot of fun and so you might be doing marketing, but it better be fun. So, having a party is marketing for us. So that was pretty important for us. And, probably the most stressful part of that was having to do work while… trying to fit in the chunks of work into all of the events and meeting up with people. 'Cause we all had a few things we needed to get done that week. We couldn't completely stop working. So, it was harder on the programmers; they had to just stay home one day and program. I had to do some promotional materials for our party, and had gotten a lot of it done on the plane ride over. But I had an afternoon off and I needed to go to a print shop and get things printed. And I had to find the print shop in the first place.	Most of this is not relevant to the design problem, but the interviewee isn't providing any pauses for the interviewers to redirect the conversation. It's sometimes better to let the interviewee go for a little while like this than to be too abrupt in redirection. At the end, she gets to an interesting point and provides an opening.
PRIMARY INTERVIEWER: How did you find that print shop?	Good follow-up.
PARTICIPANT: Yelp. [yelp.com]	
PRIMARY INTERVIEWER: Yelp? Okay. Did you have a rental car while you were there?	Follow-up opportunities: — Why Yelp.com? — Did you know the name of the print shop to begin with, or were you trying to identify one as well as figure out how to get to it? A better question than "Did you have a rental car?" would be, "How did you get around while you were there?"

Interview transcript	Comments
PARTICIPANT: No, there was no rental car. Austin *[Texas, the location of the conference]* is thankfully pretty small, though, and a lot of cabs and stuff too. And there's also the "Dillo," like a free shuttle that runs down one of the main streets. And our house wasn't very far from one of the stops. I believe it's short for Armadillo.	Follow-up opportunities: — Which of these did you use? — How did you discover them? — What questions did you have about using them?
PRIMARY INTERVIEWER: So, after all of that, did you have any free time left to explore Austin?	Closed-ended again.
PARTICIPANT: There wasn't a lot of personal free time. It's one of those events where, if you're by yourself, you might have done something wrong. But I did end up walking to a park with a friend, and walking down the shopping street at one point. I never buy anything, but I always end up at the shopping streets. There's a lot of stuff to look at.	Follow-up opportunities: — How did you decide to do these things? — How did you know where the park and shopping street were?
PRIMARY INTERVIEWER: Just window shopping…	
PARTICIPANT: Yeah, exactly.	
PRIMARY INTERVIEWER: How are we doing on time?	It's often important to watch the time, and this kind of sidebar conversation is usually fine unless it happens too often.
SECOND INTERVIEWER: I've got about 10 minutes… We could start wrapping up.	
PRIMARY INTERVIEWER: Yeah, do you have any follow-ups on business?	
SECOND INTERVIEWER: How much of it did you plan ahead of time, before you went out there?	The interviewers asked this earlier about personal travel, so it's good to see to what extent business travel differs.

Research

Interview transcript	Comments

PARTICIPANT: Oh, for South by Southwest? A lot of the planning around that was connecting with people, and making sure that we could meet up at some point. So it was a lot of e-mailing people before I got there saying, "We're going to be here and..." And most people had set up Google calendars specifically for South by Southwest, and had started filling in all their time blocks. Like, "I'm going to go to this event at this time, maybe we can meet there." Or, "I'm going to this panel," so you could actually just... It was an interesting upsurge of all these connection tools, too. So I was keeping a calendar and checking other people's calendars a lot. E-mailing. Figuring out when we could meet up. Making sure that we had kind of set something aside, otherwise it wouldn't happen. 'Cause once you get there, it's one of those events where you sort of... the entire week just goes. It's this huge flow forward of events and people and music.

> If the interviewers are interested in potential conference uses, this might inspire ideas about potential social uses of the LocalGuide at large events and possible extensions to a Web-based service.

PRIMARY INTERVIEWER: It was during the music festival? Or was it...

PARTICIPANT: There's no overlap, but there's still a lot of parties and stuff. And it's really interesting because the whole geek sphere is funny, because you're out partying but you always end up talking about tech stuff. It's the weirdest form of business, but there it is.

PRIMARY INTERVIEWER: Yeah, it is kind of... all consuming. I'm curious if you've ever taken any solo vacations to places you don't know? It sounds like a lot of those places you don't know you've gone with other people...

> The first sentence is the sort of brief acknowledgement of shared experience that can help build rapport. The question seems oddly timed, but it's probably the result of the interviewer either looking at his notes or doing a mental inventory of topics that still need to be covered. This is a good thing to do toward the end of an interview.

Interview transcript	Comments
PARTICIPANT: Yeah, this is interesting. I never really realized that I don't take that many solo trips to places that I... I'm trying to think of... Yeah, I have never stayed at a hotel by myself, for example, I don't think. I'm trying to remember if I have... I maybe have while traveling from one place to another. I stayed a couple extra days in Osaka at one point by myself, and stayed in a hotel by myself at that point. So, I guess that would be... that's what it is basically, if you stayed somewhere by yourself. But that was because I had a little extra vacation time compared to everyone else. And then at that point I really didn't have destinations. I had parts of the city that I hadn't been to yet and wanted to explore. So, I went to two different neighborhoods basically.	
SECOND INTERVIEWER: Did you think about deciding what you were going to do during that part of the trip when you were alone any differently than you thought about it when you were with other people?	Awkwardly stated, but essentially a good question.
PARTICIPANT: Um, definitely less planning than I even normally do, which is pretty minimal in the first place. I had wanted to go to an area that had a bunch of cooking stores, and then I kind of looked to see if there were things that were interesting around it. And I ended up at some of those places, but I definitely didn't map out how to get there or anything like that. The only thing I really kind of mapped out for myself was, ok, here's my hotel and here's the closest train station, and then when I got to that neighborhood, I made a note of where that train station was, and tried to stay... and keep its location in my mind.	More good information on how she navigates; again starting with the hotel, identifying an area where she wants to go, and using the train station as another sort of anchor for subsequent navigation. It's also interesting to note that she chose a general area that seemed likely to be interesting, then looked for things to do once she was in that area.
SECOND INTERVIEWER: But it was more serendipitous...?	Fine clarification. Note that the second interviewer has again stepped into the primary role; she opened the line of inquiry about how the interviewee makes decisions when traveling solo, so the primary interviewer appropriately steps back and lets her lead the follow-up on that topic.

Interview transcript	Comments
PARTICIPANT: Yeah. This is making me want to go on a trip by myself now.... That's something I really haven't done. Interesting.	The interview process prompts people to reflect on their behavior in unusual ways. Most people enjoy that aspect of being interviewed.
SECOND INTERVIEWER: That's the fun part about these things, is that ... we've heard from a couple of people that have been through the [interview] hour, contemplating their vacations and they're like, "I'm realizing some things, hmmm..."	A better response would be a brief acknowledge-ment of the statement, then some follow-up to get more detail on the behavior just mentioned.
PRIMARY INTERVIEWER: Well, I think I'm all set. Do you want to ask your favorite question?	The primary interviewer indicates that he has no more questions, but knows from prior interviews that his partner probably has at least one more.
SECOND INTERVIEWER: Yeah, I have a question that I like to end with...	
PARTICIPANT: What's that?	
SECOND INTERVIEWER: When you look back on a trip, how do you know if it was a good trip or not such a great trip?	This is a good question designed to uncover goals, and would be good to ask even earlier in the interview.
PARTICIPANT: Hmmm... It feels like the only thing that ever makes it a bad trip is people.	
SECOND INTERVIEWER: Any kind of people?	
PARTICIPANT: If someone was upset or hurt by the trip, then it was not a good trip. I'm trying to think of what makes it a really, really good trip, though, because that's independent of other people really. Hmmm. There's something to, like, having some sort of new perspective. Basically, did I learn something new on the trip? I probably wouldn't enjoy going some-where and seeing things that I've already seen before, or already knew about.	This point is worth a bit more exploration.
SECOND INTERVIEWER: Interesting, new perspec-tive. Okay.	
PARTICIPANT: That's a good question.	

Interview transcript	Comments
PRIMARY INTERVIEWER: Okay, well, I guess we're done. Thanks for your time!	Always thank the interviewee. Also be sure to establish a means for future communication (even though you might not use it), including a way for the interviewee to share any further thoughts.

Summary

You can probably see that the interviewers worked together pretty well, catching a couple of one another's misses and making a fairly smooth switch in interview leadership on a couple of occasions. They asked a number of good questions including some effective follow-up. They missed several good opportunities they had the time to pursue (the transcript covers 49 minutes). There would have been even more time for follow-up without a couple of digressions. Perhaps the biggest missed opportunities involved getting more detail about what caused the interviewee to choose destinations other than the ones she initially planned on, what information she used to make decisions and find places, and what information she needed when she got there. If other interviews don't provide this information, the team will find themselves making guesses about too many things as they start designing.

However, hopefully you can see that even a far-from-perfect interview can be packed with useful information. Don't let concern about mistakes keep you from conducting interviews. It takes considerable practice to develop your skill, and even the most expert interviewer will sometimes ask the occasional clumsy question or miss a follow-up opportunity. Also, there is seldom time to cover absolutely everything in a single interview, which is a good reason to reflect on interviews and discuss approaches to subsequent ones as you go.

To work on your interview technique, ask a colleague to give you feedback. If that's not an option, videotape or audiotape an interview, wait a few weeks to get distance from it, then dissect it yourself as I've done here. See what you could have done better, do some more interviews, then record another one to see how you've progressed. If you don't have much confidence in your interviewing yet, wait until you develop some before taping yourself; it can be a humbling experience.

CHAPTER 9

Other Sources of Information and Inspiration

The user research methods described in previous chapters are ideal for most circumstances because they provide detail about behaviors and attitudes in a relatively short time. No single method can do everything, however; you may have less time or be forced to work with data gathered by others, or you may have the luxury of supplementing your research with additional methods designed to get deeper or different information. There's room for creativity in research methods, as well as in design, as long as you're aware of any given method's limitations.

When You Have Less Time

Efficient as qualitative interviews are, even a week or two of research won't be the best way to deliver value when the product's ship date is just around the corner. If stakeholders see design or usability as something that gets spread on top instead of baked into the cake, you'll need to get the best information you can while still building some degree of consensus about the users and their needs. You'll also want to set expectations with stakeholders about the challenges of working with limited data.

When possible, try to squeeze in at least one or two days of user interviews. It's true that you risk getting unusual interview participants who could skew your thinking, but this is rare, and the risk is limited as long as you compare what you see to what you're hearing from stakeholders. Focus on the kinds of users who are most critical to the product's success or the ones you suspect are the least understood. If you're not allowed to recruit users on your own, use the friends-and-family method (see the "Desperate measures" section of Chapter 6) to find a few potential consumer users, or tag along on a sales or customer support visit if you're working on an enterprise tool. Even a small amount of firsthand exposure is invaluable.

Stakeholders are usually the best source for understanding users without direct research. Get your project owner and others who know the users best in a room for half a day. Subject matter experts, enterprise sales people, marketing staff, and customer service or technical support people tend to know the most. Use the example interview questions in Chapter 7 as the starting point for your discussion. This will help you cover essential topics such as process, mental models,

A larger interview sample allows for some quantitative analysis of the data, but is unlikely to result in better design.

frustrations, skill level, goals, and environment. Consider sending a list of topics to stakeholders in advance to get them thinking. You could even have them write down some thoughts beforehand if you only have time for a short meeting, but be very clear that written input cannot replace discussion, which allows you to ask follow-up questions and lets everyone reach agreement on the fundamental user characteristics.

Any existing focus group or survey data may also be useful. Don't limit your requests for such information to the product team; corporate marketing groups frequently conduct research that isn't disseminated. Product managers or professional services staff may also have trip notes from customer site visits that are worth perusing. If possible, review these before the stakeholder meeting so you can use the data to move things forward.

The output of this kind of compressed research is a set of abbreviated user models called provisional personas; see the section "When Time Is Limited: Provisional Personas" in Chapter 11 for more on developing these tools.

When You Have More Time

If you're revising an established product with an enormous audience—such as an operating system or widely used office product—stakeholders often want to minimize the risk of any change, so they want a lot of detail and a high degree of confidence in the data. They're probably willing to invest accordingly, which gives you the luxury of a larger sample, more time with individual users, or both. More time may also allow you to use some of the supplemental methods described later in this chapter.

A larger interview sample allows for some quantitative analysis of the data, which can be persuasive or comforting to many people. However, a larger sample adds considerable analysis time and is unlikely to result in better design, except to the extent that it lets you catch an edge case you otherwise might have missed. For these reasons, I often advise clients against a big sample if their budget is at all limited, because I know other expenditures will have a bigger impact on the value my team can deliver.

More time with individual users may or may not be beneficial. More than an hour is unlikely to shed much light when user tasks are straightforward and similar from day to day. Extra time is advantageous for intricate and highly variable tasks such as surgery, complex data analysis, and accounting. It can help you see important situations that are difficult to stage, such as an air traffic control crisis or a sudden flood of patients in a hospital emergency room. With each individual, you might choose to conduct one long session or several shorter ones spread out over time to account for seasonal variations in tasks. It may not be useful to conduct extra research with every participant, though; see which people are the most helpful, then ask those individuals to spend more time with you. Be prepared to offer significant compensation or to persuade the participant's manager to allow more time.

A long session should include an initial interview using the techniques described in Chapter 7, followed by some mixture of quiet observation time with opportunities to ask more questions about what you observe. If activities cannot be interrupted, use a small video camera; replay interesting segments for the interviewee later so you can ask questions about specifics. Consider whether it's better to have the whole team observing or to have just one person follow the informant with a video camera; surgeons are accustomed to working with large audiences, but most office workers are not.

Supplemental Research Methods

You can't beat individual interviews combined with observation as a foundation technique, but it's sometimes useful to supplement this approach. Other methods can reveal additional information or help validate what you learn in interviews. None of these techniques is a substitute for firsthand interviews and observation, however, since none of them combines the ability to get detailed, individual data with the ability to clarify the reasoning and thought processes behind that behavior.

Public-space observation

If you're designing a physical environment such as a store or an airport lounge, you obviously need to observe how people use similar environments. Public-space observation is also informative if you're designing an information kiosk or mobile device. Physical-space behavior can inform virtual-space behavior, so watching people in a bricks-and-mortar store can provide useful insights for designing an e-commerce store selling similar products. Casual observation (such as hovering near the information desk in Figure 9.1) can even be useful for certain types of enterprise systems, especially if you're having difficulty getting formal interviews in certain settings. For example, on a project involving a new generation of business telephones, my team was struggling to get interviews in specialized settings such as retail stores and hotels. We all dropped in on stores in the area and casually observed employees using telephones or radios, briefly chatting with any staff who seemed amenable and not too busy. We also took advantage of opportunities to check out phone use at hotels during our travels. These opportunistic observations weren't as useful as in-depth interviews, but still provided information that had a substantial influence on the design.

Figure 9.1. If you were designing wayfinding or an information kiosk for an airport, it would be informative to hang out at the information desk for a while.

Anonymous observation in public places raises an ethical consideration not found in interviews: informed consent.

Anonymous observation in public places raises an ethical consideration not found in interviews: informed consent. There is long-standing debate among social scientists about whether it's acceptable to observe human behavior without identifying oneself as a researcher and obtaining the consent of the observed. The issues are exemplified in a classic debate between Kai Erikson[1] and Norman Denzin[2], two sociology professors who published opposing views in the journal Social Problems in 1967 and 1968. One of Erikson's primary arguments is that such observation may cause distress to the people being observed. The examples he uses are of researchers who adopt "disguises" to gain access to closed communities, such as a support group for alcoholics. Denzin argues that such observation is not an invasion of privacy if it occurs in a public setting; he qualifies this by acknowledging that public and private spaces cannot be defined in absolute terms, but must be determined based on the expectations of the people being observed. Certainly, an alcoholism support group is not private in the sense that someone's home is, but the participants may have an expectation of not exposing themselves to others who don't share similar experiences. An airport or shopping mall, on the other hand, is open to all and thus does not create the same expectations.

The debate and uncertainty continue in the literature today. The guidance in professional codes of conduct is vague at best. With the exception of those in academia, whose work must be reviewed by a human subjects committee, most of us have to decide for ourselves where the ethical line is. My personal opinion is that it's acceptable to observe behavior and even ask a few questions in settings where people are unlikely to expect privacy, such as in a store or hotel lobby, so long as I don't misrepresent myself, capture or share data in a way that makes that person identifiable, or cause any harm or discomfort. To my mind, there's a big difference between anonymously observing how people use mobile devices on a commuter train and lying about who I am to get someone to share very personal information.

One way to minimize your impact is to observe without interacting. Unfortunately, this means you don't have the opportunity to clarify what you're seeing by asking questions. If you're comfortable doing so, start by observing, then see if there's a good opportunity to ask a question or two. It usually helps to be straightforward about why you're asking. I've also found that I get better cooperation if I approach people who have

1. Erikson, K. "A comment on disguised observation in sociology." Social Problems, Vol. 14, No. 4. (Spring, 1967), pp. 366-373.

2. Denzin, N. "On the ethics of disguised observation." Social Problems, Vol. 15, No. 4. (Spring, 1968), pp. 502-504.

at least seen me around. When studying telephone use in smaller stores, for example, I started with places where I thought the staff might know me well enough to chat for a few minutes.

Exercise

1. Would you be comfortable conducting research in the following ways? Why or why not?

   — You're designing a café. Is it acceptable to buy coffee in a competitive café, then sit at a table and watch what people do there, how long they stay, and what seems to encourage them to spend money?

   — You're designing a children's game. Is it acceptable to sit near an elementary school and watch how children play? How about wandering over and asking questions of some of the children? What about looking at their pages on MySpace or another social networking site?

   — You're attempting to improve the patient experience at a hospital. Is it acceptable to sit in a waiting room observing how people behave there?

   — You're designing a patient Web site for a new diabetes drug. Is it acceptable to sit in an endocrinologist's waiting room and chat with people about their conditions, not claiming to have diabetes but also not identifying yourself as a researcher?

2. Provided you're comfortable doing so, conduct some informal observations in a public space for the LocalGuide or RoomFinder. What behaviors do you see in this context that you did not see (or don't think you would have seen) in an interview? What did you see that provided an interesting insight?

Mystery shopper

A variation on public-space observation is being a "mystery shopper," someone who tries out the customer experience without being identified as a researcher. Anonymous usage is an important research tool because the story you get during explicit research may be sanitized; this is why good restaurant reviewers don't tell the staff who they are. The insider's view is also limited; a customer service rep may know that callers are often surly, but may not realize that it's because they have to jump through a dozen silly electronic hoops before talking to a human. This technique is a powerful tool for convincing executives of the need for change; many become passionate advocates for improvement after seeing their own products or services through a customer's eyes. I'm convinced that more products and services would be better if more executives, as one of my clients put it, "ate their own dog food."

Clearly, the informed consent question arises: Is it ethical to pretend that you're buying or using a product or service when you're not? Again, I believe the answer comes down to the potential harm or benefit to the unwitting participant. A customer service rep paid by the hour suffers no harm if you call with a typical problem or question, and the company that pays him isn't harmed if you're trying to improve their system. If he's paid on commission or measured by sales, you might consider actually making a purchase so his income doesn't suffer, particularly if it's not just a two-minute conversation. This gets difficult with major purchases, though. A client who had never seen a competitor's expensive business system once asked me to pose as a prospective buyer to get a demonstration. I said I was uncomfortable with this because there was no possible benefit to the sales people who would be spending hours of their time with me; fortunately, the client thought about it and agreed with my point.

Research

Exercise

If you work for a company that sells products or provides customer support, try using the service as an ordinary customer. Alternatively, try using a service you're not familiar with but might ordinarily use anyway (such as a physical store, online service, or telephone customer support center). What makes you feel good about the service and the company providing it? What gives you a negative opinion?

Diaries

In interviews, it can be difficult to get a sense of behavior over time because you have to rely on the participant's memory of past activities or circumstances, and artifacts can only do so much to prompt that. One way to widen your view of someone's activities without shadowing them 24/7 is to ask them to keep a diary. This can be somewhat structured, much like a survey taken several times, or can be free-form entry guided by a few questions. A diary can take almost any form: written responses to a periodic e-mail reminder, a handwritten notebook, a narrated video, or photos with written commentary.

It's important to keep the diary task simple, so don't ask respondents to keep track of more than a few things. An example list of things to track would be relevant tasks, problems they encounter, documents they create or use, and any random thoughts they may have related to the research topic. People may be reluctant to write about times they feel inadequate, so phrase any questions in ways that let them blame the system; for example, "Tell us about any occasions when the system made information hard to find," as opposed to, "Tell us about any time when you had difficulty finding information."

The length of a diary study depends on the length of time it takes to observe meaningful patterns. If someone uses an application four times a day and makes an entry each time, two or three days of entries should provide plenty of information. If entries occur once a day, it may require a week to learn much. Weekly entries might mean it takes a month or two, but you may not have much luck retaining participants' interest that long.

Recruiting for a diary study should be along the same lines as recruiting for your interviews. It's easiest to identify helpful people among your interviewees and ask them to keep diaries, rather than recruiting a separate group. Dropout rates in diary studies are high, though, so do what you can to make it fun, and be sure to provide a substantial incentive. A few reminders along the way won't hurt, either.

Keep in mind that a diary has limitations: Self-reporting error is likely. If possible, sit down with each participant and conduct a follow-up interview using the diary as a basis for questions.

Surveys

If your qualitative research identifies a behavior pattern that requires some unique and expensive feature, it's worth determining how much potential revenue that behavior pattern represents. Knowing how many people listen to music while they drive won't help you create a better car stereo design, but it will help you determine whether a feature or even the product itself will be worth its cost; if only five percent of people listen to cassettes in the car, perhaps it's not worth putting a cassette deck in every vehicle. Strictly speaking, it's usually not a design team's responsibility to determine whether a product or feature is financially viable, but designers who don't at least consider potential return on investment are doing their clients a disservice.

I've also found numbers helpful in disabusing stakeholders of pet beliefs. I once had an e-commerce client who insisted that the design be geared toward very old browsers at low resolution. My opinion alone wouldn't have been persuasive, but quantitative data helped stakeholders see that they'd be limiting the experience of their most important audience to serve a few people who were unlikely to spend much money anyway.

Surveys are the most common method for gathering quantitative data. A survey consists of a fixed set of questions to be answered by an individual. The questions usually have constrained answers, such as multiple choice or a Likert scale (see Figure 9.2), but may sometimes require short answers (e.g., a list of the consumer electronics brands the respondent buys). A survey can be administered on paper, electronically, or verbally.

Figure 9.2. An example of a survey with a Likert scale.

Surveys are best used to gather **descriptive** information, i.e., the characteristics of a population, which may include anything from ages and incomes to attitudes and beliefs. Survey data can also identify potential relationships among characteristics, such as whether people in a particular region or age group are more likely to vote a certain way, but are far less useful in explaining why those relationships exist.

FINDING EXISTING SURVEY DATA

The most efficient way to get survey data is to look at what other people already have. You can often get the most specific and useful data from the marketing department, unless you're working with a very small company. A Web search will usually yield at least one or two interesting studies from credible sources. Some studies may be available free online or at the local university library, but many reports focused on questions of commercial interest (such as market size or spending) are only available from commercial research organizations. If you're hesitant about buying an expensive report, ask the marketing people how good the reports from that source usually are.

While findings from universities and professional research firms are more often reliable than not, it's important to assess how the data were gathered so you can determine what conclusions are safe to draw from the results. Many online surveys depend on people who visit a specific site or are members of a particular organization, which means they may not represent the market at large. Be sure to look at the number of people surveyed, too, since 75 percent of a large sample is more meaningful than three out of a total of four people.

DEVELOPING YOUR OWN SURVEY

When the information you need is nowhere to be found, it's time to conduct your own survey. As with most research techniques, how thorough and careful you are depends on the importance of the decisions you're trying to inform, as well as the time and budget you have available. However, quantitative studies are easy to mess up if you don't know what you're doing—and most designers don't—so I advise working with a statistician or other professional who does quantitative studies for a living. If this is out of the question, free or inexpensive Web-based survey tools (such as www.zoomerang.com and www.surveymonkey.com) make it easy to administer a survey, but I strongly recommend at least picking up a good basic book on survey design and analysis, such as Rea and Parker's *Designing and Conducting Survey Research*.[3] *Designing and Using Organizational Surveys*[4] by Allan Church and Janine Waclawski, which is focused on surveys within organizations, is a good primer on managing the process of crafting a survey and sharing the results with stakeholders. The following basics will also help you get the most out of your survey effort.

Step 1: Identify your audience and goals

First, work with your teammates (and probably the stakeholders) to determine what you're trying to learn. Is this a single survey to understand demographics and attitudes to inform interview planning? Are you trying to assess how many people fit the various behavior patterns you've already observed? Or are you trying to assess the impact of your design with a before and after comparison?

Define your anticipated audience as best you can, just as you would for qualitative interviews (see Chapter 6). Brainstorm possible questions without worrying about their exact phrasing or appropriateness, then weed out any that aren't suited to multiple choice or other constrained answers. You may have to prioritize, since participants are often unwilling to complete a survey in excess of 20 or so questions without some substantial reward.

Step 2: Craft questions and instructions

The next thing to do is craft the actual survey in a way that maximizes participation, minimizes bias and error, and makes analysis as easy as possible. The way you construct the questions is the same regardless of whether you're administering

the survey verbally, on paper, or online. Church and Waclawski suggest that once you've determined what you want to know, it's best to determine how much coverage of a topic you want, with three to five questions on a topic generally being ideal. From there, you can decide whether a Likert scale, multiple choice, or other question structure is appropriate.

Keep your instructions brief. Include an estimate of how long the survey will take to complete. Also tell the participant (briefly!) why he should care about the survey; for example, state that you'll use his responses in improving your customer service or designing a new product. Be sure to explain any privacy or anonymity considerations, such as, "Your answers will be anonymous and confidential. We will never share the results outside of GizmoCorp or use them to try to sell you anything."

You might include a few open-ended or simple text-answer questions, but keep in mind that these will be harder to analyze. Most questions should be possible to answer in a constrained way. Here are some tips for constructing effective questions:

— **Ask only one question at a time.** For example, "If you own a camera, who is the manufacturer?" is really asking two questions. It would be better to ask whether the participant owns a camera, then ask who the manufacturer is only if the first answer is yes.

— **Be specific.** "Do you ever use the Web?" won't really tell you much, and a respondent who's used it once may not know how to answer. "How often do you use the Web? Daily / Two or more times a week / Two or more times a month / Less than twice a month / Never" would be better. Offer quantity or

3. Rea, L. and Parker, R. *Designing and conducting survey research: A comprehensive guide.* 3rd edition. Jossey Bass, 2005.

4. Church, A. and Waclawski, J. *Designing and using organizational surveys: A seven-step process.* Jossey-Bass, 2001.

frequency choices with specific numbers, since terms like "often" and "seldom" are relative.

— **Make the options for any single-answer question mutually exclusive.** For example, if you're asking about income, don't have a $50,000-$60,000 category and a $60,000-$70,000 category, because the person whose salary is $60,000 won't know what to pick; $50,000-$59,999 is better.

— **Make lists as complete as possible.** If someone who drives a minivan has to choose either "car" or "truck," she will either abandon the survey in frustration or be forced to choose an answer that doesn't really fit, thereby introducing error.

— **Allow for participants who can't provide definitive answers.** Include options such as "other," "not applicable," or "I don't know" when possible, so you don't get incorrect answers or cause people to quit in frustration.

— **Avoid negative construction for multiple choice questions.** For example, "which of the following do you not use" is likely to be read as "Which of the following do you use." If you absolutely can't avoid it, visually or verbally emphasize the negative word.

— **Limit the options in a Likert scale to five.** A scale of 1 to 5 lets people differentiate between good and great, but a scale of 1 to 10 causes confusion. Having an odd number of choices allows for a neutral answer, which generally provides a more accurate picture of attitudes. Make sure the high/low or positive/negative values are always at the same end of the scale.

— **Use both positive and negative phrasing within your sample.** When asking if people strongly agree or strongly disagree whether something is good, help minimize bias due to a desire to please by using positive phrasing with half the group and negative phrasing with the other half. For example, if you present a Likert scale with a statement like, "Product X is affordable," you will get an artificially high level of agreement. Balance this by phrasing it as "Product X is expensive" for the other half of the group.

— **Vary list sequences.** If possible, vary the sequence of items in lists; this helps minimize any bias due to people picking things at the top of the list and skipping the rest. Don't randomize the elements in any list that has a natural progression to it, such as income or age ranges.

Carefully consider the sequence of your questions. Start with questions that are likely to engage the respondent without being threatening. Put sensitive or boring topics (including demographics) toward the end. Mix up question formats; if you put too many Likert scales in a row, for example, people are likely to pay less attention to what they're selecting. Consider doing a dry run of your survey with a few colleagues to get feedback on flow and clarity.

Also find some way to indicate progress, such as "question 3 of 10," especially in long surveys. This will help reduce the number of people who drop out (unless, of course, your survey is much too long to begin with).

Step 3: Determine your sample size

The necessary sample size depends on a number of factors, including the degree of confidence you want in the results, the amount of error you're willing to tolerate, whether you expect responses distributed across a normal bell curve, the size of the population you're trying to understand, and whether you plan to subdivide your sample for analysis in any way. In other words, the number of people you need to survey is a complex question best answered with professional help; the concepts and calculations involved are beyond the scope of this book.

If you're content with an approximation, there are a number of simplistic sample size calculators online; just search on "sample size calculator." These ask for assumptions about your desired error and confidence interval. In simple terms, these two values describe the chances that the survey responses will be accurate; an error of plus or minus five percent with 95-percent confidence means you have a 95-percent chance that the "real" answer is within five percentage points above or below what you'll see in your survey responses. Desirable sample size increases with the size of your population, but the relationship is not a linear one; the sample you need for a population of ten million isn't much bigger than for a population of ten thousand. Table 9.1 includes examples of sample size for different populations and desired error and confidence. Chapter 10 describes the uses of these values in more detail.

The other critical consideration in defining your sample size is whether you plan to subdivide your data for analysis, such as comparing responses by age group or geography. In that case, you need to determine sample size for each subgroup; you can't just take a group of 384 respondents and break it into men and women without affecting the error and confidence. Instead, to keep the same error and confidence, you have to calculate the sample size separately for men and women (which would probably be 384 each, for a total of 768). For this reason, it's important to figure out how you'll want to analyze the data (see Chapter 10) before you conduct your survey.

Also keep in mind that your sample size is far less than the number of people you should *invite* to take the survey, since there will always be some percentage of people who don't respond. Your response rate could easily be in the single digits if you're targeting a broad population with whom you don't have an existing relationship. You may be able to plan on a higher response rate (such as 50 percent) if you have a motivated audience and offer a good incentive; ask the marketing department what response they've gotten to any similar surveys.

Step 4: Decide how to recruit participants

Once you've identified how many people you need to recruit, you have to decide where to find them and how to invite them to participate.

Table 9.1. **Sample size examples.**

Size of population	5% Error 90% Confidence	5% Error 95% Confidence	5% Error 99% Confidence	3% Error 99% Confidence
1,000	214	278	399	648
10,000	265	370	622	1556
100,000	272	383	659	1810
1,000,000	272	384	663	1840
10,000,000	272	384	664	1843

Many companies recruit users online through invitations on discussion lists, pop-up invitations on their own Web sites, or e-mail invitations to existing customers. Depending on the characteristics of your audience, there may be a selection bias problem with any of these approaches.

Inviting only your existing customers limits you in two ways. First, it won't tell you anything about the people you're not reaching. Second, it tends to bias the results toward favorable responses, since the least happy people have probably switched to a competitor. Of course, inviting only ex-customers provides an unfavorable bias, since they're likely to be unhappy. A mix of current customers, former customers, and those who have never been customers is the best bet for most studies; proportion depends on the goal of the survey.

Inviting people using e-mail, discussion groups, and Web sites is fine if you're targeting people who spend much time online, but could be missing an important segment. Telephone, advertising, or direct mail may work best in some circumstances. However, opt-in invitations, such as permanent links on a Web site, may create a bias toward extreme views, since people who are very happy or very unhappy are the most likely to seek out those opportunities. Opt-out invitations, such as pop-ups and phone calls, minimize this bias.

For assistance with recruiting, see the section on market research firms in Chapter 6.

Step 5: Decide when and for how long to conduct the survey

The timing and duration of your survey can have a tremendous impact on your sample. Certain audiences are either more or less available at particular times of year, days of the week, or times of day. If you conduct a telephone survey or in-store study during a weekday, your results will be skewed toward people who don't work

outside the home. Even online, some people may be less likely to spend time on a survey during the work week or during a busy season. Make sure your data collection window spans enough time to gather data from people with varied habits.

Exercise

Imagine that the stakeholders for the LocalGuide (see Chapter 6) are trying to determine how many of a possible ten million business travelers are likely to use it. What questions would help you understand this? Develop a survey. How large does the sample need to be, assuming a high degree of confidence is critical? How would you recruit?

Web analytics and customer support data

If you're redesigning a Web site, you may be in luck; most IT groups have some sort of Web analytics and logs that can help you find important issues. Customer support departments for many products and services track common issues, and CRM (customer relationship management) systems may have other useful statistics about current and former customers. All of these sources provide potentially useful ways to identify problems, as long as you keep in mind that they describe symptoms rather than root causes.

How much data you have and how useful it is depends on how sophisticated your systems are. Free or inexpensive tools can help you see basic statistics, such as how many unique visitors your site has and what pages they mostly visit. Figure 9.3 shows an example of this sort of data. High-end Web analytics and CRM data can tell you much more. Commonly available information includes:

- When during the day people are visiting your site or particular pages
- How often people visit (if you use identity cookies)
- How long people stay on the site or particular pages
- What percentage of users makes purchases (if applicable)
- Which types of customers are worth the most revenue
- What percentage doesn't purchase the items in their shopping carts
- Where frequent page errors occur
- What sites are referring people to yours
- What terms people entered into a search engine if it's the referring page
- What people search for on your site
- What operating systems and browsers people are using
- The most typical paths through the site (though cached pages can throw this off)

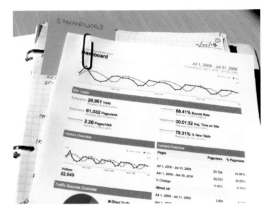

Figure 9.3. Web analytics can help you identify where there might be a problem, but won't explain why the problem occurs.

What this kind of data can't tell you is why people behave as they do or why something appears to be a problem. Are they spending a lot of time on a page because they want to or because they're hunting for the right button? Did they intend to load that page or was it a mistake? Are they giving up on a purchase because checkout is a pain or did they intend to leave that item in the shopping cart to consider for later? Why is this particular function resulting in so many support calls? Most Web analytics data also can't tell you when people are researching a product online but buying it through another channel; what looks like a failure to convert might not be. This is why you should think of Web logs and customer data as a source of useful questions, rather than a source of answers.

Customer support data can tell you what the most frequently reported problems or complaints are and which problems take the most time and effort (and the most money) to solve. Combining support data with purchase data can show you whether the customers who take up most of your support time are generating enough revenue to be worth the cost. Unfortunately, customer support data may not point to the very worst problems, since these may result in people returning products, cancelling services, or choosing a competitor from day one.

Focus groups

A focus group is a facilitated, usually 60- to 90-minute meeting with anywhere from five to a dozen members of a target market. Some marketers swear by focus groups, while others merely swear about them; I've heard multiple researchers refer to them as "the F word." Like any research tool, focus groups can be helpful when they're used appropriately (as a starting point for more research) and disastrous when they're not (as a substitute for interviews or usability tests). You may choose to conduct a focus group for your own purposes or you may need to assess and use the data from groups chartered by stakeholders.

The best use for focus groups is when you have a new product idea and know very little about the people you think might buy and use it. A group can help you learn more about the various roles and processes in an industry or the different usage characteristics in a consumer domain. If you already know enough to plan your research, though, focus groups have little to offer; the unrealistic context and group dynamics can result in a limited or even distorted view of behaviors and attitudes. Online or telephone focus groups may be cheaper, but still suffer from the same problems.

If you do plan to conduct a focus group, begin by defining what you want to learn. Industry trends? General work processes and relationships among roles? Consider whether it's more interesting to get the range of views within a particular set of people or to see how views differ across roles or perspectives. It's generally a good idea to conduct two to four similar groups; as with interviews, this helps you see if one group could be an outlier.

Limit yourself to a handful of objectives, since meaningful discussion usually takes at least ten to 15 minutes on each topic. Preparation for a focus group is similar to that for an interview (see Chapter 7), but generally involves a more formal discussion guide. The body language, open attitude, and active listening skills (see Chapter 4) are the same for both: ask open-ended questions, clarify and reflect back what you're hearing, follow up on interesting comments, and minimize how much you speak. Both interviews and focus groups absolutely require an unbiased approach and the ability to avoid leading participants.

What's unique about a focus group is the group dynamic. Some people are likely to dominate the discussion while others fade back; part of the facilitator's job is to engage everyone in the discussion and make sure dissenting views aren't smothered. Hire a skilled facilitator if you're not sure you're up to the job. If you do decide to facilitate yourself, consider asking each participant write down his thoughts on each topic before discussing it; this can help ensure that you get the full range of opinions. You should also consider having a second person be your deputy or assistant. This person can wrangle any observers and help deal with the rare difficult participant.

The best use for focus groups is when you have a new product idea and know very little about the people you think might buy and use it.

Research

If you need to use data from focus groups you had nothing to do with, ask for videotapes of the groups themselves rather than taking a written report at face value. This will allow you to interpret the data for yourself and see whether the facilitator introduced any particular bias or glossed over any minority opinions.

Card sorting

Card sorting is an organizing exercise in which participants are given a set of topics and asked to create groups that make sense to them, as shown in Figure 9.4. The technique is useful for Web sites or other applications with large amounts of content. It's not a good tool for initial research because you have to know what the content is before card sorting becomes useful; I list it here because it is a type of research, though in practice it's most useful during the framework definition phase (Chapter 16) or when you're rearranging content on an existing site.

Card sorting is best suited to relatively small Web sites with users who understand most of the content. As with other approaches, it's meant to help you gain insight, not to provide the answer for you—the average of all the card sorting responses is not the "right" information architecture. Rather, sorting will help you see that some users organize mentally based on one criterion while others start from a different entry point altogether.

Although card sorting can provide useful insight, beware of taking the results too literally. In real life, users don't look at a site and think about its content in terms of abstract relationships; they're generally looking for content in the context of some task. A good interview should reveal the biggest patterns you would see in a card sorting session, so card sorting may not be necessary, particularly if you're doing both interviews and a paper-prototype usability test of your navigation.

Figure 9.4. In card sorting, participants arrange and sometimes edit category names to fit their mental models.

Recruit participants for card sorting as you would for interviews (see Chapter 6), but using what you learned in your field research. You can do sorting with individuals or with small groups of people in the same role.

To prepare, make a list of all the topics you expect to cover on the site. These can be individual articles or, for somewhat larger sites, they can be categories of content that are fairly self-evident (e.g., you could use "executive biographies" as a topic rather than listing individual executives). Write or print each one on an identical note card, sticky note, or piece of paper, then put them in a randomly ordered pile. Use concise labels that are large enough to see from a distance. If you're adding new content to an existing site and can't affect that structure, you can provide the participant with the existing structure and only ask her to categorize the new content. The exact number of topics doesn't matter, though there are practical limits to how many topics people can deal with; a few hundred would take a very long time, but a dozen probably won't give you enough information to be useful.

Tell the participant that these are all topics that will appear on a Web site and ask her to group things she would expect to find together. Make sure there's plenty of table or wall space to work with. Tell her it's okay to make subgroups if that seems like the right thing to do. Consider having a few blank cards on hand in case the participant feels like something is missing (which shouldn't happen often) or wants to make a duplicate card and put a topic in two areas. If you have time, you can provide longer descriptions of the content on the back of each card; otherwise, be prepared to answer any participant questions about what labels mean (which can be instructive, as well). Invite her to change any labels that don't seem right to her. Once she's done categorizing, give her a marker and some sticky notes and ask her to label each category.

Competitive products and services

Companies that spend more time analyzing their competitors than understanding their customers are likely to be followers rather than market leaders. That said, a good designer should spend enough time on the competitors to understand their vulnerabilities and any opportunities for differentiation.

Start by identifying who the competitors are. The marketing team usually has a good list, but you can also look at who else shows up on a Web search, use a survey question, or ask interviewees what products or services they view as competitors. Keep in mind that a competitor isn't just someone selling a similar product or service; it's *any* other solution a customer could choose. This includes homegrown systems, which are particularly common in large-enterprise IT departments. (Some companies may be reluctant to show you homegrown systems because they don't want you selling their great ideas to their competitors; work with the sales person responsible for each account to see if you can come up with a mutually beneficial arrangement.) Niche competitors may not have entirely comparable products, but can steal customers if the part of the solution they offer is especially compelling. Ignoring the problem entirely is another sort of competition, which tends to occur when the cost or pain involved in solving the problem outweighs the difficulties of living with it.

Looking at the design language used by competitive products and services may uncover an opportunity to differentiate. If all the competitors use a similar design language, is there a way to appeal to a different or wider audience by taking an entirely different approach (e.g., the bright colors of the original Apple iMacs versus the almost universally beige or gray PCs)? Sometimes, of course, there's

> Look at competitors to understand their vulnerabilities and any opportunities for differentiation.

Research

a reason why a design language is universal; for example, most medical devices are white because that implies they're clean.

The Web and trade publications are useful sources of product images, details, and reviews. You can also set aside a small budget for getting firsthand experience with consumer products and services. It's often nearly impossible to get direct experience with competitive enterprise systems, though; see Chapter 6 for tips on gaining access.

Literature and media

Reviewing both academic and popular literature makes a poor substitute for interviews and observation, but can be a great way to use your time during empty slots in the interview schedule.

Most specialized fields have their own literature, which makes it possible to find textbooks or papers on anything from commodities trading to golf course turf management. If possible, ask a subject matter expert to help you choose the most accurate and informative publications. Professional training courses can provide insight into a technology or field, as well as what aspects of it people struggle with. The literature in various human-focused fields (such as psychology, anthropology, medicine, and education) is filled with useful insights on various populations; if you're designing an application for children, for example, look for books and articles on the social and cognitive development of your target age group. Subject matter experts are often a more efficient way to get access to this kind of information, but the literature is a good supplement and may be essential in the absence of an expert.

You can also learn a lot about emerging trends or hot topics in an industry by attending conferences, lurking on discussion boards, and reading popular or trade publications. These might also help you understand how professionals in a given field see themselves and what kind of vocabulary they use. When targeting consumers, look at the products, brands, colors, and styles that seem to resonate with them. Whether someone reads *Metropolis* and *Dwell* or *Cottage Living* and *Better Homes and Gardens* says a great deal about their aesthetic sense and even their self-image. A practical, cost-conscious appearance won't appeal to users who drive luxury cars, shop at premium stores, and buy only premium, brand-name products. Also, take a look at the advertising on Web sites or television networks that target your audience to get a sense for trends.

Most fictional books, movies, and television shows are poor sources of information, since any technical content generally involves a lot of creative license. However, science fiction, spy movies, and television shows that employ medical or forensic "science" to solve mysteries can feature imaginative solutions that offer design inspiration. Of course, some stories show cool-looking interfaces that would be dreadful to use, but three-dimensional holographic displays, tactile interfaces, and intelligent cars are a reminder that technology can do all sorts of fabulous things.

Fiction is also a way for designers to access the zeitgeist that affects how people respond to new technology products and new interaction paradigms. Media can set consumer expectations about what technology can do and how it works; after all, if Captain Kirk's communicator can reach Spock without a phone number, shouldn't we be able to dial our telephones by saying someone's name, too? Fiction can also express our fears about technology; what happens when computers take over, or we have no privacy, or our engineered genes determine our futures? You must understand any ambivalence people have in order to overcome it. (Will these arguments convince your boss that you should spend the afternoon at the movie theater watching the latest science fiction blockbuster? Only if your boss wants to see it, too.)

Summary

Interviews and observation are almost always the most valuable design research technique, but keep these other techniques in mind if you're either short on time or have the ability to spend a few extra days. The more data sources you have, the more reliable and credible your data will be. There's no reason you can't adopt or create other research techniques to fit a particular situation, so long as you consider the ethical implications and make sure that you—and your stakeholders!—understand what each technique can and cannot provide.

land what
go to

Gillian &
tech artist
high tech

John Mooney

Chris's —
push for pushes for ne
ultimately
we need & this & why

A Million of Us —
using virtual worlds
consultation agency
production house
e.g.? alternate reality gaming
movies / TV shows.
dev like 2nd life
GIAA online...
40 people. here since 03
SW?
Maria

CHAPTER 10

Making Sense of Your Data: Modeling

At the end of a typical research phase, your brain will be very full. Your hard drive might be, too, with dozens of pages of notes, dozens or even hundreds of photos, and possibly many hours of video or audio recordings. All that information can be overwhelming and hard to use, so you have to condense and massage it into some kind of structure that makes sense. Models are excellent tools for doing this.

A **model** is a description that helps people understand and communicate about observed behavior. Bohr's model of the atom and Freud's ego, superego, and id, for example, give us frameworks for understanding the complex ideas they stand for. Similarly, modeling the results of your research will help you condense and visualize information to understand human behavior patterns, workflows, and trends.

The primary objective of modeling (and the subsequent phase, requirements definition) is to *enable informed action*. You're not only trying to crystallize your own understanding; you're also trying to help the entire product team build a shared view of the problems, opportunities, and potential next steps.

Like design research, analysis should be rigorous yet efficient, focusing on the aspects of the data that will facilitate design and business decisions. The time you spend on analyzing and modeling should be commensurate with the size of your data set; it would be absurd to spend three days doing elaborate analysis of three interviews. Your degree of thoroughness should also be determined by the scale and importance of the design and business questions you need to answer.

Barney Glaser, one of the originators of a widely used analytical approach called grounded theory, argued that "all is data," meaning that your analysis should take advantage of every bit of available information in your brain, not just what you see in your set of interviews. Likewise, you should take advantage of whatever analytical approaches seem most likely to provide insight. No single technique can accomplish everything, and the right techniques to use can vary from project to project. I focus here on qualitative techniques for use with qualitative data because they work well for most projects. You can supplement these with quantitative techniques as needed to inform business decisions; this chapter also contains a brief description of some key concepts involved, but assumes you will leave all but the simplest quantitative analysis to the statisticians.

Figure 10.1 provides an overview of the modeling phase, which begins with a review of your stakeholder findings. This activity is straightforward because you can take what you heard largely at face value. The most important thing is to develop a shared view of the stakeholders' comments among the members of the design team, then determine the implications for the project. Once you've accomplished this, the bulk of the analysis then focuses on behavior and attitudes among potential users; this includes developing a set of personas. Finally, it's essential to look at the overlap between your user data and what you heard from stakeholders, since this tends to highlight risks and opportunities.

This chapter outlines techniques for analyzing your stakeholder data and beginning to analyze your customer and user data. Chapter 11 covers personas, which are the primary models used for design.

Synthesizing Stakeholder Findings

It's important to review what you heard from stakeholders and understand what it means for your work, whether this involves controversies you can help resolve with user data or presumed constraints you'll need to consider in the design. It's best for some of this to take place before the user and customer research. You can begin debriefing informally between stakeholder meetings or on the way to user interviews and then spend a half day or so doing a more formal summary later. That summary serves another critical purpose: reflecting back to stakeholders what you heard, both so they know you understood their visions and concerns, and so they understand where the disagreements among them are.

Topics to cover

If you're debriefing about stakeholders before doing user interviews, focus on the topics that will affect what you're looking for in the rest of your research, such as pet features or assumptions about user and customer needs. When you have more time, make sure the members of your team all have a shared understanding of the political

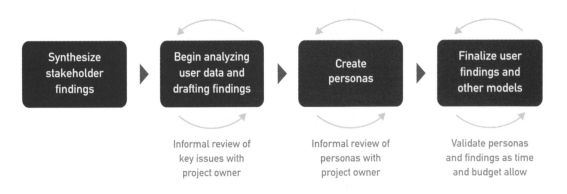

Figure 10.1. Overview of activities during the modeling phase.

landscape, potential barriers to success, and other more complex issues. In addition to making sure you all understood the same things from each stakeholder, try to answer these questions as a team:

— What kinds of users and customers do stakeholders think are most important?

— What do they think the product is?

— What do they expect to ship and when?

— What presumed constraints exist, and which may be flexible?

— What should the project accomplish for the business?

— What do stakeholders think success is and what do they think will be required to achieve it?

— What barriers to success do stakeholders expect?

— What brand values should the product or service communicate?

— How are the organization and the product or service positioned versus the competition?

— What concerns do you have about the answers to the above questions and what should you do about them?

— What disagreements about any of the above topics can you help resolve?

— What unrealistic expectations, if any, should you discuss with the project owner?

— What else did you hear that might affect how you proceed?

— Who are the most influential stakeholders and what will you (and the design) need to do to satisfy them?

Next, you must decide which of these things to discuss privately with your project owner and which to summarize and reflect back to the entire group of stakeholders. Unrealistic expectations or major disagreements about the scale or timeline of the project are best raised with your project owner.

Handling controversy

A certain amount of disagreement about project scale or timeframe is normal. If everyone's idea of the ship date falls within a range of about three months, I generally find that it resolves itself; disagreements of six months or more are almost certainly a problem. Engineers will usually be more pessimistic than others about how many features they can squeeze into a release or how small they can make the hardware, but

Mention unrealistic expectations or major disagreements about the scale or timeline of the project to your project owner.

Modeling

that's seldom anything to worry about unless the marketers are expecting something the size of a cell phone and the engineers don't think it can be smaller than a laptop.

Where there is controversy about product definition or user needs, you should be able to address that with your user data. If you can't, you probably need to improve the quality or expand the scope of your data collection. Again, some disagreement in emphasis is typical, especially when someone is overly optimistic about the importance or potential of the product. For example, a stakeholder on one project expected that executive users would just read monthly reports prepared by staff, while another thought the information was so vital that executives would log in and check it daily. This sounds like a huge disagreement, but the field study data made it easy to resolve. Completely opposing ideas about who the target audience is or which audience to address first can be a bit trickier, but data can still help.

Exercise

Imagine that you heard the following from LocalGuide stakeholders. What are the key issues you need to look out for in user research? What concerns do you have about how stakeholders view timelines, success criteria, and other issues, and how would you proceed?

CEO and cofounder

She has worked with city governments and chambers of commerce to promote tourism in Los Angeles, San Francisco, and Seattle. She found that all three struggled with getting government agencies and businesses to work together. All three were willing to invest in promoting tourism and did not expect a specific return on that investment;

they assumed it would come through generation of jobs and additional sales tax. She believes other cities have similar needs.

She envisions that the LocalGuide product will provide maps, directions, information, and a directory of restaurants and shops. It will generate revenue through some combination of setup and licensing fees paid by the local organization, rental fees (if any) paid by end users, and advertising fees paid by local businesses (which could be higher when users act on ads by patronizing attractions or stores). She expects that tourists would rent or borrow the device at their hotel or an airport kiosk, and perhaps at major attractions. She does not expect business travelers to be a major audience.

She envisions a touch screen device no bigger than a deck of cards, thinks it should have a physical keyboard, and doesn't want users to hassle with charging batteries.

Success would be five cities signed up for pilot projects before the product ships six months from now, plus another ten in the first year. Her biggest concern is running out of venture capital before starting to generate revenue.

CTO and cofounder

He's a GPS technology expert who has worked on a couple of in-car navigation systems and mobile phones. He imagines that LocalGuide will provide information specific to each user's location, such as shops or restaurants within a few blocks, or nearby public transportation options and schedules. He's concerned that getting detailed information and keeping it up to date will be difficult and costly.

He expects it will take about nine months to develop a pilot product that will have some subset of the eventual functionality. He believes the last in-car navigation system he did is very similar to what the LocalGuide will need to be, so the design problem seems straightforward to him. He wants the design finished two months from now. Success to him would be a solid pilot project with one city in the next eight months.

Director of Engineering

He followed the CTO from their last company. His experience with designers is limited primarily to graphic design focused on icons and such. He is experienced with multiple development environments including embedded systems. He's a software guy who has generally worked with predefined hardware platforms.

The software team consists of two people so far: a database specialist and a guy who has written other GPS applications. He's hoping to find a GUI engineer soon. He's also hired a mechanical engineer and electrical engineer. He agrees with the CTO that the design problem is straightforward. He also wants a detailed specification in a couple of months, but would like a rough outline of the design a month from now. He expects to ship a pilot product in nine or ten months.

Success would be a pilot project that doesn't have any big technical failures. He's concerned that the Director of Marketing doesn't understand software; he thinks her experience with identifying new toothpaste flavors won't translate well.

Lead Mechanical and Electrical Engineers

Both joined about three months ago. The ME has done mostly mobile phones. The EE has done GPS and medical devices. Both are concerned that no one else understands how difficult and expensive it is to build hardware, with the exception of the product manager. The budget they've been given for components won't allow for both a touch screen and a keyboard, and will limit their choice of components to those that are widely available. It will be difficult to get the device much smaller than a paperback book (but with a very small screen) without some changes in the budget or expectations. Neither believes it will be possible to ship in less than a year.

Director of Marketing

She's a veteran of product marketing for consumer packaged goods (toothpaste, shampoo, and several pet products). She has little experience with brand strategy or corporate communications, so she's hiring an ad agency to develop the identity and brand strategy.

She expects that tourism will be the initial market, but thinks there are opportunities to sell to large conferences, universities, and other specialized markets. She wonders if other stakeholders understand the market correctly.

She believes design will provide clarity in direction, since everyone is having difficulty visualizing the product right now. She's frustrated by her communication with the technical team; she has insufficient visibility into what they're doing and thinks they're throwing techno-speak at her to keep her at arm's length.

Continued

Near-term success would be a couple of successful pilots with results they can publicize. Long-term success would be recognition as the market leader. Her biggest concern is the lack of a five-year plan.

Director of Sales

He's mostly worked in retail channel sales, but compares LocalGuide to his experience selling to hospitals, which are political environments with various demanding constituencies. He's concerned that the CEO expects multiple cities to sign up for pilot projects in the next six months, since he expects it will be a long sales cycle. He's frustrated with the product manager because he doesn't have anything concrete to sell; he wants some kind of demo right away even if it's not what the product will really be.

Product Manager (designated project owner)

He has limited experience, all with handheld GPS systems for consumers. He's spent a lot of time with engineers, less with defining markets and financial models. He says that until they can staff up, his job is half project management, making sure everyone knows what everyone else needs and when. He's supposed to develop the final requirements and doesn't really expect the design team to affect more than aesthetic and usability issues. He's taken a course from a marketing consultancy on writing requirements documents, but doesn't know how to make sure the engineers translate that into something good. He hopes the design team can help with that.

Preparing to communicate stakeholder findings

Eventually, you'll want to communicate a summary of what you heard back to the full set of stakeholders. This may be a set of bullets on a presentation slide that you provide commentary on, or a set of points in a written document with a paragraph or two about each. For example:

Analysts will prepare information; executives will mostly consume it. Because analysis takes considerable time and expertise, no matter how clear the interface, stakeholders expect that the bulk of the work will continue to be done by analysts who clean the data, select appropriate queries to run against it, format it for easy consumption, and perhaps point out interesting issues. Executives are the primary consumers of the data, but can only engage with it through static reports today. The next release is expected to provide some ability for executives to sort, filter, and format the post-analysis data on their own. Stakeholders believe this is important because younger executives are more accustomed to tweaking documents or slides for themselves.

Don't be afraid to mention points of disagreement. It's better to get these out in the open, though you should avoid attributing comments to specific stakeholders. Here's an example:

Hopes for executive user engagement vary. We heard a wide range of views regarding how central the tool would be to executives' work. Some stakeholders expect executives to view reports every month or so, while others envision daily use even when executives are out of the office.

Modeling

It's seldom worthwhile to spend more than a day or so discussing and documenting stakeholder findings, since much of their value is in their overlap with the user and customer findings and in the understanding you gain about how to work with these particular stakeholders.

Analyzing Customer and User Data

The next step involves combing through your user and customer data to see what it can tell you. Trying to consume the raw data from your customer and user research would be like trying to eat raw flour, sugar, and butter before they were transformed into a cake—difficult and unpleasant, at best. A summary is more helpful, but to continue the analogy, a simple summary of the data is no more sufficient than a combination of ingredients to make batter; true analysis, like baking, transforms the ingredients into something much more palatable. An effective analysis also identifies the relationships among pieces of information, then explains the reasons for those relationships. Finally, most social scientists would argue that a good analysis also includes some way to validate the accuracy of your interpretation; this point is covered in Chapter 11. Figure 10.2 provides an overview of the analysis process.

The analysis process involves understanding what you've heard and observed, condensing the entire set of data into something more manageable, organizing it to identify patterns and relationships, and interpreting what those patterns and relationships mean. The process is iterative rather than linear; each act of condensing and organizing can help you identify and explain a pattern that, in turn, may point you to still other ways to parse your data to glean insight. The techniques you use may vary from project to project, but one thing is true for every project: Insight comes from spending time with your data and looking at it in multiple ways.

Qualitative analysis

Qualitative analysis is critical for design because it excels at explaining *why* and *how*, as well as *what*. Human intuition does play a role; there's nothing wrong with making intuitive leaps as long as you pause and examine the data to see if it actually fits the structure your subconscious has proposed. Good qualitative techniques make those intuitive leaps easier *and* help you determine whether your leaps are correct.

On every project, you should also be looking at the data at varying levels of granularity. Just as you can't understand an animal without understanding its ecosystem, or an ecosystem without understanding the organisms that comprise it,

Modeling

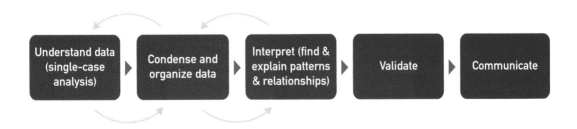

Figure 10.2. Overview of analysis process.

you need to know the individuals, as well as the whole data set, to understand what your results really mean. This is why it's best to start with **single-case analysis**, which is just what it sounds like: focusing on understanding what you heard and saw with one individual at a time. This helps ensure that you and your teammates not only understand *what* you saw and heard, but also have a good idea of *why* each person thought and behaved as he did. Once you're well grounded in the individual cases, you can move on to **cross-case analysis**, which involves grouping and comparing the individual cases to identify trends and behavior patterns. This involves comparison of individuals in most instances, but you may aggregate further to compare types of organizations (such as small versus large companies) if you're designing enterprise software.

TECHNIQUES COMMON TO SINGLE-CASE AND CROSS-CASE ANALYSIS

Most analysis at either level of granularity employs both deductive and inductive reasoning. **Deductive reasoning** starts with an existing general principle or hypothesis and compares the data to it. For example, if you assumed in your interview planning that having small children would give people more reason to take and share photos, you would be looking at your interview notes to see if the observed behavior supported your hypothesis. Clearly, it's important with deductive reasoning to avoid bending the data to fit your hypothesis. **Inductive reasoning**, on the other hand, involves trying to derive a general principle from specific data. If you saw in your data that serious photographers tend to delete a larger percentage of their images than casual photographers do, you would look in the data for explanations of why that might be the case and try to turn it into a general statement, such as, "Serious photographers tend to take many photos to make sure they capture a scene as they 'see' it. Their quality standards are exacting, so

they delete any photos that don't meet them." The primary danger with inductive reasoning is that it's easy to get false positives; just because every serious photographer in your sample owns a particular camera does not mean that all serious photographers do.

Displaying your data in various ways will also help you understand it, derive insight from it, and communicate with your teammates and stakeholders about it. While displaying your data is probably most useful in cross-case analysis, it also helps you be honest with yourself in single cases; if you can't find a way to express a process or relationship in concrete terms (whether visual or textual), that means you probably don't understand it well enough to proceed.

Finally, while it's not a good idea to force your data into a **simile or metaphor**, you might find yourself using one to describe a process, place, role, or mind-set in either single-case or cross-case analysis. If you do, stop and examine it, because metaphor is a type of model we apply to understand and explain the world around us; chances are, your subconscious has drawn some connection that you need to examine. For example, if one of your teammates compares the corporate help desk intake role with an emergency room triage nurse, his subconscious has probably just condensed that person's work process into a clear model: Hear what the symptoms are, determine how quickly they need to be addressed in order to assign a priority, and identify what skills it will take to address them to determine where to assign it. You need to articulate the assumptions inherent in that and determine whether they're true.

SINGLE-CASE ANALYSIS

Single-case analysis is primarily about ensuring that you and your teammates have a thorough (and shared!) understanding of what you've seen and heard. You probably don't need to communicate about single cases with anyone outside the design team except as examples to illustrate trends, so this part of the analysis can be entirely informal.

To walk through a single case, review your field notes with your fellow interviewer(s), discuss what you think the behavior and comments mean and why (with particular attention to anything that was puzzling or unexpected), and note any disagreements or alternate explanations. If possible, start this type of analysis on an informal basis between interviews so you can use it to guide subsequent interviews. Ten or 15 minutes between sessions and a few minutes at the end of an interview day are enough for an experienced team to do this preliminary analysis; less experienced teams may need a dedicated hour or two a day. Continue single-case analysis after the interviews are done.

Reducing and organizing your data (coding)

Social scientists begin single-case analysis by categorizing each comment or observation. They call this **coding,** but you won't hear many designers refer to it this way because of the association with writing software code. The formal version involves assigning a category to every respondent statement or observed behavior. **Check-coding**, in which two researchers individually code the data and then compare and merge their work, is generally accepted as more accurate and objective than a single researcher coding alone. Although it's far less formal, this is essentially what happens in a design team meeting in which everyone reviews her own notes and discusses her thoughts about an interview.

This categorizing process is both deductive and inductive, in that there are certain categories of information you would expect to find in your notes, while the data itself may suggest other categories. These category codes and the quantity of data can become hard to manage in large

academic studies, so it's common for ethnographers or anthropologists to use spreadsheets or specialized software to help them sort individual quotes or observations by code. The average design project involves less data and fewer categories, so the organizing tool may be no more sophisticated than scribbles in the margin of your notebook. For the most part, the codes you're likely to use on every project mirror the questions you ask in research, such as:

— Goals

— Frustrations

— Skills

— Frequency

— Quantity

— Priority

— Interactions with others

— Mental models

— Demographics

— User physical characteristics

Of course, there are always categories unique to each project, such as particular process steps or types of documents used. For an enterprise purchasing application, for example, your notes might also include the following categories:

— Requisition

— Hard goods

— Services

— Vendor selection criteria

— Payment terms

— Delivery terms

— Negotiation

— Follow-up

Here's an example of how part of a formally coded interview transcript might look, using the LocalGuide interview from Chapter 8.

Interview transcript	Codes
PARTICIPANT: Or I end up traveling somewhere that someone else I know has traveled recently.	— Choice of destination (driven by trusted guide)
SECOND INTERVIEWER: Why is that better?	
PARTICIPANT: It's just so much easier when somebody can give you a few pointers to get started. I tend to travel in such a way that I have a couple destinations that I'd like to go to and maybe they helped me figure out, oh, you should go to this landmark because there's that, plus there's other stuff around it if you don't like that. And then I tend to … "Ok, we're going to go somewhere." But I never really stick to going there, so if something else more interesting shows up or whatever, I like to be very flexible, but still a destination to at least get started towards.	— Reliance on trusted guide — Part planned, part flexible
PRIMARY INTERVIEWER: When you're traveling like that, how do you decide what other things to do? So if you planned to go one place, how do you find other things to do?	
PARTICIPANT: Yeah, I guess it depends on how you're moving about. So I had gone to Venice last November, and my friend and I had both looked in some tour books. So we went to Venice, which is a pretty small place, and so we had picked out a couple of things like, "Oh, we really need to go see this, and this." And we were there for an event. Again, this is like, I like going somewhere where there are people involved.	— Tour books — Part planned, part flexible — Choice of destination (driven by business trip)
PRIMARY INTERVIEWER: What was the event?	
PARTICIPANT: Architectural Biennial show that was put on by one of the universities there. So, we knew that that event was going to take most of the time, and so we had a little standing list of things that when we had free time, we should do. Check out the major square there. Go to the major shopping street. There was a glass blowing … island actually. An island with glass blowing workshops, which we did not make it to.	— Part planned, part flexible
SECOND INTERVIEWER: But you wanted to?	
PARTICIPANT: Yeah, it was definitely on the list. But I guess that's the thing. I don't like making the list solid because then I regret if we didn't get somewhere. But maybe there's something more interesting.	— Part planned, part flexible
PRIMARY INTERVIEWER: So once you had some free time, and you wanted to get to one of these places, how did you find it?	

Modeling

Interview transcript	Codes
PARTICIPANT: We were looking at tourist maps in tourist books for the most part.	— Navigation (maps, books)
PRIMARY INTERVIEWER: Guidebooks that you brought with you?	
PARTICIPANT: Yeah, guidebooks. And attempting to ask directions.	— Navigation (books, asking directions)
PRIMARY INTERVIEWER: Neither of you spoke the language?	
PARTICIPANT: No, not really.	
PRIMARY INTERVIEWER: How did that work out?	
PARTICIPANT: We'd usually figure out where we were going eventually. One of the people who had … so I went with a friend and there was another group of people who met us there. And when we finally connected with them, one of them spoke better Italian and had been to Venice before. Again, using people is the easiest way. So he would direct us. I think the hardest part became that you'd get somewhere, and then getting back was usually the hardest part.	— Language — Trusted guide — Navigation

Modeling

Using Microsoft OneNote on a tablet PC is an easy alternative to coding detailed transcripts. If you're recording interview audio as you write notes, the application associates the audio track with what you're writing at the time. This makes it easy to replay interesting snippets during analysis without the cost or tedium of transcription.

Another approach is to type up your handwritten interview notes using categories, rather than trying to represent your notes in a sequential fashion. This is labor-intensive—requiring about as much time to document each interview as you spent doing it—but some people find it etches the interview into their brains in a way that nothing else does. Summary notes are also useful if you have many people doing separate interviews or if you're expected to share interview details outside the design team. A summary of the interview segment above might look more like this:

Choice of destination: Chooses destination opportunistically (if she's there on business) or because people she knows and trusts have visited and enjoyed it.

Planning: Favorite source is a trusted human guide who is from the destination or has visited it. Also looks at travel books and Web sites for ideas. May read fiction related to the area. Makes a tentative list of activities to ensure that she doesn't waste time deciding what to do, but assumes it's flexible.

Selecting activities: Uses her list as a starting point. Chooses other activities that look interesting once she gets there. Prefers activities involving people. May walk by an interesting place, see an ad, or hear about it from a local.

Your team should be able to illustrate the basic activity flow you observed and describe the criteria involved at each decision point.

Navigating: Uses local tourist maps and tour books to get around. Often asks locals for directions, but language can be a barrier. Uses hotel as primary reference point.

On a project with a small team and a tight timeline, this case-by-case review may not result in any detailed artifacts or summaries at all, but might just involve informal discussion among the interviewers. The way you go about it isn't critical, so long as you go through the thought process and develop a shared view of the data. Detailed codes or categories aren't necessary unless you have a big team, a huge data set, or the need to trace requirements back to individual interviews (which may be important for some products used in medical diagnosis and treatment). Some teams find it helpful to plaster the walls of an office or meeting room with photos of the interviewees and their environments as memory aids, as in Figure 10.3.

Figure 10.3. A design team using interview photos to help with single-case review.

Articulating models within a case

Modeling the contents of each interview can help you understand and interpret your observations. After an effective interview, your team should be able to illustrate the basic activity flow you observed and, when relevant, describe the criteria involved at various decision points. **Activity diagrams** and **decision trees** like those illustrated in Figures 10.4 and 10.5 can be good ways to do this. Such diagrams include the kinds of documents, objects, or pieces of information the respondent uses and what the respondent does with them in what sequence. It's usually not critical to cover every tiny detail.

If activities are complex, you might try sketching out this kind of model toward the end of a user interview and reviewing it with your respondent to make sure you haven't missed or misunderstood anything. This is a good technique for novice interviewers, in any case.

The other thing you should be able to articulate is each respondent's **mental model** of the world as it relates to your design problem. This includes what the respondent calls various objects, how he defines them, and how he views their relationships; this is often called a **taxonomy**. For example, an individual shopper's taxonomy of housewares might look like the one in Figure 10.6. Note how some items, such as mixers, fit in multiple categories—categories in a taxonomy need not be exclusive. Card sorting, described in Chapter 9, is a useful way to extract a taxonomy, though it's often possible to do so implicitly during the course of an interview.

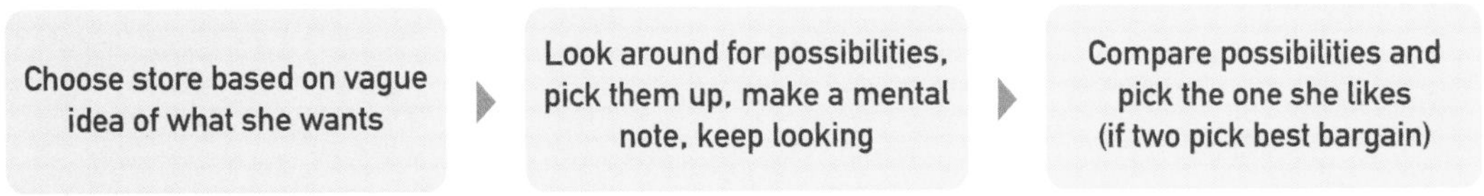

Modeling

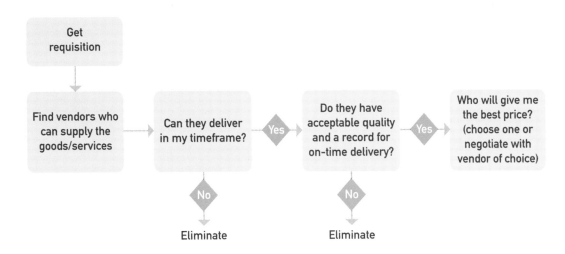

Figure 10.4. This simple diagram illustrates the process a shopper goes through before making a purchase.

Figure 10.5. This diagram illustrates the process a purchasing agent goes through to choose a vendor. Note that he considers timeline first, then a combination of two factors (quality and past performance), with price coming last.

Modeling

Kitchen Things

Appliances

Mixers
- Stand mixers
- Handheld mixers

Food processors
- Big ones
- Little ones

Blenders

Cooking Things

Pots and pans
- Skillets
- Saucepans
- Pots

Utensils
- Spatulas
- Spoons
- Tongs

Knives

Gadgets
- Garlic press
- Grater

Baking Things

Pans
- Cookie sheets
- Muffin tins
- Cake pans
- Loaf pans

Utensils
- Spatulas
- Measuring spoons
- Measuring cups

Mixers
- Stand mixers
- Handheld mixers

Dining and Entertaining Things

Dishes

Dishes
- Dinner plates
- Dessert plates
- Bowls
- Mugs

Serving pieces
- Platters
- Bowls
- Tureens

Glassware

Wine glasses

Champagne glasses

Water glasses

Juice glasses

Utensils

Silverware
- Knives
- Forks
- Teaspoons
- Soup spoons

Serving pieces
- Serving spoons
- Ladles
- Cake servers
- Serving forks

Linens

Napkins

Placemats

Tablecloths

Runners

Figure 10.6. An example taxonomy.

A mental model is a bit more than a taxonomy, though; it also includes the way that someone imagines a process or structure to work (as opposed to what actually happens). For example, most of us think about files on a hard disk existing in a single location, like a physical book on a shelf, when in fact one file may be stored in fragments across several sectors of the disk. Any application that didn't represent files as single blocks of data would be terribly confusing.

Note that the example activity diagram, decision tree, and taxonomy shown here aren't particularly formal; they're just thinking and communication tools for members of a small team with shared experiences, so there's no need to whip out Visio or concern yourself with the rules of UML. Also note that *being able* to articulate these things for every interview doesn't necessarily mean you need to spend the time to *do* so; a skilled team that's used to working together probably doesn't.

If you're not sure, you can try it for your first few interviews; if you're able to do it easily and you're not finding disagreements among interviewers, then it's probably not the best use of your time. If you're not able to outline workflows and mental models or if you have significant disagreements, you need to sharpen your interviewing skills.

Exercise

Begin single-case analysis with your interview notes for the LocalGuide or RoomFinder. If you did not do interviews, refer to the example interview transcripts on the Web site.

CROSS-CASE ANALYSIS

Cross-case analysis helps you identify behavior patterns and trends. A sociologist doing a multi-month project would begin this during research, but this is impractical for design research on a tight timeline, so most if not all of your cross-case analysis may take place after your interviews. You'll probably bounce back and forth between cross-case and single-case review to some extent.

Make sure you understand the individual cases very well before comparing them or beginning to aggregate data. Otherwise, you may equate two behaviors that seem similar at a superficial level, but may be very different in intent. One person who keeps switching stations on the car radio may be doing it to stay awake, while another is trying to find a particular station. You would design different solutions for each problem.

For design, the richest form of cross-case analysis results in **personas**, which are composite models of user behavior patterns (see Chapter 11). However, you will also want to identify trends and general issues in your data to help yourself and stakeholders understand in general terms how processes work, what kind of data you're dealing with, what potential users often struggle with, and

so forth. These themes become your user and customer findings, which lay the groundwork for people to understand and accept the personas and requirements.

In the broadest terms, the question you're trying to answer is, "What did we learn that's potentially important or useful?" Experienced team members who excel at identifying patterns can often develop user findings from a small data set through fairly unstructured discussion. If you're uncomfortable with this approach or it's not getting you very far, consider trying a more structured technique. You can use an entirely inductive approach ("These three people all demonstrated a behavior that seemed similar; what exactly is similar about it?") or start with deduction by comparing and summarizing the responses to your various interview questions ("What different kinds of photo sharing behavior did we see?"), and then use an inductive approach to categorize the rest of the data.

One manageable way to start is to select two or three respondents who strike you as similar to one another, then discuss exactly what is similar or different about them. Affinity diagrams and composite models are also common tools.

Affinity diagrams

The most common inductive approach is to build an **affinity diagram**. There are varying points of view about the best way to develop an affinity diagram, from whether it's done in silence to how many colors of sticky notes are required; there are even software packages for managing affinity diagrams. There's really no need to make a big production of it because the essential concept is simple: Each interviewer gets a pile of index cards or sticky notes and writes one respondent comment or behavior on each. The design team then clusters those notes with others that seem similar and tries to derive a category, underlying issue, or concept that describes each cluster, as the team in Figure 10.7 is doing.

Figure 10.7. Sticky notes make it easy to create and rearrange clusters.

You can also divide each cluster into subclusters or aggregate them into a supercluster defined by an overarching idea. For example, imagine that you've grouped part of your data as in Table 10.1.

You might then realize that in the "organizing" cluster, there are really two different subsets (people who organize by time and people who organize by topic), so you'd divide those into subclusters. You might also see that "sending via e-mail" and "posting to Web sites" are both forms of sharing, and so relate those in a supercluster.

When you are dealing with an enterprise system and roles that are clearly distinct (such as receptionists versus average office phone users, or nurses versus accountants), it's generally more

Table 10.1. **Example affinity clusters.**

Data points in the cluster (individual sticky notes)	Idea or category that ties them together (cluster of sticky notes)
— Alice sends photos of her little boy to her parents at least once a week via e-mail — Jorge e-mails pictures of the new baby to grandparents in Mexico	Sending via e-mail
— Ben posts photos of the twins on Flickr every few days for his sister — Alice posts pictures on her Web site for friends to see if they're interested	Posting to Web sites
— Alice organizes photos by date — Ben organizes by date, sometimes with an event name (like "Christmas") — Dan assigns attributes to each photo that describe contents, lighting, or other aspects of the image — Stacy stores photos in folders by year, then by month — Ellen puts photos in folders by subject (birds, mammals, plants, etc.), then by subtopic (seagulls, songbirds, etc.)	Organizing

manageable to do this exercise separately for each role; otherwise, you'll spend a lot of time dividing each cluster by role, anyway.

Keep in mind that *the diagram itself is not the point* of the exercise; *insight* is. The idea is simply to help your team understand the range of user characteristics and begin to identify patterns. An affinity diagram won't usually identify your personas, but serves as a useful basis for identifying behavioral variables (see Chapter 11), such as recognizing that among your interviewees, there were two different ways to organize. Don't worry about grouping people or what to do with outliers yet; other techniques are better tools for this.

In practice, I wouldn't suggest spending more than a couple of hours on affinity diagrams. They're important tools if you have a large team that didn't attend all of the interviews, but since at least two people on your team probably did attend each one, it's usually possible to do much of this synthesis in simple conversation. If you're not finding that you gain anything from this technique, skip it and move on to another one.

Composite models

You may also find it useful to develop composite activity diagrams, decision trees, taxonomies, or other illustrations of behavior across cases. These are most useful in communicating about the behavior of different personas, so they are covered in Chapter 13.

> ### Exercise
>
> Do cross-case analysis (and revisit single-case analysis as needed) with your interview notes for the LocalGuide or RoomFinder. If you did not do interviews, refer to the example interview transcripts on the Web site (www.designingforthedigitalage.com).

Quantitative analysis

Although quantitative analysis is not that useful in explaining behaviors and relationships, it is good for assessing the size of your potential market, the probability that people in your audience possess a particular characteristic, or the likelihood that two characteristics occur together. Most people think of quantitative analysis as something used solely on quantitative data such as survey results, but you can also apply quantitative methods to qualitative data. To distinguish this approach from a purely quantitative one, some people refer to quantitative analysis of small qualitative samples simply as "counting."

Quantitative analysis is good for assessing the size of your potential market, the probability that people in your audience possess a particular characteristic, or the likelihood that two characteristics occur together.

Modeling

PREPARING YOUR QUALITATIVE DATA

Qualitative samples are usually much smaller than those in quantitative studies, so it's important to represent your findings in a way that isn't misleading. Saying that 12 of your 16 respondents did a certain thing lets people decide for themselves whether they think that's true of the general population; expressing that number as a percentage hides the fact that it's a small sample and may imply that you did a quantitative study.

If you do decide to look at your sample in numeric terms, explicit coding becomes more important. With the LocalGuide interviews, for example, you might count the number of people who planned ahead, did no planning, or did some combination of the two. You might also count the number of men versus women, the number of people in various age ranges, or just about anything else.

This kind of primitive quantitative analysis may also point to the need for quantitative data. If you're designing an e-commerce Web site and you find that most of your interviewees spend very little money and a few interviewees spend a lot of money, a quantitative study can help you determine whether it's more lucrative to focus on one or the other.

UNDERSTANDING QUANTITATIVE DATA

For the purposes of this book, I assume that you will either leave the finer points of quantitative analysis to the statisticians or pick up an appropriate textbook. However, even if you're using statistics generated by someone else, it's important to understand a couple of concepts so you know just how conclusive the results are.

Most people take the results of quantitative studies at face value, but this can be misleading. For example, whenever there's an election coming up, there's always a news story when one candidate or another is gaining in the polls. The news agen-cies may report that 31% of likely voters favor candidate A and 32% favor candidate B. Even disregarding the fact that many people change their minds when they get to the ballot box, these numbers may very well be wrong because the difference (1%) is less than the potential for error in the sample.

The **standard error** (sometimes described as the **margin** of error) is an estimate of how far your answer is from the "real" answer due to sampling error in a random sample. If the standard error in the poll is 3%, then what the poll really says is that 28 to 34% of people favor candidate A and 29 to 35% favor candidate B, so either one could really be ahead by several points.

Standard deviation is a measure of confidence in the data; in other words, it describes the probability that the data can be used to predict future results. A large standard deviation means the measured values are spread far from the mean (also known as the average), so the probability of accurate prediction is low. A small standard deviation tells you that the measured values are clustered closely around the mean, so predictability is high. Let's use income as an example. If you surveyed people with similar education and experience in similar jobs at similar companies in one city, you'd have a low standard deviation because the individual responses are within a narrow range, which means you have a good chance of accurately predicting the salary of someone similar to your respondents. If you used a truly random sample of people across an entire country or region, then the values would vary much more, so you'd be much less able to make an accurate guess at an individual's real salary. Figure 10.8 illustrates this concept.

Determining confidence for a **normal distribution** (the classic bell curve where values cluster around the mean and taper off toward the high and low ends) is easy: There's a 68% probability of a value being within the range defined by the

Modeling

Smaller standard deviation

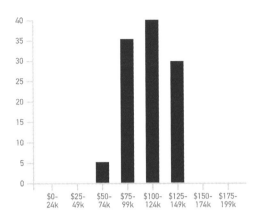

Larger standard deviation

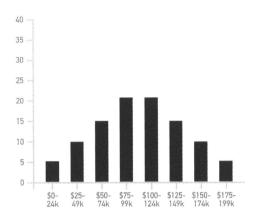

Figure 10.8. In the figure on the left, the standard deviation is relatively small because nearly all of the values are in a narrow range. In the figure on the right, the values are more spread out, which means the chances of predicting an individual's salary are lower.

standard error and a 95% probability of a value being within twice that range. In other words, if you measured an average income of $100,000 and had a 5% error with a normal distribution of results, it would indicate there's a 68% chance that someone's income is between $95,000 and $105,000 and a 95% chance that it's between $90,000 and $110,000. With a bimodal or other type of distribution, it gets more complicated, so you'll want to call up an expert or pull out that statistics textbook. Figure 10.9 shows the difference between a normal and bimodal distribution.

So, what does this mean for your analysis? For one thing, it means you should always look for the error and standard deviation in any third-party study you use so you know how much to rely on that information. If these are not provided, look at the sample size and, if possible, the range of values; a larger sample with a narrow range of values is likely to be more accurate than a small sample with a wide range of responses. You should also help stakeholders understand what the numbers actually mean or where you may be uncertain about how good they are.

Normal distribution   Bimodal distribution

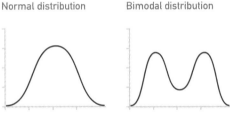

Figure 10.9. In a normal distribution, values cluster around the mean and taper off on either side. In a bimodal distribution, there are two clusters; for example, you may find a certain behavior exhibited by the very young and the very old, but not by adults in their middle years.

GAINING INSIGHT QUANTITATIVELY

Without getting into complex statistical analysis, visualization and comparison are usually the best ways to gain insight using quantitative methods. Tables may point to possible relationships among variables, while graphs can help you understand where there may be trends or clusters. You may not need to visualize your data if you have a small

219

sample, since the trend will be pretty obvious if eight out of ten people did one thing and only two did another.

Cross-tab analysis

Insight generally comes from comparing variables in a table, such as age versus attitude or geography versus access to services. This is called **cross-tabulation** or cross-tab analysis. The idea is to look for any apparent correlation between two or more characteristics, such as age, income, or region versus time spent online. You can compare pretty much any variable to any other, but use your intuition as a starting point. If you're wondering whether A and B are related based on a hunch

from the interviews, a quick cross-tab can help you figure that out. The common variances that are useful in interview planning—such as variation by environment (geography, company type, or family structure), age, or experience—are often good starting places. A bit of trial and error can also help you identify unexpected correlations. For example, in Table 10.2, there's nothing at all interesting about comparing the behavior of men and women, but you can see some clear trends when you compare the behavior of people with different primary reasons for taking photos in Table 10.3. (Note that the examples below imply that the researchers actually counted and didn't just use approximations, which are more common in qualitative research).

Table 10.2. **Men versus women.**

	Photos taken in a day	Times per year photos are taken	Photos shared at a time	Times per year photos are shared
Men	25	16	21	13
Women	27	14	17	12

Table 10.3. **People with different reasons for taking photos.**

	Photos taken in a day	Times per year photos are taken	Photos shared at a time	Times per year photos are shared
Watching children grow up	4	75	12	31
Capturing vacation and special events	35	6	43	6
Creating perfect, expressive images	276	24	2	3

As in qualitative analysis, vary the degree of granularity you're using; comparing behavior by age range, company, or region can be more informative than just totaling up what individuals do. Be aware that if you subdivide your data in ways you didn't anticipate when planning your study, the error and confidence interval you intended to use may no longer apply, since you're effectively reducing your sample size. Don't let it stop you from making a comparison, though, because it's more important to learn from the data than it is to maintain a particular margin of error—you're trying to gain insight, not prove a hypothesis.

Graphs and charts

People often use line or bar graphs to represent aggregate data (such as the relationship between education and income, or number of customer support calls versus time spent with a product) because their visual nature makes it easier for some people to grasp trends. Scatterplots, which represent individual data points in a graphical fashion, may point to relationships that are particularly hard to see in textual format. If you label each point, you may realize that people of certain types are clustered together and may be related in some way you didn't anticipate.

In the example scatterplot shown in Figure 10.10, each respondent is mapped on a grid with the y-axis being the number of photos taken per day and the x-axis being the frequency of sharing. By labeling each dot with a respondent name, the design team can see that certain people are clustered together, which makes it easier to ask what they may have in common that causes that clustering. In this case, Alice, Ben, and Jorge probably show similar behaviors because they all have small children; they take a few photos several times a week, and share them every week or two with out of town relatives. Dan, Li, and Hans are all serious photographers who are motivated by capturing perfect images; they take a lot of

images at once, but aren't motivated by sharing. Carla, Ellen, and Peter all take a fair number of photos on trips a few times a year, and share those with friends and family.

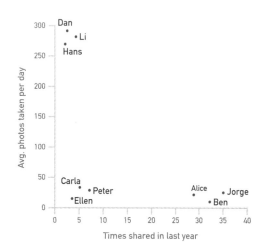

Figure 10.10. An example scatterplot.

Exercise

See what insights you gain from your LocalGuide or RoomFinder data (or the LocalGuide data on the Web site) using quantitative techniques. For example, is there any relationship between mental models or frustrations and the frequency of certain behaviors?

When qualitative and quantitative findings conflict

Qualitative results that seem a bit off from quantitative ones are not necessarily wrong. The explanation for the difference is often that surveys rely on self-reporting and may ask speculative questions, whereas qualitative studies dig deeper into actual behavior and motivations. For example, one company's quantitative survey seemed to

In any attempt at explanation, all we can do is be as objective as possible, show our work to others, and proceed based on the best theory we can assemble.

indicate that a large percentage of people would be interested in a particular service. The design team's qualitative study showed that this percentage was probably nowhere near as big as it seemed. When the design team and client did a careful review of both studies, it was clear that the quantitative study was asking people to speculate about their future behavior, whereas the qualitative one demonstrated that most people had no particular need that the new service could address. While there were clearly some people who would be interested, the indication that the percentage might be misleading led the client to reconsider the size of their investment in the new service.

Explanations and relationships

As you bounce back and forth between types of analysis, you'll begin formulating explanations for why your respondents behaved as they did and how various aspects of their attitudes, goals, and behaviors are related. Drawing meaning from your data is the whole point of analyzing it; mere summary won't accomplish much. Sometimes you can draw those explanations from within a single interview, but in most cases you'll gain more insight from comparing respondents to one another.

Of course, there is plenty of room for bias in any attempt to *explain* what you see. We humans like to believe the world is a systematic, rational place, so we tend to fill in gaps with assumptions and causal structures that may or may not be accurate. This tendency toward explanation exists in nearly every discipline and is in no way "unscientific." Everything you learned in physics class about the nature of gravity or the types and behavior of subatomic particles is simply a theory about causal structure; there is considerable evidence that makes that theory plausible, so until someone disproves it, we rely on it as truth. In any attempt at explanation, all we can do is use techniques that help us be as objective as possible, show our work to others who can tell us whether it also sounds like truth to them, and proceed based on the best theory we can assemble.

Any attempt at explanation should rely in part on the classic rules for determining causality:

1. **A precedes B.** If A is the cause, it exists or occurs before B. In the case of human behavior, this would mean that a goal, attitude, or condition exists before the demonstrated behavior exists.

2. **When A, always B.** If A causes B, in theory, B should occur any time A occurs. In reality, human behavior is very complex, so don't stop looking if it seems that B doesn't *always* follow A; sometimes it doesn't happen because some other condition exists. For example, it might seem that skilled photographers always throw out any photo that doesn't meet their standards, but one respondent kept some bad images of his son. Does that explode your theory? Not really; that photographer kept those awful photos because they were the only documentation of an important event in his child's life, so you can say, "When A, always B, except when C."

3. **A plausible mechanism links A and B.** If there is a believable connection between A and B and the other conditions are met, it's reasonable to assume that A causes B. "Enjoyment of shopping leads to more frequent shopping" makes sense, but "having blue eyes leads to more frequent shopping" doesn't make sense, so it's probably a coincidence if your data shows that people with blue eyes shop more than others.

In practice, design teams aren't making such formalized arguments, but this is essentially the thought process behind the discussion of causes and relationships among different attitudes, goals, and behaviors.

When examining the evidence, you must also consider how much weight to give any statement or observation. If a respondent said he does things one way and you observed another, the accuracy of his self-reporting is questionable, so for the sake of your analysis you should rely more on his behavior than on his statement. This is especially important when considering anything that someone says he "wants" to do. If your respondent says a magic tool would let him tag every photo in multiple ways to be able to find each one later, you should take that statement more seriously if he currently spends a lot of time filing copies in multiple folders than if he currently dumps all of his photos in a single folder. In the first case, he cares enough about finding specific photos that he's already investing a lot of effort; in the second, he's just speculating about something that might be nice, but doesn't seem to have much existing pain.

Don't expect to identify and explain every relationship right away. You'll want to revisit this step once you have personas, but persona creation will go more smoothly if you've already begun identifying relationships among various goals, behaviors, and characteristics.

> If a respondent said he does things one way and you observed another, your analysis should rely more on his behavior than on his statement.

Modeling

Risks and opportunities

By the end of your analysis time, you may find that you've uncovered previously unidentified risks or opportunities. This is one way in which design research can form a basis not only for product design, but also for product and business strategy.

Opportunities usually appear in the form of unexpected customer and user needs. Sometimes combining what you heard from stakeholders with what you've observed in user interviews can help you make a critical connection. On a health care project when the managed care model was just starting to sweep the United States, I recall an executive stakeholder saying that within a few years, every care provider's biggest problem would be figuring out how to deliver appropriate treatment within the complex reimbursement structures of managed care. Later, during user interviews, my team encountered one facility with mostly managed care patients that had created a role specifically to address that problem; we realized that creating tools for such people would be a huge opportunity for our client to jump ahead of the market.

Many of the risks are already evident to stakeholders, but it's not unusual for design research to reveal significant business problems. I've seen cases where stakeholders misunderstood who the potential users were, severely overestimated the demand for a particular type of product or service, or had already invested in technologies that would prove limiting. In each case, the stakeholders weren't happy to hear the bad news, but they were grateful to have intelligence that helped avert potentially costly mistakes. Before jumping to the conclusion that a particular course of action is bad, though, remember that stakeholders may still know something you don't. Pull your project owner aside and discuss anything you believe might be a major problem before taking it to the full product team. It's best to present your findings and help stakeholders see the implications, but let them draw their own conclusions.

Preparing to communicate your user findings

Just as thinking through the trends and relationships in your data will prepare you to identify behavior patterns and turn them into personas, walking through your findings before you introduce the personas will help stakeholders understand how the persona set emerged from your data and why it makes sense. This also gives you a chance to address questions and concerns based on examples from the data, so that once you introduce the personas, nothing in them should be controversial.

As with stakeholder findings, you can communicate user findings in a presentation, in a detailed written report, or both. Try to distill each issue to a simple statement with supporting commentary or text. Here's an example:

Buyers chose their automobiles in widely varying ways, but most decisions involved emotion to some degree. Some people selected a car because they felt it expressed something they wanted to convey about themselves, whether because they liked its design or identified with the attributes of the brand. These buyers tended to be decisive and not very research oriented; one said she purchased a Jaguar because she "liked the kitty on the hood." Most people said they choose their vehicles for various practical reasons, such as cargo capacity, safety, fuel efficiency, or budget. Some of these buyers said they may have started with a leaning toward one model for emotional reasons, but would not have bought it if it did not meet their other criteria; they seemed to feel that emotional reasons were not a valid basis for making such a decision. This group varied with respect to the amount of research they did; research orientation did not appear to be related to any particular factor. A small group, which mostly consisted of men under age 40, was very focused on performance characteristics, such as engine size and handling.

You must decide how to focus your findings, since a complete list of everything you learned will bore most stakeholders and cause critical points to get lost among trivial ones. It's fine to talk about how everyone was confused by the instructions on a specific screen if you're doing a constrained redesign. If your scope is more ambitious, though, it's best to focus your findings on things that will have the greatest effect on the product definition or accompanying business strategy, along with anything that will have major implications for design (such as major flaws in the current hardware form factor or software navigation). Common topics for a findings discussion include:

— User mental models, especially where they differ from current implementations

— An overview of existing processes and major points of pain within them

— Trends, behavior patterns, and the factors that influence them

— User skills or characteristics, especially if they differ from expectations

— Comparison of customer and user needs

See Chapter 13 for how the findings come together with personas and requirements in the User and Domain Analysis document.

Project Management during Modeling

Although you may wish to spend a lot of time working with your data, it's seldom worth more than a few days of effort. On a relatively tight project of, say, eight to twelve weeks total, you may need to limit the pre-persona modeling to no

more than a day. Make sure your approach is consistent with the amount of time you have; detailed coding of every interview, for example, could take you several days and is seldom worthwhile for small data sets. Set goals for what you want to be able to articulate at the end of each meeting, so you don't just wander aimlessly through your data. Have patience if big insights don't appear just yet, though; things may be much more clear once you have personas to help structure some of the other models. Move on to persona creation if you don't feel like you're getting anywhere, then revisit these techniques afterward.

Avoid including people from outside the design team in these activities, since it's exceedingly difficult to interpret what you didn't observe, and this type of analysis generally looks messy (and not very confidence inspiring) to an outsider. However, all design team members should ideally be present. It's often more efficient for the interaction designers to do most of the modeling by themselves, then get additional input from other design team members. Only do this when your budget requires it, though, because it's less effective in building consensus on the design team, and the other designers' perspectives can add value at every stage. Any writing during this time is generally shared among team members, though the visual designer may be primarily focused on creating polished process or concept visualizations.

It's wise to have an informal team check-in once you have some preliminary models and findings outlined. This may just be with the team lead if he or she has not participated much in developing the findings and models. It could also be with the project owner; it's fine to wait until you have draft personas if you don't want to have multiple meetings or feel that the project owner won't respond well to findings alone. Ask whomever is reviewing the work to give you feedback on the following:

- Do the findings and models cover everything stakeholders expect to see?

- Where the findings differ from stakeholder assumptions, have you provided sufficient evidence to be compelling, and have you been clear but diplomatic?

- Have you jumped to any conclusions that seem incorrect or are not supported by what you observed?

- Are your findings detailed enough to make sense, but at a high enough level that it won't take you two hours or 20 pages to explain them?

Summary

The whole point of modeling is to make sense of your data so you and the stakeholders can understand and use it to make informed decisions. Almost any approach that helps you gain insight will do, so long as it also helps ensure that conclusions come from your data and not from your imagination. Regardless of the techniques you choose, always make sure you have an in-depth understanding of each case before attempting to aggregate the data or draw any general conclusions. Examine your data from multiple points of view. Don't just summarize: Explain, and make sure your explanations account for any outliers. Finally, address any controversy head-on, because disagreements left unresolved at this stage will hinder your progress later on.

CHAPTER 11

Personas

I often speak with people who tell me they have a good understanding of their users, but are puzzled because they can't seem to agree on what the product should be or do. In order for your efforts as a designer to succeed, you must ensure that every member of the product team understands at least the fundamental characteristics and needs of your customers and users, or you'll spend a lot of time talking in circles. The research methods described earlier in the book will help you gather the right information; personas will help you determine what that data means, convey that meaning to product team members in a compelling and memorable way, make better design decisions, and build consensus around a direction.

Definition and Uses

Personas are archetypes that describe the various goals and observed behavior patterns among your potential users and customers. In the terms introduced in Chapter 10, personas are a specialized type of composite model resulting from cross-case analysis, using primarily inductive reasoning.

A persona encapsulates and explains the most critical behavioral data in a way that designers and stakeholders can understand, remember, and relate to. Unlike simple lists of findings or other types of models, personas use storytelling to engage the social and emotional aspects of our brains, which helps each team member either visualize the best product behavior or see why the recommended design is good. The very name "persona"—from the Latin term for a character in a play[1]—emphasizes their roles as storytelling devices.

Regardless of the sort of product or service you're designing, you will almost always find two or more distinct types of thought or behavior among potential users. The persona description that represents each user type includes a name, a photo, and a set of goals, as well as a narrative that covers mental model, environment, skills, frustrations, attitudes, typical tasks, and any other factors that seem critical to understanding the behavior pattern. The following narrative, Katie Bennett, is an example of a simple persona description for a digital camera user.

---

1. Yes, the correct Latin plural is *personae*, but popular usage made the argument moot long ago.

Katie Bennett

Thirty-two-year-old Katie would have gone into fine art if she felt she could have made a living at it; now she runs the business side of her husband's small landscaping firm and saves her creative ambitions for the weekend.

A couple of years ago, Katie bought a pocket digital camera so she could post photos of completed jobs on the company's Web site, which she put together using iWeb on her Mac. As she started experimenting with getting the best images, Katie realized that photography offered many of the creative opportunities she enjoyed in painting. She was hooked. Looking for a more capable camera that wouldn't break the bank, Katie went to CNET.com for advice. After looking at a few comparisons but not reading detailed reviews, she went to the nearest Best Buy and bought a Nikon D70 with its kit lens and an inexpensive tripod, relegating her compact camera to snapshots at family events. She also considered Canon's Digital Rebel, but chose the Nikon because it "felt more like a professional camera."

Katie got home and sat down with her new camera and its somewhat intimidating manual. After half an hour of fiddling, she was overwhelmed by the options and decided to give the auto mode a try. Katie started hiking about on weekends to shoot landscapes, from sweeping skylines to dew-covered flowers. She was pleased with some of her shots, but wondered why some weren't much better than what she could do with the pocket camera; many did not meet her expectations. After reading a few issues of *Outdoor Photographer*, she decided she might do better with different lenses. Confused by all the letters, numbers, and lens specifications, Katie went to the local specialty camera shop for advice on which macro and wide-angle lenses to buy; she did not expect the staff at Best Buy to provide good advice. She was reluctant to buy the cheaper lenses made by other manufacturers because surely Nikon would make the best lenses for their own cameras.

Katie is thrilled with her new ability to capture images of the local flora as she would have composed them on canvas. Though Katie enjoys it when people admire her photos, she's more motivated by the satisfaction of achieving her own creative vision. She can now capture the compositions she wants, but still isn't quite happy with some of her photos.

Katie gets up early on Saturdays to catch dramatic sunrises, frequents every park and beach in the area, and takes the occasional day trip. She loves the excuse to get out into nature. She goes out equipped with her camera, lenses, tripod, and a couple of 4 GB memory cards. Katie takes 100 to 300 shots on the average outing. She can often take her time composing a shot because plants and scenery don't move much, but sometimes needs to move quickly to capture a butterfly perched on a flower, or a shaft of light coming through the clouds just so. She usually takes a photo on the auto settings first, pointing the auto focus at the area where she wants to capture detail in the hope that this will set the correct exposure. She then dials the aperture up and down and takes a couple of shots to bracket the exposure; she read about this technique in her magazine. She still gets overly dark areas or blown-out highlights in many photos; she's increasingly frustrated by the intricacies of correct exposure. She deletes the worst photos from the camera on the spot.

Katie brings her camera home and plugs it into her Mac using the USB cable. She dumps the images into iPhoto and sees what she can learn from the bad ones before deleting them. She makes a few minor adjustments, but is generally reluctant to manipulate her photos, believing she should be able to get the right image in the camera to begin with. She posts her favorites on her personal Web site, uses them on her computer desktop, and occasionally orders large prints of especially good images via iPhoto. Katie feels a bit limited by iPhoto's organization options, but appreciates its ease of use and integration with other tools.

Katie is considering upgrading to a higher resolution camera, but is reluctant to spend the money unless she knows she can get the results she wants.

KATIE'S GOALS:

— **Be able to capture what she sees in her "mind's eye."** Katie knows she has an eye for composition, but is frustrated when her inability to master difficult lighting makes for a lackluster photo.

— **Enjoy the scenery.** Katie takes photos of nature as a way to enjoy its beauty. She doesn't want to be so focused on the mechanics of using her camera that she forgets to enjoy what she sees.

— **Feel like a "real" photographer.** Katie is proud of some of her images, but hesitates to think of herself as a photographer because she feels she hasn't mastered some of the fundamentals.

If you read carefully, you can see that nearly everything in the description conveys or reinforces something important about Katie's attitudes, goals, and behaviors. Even the mention of specific store, Web site, and product names has a purpose: They reinforce that Katie has ambitions but isn't sure where to get the best advice. Although the fact that she runs a landscape business is clearly fictitious and not directly relevant, one or two such details can make a persona seem like a real human being instead of a sterile set of characteristics.

What personas are good for

Personas can help you design pretty much anything that will be used or experienced by a human being, such as enterprise and consumer products, Web sites, services, internal business processes, organizational structures, events, advertising campaigns, documents, courses, and environments. The contents, structure, and design of this book have been driven by several personas. I've even heard from people using simple personas to design employee benefits packages and church picnics.

Personas are helpful in accomplishing a wide range of activities, including defining and designing the product, communicating with stakeholders about your audience, building consensus and rallying a team around a goal, marketing the product, developing documentation, and even prioritizing bug fixes.

> **Personas are helpful in creating and iterating a design, building consensus, marketing the product, and even prioritizing bug fixes.**

Modeling

GENERATING AND ITERATING SOLUTIONS

Personas are, above all, product definition and design tools. In the early stages of product definition, personas and scenarios will help you envision what users most need from a product or service. Later on, they'll help you generate and iterate specific solution ideas. Personas influence every aspect of the design: Navigation and workflow, color and typography, terminology, information architecture, Web site copy, and hardware form factor are all informed by what will work best for each persona. Non-designers may be surprised to see how much personas can help with technical decisions and business choices such as feature priorities and service options.

During design meetings, each persona serves as a surrogate for the thousands or millions of potential users who have similar characteristics and goals. Designers start by determining what each persona needs to accomplish. When one designer proposes a solution that seems likely to satisfy the persona's goals, the others ask questions and look for potential problems from each persona's point of view. The team iterates the solution until they all believe the personas will find it useful, useable, and desirable. Stakeholder and user feedback may drive additional iteration, but a skilled team using good personas and scenarios will only have to fine-tune the design instead of completely reworking it based on surprising feedback.

Personas help designers make decisions with a shared picture of "the user" in mind. If that understanding isn't both clear and shared, the user is an elastic being who encompasses an improbable range of needs: one minute a novice who needs wizards and extensive instructions, the next an expert who wants macros or a command-line interface. Because a persona is such a specific target, it's easy for team members to say, "Jean wouldn't know what to do with a command line, but she'd feel insulted by a wizard." Personas

also help prevent self-referential thinking, in which designers make decisions based on their own preferences or usage patterns, even though their goals and behaviors probably differ from those of the target users.

COMMUNICATING AND BUILDING CONSENSUS

Personas aren't just about creating and iterating solutions. They also help with the other critical part of your job: helping the entire product team understand what users and customers need and why your design solution is a good way to provide it. Personas are excellent tools for summarizing your research data because they let stakeholders "meet" the interviewees by proxy. They also give the entire team a common language to use in discussing solutions and trade-offs; "the user" is generally an ill-defined and ever-changing type of person, but everyone knows what others mean when they refer to "Brenda" or "Ted."

Personas, once accepted by other members of the project team, also provide an effective means to defend your design decisions. Arguing for a solution based on your opinion seldom works well because there's always someone in the room with greater authority; you're pretty much doomed in an opinion-based argument with the CEO, no matter what graduate degrees or experience you have. Arguing based on design principles can work but may not offer as much credibility as you expect. Most people who have been around product development for any length of time have seen less capable engineers throw techno-speak at people to beat them into submission, so quoting obscure cognitive science and ergonomics principles may leave the impression that you're sandbagging. However, there's tremendous power in being able to say, "Yes, I can see how that approach would make sense, but we did it like this because it fits how Ted sees the world." Provided you've convinced people that the personas are an accurate picture of potential users and customers—and provided your argument is believable based on the personas—stakeholders will usually nod their heads and move on. This is especially powerful when stakeholders are thinking self-referentially.

An entrenched set of personas can act as defenders of the design in your absence, as well. In companies where design is still relatively new, it's not unusual for software engineers to deviate from specifications when they don't see the value in something that's hard to build. Programmers who understand the rationale for the solution based on a persona's needs are more committed to building the product as designed. Once you hear the engineers and other product team members using the personas' names in discussion without being self-conscious about it, there's a good chance this kind of thinking is starting to happen.

Personas are also powerful tools for getting people to see a service or business in a new light. Most companies have separate departments or people responsible for each aspect of a customer relationship, and many of those departments don't talk to each other. Each group sees the world from its own limited perspective, so customers experience the company in disjointed and unsatisfying ways. For example, I was having problems with static on my telephone line and outages on my DSL connection. The giant telecommunications company that provides my service has a phone department and a DSL department, so they kept sending phone technicians and DSL technicians separately. Neither could deal with the whole problem, so their independent efforts could not resolve the issues. Multiple frustrating conversations revealed that their two information systems were entirely separate, so technicians in one silo didn't have any access to information about the other half of the problem, and there was no way in the system to specify that I needed both types of technician. I was literally looking up the competition's service plans when a manager finally walked across the hall and talked to someone in the other

department. Had this company used personas to examine its processes from a customer's perspective, I wouldn't have run screaming to their competitor or, worse yet, ranted about their poor service to everyone I knew.

It's also amazing to see the way personas can help a team develop a shared sense of purpose. Some teams adopt their personas almost as mascots: printing T-shirts, bringing life-size persona cutouts to meetings, and even celebrating a persona's birthday as a reminder of what they're trying to accomplish. Not every organization's culture is conducive to this kind of cheerleading, but the more people understand and identify with the personas, the more unified the team seems to be.

OTHER USES FOR PERSONAS

Although personas exist primarily to support design and communication, they have a few other uses. Marketing is the most common of these. Many marketers adopt personas with great enthusiasm; after all, knowing what makes customers tick makes it easier to convey the value of the product or service. Some even use the personas (or some approximation of them) as the stars of a marketing campaign. The point of such campaigns is generally to say, "See? We really do understand you." I've seen numerous companies use their personas as characters in trade-magazine articles, on their Web sites, and at user conferences. One client even hired actors to portray the personas at a product launch party; the actors bemoaned their problems, then the CEO showed off the new solution and explained how it would make their lives easier. The audience loved it.

Employee training is another way to squeeze value out of your research and synthesis efforts. Personas help new employees learn about the characteristics of your customers. Better yet, they help employees see the world from a customer's point of view, which can result in better customer service, better products, and a stronger brand.

Personas work not just because humans are accustomed to using models, but also because they encourage us to relate to users in uniquely human ways.

Technical writers can use personas to determine what's important to emphasize in a user manual and how to approach writing help text. This is important not only to keep the cost of user manuals low, but also because few users are likely to pick up a thick book to figure out how to turn on the new gadget or log in to the application. Users are more likely to be satisfied with their out-of-box experience (and less likely to return a product) if a compact, approachable document gets them started with the basics.

Some companies have begun using personas to prioritize bug fixes. The bugs that have the greatest impact on the most important personas get fixed first, while those the personas are unlikely to care about drop lower on the priority list. This is a significant shift for many organizations, since engineers have long viewed "UI" or "design" bugs as less important than others.

Personas can also help prioritize customer feedback. Some companies expend tremendous resources addressing nearly every comment they get from a user or customer. This is laudable, but not always wise, since a fair number of the people who feel compelled to comment are edge cases. Comparing user feedback to the personas can help product managers assess whether a customer request is really something worth investing effort in.

Why personas work

To make the best use of personas, it's helpful to understand what makes them so effective. Personas work not just because humans are accustomed to using models, but also because they encourage us to relate to users in uniquely human ways, while mitigating the disadvantages of designing with live humans.

Human beings, by our nature, classify the world around us so we can understand it, predict its behavior, and respond accordingly. A child, for example, might start out thinking of every furry, four-legged animal as a dog, then learn to distinguish between dogs and cats because the cat scratches when it doesn't want human attention. We create and act on categories as easily as we breathe. We classify our fellow humans as archetypes in the same way. We use those archetypes to communicate; when we describe someone as an entrepreneur, geek, or class clown, we know that others will associate a certain set of attitudes and behaviors with that person. (When done in ignorance or taken to extremes, of course, this can become negative stereotyping, but this is easy enough to avoid if you stick to your data.) Expressing customer and user behaviors and attitudes as archetypes is a natural way to help others understand them.

What makes personas a particularly effective sort of archetype is their presentation as people rather than as abstract ideas. We recognize the hero archetype in an intellectual way, but relate to the characters of Achilles or Harry Potter in an emotional way, so we try to see the world from their point of view. The same is true of personas; where a list of bullet points about user characteristics gets an intellectual response, a persona presented as a real person engenders empathy in designers and stakeholders alike.

If the anecdotal evidence doesn't convince you to present user models as though they were people, designer Chris Noessel[2] points to a 2003 experiment by Gallagher and Frith,[3] in which MRI scans showed people using different parts of their brains depending on whether they thought they were playing a game against a human or a computer. A similar experiment comparing how we think about dogs versus people[4] supports the idea that other humans engage our minds in unique ways. This ability to help people think differently is one reason personas have been so widely adopted by design practitioners. Personas have names and photos and stories not to be touchy-feely and cute, but to help designers and stakeholders think with a more human point of view.

Unfortunately, the storytelling aspect of personas is frequently misunderstood. Novice persona enthusiasts and critics alike confuse the *presentation* of personas with their *content*. People who are new to personas may get carried away with photos and fictitious biographical details at the expense of the data; don't confuse such creative writing exercises with real personas. Others expect that appending a name and photo will turn their bullet list of characteristics into a persona, but such dry presentations lack the power of storytelling and fail to engage our human empathy. Good data, rigorous analysis, *and* compelling, human presentation are all essential to making personas work.

Of course, all this begs the question: If humans engage our empathy, why not just have real users in design meetings? Personas provide much of the value of having real users in the room, but without the drawbacks. Unlike real humans, personas don't slow the process, start to think like members of the product team, or have idiosyncrasies such as a distaste for the color blue.

> Unlike real humans, personas don't slow the process, start to think like members of the product team, or have idiosyncrasies such as a distaste for the color blue.

Modeling

2. Noessel, C. "Ignore that designer behind the persona." *Cooper Journal of Design*, 2006. http://www.cooper.com/insights/journal_of_design/articles/ignore_that_designer_behind_th.html.

3. Gallagher, H. L. and Frith, C.D. "Functional imaging of 'theory of mind.'" *Trends in Cognitive Sciences*, February 2003, volume 7 issue 2.

4. Mason, M.F., Banfield, J.F. and Macrae, C.N. "Thinking about actions: The neural substrates of person knowledge." *Cerebral Cortex*, February 2004.

Human idiosyncrasies are a challenge to filter out of the design process, whether you have a real user in the room or you're reviewing customer feedback. Some well-intentioned teams err on the side of incorporating every piece of feedback, but a knee-jerk response can increase development time and costs with zero (or negative) return on investment. It may also drive your development team crazy. A good set of personas can help you determine whether each customer request or suggestion is broadly applicable; if it is, it will help the personas accomplish their goals. If the suggestion does not help the personas, you can call back that customer and try to find another way to solve the problem.

Because they're constructs that "live" in the heads of the design team, personas don't struggle with understanding crude sketches that aren't yet suitable for usability testing; this allows exceptionally fast iteration. This is not to say that you should use personas as an excuse to eliminate real user feedback; rather, personas will help you get the most out of your precious time with real users by helping catch the obvious problems early on, so the real users can help you see the tricky bits you would otherwise miss.

What personas are not

Personas bear enough similarity to other sorts of models that some confusion is common. Marketers may assume that personas are just another form of market segmentation. Design and usability practitioners who are inexperienced with personas may believe they are simply roles with names and photos attached. Some stakeholders may believe that personas represent "average" users. Any of these assumptions can lead to problems.

PERSONAS VERSUS MARKET SEGMENTS

There are many ways to segment the potential market for a product or service. Most consumer segments begin with demographics, such as age, gender, race, income, and household composition. Some more sophisticated segmentation models include attitudes, values, and perhaps even preferences or self-reported buying behavior. A good segmentation model will also include an estimate of the number of potential customers represented by that segment and the amount of money they can be expected to spend. However, as discussed in Chapter 4, market research (and therefore market segmentation) tends to focus on what messages will sell a product rather than on how people will use a product over time.

Although personas can provide valuable information about attitudes and can help focus marketing messages, they also contain a great deal of information about behavior, mental models, skills, and other topics that are critical to product definition and design. Personas may still contain some demographic data, though, particularly when such data is closely tied to behaviors. Figure 11.1 illustrates the overlaps and distinctions.

A market segment often contains multiple personas. For example, two potential car buyers may have identical household demographics, attitudes, and values, but one may constantly switch radio stations, need help with directions, and seldom transport anything other than groceries, while another might ignore the radio, never get lost, and carry ski equipment every weekend. These two people may respond to the same marketing messages, so it makes sense to represent them as a single market segment, but the detailed distinctions in their behavior are necessary for informed design.

The desire to consolidate personas and market segments is common because it's easier if everyone thinks about customers or end users the same way. Clearly, it's possible to stretch market segments more in the direction of personas or personas more in the direction of market segments. Merging the two models may even work in some circumstances when buying and usage

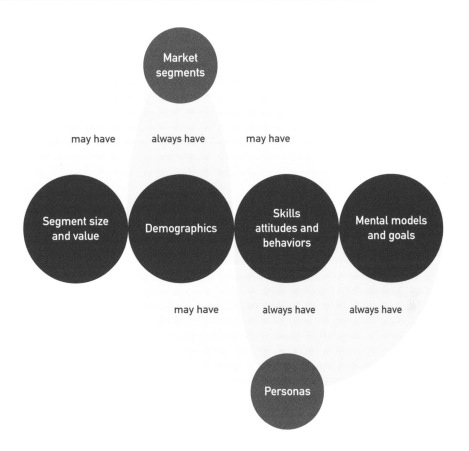

Figure 11.1. The degree of overlap between personas and market segments can vary. It's possible to stretch either tool in the other direction, but they're not entirely interchangeable.

behavior are aligned; this has been the case for some e-commerce Web sites. If there isn't a clear relationship between response to marketing messages and actual usage, though, don't force the fit and risk compromising your design tools. Also, never give up control of your design personas to the marketing department, lest they lose their utility for design.

PERSONAS VERSUS ROLES

Roles are familiar constructs in the world of enterprise software, where system permissions differ based on job descriptions and levels of authority. As discussed in Chapter 6, a role is defined largely by tasks; if there are users whose tasks will differ widely, chances are the system involves distinct roles.

The confusion between personas and roles arises because in a setting where roles are fairly specialized, it's entirely possible to have a one-to-one mapping between them. The more specialized the user population, the greater the chance that a single persona can represent a role. More often, though, two or more personas are required to represent the range of behavior within a role. For example, you might think a group of surgeons implanting the same medical device would be about as specialized as it gets, but the design

You need as few personas as possible, but as many as it takes to express the unique behavior patterns and goals you observed.

team observing them saw two distinct approaches. The surgeons who were primarily focused on ensuring the longevity of the implant always started the procedure with a particular set of tasks and made a lot of meticulous adjustments along the way. Those who were more concerned with getting the surgery done quickly—a metric for which surgeons are rewarded in some settings—performed the tasks in a different sequence and made fewer small adjustments. Their differing philosophies were based on how they first learned to do the procedure. A design that didn't accommodate the two distinct approaches would be a failure.

There are also cases where a persona may represent more than one role. This most often happens due to differences in small companies versus large ones. In purchasing, for example, a buyer in a large company places the order but doesn't process the arrival of the shipment or pay the invoice, whereas an administrative assistant in a small company may do all three. The design should recognize the expertise of the specialists and not clutter up their workspace with tools for tasks they don't perform, but shouldn't create such strict separations in functionality that it's hard for generalists to work.

PERSONAS VERSUS "AVERAGE" PEOPLE

Personas must be typical of your audience, but this doesn't mean they're "average." An average hides important differences in the data; someone with no income and someone with a $100,000 salary may average $50,000 a year between them, but their lives are drastically different. Real families don't have 2.4 children (though this fact seems to have escaped many automakers, who seem to design back seats for about 2.4 people). This is not to say that personas should represent the extremes, but it does mean they should represent the range of needs and behaviors exhibited by most of your audience.

How many personas do I need?

Personas are meant to help you hold the different kinds of users in your head; the fewer personas you have, the easier this becomes. A cast of thousands makes it hard to remember behaviors, goals, and motivations. That said, you need to have as many personas as it takes to express the unique behavior patterns and goals you observed. Single-role products or services tend to involve fewer personas, typically somewhere between two and six, but more are possible. A complex, multi-role enterprise system could easily require 25 or more legitimate personas, but because the design work generally focuses on one role at a time, you wouldn't have to worry about more than a handful of those at once. There's no magic number of personas; the right number is dependent on the data. It's impossible to ascertain exactly how many you'll have beforehand, though a designer experienced in this method makes an educated estimate in order to plan the research phase (see Chapter 6).

Keeping your persona set to a minimum doesn't mean you should try to recycle your personas. It's almost always necessary to have distinct sets of personas for each product or service. An effective persona is focused on the goals, behavior, and characteristics most relevant to a particular type of product, which makes it useless for designing most other things. If you look at the example description at the beginning of this chapter, you can see that it's focused on Katie as a camera user. It would be difficult to design even a somewhat-related product, such as photo organizing software, based on that description. If you pack too much into a single persona to use it for multiple diverse products, you'll have to wade through irrelevant information to use it for any one product.

However, it's important to use the same personas for closely related products that are meant to provide a seamless experience, such as a portable music player and the desktop application that manages the music collection. You should also use the same personas for cross-channel experiences, such as many retail or customer service applications in which the interaction could be by mail, via telephone, in person, or online. This helps ensure that the transition from one to the other is painless.

How often do I need to create personas?

Although it doesn't take that long to do qualitative research and turn it into personas, it would be a big investment if you had to repeat that effort every time you did a new release of your product. The good news is that personas can last a long time. Because personas are focused on fundamental behaviors and goals, minor changes in procedures and technologies have almost no effect on them.

Contrary to popular belief, most technology and regulatory changes are evolutionary rather than revolutionary when it comes to influencing human behavior; for example, the fact that something used to be done in Java and is now done in .NET really doesn't matter. I recently had the opportunity to revisit some health care personas my team and I had developed about nine years earlier. Since the original personas were created, the American health care industry has been set on its ear by a privacy regulation called HIPAA, but we found that other than an increased awareness of information security issues, it hadn't affected the behavior of nurses. We also found generally higher expectations of technology based on experience with consumer products, but the behaviors and attitudes were otherwise identical to what we'd seen years ago.

This is not to say that all personas are good for a decade or more; they're not. Although technology that does the same things better seldom leads to major shifts, any disruptive technology that enables entirely new behavior can cause fundamental changes in how people see the world, and things tend to change rapidly between the time such technology emerges and the time it matures. Before mobile phones became widespread, people struggled to be accessible; now, people can be as accessible as they want to be, and we as a society are trying to figure out an entirely new set of manners. It's a good idea to do a little research now and then to make sure your personas are still in sync with reality, but you can judge the need for such efforts by the pace of disruptive change in your industry.

Modeling

Because personas are focused on fundamental behaviors and goals, minor changes in procedures and technologies have almost no effect on them.

Personas who aren't users

Nearly all of your personas should exist because they represent a distinct behavior pattern observed in your user research. On occasion, though, it's useful to round out your set of user personas with one or more personas representing customers or served populations.

CUSTOMER PERSONAS

Consider adding a customer persona when you're designing a product or service that is purchased by someone other than an end user. This is most common in enterprise settings, where an executive or IT manager selects a system he will never actually use. Such people are concerned with things like ease of configuration and maintenance, total cost of ownership, scalability, and integration with other systems, though user efficiency is also a factor. The customer/user relationship can also occur among consumers, such as when a parent buys a mobile phone for a teenager but wants some way to limit its use. In either case, you won't succeed by designing the product's behavior for the customer, but you must address the customer's concerns by either including or limiting certain features and capabilities.

We first developed customer personas at Cooper in response to a client who had frequent contact with customers and very little with end users. They were having a hard time distinguishing between the needs of IT people (who wanted infinite configurability) and those of end users (who struggled with the product's complexity). The contrast between the customer and user personas helped them see how far astray the customers were leading them. Since then, we've also found that customer personas can help designers keep from focusing entirely on the end user at the expense of the customer.

Because the customers are not users of the product, you won't be designing the product's behavior with them in mind; instead, you'll be checking what you design against their needs and adjusting it if needed. For this reason, customer personas are less detailed than user personas and are focused primarily on concerns and goals rather than on behavior. *Tim Wilson, CEO,* presents an example of a customer persona for a phone system targeting small to medium businesses.

Tim Wilson, CEO

Five years ago, Tim turned his favorite pastime into a full-time job: BeSpoke Bikes, which is now a fast-growing custom cycle shop in Berkeley, California. BeSpoke's 36 employees include a small management team, a couple of designers, a few support staff, a half-dozen customer service reps who take orders and other inquiries, and the crew of the small manufacturing facility across town.

BeSpoke's office phone system is separate from the manufacturing facility, which makes for some awkwardness in forwarding calls. The customer service team is set up on a hunt group for incoming calls (though Tim doesn't know that's what it's called), but the increasing volume of calls is overwhelming this simple solution. The existing system is also expensive to maintain because Kevin, the jack-of-all-trades IT manager, is no expert in telephony; he has to place a $75 service call just to move an extension.

Tim knows it's time to replace the phone system but wants to make a good investment. Tim has heard that IP phone systems are cheaper and more flexible. He knows that quality products and good service can cost a little more, though, so he's looking for the best investment rather than the cheapest option. Kevin is investigating vendors, but Tim is as hands-on with his business as he is with his bikes—he doesn't trust such a critical decision to anyone else.

TIM'S GOALS:

— **Invest wisely.** Like many small business owners, Tim is torn between investing for the long term and keeping today's costs low. He wants a good system BeSpoke won't outgrow in a couple of years, but doesn't want to pay for capabilities or components he doesn't need yet.

— **Maintain flexibility.** Tim thinks he knows what features are important, but is aware that his communication needs could change as his business changes.

— **Minimize business disruption.** Tim wants to avoid the painful installation and the week or so of technical problems they had when the current system was installed.

Note that the description above is shorter than the user persona example presented earlier because it's focused only on Tim's concerns and goals, not his behavior.

SERVED PERSONAS

Some products exist to help users provide efficient (and hopefully pleasant) service to other humans. Examples include electronic medical records, cash registers, airline and hotel check-in systems, and the telephone and computer systems used by customer service call centers. No doubt you've experienced the result of systems that weren't designed with customer service in mind, such as when a customer

Creating personas involves identifying the critical behavior patterns and turning them into a set of useful characterizations.

service rep passes you along to someone else who asks you the same questions over and over again, or tells you that her system won't let her do that. Systems that make things difficult for users also make things difficult for the people those users are supposed to help.

Served personas help prevent this kind of shortsighted solution by reminding the whole product team of the reason for the product's existence. You won't find a need for a served persona on most projects, but there are times when one can make a big difference. The first served persona was "born" when my team was designing an electronic medical record and management system for long-term health care facilities. We created Gerta, an elderly woman with Alzheimer's, to help us avoid solutions that made life easy for nurses at the expense of patients; zapping the pill bottle and the patient's wrist with a bar code gun would make medication record keeping easy, but would be neither comfortable nor dignified for Gerta. As it happened, Gerta also served as a rallying point for the product team, who even celebrated her birthday for years after.

Served personas are much like customer personas: they're mostly focused on concerns and goals rather than detailed behavior descriptions. You won't be designing primarily for them, but you'll check each solution against their goals to make sure it won't be a problem.

Creating Personas

Creating personas involves identifying the critical behavior patterns and turning them into a set of useful characterizations. A methodical analysis of the data is essential when those patterns are difficult to identify, and is worthwhile even if those patterns seem to leap, fully formed, from the data. It's entirely possible that your initial impression of the pattern is correct, but in many cases the obvious pattern is based on demographics rather than behavior, or is otherwise missing some critical factor. Even the most experienced persona creators can benefit from a rigorous approach, which usually requires only a day or two of effort.

Like most aspects of the design process, persona creation is not strictly linear, but does follow an approximate sequence, which is detailed in the following sections and illustrated at a high level in Figure 11.2. If there are clearly defined roles among your respondents, begin the process by comparing the interviewees in only one role at a time. From your data, identify behavioral variables—ways in which user behavior differed—and any demographic variables that seemed to affect behavior. Map the interviewees against the variables, then

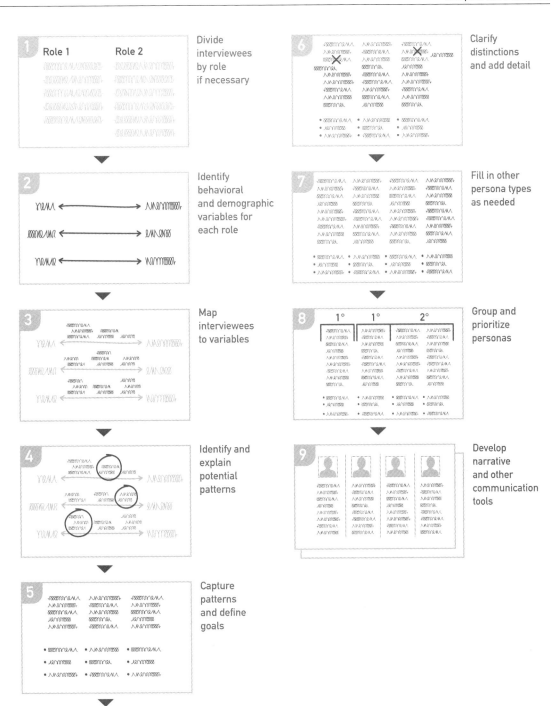

Figure 11.2 Overview of the persona creation process.

1 Divide interviewees by role if necessary

2 Identify behavioral and demographic variables for each role

3 Map interviewees to variables

4 Identify and explain potential patterns

5 Capture patterns and define goals

6 Clarify distinctions and add detail

7 Fill in other persona types as needed

8 Group and prioritize personas

9 Develop narrative and other communication tools

Modeling

look for people who cluster together across multiple variables. Formulate explanations for that clustering to see if it really is a valid behavior pattern, then keep looking for any other patterns. Once you've exhausted the patterns within a given role, do the same for the other roles. Turn each behavior pattern into a persona by articulating goals and adding detail from the data. Fine-tune the personas as a set by clarifying the distinctions among them. Consider whether you need any other personas for political reasons before reviewing your rough drafts with stakeholders. Finally, prioritize the personas and develop the narrative and any other artifacts needed to describe them.

Simple as this all sounds, there are a hundred things you can do along the way that will make your personas either indispensable or a waste of time. That's not to say you can't experiment with how to create personas—after all, that's how they evolved as design tools in the first place—but when you're creating a real product or service with stakeholders who are skeptical, hurried, or otherwise not disposed toward design, you may only have one chance for your personas to succeed. The advice in this chapter should help you get them right the first time.

Step 1. Divide interviewees by role, if appropriate

As discussed in Chapter 6, roles are largely defined by *what* tasks people perform, rather than by *how* people perform those tasks. Roles usually seem clear in enterprise settings, such as end users versus system administrators. You can expect them to be less clear outside of a work environment, but they may still emerge; in some families, for instance, one family member primarily pays the bills, keeps in touch with relatives, or takes most of the photos.

It's often necessary to do your initial research recruiting based on job titles, which sound like roles but may differ widely among organizations. Don't be surprised, however, if it turns out that your research participants can't immediately be slotted into neat categories based on tasks. Job titles can hide specialization; for instance, a human resources manager might do a little of a lot of things, or might be focused on recruiting, staff development, or compensation and benefits. Sometimes the specialization is even less clear than this and may not be crisp enough to define separate roles. On a couple of projects involving financial analysts, for example, my team saw that some analysts were focused on routine tasks, such as monthly and quarterly roll-ups across various lines of business, while others did less predictable work, such as responding to unexpected changes or modeling various future scenarios. Many analysts did some mixture of all three, so treating these overlapping responsibilities as separate roles would have been problematic.

When the division between roles is very clear, such as between a surgeon and anesthesiologist or a loan officer and bank teller, it's best to treat the research participants in each role as a separate group for the purpose of identifying patterns. This is because large differences tend to obscure smaller differences; when you're comparing apples and oranges, for instance, it's harder to see that the apples are two different varieties, because the difference between the two types of fruit is so glaring. When you take the oranges away, you can see that one variety of apple differs slightly from the other in size, shape, and color. (See Figure 11.3.) For the same reason, customers and served populations should always be treated separately from potential users, as well. When the distinctions are muddy, as with the financial analyst example above, treat those interviewees as a single group. Table 11.1 illustrates this idea using the examples from Chapter 6, as if we've just completed the interviews.

Figure 11.3. Glaring differences, such as between the apples and oranges, tend to obscure more subtle differences, like those between the two varieties of apples.

Table 11.1. **Examples of how to divide interviewees to begin persona creation.**

Product	Expected roles	Observed behavior and next steps
E-mail system	— System administrator — E-mail account holder — External e-mail recipient — Purchase decision-maker	System administrators, purchase decision-makers, and typical account holders were clearly distinct. All account holders were also external e-mail recipients, so they should be treated as one group.
Consumer digital camera	— Photographer — Buyer (usually the photographer)	The people who bought cameras for others also used cameras themselves, so they're not distinct enough to separate.
Camera company Web site	— Potential buyer — Current camera owner — Camera dealer — Investor — Press — Job seeker	Distinctions between buyers and owners were fuzzy, so they should be treated as one group. Dealers, investors, press, and job seekers were all distinct enough to treat as separate roles.
Inbound call center software	— Call center agent — Escalation agent — Call center supervisor — System administrator — Customer on the phone — Purchase decision-maker	Most roles were distinct, but agents and escalation agents seemed to overlap quite a bit, so it's safest to treat them as one role.

Continued

Modeling

Product	Expected roles	Observed behavior and next steps
Complex purchasing application	— Person who requests things — Person who processes requests — Person who authorizes purchases — Person who receives shipments — Person who pays bills — System administrator — Purchase decision-maker	Many interviewees were clearly in one of these roles, while others overlapped two or more roles. You could include the multi-role interviewees in each of the distinct roles that applied.
Family calendaring system	— Family member — Perhaps one adult manages calendar	Some adults clearly managed the calendar, but most shared management to some extent. Children and teens did no management, so it might be best to treat them as a distinct role.
Device used to deliver intravenous medications in a hospital	— Person who administers medication — Person who prescribes medication — Person who dispenses medication — Person who monitors patients — Patient — Purchase decision maker	Patients and purchase decision makers are clearly distinct roles, as are the pharmacy staff who dispense medications to physicians and nurses. Nurses monitor patients and administer medications. Doctors may do those things once in a while, and only they can prescribe. There's a lot of overlap between doctors and nurses, but enough distinction that it's probably best to treat them separately.
Clothing store targeting women aged 25 to 40	— Woman shopping for her own clothing — Someone buying a gift	Many gift shoppers also wound up shopping for themselves once they were in the store, so it's probably best to treat all interviewees as one group.

As you can see from the examples, whether to separate interviewees at this stage is really a judgment call. When in doubt about whether a role distinction makes sense, it's safest *not* to separate interviewees by role. It's easy enough to try a different approach if your grouping doesn't work well for subsequent analysis.

When roles are so specialized and consistent that every interviewee seems like a clone of the others, you might be able to skip steps two through four, though I recommend walking through them anyway. Often, you will find two or more important differences within each role. When the roles are very broad, as with consumer products and services, I strongly recommend not skipping any steps. Identifying good personas in large, diverse audiences is sometimes more difficult than for most enterprise products because roles don't provide a convenient starting point.

WHAT YOU SHOULD HAVE AT THE END OF THIS STEP

Before proceeding to the following step, you should have a set of roles (if you have more than one) and a determination of which interviewees fit which roles.

> **Exercise**
>
> Determine how to separate interviewees by role, if at all, for the RoomFinder or LocalGuide. Use your own interview data or the data on the Web site.

Step 2. Identify behavioral and demographic variables

For each role, begin the cross-case analysis by identifying **behavioral variables**, which are aspects of behavior and attitude that seemed to differ across interviewees. Task frequency, mental models, and goals are all common types of behavioral variables. (If every interviewee demonstrated an identical concern or behavior, that's important information, but not useful at this stage.)

Once you have covered the behavioral variables, add any **demographic variables** or other facets of your interview data, such as environment, that seemed to affect behavior. Using the biggest writing surface you can find, lay each of these out as a spectrum or, occasionally, a set of multiple-choice options. This serves as an organizing structure for comparing individual interviewees in the next step, so leave plenty of room to write respondent names. Figure 11.4 is an example of such a variable set for people interacting with the health care system.

Almost any behavioral variable can be expressed as a continuum, whether this is a range from low to high or a contrasting pair, such as liberal to conservative. When the variable is quantifiable, label one end something like "many x" or "often does x" and the other as "few x" or "seldom does x." Don't worry about specific quantities while brainstorming variables; it slows the process. You can quantify later when mapping the data to the variables. To avoid confusion, always put the low end of any quantifiable variables on one side of the spectrum (usually the left) and the high end on the other. Table 11.2 shows some examples of how you might express behavioral variables related to shopping.

Begin the cross-case analysis by identifying *behavioral variables*, which are aspects of behavior and attitude that seemed to differ across interviewees.

Modeling

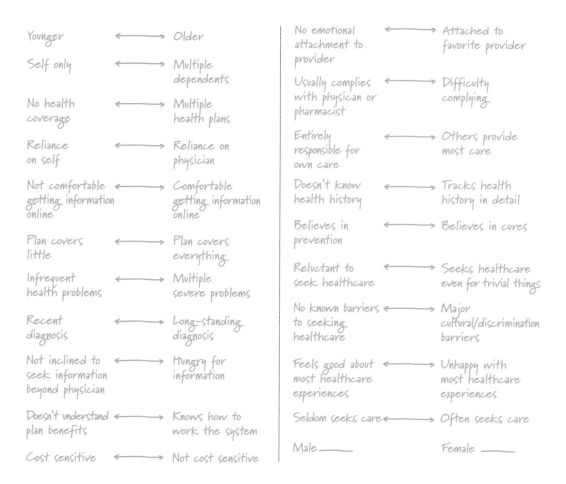

Figure 11.4. A typical display of continuum and multiple-choice variables.

Table 11.2. **Continuum behavioral variables.**

Variable	Ends of spectrum	
Frequency of shopping	Seldom	Often
Price and brand sensitivity	More concerned with price	More concerned with brand
Price and quality sensitivity	Always chooses cheapest	Always chooses best quality
Attitude toward shopping	It's fun	It's a chore

There are sometimes a few variables, such as goals, that are difficult to express as a continuum, or for which a continuum doesn't make sense because the values are mutually exclusive. Express these as multiple-choice variables. For example, if you heard that people shop primarily to buy something they need, to spoil themselves, or to enjoy the challenge of finding a bargain, each of these reasons would become a choice. Table 11.3 shows some other examples of multiple-choice variables.

It's unusual to have more than a couple of multiple-choice variables in the whole set. If you find yourself wanting to express many variables as multiple choice, or if your multiple-choice variables have more than three or four choices, you're probably focused on the *tools* people use to accomplish the behavior rather than on the behavior itself. For example, it might be tempting to list many methods for sharing photos, such as sending e-mail, posting to personal Web sites, posting to online photo-sharing services, mailing hard copy prints, showing off physical albums, showing people photos on a mobile phone, and running slideshows from a laptop or set-top box. People use such a wide variety of tools that the choices quickly become bewildering. Instead, examine what people are trying to accomplish with those tools. Some are sharing photos in a nonsocial way with people who aren't nearby, while others turn sharing into an interactive or social event; these could be characterized as remote sharing and local/social sharing.

In addition to focusing on behaviors rather than tools, good variables minimize subjective judgment by focusing on a single aspect of behavior. For example, whether someone is "very organized" or "not very organized" is somewhat subjective. I work with someone whose desk always looks like a disaster to me, but who can always put her hands on the desired information in about ten seconds or less, which makes it hard to argue that she's not organized. It's better to break the complex idea of "organization" down into several more objective variables, such as how many different systems someone has, how consistently he applies those systems, how much time he spends on staying organized, how often he misses deadlines, what the basic structures of his organizing system(s) are, and how quickly he can find a specific bit of information he needs.

Table 11.3. **Multiple-choice behavioral variables.**

Variable	Options			
Reasons for taking photos	Artistic expression	To share events with friends and family	To remember people and events	For business and insurance purposes
Most important criteria for choosing a car	Overall cost	Features	Emotional appeal	Environmental responsibility
Organizes messages by	Date and time	Sender or recipient	Topic	
Surgery starting point	Femur	Tibia		

By the time you're done identifying behavioral and demographic variables for a role, you'll probably have somewhere in the neighborhood of 20 variables, perhaps a few more or less. If you have considerably fewer, you may be missing important behavior. If you have a lot more, you're probably focused on mechanisms or trivial behaviors rather than fundamentals, which is problematic because it will make the critical behavior patterns harder to identify among all the noise. However, it's safer to err on the side of including a variable rather than excluding it. You'll see in subsequent steps that not every variable will be critical to identifying the behavior patterns.

TYPICAL BEHAVIORAL VARIABLES

Behavioral variables differ considerably from project to project and from role to role, so you'll have to identify many of them inductively from your data. One good way to do that if you haven't done a thorough job of coding is to pull out the notes for a couple of interviewees who struck you as very different, list the ways in which they differed, and then expand the list using other interviewees who seemed much different from the first two. In a sense, listing variables is like summarizing the answers to the questions you asked, along with the answers to questions you didn't ask. You can also get started by listing the following variables, which are almost always useful.

Mental models

As discussed in Chapter 7, understanding users' mental models of data and processes is critical to designing a system they can understand and use. Mental models are often one of the key distinguishing factors among personas. Such distinctions are usually most evident in how people organize their tasks or information. For example, an audiophile might think of albums as the fundamental organizing unit for music, since an album may tell a particular story or capture a point in an

artist's career. Others might not think of albums at all, except as the inconvenient way they had to access music when their collections were stored in cabinets rather than on hard drives. Chances are this mental model difference is related to other distinctive behaviors and attitudes.

Motivations and goals

The reason someone bothers to perform a task in the first place often leads to tremendous differences in behavior, so goals and motivations are almost always important variables for identifying patterns. Self-image and relationship to brands tend to fall in this category; someone's goal for buying a certain brand might be related to status, perceived quality, or other factors. If you find only two primary motivators, whether you represent this as a spectrum or multiple choice depends on whether some people are motivated by a little of each; people who are a little of both can be represented in the middle of the spectrum. Goals are usually best expressed as multiple choice unless you saw only two.

Frequency and duration of key tasks

Identify the common and important tasks in a broad sense. If you're designing a music library, for instance, these key tasks might be listening, organizing, sharing, and acquiring new music. Consider how often your various interviewees performed each task and for how long at one sitting. If the respondents differed much with respect to any of these behaviors, turn it into one or more variables, being sure to distinguish frequency from duration, such as "listens seldom/listens often" and "listens for short periods/listens for long periods."

Quantity of data objects

Users who deal with high volumes of data often have skills, behaviors, or needs not shared by people who handle smaller quantities. It's often helpful to consider total quantity of data as well as quantity handled at one time. For example, someone importing music from a big pile of compact discs is handling a lot of data at once but may have a small library, while someone who only downloads one or two tracks a day may have an enormous library overall. Like frequency, quantity may or may not be critical to identifying the behavior patterns, but can often make those patterns more clear because of its relationship to other variables.

Attitude toward tasks

Does someone perform a task because she enjoys it, because it's her job to do it, or because it serves some higher goal? This variable is often revealing; without considering attitude, it would be easy to assume that two people who both spend a lot of time on a task are similar, even if they perform the task for entirely different reasons.

Technology and domain skill

Skill and experience may be primary drivers of behavior, but sometimes they're incidental to it. Be sure to separate skill or comfort with technology from skill or comfort with the domain; a nurse, for example, might not be comfortable with a computer, but she is expert at being a nurse, whereas a call center agent—who is unlikely to have much training—might need help doing his job.

Tasks people perform

While a role is defined by similar tasks, not everyone within a role will perform exactly the same tasks. In a work setting, some users may focus more on particular stages of a process, have more freedom in how they execute their tasks, or be more likely to do ad hoc tasks rather than the strictly routine. These factors tend to be affected by environment, skill, or seniority. In a consumer setting, tasks people perform may be more related to goals; someone who isn't worried about bouncing a check or motivated to save money, for instance, may be less likely to track every expenditure.

DEMOGRAPHIC AND OTHER VARIABLES

Once you think you have the important behavioral variables covered, consider whether there are any demographic or environmental factors that seemed to affect behavior. It's rare for more than a few demographic factors to matter, so including too many will add distracting

> **Behavioral variables differ considerably from project to project and from role to role.**

Modeling

clutter to your variable list, but feel free to include any that your gut tells you might be important. If you're listing multiple demographic variables, it might help to put them together at the bottom of your workspace.

The demographic variables that most often affect behavior are the ones described as recruiting considerations in Chapter 6: age, family structure, and geography for consumer products, and seniority, company size or industry, and geography for business environments.

Your user's height and physical strength seldom make much difference in the design of a Web site, but physical characteristics and abilities matter a great deal in designing physical products that are ergonomically appropriate. Physical characteristics should be included as a variable if you have a broad audience, but need not be considered a variable if your target population is within a narrow range of size and strength.

Physical environment is likewise a common variable for many physical products; does the respondent have a lot of space or a little, a cluttered space or a neat one? Again, use these factors as variables only when you saw distinctions.

WHAT YOU SHOULD HAVE AT THE END OF THIS STEP

Before proceeding, you should have a list of 20 or so variables that cover most of the codes in your notes, with most expressed as continua and perhaps a few as multiple choice. If you have any codes in the interviews that aren't reflected in your variable list, consider whether they should be included; you might have some codes that simply aren't useful. Compare a few pairs of respondents to one another and see if they have any differences, other than trivial ones, that aren't reflected on your list. If you have someone available to you who is experienced with this technique and at least somewhat familiar with your research, ask them to review your work for possible miss-

ing variables, variables that are too complex or subjective, variables that are really tools, and any other issues.

Step 3. Map interviewees to variables

The next step is to map the individual respondents to your variables as in Figure 11.5. This is easiest if you've coded your data, but not terribly difficult as long as you have a manageable data set and at least two people on the design team who've attended every interview. Team members who have attended a subset of the interviews can contribute to this discussion, but since it involves comparing each interviewee to every other, the most informed team members are ultimately responsible for the mapping.

The idea is to place each interviewee relative to the others along each spectrum (and in the appropriate multiple-choice categories, if applicable). Your placement need not be precise; this is not an exact science, so it really doesn't matter if respondent A is five or ten percent further along the scale than respondent B. What does matter is if respondent A is at one end and respondent B is toward the middle. This technique is similar to using a Likert scale, in that trying to break each continuum into more than about five zones is unlikely to be helpful. You'll find that some variables are polar, with people clustering near one end or the other and no one in the middle. Others may show clusters across the whole spectrum. If every interviewee is clustered around the same part of the spectrum, it means that variable won't be useful in distinguishing the patterns, so you can erase it from the board.

Figure 11.5. Example of interviewees mapped to continuum and multiple-choice variables.

APPROACHES TO MAPPING

There are two common approaches to mapping interviewees, both illustrated in Figure 11.6. Some people prefer to focus on one case at a time, placing a single interviewee on every variable before moving on to the next interviewee. This prevents digging through the notes for every interviewee as you consider each variable, but may mean you have to move a few interviewees you placed incorrectly. For example, you might think respondent A was close to the extreme end of a spectrum, but realize later on that he's closer to the middle when compared to respondent G. This need to erase and reposition is one of many reasons a giant dry-erase board makes a good tool for this activity. This approach can be challenging if the whole team doesn't have practice with making quick mental comparisons to other interviewees; if you're erasing and moving most people around as the process goes on, try the other technique.

You can also place every interviewee on a single variable at a time, so every variable is filled in before you move on to the next. This may prevent a lot of erasing names and moving them around, but can require more flipping through interview notes for detail on each interviewee. This approach may be slower for experienced persona creators, but seems to be an easier starting point for most people. Consider trying both to see which works better for your team.

In either case, place interviewees on each scale relative to one another, not to what you believe of the population at large. Ensure that the placement is based on the data rather than your instincts or memory alone. An interview participant who felt strongly that she did something often might also leave you with that impression, whereas an objective comparison might show that she was about average in your sample. Look for some objective observation or statement to help you judge each quantifiable variable. Look for verification of any self-reported numbers; rely on your observation over the interviewee's statement unless you heard an explanation for the mismatch during the interview.

Place interviewees on each scale relative to one another, not to what you believe of the population at large.

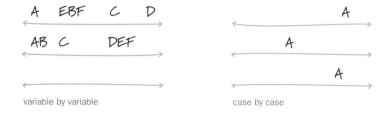

variable by variable · case by case

Figure 11.6. You can place every interview on one variable at a time or place one interviewee at a time across every variable.

For variables that are less quantifiable, such as skill or attitude, consider any work product you saw, the terminology someone used, body language, and any other clues. For example, you can tell from an interview whether a camera user has no idea what aperture means, knows what it means but struggles with getting it right, or lives and breathes exposure without thinking hard about it. Ignore the interviewee's own assessment of his skill or comfort relative to other people; his points of comparison differ from the ones in your interview set.

When one designer proposes a placement for an interviewee, refer to your notes and see if you agree with the proposed position relative to other respondents. The discussion should continue until all team members agree. At least two of you presumably sat through all of the same interviews, so if there's much controversy, this is usually a sign that either someone is relying on memory rather than referring to the data, or something is wrong with the choice or expression of the variable. Sometimes there's disagreement about the meaning of the words you've used to label the variable; you can solve this by asking what each team member thinks is meant and not meant by the term. It's also possible that your variable is too complex or subjective, as discussed earlier in Step 2; break it down into more granular behaviors.

If you feel it might be helpful to go through this process partway through your interviews, give it a try. Because each part of the analysis and design process builds on the earlier ones, it can shed light on what you could have done better in the previous step. If you find you're unable to map every interviewee to nearly all of the variables, it's a good indication that your interviewing or data-capture skills need work.

TRICKY MAPPING SITUATIONS

Not every mapping situation is straightforward because there's no such thing as a perfect data set. The following sections outline how to deal with some tricky (but common) situations.

Behavior that varied by circumstance

If can be difficult to place an interviewee on a spectrum if her behavior varied by circumstance. What to do about that depends on whether one behavior was clearly dominant. If someone almost always behaves one way, but there are very rare exceptions, it's usually best to ignore the exceptions. For example, imagine that your multiple-choice variable is "motivation for taking photos" and the options are "artistic expression," "memories," and "sharing." Someone who sends photos of the kids to relatives once a month is clearly motivated by sharing. Someone who never shares, except for giving a framed landscape photo as a gift every few years, really doesn't belong in the sharing category; yes, she does share once in a great while, but it's not the reason she takes photos.

If the interviewee's behavior is consistently varied by circumstance, though, it's sometimes useful to note that interviewee on the scale in two positions, with a note about the circumstance that drives that behavior. Figure 11.7 is an example of this. If your spectrum ranged from "organizes photos by content" to "organizes photos by time or event," for instance, you could put me in the middle because I do some of both. However, it would be more informative to put me in two

places because I always assign attributes (such as species, location, and the pose or behavior) to my wildlife photos, but I always organize photos from family events by time. Thankfully, this sort of thing isn't that common because it can clutter up the display. If it happens with more than one or two interviewees, consider dividing the problematic variable into some finer categories.

Speculation about behavior

At some point, you probably heard interviewees describing what they would *like* to do if they had more time, if their tools were better, or if they themselves were better in some way. The emphasis in mapping is on each interviewee's real, current behavior, not on speculation or wishful thinking. People who are strongly motivated to do a certain thing find ways to do it, regardless of their tools or the time they have available. Someone who only wishes your Web site made it easy to compare prices with other sites doesn't belong in the same category with someone who spends the time to look up multiple sites, bookmark them all, and make a spreadsheet comparing prices and shipping costs across all of them. Mind you, she also doesn't belong in the same category as someone who didn't seem to care about price at all; words carry some weight, but not nearly as much as behavior.

Third-party behavior

As a general rule, you should exclude the behavior of third parties from consideration. If someone

Figure 11.7. You can note behavior that differs by circumstance this way.

tells you his wife performs a certain task, that's not helpful in profiling *his* behavior. The exception is when multiple people, such as the members of a family, will share a single device or application. Don't record this behavior on the spectrum as if it were your interviewee's, but consider how you might incorporate it if it seems to have a significant impact. One way might be to add another variable or two dealing with whether a device or application is shared, and the extent to which a third party's data or preferences interfere with your interviewee's tasks.

Missing data

It's possible that you will encounter missing data, especially in your earliest interviews or as your interviewing skills improve. If your notes don't contain the right information to help you place an interviewee on one of the scales, the best option is to avoid introducing potentially incorrect assumptions by not placing that interviewee on that spectrum at all. You might feel the need to fudge this a bit if your interview set is thin. Only do so if you're very confident in your conjecture and know that no major business decisions are dependent on the personas; otherwise, consult with your stakeholders to decide whether to get a little more data or go with your best guess. If you feel you must speculate about where to put an interviewee, indicate this visually, as shown in Figure 11.8; this will help you see what parts of your conclusions are built on shaky data.

Figure 11.8. If you must incorporate questionable data, indicate it visually so you can see where your analysis may be weak.

WHAT YOU SHOULD HAVE AT THE END OF THIS STEP

Before going on to identify patterns, make sure your display captures every interviewee in this role in relation to every variable you can fill out. If your data has a lot of holes in it, consider whether you need to do more research. Be sure that the whole team agrees with the placement of each interviewee. Capture the current state of your diagram; a digital camera is a convenient way to capture the contents of a whiteboard without doing a lot of tedious copying.

Step 4. Identify patterns

The whole point of developing a set of variables and mapping your interview data to them is to facilitate the identification and verification of potential behavior patterns. What comes out of this step is a set of proto-personas: two or more behavior patterns defined by the correlation of multiple variables. Patterns are usually easy to spot in narrow roles (especially with a small set of interviewees) and more difficult to identify in unspecialized ones.

SPOTTING POTENTIAL PATTERNS

You might have a hunch about what the patterns are, but you might also have to look hard. Look at your entire set of variables at once. Rather than trying to find large clusters of people, start by looking for two or more people who frequently occur together. As in Figure 11.9, circle them with a colored marker so it's easy to see where their behavior and attitudes coincide. They almost certainly won't occur together on every variable, but if

Modeling

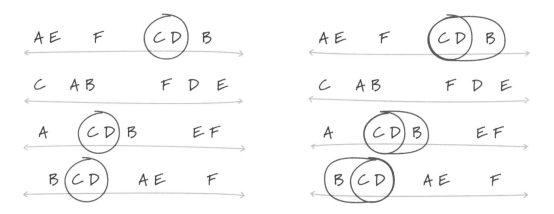

Figure 11.9. Start by circling the two people who show up together most often. Next, expand your circles to include anyone else who seems to appear with them most of the time.

they show up together on more than a third of the variables, they might represent a pattern. Step back and see if anyone else seems to be occurring frequently with your first pair. If so, expand your initial circles to include them. You might then find that these people appear with one of your original pair, but not the other, on some variables; circle these, too.

If the people in your possible pattern don't show up exactly together, but aren't all that far apart on the scale, these variables might still provide insight. Indicate these more tenuous relationships in a way that lets you see them, but with less emphasis. A dotted line is one good way to do this, as shown in Figure 11.10.

Figure 11.10. Use a dotted line to indicate more tenuous relationships.

Once you've circled everything that looks like it might be part of this first pattern, look at all of the variables where these people occur together. Try to explain how the variables are related (see Chapter 10, the section "Explanations and relationships," for more on explaining relationships in your data). Do you see one or more of the variables that seem like they might be the root cause for the other behaviors you observed? How is each variable related to at least one other? Is there a plausible explanation for that relationship, or does it seem like a coincidence due to your small sample? For example, it makes sense that a shopper's budget would affect how much time she spends comparing car models, but it's harder to believe that the amount of time she spends would be affected by the city she lives in.

After you've identified the variables that are legitimately related, consider the variables where these people did not appear together. Do any of them seem like they should be related, even though the results seem inconsistent with the rest of the pattern? If so, does that mean your potential pattern isn't really valid, or is there some reasonable explanation for the apparent mismatch?

Let's look at an example to see how this works. The mappings in Figure 11.11 are from interviews with investment advisers. As is often the case with narrowly defined roles, an apparent pattern is easy to spot: Sandra and Anton appear close to one another more often than not. Carlos and Tom are often close by, as well, but differ with respect to several variables, so their relationships to this possible pattern are unclear so far. Both Sandra and Anton:

— Are less inclined to do extensive, independent research on stocks

— Rely on a small number of tools for the research they do

— Believe it's important to speak in terms clients understand

— Spend more time educating their clients

— Are well versed in Modern Portfolio Theory (MPT), which focuses on optimizing portfolios through the weighting of various assets

— Are experienced

— Have a small number of large accounts

— Tend to focus on diversification and risk management rather than riskier, potentially higher-return investments

— Focus more on the client's goals and relationship than on constant portfolio tweaking

— Use a handful of portfolio structures with limited customization

— Trade less often

— Communicate less often with their clients

— Are likely to provide advice beyond the allocation of the assets they manage

— Are inclined to argue with clients who want to act on "hot stock tips"

So, how might these variables be related? These two interviewees see themselves as stewards of their clients' wealth, and their grounding in MPT leads them to believe that proper allocation of assets across a diverse portfolio is the best way to balance risk and return. Their focus on a client's life goals allows them to find the proper allocation of assets. Given their long-term view, it makes sense that they would be reluctant to make frequent trades in response to client worries about short-term market fluctuations. Less frequent trading also explains why they're less likely to communicate often with their clients. They don't feel the need to do constant research because they're responding to trends rather than individual bits of data, so the analysis they have access to covers most of what they feel they need to know. They believe educating their clients and talking about financial matters outside the portfolio encourages long-term thinking. Clearly, there's a strong relationship among most of these variables.

Two of the variables are a bit more difficult to explain. Does having a lot of experience lead Anton and Sandra to take the long view? Maybe, but maybe not. Denise is also very experienced but has a different philosophy. Carlos seems to share many similar views in spite of his much shorter tenure. This variable doesn't really seem to fit. The fact that Sandra and Anton each have only a few, large accounts might explain how they have the time to look beyond the portfolio, but this variable also seems to have a tenuous relationship with the rest of the pattern.

The differences between Sandra and Anton don't seem to contradict anything in the pattern. There's no clear reason that working in a team would affect the behaviors and attitudes they have in common. Their differing views on technology don't seem related, either.

When you're confident you've got a solid pattern, capture the characteristics of that pattern based on the variables that define it. Don't worry about the variables that aren't included in the pattern. This list of common characteristics is your first proto-persona. In the preceding example, the list

Modeling

minus the two characteristics that don't seem to have a clear relationship would be your proto-persona.

Once you have one pattern captured, look at your mapping and see if you can identify another pattern. The things that define the other patterns are often based on the same variables that defined the first, so it's easiest to start by looking at those. Find another pair and circle them in a different color. Look for others who might be part of the pattern, see if you can explain how the variables are related, and turn this into another proto-persona.

In the financial adviser example, the obvious thing to do is to see which people occur together and are clearly different from Sandra and Anton. Again, it's pretty easy to see in Figure 11.12 that Denise and Hugh appear close to one another more often than not.

Both Denise and Hugh:

— Are inclined to do extensive, independent research using many tools

— Use a fair amount of jargon, even if clients don't understand it

— Spend little time educating their clients

— Are only somewhat versed in Modern Portfolio Theory

— Tend to focus on higher-return investments over diversification and risk management

— Focus less on the client relationship and more on constant portfolio tweaking

— Customize extensively

— Trade often

— Communicate often with their clients

— Seldom provide advice beyond the allocation of the assets they manage

— Are inclined to make portfolio adjustments at the request of clients

Unlike Sandra and Anton, Hugh and Denise believe clients hire them to make the most lucrative investment choices by picking the right stocks and buying and selling at the right times. They use plenty of jargon to reinforce their expertise. They know some diversification is a good thing, but they're reluctant to buy mutual funds and index funds, as these don't require their skills. Denise and Hugh use a variety of sources for extensive research. They have little time or inclination to educate clients or deal with broader financial issues. They do communicate often with their clients, though, since frequent trading makes this necessary.

> # The list of common characteristics that define a clear pattern is your first proto-persona.

Modeling

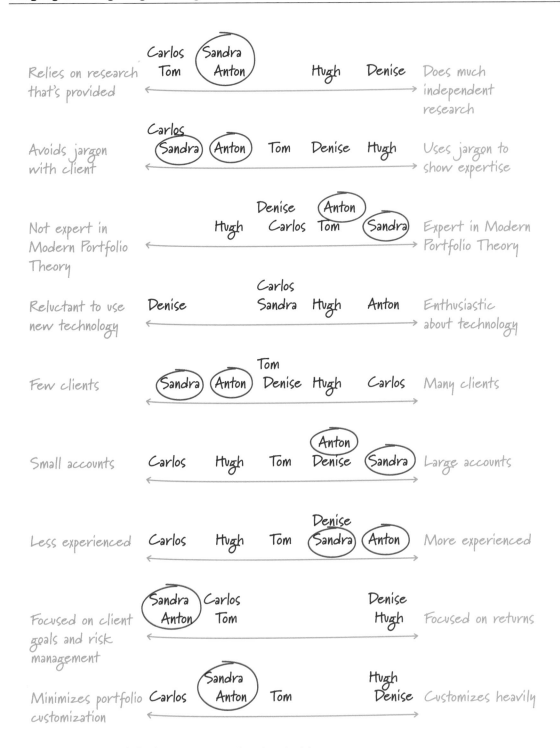

Figure 11.11. A possible behavior pattern among investment advisers.

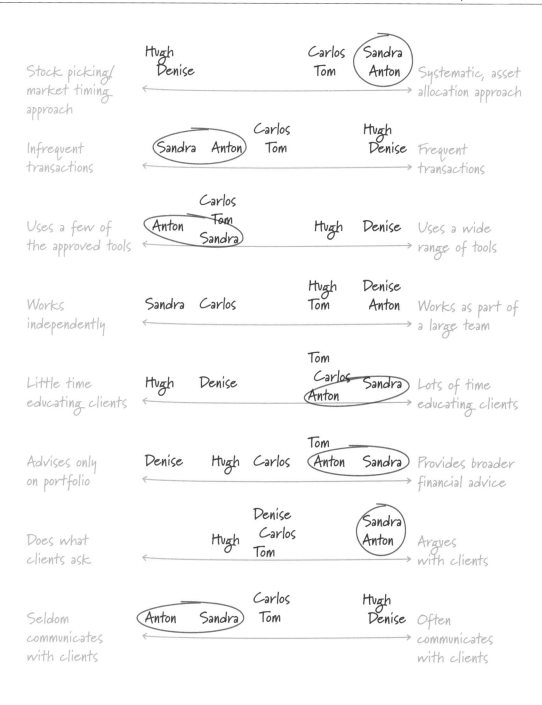

Stock picking/ market timing approach — Systematic, asset allocation approach

Infrequent transactions — Frequent transactions

Uses a few of the approved tools — Uses a wide range of tools

Works independently — Works as part of a large team

Little time educating clients — Lots of time educating clients

Advises only on portfolio — Provides broader financial advice

Does what clients ask — Argues with clients

Seldom communicates with clients — Often communicates with clients

Modeling

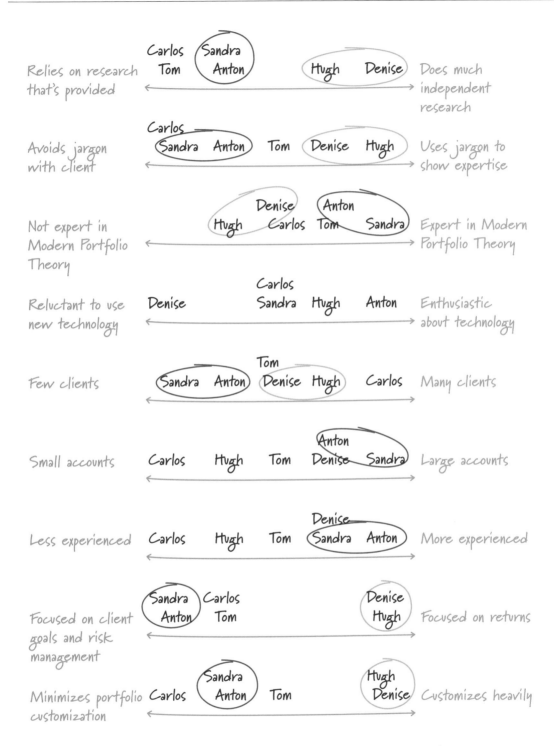

Figure 11.12. A second potential pattern among the financial advisers.

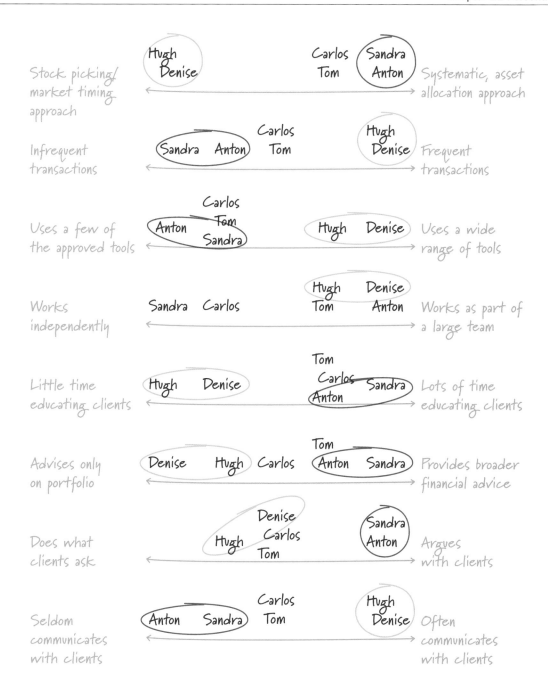

There's a clear explanation for most of the ways in which Hugh and Denise are similar. The fact that they both work in a team setting doesn't seem particularly related to the rest, however, so that may not be essential to the pattern. Denise's reluctance to use new tools doesn't seem to invalidate the pattern. Hugh is a bit less experienced than Denise, but because the difference in experience doesn't seem to affect either person's behavior, perhaps it's not essential to the pattern, either.

Keep going until you don't find any more potential patterns. It's common to find only two or even one in a very narrow role, but you might find several in a broader role. If you have some interviewees who don't quite fit any of the patterns, it may not be a problem, but it is cause for closer examination.

HANDLING OUTLIERS

If you have an outlier who appears completely unlike the other interviewees, consider the composition of your interview sample. It's safe to ignore any outliers who simply don't fit your target market. These are recruiting errors; it's best not to map such people at all unless you're truly desperate for data. If the outlier fits your recruiting criteria but is simply very different from your other participants, talk with your project owner to determine whether such people are interesting enough to warrant extending your research. Your project owner should include other stakeholders in the decision as needed.

It's normal to have a couple of interviewees who mostly fit a pattern but have one or more unique needs. For example, imagine that you interviewed a group of managers who travel a lot and depend on constant access to their communication tools. If you have one or two people who are mostly like that pattern but have assistants, this introduces some significantly different behaviors and needs with respect to telephone communication, so this should be a separate persona.

Carlos the financial adviser is another, more complex example. He seems philosophically aligned with Sandra and Anton, and most of his actions are consistent with this. However, he's more likely than they are to act on a specific stock purchase request from a client, which also makes him more likely to trade often and communicate with his clients about that trade. This happens because he has many more accounts and less experience than Sandra and Anton, so he doesn't have the confidence, skill, or time to argue his clients out of short-term thinking. Does Carlos represent a distinct persona? Big differences in skill level and quantity of data objects are usually significant design considerations, so as long as you're confident that Carlos isn't a fluke, it would be best to develop an additional persona.

It's also common to have one or two interviewees who are a little like one pattern and a little like another, but don't have any unique characteristics. Such people would be completely happy with a product or service designed for the people who fit the patterns, so they don't need to be represented as distinct personas. For example, Tom is a financial adviser whose philosophy and behavior seem like a blend of Sandra and Anton with Hugh and Denise. Unlike Carlos, he doesn't appear to have any unique needs that wouldn't be satisfied by designing for the others, so you wouldn't need another persona to represent people like Tom.

WHAT YOU SHOULD HAVE AT THE END OF THIS STEP

Identify patterns for each role before moving on to the next step. At this point, you should have a set of pattern descriptions, each comprised of perhaps a dozen characteristics. Make a note of any characteristics that seem questionable.

Table 11.4. **Example summary behavior patterns for financial advisers.**

Senior asset allocators	Junior asset allocators	Stock pickers
— Limited research with a few tools	— Limited research with a few tools	— Lots of research, many tools
— Speak in terms clients understand	— Speak in terms clients understand	— Lots of jargon
— Spend time educating clients	— Spend time educating clients	— Little client education
— Understand Modern Portfolio Theory	— Understand Modern Portfolio Theory	— Somewhat versed in MPT
— Experienced	— Relatively inexperienced	— Focus on higher-return investments over diversification and risk management
— (Small number of large accounts?)	— Many small accounts	— Extensive portfolio customization
— Diversification and risk management focus	— Diversification and risk management focus	— Frequent trades
— Relationship focus	— Relationship focus	— Frequent client communication
— Minimal portfolio tweaking or customization	— Minimal portfolio tweaking or customization	— Seldom advise on anything but portfolio
— Infrequent trades	— Somewhat frequent trades	— Don't argue with client requests
— Infrequent client communication	— Somewhat frequent client communication	— (Variable experience?)
— Advice beyond portfolio	— Little advice beyond portfolio	— (Work in a team?)
— Argue when necessary	— Argue when time and skills permit	

If you have a large number of proto-personas, you might want to give each one a temporary descriptive designation (such as the bargain hunter, reluctant shopper, social shopper, and so forth); this will make it easier to keep track of them while you flesh them out.

Exercise

Use the mapping from the previous exercise to identify the behavior patterns.

Step 5. Define goals

Engineers, product managers, and designers often spend so much time thinking about tasks that it's easy to lose sight of users' goals. You can spend a lot of time improving the usability of your file-management dialog, or you can realize that managing files has nothing to do with your user's goal and get rid of the task altogether. That's why the method in this book is called Goal-Directed Design; persona goals drive every solution.

Goals are an integral part of personas; the clear focus they provide is a big part of why personas are so effective as design and communication tools. An explicit statement of a persona's goals is useful in everything from prioritizing features to determining what piece of information gets emphasized on the display.

For each of the proto-personas, there's usually at least one goal evident from the mapping exercise. To fill out the rest, you'll need to refer back to your notes for the interviewees who are the basis for the persona; see the "Goals" section of Chapter 7 for more on identifying goals from an interview. Frustrations, observed behavior, and answers to questions about what makes a good experience are all good sources for goals. Most personas have three or four goals. You can articulate these either before or after you outline each persona's characteristics in detail.

GOAL TYPES

Getting goals at the right level is tricky. Overly ambitious goals are hard to design for, but if a goal isn't ambitious enough, it won't cause you to stretch the design. One way to help get your goals at the right level is to think about them by type. The boundaries between these types are fuzzy, but they're meant as a way to calibrate your internal "goal-appropriateness meter," not as a strict classification system.

Nearly all of us share a set of **basic human goals**, such as being safe and healthy, being treated with respect, being comfortable, and feeling good about ourselves. It's reasonable to assume that these are true of any persona, but because knowing that people want full bellies and warm feet doesn't help you design a better e-mail application, it's seldom necessary to state them explicitly. Once in a while, though, you may have a persona who feels more anxiety about one of these goals than most people do. For example, someone unfamiliar with technology might be uncomfortable using a computer in a public place for fear or embarrassment.

In these cases, stating "avoid embarrassment" as an explicit goal underlines a fear that will influence how you design.

Most people also have certain **life goals**: retire at age 60, raise wonderful children, be a movie star, graduate from college, be the best chess player in school, discover a new species of plankton ... the list is as varied as you can imagine. Fascinating as such goals are, they're seldom relevant unless the product or service has the potential to help accomplish them. A financial-planning product, for example, could help someone retire at a particular age, but wouldn't do much to help her improve at chess or find an undiscovered protozoan. It's unusual to have more than one persona goal at this high level, and many personas don't require a life goal.

Most persona goals should be just a notch below life goals. Since "product goals" would be a confusing term, I call these **end goals**: aims the personas could accomplish, at least in part, by using the product or service. Examples might include things like taking better photos, beating a sales target, or seeing trends before they become problems. It's typical to have two or three end goals for each persona.

A good end goal is usually something the product can *help* people accomplish, but can't entirely accomplish *for* them. For example, a product can help someone be more organized by providing reminders, tools for managing lists, and so on, but it can't accomplish that without some effort on the user's part. If the product can accomplish the goal entirely on its own, there's a good chance (though not a guarantee) that the "goal" is really a task or a product feature.

To determine whether what you've articulated is really a goal, ask yourself, "Why?" For example, imagine that your teammate has proposed that Ted's goal is to "get driving directions verbally." You ask, "Why does Ted want to get driving directions verbally?" Your teammate says, "So he doesn't have to look at the screen while he's driving." When you ask why Ted doesn't want to look at the screen, your teammate says, "So he can keep his eyes on the road and not get into an accident." Now you're getting somewhere! Keeping Ted's eyes on the road is something you can help with, but can't be entirely responsible for.

Phrasing can be a clue that you don't have an effective goal. Any statement that specifies a mechanism, such as "Do X wirelessly," is probably both a task and a feature but not a goal. Anything phrased as "Do X more easily" is almost certainly a task.

In addition to end goals, it's often a good idea to articulate an **experience goal** for each persona; this describes how the persona wants to feel while using the product or service. This is arguably an end goal, but I find that describing it as a separate type helps people remember to consider feelings and aspirations. This is especially important in branded visual or industrial design. Someone who wants to feel like her money is safe, for example, will respond better to a bank Web site that uses navy blue and white than to one that uses orange, purple, and lime green.

Goals are most memorable and effective when they're short, pithy, and expressed in words the persona would use. Feel free to quote directly from your interviewees if someone phrased something in a memorable way. Start each goal with a verb, and make it a sentence; "avoid hassles" is much more clear than "no hassles." Try to convey the hope, frustration, or other emotion behind the goal. "Maintain a good work/life balance" sounds clinical. "Have a life" hints at a touch of frustration and implies that the balance is skewed too far toward work right now. "Clear my desk by 5:00" implies that most tasks can be accomplished in a day and illustrates a nine-to-five, work-stays-at-the-office attitude. "Get everything done," by contrast, lacks this nuance.

WHAT YOU SHOULD HAVE AT THE END OF THIS STEP

When you're done, you should have about three or four crisp, memorable goals for each persona, including any customer or served personas. If you have a lot of goals, consider whether they're really tasks, or if they're all necessary. If you only have one or two, keep looking, because you're probably missing something.

> End goals are aims the personas could accomplish, at least in part, by using the product or service.

Exercises

1. Develop goals for your LocalGuide or RoomFinder personas.

2. Critique and improve on the following sets of goals:

FOR AN ONLINE SHOPPER:

— Register easily

— Save money

— Fun

FOR A RECEPTIONIST:

— Answer every call

— Transfer calls easily

— Be seen as a professional

— Get that modeling gig

FOR A TEENAGE MUSIC LISTENER:

— Keep my music organized

— Enjoy my music

— Rebel against my parents

Step 6. Clarify distinctions and add detail

You can see that it will take some effort to turn your proto-personas into the real thing; they still lack details about behavior, frustrations, environmental factors, and other information needed to make them effective design and communication tools. This next step involves not only filling out such details, but also sharpening the distinctions among the personas; the more distinct they are, the easier they are to remember and use.

Start by referring once more to your mappings. You'll see at least a few variables that weren't critical to defining the patterns, but may still represent important information. Demographics, such as age or gender, are often among these

leftovers, but comfort with technology or a few other behavioral variables might also be unaccounted for. Because there was variation with respect to these behaviors, that range should be represented in your persona set. You need to determine which of these various characteristics best matches which pattern. There are two criteria that drive these decisions: which characteristic is most believable with which pattern, and what choices will make the personas the most distinct and useful as a design tool.

For example, which of the following should be female: someone who frequently sends photos of the kids to relatives, or someone who seldom does? Even if the data doesn't show any strong link to gender, most people would assume the persona sending photos is female, since women are generally seen as more likely to stay in touch with family. The other persona will therefore be more distinct (and easier to remember) if it's male.

This is where the research purists usually jump out of their seats in shock and say, "But...you're just *assigning* these characteristics with no regard for the data?!" Yes and no. Yes, you are just assigning these characteristics based on what will make your characters more believable and memorable, but no, it's not without regard for the data. These characteristics aren't coming out of nowhere—they're typical of the sample. Your data is what told you there's no apparent relationship between the assigned characteristics and the ones that are essential to the behavior pattern, so there's no contradiction. It's important to remember that although personas do represent key patterns in the research, their function is to promote empathy for users and to facilitate discussion about design decisions, not to be exact statistical representations of the user population. It's entirely possible that men are two percent more likely to be the ones keeping in touch with families by sending photos, but this is irrelevant for the purposes personas are meant to serve.

You also have to think about any potential problems with an assigned characteristic, which may involve consultation with your project owner. In the financial adviser example in Table 11.4, the stock-picker pattern indicates variable experience because there was inconsistency with respect to this characteristic. The fact that experience level doesn't seem to cause differences between Denise and Hugh means it can be an assigned value. What experience level will be more believable and more useful as a design tool? The other two patterns cover the range of experience from low to high, so there's not a gap to fill, and industry demographics don't provide a clear answer. However, if you imply that anyone who relies on market timing is inexperienced, it may make stakeholders less inclined to take that part of the user population seriously, so it might be best to lean toward experience.

After you've accounted for all of the variables, fill in additional details. Review your notes for the interviewees who contributed most heavily to the pattern. Start with anything that's common to all of the relevant interviewees. You probably won't find 100 percent overlap, so you will again have to fill in gaps by deciding which details are most typical of the pattern and most distinct from other patterns.

As with every step of this process, collaboration will help you stay as true to your data as possible. Each team member should have interview notes available. One team member should have a marker in hand to capture the agreed upon characteristics. When someone proposes a characteristic, consider how well it fits the data or, for assigned characteristics, what is most believable based on other data sources and stakeholder perceptions. Also keep your eyes open for anything that crosses the line into negative stereotyping.

COMPONENTS OF A PERSONA

The idea is for each persona to answer every research question described in Chapter 7. There will be details unique to the personas for each design problem, but several categories of information are important in any good persona. Whether you capture these as bullet points or prose is up to you; bullets are usually a better starting point for team collaboration, since crafting a sentence by committee can be contentious.

Behaviors

To understand how a product or service can improve someone's life, you have to understand what that person's life is like now. Every user persona (but not customer or served personas) should incorporate a "day in the life" description of current behaviors relevant to the design problem. Note that "day in the life" is a loose term; the relevant behavior might only happen during the course of an hour. What tasks did people like this perform? How? Where do they start, what are their subsequent actions and decisions, and what affects those? What reasons can you provide for this behavior? Some of the details presented earlier in this chapter for camera user Katie Bennett, for example, would look like this:

— 100 to 300 shots per outing
— Takes time composing most shots
— Occasionally captures subjects that might move or change (animals, light)
— Starts with auto settings (auto focus, metering)
— Brackets exposure if she has time

Chances are good that the interviewees who contributed most heavily to the pattern weren't quite identical in their process, so use the behavioral details that best reinforce the rest of the pattern. For example, imagine that your persona is a car buyer who tends to do a lot of research. Of the five interviewees who contributed most to the pattern, all read articles from a variety of sources. Three only read information online. The other two also bought automotive magazines. Which detail best fits the behavior pattern? If what you're trying to

It's important that people accept the personas as a description of the current state before you start talking about the implications for the future.

convey is the extensive nature of the research, then mentioning both online reading and purchased magazines will be more effective.

The exact situations you describe for your personas don't have to be identical to those in your data as long as they're consistent with the behavior and motivations. For example, parents in your sample may have mentioned taking photos of soccer games and school plays, but it doesn't matter if your persona's child is on the baseball team and giving a piano recital—in either case, the persona is recording important events that other people can relate to.

Cover each type of current persona behavior that the product or service *could* accommodate; just as in your interview questions, don't limit yourself to current functionality. Describe the whole ecosystem of which your product is a part. If your current product is an e-mail system but the persona's conversations are usually carried out over e-mail, voicemail, and live conversation, describe the interaction among these tools. However, don't turn this into what the persona would want from a new product. It's important that people accept the personas as a description of the current state before you start talking about the implications for the future.

When you're developing an entirely new product category, describe behaviors that are as close to the purpose of the product as you can get. For example, if you were designing a tiny handheld television device and content service before anything similar existed, you would describe the related behavior you observed in your interviews: how your personas watched television at home, what kind of information or entertainment needs your personas had when not at home, and how your personas used other mobile devices.

If you have difficulty coming up with these descriptions, it's a sure sign you didn't get enough detail in your interviews. You will need to fill in any gaps by calling up your interviewees or at least talking to a subject matter expert.

Frustrations

Along with every set of behaviors comes a set of frustrations. Even if their processes differ a bit, the people who make up a behavior pattern usually have similar problems. Review your notes for each person to see what they mentioned. Look over the description of the behavior and recall what about the process annoyed your interviewees.

Environment

It's usually worth mentioning (and sometimes illustrating) anything about the persona's surroundings that might affect usage. For business tools, this sometimes includes the industry or size of company where someone works. Factors for most products include interruptions or lack of privacy, as well as noise, lighting, distance from the screen, or other ergonomic challenges. Environments involving temperature extremes, moisture, and mess may be important to mention if you're designing a physical product. The personas aren't the only opportunity to represent such things, but they're a good way to highlight problems in any of these areas.

As with behaviors, you may have seen variation in environments among the interviewees contributing to each persona. Consider which environment details are most believable and best reinforce the persona's other characteristics.

Skills and capabilities

Each persona includes some description of skills, experience, and, when useful, physical capabilities. This often includes a mention of relevant education or where someone worked before coming to his current position. You can also describe specific tasks or concepts someone has difficulty with. Your field study data should give you a good idea of what's typical, but consult quantitative studies or subject matter experts as necessary.

Feelings, attitudes, and aspirations

When you did the user research, you got a visceral sense for whether interviewees enjoyed various activities or viewed them as chores. You might also have a good idea of what their hopes are, how they see themselves, and how they want to be seen. This information can help stakeholders understand that an existing product or service is making people miserable. It can also help everyone on the product team see how emotions, self-esteem, and other "touchy-feely" qualities affect how people perceive brands and interact with products. This understanding is important to interaction design and essential to visual and industrial design. You can describe feelings and aspirations directly. You can also mention well-known products and services to reinforce those feelings, or use a collage to depict the persona's interests and personal style.

Interactions with other people, products, and services

Outline the ways in which the persona's tasks involve other people, products, and services. If you can't think of any, keep thinking; the vast majority of products and services involve some negotiation or interaction with other human beings, whether this is as complex as online collaboration or as straightforward as opening a document sent by another person. Even the lowly alarm clock may involve negotiation about what time you're going to get up and what music you and your significant other can both tolerate at six in the morning. Describe shared information and tasks, dependencies, and the ways in which other people drive your persona crazy. Diagrams can sometimes be useful for explaining relationships.

Demographics

It's impossible to look at another human and not have some mental estimate of age, gender, ethnicity, and perhaps other demographic data. For this reason, your personas won't seem real if they lack this information. You may have a good sense for the demographics from your field studies, but don't hesitate to pull in whatever quantitative data you have available.

You may be tempted to use the persona set to paint the world as it "should" be. For example, most people expect a CEO in any Western country to be a white man over 50, and they'd be correct more often than not. Much as I believe this shouldn't be the case, I know that many people will have more trouble accepting a persona who does not fit this profile. Any part of your persona that feels wrong to stakeholders will cause them to question the validity of every other part, which can make the whole design process more difficult. You should certainly make your persona set as diverse as possible, but use demographics that are typical of the market.

If you, like many designers, feel strongly about accessibility, you may be wondering how your persona set can account for differing abilities. It may sound insensitive, but personas are seldom the right tool for this unless accessibility is a problem for a large number of your users. It would take so many personas to account for the range of differences (such as in sight, hearing, speech, dexterity, learning, and mobility) that these would overwhelm the number of personas for most projects. Incorporating those differences into the other personas would also make them demographically atypical, causing them to become ineffective. It's better to incorporate these important issues into the design process in other ways, such as by following appropriate guidelines, having your design reviewed by accessibility experts, and incorporating a wide range of users in testing.

Relationships among personas

No doubt you've noticed that every persona example used so far has been an individual. This is because humans think and act as individuals, and most products are used by only one person at a time. However, there are instances when multiple people use a product together, or at least attempt to; battling over the television remote may come to mind. Technology also serves to mediate some interactions between people, such as on a social networking site or video chat. In these cases it's important to acknowledge that more than one mind, and perhaps more than one hand, guides the interaction with the product, and that the relationships among people can affect their behavior.

This issue was especially vivid on a project for the J. Paul Getty Museum. The design team found that for many visitors, a trip to the Getty Center was partly a social occasion; friends and families visited not only to enjoy and learn from the art, but also to take in the beautiful architecture and gardens together. If one visitor stopped at a kiosk, the others would be likely to stop, too. The interests of the group would drive the interaction. Two adults together might enjoy wandering through the digital collection at length, while an adult visiting with her family might be distracted from browsing by a squirming child. To address these different group dynamics, the team arranged their personas to represent typical groups of visitors: a young couple, a small group of women at the Getty for a leisurely outing, and a family with two children. The resulting scenarios could then address, for example, the tug-of-war between a parent hoping for an enriching cultural experience and a child who wants to find the nearest food.

You might consider putting your personas in the same family or company if your product will be shared among family members or span several roles. There are pros and cons to this, of course. Having the personas exist in a shared environment makes it easier to express relationships. It's also convenient for storytelling later on, as you develop scenarios to drive the design process. Shared environments can also help emphasize the contrasts in user needs among companies of different sizes or types (for more on this, see the sidebar on **organizational archetypes**).

However, putting all your personas in one group can be limiting if you saw variation in your data based on things like family structure, industry vertical, geography, or company size. Sometimes it's possible to address company size and geography issues by having the personas in different offices of the same company, but don't obscure important differences in your data for the sake of easier storytelling.

Organizational Archetypes

Just as there are patterns in human behavior and demographics, there are patterns in organizational characteristics and needs. You might have found, for example, that government agencies and private businesses handle their accounting rather differently, and that this has led to some important behavioral distinctions in your personas. In such a case, you'd place your personas within two distinct **organizational archetypes**, which are simply persona-like models representing types of organizations. Each organizational archetype generally gets a name and a brief one- or two-paragraph description covering the topics most relevant to persona behavior. Organizational archetypes are not always necessary, but when they are, you'll always have at least two.

Here are examples of two brief archetypes for a restaurant reservation-and-table management system; it's possible to do slightly more elaborate archetypes for complex design problems:

Pizette

Pizette is a small but hip neighborhood restaurant run by its founding chef. To keep up with popular demand last year, Pizette had to institute a reservation policy for its 15 tables, but its ten bar seats remain available on a walk-in basis. The hostess and three servers all work from a paper reservation book, wait list, and laminated-paper seating chart to estimate table availability. The bartender, who also serves food for those seated at the bar, doesn't use the system. Although the regular hostess has things under control, chaos ensues if she's out sick or away from her post and someone else tries to handle a reservation or table assignment. All tabs are figured manually and rung up on the cash register.

Down Home

Down Home is a fast-growing regional chain of 56 family-oriented restaurants in six states. Each restaurant has between 30 and 50 tables with a manager, one or two hostesses, and three to six servers on duty at any time. Most accept reservations only for large parties; the hostesses use a paper wait list when things get busy. The current touch screen system allows the hostesses to assign tables and estimate wait times. The servers use one of two touch screen kiosks to enter orders and ring up tabs.

Note how these two examples contrast: The organizations are different sizes and have entirely different issues with managing reservations and table occupancy. Quick organizational sketches like these help provide context for a set of personas so you don't have to explain the environment in each persona's description. More than this, they serve to highlight for stakeholders the connection between organization type and user behavior.

> Organizational archetypes are persona-like models representing types of organizations that drive difference behavior.

Modeling

Names

Every real human has a name; most of us, except for the occasional eccentric rock star, have at least two. Personas are most effective when they seem like real people, so each persona should have a realistic first and last name. Never use silly or alliterative names, such as Eagle-Eyed Ed, Shirley Shopper, or Fannie the First-Time User. These undermine the value of your personas by emphasizing that they're not real. If you don't take the personas seriously, no one else will.

That said, you can use a name to reinforce something about a persona's personality as long as you're subtle about it. People will be surprised if a construction worker goes by William Smith III, but not if the head of a successful law firm does. A persona meant to seem like the friendly and approachable sort might be Tom or Tommy rather than Thomas. This is a fine line to walk; be careful not to use stereotyped names. Also consider whether a name is appropriate to the age of your persona; Madison was a popular name for American girls starting in the 1990s, but Edith was far more popular in the 1950s.[5]

Baby-name books are one source of name ideas. The local telephone directory is even better, but may not be a good source of names from other countries. Searching for international names online (e.g., typing "Finnish baby names") generally yields plenty of options. Choose names that are easy for your team and stakeholders to remember, though; names that are long or difficult for team members to pronounce tend not to be adopted. Western audiences may get confused when family names come before personal names, so you may want to transpose these.

Don't use the names of any product team members, interviewees, or anyone whose name carries strong associations; a persona at Microsoft shouldn't have either Bill or Gates in its name. Also avoid names that might be confused with states or cities (such as Georgia or Savannah), or have strong associations (such as Disney, Porsche, or Clinton).

What not to include

Persona creation can be fun, so it's easy to get carried away. Don't insert a bunch of fictitious details about your personas unless you have a clear argument for why they're important; for most products, it almost certainly doesn't matter what color the car is, what the dog's name is, or what show is currently on the television. One or two of these touches can be helpful in polishing the narrative later, but this sort of thing can take over your persona descriptions if you start adding it now.

WHAT YOU SHOULD HAVE AT THE END OF THIS STEP

When you've filled out each persona, you should have a longer bullet list for each that includes activity descriptions, frustrations, skills, environment, demographics, feelings and attitudes, and names. Customer and served personas should have frustrations, concerns, and company or family demographics, but not activity descriptions. Some people may be most comfortable beginning to express some of this detail in prose.

Exercise

Fill in details for your RoomFinder or LocalGuide personas. Be sure to cover behavior, frustrations, skills, environment, relationships, feelings, and aspirations. Give each persona a name.

---

5. If your personas are American, there's a great source for this information (and a nice bit of information design) at http://www.babynamewizard.com/namevoyager/lnv0105.html.

Step 7. Fill in other persona types as needed

Once you have a rough outline of every persona that seems necessary from a design perspective, stop and ask yourself how stakeholders will receive your persona set. If stakeholders tend to confuse customers with users, then a customer persona may be necessary if you don't have one yet. You might need a served persona if you're worried that product team members may forget about the people their users are supposed to help.

The more difficult situations arise when stakeholders expect to see types of users you haven't represented as personas. If you're lucky, these are just people who differ slightly from your personas with respect to job title or some other characteristic. Otherwise, you might find yourself arguing about a type of user who simply didn't exist in the data, or who is so different from other users as to be a bad design target.

SUPPLEMENTAL USER PERSONAS

Stakeholders occasionally have strong assumptions about the importance of certain types of people, even though your research shows that such people don't have unique characteristics from a design point of view. Although it's best to limit your persona set to the smallest number of personas you can use to express the behavior patterns you observed, you won't get anywhere if people believe your persona set is missing critical parts of the user population.

Consider adding a **supplemental persona** or two if you believe you won't convince stakeholders that your personas cover the necessary ground. Though they're not useful from a design perspective, these are still realistic portraits drawn from the data. For example, I've designed multiple health care products that were used primarily by nurses, but also used occasionally by physicians who did exactly the same things in the same ways. In each case, there was a strong belief among some stakeholders that it was important to consider physicians in the design, so my team trotted out a supplemental physician persona to demonstrate that we were considering his needs. We quietly ignored the unnecessary personas during design meetings, and everybody was happy.

Of course, supplemental personas introduce a small risk that stakeholders will want the wrong users to be the design focus, so think twice before introducing them, and make sure they're based on good data just in case.

NEGATIVE USER PERSONAS

If stakeholders are focused on a type of user who is so unlike the rest of the market that designing for them would make the product unappealing, you may need to develop a **negative persona**. With enterprise systems, your internal users might be very loud (and hard to ignore because they're just down the hall), but their needs are often quite different from those in the mass market. In the consumer realm, such problematic users are typically at the extremes of the user population, such as very technically skilled users. For example, my team once created a negative persona when an executive wanted to ship a mass-market consumer product but insisted that we please people who could build their own computers. The negative persona made the contrast so clear that the executive immediately agreed it would be a mistake to design for him.

Negative personas are seldom necessary because most groups of stakeholders understand the difference between a reasonable design target and a bad one. If you do decide to use a negative persona, base it on data just as you would your other personas, and make sure it's not a caricature. Present the negative persona as a choice, i.e., "Here are the trade-offs we'd be making if we focused on this persona," rather than,

Modeling

"We can't focus on this persona because it will kill the product." Stakeholders can see that for themselves.

NONEXISTENT PERSONAS

At some point, you may run into a stakeholder who insists on a persona you couldn't find in your data. This usually happens because someone got attached to a product idea before doing any research, and is trying to justify the idea by retro-fitting personas to it. On one project, for example, a client wanted to build a software development application for users who were deficient in a particular skill. The team couldn't find any such people in their research; new programmers were all being trained in that skill, and experienced pro-grammers had either gotten training in it or gotten out of programming entirely. Even if there had been a market window at one time, it appeared to be closed. The design team expanded their re-search at the client's suggestion and still couldn't find any such people. However, they found types of users who provided other opportunities, so the client was eventually persuaded to shift the focus of the product.

When a stakeholder insists on a persona you be-lieve doesn't exist, say that although you haven't found any such people, perhaps you simply need to expand your research. Review what you've done so far to find them and ask where else the stake-holder suggests you look. If you still don't find them, any reasonable stakeholder will see that his assumptions were wrong.

WHAT YOU SHOULD HAVE AT THE END OF THIS STEP

If you're lucky, your set may be unchanged at the end of this step. Otherwise, you'll have an extra persona or two that you'll need to present very carefully to avoid having the design get sidetracked.

Step 8. Group and prioritize user personas

By the time you're done outlining your personas, you might have just two or three, or you might have a dozen or more. Now imagine trying to de-sign with all of these personas in mind. Even with just two personas, you may face a dilemma when they each need slightly different solutions. If you've decided beforehand that one persona will win such arguments, the dilemma goes away. This is why it's important to prioritize the personas within each role.

Personas are prioritized within roles because each role needs its own **interface**, with a distinct set of tools and data laid out in a specific man-ner. Users are most effective when all of the tools they need for a task are close at hand, but none of the tools they don't need is in the way. This is why most people keep the mixer and food processor in the kitchen and the drill and jigsaw in the garage; you'd never use a food processor to build shelves, and hopefully your baking ef-forts don't require a jigsaw to cut through. The same basic idea is true in software: People who have clearly distinct tasks should have their own sets of tools and not be forced to stumble over everyone else's.

A **primary persona** is the best design target within a role; if you designed a product for the primary, the other personas would be mostly (but not completely) satisfied. You will generate your initial design ideas from the primary persona's point of view. **Secondary personas** have similar needs but require some small difference, such as an extra tool or a different level of sophisti-cation. Once you have a design solution for the primary persona, you'll modify it as needed to accommodate each secondary persona, as long as your modification doesn't cause problems for the primary persona. Supplemental personas (which you might also consider "tertiary") are not considered in the design because they have no distinct needs.

Modeling

Multiple factors will affect your choice of primary. The first consideration is how representative the primary's needs are. You can follow a process of elimination to determine which persona best satisfies the range of needs. For example, if you design first for persona A, persona B will be mostly happy, but persona C will be unhappy. If you design first for persona B instead, personas A and C will mostly be happy, so persona B is the better candidate. Skill and experience are often factors in this comparison. If you're designing an airport check-in kiosk, should you think first about frequent fliers or about people who have never seen a check-in kiosk before? If you start with frequent fliers, they might swipe a membership card and immediately get a boarding pass based on their usual seating preferences. It could be difficult to add on to that process for a novice. If, on the other hand, you start with the level of instruction and reassurance a novice needs, it's easy to streamline for frequent fliers from there, so the novice is the better target.

However, starting with the lowest skill level can be a bad idea. If you're designing a tool for customer service agents in a call center, efficiency is important because the more calls an agent can handle, the fewer agents are needed. Designing for a brand-new agent would place the emphasis on instruction and support over speed. It would be hard to streamline such complex activities for more-experienced users. Also, agents don't stay new for very long; even if they only stay for a year, they'll be using the system like pros in less than a month.

Also consider breadth of tasks in designating your primary. Sometimes the persona with a slightly broader set of tasks makes the better choice. Consider a nurse persona who works in a general hospital ward, where patients might have nearly any condition, versus one who works in an oncology ward, where she treats only a limited set of conditions. If you were designing a medication delivery system, the nurse persona with

the broader tasks would make a better starting point for design because her solution would need to be more flexible. You could then satisfy the oncology nurse by stripping out the options she doesn't need.

Of course, the broadest tasks don't always make the best primary, either, particularly when the person with broad tasks crosses roles. When we redesigned a purchasing system, for example, my team designated the specialized users as primary for each of three interfaces (purchasing, receiving, and accounting). The generalist persona, an administrative assistant who sometimes placed orders, verified their receipt, and approved invoices for payment, was designated as secondary for all three. Starting with her would have put too many useless tools in the way of the specialist users and would have focused us on occasional use instead of intensive, daily use, which was more important to optimize for.

Market proportion or value can also be a consideration. A persona who sounds like a good primary target from a design point of view might be a poor choice if only five percent of the target market is like that persona. If those five percent are potentially worth 80 percent of your revenue, though, perhaps that persona would be a wise choice of primary, after all. However, remember that your personas represent the range of behaviors in your market; some real users will be partly represented by persona A and partly by persona B, so this kind of assessment can be problematic.

Timelines and budgets ideally should not drive your choice of primary. However, in rare cases, it may be that your budget prevents the inclusion of functionality critical to satisfying an otherwise likely primary persona. This might (or might not) mean it makes better sense to target a persona who is easier to satisfy so the product gets traction in the market.

Modeling

As seems to be the case with most aspects of persona creation, this step is often easier for enterprise applications than with a set of consumer personas. This is partly because tasks and skill level can provide easier decision criteria than attitudes and more subtle behaviors, and partly because the breadth of a consumer persona set provides so many more options. If you can't find a single primary whose needs mostly overlap with every other persona, it's possible that you need more than one product.

If you're designing a Web site, you may be able to find a single primary, but this can be a challenge. Instead, you might need to designate an overall primary for the site, but have distinct primaries for particular sections. For example, consider the following personas for a mid-range auto manufacturer's Web site:

— Lydia, a middle-aged buyer who doesn't want to make a bad deal, but isn't overly concerned about cost. She wants to get a car she loves without putting too much effort into the process. She tends to make buying decisions based on aesthetic and emotional appeal.

— Jake, who reads automotive magazines and wants a new car with tight handling and more valves and horsepower than his buddy's. He sees himself as a rational decision-maker who likes data, though he focuses only on performance information.

— Ryan, a young adult buying his first new car. He's tired of trying to haul his mountain bike and other outdoor gear in the ten-year-old compact car he bought in college. Cost is an important consideration, but he doesn't want to feel like he's getting the budget model.

(Note that in reality, there would be more personas than this, but I'm trying to keep the example simple.) Lydia would make a good **site primary**

because nothing about her needs will annoy the others, and her emphasis on emotion and aesthetic will be a good guide for the site's visual design, which has to feel consistent and coherent throughout. Jake's focus on performance data would overwhelm the others. Focusing on cost would annoy Jake and Lydia, and wouldn't even make Ryan entirely happy. However, any specification pages should be aimed primarily at Jake, and cost comparison or financing information could target Ryan as primary.

As you can see, there's no easy formula for selecting your primary. It's a matter of comparing the personas and thinking through the design and business implications of focusing on each. On some projects, the choice of primary persona is really about which is the easier starting point for design. In such a case, the design team should choose the primary, then confidently present that choice and rationale to stakeholders. If, however, choosing one primary or another has significant business implications or will lead the product in different directions, it's imperative that stakeholders participate in the decision. (See the section "Delivering the presentation and leading the discussion" in Chapter 13.)

WHAT YOU SHOULD HAVE AT THE END OF THIS STEP

Before you move on, you should have either prioritized your personas as primary, secondary, and supplemental, or come up with a clear set of consequences for stakeholders to consider if the choice of primary persona(s) is unclear.

Exercise

Prioritize your LocalGuide or RoomFinder personas. Discuss the rationale for your decisions.

Step 9. Develop the narrative and other communication

Because personas are in large part communication tools, you're not done until you've put together the materials you will need to communicate about them. The persona description is the essential communication tool, but there are several others that can be helpful.

DESCRIBING INDIVIDUAL PERSONAS

An effective persona description includes, at minimum, a name, a photo, and a one- to two-page narrative that encompasses each persona's important behaviors, frustrations, environment, skills and capabilities, feelings, attitudes, aspirations, relationships, demographics, and goals. Each persona may also include illustrative quotes, diagrams, or other information.

Photos

The right persona photo can help make the difference between a cold, static profile and a seemingly real person. The photo should, of course, be acceptable from a technical perspective: in focus, well composed, and with good contrast. Just like the persona description, the photo should portray the persona in a sympathetic light and not seem to poke fun in any way. An effective photo shows a likeable, normal person in an appropriate context of use, not a perfectly groomed model in an artificial pose against a white backdrop. While some graphic designers might argue for the latter, it's clearly stock photography rather than a "real" person captured in the course of her normal activities.

It's important that the photo includes a good view of the person's face, since we humans tend to imprint on faces. The image also should not contain anything that doesn't make sense in relation to the persona description. For example, an image that's supposed to be of a physician would seem false with a row of test tubes in the background. Careful cropping can sometimes turn an unsuitable photo into something believable by eliminating the inappropriate elements. Table 11.5 shows some good and bad examples of health care persona photos.

It's usually possible to find a reasonable set of persona photos using a stock photography service, though you might need to look in more than one place. (You won't always be able to get a perfect persona photo, though; the photo of Katie Bennett earlier in this chapter, for example, would ideally not show her face partly obscured by her camera.) Your team or marketing department may already have a stock collection licensed, so start there. Traditional stock services like Getty Images can

> The right persona photo can help make the difference between a cold, static profile and a seemingly real person.

Modeling

Table 11.5. **Good and bad persona photo examples.**

 This is not a sympathetic portrayal of a persona; it looks like someone you'd make fun of.

 This woman is more believable, but having trees in the background is strange; does she practice medicine in the park?

 It's better without the fisheye lens effect, but the exaggerated expression is still a bit much.

 Watch for elements that just don't make sense. There's no reason for doctors to wear masks while reviewing films.

 This image doesn't work because you can't see the persona's face.

 This one isn't bad. The background is more realistic. It would be better if she weren't so obviously posing for the camera.

 "I'm not a doctor, but I play one on TV." This woman is too beautiful, polished, and posed.

 This woman is in a realistic environment, her hair is a little mussed, and she's in the middle of a task instead of posing. The composition is a little distracting, but might be salvageable with cropping.

 This looks like someone's fantasy of a hospital, not the real thing.

 This is a good persona photo. The doctor's face is visible, she's in a realistic environment but without a lot of distractions in the background, she's attractive but not perfect, and she's engaged in a realistic task instead of smiling for the camera.

Modeling

be expensive to license image by image, generally ranging from about $50 to $300 for royalty-free images. Microstock sites such as iStockPhoto offer less-expensive licenses of anywhere from $1 to $10 or so. In either case, use is nonexclusive, so you might see your persona advertising a product on the side of a bus. If you plan to make use of your personas outside the product team, consider using rights-managed or commissioned photos for which you can get an exclusive license.

Avoid using photos of your interviewees. They're real people whose quirks you will remember, so they're not terribly effective as archetypes. Also, you would need to get a model release allowing you to publish any such photos outside your team.

If you're having difficulty finding the perfect photo, you might have to consider changing the gender, age, or ethnicity of your personas unless these characteristics are essential.

Illustrations are usually not the best way to represent your personas because they seem more abstract and less realistic; remember that the more real they are, the more they will engage the empathy of product team members. (Yes, people empathize with illustrated characters, such as Bambi or Buzz Lightyear, but only after they've seen at least a few minutes of anthropomorphized behavior.) Doing reasonable illustrations may also take more time than finding a handful of photos. However, there are two situations where you might consider illustrations. One is when you're designing a tool for a group of internal users who will all be exposed to the personas. Such people may accept the personas more readily if they are slightly abstracted. The other situation is when you anticipate drawing a lot of storyboards showing the personas moving around in a physical environment. In that case, it's easiest if the people reviewing the storyboards don't have to translate between the persona photos and the drawings. Figure 11.13 shows an example of a persona illustration.

Figure 11.13. An example persona illustration.

Depicting your personas as cartoon characters or dolls moves them even further from reality. One user experience team tried depicting their personas as custom-made action figures because they believed these would be more memorable. While people seemed able to remember the personas, probably due in part to alliterative names like Multitasking Millie, the team was not able to demonstrate whether the personas were effective at helping people think differently. In the long run, I suspect these representations will not have the desired effect, and that they will do more harm than good.

However you choose to depict your personas, try for a consistent style and dimensions across the images. If some photos are head shots and others are full body, or some are on white backgrounds while others are not, it can be distracting when you lay out the photos on a summary page or other materials. This is not as important as getting the right images, but is nice to consider if you can.

Narrative

A good
description is
mostly comprised
of narrative
because
storytelling is
what breathes
life into the
personas.

A good description is mostly comprised of narrative because storytelling is what breathes life into the personas. You can say that someone is busy and frequently interrupted, but this dry statement of fact doesn't have the same impact as saying that the sandwich her assistant brought her for lunch two hours ago is still sitting, uneaten, on her desk. The first invokes our intellect, while the second invokes our empathy. Think about the details you observed in user interviews that helped create your impressions of the interviewees, then use similar details to reinforce those impressions in the persona descriptions. A great persona description manages to pack tremendous meaning into nearly every sentence. Read the bullet-list persona description below and then compare it to the narrative version that follows.

Carla Ramirez

— 32

— Graphic designer

— San Francisco

— Last car: Honda Civic hatchback base model

— Computer: Mac

— Media influence: Metropolis

— Web site influence: Amazon

— Reasons to shop now: current car is paid off

CURRENT CAR: 2006 MINI COOPER

— Likes that it: gets good mileage, has cargo space, is easy to park in small spots

— Also considered: Ford Focus, VW Beetle

— Financed for: 2 years

— Started looking when: Saw car in movie

— Test drove after: 1 week

— Purchased after: 2 weeks

— Picked up after: 3 weeks

— Decision criteria: Finds reasons to rationalize emotional choice

— Desired features: sun roof, stereo upgrade, leather seats

— Purchased features: sun roof

— Research tools: MINI Web site, others recommended by boyfriend

MANUFACTURER WEB SITE USE

— Visits before purchase: 3

— Reasons: explore, reconfigure for lower cost, find dealer stock

— Time of day: lunch, evening

— Likes: attitude, initially playful experience

— Dislikes: slow loading, less fun the second time, no maintenance suggestions, no dealer inventory, not sure when car was arriving

— Visits after purchase: 1

— Reasons for visit after purchase: maintenance recommendations

GOALS

— Have reasons to get the car she wants

— Get it now

— Enjoy the buying experience

— Be taken care of after she buys

The bullet description is compact and makes for a nice reference, but it helps you understand Carla only on an intellectual level. This kind of thing is suitable for a slide presentation or persona cheat sheet because you can cover the storytelling aspect verbally. The narrative description that follows is much more effective for a document because it helps you get inside Carla's head.

Carla Ramirez

The last time 32-year-old Carla Ramirez decided it was time for a new car she bought one within two weeks. Not long after she paid off her first car—a base model Honda Civic hatchback—in 2006, she watched *The Italian Job* on DVD and fell in love with the MINI Cooper's spunky design. Driving around San Francisco the next week, she found herself looking longingly at every MINI she passed.

Taking a lunch break at the office after laying out the latest batch of ads, Carla decided to check out the MINI Web site instead of reading *Metropolis* as she usually did. The site's attitude encouraged her to keep looking; it felt like play rather than research. She began to find reasons that the car she was drawn to would be a rational choice, too. It was small enough to make city parking less painful, had enough space to fit several bags of groceries, and had good enough mileage that she wouldn't have to feel guilty about not getting a hybrid. As she assembled her dream car online, though, she realized that it might be a little much on a graphic designer's salary.

When she mentioned her disappointment to her boyfriend Todd that evening, he booted up her Mac and looked at several automotive sites, then suggested other cars with comparable features, including the Ford Focus and VW Beetle. Carla dutifully looked at the others, but found herself back on the MINI site before long.

A great persona description manages to pack tremendous meaning into nearly every sentence.

Modeling

Goals shouldn't be just tacked on at the end of the description; they should be implied throughout it, as well.

She tried another configuration without the sun roof, stereo upgrade, and leather seats. When she saw that the new total wasn't much more than the Ford, she decided to test drive the MINI that weekend. She saved the configuration for later to avoid going through the process again; what had seemed fun the first time was annoying the second.

A test drive convinced Carla she had to have the car (and the sun roof). Ready to buy, she was frustrated that the dealer didn't have many cars in stock. She went back to the Web site to see what other nearby dealers had. If Amazon could tell her what's in stock, surely a car dealer's Web site could do the same. Unfortunately, the dealer sites didn't have much information, so she called the one with the least annoying page. They told her they were getting a shipment in a few days, and that most dealers had very few cars in stock. Carla hung up, wondering whether she should take another look at the Beetle. Eventually she called back and gave them a credit card number to hold the red one with the sun roof. When the dealer finally called to say that her car was there, she waited to pick it up until Friday afternoon so she and Todd could celebrate with a drive down the coast.

A couple of months later, Carla wondered when to get her car serviced, so she logged on to the owner section of the site. She was disappointed to find that even when she entered all the information about her car, it did not recommend what service to have performed and when. She has not returned to the site since.

Much as she has enjoyed her MINI, it's been paid off for six months and Carla's eyes are starting to wander again.

CARLA'S GOALS

- **Have reasons to get the car she wants.** Even if her decision is about the style or emotional appeal of the car, Carla likes to see herself as a rational person.
- **Get it now.** When Carla is ready for a new car, she's going to act quickly.
- **Enjoy the buying experience.** Car shopping should be fun, not work; a new car is a treat.
- **Be taken care of after she buys.** Poor support regarding delivery or ownership issues can tarnish the experience.

The narrative description puts the actions in sequence and in context, portrays Carla's emotions at various points in the process, and uses other clues to reinforce aspects of her attitude and behavior. Every sentence and every detail has a purpose. Note that the description captures key points in the action, but not every tiny detail. It would take a lot of space to describe every click. It's also difficult for a persona to serve as an archetype if you get too specific. When possible, explain the reason for the behavior, especially if it differs from what you or the stakeholders might expect. Goals shouldn't be just tacked on at the end of the description; they should be implied throughout it, as well. Table 11.6 dissects the persona description in more detail.

Be unapologetic in your description; don't be afraid to say that Carla makes decisions based on emotional appeal rather than logical criteria. However, never use any language that implies a negative view of the persona; perhaps your car shopping process differs, but that doesn't make Carla flighty or silly. Describe each activity, frustration, and goal in terms the persona would use. A technology expert might say there was a problem with the Web browser's cache, while a novice would say the Web page was very slow to load when she used the back button.

Table 11.6. **Analysis of a persona description.**

What it says	Why this is useful
The last time 32-year-old Carla Ramirez decided it was time for a new car, she bought one within two weeks.	The first sentence sets the stage for what to expect from this persona: She bought a car because she felt like it, and she moved fast.
Not long after she paid off her first car—a base model Honda Civic hatchback—in 2006, she watched *The Italian Job* on DVD and fell in love with the MINI Cooper's spunky design.	Implies that she feels the need for a new car almost as soon as she can afford it. Anyone familiar with cars knows that a Civic is a common first car, so she's ready to move up to something less generic. She responded to the emotional appeal of the car, and it was opportunistic; another car could have grabbed her attention.
Driving around San Francisco the next week, she found herself looking longingly at every MINI she passed.	Tells you she didn't look long before acting, and an immediate, emotional bond has formed.
Taking a lunch break at the office after laying out the latest batch of ads, Carla decided to check out the MINI Web site instead of reading *Metropolis* as she usually did.	Tells you that she browses opportunistically, not in some long-planned research session, and that she responds to good, modern design.
The site's attitude encouraged her to keep looking; it felt like play rather than research.	Reinforces her response to emotional appeal.
She began to find reasons that the car she was drawn to would be a rational choice, too.	Tells you what function the Web site served for her.
It was small enough to make city parking less painful, had enough space to fit several bags of groceries, and had good enough mileage that she wouldn't have to feel guilty about not getting a hybrid.	Tells you what features appealed to her and why.

Continued

What it says	Why this is useful
As she assembled her dream car online, though, she realized that it might be a little much on a graphic designer's salary.	Implies that she had a level of commitment to the product before she saw the price tag, and that cost is a concern but was not her first thought.
When she mentioned her disappointment to Todd that evening, he booted up her Mac and looked at several automotive sites, then suggested other cars with comparable features, including the Ford Focus and VW Beetle.	Describes how someone else influenced her search and what other brands seemed comparable.
Carla dutifully looked at the others, but found herself back on the MINI site before long.	For all their logical value, the others lacked the same emotional appeal.
She tried another configuration without the sun roof, stereo upgrade, and leather seats. When she saw that the new total wasn't much more than the Ford, she decided to test drive the MINI that weekend.	Tells you what features appealed to her, what she was willing to get rid of, and how she was able to rationalize the cost.
She saved the configuration for later to avoid going through the process again; what had seemed fun the first time was annoying the second.	Indicates frustration with the experience over time.
A test drive convinced Carla she had to have the car (and the sun roof).	Reinforces the emotional nature of her decision-making.
Ready to buy, she was frustrated that the dealer didn't have many cars in stock. She went back to the Web site to see what other nearby dealers had.	Another roadblock provides another opportunity for the Web site to help.
If Amazon could tell her what's in stock, surely a car dealer's Web site could do the same.	E-commerce sites have set her expectations for the information that should be available...
Unfortunately, the dealer sites didn't have much information, so she called the one with the least annoying page.	...and the site failed to meet those expectations.
They told her they were getting a shipment in a few days, and that most dealers had very few cars in stock. Carla hung up, wondering whether she should take another look at the Beetle.	Another roadblock tests her resolve. This is not strictly a design issue, but is the kind of service issue you should still be pointing out.

What it says	Why this is useful
Eventually she called back and gave them a credit card number to hold the red one with the sun roof.	The emotional attachment to the product overcomes it. The transaction takes place entirely outside the Web site.
When the dealer finally called to say that her car was here, she waited to pick it up until Friday afternoon so she and Todd could celebrate with a drive down the coast.	Picking up a new car is a special event, and the Web site doesn't take part in that event right now.
A couple of months later, Carla wondered when to get her car serviced, so she logged on to the owner section of the site.	It took a while before she thought to check the site again.
She was disappointed to find that even when she entered all the information about her car, it did not recommend what service to have performed and when. She has not returned to the site since.	She put in effort in anticipation of a certain value in return. Failure to meet that expectation effectively ends her relationship with the Web site...
Much as she has enjoyed her MINI, it's been paid off for six months and Carla's eyes are starting to wander again.	...and the brand has failed to win her loyalty.
Have reasons to get the car she wants. Even if her decision is about the style or emotional appeal of the car, Carla likes to see herself as a rational person.	Reinforces the need for rationalizing the emotional decision.
Get it now. When Carla is ready for a new car, she's going to act quickly.	Reinforces the impatience.
Enjoy the buying experience. Car shopping should be fun, not work; a new car is a treat.	Reinforces the desire for specialness and fun.
Be taken care of after she buys. Poor support regarding delivery or ownership issues can tarnish the experience.	Reinforces how to win her loyalty.

It's essential to keep your persona descriptions firmly grounded in the present. You need to get agreement that the personas are good representations of your users, and that they're the people you should target. Introducing interpretation of what the personas need from the product only weakens the persona's perceived basis in data (rather than opinion) and may introduce controversy. Save any projection into the future for your scenarios.

Quotes, collages, and diagrams can enrich your persona descriptions and make them more memorable.

Here's an example of what *not* to do:

> When she mentioned her disappointment to Todd that evening, he booted up her Mac and looked at several automotive sites, then suggested other cars with comparable features, including the Ford Focus and VW Beetle. Carla would have appreciated having comparisons on the MINI site. She dutifully looked at the others, but found herself back on the MINI site before long. Carla tried another configuration without the sun roof, stereo upgrade, and leather seats. She would like a more flexible way to try turning different combinations of options on and off. When she saw that the new total wasn't much more than the Ford, Carla decided to test drive the MINI that weekend. She saved the configuration for later to avoid going through the process again; it would be nice if the site just did this for her using a cookie.

You can also add other touches to make your personas more memorable. One common addition is a quote that embodies each persona's top frustration, goal, or view of the world. For example, a persona challenged by money management might have a quote under his photo that says, "My whole paycheck seems to be spent before I get it." Another persona who's great at saving money might say, "Credit cards are for convenience, not for credit."

Adding a collage of photos depicting each persona's environment and activities can also enrich a description (see Figure 11.14). These hint at the types of visual and industrial design language that resonate with the persona; someone whose environment consists of pale pink walls and wicker furniture clearly values a different aesthetic from someone whose house is filled with modern art and Eames plywood chairs.

Diagrams

Though not necessary for many personas, visual representation of particular persona characteristics, such as workflow, data needs, or physical environment, can also further everyone's understanding of the behavior patterns and the differences among them. See the examples in Figures 11.15 and 11.16.

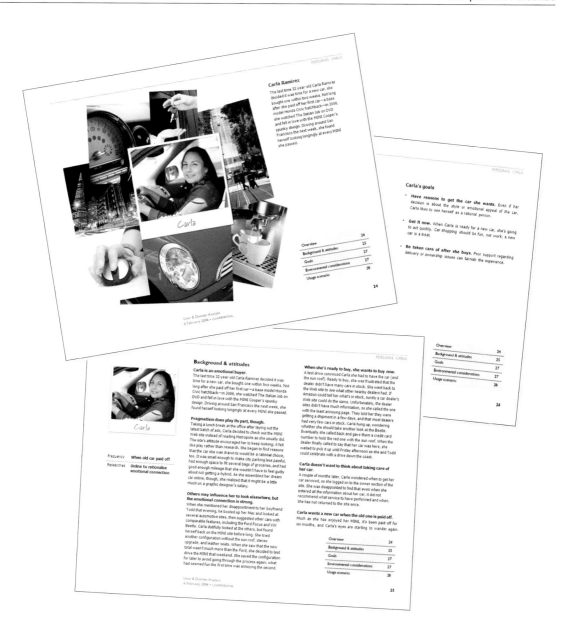

Figure 11.14. This persona description is enriched with a photo collage depicting her usage environment and activities.

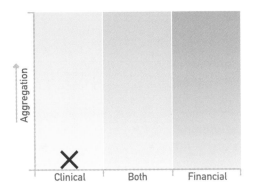

Figure 11.15. This very simple diagram shows what type of data a persona in a health care facility needs.

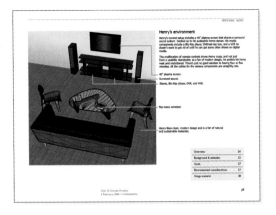

Figure 11.16. This illustration shows the persona's home, which provides context for how a product will fit in.

Exercise

Write a description for one or more of your LocalGuide or Roomfinder personas.

HELPING PEOPLE UNDERSTAND THE PERSONAS AS A SET

In addition to helping everyone understand the personas as individuals, you should develop ways to communicate about them as a **set** that represents a range of behaviors and needs. The first artifact to consider is some kind of persona summary document that serves as a quick reference. The design team may know the personas so well that they don't need such references, but other project team members find them helpful. The simplest version of this is a persona summary table laid out on a single sheet (or two, if you have a large persona set). Each column represents one persona and typically contains the persona's name, photo, goals, and a few key points (generally the ones that distinguish each persona from the others). It's helpful to group large persona sets by role, with each primary persona visually emphasized. More elaborate versions of this idea could include tri-fold brochures, table tents, or rings full of persona "trading cards," but simplest is usually best. Figures 11.17 and 11.18 offer some quick-reference examples.

Figure 11.17. Several examples of persona quick-reference-material formats.

West Valley Veterinary Hospital				Springfield Small Animal Clinic	
Clinical		Administrative		Clinical	Administrative
Maureen Keller DVM	**Amanda Lee** Vet Tech	**Tina Lopez** Office Manager	**Carol Martin** Receptionist	**Pete Harvey** DVM	**Laura Brown** Office Manager and Receptionist

Co-founded clinic. Prides herself on having specialists and the latest equipment. Sees 10-20 patients a day. Thinks 10 minutes of charting is too much. Missing chart info is a pet peeve.	At WVVH for 3 years. Preps pets for vets. Takes care of up to 25 hospitalized pets a day. Has difficulty tracking what treatments and measurements to do when. Sees herself as a nurse for animals.	8 years at WVVH. Has to satisfy 4 vets who own clinic (and 8 who think they do). Knows everything. Has accounting and purchasing under control. Current focus is maximizing appointment efficiency.	2 months at WVVH. Mostly makes appointments and collects payments. Feels out of her depth when callers ask for advice. Still learning her way around. Wants to feel like a healthcare pro, not an admin.	Bought the practice 4 years ago. Hasn't entirely mastered running a business, is grateful for Laura. Not comfortable with picking the right computer system. Has little patience for charting.	Joined SSAC shortly after Pete bought it and has become his right arm. Does everything from taking calls to purchasing and basic bookkeeping. Likes that every day is an adventure, but could sometimes use less excitement.
Maureen's goals · Focus on care, not record keeping · Know she has the right information · Minimize adminis-trative time · Feel like she has a world-class clinic	**Amanda's goals** · Provide the best care · Know she's doing the right thing at the right time · Avoid mistakes	**Tina's goals** · Keep the vets happy · Maximize billing per hour · Keep track of all the details	**Carol's goals** · Keep clients happy · Keep her cool · Avoid mistakes · Feel professional	**Pete's goals** · Minimize adminis-trative time · Have instant access to information · Know the practice is running smoothly · Have confidence in his tools	**Laura's goals** · Stay calm · Keep clients and clinical staff happy · Keep track of all the details

Figure 11.18. A good example of an easy quick-reference sheet.

When a room full of experts in an industry can review the work you've done and think it makes sense, that's a pretty good sign that you're on the right track.

A quick reference is always a good idea, but may not be enough to help people grasp the relationships among the personas. It may be necessary to include diagrams that illustrate the relationships and differences among your personas, or between your personas and market segments. See Figures 11.19 and 11.20 for examples.

Validating your personas

One question I sometimes get from designers is, "How do you know your personas are right?" It's reasonable to be anxious that your persona set will somehow miss the mark and cause a product disaster; this is why you should take a rigorous approach to crafting your personas. If you follow the process outlined here, chances are good that your personas will be true to your data, so the better thing to worry about is, "How do I know I got the right kinds of people in my research sample?" The short answer is: by getting as much background and stakeholder participation in interview planning as you can, and by keeping your eyes open during the research for things you didn't expect. (For the long answer, read Chapters 6 and 7.) No amount of rigor in persona creation can make up for an overly narrow research plan.

The most common form of validation is a simple gut check. When a room full of experts in an industry can review the work you've done and think it makes sense, that's a pretty good sign that you're on the right track. If the outspoken skeptic in the room agrees, that's even better. This level of validation is usually good enough for most stakeholders, including top executives at the biggest companies. Perhaps this is because most business people know that sometimes you have to make decisions with the best data available, and the results of qualitative research usually provide better, more actionable data than they've ever had. People who balk at the accuracy of the data are often balking about something else entirely, such as a failure to include them in the process, or evidence that an idea they've championed may be wrong.

There are a few authors, including Steve Mulder and Ziv Yaar,[6] who argue that you can't be certain you have good personas unless you validate them with quantitative data. This point of view represents a fundamental misunderstanding about personas: A survey cannot tell you whether your personas are effective design tools. It can only tell you whether your personas are good market segments, which is not what personas are intended to be. That said, if you're designing

---

6. Mulder, S. and Yaar, Z. *The user is always right: A practical guide to creating and using personas for the web.* New Riders, 2007.

Figure 11.19. This diagram illustrates how the personas cover the full range of needs in the market.

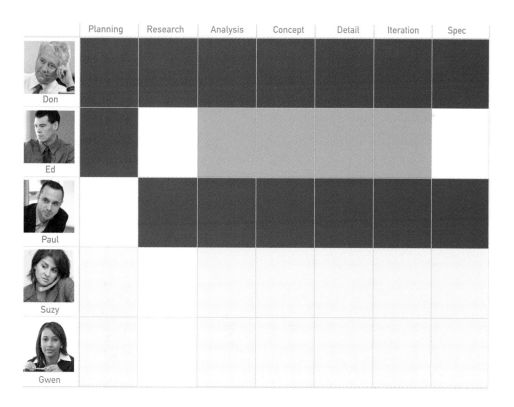

Figure 11.20. A chart showing what parts of a business process the various personas cover.

an e-commerce site, there is value in knowing whether a particular persona is insignificant from a revenue standpoint; if so, why build an expensive tool just for that persona? Don't hesitate to draw on any quantitative sources you may have, but don't obsess over quantifying your personas; mathematical cluster analysis is as reliant on human interpretation and explanation as any qualitative analysis.

The only real validation of your personas is the success of your design, as measured by usability tests and, more importantly, by success in the market. By that measure, any persona that helps you get a better product to market in a more efficient way is a good persona.

When Time Is Limited: Provisional Personas

This whole process works well when you have a data set from which to extract patterns, but designers are all too often asked to create or improve something with no time or budget to gather data. This doesn't mean you have to give up on personas altogether; it just means you'll have to create cruder versions of them.

Gather some knowledgeable stakeholders (and especially subject matter experts) in a room for an afternoon. Ask for their hypotheses about how users differ, using much the same questions you would ask in user interviews. To the extent you can, get stakeholders to tell you specific stories about any processes, frustrations, and so forth. As agreement emerges, develop a list of characteristics and goals for each presumed type of user. These lists serve as **provisional personas**; see Figure 11.21 for an example.

Katie

— Hobbyist photographer with a prosumer camera she hasn't fully mastered (especially exposure)

— 100-300 landscape and macro shots per outing

Goals

— Be able to capture what she "sees"

— Enjoy the scenery

— Feel like a "real" photographer

Figure 11.21. An example of a provisional persona description.

Clearly, provisional personas comprised of stakeholder knowledge and assumptions can't give you the kind of solid foundation for design that real personas do, but they still provide two important benefits. First, a provisional persona still gives you a target, even if it's a little off; you'll never hit anything useful if you don't aim at *something*. Second, the process of developing the provisional personas helps build consensus; by getting the stakeholders together to talk about user characteristics and goals, you're probably encouraging discussion that hasn't happened yet. Even if two stakeholders disagree, they can at least agree to make a reasonable assumption and let the process move forward.

Naturally, you don't want people to confuse provisional personas with the real thing. It helps if your communication about provisional personas is much lower fidelity. Use an empty oval or a quick sketch instead of a photo, use only a first name, and limit the description to a list of points without the detailed narrative. The distinction is helpful when you introduce real personas later, or when you have to use both real and provisional personas on the same project; see Figure 11.22.

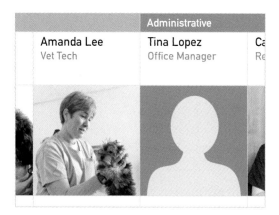

	Administrative	
Amanda Lee	**Tina Lopez**	C
Vet Tech	Office Manager	Re

Figure 11.22 The visual distinction between data-backed personas and the provisional one clearly indicates the lower level of certainty.

Exercise

Develop a set of provisional personas for a product and service that compete with iTunes and the iPod product line.

Persona Pitfalls

Like any other tool, personas are subject to misuse. Sloppy or biased personas can be abysmal failures that sour every project participant on the very idea of user archetypes. Some people use this as a criticism of the method, but this is like saying no one should use desktop publishing just because some people do horrible things with page layout tools. Any professional has to take responsibility for mastering any tool he uses.

You should be able to avoid the most common mistakes in persona creation if you follow the methods described here, but there are still a few things you can do that would endanger the acceptance of personas on your project.

One common mistake is to introduce requirements or wish list items into the personas. Remember that personas represent current behavior, frustrations, and goals, regardless of whether your product ships in ten days or ten years. It's essential that people accept the personas as accurate user and customer representations *before* you start debating features and functions.

Getting carried away with biographical detail is another typical error. Including a lot of clearly fictitious detail about irrelevant topics will make it hard for people to accept the persona, and it can ruin your credibility. Focus on the behaviors and goals derived from your data.

The third problem is a disturbing trend in the industry to treat personas as either panaceas or as ends in themselves. People approach me at conferences and tell me they know everything will be great now because they finally have personas at their companies. I congratulate them on their progress, but remind them that scenarios, design skills, and various issues beyond the control of the design team are still essential to success. Personas are expected to solve every problem, so people are inevitably disappointed in them when they fail to do so.

Some practitioners also invest unreasonable amounts of effort in their personas. I know of at least one company that created a department just to manage their ever-expanding persona collection. One Web consultancy even went so far as to create actual living rooms that are decorated according to each persona's tastes and constantly updated with whatever magazines the personas are "reading" this week.[7] No doubt the novelty of the rooms generated some attention and excitement, which is always a good thing. In the long run, though, this kind of three-dimensional mood

Modeling

7. Manning, H. "*Persona rooms: What, why, and how.*" April 5, 2006. http://www.forrester.com/Research/Document/Excerpt/0,7211,39260,00.html.

board seems like a poor investment for designing a Web site; at San Francisco rents, that's about $20,000 a year just for space, not to mention the furnishings and effort to keep them up. Cost aside, portable artifacts are more effective because you can share them with distributed teams who can't hang out for a beer on the persona's couch.

This trend toward gold-plated hammers is a problem for a couple of reasons. First, it eats up resources that would be better applied to research or design. Second, this trend indicates that people are thinking of personas as the whole point, and not as convenient tools we create in service of design. Even Alan Cooper, who originated the persona concept, calls personas "the bright lights under which we do surgery." In other words, they help us see more clearly, but they're no replacement for a sharp scalpel and a skilled surgeon; no patient was ever healed by sitting under the lights in the operating room.

By all means, get excited about your personas and market them internally to get others excited, too. Print mouse pads or posters, play persona trivia, send people e-mail from your personas… whatever works. Before expending a lot of effort and money on a novel communication method, though, ask yourself what that method will accomplish that text, photos, and illustrations won't, and whether the gain is really worth it. Also ask yourself whether that method will obscure the behaviors and goals, which are the most important aspects of your personas.

Project Management for Creating Personas

Involved as the persona creation process sounds, it generally happens in anywhere from a day to a week, depending on the number of roles and amount of data you have. The initial mapping and pattern extraction seldom take more

than a couple of days; developing the descriptions and any other communication tools takes another two or three.

If you were to observe a design team meeting at this stage, it would be hard to distinguish between the two interaction design specialties (the generator and synthesizer). These two roles generally drive the persona creation process largely because they're usually the only ones who attended every user interview. The visual designer, industrial designer, and team lead may or may not be in the room for most of these discussions, depending on their level of participation in the interviews. At a minimum, all team members should have a chance to review and suggest improvements to the personas before they're shared with anyone outside the design team.

The team lead should review how the designers arrived at their conclusions, and should look for any missed or questionable patterns or personas that are not very distinct from one another. She should also help the team consider how stakeholders will receive the personas, ensure that the details are credible, and offer suggestions for improvement on any details such as names and goals.

Both visual and industrial designers tend to have a strong interest in the goals, especially any experience goals, and any details about how the personas relate to various aesthetics or brands. They're also good at making sure the persona descriptions include any important ergonomic issues, such as poor eyesight, arthritis, or unusual lighting. Both may also identify the same kinds of opportunities for improvement that the team lead does. Visual designers can often come up with elegant solutions for depicting the relationships among the personas, as well.

Once you have rough outlines of your personas, run them by your project owner in an informal meeting before spending time on the detailed descriptions. The project owner can usually provide a useful validity check and may anticipate stakeholder concerns you haven't considered. Even if the project owner doesn't identify any issues, he will be better prepared to back you up in a meeting with the larger group of stakeholders. If for some reason your project owner feels the persona set is off, you'll need to have a discussion about whether this is a flaw in your research set, or whether the project owner's concern is based on assumptions that simply aren't borne out in the data.

The IxD synthesizer usually takes the lead on writing persona descriptions, but unless the IxD generator is spending a lot of time on visualizations, it's probably a good idea for her to pitch in. A visual designer is often responsible for identifying potential persona photos and any collage photos, which are reviewed by the whole team. He generally puts together any visualization of persona relationships, environments, and tasks, as well, though this is usually in close collaboration with the interaction designers.

Summary

Done well, personas are incredibly useful tools for product definition and design. There are many ways to encapsulate the key findings from your user research, but only personas effectively engage the parts of your brain that think in human terms. That unique way of thinking results in better decisions and faster consensus than most product teams would otherwise achieve.

The key to doing personas well is to focus on finding and expressing the behavioral patterns in your data, and then expressing those patterns in ways that are clear, memorable, and likely to invoke empathy. It will probably take you several persona sets before you're getting the most out of the technique.

Important as personas and their goals are, remember that they're just one of many tools you need to be an effective designer. Put in the time and energy to do them well, but don't confuse the means with the ends.

Modeling

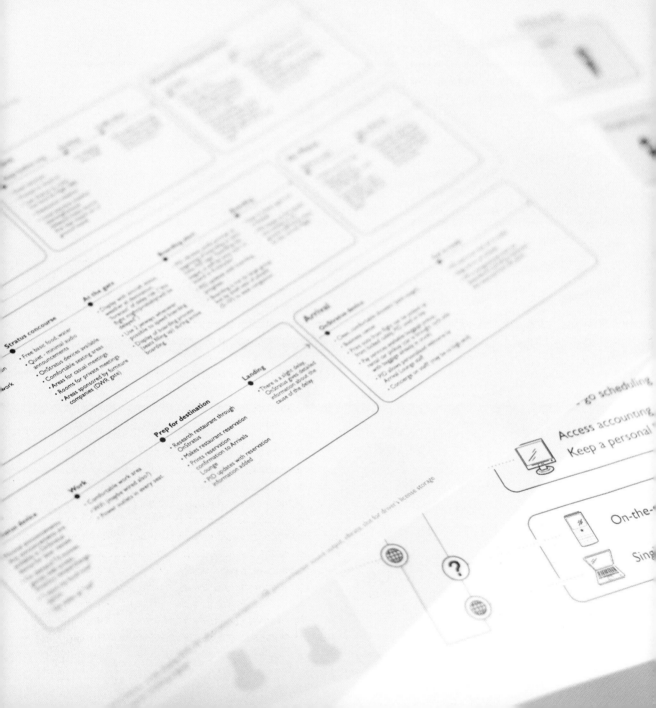

CHAPTER 12

Defining Requirements

Once you have analyzed your data and represented your findings as models, you have finished the necessary description of the world as it is today. The next step is to begin thinking about the future: what the product or service must do in order to succeed. In the language of product development, these needs are expressed as **requirements.** Using this term tells all project participants that you're talking about product definition and not just hardware styling or the arrangement of widgets on the screen. Unfortunately, this little word carries a great deal of baggage with it.

The Problems with Requirements

Most requirements processes are fraught with problems. Marketers or product managers spend prodigious amounts of time developing requirements and are disappointed when a stellar product does not result. This is partly due to how requirements are generated, how they're communicated, and a problematic view of their role in the process.

Requirements cannot be "gathered"

Ask the average engineer how the marketing team develops requirements, and he'll probably say (only half facetiously) that the product managers lock themselves in a room with a bunch of competitive products and a lot of beer. Believe it or not, I have seen companies where this was the case, though most take requirements far more seriously. Even in the most structured process, many requirements are based on executive opinion, engineering technology preferences, or customers' stated desires, all of which can be red herrings.

Ask the average product manager, and he'll tell you requirements are gathered from a variety of sources, ranging from customer requests to competitor reviews, regulatory agencies, and executive intuition. It sounds as if each of these sources provides requirements as ripe fruit that can be plucked from the tree and eaten. Of course, most product managers don't transcribe every competitor feature and customer request directly into the requirements list. In the absence of good tools for evaluating possible requirements, though, what goes in and what doesn't tends to be a

Design research and personas can help generate, filter, and prioritize requirements.

matter of opinion, which can result in endless wrangling or bad political compromises. At best, it can mean that the requirements process takes far longer than it should; in the time that most companies take to complete requirements, a skilled design team could have developed a blueprint and gotten the engineers started.

This is where you come in. Although most product managers assume that the design team's job is to provide the visual or physical *expression* of the requirements, your design research and personas can help them generate, filter, and prioritize requirements. In other words, design methods are excellent tools not just for design, but also for product definition. Many product managers are delighted to have such effective help, though some view designer involvement in requirements as an encroachment on their territory. Initial reactions may range from polite disbelief to outright hostility. I've found that referring to *"design requirements"* or even "user needs" tends to defuse the problem, even when the design team discusses issues that are well beyond what most people view as design.

Requirements are not features

All too often, requirements conflate needs with solutions. The one I hear most often is, "It has to be Web based." This is a solution, not a need. When I ask what making it Web based will accomplish, the answer is usually something like, "IT managers won't have to install the software on every machine." Ah, now *that's* a need: avoid the time and effort involved in installing individual clients on each desktop. There are multiple ways to accomplish this, though; putting the software in a browser is only one of them.

Jumping to the "obvious" solution too early is a common mistake that can eliminate great opportunities. Sure, it's obvious to let people share digital photos by e-mailing them to friends, but doing the same thing via a Web-based service has the potential to generate revenue through advertising, membership fees, or merchandise orders. By stating the need first, you give yourself and other members of the project team a chance to see such opportunities and come up with more innovative solutions. It's true that the best solutions for most needs are the obvious ones, but separating needs and solutions has yielded at least one big idea on almost every project I've seen.

Needs are so often combined with solutions because someone heard a customer request and didn't dig any deeper, because executives often communicate needs by suggesting solutions, or just because someone thinks being buzzword compliant will lead to success ("We need to be

Web 2.0!"). As in stakeholder and user interviews, your job is to get everyone focused on the needs behind these presumed requirements, rather than taking them at face value.

Requirements are not specifications

In most companies, the word "requirements" means a big list of capabilities generated by product managers and handed to the engineers as a marketing requirements document (MRD) or product requirements document (PRD). These hefty tomes may include everything from vague ideals ("should be visually appealing") to extremely specific detail ("the address screen must include a list box for selecting a state"). Many smart people put months of hard work into these documents, but in the end, most aren't worth the effort. I often take calls from companies asking for help because they've been working on requirements for a year or more, but can't seem to get a decent product prototype. These immense piles of text don't work well as consensus generators because they're hard for engineers (or anyone else) to decipher.

Both the people creating requirements and the people consuming them are hoping they'll help control the product development process. Product managers drive toward detail because the engineering process, especially with respect to software, can be a black box; product managers figure that if item 13.2.5.b says the product has to be easy to use, then they have a way to hold the engineers accountable for that. Engineers, on the other hand, are frustrated because the requirements are vague and difficult to satisfy, so they push for UML diagrams or other highly structured ways of communicating. Many software engineers throw up their hands and say it's impossible to understand the requirements until you start building the thing, so we should all just use agile methods to iterate until we get there.

Both parties are right, in a way. Product managers' inclination toward specificity is absolutely correct; they do need specific documents that provide both visibility into the process and accountability for the end result. However, handing a textual set of requirements to the engineers is like handing the actors and movie camera crew a few snippets of dialog and telling them you need a love scene, a chase scene, and a few things exploding; the end result isn't likely to win any awards, but is likely to cost far more and take far longer than it should.

The engineers who think a textual requirements document can never provide a complete or accurate picture of the eventual product are also correct; there's no way to have stakeholders agree on a complete and accurate list until they have something to look at. It's not necessary to build the product to figure this out, though; it's cheaper, faster, and more effective for designers to "build" the product in sketches. This is why filmmakers develop scripts and detailed storyboards long before the actors and crew arrive on the scene; things might evolve a little as they shoot the movie, but they know the only way to achieve their vision within a budget is to start with a clear idea of the camera angles and action they want to end up with.

Mind you, some software engineers don't want product managers drawing screens; they believe engineers can do a better job. They're often right. However, programmers who have worked with competent designers recognize that competence and are thrilled to have someone else worry about the product's form and behavior.

To improve the product development process, participants have to realize that requirements are the wrong tool for the job. It's a waste of effort to attempt to produce exhaustive, final requirements intended for direct engineering consumption. Instead, early requirements should be high-level needs that help project stakeholders make business decisions. These generally won't exceed a few document pages or a handful of presentation slides, and won't take more than a few days to develop. Additional requirements should then be developed iteratively through the design process and expressed in the final specifications. In other words, requirements definition isn't entirely finished until the design is finished.

Generating Effective Requirements

The trick to getting the right set of requirements is finding the best balance among competing factors. What will help make the initial sale? What will ensure long-term loyalty? What will be too much time or money to spend? Before you've started designing, you can only begin to answer these questions at a high level, but your design will be closer to the mark and your efforts more efficient if you can at least get consensus on key points.

Sources of requirements

To begin defining requirements, you will need to draw on multiple sources, as shown in Figure 12.1. Personas and the scenarios derived from them are your primary tools for generating requirements. Others include business objectives, customer goals, and external influences such as regulatory agencies, competitors, and influential media. Good design principles, such as those that promote accessibility or readability, are another source. Plain old brainstorming might also generate a few good ideas.

However, not every need and want implied by these various sources belongs in your list of requirements. Persona goals serve as both a lens to focus the potential requirements and a filter to remove problematic ones. If a potential requirement is contrary to your personas' goals, it usually shouldn't be a requirement. This helps resolve

opinion-based wrangling and arguments over pet features. Personas can also help you mitigate the problems with unavoidable requirements such as cumbersome regulations.

Types of requirements

Essential requirements include at least an approximation of what data the system must handle, what users must be able to do with that data, the qualities the product or service must possess, and any constraints on the solution.

DATA NEEDS

Any interactive product or service involves some exchange of information between human and system (or between human and human, mediated by a system). That information exchange could be short and simple, such as a human providing a business name or address for which a Web site delivers a map and directions. That exchange could also be complex and ongoing, such as when a financial analyst uses software to support business decisions. Even video games and music players involve data, such as how many lives your character has left or what song is playing. The bits of information a user needs to consume are called **data needs.**

Data needs are best described as a list of the data objects in each persona's mental model (see the section "Mental models" in Chapter 7), plus important attributes of those objects. Data objects are the *nouns* in your personas' mental models: the things they look for, read, or manipulate, such as e-mail messages, spreadsheets, or contacts. Attributes are either components or descriptors of each object. Attributes of an e-mail message, for example, include its subject, who sent it, when it was sent, who else was copied on it, and what action was taken in response. Those attributes may or may not be connected to other objects; a sender, for example,

Figure 12.1. Persona goals serve as a filter for requirements from a variety of sources.

may or may not exist as an independent object in the contact list.

It's important to identify your entire list of data objects early on because they can have a profound effect on the design; adding more objects later can cause your interface structure to break down. For example, iTunes worked nicely as a music library, but some of its data structures and interface conventions didn't work as well once video was added to the application. Using iTunes to manage the photos and contacts on a mobile device is even more awkward, because

the application isn't set up to handle those; you have to open another program to see what photos are in each folder you want to synchronize with a device. The initial design should account for data objects you plan to add later, even if they're not going to be available in a near-term release.

A comprehensive list of attributes is less important at this stage. Be as thorough as you can, but don't worry if you're missing some detail; there's plenty of time to catch that when you start doing detailed design.

FUNCTIONAL NEEDS

If data objects are the nouns in a user's mind, then **functional needs** are the *verbs* that describe what users should be able to do with or to those objects. With an e-mail message, for example, your persona probably needs to be able to read it, delete it, keep it with other messages that are related in some way, respond to it, or share it with someone else. She probably doesn't need to know how many characters it contains or what servers it passed through to get from there to here. Functional needs also include actions users must be able to take on the "object" that is a physical product: Users need to be able to charge it, carry it, clean it, and so forth.

It can be tempting to describe functional needs in terms of technology solutions, such as "print photos" instead of "get hard copies of photos." Sending the files to a connected printer may seem like the obvious solution, but you could also offer the ability to order prints through an online service. Each possible solution involves significant implications for both design and business; some solutions cost too much, while others create new revenue opportunities. The idea is to surface these possibilities to stakeholders so the business decisions are in their hands.

As with attributes of data objects, it's best to get as thorough a list of functional needs as you can, but don't worry if you're missing some. You'll generate additional functional needs through the design process.

PRODUCT OR SERVICE QUALITIES

Data and functional needs can't describe everything important about a product or service. It's usually important to ensure that the product has certain attributes related to brand, persona skills, environments, or other considerations. Some people refer to these as design requirements, but since the design team is discussing

requirements in a broader sense, this term could be confusing, so let's call them **product qualities**. Some of these are pragmatic, quantifiable requirements, such as the sort of abuse a device has to withstand or how quickly the system should process a file. Others are emotional qualities, such as what brand messages the product should reinforce and what emotions it should invoke; these **experience attributes** will drive the initial visual language explorations for both visual design and hardware.

CONSTRAINTS

There are always **constraints** in design. These may include the time at which the product must ship, the cost of development and manufacturing, or regulations with which a system must comply. The important thing at this point is to capture all of the presumed constraints for discussion so you can determine which ones are firm and which may be flexible. Timeframes and cost constraints can often shift a bit if the design is compelling enough. Regulations may be unavoidable, but people might be making assumptions about the way in which a regulation must be satisfied.

The process for generating requirements

Developing requirements involves two fundamental activities. One is analytical: looking at the requirements directly implied by various sources, then filtering them through persona goals. The other is generative: creating scenarios that describe idealized product or service use, then drawing requirements from those. Figure 12.2 outlines the overall process.

Some people like to track requirements and their sources in a table. This isn't usually necessary unless you are required by law to trace every requirement to its source (such as for a medical device) or your organization is inclined toward

Requirements

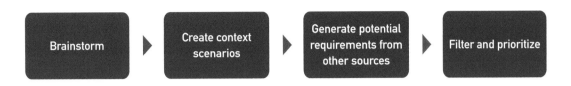

Figure 12.2. An overview of requirements definition.

doing so. However, you may find that it helps you be thorough, since it serves as a reminder of all the tools you should be using to develop requirements. This doesn't mean you'll fill in something for every cell, however. You might also find that some requirements fit more than one cell. Table 12.1 is a sampling of what you might have in a table of requirements from all sources; note that there would be more content in a complete table for a real product.

Table 12.1. **Example requirements matrix.**

Source	Data needs	Functional needs	Product qualities	Constraints
Katie (primary)				
Scenario #1	— Shots remaining — Battery sufficient for how many shots — Recommended and actual exposure settings — Photos and settings at which they were taken	— Select auto focus area with fair precision (probably at least 9 zones, preferably more) — Auto exposure settings — Ability to bracket and adjust exposure — Ability to review photos and settings in camera — Ability to delete photos in-camera		
Scenario #2	— Number of photos on the card — How long they will take to load	— Some kind of automatic backup — Ability to connect to PC		

Continued

Requirements

Source	Data needs	Functional needs	Product qualities	Constraints
Mental model		— Understand the effect the setting will achieve		
Goals		— Easier, more effective ways to teach her about exposure — Auto modes for dealing with sharp contrast	— Easier, more effective ways to teach her about exposure — "Professional" camera look and feel ("crisp" shutter, "solid" body)	
Environment			— Screen visible in bright sunlight — Tolerant of dampness, temperatures from below freezing to inside a car on a hot day	
Skills and abilities		— Easier, more effective ways to teach her about exposure — Auto modes for dealing with sharp contrast	— Fit comfortably in average woman's hand	— Fit comfortably in average woman's hand
Jorge (secondary)				
Scenario #3		— Ability to stabilize image for handheld use — Fast auto focus within a focal length range		
Mental model				

Requirements

Source	Data needs	Functional needs	Product qualities	Constraints
Goals		— Quickly access his own shooting modes with custom settings	— Lightweight body	
Environment			— Able to repel dust from sensor	
Skills		— Total control of shutter, aperture, ISO, white balance		

Marina (camera dealer, a customer persona)

Goals			— Clear differentiation from models above and below it in product line	— Small packaging

Stakeholder interviews

Jim		— Must provide easy transition for users upgrading to/from other products in same line	— Appeal as primary camera for novice SLR users, cheap second camera for more advanced users	— Price point between $400 and $600

Competitors

Acme Camera		— At least 6 megapixels		

Influencers

Analyst A		— Full frame sensor		

Regulations

FCC

Brainstorming

Brainstorming—gathering a group of people in a room and generating a bunch of possibilities—is a popular way to begin defining requirements. Because an effective brainstorming session encourages creative thinking, it can result in some great ideas. However, many of the ideas that come up in brainstorming are built on faulty assumptions, personal biases, and other flimsy foundations; getting these written down early makes it easier to set them aside and clear your mind for a more data-driven approach.

This is the one exercise in the requirements process that doesn't rely on research data. This makes it a good way to involve the larger product team in ideation. You can even order pizza and make an event out of it. Just be aware that if someone's favorite idea doesn't wind up in the product, you may need to explain why.

An effective brainstorming session gets a little crazy. It should be a safe place for people to have silly ideas because sometimes those silly ideas lead to fantastic ideas. Whatever you do, don't start critiquing ideas; nothing will squash creativity sooner. Don't worry about whether what's proposed is a requirement or a solution, whether it's feasible, or whether it makes any sense at all for the personas. Encourage shy people to chime in even if they need to preface their ideas with disclaimers.

Make sure someone with decent facilitation skills is at the whiteboard capturing ideas. With a big group, you may want to split facilitation and capturing duties so one person doesn't get overwhelmed and miss anyone's contribution. You'll know the brainstorming meeting is winding down when people start repeating ideas, running out of ideas, or suggesting things that are just plain dumb. The session should take an hour or two at most.

When you're done, you'll be able to see that some of the thoughts on the list are just too far out there. Others might be interesting; set these aside to consider later in the process (see Chapter 16).

Scenarios

A **scenario** is a plausible description of the future based on a coherent set of assumptions. Scenarios of one kind or another have long been used in many fields, such as military tactics or urban planning. In these arenas, a scenario is some combination of circumstances that *might* happen; by imagining a range of possible scenarios, leaders can ensure that they are prepared for any eventuality. Scenarios are among the most powerful tools in product and service design, with uses ranging from developing requirements to ensuring that a design accounts for the full range of possible interactions.

A Goal-Directed scenario is a textual description of a persona's interaction with the future product or service. Each scenario begins with a specific situation, then describes the interaction between persona and system from the beginning of a task or session through its completion. A scenario describes the actions of the persona and any system behaviors or actions evident to that persona, but does not describe any system behavior that's invisible. Along the way, a good scenario explains the persona's motivations for particular behavior and indicates what persona goals the system's behavior achieves. In this way, scenarios are essential to realizing the value of personas; personas without scenarios would be like characters with no plot.

The early scenarios used in requirements definition, called **context scenarios**[1], are high level and optimistic, focusing on ideal system behavior in

---

1. Although used somewhat differently in Goal-Directed Design, the term is borrowed from John Carroll (*Scenario-based design: Envisioning work and technology in system development*; John Wiley, 1995).

situations that *will* happen. Context scenarios do not include specific solutions. Later in the design process, increasingly detailed scenarios account for each constraint and for less common situations that *might* happen. These other scenarios—called key path, validation, and communication scenarios—are covered in later chapters.

Why use scenarios?

Context scenarios are the first activity in which you'll begin to imagine what the product or service could be like. If you're like most people, you learned to put away your imagination as you grew up, so these days you probably see an empty cardboard box as a recycling chore. A child, on the other hand, can see that box as a castle, a spaceship, or a bus. A favorite teddy bear might be anything from a hospital patient to a superhero. Each idea is inevitably accompanied by a story. By making use of these childhood tendencies, storytelling can help us imagination-impaired grown-ups remember how to see the possibilities in any situation. Like personas, scenarios can also help you evaluate whether your proposed solutions make sense.

Some people object to scenarios on the basis that they are invented. In truth, scenarios are more extrapolation than invention; they rely on our human understanding of a particular sort of person. You know a persona would behave in a particular way because you know what makes him tick. It's just like buying a gift for someone; the better you know that person, the more likely you are to find something they'll love. It may not be science, but it works all the same.

The third important virtue of scenarios is that they involve a *sequence* of events. Many talented but inexperienced interaction designers are inclined to draw screens and controls based on conceptual relationships rather than flow. Interactive products change state over time, though, so a sense of what comes first and what comes next is as essential here as it is to filmmaking.

Finally, scenarios provide a concrete way to think about human behavior and needs and their implications for system behavior. It's possible to argue forever about abstract concepts, but getting to specific examples can cut the argument short. When someone says, "The mobile phone should accept input from the television remote control," you can respond by asking, "Can you describe a scenario in which that would be useful to one of our personas?"

How Goal-Directed scenarios differ from similar tools

Scenarios and their close cousins, use cases, have seen increasingly widespread use in the last couple of decades. This is a good thing, since thinking about human behavior in sequence facilitates clear thinking about product behavior. Unfortunately, it also means that people are using similar terminology to mean slightly different things, so it's important to clarify how Goal-Directed scenarios differ from similar tools.

The term "scenario" is used in a variety of ways. Some people describe existing workflows as scenarios. There is disagreement about how detailed scenarios should be, whether they include system behavior that isn't visible to users, and how they should be documented. It's also a common misconception that scenarios, use cases, and user stories are interchangeable.

As originally defined by Ivar Jacobson and others, **use cases** describe the interaction between an "actor" and a system. An **actor** may be a person or another system, such as a bank database providing information to an automatic teller machine. Use cases are generally described in the form of diagrams, often using specific conventions such as those outlined in UML (Unified Modeling Language). "Goals" in use cases are typically at a lower level than persona goals; some may be end goals, but most are tasks. Use cases do not incorporate how users feel about the interaction or why a particular behavior is good. They also don't employ personas; even a human actor is likely to be defined as a role.

Agile programming methods such as Scrum advocate another tool called a **user story**. On the surface, this sounds similar to a scenario, but user stories are much more like requirements than scenarios. They're typically no more than a couple of sentences. For example, a user story titled "Login" might say, "When a user logs in, the application asks for a user name and password. It offers the option to remember both." User stories don't describe a user's entire flow from start to finish—a scenario, in contrast, would describe login as something that happens along the way to accomplishing an end goal. They don't use personas. Like use cases, they also don't focus on how users think and feel.

A SCENARIO DESCRIBES THE FUTURE, NOT THE PRESENT

Correctly or not, many people documenting how users interact with existing tools refer to such descriptions as workflows, scenarios, or use cases. For the sake of clarity, in the Goal-Directed lexicon, scenarios are always focused on use of the future product or system. Current behavior is described in the personas and other models.

A SCENARIO DESCRIBES A PERSONA'S POINT OF VIEW

A scenario represents the world as *users* will see it, deliberately excluding any behind-the-scenes work the system does. Describing the fact that the ATM checks with the central bank computer to determine how much cash a user can withdraw, for example, is problematic for a couple of reasons. First, it pulls the focus of the story away from visible behavior and into implementation, which is not within your purview as a designer. More important, it forces the people generating

and reading the scenario to think in system terms instead of human terms; as discussed in Chapter 11 with respect to personas, thinking in human terms engages a different part of our brains. The fact that the ATM has to talk to the bank is a requirement—an implication of the story—but not part of the story itself. Just as you want people to agree that the personas are correct before you introduce controversial topics like what the personas require, you want people to see the possibilities in the story before they worry about what it takes to make the story come true.

Emotions and motivations are also part of a persona's point of view. If you are describing a parent uploading precious baby photos from a digital camera, it's important to understand that person's anxiety about making sure the photos are copied before deleting them from the camera. Describing this sort of thing helps ensure that the design team is using persona goals and characteristics to drive the system's behavior, while also ensuring that people who read the scenario understand why certain system behavior is important.

A SCENARIO IS A STORY WITH A BEGINNING AND AN END

Since they're stories, scenarios are generally expressed in narrative form (though it's not necessary to document every tiny scenario used in the design process). Users don't think, "I'm going to use the print function now," so scenarios don't describe the product in those terms. Rather, they describe an entire session or typical task based on what the persona would see as the task's beginning and end; this could involve a single function or several dozen, and might cover a few minutes or an entire day. A scenario might even describe interrupted usage, such as a task that someone starts in the morning and has to pick up again after half-a-dozen interruptions.

Crafting effective context scenarios

Context scenarios are the most ambitious and least detailed scenarios in the design process. A context scenario begins with some kind of triggering event, such as the receipt of a purchase requisition, the need to upload images because a camera's memory card is full, or the need to withdraw cash for the bus. From there, it describes the sequence of information exchange between persona and system, decisions made or actions taken by the persona, and the results the persona sees. Here's an example of a context scenario for a mobile smart phone and personal organizer:

> After a long meeting, Anne pulls out her Personal Assistant to note a couple of items she needs to follow up on, confirm the location of her next meeting, and see if anything important has come up in the last couple of hours. When she turns on the screen, the PA shows her the subject and location of her next meeting, which is in 25 minutes. There's also an indication that she has three messages marked urgent (including one from her boss), one message from a client whose messages she's told the PA are top priority, and a dozen others that can probably wait.

> After noting her to-do items before she forgets them, Anne selects the urgent message from her boss, which is a voicemail, and listens to it as she walks to the parking garage. His question about a recent contract is time sensitive, so she selects the option to call him back. As soon as she's done answering his question, she looks to see who the other urgent messages are from and decides to ignore them for now. She selects the message from the important client. It's an e-mail, but she wants it read to her because she's fumbling to find her car keys. Deciding it doesn't need an immediate response, she tells the PA to remind her to follow up later today; she juggles so many things in a day that she needs help keeping track of the details.

> Getting into the car, she sees that she has 15 minutes left to get to her next meeting. It's potentially a large account, so she's anxious to arrive on time. She asks the PA for the fastest route from her current location. The PA shows her the best option based on current traffic conditions. Pulling out of the garage, she tells the PA to give her audio directions so she can keep her eyes on the road.

A context scenario begins with a triggering event and goes on to describe the sequence of information exchange, actions, and results.

Requirements

It's essential to take a solution-agnostic approach in context scenarios to avoid unconsciously eliminating options.

Arriving at her destination right on time, Anne reviews the meeting participants so she can greet them by name; the personal touch is everything in sales. When she's escorted into the conference room, she sets her PA on the table in case she needs it. She knows the device won't interrupt her meeting, even by vibrating, unless someone tells her voicemail it's an emergency. Anne realizes a few minutes later that she needs some information from her desktop PC back at the office. She uses the PA to access the spreadsheet she needs.

After wrapping up another successful meeting, Anne checks her PA again. With an hour until her next stop, she asks it to show her the way to the nearest café so she can grab a bite. The PA shows her a couple of options. Anne chooses the nearest and walks there using the PA's directions. She has a sandwich and a cup of tea as she uses the PA to check out the latest news headlines. Knowing it will take her 20 minutes to get to her next appointment, the PA interrupts Anne's reading when she has 30 minutes to go.

After an afternoon of meetings, Anne checks for messages from her family. She sees an e-mail from her husband, Ted. She checks it in case there's something he wants from the grocery store. He wants her to pick up a pizza, but didn't specify what kind. She chooses the option that lets her respond to the message with a phone call. After a quick conversation, she hangs up and adds a veggie supreme to the grocery list on her PA. One more stop and she can go home.

You can see that the scenario is high level; it specifies a few key bits of information, but doesn't go into detail about whether each message has a subject line or whether driving directions are shown alongside a map. You can also see that the scenario doesn't specify mechanisms; instead, it treats the interaction between Anne and her Personal Assistant as a conversation. Phrases like "chooses an option" or "shows an indication that she has messages" imply what the functionality is, but don't specify a particular way to accomplish it. This solution-agnostic approach is essential in context scenarios, because jumping to solutions too early means eliminating options, often without even realizing you're doing that. In the PA example, it's tempting to specify that she uses a touch screen or a thumb keyboard. However, both of these choices have design and cost implications, so it's better not to make that assumption yet.

The following sections describe how to go about creating your context scenarios.

STEP 1: IDENTIFY WHAT CONTEXT SCENARIOS YOU NEED

You will almost always need at least a couple of context scenarios for any product or service. Complex authoring tools or multi-role enterprise products may involve a dozen context scenarios. It's rare to have much more than that unless you're designing something truly immense, such as an entire ERP system that covers nearly every function in a business; even so, you'd still be unlikely to have more than a double handful of scenarios per primary persona's interface. These small numbers may be shocking to people accustomed to documenting every possible use case. Not to worry: The design will eventually address even the more obscure possibilities. The idea with context scenarios is to focus on the big issues first and get agreement on them so you can start designing, rather than getting bogged down in analysis paralysis by trying to cover everything.

Your context scenarios should include a typical example of each major activity your personas are likely to engage in. Activities that tend to occur together should be combined in a single scenario. Scenarios for multiple small tasks, such as processing invoices, should cover several examples to illustrate how the persona would want to manage the flow from one invoice to another. Activities that occur in separate sessions or are not at all related are best addressed in distinct scenarios. Infrequent activities, such as configuration, are usually straightforward enough to address later. The exception is when the out-of-box experience is crucial, such as for a consumer gadget, or when painful configuration is one of the critical problems with an existing system.

Start by listing the critical activities of your primary personas. Determine whether any of those key tasks tend to occur together; if they do, assume that you should combine those in a single scenario. Once you have a list based on your primary, consider what additional activities you'll need to cover for any secondary personas. This includes not only additional tasks not performed by the primary, but also tasks that your secondary personas approach differently. For example, if two surgeon personas start the same surgery at different points, you would need to describe a context scenario for each. There's usually at least one scenario per secondary persona, even if it's a simple variation on an activity performed by the primary persona. Supplemental, negative, served, and customer personas do not appear in context scenarios (except to the extent that served personas are being helped by a primary or secondary). Table 12.2 outlines some example lists of context scenarios that should be outlined for various products.

> Nearly every product or service involves multiple context scenarios.

313

Table 12.2. **Example lists of context scenarios.**

Product	Persona	Scenarios
E-mail system	A system administrator with simple needs (primary administrator)	— Set up the system — Add an account — Change settings — Delete an account — Upgrade the system
	A system administrator who makes complex connections to other systems (secondary administrator)	— Set up the system
	Someone who uses e-mail in a single location (primary end user)	— First use at the beginning of the day — Use throughout the day
	A mobile e-mail user (secondary end user)	— Remote use
Consumer digital camera	A family photographer of average skill (primary)	— Out-of-box experience — Taking photos at an event — Taking photos here and there — Uploading photos
	A hobbyist photographer with high standards who takes a lot of photos (secondary)	— Photo shoot — Uploading photos
Camera company Web site	An uninformed point-and-shoot buyer who doesn't want a lot of detail (primary for point and shoot content)	— Find a point-and-shoot camera that meets some basic needs and learn where to buy it
	An uninformed SLR buyer who needs help making a good choice (primary for SLR content)	— Find the right SLR and accessories and learn where to buy it
	A knowledgeable SLR buyer who wants to know a lot of technical detail (secondary for SLR content)	— Find the right SLR and accessories
	A current owner (primary for support content)	— Find a lens or accessory — Get help with a problem

Product	Persona	Scenarios
	A camera dealer (primary for dealer content)	— Learn about the latest models — Set up a dealer account — Place an order — Handle a problem with an order
	A job seeker (primary for career content)	— Learn what's available and apply
Inbound call center software	An experienced call center agent (primary agent)	— Handle basic calls — Escalate a call
	An inexperienced agent (secondary agent)	— Handle basic calls — Escalate a call
	An escalation agent (secondary agent)	— Handle calls
	A supervisor in a small call center (secondary manager)	— Monitor call flow — Optimize operations — Coach an agent
	A manager of a large call center (primary manager)	— Monitor call flow across multiple units — Optimize operations across multiple units
Complex purchasing application	A person requesting a purchase (primary requester)	— Request a purchase
	A specialized purchasing agent for a manufacturing supply chain (primary purchasing agent)	— Process requests — Follow up on orders
	A specialized purchasing agent for miscellaneous corporate needs (secondary purchasing agent)	— Process requests — Follow up on orders
	A specialized goods-receipt clerk (primary for goods receipt)	— Process received shipments
	A specialized accounts-payable clerk (primary for accounts payable)	— Pay invoices, including a problem invoice
	An office manager (secondary for all three)	— Process purchase requests — Process received shipments — Pay invoices

Requirements

Product	Persona	Scenarios
Family calendaring system	An at-home parent who manages a calendar (primary)	— Reviewing everyone's commitments and planning the day — Entering an upcoming event for a child — Finding a time when the whole family can do something with friends
	A working parent who manages the calendar (secondary)	— Accessing the calendar remotely
	A twelve-year-old (secondary)	— Adding an event
Device used to deliver intravenous medications in a hospital	Nurse in a general ward (primary)	— Administer a medication (simple case) — Administer multiple medications at a time (complex case) — Adjust dosage — Respond to a problem
	Nurse in a neonatal intensive care unit (secondary)	— Administer a medication
	Nurse in an oncology unit (secondary)	— Administer a medication
	Anesthesiologist in an operating room (secondary)	— Administer a medication while constantly monitoring vitals
	Nursing aide (secondary)	— Monitor — Respond to a problem
	Person setting up medication lists and safety parameters (primary administrator)	— System setup
	Person cleaning and servicing the device (primary maintenance)	— Clean the device — Replace parts
Clothing store targeting women	A brand-focused shopper (primary)	— Browse the store, try some things on, buy some — Look for a specific item — Return an item — Order an item that's not in stock

Product	Persona	Scenarios
	A price-conscious shopper who can only afford sale items (secondary)	— Find items on sale
	A man shopping for a gift (secondary)	— Get help finding the right gift

STEP 2. DEVELOP EACH STORY

For each situation you've listed, the next step is to tell the story of the persona using the product or service. This requires a combination of imagination, empathy with the persona, and an understanding of some fundamental design principles; although you are not yet drawing solutions, you are beginning to make design decisions by describing the overall flow.

Answer the right questions

A context scenario answers most of the basic journalistic questions: who, what, where, when, why, and how. *Who*, of course, is the persona, but might also include other people with whom the persona interacts to accomplish a task. *What* is the data exchanged among the persona, other people, and the system, and the actions the persona takes as a result. *Where* is the setting in which the product or service will be used, such as in a typical office, in a meeting room, at home, or in someone's car. It could also include a description of a virtual workspace, such as a workstation or task queue shared by multiple people. *When* is an indication of whether this activity is common, how long it lasts, and whether it's interrupted. *Why* is the persona's reason for performing the task and his motivation for various behaviors along the way.

How is the problematic question; the scenario should outline the *process* the persona follows to complete the task, but not specify the

particular *tools* used during that process. In other words, we need to know that she somehow gets the nail into the piece of wood, but don't care if it involves a hammer, a wrench, or the heel of her shoe.

Use the right level of detail

The trickiest part about context scenarios is judging how much detail is too much. Here's an example of a description that's not detailed enough:

> After a long meeting, Anne pulls out her Personal Assistant to note a couple of items she needs to follow up on, confirm the location of her next meeting, and see if anything important has come up in the last couple of hours. She checks her messages and responds to one from her boss but ignores the others. Getting into the car, she asks the PA for the fastest route to her destination.

It's difficult to tell from this description what the implications of the design will be. In the good example provided earlier, it was evident that voicemail and e-mail were both listed in one place and that the PA was aware of her current location as well as traffic conditions. Both involve considerable business and technical issues, so it's best not to gloss over them. Also, it's hard to see how Anne makes a decision about what message to respond to. Overall, you begin to get a sense of bare bones functionality, but not of how the system should behave.

Context scenarios should be compelling; they need to engage the imagination and help people see possibilities, not bog them down in detail.

Too much detail can be equally problematic. Here's an example:

> When Anne turns on the screen, the PA shows her the subject and location of her next meeting, which is in 25 minutes. There's also a list of messages that includes information about the sender, time, and subject; at the top are three marked urgent (including one from her boss). Under those is one message from a client whose messages she's specified as top priority in her address book, and a dozen others that can probably wait.
>
> Anne selects the urgent message from her boss, which is a two-minute voicemail, and listens to it as she walks to the parking garage. His question about a recent contract is time sensitive, so she selects the option to call him back; she could also send voicemail, send e-mail, delete his message, or flag it to follow up on later. As soon as she's done answering his question, she looks to see who the other urgent messages are from and decides to ignore them for now. She selects the message from the important client. It's an e-mail, but she wants it read to her because she's fumbling to find her car keys. She selects the "read aloud" button. Deciding it doesn't need an immediate response, she adds it to her to-do list for later follow-up.

The first thing you probably noticed is that this version is tedious to read. Context scenarios should be compelling; they need to engage the imagination and help people see possibilities, not bog them down in detail. Some of the information is irrelevant at this point; it may eventually be important to know all of the options available at the end of the message, but this is a trivial issue compared to unified messaging and traffic-aware driving directions. You might also see that at this level of detail, it's almost impossible not to delve into solutions; the text is beginning to describe screen layout, navigation, and buttons.

As with most aspects of the method, using the context scenarios in subsequent steps will help you create better ones the next time. However, you'll avoid the most common mistakes if you keep the following tips in mind.

Start with an optimistic mind-set

Looking ahead can sometimes change how stakeholders think about timelines, so think of the long term even if you're working on a near-term release or constrained redesign. If you're working on a product that will launch in the next year, consider what another year or two of effort might make possible. For a product three years out, think about what four or five years might accomplish. In other words, you should always be somewhat more ambitious than you think your timeline allows, but not so much more ambitious that you will lose credibility and frustrate other product team members. The work isn't wasted in any case, because you can use it again when the next version of the product ships or the service is expanded.

One way to ensure that you're thinking optimistically is to pretend that the thing you're designing is either magic or human. This gives you permission to forget about technology and constraints. You can see the results of this kind of thinking in the Personal Assistant example scenario described earlier. Take this sentence, for instance:

> There's also an indication that she has three messages marked urgent (including one from her boss), one message from a client whose messages she's told the PA are top priority, and a dozen others that can probably wait.

A helpful human assistant would prioritize messages so time-sensitive or important issues get dealt with sooner. Having senders mark messages as urgent is insufficient because the recipient may have different ideas about what is and isn't time-critical. It would take a lot for an electronic assistant to prioritize messages based on content, but it wouldn't be terribly hard for a system to give special treatment to messages from certain senders.

Exercise

What would the following things do if they were magical or replaced by a helpful human?

— Your e-mail application
— An automatic teller
— An airline reservation system
— A clothing Web site

Stay true to the personas

Typically, one team member sits at a keyboard (with the document projected on the wall) or stands at a whiteboard to capture and facilitate. Another team member drives the story forward. Any team member not proposing the scenario elicits more detail, throws in an occasional idea, and watches for constrained thinking or excessive specificity. Any team member might play either role, but most often the IxD generator or ID is inclined toward ideation, while the IxD synthesizer facilitates and acts as a backstop.

Team members also share a responsibility to challenge anything that's inconsistent with the persona's goals, attitudes, or behavior. Here's an example of how such a conversation might go:

Designer A: Anne orders a sandwich and a cup of tea, then uses the Personal Assistant to read her other messages while she eats.

Designer B: Why do you think she reads her other messages during lunch?

Designer A: It's her first chance to look over the non-urgent ones.

Designer B: Sure, but one of her goals is to maintain some balance between work and life. It seems like she'd want to take a break and not be all about work, even if it's just for a few minutes.

Designer A: Hmmm … good point. She'd probably read the newspaper or a magazine. Maybe the PA should make that kind of thing available to her.

Before moving on from one scenario to the next, see if anything in the scenario causes problems for other relevant user personas (either primary or secondary) or for your served or customer personas. If so, consider how you might modify it without making the star of the scenario unhappy.

Apply important design principles

As you describe the behavior of the system, you're beginning to design even though you're not getting specific about solutions. The important design principles to consider at this point are essentially descriptions of good product manners,[2] such as these:

— Do no harm, whether that's actual injury or just wasting someone's time.

— Provide all the tools your persona uses at the same time in the same place.

— Don't ask for confirmation of actions; make them possible to undo instead.

— Don't interrupt users to report events they don't care about.

— Make errors impossible; don't offer choices that won't work.

— Don't ask users to remember things if you can avoid it.

— Remember and learn from user behavior.

— Make reasonable assumptions instead of forcing users to customize or make a lot of unnecessary choices.

— Don't confuse what users will always do with what they might occasionally do.

Teammates should also be on the lookout for bad design decisions implied by a scenario. Here's an example:

Designer A: Anne listens to the urgent message from her boss. She decides she needs to reply, so she opens up her address book to find his number and call him back.

Designer B: Why would we force her to go to an address book application? Shouldn't we anticipate that she might want to respond either via e-mail or voice and make the option available right there?

Designer A: Hmmm … yeah. You're right.

Have someone review your scenarios

It's easy when you develop the scenarios to get nearsighted about them, so have someone review your scenarios after you've completed them. A team lead who is knowledgeable about good scenario construction and has participated in part of the research is the best person for this. You may also want to have a subject matter expert or the project owner look over the scenarios before you extract requirements from them and share them with other stakeholders.

---

2. For good examples of this kind of principle, see *About face 3: The essentials of interaction design*, by Alan Cooper, Robert Reimann, and David Cronin. Wiley, 2007.

Exercise

Critique the following context scenario for Carla Ramirez, the car buyer persona described in Chapter 11. Where is there too much detail, and where too little? What premature design decisions do you see? Where are good design principles not being followed? Where is the scenario not true to the persona?

CARLA LOOKS FOR A NEW CAR

Carla's MINI Cooper is starting to experience the mechanical problems that come with age, so she thinks it's time to buy a new car. She's torn between the CarCo Alpha and that little MegaMotors car she can never remember the name of (it's all numbers and letters). When she sits down at her home computer and opens up the MegaMotors Web site, she instantly recognizes an image of the PC3. She decides to look at more detail to see if it's the right car for her.

Carla goes to the PC3 page, which has several menu items across the top, including a gallery, specs, reviews, features, and accessories. First, though, she's drawn to the little widget that lets her spin the car around and change its color. After a minute of noodling with that, she thinks it's time to get down to business, and looks for more information on the car's interior by clicking the "features" menu item. When she finds her way to the interior specs, she sees that the trunk has eight cubic feet of cargo space; when she rolls over this, she sees that it translates to about four bags of groceries or a small roll-aboard suitcase and carry-on bag. It gets 30 miles to a gallon on the highway, which isn't bad.

Her patience for specs exhausted, Carla moves on to the "build your PC3" feature. She picks red paint, a tan interior, and a sun roof. The tool tells her the tan interior is not available with a red exterior, so she goes back to the previous step and picks a black interior. She adds a stereo upgrade, leather seats, and alloy wheels. Ouch, it's a little expensive. She sees an option to compare the PC3 to competitor's cars, so she decides to see how a comparably equipped Alpha would be priced. It's not much less, so Carla decides to see where the nearest dealer is so she can take a test drive this weekend.

Review your scenarios with your team lead and subject matter experts before extracting requirements.

Requirements

321

STEP 3. PREPARE TO COMMUNICATE YOUR SCENARIOS

Most of the work in scenario creation happens in team meetings. However, the rough outline still has to be turned into a compelling narrative. Any team member may take on this task depending on who has time for it, but it's generally the province of the IxD synthesizer because crafting each sentence by committee would be painful. However, each team member should take a look at the draft narrative and comment on it before it gets shared outside the design team.

It's almost always a good idea to share your context scenarios with stakeholders, since they will be the basis for many of your requirements. There are rare stakeholders who don't respond well to scenarios due to a discomfort with things that aren't concrete. Verbal descriptions can create anxiety in people who aren't accustomed to imagining things they can't see. You generally have three choices for handling this situation. One is to provide lots of disclaimers about what scenarios can and can't do and encourage the anxious stakeholders to sit tight for a week or two until you have sketches. This can be uncomfortable, but doesn't usually result in big problems. Another is to jump straight to requirements without directly communicating the scenarios. This can work, but it's harder to justify how you arrived at your conclusions.

The third option is to illustrate your scenarios to make them more concrete. High-level storyboards can work well with scenarios involving movement through physical space, such as the use of a mobile device with another system. This is seldom a good idea with software interfaces, because it's hard to do without representing navigational structures and other details you haven't considered yet. If you believe you'll need to illustrate your scenarios, try to delay the

stakeholder meeting for discussing requirements until you've had at least a few days to start the design framework (see Chapters 14 and 16).

A good storyboard at this level shows only the highlights of the interaction and deliberately glosses over (or crops out) anything you can't be specific about yet. If you don't have a good illustrator on your team, you can take photos of your teammates in the right poses, then use an application like Adobe Illustrator or Photoshop to draw a silhouette on top of the image. The one in Figure 12.3, for example, shows the context and the high points of Anne's "conversation" with her Personal Assistant, but it hand-waves the form factor and screen contents.

Exercise

Make a list of the context scenarios you need for the RoomFinder or LocalGuide, considering each of your personas. If you haven't created those personas, use Katie Bennett, the photographer persona from Chapter 11. Develop and document at least two context scenarios.

Extracting requirements from scenarios

Finally, you need to extract requirements from your scenarios. Even if it feels a bit repetitious, most stakeholders have an easier time digesting requirements that are called out in a list rather than hidden in a narrative. One effective way to do this is to put the scenario in a table and list the relevant requirements alongside it. You can then duplicate those requirements in a centralized list, if you have one. See Table 12.3 for an example.

Figure 12.3. An example storyboard for Anne's Personal Assistant scenario.

Table 12.3. **Example requirements from a context scenario.**

Scenario text	Requirements
After a long meeting, Anne pulls out her Personal Assistant to note a couple of items she needs to follow up on, confirm the location of her next meeting, and see if anything important has come up in the last couple of hours.	— Ability to enter text — Ability to track appointments — Ability to see a list of messages — Portable form factor
When she turns on the screen, the PA shows her the subject and location of her next meeting, which is in 25 minutes.	— Ability to turn off the screen without the turning off the device — Ability to count down to the next event
There's also an indication that she has three messages marked urgent (including one from her boss), one message from a client whose messages she's told the PA are top priority, and a dozen others that can probably wait.	— Ability to see both e-mail and voice messages in a single place, along with next event — Ability to auto-prioritize some messages based on simple criteria specified by users, as well as based on urgency indicated by the sender

Continued

Requirements

Scenario text	Requirements
After noting her to-do items before she forgets them, Anne selects the urgent message from her boss, which is a voicemail, and listens to it as she walks to the parking garage.	— Ability to enter and track tasks — Ability to select a message from a visual list — Ability to listen to voicemail
His question about a recent contract is time sensitive, so she selects the option to call him back.	— Ability to initiate various types of return communication directly from a message
As soon as she's done answering his question, she looks to see who sent the other urgent messages and decides to ignore them for now.	— Ability to return to what she was doing last
She selects the message from the important client. It's an e-mail, but she wants it read to her because she's fumbling to find her car keys.	— Ability to hear e-mail messages hands free
Deciding it doesn't need an immediate response, she tells the PA to remind her to follow up later today; she juggles so many things in a day that she needs help keeping track of the details.	— Ability to schedule action items or reminders from a message
Getting into the car, she sees that she has 15 minutes left to get to her next meeting. It's potentially a large account, so she's anxious to arrive on time.	— Ability to count down to the next event
She asks the PA for the fastest route from her current location.	— Ability to approximate current location closely enough to provide driving directions Ability to calculate fastest route from current location
The PA shows her the best option based on current traffic conditions.	— Ability to factor in current traffic conditions when calculating fastest route
Pulling out of the garage, she tells the PA to give her audio directions so she can keep her eyes on the road.	— Ability to get audio directions — Ability to provide appropriately timed driving directions
Arriving at her destination right on time, Anne reviews the meeting participants so she can greet them by name; the personal touch is everything in sales.	— Ability to review information about meeting participants

Requirements

Scenario text	Requirements
When she's escorted into the conference room, she sets her PA on the table in case she needs it. She knows the device won't interrupt her meeting, even by vibrating, unless someone tells her voicemail it's an emergency.	— Ability to select parameters for interruptions and to apply them automatically during scheduled meetings
Anne realizes a few minutes later that she needs some information from her desktop PC back at the office. She uses the PA to access the spreadsheet she needs.	— Ability to connect to a remote computer with appropriate permissions — Ability to view common document formats
After wrapping up another successful meeting, Anne checks her PA again. With an hour until her next stop, she asks it to show her the way to the nearest café so she can grab a bite. The PA shows her a couple of options. Anne chooses the nearest and walks there using the PA's directions.	— Ability to count down to next event — Ability to locate common services such as food, fuel, etc.
She has a sandwich and a cup of tea as she uses the PA to check out the latest news headlines.	— Ability to get various publicly available content
Knowing it will take her 20 minutes to get to her next appointment, the PA interrupts Anne's reading when she has 30 minutes to go.	— Ability to get proactive reminders that are intelligent about accounting for travel time
After an afternoon of meetings, Anne checks for messages from her family. She sees an e-mail from her husband, Ted.	— Ability to view messages
She checks it in case there's something he wants at the grocery store. He wants her to pick up a pizza, but didn't specify what kind. She chooses the option that lets her respond to the message with a phone call.	— Ability to initiate a message response from one channel in any other channel, directly from the message
After a quick conversation, she hangs up and adds a veggie supreme to the grocery list on her PA. One more stop and she can go home.	— Ability to track various lists

As you can see, these requirements are framed in terms of what Anne needs to do. They're solution-agnostic and not terribly detailed. "Ability to approximate current location closely enough to provide driving directions," for example, doesn't specify that the device must know a location to within two meters, because it will take some experimentation to see just how much imprecision you can get away with. It also doesn't specify GPS technology, since it might be possible to triangulate an approximate location using cell phone towers or some other method.

You might also notice in the example that the ability to count down to the next event is listed more than once. You could certainly stop after you've listed a need once, but multiple listings can help people see that a certain capability has multiple uses and may show up in multiple scenarios. It also helps with making your requirements traceable.

Exercise

Extract requirements from your RoomFinder or LocalGuide scenarios, or from your rewritten scenario for Carla's car-buying experience.

Other Requirements from User Personas

The majority of your requirements will come from the scenarios, but persona goals, skills, environments, physical attributes, and mental models are all helpful in identifying additional needs. The list of requirements from each of these sources tends to be much shorter than the list generated from the scenarios.

Mental models

As discussed in the "Mental models" section of Chapter 7, a mental model describes how someone thinks about objects, relationships, and actions. A design that's antithetical to the personas' mental models will be difficult to learn and use, so mental models are often an important source of requirements. A photographer who thinks of her photos as belonging to a particular event, such as a holiday or vacation, will be frustrated if she can't group her photos based on events. On the other hand, someone who takes photos to create aesthetically pleasing images will be annoyed if

he's forced to organize those into mutually exclusive albums. This example might also occur naturally in a scenario, but it's worth asking yourself whether you've missed any other requirements implied by the mental model.

Environments

Some requirements are suggested by the virtual or physical environment in which a product will be used, as well as the personas' expectations of what is normal for that environment. For example, hospital staff would be surprised if a medical device couldn't survive being scrubbed with soapy water and sprayed with bleach, whereas most reasonable people don't expect a mobile phone to work after it's gone through the washing machine. Typical environmental considerations include:

— Lighting conditions under which a screen should be comfortably viewable

— Viewing angle from which data on a screen should be readable

— Distance at which text or indicators must be readable

— Physical abuse and temperature variation a device should be able to survive

— Privacy needs for data viewed in public places

— Need to share task lists or other virtual spaces with other users

— Frequency of interruption

— Portability needs

— Whether input will be hampered by gloves

— Ambient noise level above which any sound should be audible

— Security needs, such as protecting settings from unauthorized changes

— Need to fit within a certain size display or storage space

Some of these requirements will evolve as the design and engineering progress, but the more specific you can be early on, the better.

Physical and cognitive characteristics

It's obvious that industrial designers need to worry about a persona's physical characteristics, such as the range of body sizes and physical capabilities a device should accommodate. However, this is also a consideration for interaction and visual design. People with poor vision will need larger text. Users with arthritis will need interactions that don't depend on a lot of manual dexterity or strength. Even users with perfect eyesight and a full range of motion need to avoid repetitive stress injuries.

The Measure of Man and Woman[3] and the *Handbook of Human Factors and Ergonomics*[4] are both useful references for understanding human physical and cognitive characteristics.

Skills and knowledge

Consider what kind of support the personas need from the product or service, whether this support is about technology or about an area of expertise. For example, an average person filling out his annual tax forms may need help understanding what deductions he can take, whereas a professional accountant would not. Someone looking up prescription drug information probably needs help spelling obscure medication names. Someone unpacking a new home computer might require help understanding how to set it up.

Goals

Goals are the other important source of persona-based requirements. Some of those requirements are intangible, such as helping someone feel confident in a financial institution. Katie Bennett, the photography persona from Chapter 11, wants to feel like a "real" photographer, which implies that the camera has to look like a professional camera and feel solid in her hands. (See the discussion of experience attributes later in this chapter.)

> Consider what kind of support the personas need from the product or service, whether this support is about technology or about an area of expertise.

Requirements

3. Tilley, A.R. and Henry Dreyfuss Associates. *The measure of man and woman: Human factors in design*. Wiley, 2001.

4. Salvendy, G., Editor. *Handbook of human factors and ergonomics*. Third edition. Wiley, 2006.

Although users should be the focus of most requirements, the organizations that develop and sell the products have needs, too.

Goals may also lead to important functional or data needs; a nurse's desire to make sure everyone gets the best treatment might suggest a requirement that a system draw her attention to symptoms of poor care. Katie Bennett's desire to capture what she sees in her "mind's eye" while still enjoying the scenery implies that she needs automated settings that help her accomplish a variety of effects.

Exercises

1. If you've been working on the RoomFinder, what needs are implied by your personas' mental models of the relationship between rooms and tools like projectors or conference phones? If you've been working on the LocalGuide, what needs are implied by how your personas think about finding a restaurant?

2. What environmental requirements would you expect for personas using an electronic recipe display in the kitchen? What about for an office phone system with two receptionists handling lots of incoming calls?

3. If your personas for a television remote control included a 10-year-old, a large adult man, and someone with arthritis, what needs are implied by these physical characteristics?

4. Imagine that you're designing an image editing application to compete with Adobe Photoshop. One of your personas is skilled with Photoshop, while the other hasn't done much image editing and isn't familiar with channels, layers, or various effects. What requirements are implied by their differing skills?

5. If you were to design an auto manufacturer's Web site for Carla Ramirez, what requirements are implied by her goals?

   — Have reasons to get the car she wants

   — Get it now

   — Enjoy the buying experience

   — Be taken care of after she buys

Requirements from Business and Other Needs

Although users should be the focus of most requirements, the organizations that develop and sell the products have needs, too. You probably have customer needs to consider if you're selling to businesses.

No doubt you will discover some conflict between these requirements and the ones based on the personas and scenarios, so you will need to strike the right balance. The design team can often determine the right balance for any conflicts that are about emphasis in the design; any that have potential business impact should be discussed with stakeholders.

Customer persona goals

You have to get your product into someone's hands before you can delight him with it, and that means making sure *customers* see its value. A decision-maker spending thousands (or millions) of dollars on a complex enterprise system probably wants to improve effectiveness and reduce costs, so he's worried about things like ease of deployment and maintenance, training time, reliability, compatibility with other systems, and the quality of support a vendor will provide. Retailers, who are manufacturers' direct customers for packaged goods, have concerns about how much shelf space something takes up. Companies incorporating another company's product or service into theirs often want the ability to customize certain aspects of it.

A good customer persona already encapsulates these issues, so it should just be a matter of extracting the relevant information and putting it in requirement form. Goals are the main source of this information, but other concerns or problems might be mentioned elsewhere in the persona description.

Apparent conflicts between customer goals and user goals are often simple to resolve if you're really dealing with goals; they're much harder to address if you're looking at solutions. For example, imagine a large corporation trying to ensure that employees aren't using more copies of an application than the company has licensed. A presumed requirement might be to prevent

employees from installing an application without approval from someone in IT, but this will frustrate a persona who needs that application right now to be productive. If you focus on the company's goal, which is to avoid getting sued by the software maker, you can come up with a solution that lets employees install the software and notifies IT that they need to purchase more licenses.

Exercise

What office communication-system requirements are implied by the customer persona description for Tim Wilson in Chapter 11?

Stakeholders

Stakeholders are the only source for two types of requirements: what the product or service should accomplish for the business and how much time and money they're willing to spend. The first you can usually take at face value. The second is typically just a stake in the ground. Product development projects are a bit like landscaping or remodeling a house—you give the architect a cost range, but when you see the difference between a $60,000 remodel and a $75,000 remodel, you might decide that the extra $15,000 is worth spending. It's hard to make those choices until you see the effect of the additional expenditure.

Most other requirements from stakeholders, such as technology platform, are really assumptions. The user and customer personas will help you filter these. A presumed requirement that's consistent with persona goals stays on the list. If it conflicts with persona goals or introduces constraints that do so, it requires deeper examination. You can also use the personas to help settle disagreements among stakeholders about whether a certain feature needs to be included.

Requirements

Exercise

If you're designing an e-commerce site with a business goal of getting shoppers to visit more often and spend more when they visit, how could you balance this with a user persona's desire not to be bombarded with e-mail from the site?

Lawyers and regulations

Whether they are trying to ensure compliance with laws or to avoid getting sued, corporate legal departments are increasingly affecting the quality of user experiences. Legal involvement is often necessary, but a lawyer's approach to solving a problem usually requires users to read and accept large amounts of text before they can install software, order a product online, or even use the navigation system in a rental car. It's often best to note "comply with regulation X" as a requirement, develop a solution that makes that compliance as painless as possible, and *then* run it by the lawyers.

Competitors and media

Many product managers put features into requirements documents because they want "feature parity" with competitors. This is often a good idea, since some people—especially members of the media—do compare products based on their feature lists. With software, in particular, it's often easier to convey that your product does a certain thing than to demonstrate that it's well designed (though good visual design is a big help). However, sometimes those extra features just make the competitor's product unnecessarily complex. Use the personas to help assess whether you really need to match the competitor feature for feature, because going there might mean you constantly play catch-up instead of coming up with something great the competitor doesn't already have.

Accessibility

Although personas aren't the best tool for ensuring that your product is accessible to people with disabilities, your requirements should reflect these needs. You don't have to invent most of these requirements, though; the U.S. government has a good starting point available at http://www.access-board.gov/sec508/standards.htm. Section 508 compliance is required for most products sold to the U.S. government. Many other countries have similar laws and standards.

Sustainability

Designers can exert tremendous influence on ecological, social, and economic sustainability efforts. By designing products that use minimal packaging and recyclable materials, for example, we can reduce the amount of waste in our landfills and the number of toxins in our air and water. This is familiar territory for architects and industrial designers—who are increasingly accustomed to considering materials based on longevity, ease of recycling, and other factors—but is not yet second nature for interaction designers; after all, it's just pixels, so how can we encourage sustainability? Chances are, we can do one or more of the following:

— Consider how to upgrade the software on an existing platform rather than starting over with new hardware

— Argue for faster start-up times so people don't feel compelled to leave devices on standby

— Find ways to minimize printing

— Offer e-commerce shoppers ways to offset the environmental impact of their purchases

— Use technology to keep people out of their cars

— Consider whether a huge color display is really necessary, or whether a small monochrome display will do

Unless you work for an unusually green company, the design team may be the only likely advocate for sustainability. You will probably need to articulate the cost (and public relations) benefits to get sustainability considerations adopted as requirements.

Experience Attributes

The companies with the strongest brands understand that their products must not only make a good impression, but should also be visually identifiable as *theirs*. Every time you see a distinctive set of white earbuds or a gray telephoto lens, for example, it reinforces the unconscious impression that Apple's iPods and Canon's cameras are everywhere and must therefore be good products. To build brand equity, the look of every knob and pixel, the tone of each piece of content, and the behavior of every product should reinforce a consistent set of brand values, such as reliability, luxury, adventure, perfection, caring, or innovation. Those attributes might be functional (such as the *quality* or *ease of use* you expect from a product) or emotional (such as a sense that the company is *trustworthy*). Brand-oriented companies are careful to emphasize such qualities in most customer points of contact, but surprising numbers don't seem to realize that rude or incompetent software—like rude or incompetent employees—damages the brand. Through this and other forms of neglect, brands may become associated with undesirable qualities that designers must strive to overcome.

> **Exercise**
>
> What positive brand values would you say are associated with the following well-known brands? What negative qualities are often ascribed to them?
>
> — IBM
>
> — Wal-Mart
>
> — Microsoft
>
> — Amazon
>
> — BMW

Most product requirements documents don't address brand because people either don't think about brand when designing their products (which is more common than you might imagine), or assume that existing brand descriptions will suffice. However, it's important to cover this topic specifically for each product because even the best corporate brands are difficult to translate directly into visual terms. What does

The companies with the strongest brands understand that their products must not only make a good impression, but should also be visually identifiable as *theirs*.

Requirements

"value for money" look like? What color is perfection? Also, different products within a brand may be targeting different markets, so there has to be some flexibility in how a brand is interpreted in visual language. Many corporate identity guidelines are also geared toward print or, at best, Web usage, and don't work well for software or physical products, where the corporate identity is often secondary to content or function.

Using persona goals allows for product-specific interpretation of the broader corporate brand. Persona goals don't define the brand, but they are the lens designers use to focus on the specific brand characteristics that are most appropriate to a particular type of user or customer. This interpretation results in a small set of requirements called **experience attributes**: visually oriented adjectives that describe the messages or personality the product should convey (see Figure 12.4).

Once the attributes are agreed upon, they serve as the basis for developing the visual and industrial design language (as well as the tone of content) in much the same way that personas and scenarios drive behavior. They're also helpful

in getting stakeholders to assess different approaches to the design language based on something more objective than personal preference; when someone says, "I prefer bright purple and gold," you can reply, "We agreed that it was important to convey sophistication. When you think of other products you'd describe as sophisticated, none of them uses such a bright palette."

The visual designer and, if appropriate, the industrial designer should lead the development of the experience attributes; interaction designers use these requirements as well, but are usually less accustomed to translating emotional qualities into a design language. The process starts with a list of potentially desirable qualities from the corporate brand materials (including a brand's legacy) and stakeholder interviews, as well as qualities that seem desirable based on the persona goals and environments. These terms are then distilled and refined using something akin to the affinity diagram technique described in Chapter 10. The end result is a set of four (occasionally three or five) experience attributes, each of which has a handful of supporting terms. Like the other

Corporate brand materials

Product brand attributes

Stakeholder views

User persona goals

Figure 12.4. Experience attributes for a product come from the overlap of corporate brand and persona goals.

Requirements

requirements, the experience attributes are intended to be discussion and decision-making tools.

Although this process is described in a linear fashion for clarity, it's actually somewhat recursive, as are most analytical processes. Take the steps as an approximation of the workflow rather than an exact prescription. People new to this sort of work may want to follow it closely, but experienced practitioners will find themselves anticipating subsequent steps and making choices in their heads. Experienced designers can do this in a day; others should allow two. Figure 12.5 shows an overview of the process.

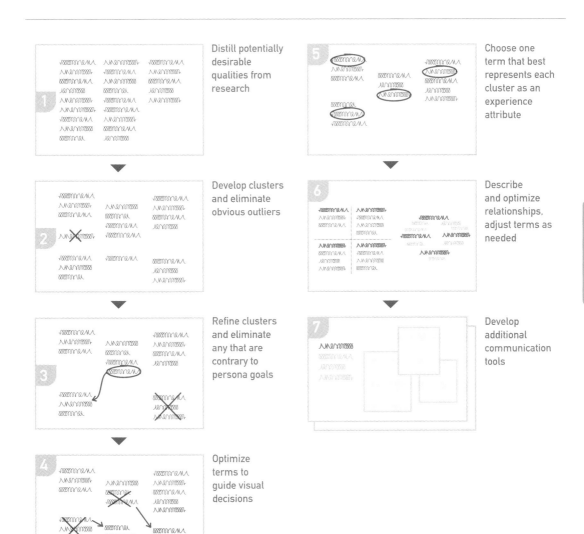

Distill potentially desirable qualities from research

Develop clusters and eliminate obvious outliers

Refine clusters and eliminate any that are contrary to persona goals

Optimize terms to guide visual decisions

Choose one term that best represents each cluster as an experience attribute

Describe and optimize relationships, adjust terms as needed

Develop additional communication tools

Figure 12.5. An overview of the process for developing experience attributes.

If you find this process more subjective than some of the other techniques in this book, you're right; it's certainly a step farther away from science than persona creation is. However, it's not meant to be science. It's merely a tool that helps less experienced designers go through the kind of thought process that the best senior designers instinctively use. It also gives those senior designers a way to explain and build consensus regarding the many decisions they make to get from point A to point B.

Step 1: Compile desirable qualities from research

The first step is to make a list of potential attributes. You'll be rearranging them, so consider using sticky notes. Start with terms drawn from the corporate brand materials, including identity guidelines, mission statements, and the brand's legacy. Review what stakeholders said about the company and how they'd like the product to be perceived. Write down exactly what they said; it's fine if these are phrases rather than individual words. Either repeat or put some sort of mark next to words you heard over and over again, as shown in Figure 12.6. There should be several clear themes if the company is at all brand oriented. If the brand is poorly articulated, hopefully you asked stakeholders to compare the product to people, cars, or other products (see the "Marketing stakeholders" section of Chapter 5) to generate some thoughts.

Look over the words you've listed and see if any of them are ambiguous. *Reliable*, for example, might mean a system that doesn't crash, or it might mean a system that's trusted to provide good results. Discuss with your teammates and agree on which meaning was intended, then replace or annotate the confusing word with a synonym. It's important to be clear on the intended meaning of each term before you try to group them.

Expert ✓✓	Familiar	Modular ✓✓
Market leaders	Insight ✓✓✓✓	At a glance
Partner	Fast (to use)	Precise
Thorough	Simple	~~Reliable~~ Trusted
The latest, greatest	Good science ✓✓	Non-threatening
~~Robust~~ Full featured	Customizable	Automated
Deep	Powerful	Rich
Knowledgeable ✓	Innovative ✓✓	Not arrogant
Comprehensive	Advanced	Cutting edge
Flexible	Helpful	Platform
Best in class	Experienced	A la carte
Structured	Component-based	Elegant

Figure 12.6. A list of attribute candidates for a complex financial analysis tool. Note that some words occurred multiple times.

Requirements

Once you've exhausted the list from the company's point of view, add terms based on the research and the personas. In a way, the persona experience goals pose questions whose answers describe a desirable product personality. Imagine, for instance, that a persona's experience goal is to feel confident in the medical care she's receiving. Think about what qualities in a care provider, such as expertise, would make her feel most confident. Add it to your list if it's not already there. Also describe the visual qualities of any products or environments that especially appeal to the personas, if they seem relevant.

Step 2: Group related qualities into clusters

Next, group terms that seem related to one another. There are usually somewhere between three and seven groups initially. You may find yourself clarifying terms further as you group them. It's common to have a couple of terms that just don't fit any of the clusters, usually from stakeholders who don't spend much time thinking about the brand. You can generally remove or ignore these. In Figure 12.7, for example, the word *structured* doesn't seem to fit anywhere, and it contrasts with terms like *flexible*, so it can be eliminated as an outlier.

(good stuff)
Expert ✓✓
Good science ✓✓
Knowledgeable ✓
Experienced
Precise
~~Reliable~~ Trusted

(and lots of it)
Comprehensive
Deep
Rich
Thorough

(seen in new ways)
Advanced
Market leaders ✓✓
Innovative ✓✓
Cutting Edge
Insight ✓✓✓✓
The latest, greatest

Partner
Not arrogant
Non-threatening

Customizable
Powerful
Flexible
~~Robust~~ Full featured
Best in class

~~Structured~~

Modular ✓✓
Component based
A la carte

Elegant
Simple
Fast (to use)
Familiar (easy to learn)
Helpful
Automated
At a glance

Figure 12.7. An initial set of clusters.

Step 3: Refine and filter clusters

With the entire design team, refine your clusters until you have four if possible, but at least three and no more than five. Fewer will not provide adequate definition but more will be difficult to manage. When deciding what qualities to emphasize, consider how important the category seemed to stakeholders, how closely it's tied to the company's core brand platform, and whether it's important in differentiating the product from competitors. Also consider each cluster in light of goals: Would a product with these qualities satisfy the primary and other persona(s)?

You should remove any cluster that seems contrary to the persona goals. In Figure 12.8, for example, you can see that the terms relating to modularity have been eliminated because, although stakeholders are excited about a modular solution, it's really about making development and sales easier and not at all about the user experience. The three clusters on the left (*good stuff … and lots of it … seen in new ways*) seem closely related. Expertise is one of the cornerstones of the brand in this case, and both stakeholders and users emphasized that the company is valued for its expertise, so dropping that *good stuff* category wouldn't make sense. The terms related to insight and innovation seem critical, as well—the majority of the stakeholders talked about the product

(good stuff)
Expert ✓✓
Good science ✓✓
Knowledgeable ✓
Experienced
Precise
~~Reliable~~ Trusted
Comprehensive
Deep
Rich
Thorough

(seen in new ways)
Advanced
Market leaders ✓✓
Innovative ✓✓
Cutting edge
Insight ✓✓✓✓
The latest, greatest

Partner
Not arrogant
Non-threatening

Customizable
Powerful
Flexible
~~Robust~~ Full featured
Best in class

~~Modular ✓✓~~
~~Component-based~~
~~A la carte~~

Elegant
Simple
Fast (to use)
Familiar (easy to learn)
Helpful
Automated
At a glance

Figure 12.8. An example of clusters being refined.

providing insight in new ways. This tool and all the competitors provide plenty of detail, so emphasizing that quality wouldn't provide any advantage. To avoid losing this quality altogether, though, you could combine it with the terms describing expertise.

Step 4: Optimize terms to guide visual decisions

To be useful in guiding design choices, an attribute has to be an adjective, has to be aspirational, and almost always has to describe a quality that can be represented visually. These are typically the kinds of words you'd use to describe the admirable aspects of another person's appearance or personality. *Easy to use* would be an unfortunate descriptor for a person; *approachable* would work better. Reword any negative constructions, such as *not arrogant*, in positive terms; *humble* sets the bar higher.

As with personas, the set should be small enough to be manageable and memorable, but not trimmed to the point where you lose all nuance. You can eliminate some terms altogether if you have a close synonym and several other good words in the cluster. You might also continue moving terms around a bit; as things progress in the list shown in Figure 12.9, for example, *rich* and *deep* seem like a better fit with *powerful* and *full-featured*. If any of the categories don't seem nuanced enough, think back to your original conversations with stakeholders and users to see if you can dredge up any other useful terms to add.

If you can't visualize what a word looks like, pull out your thesaurus and try out some synonyms. *Intelligent* might be hard to envision, but *brilliant* evokes a certain sense of sparkle and liveliness. *Smart* brings to mind the crisp, classic lines of a tailored suit. You might not be able to envision what brilliant or smart looks like, either, but visual and industrial designers are accustomed to representing such qualities in a design language by manipulating color, texture, material, shape, line, and other visual properties.

In Figure 12.9, *good science* is replaced by *scientific*, but it and *precise* are very similar terms. It's not entirely clear yet which will work better. It is clear that *rich* and *deep* are much more visual terms than *comprehensive* or *thorough*. *Expert* is the superlative term; an expert commands more respect than someone who is merely *knowledgeable*.

There are some cases when a word that's hard to visualize should remain untouched. Stakeholders are likely to balk if you replace a word that's one of the company's core brand values, or that has been

A useful experience attribute is an aspirational adjective that can almost always be represented visually.

Requirements

widely adopted because a senior executive has been evangelizing it. This is a bit like using a supplemental persona: You have to trot it out in public, but within the design team you know you'll be relying on the more visual words in the cluster to guide your design choices. In the example, you can see that *insight* (which has been turned into an adjective) remains on the list even though it's not a very visual term. The other words in the category are better; they imply a clean, modern look with, for example, thin lines and sharp corners. *Expert* is hard to eliminate for similar reasons.

A term that isn't obviously visual can be helpful, though. *Familiar* would be hard to draw, but it implies that the design should take advantage of idioms, icons, and visual elements that the personas are accustomed to. *Best in class* says it's important to pay attention to fit-and-finish details. *Helpful* and *flexible* may or may not

directly drive visual design, but are worth keeping because they're important qualities of the product's functionality and behavior. A term like *witty* would be a good guide for writing Web site copy.

You might also find words that are still somewhat at odds with the personas or with other terms in the set. The example set contains the word *simple*, but a financial analysis product is an inherently complex tool that's also *powerful, flexible, rich,* and *deep*. *Simple*, to some, implies a lack of power. *Clean* might be a better choice. *Elegant*, which is intended to say a similar thing, may connote a certain daintiness that's less desirable.

Step 5: Choose the best term from each cluster

As you winnow your set, choose the term from each category that best represents the concept.

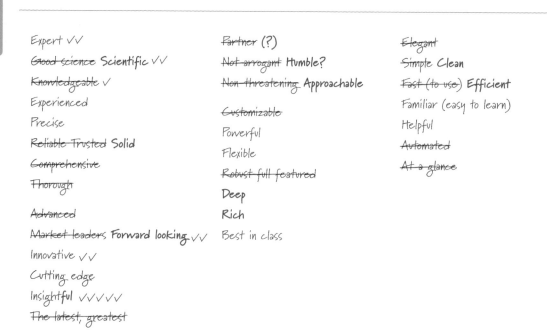

Figure 12.9. The less visually evocative terms in this example are replaced with more useful words.

These are the experience attributes. Keep the other words in each category as **supporting terms**, though; they're necessary to provide an accurate sense of the concept. Ideally, the attributes are among the more visual terms, but you may also choose a word because it's closest to the brand values, best suits the needs of the primary persona(s), or helps differentiate the product from competitors. Which factor you emphasize depends on the situation you're in.

In Figure 12.10, experience and insight are the key value propositions for the product, and both have a lot of traction with stakeholders, so it's difficult to choose anything else from those clusters. The related supporting terms will provide more help with design language choices. *Efficient* and *powerful* aren't the most visually expressive terms in their categories, but a clean, familiar look and helpful behavior are all about promoting efficiency, and depth and flexibility promote power. If the product is expert, insightful, powerful, and efficient, *humble* might be tough to pull off, but *approachable* brings to mind a laid-back college professor who says there's no such thing as a dumb question.

You may have noticed that one of the clusters in Figure 12.10 contains only two terms. If you can't find the right way to add nuance to a category, the next step might provide some ideas.

Step 6: Describe and optimize relationships

Your chosen attributes may sound right for their categories, but they also have to work well as a set. Together, these terms define the boundaries of the future visual language. A good set creates tension and balance among the attributes to keep the design language from going to inappropriate extremes. *Approachable*, for example, might lead to an overly simplistic visual language with bright or warm colors, but if it's balanced with *scientific* and *precise*, you'll know not to draw cartoon-like brown and gold buttons.

Even though *approachable* helps offset the other attributes, they still seem like overkill; a tool that comes across so strongly as *expert*, *insightful*, *powerful*, and *efficient* has the potential to be intimidating. Financial analysts view a powerful tool as one that helps them gain insight in an efficient way, so there's no good reason for the

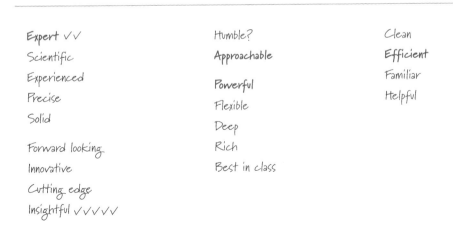

Expert ✓✓
Scientific
Experienced
Precise
Solid

Forward looking
Innovative
Cutting edge
Insightful ✓✓✓✓

Humble?
Approachable

Powerful
Flexible
Deep
Rich
Best in class

Clean
Efficient
Familiar
Helpful

Figure 12.10. Tentative choices for experience attributes that represent each group.

Diagrams can help illustrate the conceptual relationships among the experience attributes and supporting terms.

redundancy. *Efficient* provides a nice counterpoint to *insightful* and *expert* because those might encourage excessive density of information and tools; more information than a user needs at a given moment doesn't make him efficient. These four terms together provide a well-rounded personality for the product: It knows a lot, it's good at extracting value from its knowledge, and it shares the wealth in an efficient way.

Removing *powerful* as one of the attributes makes it possible to rearrange some of the supporting terms in useful ways as shown in Figure 12.11; as you can see, this is an iterative process.

Many designers find it helpful to illustrate the conceptual relationships among the attributes using diagrams, such as those in Figure 12.12. The word cloud diagram in Figure 12.13 is also an effective storytelling tool, accompanied by an explanation. By establishing a visual hierarchy, it illustrates the relationship between the experience attributes (the largest words) and the supporting terms (which are the two intermediate sizes, with the larger being the more important). In a way, it also explains the origins of the terms that are being emphasized by surrounding them with a cloud of the original words. Spatial arrangement indicates that these concepts are not rigid boxes. Either sort of diagram needs to be accompanied by explanation to make sense to anyone but the design team.

Figure 12.11: Rearranging the attributes.

Figure 12.12. These diagrams illustrate the balance and tension within the set of attributes. The quadrant approach provides a more direct contrast, but might incorrectly imply that the terms are meant to be opposites.

Figure 12.13. This word cloud diagram illustrates the hierarchy of attributes and supporting terms, their relationships with one another, and their origins.

Step 7: Develop additional communication tools

Communicating about the experience attributes in several different ways helps stakeholders understand and engage in fruitful discussion about them. The diagrams in Figures 12.12 and 12.13 are a good starting point and may suffice if your stakeholders are good at visualizing. Whenever possible, though, you should also communicate visually because it helps stakeholders connect the dots. There are two typical approaches to this.

The first involves developing a collage of images (such as the one in Figure 12.14) that represent each attribute and its associated supporting terms, using products (or details of product finishes and materials), environments, or even people.

341

These are sometimes called "mood boards." When possible, the images should communicate on multiple levels, not only demonstrating aspects of appropriate design language, but also taking advantage of qualities associated with the image. For example, a photo of San Francisco's famous Golden Gate Bridge carries with it a certain aura of great human achievement that, say, the many other bridges around San Francisco Bay do not. An image of an iPod selected for its clean lines also conveys the status of a category leader and huge commercial success.

This exercise is not as easy as it sounds, because the images have to be free from unwanted associations. An image of a failed product with a perfectly appropriate design language won't instill confidence in stakeholders; it will only confuse the discussion. A photo that contains too much clutter makes it hard for viewers to know what quality you're trying to communicate. Avoid images that contain conflicting qualities; if you're trying to say *simple*, then it doesn't work to have an object with an uncomplicated shape but a very busy texture, or one that looks simple but is associated with a very complex activity. It's better to skip the images and communicate with just the words if you can't take the time to do it well. If you're having a lot of difficulty finding images that communicate what you want them to, you should also consider whether you have quite the right words in each cluster.

Consider the examples in Figures 12.14 and 12.15. Figure 12.14 is not successful because it was approached from an intellectual rather than an emotional point of view. The image of the stone wall and even the heavy door wouldn't be bad by themselves, but walls and fences viewed from the outside say *go away*. Guns, traps, snarling dogs, and fighter jets are all tools people use to create security, but they don't evoke the *feeling* of security—they inspire anxiety, which is the opposite of the desired effect. In Figure 12.15,

on the other hand, visual designer Jayson Mc-Cauliff used images that evoke a sense of safety, shelter, and protection. A walled garden, for example, is private from the outside world without being unpleasant. The polished, precise-looking safe implies mass, quality, and a sense of control. The rock evokes strength and solidity. The suit of armor and the armor-like texture are defensive rather than offensive, so they're not off-putting in the way the more aggressive images from Figure 12.14 are. The armor texture is also reminiscent of a roof's shingles, which provide shelter.

Beyond the emotional content, the images in Figure 12.15 form a better basis for the eventual design language (see Chapter 18). The dog, chain-wrapped safe, and most of the other elements in Figure 12.14 would be difficult to translate into a visual direction. The metallic color and finish of several of the images in Figure 12.15, along with the heavy incised lines on the safe's combination lock and the geometric precision of the garden, all hint at a possible palette and an approach to lines and shapes. The warmth of the human elements and the color in the garden forecast that the design language can't be entirely cold and metallic, but needs a hint of some warmth and softness to avoid being off-putting.

Another useful communication tool helps define the boundaries of the experience attributes by contrasting them with other terms that are either extreme versions of the attributes or synonyms with distinct connotations. For example, a Web site might be witty but not cheeky, smart but not intellectual, or polished but not slick. These are ideally illustrated with photos that embody the quality described, as designer Jayson McCauliff illustrates in Figure 12.16. You may also find that this exercise helps clarify your thinking. As with the collage in Figure 12.15, these should ideally hint at possible design language elements.

Figure 12.14. An unsuccessful collage.

impenetrable
protected
safe
solid
fortified
sheltered
massive
private
SECURE
stable
trusted
strong
tight
anchored

Figure 12.15. A successful collage.

Youthful NOT Young

Clean NOT Sterile

Innovative NOT Bleeding edge

Figure 12.16. Using words and images with different nuances can help define the boundaries and focus of the experience attributes.

Requirements

Expressing the experience attributes in visual terms helps stakeholders understand their relationship to the design.

Regardless of how you express the experience attributes, remember that the idea is to provide a sharp focus on the product's personality and appearance and help less visually-inclined stakeholders understand its significance.

Exercise

Imagine that you heard the following terms in relation to the Local-Guide experience; feel free to add your own from any research you did. Develop a set of experience attributes and supporting terms, along with appropriate communication materials.

FROM THE LGS BRAND MATERIALS:

— Experienced

— Enabling commerce

— Trusted partner

— Reliable

— Flexible

— Helpful

FROM STAKEHOLDERS:

— Durable

— Customizable (for individual cities)

— Users "get it" instantly (from three stakeholders)

— Compact (has to look like it won't be a pain to carry around)

— Local expert (from four stakeholders)

— Simple but not childish

— Rugged

— Comfortable

— Easy to use (from three stakeholders)

— Cool

— Not intimidating

— Up to date

FROM POTENTIAL-USER DATA:

— Unobtrusive (several users did not want to look like tourists)

— Trusted guide (from most users)

— Not flashy

— Rich (in the informative sense)

— Helpful

— Useful

— Fun

Project Management for Developing Requirements

Involved as this phase may sound, it seldom takes more than a week to develop scenarios and requirements for even the most complex projects. Projects with a single primary persona and a narrow scope (such as three or four context scenarios) might need only a day or two.

The interaction designers generally drive the scenario creation and the translation of scenarios into requirements. The visual designer (sometimes with an industrial designer) works on the experience attributes in parallel. If there are many context scenarios, the visual design work may take less time than the interaction design work, which may mean the visual designer is not full-time during this phase. Any industrial design time is most likely split between these two activities. Both the visual and industrial designers are also responsible for developing any requirements specific to their disciplines, though some of these may also arise from the scenarios.

As with most parts of the process, each design team member needs a few opportunities to review the work of the others and provide input. Good topics for informal check-ins with the team lead and other designers include the:

— List of context scenarios

— First draft of each scenario

— Clusters of experience-related terms

— First draft of the requirements list

— Proposed experience attributes and supporting terms

— Visual communication related to the experience attributes

During these check-ins, each team member looks for potential issues, such as deviations from the personas, inappropriate breadth or depth, unjustified conclusions, and stakeholder concerns that aren't addressed. Each contributes missing pieces or suggests improvements.

Table 12.4 outlines a typical schedule of team member activities during this phase.

Initial requirements definition seldom takes more than a week.

Requirements

Table 12.4. **Example team member schedules.**

	Interaction designers	Visual designer	Industrial designer	Design team lead
Day 1 morning	Develop context scenario list, review with team lead	Begin experience attributes	Develop context scenario list, begin experience attributes	Review scenario list
Day 1 afternoon	Draft scenarios #1 and #2, collaborate with ID	Continue experience attributes	Continue experience attributes, collaborate with IxDs	
Day 2 morning	Team check-in on scenarios and attributes	Team check-in on scenarios and attributes	Team check-in on scenarios and attributes	Team check-in on scenarios and attributes
Day 2 afternoon	Draft scenarios #3 and #4, collaborate with ID	Refine attributes and begin assembling communication tools	Refine attributes, collaborate with IxDs	
Day 3 morning	Brief team check-in, refinement, prep for project owner check-in	Brief team check-in, refinement, prep for project owner check-in	Brief team check-in, refinement, prep for project owner check-in	Brief team check-in, refinement, prep for project owner check-in
Day 3 afternoon	Informal check-in with project owner	Informal check-in with project owner	Informal check-in with project owner	Informal check-in with project owner
Day 4 morning	Refine scenarios, draft requirements list	Refine attributes and communication tools, draft requirements list	Refine attributes and communication tools, draft requirements list	
Day 4 afternoon	Team check-in on requirements list, refine	Team check-in on requirements list, refine	Team check-in on requirements list, refine	Review requirements list

Summary

Requirements definition connects the dots between research and design, so a rigorous process continues to be important. While you should certainly use every source at your disposal, including your imagination, be sure to check your ideas and assumptions against the personas, business goals, and other objective tools. Spend plenty of time on your scenarios, since these will be a critical design tool in the next phase.

Remember that stakeholders, not engineers, are the audience for these requirements. The whole point of the exercise is not to generate an exhaustive list or a stack of documents, but to stimulate discussion and facilitate informed decisions. Your ability to see through the eyes of the personas and clearly define needs before seeking solutions will provide tremendous value in product definition.

Requirements

Carla

CHAPTER 13

Putting It All Together:
The User and Domain Analysis

As you've been conducting your research and figuring out what it all means, you've probably been having plenty of informal communication with your project owner or other stakeholders. E-mail, hallway conversations, and brief check-ins help everyone feel informed, get necessary support, or review ideas in a low-risk environment. Design team intranets and other shared virtual workspaces can give others easy access to work in progress. However, these informal methods are seldom effective for resolving big issues, and they don't ensure involvement and understanding on the part of the necessary people. More formal communication is an essential part of the design process because it promotes common understanding, shared expectations, and commitment among stakeholders in a way that no other approach can. The **User and Domain Analysis** (U&DA, for short) is a critical milestone that helps ensure you have all three before you start designing.

There are several important reasons for formal communication at this point. The first is to have all the relevant stakeholders review your work for potential flaws. Experienced design teams rarely need major corrections, but no one is infallible. Any issues stakeholders can spot now will save

you time and grief later. This review is especially important if you've had to compress your research due to limited time or budget.

This is also an opportunity to build your credibility with stakeholders. It may be less important if you've worked with them for a while, but consultants and new designers often have to demonstrate that they can grasp the complexities of a new industry or complex process. Stakeholders will be impressed if you can help them see more clearly or in a new way. However, it's enough if they leave the meeting convinced that you understand the fundamentals and have the beginnings of a vision for the product. Some may be a little disappointed if you don't have any game-changing revelations to offer, but they'll also be happy to know that they haven't been missing something important all along.

Of course, one of the main reasons for doing research in the first place is to enable informed action, so the U&DA should provide a set of clearly articulated choices and, to the extent possible, the information and tools to help stakeholders make them. There may very well be business or technical information you can't provide, but you

Formal communication is about building consensus and getting commitment from stakeholders.

can offer a clear understanding of users and customers and their needs, the opportunities and problems to be addressed, and the constraints and challenges involved in doing so. Your personas and goals will also provide a framework for making decisions, and your scenarios will begin to provide a vision for the product or service so stakeholders have a better idea of what they're giving up when they make certain choices.

Finally, formal checkpoints are meant to build consensus and get commitment from each and every stakeholder before you proceed. A live presentation with everyone in the same room allows stakeholders to ask questions (which builds their confidence in you) and to see how their colleagues are responding. It also means they're all looking you and one another in the eyes when they say, "Yes, these findings and personas make sense, and I agree that we should focus on these requirements and not those." This minimizes feature creep and thrashing about product direction later on.

Senior business decision-makers are the primary audience for the U&DA, since you will be asking them to make choices about product positioning, priorities within the target market, and time and cost versus functionality and polish; in most cases, neither the marketing stakeholders nor engineering leads should be making this kind of call on their own. However, it's essential that other stakeholders are involved, both to build consensus and to make the decision-makers aware of issues related to their specialties. A presentation and discussion are essential; a detailed document is also useful if time permits, especially for large, distributed teams or major projects.

Typical Structure

Whether you're developing a presentation or a document, the idea is to make the case for your conclusions by bringing the audience through your thought process. How much detail to provide depends on the temperament of your audience—some will be happiest if you skip the *how* and go straight to the *what*, but more analytical stakeholders will want to see if your logic makes sense.

Because you're essentially building an argument, presentations (and documents, when applicable) consistently work best when they follow a rhetorical structure something like this:

— An introduction that includes the project parameters
— A description of the research methods and activities and why you chose them

— A summary of findings that describe general issues and patterns

— The set of personas that encapsulate those patterns

— Several scenarios describing how the personas would like things to be

— The requirements implied by those scenarios and your findings

— A discussion of how you'll move the process forward

If you're in a small organization with easy access to all the right stakeholders, you might consider splitting this milestone into two: one that's purely focused on describing the world today, which includes your research findings and personas, followed by another focused on your scenarios and requirements. This is a good idea in that it allows everyone to agree on the problem definition before you spend any time thinking about solutions.

However, there are a few reasons not to split this content. One reason in large organizations is simple logistics: Getting all the stakeholders in a room twice within a week or two can be all but impossible. Also, because scenarios and requirements take just a few days, and because you can do an informal check-in with your project owner, there's little chance of the time you spend on those activities being wasted. The most important reason is a little bit of psychology: Whether they're conscious of it or not, most people don't respond well to being shown a problem without at least the hint of a solution. By outlining scenarios and requirements immediately after discussing the problems to be solved, you will leave stakeholders with a sense of possibility and an eagerness for action, rather than a feeling of helplessness and a fear that you won't come up with good solutions.

The following sections walk you through each part of the content in more detail; specifics related to documents versus presentations follow the content discussion.

Introduction of the project parameters

The main points in your introduction should include:

— Project mandate and objectives

— Timeline

— Overall approach

— Contact information

Each document or presentation should begin with an introduction that includes a brief description of your mandate, your timeline, and your

> Leave stakeholders feeling empowered, not staring helplessly at a list of problems.

Requirements

approach to the project. Stakeholders who have been involved all along can use the reminder, and you never know when someone new may show up at a meeting. Documents and presentations can have a long life, too; someone three years from now may need that information to figure out how to approach a similar project.

Your mandate is a statement about why the company is undertaking the project and what you've been asked to accomplish. Surprisingly enough, not everyone who sees your work will be informed about these basics, so including them can prevent a lot of unnecessary questions about why you're not doing this or that.

Your timeline and approach to the project can help put your document or presentation in context. People will be less likely to express concerns about the level of detail or the breadth of research if they can see how much—or how little—time you've spent. They'll also be more

comfortable with what's *not* in the U&DA if they know they're going to see design concepts in just a couple of weeks.

You'll also do your audience a favor if you include some basic quick-reference information, such as how to reach the members of the design team or where on a corporate server to find related documents.

Keep this section simple; a couple of slides or pages should do. See Figure 13.1 for examples.

Research activities: what you did

The main points under research activities should include:

— Research methods and why you chose them

— Description of field data set

— Other information sources

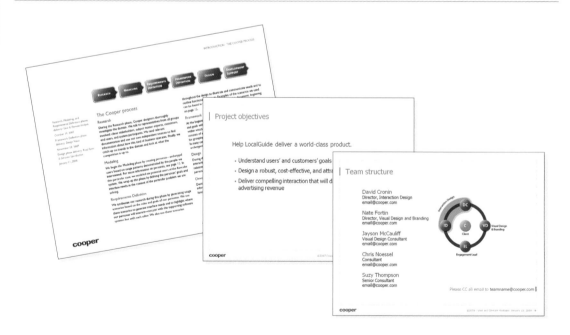

Figure 13.1. Some examples of introductory U&DA document and presentation content.

A research summary describes both your methods and the composition of your data set. This helps stakeholders assess how much weight to give your data and conclusions. This is not the place for results or analysis, but is simply a record of what you did and why. It is also, implicitly, a record of what you did not do.

Briefly explain what research methods you used, why they were appropriate, and—if applicable—what makes them different from previous approaches to research in this organization. You may have to sell the methods to some extent. If your audience includes any stakeholders who were not involved in the research planning, it's often essential to discuss the difference between qualitative and quantitative methods. However, don't over-sell; be clear about what any research method is and isn't good for. A paragraph of text or a slide on each method should be plenty; the stakeholders who care to know more were probably involved in that part of the process anyway. Here's an example description of the interviewing techniques from Chapter 7, outlined at an appropriate level of detail for most stakeholders:

We conducted individual interviews using primarily ethnographic techniques that combined observation and discussion. Instead of asking users what features they wanted, we asked about their behaviors, frustrations, and goals. Conducting interviews in the context of use provided clues about workarounds and unacknowledged tasks. These techniques are effective at uncovering attitudes and motivations, as well as unconscious behaviors, and are well suited to identifying the range of needs the product should accommodate. However, because the approach is qualitative, it's only of limited use in determining the prevalence of each type of behavior.

You might also want to list every credible source of information you used, such as documents you read, forums you lurked in, surveys you conducted, trainings you attended, people you interviewed, and competitors you assessed. (The comic books and science fiction movies may not help your case, though.) A long and detailed list like the one in Figure 13.2 is reassuring for stakeholders

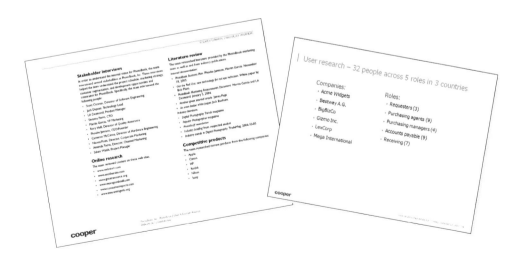

Figure 13.2. Slide and document examples of information sources.

and potentially helpful when you need to track something down later on. Don't worry about the tedium of reading these aloud in a presentation; you can either tell people to see the list in the document, or briefly flash a slide and say something like, "We read a lot of documents ... <click> ... and we talked to 19 stakeholders, including most of you ... <click> ... and we interviewed 25 users."

It's a good idea to list each stakeholder you interviewed by name and ideally by job title, so each person can see that you've involved the right people. It's probably better to omit job titles than to annoy people by getting their titles wrong. Always be sure to double-check the spelling of names, too. Consider alphabetizing the stakeholder list so no one worries about whether someone higher up the list is seen as more important (it sounds silly, but people can get hung up on things like this).

For consumer products, stakeholders usually have questions about key demographic characteristics and geographic locations of the interviewees or survey participants, so describe your sample in these terms, such as in this example slide text:

We did 25 driver interviews:

— Chicago, New York, and Sacramento

— 12 men, 13 women

— Ages 17 to 64

— 10,000 to 130,000 miles per year

— In-home, at dealerships, in-vehicle

A map with locations highlighted can make a nice visual aid for this topic. For enterprise products, stakeholders usually want key facts about each of the companies you visited: what product or version they use, what industry they're in, or how big they are. Also list how many people you interviewed and in what roles. For example:

Acme Widgets, Savannah, Georgia

— Second-largest widget manufacturer in U.S.

— 1,200 employees

— Purchases for supply chain and general business needs

— Using Purchase Pro 2.0

— Interviewed 3 purchasing agents and 1 accounts payable clerk

You may not want to name every person you interviewed, though; this information is usually meaningless and boring to your audience and might violate any promises of anonymity you made. However, stakeholders who are well acquainted with specific customers may want to know that you spoke with Bob Smith at Acme Widgets.

Research findings: what you learned

Your research findings should include:

— What you heard from stakeholders

— What you learned about the industry

— What you learned from potential customers and users

— What you learned about the current product or service

To many stakeholders, the research findings are the whole point of attending a presentation or reading a document. This summary helps others learn from your research insights. Some in your audience may be learning about their potential customers and users for the first time; a good U&DA also makes an excellent employee training tool. Most stakeholders are at least somewhat familiar with their market, though, and are hoping your research will highlight unforeseen opportunities, help them avoid mistakes, or validate a direction they've tentatively decided upon. While

Requirements

stakeholders sometimes don't realize it, the findings are also your chance to help end disagreements and clear up misconceptions.

WHAT YOU HEARD FROM STAKEHOLDERS

Stakeholders don't want you to spend a lot of time regurgitating what they told you; they just want to know they were heard. Of course, a recap of stakeholder findings may be your chance to point out where there is disagreement that the research findings can clear up or that you need resolved soon. However, it's best to involve your project owner in determining whether a group meeting is the right way to handle controversy; it's usually unwise to contradict a senior executive's dearly held belief in a public forum.

Provide a brief summary of what you understand about the following points, using just a few document pages or slides:

— What kinds of users and customers the stakeholders think are most important

— What stakeholders think the product is

— What they expect to ship and when

— What presumed constraints exist, and which may be flexible

— What the project should accomplish for the business

— What stakeholders think success is, and what they think will be required to achieve it

— What barriers to success they expect

It may seem like you can omit this content if you're working on an internal team rather than as a consultant, but nearly every set of stakeholders needs to discuss at least one of these topics as a group.

WHAT YOU LEARNED ABOUT THE INDUSTRY

A brief summary of what you learned about the industry may be old news to many stakeholders,

but will at least confirm that you've understood the important points if you need to establish credibility (see Figure 13.3). It's also helpful for any future product team members. In six months, you might also be glad you put a glossary of the more obscure terminology in a document appendix. The following topics are typically of interest to stakeholders, though in-house designers may be able to gloss over them:

— How business relationships are structured

— What regulations and standards affect needs and behaviors

— What emerging technologies and related issues are generating buzz

— How various brands and competitive products are positioned

Figure 13.3. An example slide illustrating industry findings.

WHAT YOU LEARNED ABOUT POTENTIAL CUSTOMERS AND USERS

The user and customer findings are not simply a summary of everything you saw; rather, they describe the patterns and insights derived from your analysis. The findings will help stakeholders empathize with the customers and users, and should help settle any open questions. They also prepare the audience for the personas—just as a movie romance is more plausible if you've seen the signs leading up to it, the personas and requirements make much more sense to stakeholders when you've used the findings as foreshadowing. For example, the following comment prepares the audience for Tim Wilson, the office phone-system customer persona in Chapter 11:

> **Small business owners have to balance long-term thinking with today's needs.** They know it's not smart to invest in any system that can't grow with the business, but they're concerned that more capable systems will be more expensive and more difficult to configure.

This finding helps lay a foundation for Carla Ramirez, the car-buyer persona from Chapter 11:

> **Emotional buyers do limited research.** Buyers who respond emotionally to a particular vehicle may conduct a small amount of research to see whether it fits a few specific criteria, such as cargo space or cost. They often don't look at other vehicles as long as the one that elicits an emotional response meets their most important needs.

User findings should not only introduce some of the key trends that make up the personas, such as frustrations, mental models, and approaches to tasks, but should also describe the world in which the personas exist, such as relationships among roles or differences between large and small companies. It's especially important to highlight anything contrary to the expectations you or stakeholders had before the research, such as roles that weren't as crisply defined as you thought.

It generally works best to start at a high level, such as by describing company types or other environmental patterns, followed by any role and process distinctions among them. Later, get down to the detail of user characteristics and, finally, frustrations.

For example, consider the following outline of findings from corporate purchasing research:

Large companies had dedicated specialists:

— Purchasing agents

— Receiving clerks

— Accounts payable clerks

— The relationship among the three roles looked like this...

Small companies had part-time generalists

— One individual performed all three roles on occasion

About purchasing agents

— Most had high school educations and 1-3 years of prior clerical experience

— Usually moved into purchasing after demonstrating administrative competence

— All were comfortable with e-mail, basic Word use, and PurchasePro fundamentals, but did not know any application's full capabilities

— Duties include placing orders, negotiating deals, following up on orders

— Typical process...

— The process for manufacturing supply chains differed...

— Most were frustrated by...

About receiving clerks

Etc.

It's often effective to incorporate quantitative data along with the qualitative findings, whether they reinforce or contradict one another. For example:

Of the 18 investors we interviewed, 14 indicated that they were not entirely happy with their brokers; this is consistent with the survey finding that 73% were dissatisfied or somewhat dissatisfied. However, our qualitative findings seem to contradict the survey with respect to how many of these would be interested in self-service investing. Nine of the 14 interview participants expected to stick with their brokers because it's more convenient, whereas 85% of dissatisfied survey participants said they were looking into self-service. While the qualitative result is not conclusive, we believe the survey result may be artificially high due to the fact that participants were recruited primarily from an online investing information site.

This is more interesting and informative than walking people through every survey question independent of the qualitative findings. However, if you're incorporating a lot of quantitative data, it's usually easier to break out the analysis of a lengthy survey into its own section.

How much detail you provide depends on the time you have and the inclinations of your stakeholders. On most projects, it's sufficient to cover the roles, a high-level workflow example for each, the behavioral trends that form the basis of the personas, and the most common frustrations with existing solutions. It's rarely necessary (or desirable) to describe every behavior or summarize each interview.

The more vivid you can make your findings, the more impact they'll have. Include some of your research photos of workspaces and workarounds, such as those in Figures 7.1 through 7.9. Showing several photos illustrating the same kind of problem makes it harder for people to dismiss an inconvenient issue. Images are likewise important in describing the physical and visual characteristics of users' environments (see Figure 13.4). Also include any of the models and visualizations you developed while analyzing your data, since they may help stakeholders gain insight just as you did. Direct quotes from interviews or user diaries can be compelling, as well.

Requirements

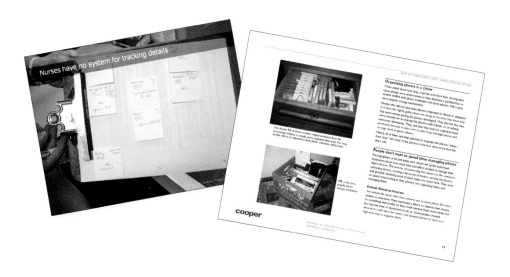

Figure 13.4. Slide and document examples of user and customer research findings.

Requirements

WHAT YOU LEARNED ABOUT THE CURRENT PRODUCT OR SERVICE

When you're redesigning an existing product, stakeholders need to agree on what's wrong with it before you can talk about how to fix it. It can be tricky to figure out just where in your narrative to do this, though. Product reviews often work best in the findings section after the discussion of roles, workflows, and trends, but there are two disadvantages to this placement. First, if it comes before you've introduced the personas, your review has to be based on general design principles and user comments, whereas you could use the personas to describe the issues if it's later in the flow. Using principles alone makes it harder to critique problems due to incorrect workflow or contradiction of user mental models. Also, a lengthy product audit between your behavioral findings and the personas can make it difficult for stakeholders to connect the dots between them. After the personas, though, it interrupts the flow from personas to scenarios and requirements. Any critique of visual design from a brand perspective also requires that you describe the experience attributes first.

The easy solution in a document is to put any product review in an appendix. In a presentation, use whatever placement feels least disruptive, and just address a handful of the most critical points. The exception is when you're doing a very tactical redesign, in which case a principle-based review may deserve more attention. An extensive overhaul will make minor issues irrelevant, though, much as knocking down a house and starting over makes it pointless to worry about whether the drapes are ugly.

Reviewing existing products requires diplomacy, since the people who developed them are likely sitting in the room as you pick apart their work. This makes it important to find positives as well as criticisms, and to ground each point in established design principles, user data, or—if you're doing the product review after the personas—in persona goals. I find that people receive critique

Follow the mental model

"Alignment and spacing" presumably deals with aligning things on the slide. Why are the controls for aligning objects under "size, rotation, and ordering"?

Figure 13.5 An example product critique shows how screen shots or product photos are essential to illustrating your points.

best when I start by stating the principle or user goal, getting agreement that it makes sense, and then pointing out how the product doesn't satisfy it. Figure 13.5 provides an example.

Personas

Your discussion of personas should include:

— What personas are and why they're useful

— An overview of the set

— Individual personas

— Relationships and priorities

Once your user findings have laid the groundwork, it's time to introduce the personas who will be the basis for the requirements and design. Unless all of the stakeholders are accustomed to using personas, begin with a brief description (perhaps a page or a couple of slides) of what personas are, how they're derived from behavior patterns in the research, and why they're useful. This is worthwhile even if you've already defined personas in your kickoff meeting because misconceptions may persist, and you may have a new stakeholder or two.

Figure 13.6. This diagram illustrates how the personas fit within each organizational archetype.

Figure 13.7. A summary of personas versus the behavioral and demographic variable mappings helps demonstrate that you took a rigorous approach.

Provide a brief overview of the entire set before getting into detail about each persona. This puts stakeholders at ease that you have the range of needs covered. You can use a quick reference like the one shown in Figure 11.18 for this. However, it's often most effective if you can start by illustrating the relationships between the personas and findings, such as by tying them to a process model or showing how they cover the range of important demographics, as in Figures 11.19 and 11.20. Include any organizational archetypes in this overview and illustrate how the personas fit within each organization, such as in Figure 13.6. This provides useful context.

Once you've provided the overview, introduce the detailed personas. A document should include the narrative description; a list of key points is fine in the presentation. A parallel structure for each description makes them easier to digest. Don't worry about having persona summary posters and a lot of other artifacts when you first introduce the set—you can work with stakeholders to determine how to promote the personas within the organization. It often works better when stakeholders are the ones saying, "Hey, these persona things are great. We should develop some more materials to help everyone adopt them."

Some further comparison of persona attributes may be useful after stakeholders have met each one, particularly if you anticipate concerns about how well you've covered certain market segments or addressed particular types of customers. Showing a distilled version of your behavioral and demographic variable mappings (using just the personas, not the interviewees) can help to illustrate your thoroughness and reinforce that the personas are not arbitrary. See Figure 13.7 for an example.

Finally, you'll need to discuss the roles of primary, secondary, and possibly supplemental personas. It's important that stakeholders understand that you'll just be *optimizing* for the primary, not excluding the other personas from consideration. Also be sure to explain the implications of multiple primaries, if you have them. Your approach to discussing priorities will differ slightly depending on whether you've made a choice of primary or whether you're asking stakeholders to do so. In either case, you'll need to explain the implications of each possibility and describe useful criteria for making the decision, such as those in Figure 13.8.

Requirements

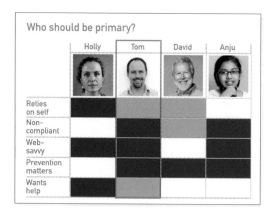

Figure 13.8. This table provides a good analysis of which persona should be primary.

Context scenarios

Your discussion of context scenarios should include:

— What scenarios are and why they're useful

— Individual scenarios

The personas are informative but seldom exciting. The context scenarios begin to demonstrate the so what of your research: how what you learned makes it possible to please customers and users. This is your chance to get stakeholders fired up about what the product or service could be.

However, some people have trouble envisioning design from reading or hearing context scenarios; it's almost always a good idea to share them, but consider ways to reduce any potential anxiety, such as by providing rough storyboards like the one in Figure 12.3. Also preface your scenarios with an explanation of what they are and are not: they're high-level, idealized descriptions of typical interactions from the personas' points of view, intended to help everyone think about what's possible. Remind your audience that you'll get to better solutions if you start by thinking optimistically and not focusing on constraints just yet.

Although it's more efficient to outline the scenarios in a table with the requirements listed alongside each point, it's important—especially in a presentation—to engage the audience's imagination with storytelling before engaging their intellect with requirements. Use a prose description in the document and a list of key points in a presentation.

Requirements

Main points for requirements include:

— The role of these requirements

— Specific functional, data, and other requirements organized by priority, persona, or source

— Experience attributes

After you've described the personas' ideal interactions and hopefully gotten your audience excited, you need to help them think through the implications of what you've just described. Start by explaining that your preliminary list of requirements (or other politically appropriate term) is meant to stimulate discussion and enable decisions about big issues, not to be exhaustive. Briefly describe that they are derived not only from the scenarios, but also from the persona goals and characteristics, business needs, and so forth.

Communicate all of your proposed product requirements—even those that are likely to be unmet in the next release—to encourage long-term thinking. However, it's often a good idea to indicate your sense of priority for the requirements, such as those that are absolutely essential to achieving persona goals and necessary tasks, those the personas could live without for a while but will appreciate, and those the personas don't especially care about. It's almost never feasible to accomplish everything in an initial release.

There are a few ways to structure the requirements discussion, any of which can work well— it's a matter of deciding which one best fits the nature of your requirements and the personalities of your stakeholders. One option is to jump straight from the scenarios to a single, prioritized list of requirements. Another is to walk through a prioritized list of ways to satisfy each persona, followed by additional needs implied by the environment, business objectives, and other factors. You can also emphasize the relationship between scenarios and requirements by listing the specific requirements implied by each scenario, usually in tabular form, then moving on to the requirements generated from other sources. See Figure 13.9 for several examples. In any case, these requirements seldom take more than a handful of slides or document pages.

The experience attributes are different enough from the other requirements—and involve a sufficiently unique thought process—that it's usually most effective to describe them after you've covered the other requirements. In a presentation, this also allows for a separate discussion, since stakeholders who are not brand oriented sometimes don't participate in productive ways (though it's better to educate them than to exclude them, whenever possible).

You need to make a case for the set of attributes you've outlined, so this brief section builds an argument much as the rest of the presentation does. Revisit your understanding of the corporate brand and what you heard from stakeholders. Explain why you need to translate that into characteristics you can express in visual and industrial design or copy style. Briefly describe how you employed the user data and personas to do so, perhaps using images from the research data to describe the environments you saw. Explain the personas' experience goals, affiliation with well-known brands that are relevant, or other important attitudes. Finally, use the communication tools discussed in the "Experience attributes"

section of Chapter 12 to explain the attributes. An attribute cloud (such as the one in Figure 12.13) makes an excellent starting point because it illustrates the relationships among the attributes and supporting terms, and even shows them emerging from specific words used in stakeholder and user interviews. Following this with a collage for each group of terms (see Figure 12.15) helps stakeholders better understand each attribute. Is/is-not illustrations (such as those in Figure 12.16) can then help sharpen the boundaries of the attribute set.

Next steps

Main points to review about next steps include:

— The date of the next discussion

— What people will see

— What you need in the interim

By the time they're done reading your document or listening to your presentation, your audience should feel like you've given them a great summary of the issues and some clues about how to address them. They'll also be itching to see concrete solutions and to know how you plan to get there, so wrap up your presentation or document with a reminder of when the next milestone is, what stakeholders should expect to see, and what you need from them in the meantime. If you can show examples of framework sketches (see Chapter 16) and design language studies (see Chapter 18), this will help reduce the anxiety stakeholders inevitably experience at this point.

The list of action items for stakeholders might include certain decisions or answers to essential questions. When something is unresolved, state the assumptions you plan to make as you proceed with developing design concepts; it's almost always more productive to make progress based on assumptions than to wait until every decision is made.

Requirements

Organized by persona

How we can help Holly

Most important:

— Show her the latest cancer research (in lay terms)

— Provide human contact with other survivors

If possible:

— Support her efforts to stay healthy with nutrition, stress, and other information

Organized by priority

Critical requirements

— Make the latest research available in lay terms

— Provide contact with others in similar circumstances

— Provide resources targeting the newly diagnosed

— Offer tools for taking action (such as personal record-keeping and discussion points for doctor visits)

— Provide reminder services

— Have a real human check in periodically, especially with the newly diagnosed

Organized by scenario

Scenario text

After a long meeting, Anne pulls out her Personal Assistant to note a couple of items she needs to follow up on, confirm the location of her next meeting, and see if anything important has come up in the last couple of hours.

When she turns on the screen, the PA shows her the subject and location of her next meeting, which is in 25 minutes.

There's also an indication that she has three messages marked urgent (including one from her boss), one message from a client whose messages she's told the PA are top priority, and a dozen others that can probably wait.

After noting her to-do items before she forgets them, Anne selects the urgent message from her boss, which is a voicemail, and listens to it as she walks to the parking garage.

His question about a recent contract is time sensitive, so she selects the option to call him back.

Requirements

— Ability to enter text
— Ability to track appointments
— Ability to see a list of messages
— Portable form factor

— Ability to turn off the screen without the turning off the device
— Ability to count down to the next event

— Ability to see both e-mail and voice messages in a single place, along with next event
— Ability to auto-prioritize some messages based on simple criteria specified by users, as well as based on urgency indicated by the sender

— Ability to enter and track tasks
— Ability to select a message from a visual list
— Ability to listen to voicemail

— Ability to initiate various types of return communication directly from a message

Figure 13.9. These slides and document pages illustrate several ways of expressing requirements.

Developing an Effective Document

A detailed document is not always necessary at this point, but can be a good idea for several reasons. For one thing, your research probably uncovered a lot of detail that may be valuable, but is difficult to convey in a presentation of reasonable length. For another, presentation slides lose a great deal when viewed out of context, which makes them less useful to absent team members or those who join the project in the future. Documents also provide a better reference several months later when memories have faded. Internationally distributed teams can benefit from having time to sit and absorb the content, since it's easy to miss detail when listening to a presentation delivered in anything other than your native language.

Research documents can be dry and difficult to read, especially when written as if for an academic audience. A User and Domain Analysis is not for an academic audience, though—it's for busy people who don't have the time or patience for piles of convoluted prose. Your document will be more useful (and will encourage more people to read it) if you make it engaging and easy to digest.

A document, like any other designed product, has to serve multiple types of people: those who are inclined to read the whole thing from start to finish and those who are either looking up a specific detail or flipping through the document to get a sense of the highlights. Use prose to create a coherent, detailed narrative that works well when read from cover to cover, but use headings, bullets, and visual communication to orient flippers and draw them in; as my colleague Steve Calde says, "Write for readers and format for flippers." Figure 13.10 shows an example of a page formatted for flippers.

Throughout the document, use plenty of headings and subheadings that stand out visually from the rest of the text. These make it easy to skim a page for something relevant or interesting. When describing findings, consider treating your headings as headlines rather than simple topic labels; "the product looks unprofessional" is more likely to catch a flipper's attention than something bland like "views on visual design."

Pull quotes—snippets of compelling text called out in larger type—also provide visual entry points on the page. These may be actual quotes from interviewees that relate to a point in the text, or may be used to emphasize especially important points drawn from the copy.

> # Write for readers, format for flippers.

Requirements

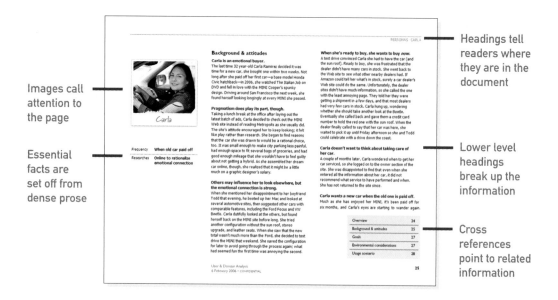

Images call attention to the page

Essential facts are set off from dense prose

Headings tell readers where they are in the document

Lower level headings break up the information

Cross references point to related information

Figure 13.10. A clean, simple layout grid with plenty of white space makes pages more accessible. Headings, pull quotes, and images draw flippers in.

Photos and diagrams are useful for illustrating important or complex concepts and relationships, reinforcing specific points, or simply breaking up walls of text. Distribute photos throughout the findings section to intrigue flippers and get them to read more about a topic. Reasonably attractive diagrams and crisp, well-lit photos are best, but clear communication is more critical than exquisite visuals. Obviously overdesigned documents can cause stakeholders to wonder if you're spending your time wisely.

Don't underestimate the importance of making a good impression, though. A clean, consistent layout and legible type make your document easier to read. Effective organization and clear, professional writing make your points more compelling and credible. Use active voice and reasonably simple sentences. Use a professional tone, but don't feel compelled to show off the entire range of your vocabulary; there's no reason to use "Brobdingnagian" when "enormous" or just plain

"huge" will do. Have someone with appropriate skills edit for grammar and spelling.

Consider asking your project owner to review a draft for stakeholder pet peeves, political gaffes, or any other potential missteps that might make stakeholders less receptive. This is not to say that you should avoid controversy, however; your job is to tell stakeholders what they need to hear, even if they don't want to hear it.

Developing an Effective Presentation

Regardless of whether you have a document, a presentation is always essential. Unlike a document, which is generally one-way communication, a presentation provides a forum for questions and discussion, which are necessary for a group to agree on difficult choices. Busy executives often won't read documents, either, so a presentation is the best way to ensure their attention.

Dense text not suited to a slide

Maureen Keller, DVM
West Valley Animal Hospital

Maureen co-founded the clinic with 3 other vets 10 years ago. She prides herself on having specialists on staff and on having the latest equipment available. She sees 10 to 20 patients on most days. Maureen thinks 10 minutes of charting is too much time to spend per patient, but dislikes it when there's information missing from the chart.

Maureen's goals

– Focus on care, not recordkeeping
– Know she has the right information
– Minimize administrative time
– Feel like she has a world-class clinic

Less text with better formatting

Maureen Keller, DVM
West Valley Animal Hospital

– Co-founded clinic with others 10 years ago
– Proud to have specialists and latest equipment
– Sees 10 to 20 patients a day
– Thinks 10 minutes of charting is too much
– Dislikes missing chart info

Figure 13.11. Minimize the text on the slide, or at least use formatting that lets your audience focus on the key points.

Plan for an hour or at most two before you lose the attention of your audience. A presentation is necessarily linear; individual stakeholders can't just skip past the things they don't care about, so you have to anticipate what those things are. Treat the presentation as a set of document highlights rather than a complete recitation of the document. Spend the minimum number of slides on introductory information and research activities. Focus most of the slides on customer and user findings, personas, scenarios, and requirements. Keep your audience oriented by providing an agenda up front, then showing an agenda slide at the start of each section to indicate where you are.

Unless slides are your only documentation, keep the text on each slide to a minimum by using bullet lists and phrases rather than complete sentences, as shown in Figure 13.11. This provides enough information to remind you of what to say but not so much that the audience is reading the slide instead of listening to you. It also prevents too much reading from the slides—a sure way to drive your audience nuts. You can use formatting to emphasize the key points and encourage

people to focus on you even if your slides are the primary document.

Photos and diagrams are especially helpful for presentations because you can explain them verbally without the need to show a lot of text. Build slides, which let you add elements click by click without changing slides, can be effective for communicating complex processes, but can be distracting when overused. Use animation sparingly for the same reason.

As with a document, make sure you've got the basics covered: Proofread, use a clean and consistent visual style, and have your project owner look it over for political land mines. However tempting it is, though, never save a controversial point for the document to avoid confrontation—the more challenging it is, the more critical it is to address in the meeting.

Exercise

Develop a User and Domain Analysis presentation based on your work for the LocalGuide or RoomFinder.

Conducting the Meeting

Slides and documents aren't the point; discussion and decisions are.

Perfect slides and documents are not the point of the User and Domain Analysis milestone; discussion and decisions are. No matter what else happens, you need to get all of the stakeholders together to share what you've learned and what you think it means and, ultimately, help them arrive at decisions about it. Failure to do so will leave the product team stuck in a never-ending requirements phase.

Before the meeting

Send an e-mail before the meeting to set expectations about what people will see and hear and what kind of participation you need from them. Ask them to be fully involved, not reading their e-mail or taking calls; important decisions about the definition of the product deserve their complete attention. Ask that they arrive on time and stay for the entire meeting. Send remote participants a copy of the slides in case you have problems with the remote-conferencing system.

Arrive at the meeting room a little early to set up your slides and relax; running an effective meeting requires the whole design team to be prepared and attentive. Determine in advance who will be presenting what content. If you're not currently speaking, be ready to take detailed notes about questions and action items. Also be prepared to clarify a point or get the conversation unstuck if needed, while allowing the current presenter to lead the discussion. Spread the design team around the room so you can each see a subset of the stakeholders.

Delivering the presentation and leading the discussion

This is your meeting, so take charge of the room once everyone has arrived. Stand up at the front of the room so everyone can see and hear you, and so you can see everyone's reactions. This also indicates to others that you have the floor. Recap expectations for the meeting and let people know you're excited to share your results. Encourage them to ask questions if something isn't clear, but let them know you may ask them to hold a question or discussion for later. Mention that you also have a document if you do, but don't distribute it until the end of the meeting; otherwise, people will be flipping through pages instead of paying attention to the discussion.

INTRODUCTION, RESEARCH ACTIVITIES, AND FINDINGS

The agenda is seldom a controversial item. Your description of the project mandate should be routine if the people in the room were all involved in the project kickoff. New product team members might question the project's parameters or the research plan. Refer these questions to the project owner, who probably determined those parameters, but field any questions about the choice of research methods yourself. Don't make a fuss over any weaknesses in your sample, but do mention them.

Thank any of the stakeholders who were especially helpful in getting customer and user interviews, or who were otherwise generous with their time and expertise. Acknowledge people who aren't in the room, too; few research efforts would succeed without an administrative assistant's help with phone calls, scheduling, or travel arrangements.

Move quickly through anything you heard from stakeholders that wasn't controversial. If there was a disagreement that the user findings will shed some light on, say so. However, don't attribute points of view to particular people or say publicly that the data proves someone wrong. Highlight any important questions that the user findings won't help resolve, but don't discuss them now; these are best saved until after the presentation.

As you describe what you learned from customers and users, gloss over anything that isn't news to your audience. Focus on the issues that may surprise them or that have important implications for design. Acknowledge anything that surprised you, too; you don't want to look smug because you've learned things the stakeholders didn't know. You're not smarter than they are—you just have better tools and perhaps more access to users. Share specific stories that make users seem like real people and not an abstraction. Help stakeholders see users as frustrated and clever for coming up with workarounds, rather than as stupid for not understanding their existing systems.

HANDLING QUESTIONS AND CHALLENGES

Make sure you understand each question before responding. Never be afraid to say you don't know and will have to get back to someone, or to defer to a teammate who is better equipped to respond. This tells stakeholders that when you do answer a question, you really do know what you're talking about. When someone asks why you didn't do this or that, acknowledge why it might have been a useful thing to do, then explain why you didn't. Ask if you've answered the question before moving on.

Be careful not to let questions and discussion become a free-for-all, though. If a question is likely to pull the conversation off track, make a note of it (preferably on a whiteboard or somewhere else visible to the audience) and say you'll get back to it later. If you see side conversations starting to happen, ask the participants if there's a question or a topic you need to address.

Make sure you've answered any questions about findings before you move on to the personas. It's rare to have stakeholders flat out dispute your findings, but it can happen. Acknowledge when there is some possibility for error due to the size of your sample, but politely ask any skeptics to support their beliefs with evidence. Are there specific companies where they've seen things done that way? Is there a study you haven't seen that contradicts what you've learned? Ask other stakeholders for their thoughts on the skeptic's point of view. Most will usually support your findings. If all agree that your findings are somehow off, say you'll discuss how to address that with your project owner later on.

Focus more on hearing people and gaining agreement than on trying to be "right."

Focus more on hearing people and gaining agreement than on trying to be "right." If someone is disagreeing with you, they have some reason for doing so, whether they have information you don't have or are simply not feeling heard. Approach the discussion not as a battle you need to win, but as an exchange of views to build shared understanding. You may also have to help others in the room do this by ensuring that stakeholders understand one another's questions and concerns; this kind of facilitation is usually best handled by a design team member who is not currently presenting.

PERSONAS

Introduce each persona as if you were talking about a real person. Don't say, "We decided to give her limited technical skills." Instead, say, "She's comfortable with most Web sites and e-mail, but nervous about trying new applications. When she got a digital camera, she watched her daughter upload the photos and wrote down each step so she wouldn't forget it."

You'll know stakeholders agree with the personas when they're nodding their heads or when they start asking questions about specific personas by name. If you're not getting a lot of questions, ask whether the personas make sense or if there are any concerns about them before you discuss prioritization of the personas. It's critical to get agreement on the personas before you move on to scenarios and requirements.

If you're trying to prioritize the personas with the stakeholders, describe the possible directions and the implications of each choice, then step back and ask stakeholders what they think. Your role will shift, at least briefly, from presenter to facilitator. Encourage stakeholders to discuss the implications with one another, but always move the discussion forward toward a conclusion. It's rare that any information not currently available will help make that decision, so there's no point in dragging it out over the next several days.

Questions, challenges, and misconceptions regarding the personas are fairly common, though you can probably anticipate many of them. Here are some of the more common ones, along with some responses that usually work well.

How can one person represent all of our user needs?

This question may be based on one of two misunderstandings. If the questioner is focused on just one persona, ask him to consider the personas as a set. Together, they represent the full range of needs and behaviors you observed, and since everyone here was involved in defining our research sample, you're pretty confident they're representative. If the questioner doesn't see how one persona can represent the needs of many people, explain how the personas are aggregated from many similar people.

Why isn't [a particular sort of person] in the set?

There are three likely answers to this question. One is that the type of person the questioner expects to see simply did not exist in your sample; either indicate that it's possible your sample just wasn't big enough, or explain why you don't believe such people exist in any numbers. Another is that people of this sort represent such an insignificant part of the market that the project owner excluded them. The most likely, though, is that the sort of person the questioner is looking for is already covered by the personas you've described, so you can respond with something like, "We saw a couple of people like that. They're basically a blend of Troy and Seth, so we believe that if we satisfy both, the people you're describing will also be satisfied." Keep an open mind, though; it's always possible the stakeholder is talking about a type of person you missed.

How do these relate to our market segments?

The question might be based on a misunderstanding about the difference between personas and market segments, which you'll need to explain, or it might be a desire to see how one maps to the other. The latter question is easier to answer if you've prepared a slide to address it. That answer is obviously dependent on your particular project, but it's usually similar to the "missing persona" question above, in that you need to explain how the persona set addresses the full range of needs.

How can you be sure these are the right personas?

Since the personas guide important product decisions, some stakeholders are understandably anxious about making sure they're on target. This concern is more rare than you might expect, because most stakeholders see (and trust) the connection to the data as long as you've explained yourself clearly. It's usually important to provide several responses to this question when it does arise. You can say that the personas are as good as the data, so as long as stakeholders are confident that you got a good sample, chances are excellent that the personas are correct. If you feel equipped to do so, offer your own assessment of how good the sample was based on your previous experience. Also ask the stakeholders how much they trust their own judgment; if a room full of industry experts with decades of experience among them thinks the personas make sense, that's further evidence they're probably right. If they're not sure whether to trust their own judgment, you can suggest some follow-up research to provide greater confidence.

What if we pick the wrong primary?

This question is driven by a similar anxiety. Additional research seldom helps with this decision, so the best answer is that there isn't really a "wrong" primary; the worst that will happen is that the product is optimized for one type of user or another. If it turns out the other sort of user would have been a better target, the differences are usually small enough that you can shift emphasis in the next release. You can also remind your audience that even if the personas are a little bit off, designing for a clear target is still better than designing for no particular target.

That persona is [someone the stakeholder knows].

Having a stakeholder mentally replace a persona with a real person, such as his wife or Bob from Acme Widgets, is problematic because that real person comes with idiosyncrasies. Say that it's great to know stakeholders can relate the personas to real people, since this means they're good archetypes, but it's important to focus on the personas because they're more representative than a specific real person can ever be.

What if another Hugo down the hall is different?

Product team members (such as programmers) who are used to dealing with infinite variation may be worried about how the personas can cover every possible use case. Remind them that there's just one Hugo; if he becomes elastic, then you'll be back to the same problems you had with "the user." Also reassure everyone that you'll address all the variants eventually, but by focusing on Hugo, you'll be able to provide a cleaner, more usable design.

I don't think this persona should be [something].

A stakeholder may occasionally object to some detail about a persona, usually something demographic. Sometimes this is entirely reasonable because your persona is a bit atypical in some way you didn't realize, so your response should be, "No problem—we'll make that adjustment." However, I've often seen stakeholders object to something about a persona for no rational reason—perhaps they don't like the photo or have an unpleasant association with the name. An executive once objected to a persona who was a divorced single mom; the fact that she was a single parent was essential to the behavior pattern, so she became a widow instead. There's not much you can do in these situations except stick to your guns about what's intrinsic to the behavior pattern and find alternatives for the rest.

SCENARIOS

Presenting scenarios is much like presenting personas: Focus on the storytelling. The questions about scenarios are also a lot like the usual questions about personas: How do you know, and how will you address all the edge cases? Explain how the scenarios are extrapolations based on your human understanding; how does a parent know where to look when a child isn't where she's supposed to be? Repeat that you're focusing on the most critical and common cases now, and you'll gradually get to the others.

REQUIREMENTS

The requirements are the most likely source of controversy, so expect vigorous discussion about them. Be sure you leave plenty of time for this part of the meeting; 15 minutes might be enough in very simple cases, but half an hour to an hour may be required in others.

Be clear that these are *proposed* requirements based on what you learned in your research; designers seldom have the authority to make requirements stick without the support of a product manager. Where you're suggesting a capability that might be hard to implement, say that you're not attached to a solution, and there might be straightforward ways to achieve something close to the desired end. For example:

> We believe that because sharing her child's development with family and friends is one of the main reasons Debbie takes photos, she won't adopt a tool unless it makes sharing easy. There are many ways we could do this, from integrating with her existing e-mail client to offering an online service. Maybe we can eventually offer several ways to share. Let's talk about the implications of various approaches for our next release.

Briefly present your case and then be prepared to facilitate the discussion in an objective fashion. Ask the product manager and the marketing and sales stakeholders whether they agree that the requirements are desirable and whether they agree with your take on priorities. Tell the engineers you're not asking them to commit to anything, but ask them to brainstorm (in lay terms for the benefit of non-technical team members) about a range of possible technical solutions. Weigh in on the expected design implications of these.

Elicit the opinions of stakeholders who are quiet; this can be challenging if there's someone who tends to dominate the discussion, especially if that person is the ranking individual in the room. Consultants are in a better position to nudge such people than in-house designers are, but it's still worth trying to have a private conversation before the meeting if you can. Point out that some stakeholders seem reluctant to express their opinions until the boss has done so. If the executive is truly interested in their opinions, he might be willing not only to hold back his own thoughts, but also to request the opinions of others. It will be hard to change the meeting dynamic (and, frankly, to have a successful project) if he's not interested in the opinions of his team.

When discussing the experience attributes in a mixed group, especially in a company that is not brand oriented, be prepared for some product team members to raise their eyebrows at the "fluffy stuff" at first. You can circumvent the problem by continuing the meeting with just the brand stakeholders, but it's often better to educate the entire team about the importance of brand and product personality. Point out examples of products and services with strong brands and discuss the loyalty (and premium prices) they command:

Products with distinctive personalities are more recognizable, and products with the right experience attributes generate loyalty and command higher prices. Apple doesn't sell technology—it sells the power of simplicity and style. Volvo sells safety. Lexus sells perfection. If we want this product to generate similar loyalty, emotional appeal is a critical part of doing that.

As with the other requirements, it's important to gain agreement on the experience attributes, especially from the brand stakeholders. This will allow a more objective discussion of visual style later on.

It's entirely possible to come to consensus on every requirement in this meeting, provided the possibilities and implications are well understood. If the range of possible solutions, and costs is broad and there are a lot of unknowns, it will probably take some work outside the meeting before the product team can reach any conclusions. This is fine, as long as you leave the meeting with a list of what needs to be figured out, who is responsible for gathering the information, and when you will meet next to discuss it. You'll also want to agree on what assumptions the design team should make to begin exploring design solutions.

NEXT STEPS

Before you leave the room, remind everyone of when the next milestone is and what they can expect from it. Any questions about this are likely to focus on what people will and won't see or why you're approaching the next steps in a particular way (which is difficult to discuss until you've read the next few chapters).

Requirements

If you remember that your job at this point is to enable informed action, it will help the content fall into place.

Developing your skills

Like it or not, anyone but the most junior designer needs to be an effective presenter. Here are some tips for developing your skills.

KNOW YOUR SLIDES.

The person presenting each section should ideally be responsible for developing the slides in that section, since this is the best way to become familiar with the content. Spend time ahead of any presentation thinking about what you want to say when that slide is on the screen, what questions your audience will have about it, and how you can anticipate those. If necessary, write down exactly what you want to say.

SCHEDULE DRESS REHEARSALS.

Don't just rehearse by yourself—deliver the presentation to your teammates exactly as you plan to do with stakeholders. This helps ensure that each team member is comfortable with what the others will say. It can also help you refine your timing; eventually, you'll learn whether you tend to take one minute per slide or five.

ASK FOR CONSTRUCTIVE FEEDBACK.

Ask your teammates to give you feedback on your dress rehearsal. Did you make the right points in a clear and compelling way? Could they hear and understand you? Did you look and sound confident? Did you do anything distracting, like saying "um" or shuffling your feet? Ask for the same feedback after the real presentation. You can also videotape yourself delivering the real thing and review it later; this is not for the faint of heart, though, because it can make you overly self-conscious.

DRESS FOR SUCCESS.

Dressing nicely isn't just about making a better impression. It can also make you feel more confident and help you turn on the charm. However, avoid clothing or shoes that you're uncomfortable standing in for an hour or two—it will show.

PRACTICE ACTIVE LISTENING.

Half of meeting facilitation is active listening: asking questions to elicit information, paraphrasing to make sure you understand what's being said, and helping others in the room do the same.

GET HELP.

If you lack either confidence or skill, nothing will do you more good than practice and coaching in a low-risk environment. You can take a class or even join an organization that provides you with ongoing practice. Toastmasters (www.toastmasters.org) is an international organization that offers resources, training, and ongoing support through local chapters.

Project Management for Developing the U&DA

The amount of time it takes to develop the presentation and document varies depending on how much research and how many personas you have to discuss. You can put something together in an afternoon if you must do so for an extremely compressed, tactical project. For a thorough set of research with half a dozen personas, it's worth taking two to three days to develop a presentation; careful communication makes success more likely. Expressing the same content in document form takes another couple of days on top of that, assuming the team takes a divide-and-conquer approach. A document that covers content not in the presentation may take a little longer. Be sure to build in time for proofreading and printing.

Since there's not much drawing to do, documentation responsibility for this milestone is shared among team members. The IxD synthesizer most often leads the effort, with other team members contributing sections. The visual designer typically leads the creation of any diagrams or elaborate slide layouts.

The team should develop the outline together, then review the draft presentation to ensure that it presents a coherent, compelling story and covers the points stakeholders will expect. Each team member should also have an opportunity to comment on a draft of the document; it's usually most efficient for the person incorporating comments (usually the IxD synthesizer) if everyone comments on the same copy. Once the design team is happy with the content of the document and presentation, give the project owner a chance to review it before sharing it with the entire set of stakeholders.

Summary

Regardless of how you choose to communicate your research findings, personas, scenarios, and requirements, it's essential to make that communication formal in order to ensure stakeholder consensus and commitment. Assume your stakeholders are busy people; capture details for posterity as you have time, but make it easy to focus on the most important points. Try to anticipate stakeholder questions and concerns. If you remember that your job at this point is to enable informed action, it will help the content fall into place.

Requirements

CHAPTER 14

Framework Definition: Visualizing Solutions

Once you have consensus from the stakeholders about what users the product should serve and what it will take to satisfy them, you can finally start to visualize concrete solutions. This begins with defining the **framework** of the design: the supporting structures and underlying concepts upon which every detail depends. Although scenarios are truly the first point at which you're envisioning the future, most people think of framework definition as the beginning of design.

Framework definition is far more dependent on design skill and experience than the previous phases. Many product managers and marketers can learn to do a decent job of interviewing users and creating personas, but most are not adept at visualizing solutions from thin air. Engineers can often visualize, but most lack the expertise to develop an elegant and desirable solution from a user's perspective.

Most stakeholders have high expectations. Some may even be hoping you can come up with a hot rod on a bicycle budget. This, combined with the natural anxiety of anyone facing a blank sheet of paper, makes framework definition one of the more stress-inducing parts of any project. It's also one of the most difficult; less-experienced designers generally need considerable guidance to develop strong solutions, and even the most expert designers need another set of eyes at some point. For all of its challenges, though, this phase is why most designers become designers: It's exhilarating to create a concrete and elegant solution out of nothing but scenarios, requirements, and your own skill.

The approach to this phase differs somewhat depending on whether you're doing novel design or incremental improvement. When you're doing a conservative redesign for an incremental software update, your goal may simply be to fix the biggest usability problems or make the interface more appealing. Parts of Chapters 16 and 18 address this situation as it relates to interaction and visual design, respectively. If your project mandate is at all ambitious, however, your objectives in the framework phase should be:

1. To provide a concrete and compelling vision of what the product or service is, how it works, and how it looks;

2. To do so as quickly as possible so stakeholders can make informed decisions with minimal investment; and

Users have only one experience of a product or service, so it's essential to focus on the entire system; failure to do so causes many of the worst usability issues.

3. To ensure that the design you envision now will accommodate all known plans for the future, even if it's modified for the short term.

Essential Principles of Framework Definition

It's easier to come up with great design when you start by approaching the problem in a broad-minded, optimistic fashion. Think of the solution as a complete system at first, even if that goes beyond your specific mandate. Try to anticipate the functionality you expect to build over at least the next three to five years. Learn through trial and error; set aside most of the details so you can do this quickly. Let stakeholders influence your thought process by showing them your ideas as soon as they're coherent.

Consider the whole system at once

The interaction framework and, in some cases, the hardware form factor describe what the product is and how it works; the visual and industrial design language describe how the product looks and feels. All these aspects of the product, as well as any related services, must come together in a coherent whole. Users have only one experience of a product or service, so it's essential to focus on the entire system; failure to do so causes many of the worst usability issues. For example, when redesigning a portable medical device for use in hospitals, my team found that nurses were constantly frustrated by dead batteries and by not having all the right supplies on hand, so we made it easy to charge the device in the redesigned case; we also designed a charging rack for spare batteries so it would be easy to swap in a new one if someone had forgotten to plug a device in.

Apple's iPhone, though it has its flaws, is a great example of what happens when you approach a product and service as a complete system. Apple knew that in order for the phone experience to be what it should be—including nonsequential access to a visual list of voicemail messages—they would need to change how each carrier's voicemail technology worked. They also realized that one of the most annoying parts of buying a new phone is standing in the store while the sales rep goes through a ridiculously long setup process, so they made it possible to activate the phone from home. Less than a year after the product was introduced, industry analyst Canalys reported that Apple had seized 27 percent of the smart phone market in the U.S.[1]

---

1. Canalys research release dated February 5, 2008. http://www.canalys.com/pr/2008/r2008021.pdf.

Framework

However, most interactive devices are obvious failures of systems thinking. Companies hire separate firms or have separate internal groups to work on the hardware and software. Often, the hardware is almost finished by the time the interaction and visual designers are asked to make the best of a screen that's the wrong orientation for the data, or buttons that don't relate well to on-screen content. Interaction design should certainly be driven by hardware budgets to some extent—after all, huge color touch screens or massive storage aren't possible for every product—but within the budget constraints, the needs of the interaction should largely dictate the input mechanisms as well as the size and orientation of any screen.

Integration isn't just essential to products that combine hardware and software, though. Well-designed software shows a seamless integration of interaction design and visual design; interaction design drives visual design by determining what data or controls should get visual emphasis, while visual design drives interaction design by determining how much data can legibly fit on the screen. The visual design system for software must also relate in a meaningful way to the corporate brand identity system. Perhaps most difficult of all, enterprise software and Web sites must often work with multiple other systems that have their own limitations; this is one reason business analysts are indispensable when it comes to redesigning legacy systems.

However, even treating hardware, software, and services as a system won't result in a completely satisfying design unless you consider the aesthetic and emotional aspects of the design language in addition to functional characteristics. While the old saying that form follows function is largely true, the way a product should look

and feel can influence its shape and behavior. An architect designing a home, for example, considers its style as she develops the floor plan. A house in the Craftsman style won't just have wood details and exposed rafter tails; it will also have a free flow between living areas and some sort of transition between indoors and out, whether this is a porch, a foyer, or both. Neither structural element is strictly necessary from a functional standpoint; both are dictated by the equivalent of experience attributes specific to the style. Similarly, if it's important for teenagers to feel cool using a handheld device, you might avoid fussy stylus input even if it were ideal from a usability standpoint.

Learn by sketching and failing

Designers learn by trying something that seems like a good idea and seeing what aspects of that idea do and don't work. Making ideas manifest in visual or physical form is essential to evolving them because it's easier to understand what you can see. No doubt you had at least one teacher in school who told you that expressing an idea in writing is a way to clarify that idea; sketching plays much the same role in design.

As Bill Buxton notes, there's an important difference between *sketching* to learn and *drawing* to document your work.[2] He quite rightly argues that early sketches (a term he applies to crude physical prototypes, as well) should be quick, timely, inexpensive, plentiful, and disposable, and should avoid distracting the viewer with unnecessary detail. Sketches aren't precious; they have more in common with words exchanged in a classroom discussion than with a term paper or thesis.

---

2. Buxton, B. *Sketching user experiences: Getting the design right and the right design.* Morgan Kaufmann, 2007.

A sketch provides a visible expression of your thoughts and invites questions, discussion, and suggestions.

Sketching is essential to design collaboration (which is, itself, essential to good design). A sketch provides a visible expression of your thoughts that others can understand. By its somewhat ambiguous nature, an effective sketch invites questions, discussion, and suggestions. A drawing that's too precise and detailed takes too much time to render and makes others hesitant to scribble on it. A whiteboard is an excellent sketching tool because anything drawn there is clearly *not* precious; it will be erased, not pinned on the wall in perpetuity. An industrial designer's prototype cobbled together from foamcore, tape, paper sketches, and found objects implies a similar impermanence.

Sketching is also a more natural extension of thinking than any software tool. When you're drawing by hand, there's no mouse, keyboard, or dialog box to get between your brain and the expression of your ideas. Experienced designers only sit in front of a computer when they need to start developing scale drawings or renderings for communication; electronic tools are better for refinement than for ideation.

This process of sketching ideas, learning from them, and throwing them out can be uncomfortable for people not accustomed to trial and error or ambiguity. This varies from person to person, though I find that roles are often a good predictor of comfort level with sketching. Some stakeholders—mostly design engineers—can be valuable additions to early design meetings. However, many can become anxious because they mistake valuable concept exploration for the designers being lost in the weeds. In the worst case, a stakeholder might ask so many detailed questions or be so obviously uncomfortable that he quells essential exploration. This is why most stakeholders are not involved in this phase until there's something coherent to show, as you'll see in Figure 14.3.

The problem with software prototypes

It seems to be widely understood that industrial design and mechanical engineering prototypes—from paperclips and tape to polished appearance models—are disposable learning tools. Prototyping is clearly distinct from manufacturing, so it would be ludicrous to think that even a late-stage prototype could be reused as part of the final product. In software, however, the tools used for anything other than paper prototyping are generally the same tools used for "manufacturing" (i.e., writing production code). For this reason, many stakeholders can't see why a detailed prototype that appears functional is still many months away from completion. It's important to educate stakeholders that prototype code is kind of like the illusion of automatic doors on Star Trek—it looks like it's working, but it's really a guy standing behind the wall pulling a rope.

Focus on structure, not details

Remember years ago when your teachers forced you to develop a detailed outline for every paper? Tedious as it may have been, you probably learned that you could save a lot of time—and write a better paper—by figuring out what to say before worrying about exactly how to say it. In the same way, making high-level decisions first will help you achieve a simpler, more elegant, and more internally coherent design.

Sketching, in addition to being a useful discussion and learning tool, is important because of the quality of thought it encourages. Low-resolution tools like whiteboard markers or foamcore and tape force designers to ignore details and focus on big issues like structure and flow. At this stage, interaction designers should focus on identifying the major screen states, sketching roughly what's going on in each, and defining how users get from one to another. Widget selection and exact screen content should wait until later, though it's important to have a sense of how much and what sort of data and tools will go on a screen. Industrial designers should focus on the approximate form: the size, shape, and relationships of major parts. Visual designers and industrial designers should establish a design language for the product, which includes identifying a range of colors, materials, typefaces, and other visual language components that will convey the right experience attributes. IxD synthesizers should ensure that all of these parts together tell a coherent and compelling story that covers the most critical issues.

Develop your ideas to the point that you and your teammates have confidence in them. After that, keep going only until you have enough detail for stakeholders to understand and evaluate your direction; Figure 14.1 shows some typical examples of such early work.

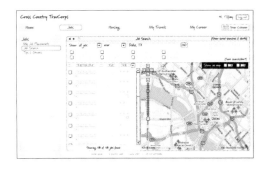

Figure 14.1. Examples of early interaction design, industrial design, and design language concepts ready for stakeholder review.

Framework

Design for the long term

Push at the constraints but don't bulldoze over them.

The trickiest part of any design framework is knowing how optimistic to be. Most of us don't live in an ideal world where we can ignore the constraints entirely, but downplaying them for this first round of design encourages creativity. Good designers constantly push at the constraints but don't bulldoze over them; think a little bit ahead if your timeline is tight, but look several years ahead if you have room to do so. For example, on one project, my team pushed for a more expensive, pixel-based display rather than the lower-cost, segment-based screen the client expected to use. It made a tremendous difference in usability because we could show step-by-step instruction and animation to explain the mechanically complex device. By the time the client had finished the necessary mechanical engineering, the cost of the pixel-based display had dropped to the point where it had become affordable.

Design for the entire system that will eventually be built. If you know you'll be adding a task list or reports next year, create a structure that will let you slot them in without reworking the navigation. If you'll be shipping hardware with a wireless capability later, build in space for the component now. This approach helps stakeholders make more informed decisions about what they want to ship and when. A design that anticipates likely changes so it doesn't have to be completely revamped every year or two also saves months of work and sometimes millions of dollars later on.

Though some engineers are very comfortable with optimistic ideation, especially those who work in design-oriented companies, many are impatient with it because they're understandably focused on near-term deadlines. Anxious engineers want to focus on the constraints and edge cases they'll have to resolve. This is why Figure 14.3 shows limited engineering involvement in this phase, often just at a mid-point review and perhaps for a couple of brief consultations on technology. If you're working with engineers who can focus on enabling desirable solutions, then by all means involve them more; they might even surprise you by telling you something is easier to build than you think it is.

Product managers who are in a hurry may want you to skip the long-term thinking for now. There may be reasons for this you can't affect, such as an external event or severely limited funding that won't increase without a demonstration of short-term value. On most projects, though, thinking long term costs a couple of weeks at most, so make sure the right people are involved in deciding whether you should do so.

Process Overview for Framework Definition

Like most aspects of Goal-Directed Design, the approach to early ideation is based on what has worked well for many designers over a wide range of projects. Years ago, the small group of designers then at Cooper were of course influenced by Alan Cooper's belief that storytelling is a powerful design-ideation tool; many of us were also influenced by the work of John Carroll and others in scenario-based design.[3] However, we were finding it difficult to help less-experienced designers succeed using this loosely articulated approach, so a handful of us sat down to figure out what we were doing in our heads so we could teach it to newer designers.[4] We all found that we used a startlingly similar process. That work is the basis for the process articulated in the next few chapters, though of course we've refined it over the years, learning as much from teaching it as from doing it.

In part, the process is about helping designers get to good solutions in a repeatable and efficient way. By encouraging rational assessment along with creativity, a clear process helps prevent bad solutions from taking root. The process is not a foolproof recipe, though; it requires a head full of design patterns and principles (a designer's vocabulary and grammar), as well as creativity, judgment, and visualization skill. Without those, it's entirely possible to follow every step and still end up with a worthless result. However, provided you have the right skills, the process provides enough structure to increase your chances of generating good ideas on a deadline; in a way, it's like cranking up the power to get a spark to jump the gap between two electrodes.

The other reason for a structured process is to bring other people across that spark gap with you. It's not enough to stand up and say, "Here's the design and it's good because I'm the expert." There's always someone else on the product team who's an expert in engineering or the business domain, so who's to say you're more expert than they are? If you can describe how you got from personas and scenarios to the pictures on the screen, you can help people see for themselves why a solution is good.

Good process helps designers get to good solutions in a repeatable and efficient way.

Framework

---

3. Carroll, J., editor. *Scenario-based design: Envisioning work and technology in system development*. John Wiley & Sons, 1995.

4. Dave Cronin, Wayne Greenwood, Lane Halley, Robert Reimann, Steve Calde and the author articulated the fundamentals of interaction framework definition. Nate Fortin, Robert Reimann, and the author developed the initial approach to defining a visual language.

Process for design on a novel platform

As you can see in Figure 14.2, the framework definition process is really two or three closely related sets of activities happening in parallel. If the design involves a device, the design team starts generating ideas for the approximate form of the device, the size and orientation of any screen, and the input methods (such as a touch screen, physical buttons and knobs, and so forth)—these fundamental decisions are the basis for one or more potential hardware **platforms**. As the team narrows this down to a small number of worthwhile platform ideas, the work briefly splits up. The interaction designers (generator or IxDG and synthesizer or IxDS) work through a representative scenario or two for each candidate physical form to see which best fits the needs of the interaction. In parallel, the industrial designer (ID) works on multiple approaches to each platform, and the visual designer (VisD) and industrial designer begin work on possible approaches to a design language. In an ideal world, there are two or three IDs and two or three VisDs working in parallel to ensure broad exploration.

As soon as each sub-team has explored enough to gain some insight, the whole team gets together again to narrow their focus and resolve problems, then splits up again to do further refinement. This continues until one or more directions are sound enough to share with stakeholders. As the functional part of the design gets more detailed, the design language can be applied to the form and an example screen; this may occur during framework definition, but is just as likely to happen at the beginning of detailed design, if framework definition isn't quite long enough to get there.

At the end of framework definition, you should have settled on a solid approach to a single platform (if applicable), interaction paradigm, and design language; proceeding into detailed design without these issues resolved would be time consuming and expensive.

Process for design on a known platform

The process is a little simpler for software running on a desktop computer or other known platform. Initial brainstorming is very brief. The interaction designers quickly draft a framework using scenarios, review this with the other team members, and keep iterating until it's coherent. The visual designer's work is much the same regardless of whether

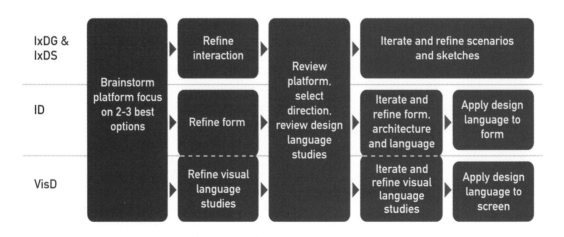

Figure 14.2. An overview of how design disciplines collaborate to create a cohesive experience.

the design involves a novel device: developing design language studies that account for the sorts of things the screen will display (assuming a good design language doesn't already exist), influencing the screen layout, and eventually applying the design language to a framework sketch. If the hardware will be slightly updated but not fundamentally changed, the industrial designer focuses on the design language along with the visual designer. An ID is typically not involved if the hardware will remain unchanged.

Process for designing services

There's an extra step involved for service design. First, the team must define the components of the service, which may include specialized products, Web sites, third-party products and services, environments, and so forth. For example, an airline service design might include a Web site for booking a ticket, a kiosk for checking in at the airport, a streamlined security process, interaction with a human to change a seat, actually boarding the airplane, and any number of other components. The team then treats each service component as they would a product, following the process above for the Web site, the kiosk, and so forth.

Project Management for Framework Definition

How long the framework takes to develop depends on how complex the product is, how much ambiguity stakeholders can tolerate, and how many directions you're pursuing. A skilled team working full-time can usually develop one framework direction in two to four weeks if they don't start with broad ideation and aren't doing extensive model making; frameworks involving hardware or multiple interfaces are generally at the high end of that range. It can take months of design team time to develop multiple directions to a similar level of detail. Most companies are not willing to spend time

or money on this much broad exploration. A good compromise between broad exploration and speed is to spend four to six weeks, with the first week or two on exploration and the remainder focused on getting one concept to the point where you're confident it will work. However, even a framework phase that's scoped for just one direction should at least involve quick whiteboard exploration of multiple approaches.

If your product team wants to think long term but has a constrained release coming up fairly soon, do the more optimistic framework first if you can, then schedule a second, shorter framework phase to strip that down to what's feasible in the near term. This increases the chance that some portion of the near-term release can be recycled.

How many directions to explore

In most design endeavors, the ideal is to pursue multiple possibilities in parallel up to a certain point, evaluate the results, then focus on refining the most successful ideas. Although non-designers often ask how many directions a design team will try, the better question is how many directions they will pursue to the point that stakeholders can see and compare them, since effective design teams may try out and discard dozens of ideas so quickly that the process is invisible to stakeholders.

Most stakeholders expect to see multiple directions for a product's design language, if only because subjective reactions play such a large part in decisions about appearance. Fortunately, it's possible to try out half a dozen visual directions in just a few days, so the cost of this exploration is limited. Companies building devices are also likely to invest initially in two or more hardware design directions because the per-unit manufacturing costs— the **cost of goods sold** (COGS) or **bill of materials** (BOM)—can vary tremendously; this makes the potential benefit of the investment obvious.

Framework

In most design endeavors, the ideal is to pursue multiple possibilities in parallel up to a certain point, evaluate the results, then focus on refining the most successful ideas.

Interaction design for desktop applications and Web sites is often a different story. Exploring multiple design directions with stakeholders or users is time-consuming, since each concept must be articulated in a fair amount of detail before it can even be explained. Many companies are reluctant to invest the extra couple of weeks required to do this, either because they're in a hurry or because they view software as easy to change later on. This belief is seldom true, since the average piece of enterprise or productivity software has more moving parts and potential failure points than a 747 jetliner; most companies spend far more on fixing bad design choices than on building the first version of an application. Fortunately, personas and scenarios make it easy to throw away unworkable solutions very quickly, without taking the time to explain them to anyone outside the design team.

For all of these reasons, the design methods described here are optimized for fast and inexpensive iteration at the whiteboard, with the design team eliminating dozens of possible directions within the first day or two of design. The downside is that this iteration isn't visible to stakeholders, but Chapter 19 describes how careful communication can alleviate this concern. Of course, you can use the same methods to develop several directions if you have the time to do so.

Planning your time

Spend a little time on the first day of the phase drafting a day-by-day plan of each team member's activities, if you don't already have one, and agree on what you need to show stakeholders. Use your first day or two to figure out the best potential platforms (form factor and input methods) as a team if you're working on a device. Otherwise, dive right into the interaction and visual design work. Spend only a few days sketching before having an informal review with the project owner and design engineer(s). Spend at least another two to three days refining the framework for a single interface product before showing it to a large group; plan on more time (and more informal check-ins with the project owner) if you have multiple primary personas. Allow two or three days on average to develop legible sketches and put together a compelling narrative (this topic is covered in Chapter 19). Figure 14.3 outlines the level of team member involvement throughout the phase.

The example project plan in Table 14.1 outlines a slightly compressed framework definition phase. For the sake of time, it's limited to two possible directions for the hardware platform (a less ambitious one and a more ambitious one) and a modest amount of design language exploration.

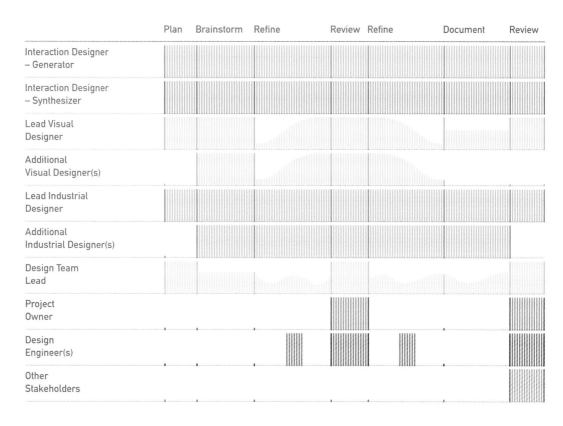

Figure 14.3 Example time commitments during framework definition.

Table 14.1. **Example project plan for device framework definition.**

Day	Interaction designer (generator)	Interaction designer (synthesizer)	Industrial designer(s)	Visual designer(s)
1	Brainstorm possible platforms, define functional elements, narrow to three or four platform possibilities	Brainstorm possible platforms, define functional elements, narrow to three or four platform possibilities	Brainstorm possible platforms, define functional elements, narrow to three or four platform possibilities	Brainstorm possible platforms, define functional elements, narrow to three or four platform possibilities
2	Throw scenarios at all and see if any break	Throw scenarios at all and see if any break	Explore various concepts for each platform, begin design language exploration	Begin design language exploration

Continued

Framework

Day	Interaction designer (generator)	Interaction designer (synthesizer)	Industrial designer(s)	Visual designer(s)
3	Review and find alternates if necessary; narrow to two or three platforms; draft presentation outline	Review and find alternates if necessary; narrow to two or three platforms; draft presentation outline	Review and find alternates if necessary; narrow to two or three platforms; draft presentation outline	Review and find alternates if necessary; narrow to two or three platforms; draft presentation outline
4	Check in with project owner and design engineer(s); narrow to two platforms	Check in with project owner and design engineer(s); narrow to two platforms	Check in with project owner and design engineer(s); narrow to two platforms	Check in with project owner and design engineer(s); narrow to two platforms
5	Refine platform #1 using scenarios	Refine platform #1 using scenarios	Work on various concepts for platform #1, work on design language	Design language studies
6	Refine, narrow ID concepts to 3	Refine, narrow ID concepts to 3	Refine, narrow ID concepts to 3	Refine, narrow ID concepts to 3
7	Refine	Refine	Refine	Refine
8	Review and refine, begin assembling sketches for communication	Review and refine, begin assembling slides for communication	Review and refine, begin 3D modeling	Review and refine
9	Check in with project owner and design engineer(s)	Check in with project owner and design engineer(s)	Check in with project owner and design engineer(s); review studies with a brand stakeholder	Check in with project owner and design engineer(s); review studies with a brand stakeholder
10	Refine platform #2 using scenarios	Refine platform #2 using scenarios	Work on various concepts for platform #2, refine design language	Refine design language
11	Refine, narrow ID concepts to 3	Refine, narrow ID concepts to 3	Refine, narrow ID concepts to 3	Refine, narrow ID concepts to 3
12	Refine	Refine	Refine	Apply preferred direction to a screen from platform #1

Day	Interaction designer (generator)	Interaction designer (synthesizer)	Industrial designer(s)	Visual designer(s)
13	Review and refine	Review and refine	Review and refine	Review and refine
14	Check in with project owner and design engineer(s)	Check in with project owner and design engineer(s)	Check in with project owner and design engineer(s)	Check in with project owner and design engineer(s)
15	Last minute adjustments	Last minute adjustments	Last minute adjustments, 3D modeling, apply design language studies to a neutral form	Apply preferred direction to a screen from approach #2
16	More polished sketches for presentation	Presentation slides	Renderings and foam models	Refine
17	More polished sketches for presentation	Presentation slides	Renderings and foam models	Design language presentation slides
18	Review, refine, and practice presentation	Review, refine, and practice presentation	Review, refine, and practice presentation	Review, refine, and practice presentation
19	Present to stakeholders	Present to stakeholders	Present to stakeholders	Present to stakeholders

The project plan in Table 14.2 outlines a software-only framework definition phase for a single interface product. The timeline is tight, but not unreasonably so for a simple product.

Table 14.2. **Example project plan for software framework definition.**

Day	Interaction designer (generator)	Interaction designer (synthesizer)	Visual designer(s)
1	Define functional elements, brainstorm possible directions, focus on most promising	Define functional elements, brainstorm possible directions, focus on most promising	Define functional elements, brainstorm possible directions, focus on most promising
2	Quickly run through all key scenarios to see if any break the framework; team review at end of day	Quickly run through all key scenarios to see if any break the framework; team review at end of day	Begin visual design language studies; join team review at end of day

Continued

Framework

389

Day	Interaction designer (generator)	Interaction designer (synthesizer)	Visual designer(s)
3	Refine scenario #1 and #2	Refine scenario #1 and #2	Visual design language studies
4	Refine scenario #3, team review and refine	Refine scenario #3, team review and refine	Visual design language studies; team review and refine
5	Refine scenario #3	Refine scenario #3	
6	Check in with project owner and design engineer(s)	Check in with project owner and design engineer(s)	Check in with project owner and design engineer(s); review studies with a brand stakeholder
7	Refine	Refine	Refine visual design language
8	More polished sketches for presentation	Presentation slides	Apply preferred direction to a screen
9	More polished sketches for presentation	Presentation slides	Review and refine, visual design slides
10	Review, refine, and practice presentation	Review, refine, and practice presentation	Review, refine, and practice presentation
11	Present to stakeholders	Present to stakeholders	Present to stakeholders

Essential Skills for Framework Definition

Skills are at least as important to successful design as good process. Along with knowledge of principles and patterns, every designer should have the skills to sketch ideas, collaborate with others to make them better, and capture the results of an effective design meeting.

Sketching and storyboarding

As mentioned earlier in this chapter, sketching—quickly expressing ideas in rough visual form—is central to the design process because it's a thinking and learning tool as well as a collaboration tool.

THE ROLE OF DRAWING SKILLS IN INTERACTION DESIGN

Sketching three-dimensional objects in an intelligible way requires, at a minimum, mastery of line and perspective, so it's hard to imagine a working industrial designer without drawing skills. Interaction designers, on the other hand, currently come from a variety of backgrounds that may or may not have involved design school, and not all of the emerging interaction design programs emphasize drawing by hand. It's true that it doesn't take much drawing ability to put a bunch of rectangles on the whiteboard; I've known some pretty good generative interaction designers who couldn't draw much more than those rectangles, but still had the requisite *visualization* skill—the ability to imagine a solution in concrete terms.

However, lack of drawing skill can leave a generative IxD at a disadvantage when it comes to expressing ideas, especially if they venture outside the ordinary on-screen patterns. Being able to draw with confidence frees you to express your ideas more fully; it also doesn't hurt your credibility with non-designer stakeholders (or with fellow designers from other disciplines, who sometimes view interaction designers who started in other fields as something other than "real" designers).

Technique is part of creating intelligible drawings, but you can learn pretty much all the technique there is in a one-semester class. The more difficult—and more essential—thing to learn is how to draw what your eyes see, rather than what your brain thinks is there; yes, the base of that lamp is flat on the bottom, but the eyes see a curved line because the base is round. Once you understand the basics of how to portray perspective and how to use line, contrast, and texture to represent what you see, the rest is practice, practice, and more practice, which you can do in more classes or on your own.

The other thing a drawing class can teach you is how to *suggest* what you see with a minimum of rendering. Reducing an image to just a few lines allows you not only to draw quickly, but also to focus attention on what's important in the image. This is the part of drawing that's analytical: What about the shape of an object makes it recognizable as that object? You can get better at this by looking at objects through nearly closed eyes, then drawing only what you still see or notice. Learning to view the world in this way also gets you accustomed to thinking this way: If you can express the fundamentals of a design with a few simple lines, it probably means the design is cleaner and easier to understand.

Exercise

If you haven't had much practice with illustration, see how few lines or shapes you can use to draw these things and still have them be recognizable to someone familiar with their context:

— An iPod

— A computer mouse

— Your operating system's desktop

— Your favorite Web browser

— A print icon

— Your cell phone's controls

Beneficial as drawing skills are, though, don't be too self-conscious if you're an interaction designer who can't do much better than stick figures. It's not essential that you be able to draw portraits as long as you can draw clearly and quickly enough to communicate your ideas in a design meeting.

REPRESENTING INTERACTION IN SKETCHES: STORYBOARDING

Because interactive products change state over time, generative interaction designers need a good way to represent those state changes in sketch form. Storyboarding is essentially a type of sketching used to portray action over time—a rough draft of the visual story. Many people credit the animation industry with being the first to develop the technique, but one might also argue that comic book artists were drawing storyboards before anyone thought to make images move. A film storyboard is an inexpensive series of still images drawn to help visualize the action on-screen: where the characters will be in relation to the set and to each other, what they will

Storyboarding a scenario with thumbnail sketches is a great way to visualize and assess flow.

do and say, and how they will move throughout the scene. There is a sketch or still image portraying each significant action, matched up with the dialogue or some other textual description. Something that sounds good in a script may not work well once it's storyboarded, so the technique helps everyone visualize and refine the end product before working in a more expensive medium.

Because interactive products and services involve a flow of action—and because coding that interaction is expensive—storyboarding a design scenario with a series of small thumbnails is a great way to visualize and assess that flow. If you try to visualize it by revising a single whiteboard sketch over and over, you'll just wind up confusing yourself and everyone else. Like the storyboards for animated films, interaction design storyboards start out fairly crude, but their fidelity increases as the details get refined.

Here are some tips for effective interaction design storyboarding:

— Use small thumbnails, especially early in the process. This will help you focus on big issues like flow and make it harder to get sidetracked by details.

— Use arrows to indicate relationships and state changes, such as when a selection in one pane on the screen makes something appear in another.

— Use short notes to point out critical issues or describe the action.

— Number each picture and corresponding scenario to make things easier to track.

— Draw the initial state before the action starts.

— Draw each major state change; don't draw a new screen every time the persona fills in a field, but represent each distinct screen, physical interaction, or other change that's essential to understanding flow.

— Draw the persona and environment only for interactions outside the software, unless you find it helpful to show a persona's thoughts as you might in a comic strip.

— See Figure 14.4 for an example using a transactional Web site and Figure 12.3 for an example using a mobile device.

Framework

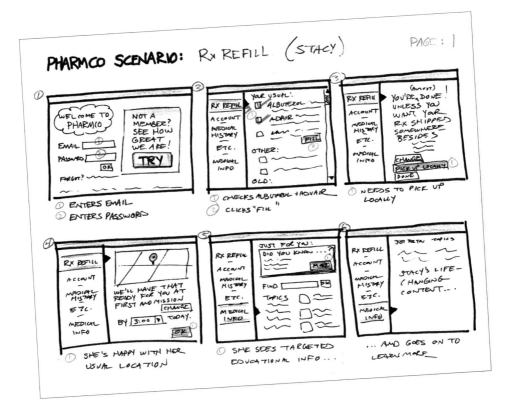

Figure 14.4. An example storyboard for a Web site scenario.

Exercise

Draw a storyboard for each of the following:

— Your last experience with airline travel, starting from any preflight interaction with the airline, such as online check-in, through retrieving your baggage at your destination.

— Your last online shopping experience, from arriving at a Web site through checkout and confirmation of your purchase and any order follow-up, such as checking order status or returning an item.

Collaboration

Like data analysis, framework definition involves a great deal of time in design meetings, usually all day for the first few days, then decreasing somewhat as the work progresses. Meetings seldom take up less than half the day for the interaction designers during this period; other disciplines may spend more solo time. This intensive collaboration is critical both because the team must form a shared idea of the direction they're taking, and because close collaboration generates more and better ideas in less time.

Framework

Each team member should be encouraged to contribute to any aspect of the design so long as her primary responsibilities are covered.

TEAM ROLES

Team roles start to become more distinct at this point in the process. The IxD generator (IxDG) and synthesizer (IxDS) are focused on scenarios and behavior on-screen as well as interaction with physical controls; the IxD generator is responsible for drawing the screens, while the IxD synthesizer generally takes more responsibility for scenario evolution, meeting time management, and narrative development. The visual designer is primarily focused on the visual language, but often contributes helpful ideas about the layout of information on-screen and offers useful review of others' work in progress. The industrial designer's emphasis is on the physical form, with some time dedicated to design language.

Each design team member is welcome and encouraged to contribute to any aspect of the design—an ID might have a great interaction idea or an IxD could offer helpful thoughts on the visual language. However, each person must first ensure that his primary duties are covered; an IxD synthesizer who is too focused on ideation will neglect his responsibility to ensure clarity, just as an IxD generator who spends too much time thinking about visual or industrial design will neglect the interface structure.

Although it works fine to have just one visual designer and one industrial designer assigned to most of the project, doubling up for this phase encourages broader exploration and greater clarity. It's not necessary to double up on interaction design because the IxD generator/synthesizer relationship serves this purpose throughout the project. As you can see in Figure 14.3, the additional visual and industrial designer(s) need not be involved for the entire phase. The lead ID and VisD (who are the consistent team members from research through detailed design) provide guidance to any temporary team members.

The team lead's role varies not only by personal style, but also based on the seniority of the team. She may need to provide explicit time management and creative direction in some cases, but with a very experienced team, she can ideally be more of a facilitator and coach. An effective lead can often help the team members see problems for themselves by asking the right questions; this encourages more skill development than pointing out problems and suggesting fixes does. However, this doesn't mean the team lead's role is unnecessary with senior designers; even the most experienced teams benefit from having work reviewed by a skilled person who isn't so close to it.

What's a lone designer to do?

Many in-house or freelance designers work by themselves. Most are strongest in one set of skills, but some can fill other roles in a pinch. If this is your situation, there are a couple of things you can do to be more effective:

1. **Find like-minded collaborators.** These might be other lone designers in different groups or companies, or they might be design-minded engineers, technical writers, SMEs, or product managers in your company. When I worked as the lone designer in a startup, I found the QA manager was good at pointing out little things I hadn't thought of, though one of the engineers was better at helping me think through workflow. What's most important is to find someone who makes you more effective by asking the right questions or providing thoughtful comments. Try to spend at least a couple of hours a week with someone like this. People may be more willing to help if you reciprocate, so offer to be a sounding board for them, too.

2. **Dedicate specific amounts of time to each aspect of the design problem.** It's easy to neglect the aspects of the design work you like the least or are least proficient in. Carve out specific time in your schedule when you're *only* focused on the behavior, the design language, or the documentation. Force yourself to work first in low-resolution tools when considering behavior; it's harder to focus on visual questions when you're drawing in whiteboard marker, for example.

3. **Ask for help.** While you're working on the design language, no progress is being made on the interaction framework, and vice versa. Tell your boss you'd move faster and achieve better results if you had help. Consider not only which aspects of the design you're best at, but also what tasks are easiest to separate from the others. Some of our clients at Cooper, for example, know they don't have the skills in-house to develop a good visual system even though they have the interaction design covered; others need help at the conceptual interaction or industrial design stage but feel equipped to manage the detailed design.

> If you're a lone designer, find someone who makes you more effective by asking the right questions.

RUNNING AN EFFECTIVE DESIGN MEETING

People in many fields describe an ideal mental state in which they are wholly focused on the task at hand, whether that task is solving a math problem, creating a painting, or simply sitting in a garden and feeling at one with the world. This mental state is characterized by an almost euphoric feeling that you can do no wrong and can go on forever. Athletes call this "being in the zone." Psychologist Mihály Csíkszentmihályi calls it "flow."[5] Csíkszentmihályi asserts that flow encourages creativity, and most designers I know would agree that they do their best work when in this state. Although most people describe this as a state that occurs when they're working by themselves, it's also possible to achieve flow

---

5. Csíkszentmihályi has many publications on this topic, the best known of which is *Flow: the Psychology of Optimal Experience* (Harper and Row, 1990).

or something much like it in a good design meeting. An effective design meeting doesn't just enable flow, though. It also:

— Encourages creative thinking

— Tests ideas and takes advantage of various viewpoints

— Allows everyone to feel heard and respected

— Accomplishes clear objectives in an efficient way

— Gives participants a clear idea of what to do when the meeting is over

Determine what you need to accomplish

Although most effective teams have a day-by-day calendar that outlines what topics they'll cover and when, this is usually not specific enough to guide a meeting. Spend the first couple of minutes in each meeting figuring out exactly what you need to accomplish, such as covering a specific scenario, answering some unresolved design questions, or drawing specific screens. This will let you focus on the design topics instead of on meeting management. Avoid discussing the topics at this point—just list them on the board, then figure out which you want to address first and which you may want to cover in another forum. Refer back to your notes from the previous meeting for any topics you needed to carry over, but always try to accomplish the work of each meeting in the time allotted; you're just trying to get to a solid concept, not worrying about perfecting it. If you're spending more than five minutes laying out your agenda, flip a coin to pick a topic and move on; you don't want the discussion of what to do to turn into a meeting itself.

Let the best idea win

Some people feel that a combative approach encourages intellectual rigor, but in my experience, competitive design meetings quickly become unproductive. If you're intent on having the best idea or looking smarter than your colleagues, then you and your teammates are no longer working toward a shared goal. Truly functional design teams often can't identify later exactly which idea is whose because no matter who proposed the original thought, others helped build upon and refine it until it belonged to the whole team. This doesn't mean everyone has to amend every idea like legislators amending a bill, though; if an idea is good as it is, let it be.

Look down the rat hole, but don't go in

Half-formed thoughts and stupid ideas can be the basis for brilliant solutions. They can also wind up being stupid after all, but you can't know that until you give someone a little time to explore. Unless your teammates are allowed a little space to be incomplete and wrong, they'll be hesitant to take risks and share their ideas. However, this doesn't mean you should allow the meeting to go down a rat hole; if it seems to be getting way off track, ask your teammate how the topic relates to the agenda item you're focused on right now.

Elicit and understand before assessing or suggesting

Great IxD synthesizers (or people with similar skills) help ideas evolve without turning meetings into competitions. As the IxD generator starts to draw an idea, a good synthesizer first elicits information to help her express the idea as completely as possible, paraphrases it and asks clarifying questions to ensure he understands the generator's intent, and only then points out concerns. The IxD generator ensures that she understands the concerns, then tries to address them. If she can come up with a good response or solution, the synthesizer again elicits detail and clarifies his understanding, and the meeting moves on to the next problem. If the generator

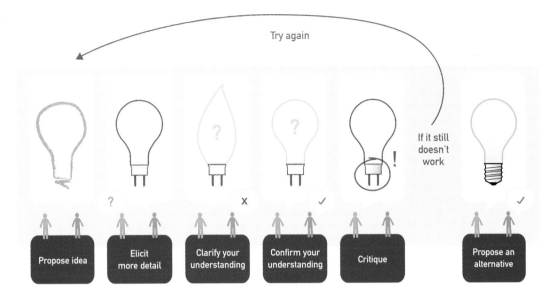

Figure 14.5. First elicit detail and make sure you understand the idea before you critique it. Offer alternatives only if your teammate can't address your concern.

can't address the concern, *then* the synthesizer may propose an alternative. If a junior generator isn't ideating at all, a skilled synthesizer might throw something up on the whiteboard just to get things moving, then step back. Figure 14.5 illustrates this concept.

Don't take this as an absolute rule, of course; it would be a shame for any team member to stifle a great idea because it wasn't "allowed." The essential point is that when a teammate is leading the ideation, you should err on the side of clarifying and improving the idea at hand before proposing a different solution. You should also stop and think about whether your solution is really better before offering it. It's a lot like being a good editor: You point out problems and help the author improve, but don't change something that works just because you would have said it differently.

Here's an example of how this sort of conversation goes:

IxDG (drawing at the whiteboard): Caroline finds the customer in the organizer pane, then selects him and the record shows up over here in the workspace.

IxDS: How does she find him in the organizer?

IxDG: Um ... She probably just types in the customer's name at the top of the organizer pane, and it shows the likely matches in the results list. She'd select the right one from there.

IxDS: So are you saying that selection in the organizer always drives the contents of the workspace?

IxDG: Yes, I think that's the right way to go.

IxDS: And she can only select one thing at a time?

Framework

If a teammate has a question or concern about something you're proposing, she probably has a good reason for it.

IxDG: Yes, that seems like the least confusing option.

IxDS: OK, I agree that makes sense most of the time, but what about when she has to compare two records, like this year and last year? It doesn't seem like what you've drawn handles that.

IxDG: Oh. Yeah, you're right—this would break, wouldn't it? Hmm … you know, she won't need to do that very often, so how about if we put some kid of "compare" button in the record, and it just shows a special side-by-side view like this? That way, we can keep the clear selection idiom between the organizer and the workspace.

IxDS: Sure, I think that works.

Although this dynamic is most evident in the IxD generator/synthesizer relationship, all team members should be practiced at this approach of "elicit/clarify/critique, elicit/clarify/critique, *then* suggest." Whoever is proposing an idea "has the board" for the moment, so other team members should play this facilitative role.

"Park" questions and comments when necessary

When you're drawing at the whiteboard and trying to give birth to a half-formed idea, you're usually the best judge of what questions will help you clarify the idea and what will break your train of thought. If a question or concern seems unhelpful at the moment, write it down in a designated "parking lot" zone of the whiteboard (or ask the IxDS to add it to his list, if he keeps one throughout the meeting). This allows the person with the concern to set it aside because she is assured you won't forget it, while minimizing interference with your flow.

Have a reason for every decision

An old colleague of mine, Josh Seiden, was notorious for asking, "Why is that good?" at least once in any design meeting. Sometimes it was his way of saying that he didn't think something was good, but he often asked it simply to ensure that team members could articulate good reasons for each design choice. Good design isn't arbitrary. If a teammate has a question or concern about something you're proposing, she probably has a good reason for it. Saying, "It's this way because I think it should be, and I'm responsible for this part of the design," is seldom productive. Explain your reasoning and be open to having someone question it; don't defend a decision as a *fait accompli*.

Make decisions in the meeting, not at your desk

If you're not accustomed to close collaboration, you may be tempted to go back to your desk and think about the design before making a decision or responding to a concern. There's nothing inherently wrong with this, but it makes for exceedingly slow progress. You should be able to make most design decisions in the meeting during this phase; later on, there are some decisions that require some solo work, such as figuring out exactly how many readable characters you can fit on a 17-inch screen at 1024 × 768 pixels. However, this shouldn't stop you from sketching a few ideas before a design meeting; many designers are more comfortable if they can propose an idea right away instead of staring at a blank whiteboard in front of their teammates.

Use the 15-minute rule

If you're simply having trouble ideating or you and your teammates have a disagreement you can't resolve, don't waste more than 15 minutes or so before bringing in another person to help you move forward. The team lead is usually the first choice for this role since she knows the project well enough to get you unstuck without too much explanation. Failing that, almost anyone will do as long as they understand how the 15-minute rule works.

Asking the third party to weigh in with yet another opinion usually doesn't help. Instead, explain what you're trying to accomplish and where you're stuck. If necessary, provide a quick explanation of who your persona is. The team lead or other helper should ask useful questions to help you find your own solution. Sometimes this is just about helping you communicate more effectively with your teammates, but it can also involve asking why your proposed solution is good, suggesting techniques for generating ideas (such as pretending the product is human), reminding you of useful principles and patterns, or asking questions that help you see the design problem from a different angle.

The 15-minute rule is generally successful in helping functional teams resolve issues. It's better to use this approach than to postpone decisions until later meetings, because your next meeting has a different topic and your ability to move ahead may depend on you resolving the open issue. If tempers are flaring to the point where you can't have a productive conversation until you've cooled off, you need to work on your team's collaboration skills (pay special attention to listening and paraphrasing back).

Capturing what happens in meetings

It's essential to capture what happens in your design meetings and make sure all team members have access to the notes. When this doesn't happen, you may all leave the room with slightly different ideas about what you decided to do, so you'll waste time later revisiting decisions you've already made. Look to either your note-taking practices or lack of clear decisions in meetings as the most likely causes if this problem happens often.

Team notes are usually the responsibility of the IxD synthesizer if he's present, both because he's less likely to be up at the whiteboard and because he's responsible for documenting the details later, which motivates him to be thorough. However, each team member should keep at least some notes about action items and things he'll be responsible for later. A generative interaction designer, for example, might not capture the text of the design scenario, but would jot down screen drawings with any notes that will help her draw screens for a check-in.

Don't wait until the end of a meeting to capture notes. Keep track of questions and issues as they come up. There's no need to copy down every intermediate sketch that goes up on the board, but when you finish a design topic, stop and document your decisions before moving on. It's usually helpful to do a clean sketch on the whiteboard instead of trying to make sense of all the intermediate scribbles. A small digital camera is handy for capturing

Framework

whiteboard contents, and it's a far cheaper and more portable solution than any sort of electronic whiteboard.

However, unless you take unusually extensive notes on the board, a snapshot seldom captures everything necessary, so an additional note-taking tool is important. A paper notebook is useful for capturing drawings, but a laptop is better for written notes because you won't need to recopy them to turn them into something you can share. A tablet PC with Microsoft OneNote provides the best of both worlds, since you can take notes and draw on it, though some of these devices are still a bit buggy; nothing breaks meeting flow like fussing with a crashing computer.

Effective meeting notes capture:

— The content of every scenario introduced or modified during the meeting

— Every design decision, including sketches and explanations of what's going on in them

— Every open question, ideally with some indication of when it will be addressed

— Every action item, including the person responsible for completing it and any deadline by which it should be done

— Any important or potentially controversial design directions you ruled out, and your reasons for doing so

Good meeting notes are as concise as possible without losing detail and are organized for later reference rather than organized sequentially. Notes ideally add value to what happened in the meeting rather than just summarizing it, though any additional thoughts, questions, and commentary should be noted in some distinct way; never insert new opinions or interpretations without drawing others' attention to them, or they won't trust that your notes are accurate. See Figure 14.6 for an example of ineffective meeting notes and Figure 14.7 for a better example.

Project X design meeting
8/8/2008

She connects camera, application automatically opens and recognizes it, says it's getting new images, shows each in the workspace and being loaded into a new temporary collection. Application says it's done with all 312 images, does not ask if it should delete from camera because she previously told it not to. Reviews each image and deletes the worst ones. Compares several similar ones to decide which is best, throws out the others. Assigns tags to each image she decided to keep. Makes some adjustments to exposure on an image that wasn't quite right. When she adjusts exposure on an image, does it keep the original available?

— Too many panes

— What's the target screen resolution?

— Not sure how viewing mode works

Figure 14.6. These notes are poorly organized, missing information, and difficult for teammates to digest.

Project X design meeting
8/8/2008

Topic: adjusting framework for Katie (secondary persona)

Present: Charlie, Suzy, Dan

Action items:

— Dan: discuss target screen resolution with client by 8/10

Open issues:

— Simplify screen layout/reduce number of panes

— How does viewing mode work?

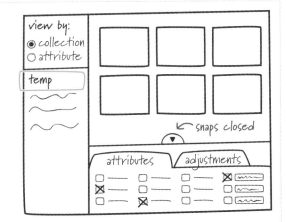

— Attribute pane shares space with adjustment pane at bottom of workspace

— Shows all available tags

— Attributes automatically saved when checked

Scenario 3: Katie loads images

She connects camera, application automatically opens and recognizes it, says it's getting new images, shows each in the workspace and being loaded into a new temporary collection

Application says it's done with all 312 images, does not ask if it should delete from camera because she previously told it not to

Continued

Framework

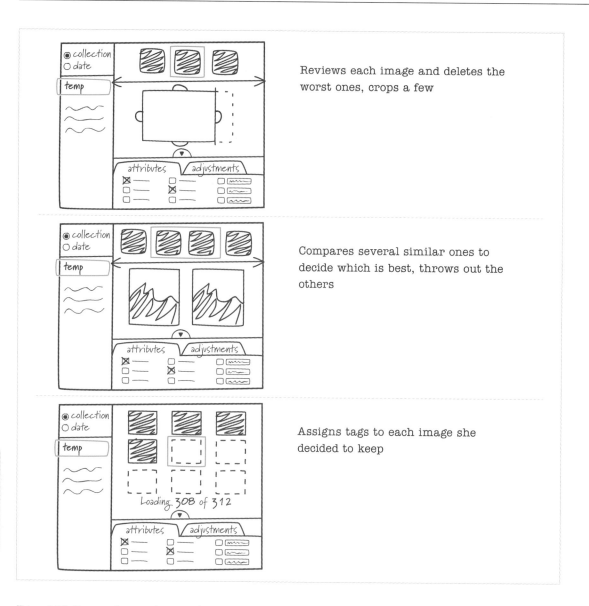

Reviews each image and deletes the worst ones, crops a few

Compares several similar ones to decide which is best, throws out the others

Assigns tags to each image she decided to keep

Figure 14.7. These notes are clear, concise, and organized for easy scanning. They include annotated sketches as well as useful (and clearly identified) thoughts that occurred to the author after the meeting.

Ideally, the description of product behavior in your notes can serve as a rough draft for the Form and Behavior Specification (see Chapter 24). However, don't spend a lot of time on making your notes perfect; more than half an hour or so a day polishing your notes is probably not the best use of your time.

Distribute notes to the other members of the design team, who should review them as soon as possible to see if there are any misunderstandings or missing points and to make sure they have all of their action items noted. Store the notes in a central place where all team members have access to them.

Framework

Summary

The object of framework definition is to show stakeholders at least one compelling, viable solution (and preferably more) to help them make business decisions with a minimal investment of time and money. The early stages of design are all about trying, failing, learning, and trying again, all in as little time as possible. This takes a design team with the right skills, including the ability to collaborate closely; allowing others to be wrong or incomplete for a little while, but always ensuring that designs are clear and coherent and that no decision is made arbitrarily.

Chapters 15 and 16 outline how to define what the product is and how it behaves. Chapters 17 and 18 describe how to develop and refine potential directions for the design language. See Chapter 19 for more on how to communicate about the design with stakeholders.

Framework

THE INNOVATIVE ENTERPRISE

Principles and Guidelines in
Software User Interface Design

Information Design   Jacobson, editor

DREYFUSS DESIGNING FOR PEOPLE

NORTON THE ICON BOOK Visual Symbols for Computer
Systems and Documentation

PAPER PROTOTYPING SNYDER MK

About Face 3 The Essentials of Interaction Design Cooper Reimann Cronin WILEY

Universal Principles of Design William Lidwell · Kritina Holden · Jill Butler

The Visual Display of Quantitative Information

Designing Brand Identity Second Edition WILEY

CHAPTER 15

Principles and Patterns for Framework Design

Process, principles, and patterns are equally important to generating good solutions. While good process tools such as scenarios help ensure that you have an appropriate workflow and some objective criteria for evaluating decisions, a designer cannot be effective without an extensive vocabulary of design patterns to use as building blocks for solutions. Appropriate application of those patterns involves an understanding of certain key design principles in addition to persona goals; both help assess the best way to apply patterns.

This chapter contains a sampling of the principles and patterns that tend to be most important at this stage of designing form and behavior. Chapter 17 covers patterns and principles relevant to design language creation. These are by no means all of the principles and patterns you should know; a hungry mind will serve you well in building your design vocabulary just as it does in learning about users.

The Importance of Context

Always consider context when applying the design principles and patterns in this chapter (or from any other source). A pattern or principle that works well for certain types of users doing particular sorts of tasks on a specific platform might be entirely inappropriate to another context, just as a chef's knife is optimized for cooking, but a multifunction pocket knife is better suited to camping. Personas and scenarios supply the necessary context to help you determine what kind of solution is appropriate, as you'll see in Chapter 16.

Alan Cooper's idea of **posture**[1] is another useful tool for evaluating what sort of solution best fits a given context. Although they certainly don't cover every case, two of the postures he introduced are worth considering with respect to framework definition.

In Cooper's parlance, a **sovereign** application is one that "rules" the screen because people use it to perform complicated tasks over long periods

1. Cooper, A. *About face: The essentials of user interface design.* John Wiley & Sons, 1995.

of time. Word processors, spreadsheets, and most specialized productivity tools, such as Photoshop, business-analytics tools, or call-center applications, fit in this category. These applications typically have many features that take some time to learn. Such tools should usually be optimized for intermediates, who will quickly master the subset of features they generally use, but probably won't explore every nook and cranny in the product. Sovereign applications typically run in maximized windows, so there's plenty of room to put lots of functionality at users' fingertips. The data or content should be the central focus, though; the interface ought to be as compact and unobtrusive as possible, making use of drop-downs, unlabeled icon buttons, and other space-saving idioms.

A **transient** application, on the other hand, is just passing through. Users open a transient application to perform a narrowly focused task, such as compressing a file, backing up a folder, or checking the weather forecast. Apple's desktop Widgets are good examples of transient applications. Users rely on these tools to perform simple (and sometimes infrequent) tasks, so they're less willing to invest time in learning what a bunch of abstract icons mean. Transient tools should express themselves in plain language, expending pixels on instruction or explanation where necessary. However, because they involve simple, temporary tasks, it would be obnoxious for most transient applications to take over the screen, especially because they're often used in conjunction with sovereign applications.

Unfortunately, these concepts can be difficult to apply because many of the products we use every day aren't really one posture or the other. Users may spend a lot of time browsing through the books at Amazon.com, and it's clear that content should use more space than controls, but no retailer wants a learning curve to get between the customer and the cash register. A kiosk in a museum completely takes over the

screen—a "sovereign" behavior—but a museum kiosk should be designed for instant learnability over efficiency. Handheld devices, car stereos, and other interfaces that don't exist on a typical computer screen likewise can't be easily classified according to posture.

It can also be oversimplification to say that an entire application is one posture or the other; not every *activity* in an application is equally sovereign or transient. Writing in a word processor is the primary focus of attention, but inserting an image and printing a document are transient activities; they shouldn't entirely take over the screen, but should include enough instruction that users don't have to think too hard about how to accomplish a simple task.

Rather than conflating multiple issues into the single concept of posture, it's more useful to break them down into a couple of fundamental questions, applied to both the product as a whole and to each task the product can accomplish:

— **Which is more important: instant ease of use or efficiency over time?** The answer determines how dense you can make the screen, how much space to expend on explanation, and how much of a learning curve is acceptable.

— **Is the focus on performing a simple task or working with rich content?** Simple tasks should use limited real estate, but some content requires space even when the task itself is straightforward.

Principles for Form and Behavior

A design principle is a guideline that can help you choose the best way to organize and portray information and tools so users can take action with minimal time and effort. Principles operate at multiple levels, from high-level values to tiny details such as the size of a touch target or the phrasing of a button label. In between these, there are a variety of principles that guide interface structure and behavior to minimize work and make the user experience more pleasant.

Design values

Most designers in any discipline are, by nature, both idealists and humanists. We do design not only for the joy of creation, but also because we want to make the world a better a place, whether on a grand scale or a small one. Years ago, Hugh Dubberly, David Fore, Jonathan Korman, Robert Reimann, and I set out to articulate these core design values. We proposed that in order to be considered "good," a design solution must be ethical, purposeful, pragmatic, and elegant.

GOOD DESIGN IS ETHICAL

A designer's primary value should echo that of a physician: First, do no harm. In the design of interactive products and services, harm could mean a number of things:

— **Physical harm.** Careless design of medical treatment devices or automotive systems can cause severe pain, injury, or death. Even bad information design on paper can have terrible consequences; Edward Tufte[2] describes how better design could have prevented the explosion of the space shuttle Challenger in 1986. Though most design mistakes won't have such disastrous results, even typical Web sites and desktop applications can do harm by causing repetitive stress injuries, eyestrain, and headaches. A device that requires users to adopt an awkward posture or exert excessive force can cause strains and other injuries.

— **Psychological harm.** While a nasty error dialog is unlikely to crush someone's ego in a single stroke, hard-to-use products can make users feel frustrated and incompetent. Cold or overbearing visual design can make people feel less at ease.

— **Social harm.** A calendaring program that's confusing can lead to embarrassing missed meetings. A system or service that doesn't accommodate a range of physical, cognitive, economic, and educational needs can perpetuate injustice and inequality.

> # Good design is ethical, purposeful, pragmatic, and elegant.

2. Tufte, E. *Visual explanations: Images and quantities, evidence and narrative.* Graphics Press, 1997.

Framework

- **Economic harm.** Poor software design can lead to costly errors in business applications or personal finance tools. An expensive cell phone with a slippery grip can cause economic harm when it falls out of a user's hand and breaks. Wasting a user's time with clumsy interaction is also a sort of economic harm.

- **Environmental harm.** Hardware that can't be upgraded leads to toxic and nonbiodegradable landfill waste. Services or applications that encourage paper use kill trees. Lengthy start-up sequences encourage users to leave devices on instead of powering them down.

Avoiding harm doesn't go far enough, however. Good design should also improve the human condition in some way. It's easy to feel like you're making the world a better place when your design has the potential to save lives, decrease electricity use, or help someone learn to read. It may be harder to see the greater good in a better accounting tool, but making the accountant's daily tasks more pleasant improves her quality of life.

As a designer, you're bound to encounter ethical dilemmas that require you to balance potential harm with potential good. These situations may be so dramatic that they affect your willingness to design the product at all. If you're asked to design a system for targeting smart bombs, for example, you might find the very idea abhorrent, while another designer might decide that it's better to minimize the harm by making it harder to aim at the wrong target. Workforce efficiency presents a more common dilemma. A colleague and I once designed a purchasing application that improved efficiency by 700 percent; clearly, this made it possible to accomplish the same amount of work with fewer people, so the new design probably cost some purchasing agents their jobs. On the other hand, it meant the people who stayed in their jobs could focus on negotiating deals instead of spending so much time on mindless drudgery. We all have to decide for ourselves whether we're

comfortable with the balance of potential harm and good inherent in any design problem.

GOOD DESIGN IS PURPOSEFUL

A well-designed product or service is optimized to accomplish what users want to do in the most natural way. Context is everything; a Web site meant to serve pharmaceutical experts will necessarily differ from one aimed at consumers. Focusing on goals also helps achieve optimization; if you know the persona's goal is to figure out whether her laptop's battery will last through the plane flight, it's easy to see that a "time remaining" display is more useful than a "percent charge remaining" display.

Being purposeful also requires being focused; as Polonius said to Laertes in *Hamlet*, "To thine own self be true." Developing a product that suits a particular niche very well requires ruthless culling of anything that doesn't fit the product's purpose; to get an ultralight laptop, you have to accept that it won't be suitable for rendering huge animation files or storing terabytes of data. Many products or services also have to be true to a company's brand; this consideration sometimes trumps others. When we were designing a Web site for a "value" brand company, for example, they told us our first attempt at the visual design looked great, but was too polished. They asked the visual designer to "make it cheesier." Startling as the comment was, it was absolutely right; a polished look didn't quite fit with the company's no-frills image. In the same way, a product that required complicated setup wouldn't fit Apple's reputation for simplicity, and a customer service system that didn't allow easy access to a human wouldn't fit a luxury brand.

GOOD DESIGN IS PRAGMATIC

It doesn't matter how ethical, purposeful, or elegant your design is if it never sees the light of day. The best design solution for any circumstance isn't always the ideal solution from a user's point of view. If a company can't make money by selling devices with color touch screens, you need to find a way to make a monochrome LCD and soft buttons work. If the product will serve a very small market, it won't be cost-effective to design custom widgets that take three times as long to build. Business models can also lead to requirements that aren't high on users' wish lists, such as the need to build advertising into an e-mail client. Your job as a designer is to find a way to accomplish business goals (such as making a profit) without unduly hampering persona goals; ideally, there's a solution that's mutually beneficial.

This is not to say you shouldn't push on constraints—the day you lose all of your idealism and acquiesce to the status quo is the day you cease to be effective as a designer. However, productive designers learn to see constraints not as hateful restrictions, but as interesting—and indispensable—parts of the puzzle.

GOOD DESIGN IS ELEGANT

Elegance is usually what differentiates the work of an experienced professional designer from the work of anyone else; non-designers often say a designer's work has that "extra something that just makes it seem right."

An elegant design is usually the simplest complete solution. A design is done when it accomplishes all that it must, but there's nothing else you can take away: You've used the smallest number of screens, widgets, and hardware buttons possible to accomplish the task. Minimalism isn't always synonymous with elegance, though; if you overload a physical control with three different functions, your solution is incomplete and therefore more complex even if it looks clean and simple. The iPod click wheel is a good example of this dilemma: It seems elegant at first glance, but if you have a large data set to scroll through, the design violates the "do no harm" principle because of the repetitive awkward motion.

Elegant designs are also coherent, possessing an internal consistency that makes all the parts of the design seem to belong together. A design with inconsistent behaviors and visual elements will seem as jarring as a rude sales person at a high-end department store or a mid-century modern couch with a Chippendale chair. Most people looking at a design that "just works" don't notice this cohesiveness because it just feels right—the design becomes invisible. Cohesiveness and blandness aren't the same thing, though; good designers make careful use of contrast to emphasize certain information or functions or to give the design a bit of life.

> It doesn't matter how great your design is if it never sees the light of day.

Framework

Though many designers lean toward modernism, elegance does not require a specific style. Elegant designs tend to be visually pleasant due to their simplicity and consistency, but a colorful child's game can be as elegant in its own way as a powerful IT application or a luxury-brand Web site.

Minimizing unnecessary work

Below the level of design values are principles that describe how to reduce harm and make solutions more purposeful, pragmatic, or elegant. Many of these are about reducing effort that doesn't get users any closer to accomplishing their goals. It's almost always a good idea to do so, though some games and other sorts of entertainment can be less engaging if there aren't obstacles to overcome. Both framework design and detailed design can affect the amount of unnecessary work users do.

FOUR TYPES OF WORK

Interactive products and services tend to require four different types of work from users: cognitive, visual, memory, and physical. To reduce them, it helps to start by understanding each type of work and what typically causes it.

Cognitive work

Most interactive products exist to enable work that is largely mental: writing, accounting, learning, reading, and so forth. However, products can require users to think hard about other things that don't help with these tasks, such as saving and finding files or figuring out whether to click yes, no, or cancel in response to a convoluted confirmation dialog. To the greatest extent possible, using a product should be more like riding a bicycle: something users don't have to think consciously about once they've learned how. Inconsistent or unpredictable interface behavior, excessive or badly written text, and opaque organization are typical causes of pointless cognitive work. The dialog in Figure 15.1, for example, requires a great deal of cognitive work just to save a file.

Visual work

Visual work includes finding a starting point on a page, figuring out what's available on the screen and how it's related, and locating the right control or object among many. Clutter, confusing affordances, inappropriate typefaces, careless use of color, and lack of visual hierarchy (see Chapter 17) lead to excessive visual work. Although visual designers clearly have a great deal of influence on visual work, interaction designers can help reduce it by managing the density of controls and information on the screen and determining what data or controls are most important in a given context.

For example, compare the ESPN and weather desktop widgets in Figure 15.2. In the ESPN widget, the background image and navigation control compete for attention; the content, which is presumably the whole point of the widget, is

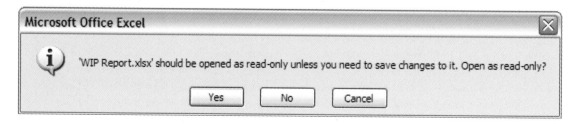

Figure 15.1. This dialog box requires unnecessary cognitive work to decipher.

difficult to read because it's very small and is superimposed on the image background. That's a lot of visual work just to see what's going on in your favorite sport. Apple's weather widget, on the other hand, makes the most important information—today's weather—abundantly clear.

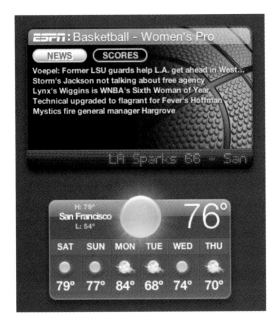

Figure 15.2. The ESPN widget creates a lot of visual work, while the weather widget is readable at a glance.

Memory work

To understand the level of effort required to remember something, it's important to differentiate between recognition and pure recall. Pure recall is the ability to dredge up a fact, such as a phone number, with little or no context. This can be especially challenging if you haven't used the number recently or often. Even in the short term, it's hard to remember long lists of items; you can probably remember the four or five things you need at the grocery store without writing them down, but most people can't recall a dozen things unaided. Recognition—the ability to identify the

desired thing when you see it—is much easier. You might forget the name of the street you need to turn left on, but you may recognize it by the color of the house on the corner.

Interactive products and services require memory work in the form of passwords, file names and locations, command names and locations, and procedures. Much of this work is pure recall, though remembering which icon on the toolbar did something is more a matter of recognition.

Physical work

Physical work related to most products involves fine motor skills, such as typing, using a mouse, or turning a dial. Some services might require other types of physical work, such as opening a DVD mailer. It's nearly always desirable to reduce physical work in interaction design because it can lead to injury. (However, it's possible for interactive products such as games to encourage healthy physical exercise that uses the whole body, rather than just the hands and wrists.)

IMPORTANT PRINCIPLES FOR FRAMEWORK DESIGN

There are a host of principles that help reduce unnecessary work. Some of the most relevant for developing the interaction framework and hardware form factor are highlighted here.

Give users all of what they need, but only what they need

I sat down at my desk the other day to work on my income taxes, only to realize that my bank hadn't sent me an important piece of information. I had to stop what I was doing and call the bank to get it. When I had the information, I returned to my task, but was thwarted again when I saw that my mortgage lender also hadn't sent me a necessary form. Again, I had to look up my account, find the phone number, and place a call. Sounds annoying, right?

Framework

Don't force users to make design decisions.

Yet this is the sort of thing many applications require users to do: enter information on one screen, review it on another, and look up an answer in yet another place.

Your interface is a user's workspace, so to the extent possible, a single screen should contain easy access to all of the information and tools necessary to perform common, related tasks. You may need to use multiple screens of data and tools for high-density applications, such as analytical tools, or for devices with small screens. However, finding a commonly used tool should be more like opening a desk drawer than walking to the storage closet down the hall. Navigating is something most people do when they're lost; no one wants to navigate any more than necessary.

Of course, you don't want absolutely everything available in all circumstances—who wants to trip over the holiday decorations when you open the closet every morning? Chapter 16 will show you how to use scenarios to decide what tools and information need to be available together, and which can be tucked away.

Don't force users to configure anything you can make a reasonable guess about

"Let's just ask users to set a preference" is a designer's cop-out. It would seem absurd if you were ordering in a restaurant and the waiter asked whether you'd like your meal cooked or raw, on a plate or in a bowl, and with or without utensils. It's likewise ridiculous for a product to refuse to make reasonable guesses about what typical users need. Don't defer design decisions to users; make reasonable choices so most users can get started with as few decisions as possible.

Rely on mental models instead of metaphors or implementation models

Data structures and product behavior are easiest to understand when they fit a user's mental model of how things work, rather than surfacing how the company is organized or how the product is built. Metaphors, which equate objects or interaction to something in the real world, are seldom successful at the framework level because they introduce too many limitations, or because the translation from atoms to pixels is imperfect enough to cause confusion.

Direct manipulation is one idiom that nearly always fits user mental models. If we want to manipulate a thing in the real world, we pick it up and move it around with our hands rather than typing commands to a robot arm. This means that the more directly people can manipulate data objects and interface elements, the easier the tool will be to understand. For example, it's much easier to sort a column by clicking on its header than by opening a menu or dialog box to select a preference.

Have a compelling reason for inconsistency

Inconsistency is usually a bad thing because it creates memory and cognitive work for users. For instance, the do-it-yourself electrician who lived in my house in the 1970s made some interesting design decisions about how the light switches should behave. There are two light switches in the kitchen, one of which affects the other's behavior. If the first switch is off, the second switch doesn't work at all. This drove everyone nuts until we put something in front of the first switch to keep anyone from using it. However, it's okay to be inconsistent if it provides a significant benefit. The dual switches that turn the light on or off from either the top or bottom of the stairs don't bother us, even though the standard "off" and "on" positions are meaningless, because it's so convenient to control the light in the stairway from either place.

Design for the probable, provide for the possible[3]

Good engineers have to consider all of the crazy things someone might do to break a product. Software engineers think about what would happen if millions of people suddenly decided to look at your Web site, or if someone had thousands of contacts in his address book application. Mechanical and electrical engineers think about devices getting dropped on the sidewalk or functioning at extreme temperatures. Considerations of this type are important, but shouldn't drive the design unless they are essential to its

function; for instance, durability should be a primary consideration in the design of a GPS device targeting hikers.

Patterns for Form and Behavior

Patterns—types of solutions that tend to be useful for certain classes of problems—are tremendously helpful at this stage of design. The patterns of interest at this point tend to focus on ways to manage screen real estate and navigation; later, you'll use many other patterns focused on lower-level interaction issues. You should never be limited by these few patterns, but recognize that they're usually a good place to start.

Organizing objects and activities

Although the range of potential interaction patterns is large, you can address most common design problems with a surprisingly small number that work not only for desktop applications, but across multiple platforms.

COMMAND LINE

Command line, a sort of textual conversation between user and machine, is the original interaction design pattern: The computer offers a prompt, the user types something in, the computer does something in response, and the computer throws up another prompt as if to say, "Now what do you want me to do?" Anyone over the age of 35 probably started using computers with a command-line interface like the one shown in Figure 15.3.

Framework

---

3. Cooper, A., Reimann, R., and Cronin, D. *About face 3: The essentials of interaction design*. Wiley Publishing, Inc. 2007.

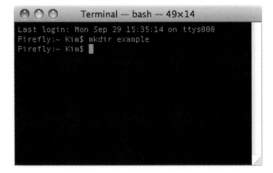

Figure 15.3. Apple's Terminal is an example of a command-line interface.

Few but programmers and some network administrators see classic command-line interfaces these days, but the idea of conversation as interface is alive and well. Customer service telephone systems that ask, "How can I help you?" are becoming more common, though some are not well done. Some games also use a conversational idiom (usually in combination with images that look anything but old-fashioned).

For those who know the lingo, command-line interfaces can be fast and powerful. For most users and applications, though, the learning curve is much too steep; the direct manipulation offered in graphical interfaces is much easier to grasp.

ORGANIZER/WORKSPACE

At its most basic, the **organizer/workspace** pattern consists of two panes: an organizer (usually either on the left or top of the screen) that allows users to find a file or other object, and a workspace (typically below or to the right of the organizer) that shows detail about the selected object. In most cases, only one object can be selected in the organizer to be displayed in the workspace, though some applications allow for multiple selections. What's shown in the workspace may vary depending on the type of object selected. The organizer may offer a flat or hierarchical list (as in iTunes), a search field and results, or more visual tools for navigating information. The allocation of space to each pane may be fixed or adjustable in a variety of ways.

As you can see in Figure 15.4, Adobe Acrobat Reader has a pane of page thumbnails that are selected to show an individual page in the workspace. iTunes also follows this pattern; selecting a playlist shows the songs it contains in the workspace, while selecting a device shows a set of tabs with various details about the device. Complex enterprise applications often make use of this pattern, as well. Monitoring applications may use a set of metrics in the organizer with drill-down reports in the workspace. The pattern also appears in some world-building simulation games.

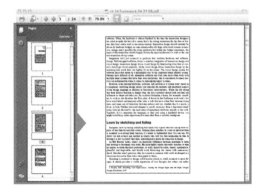

Figure 15.4. The organizer/workspace pattern exemplified in iTunes and Adobe Acrobat Reader.

Framework

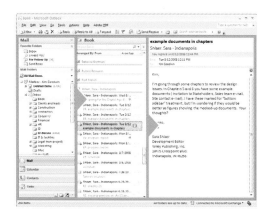 

Figure 15.5. Microsoft Outlook and Apple iPhoto use multi-pane variants of the organizer/workspace pattern.

This pattern is helpful when users have many files or objects to manage, need to see detail about individual objects, and frequently switch from one object to another. If switching is infrequent and the objects require considerable screen real estate to display, then the organizer may be in the way unless it behaves like a drawer that slides shut when not in use.

One common variant, shown in Figure 15.5, involves three levels of detail, with one pane showing the highest-level data objects such as folders, another showing individual objects, and a third showing detail about an individual object. Selection in the first pane drives the second, which in turn drives the third. Mail applications (such as Microsoft Outlook or Mac Mail) typically follow this pattern. Some photo management applications show albums or folders in the first pane, photo thumbnails in the second, and a zoomed-in view of an individual photo in the third.

HUB-AND-SPOKE / HIERARCHICAL MENU

In the **hub-and-spoke** or **hierarchical menu** pattern, users must return to a central hub such as a main menu screen to transition from one

activity or record to the next (see Figure 15.6). The pattern may include a nearly flat hierarchy or multiple levels. Each menu option may be represented by text, an icon, or both, or may be spoken in an audible interface. However, the pattern isn't limited to transaction or activity choices; it also works for progressive disclosure of information (such as drilling from artist down to album down to a particular song on a music player).

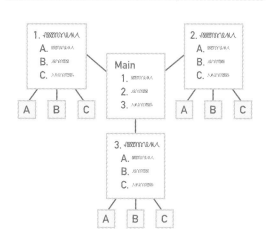

Figure 15.6. The hierarchical menu or hub-and-spoke pattern.

Framework

415

This pattern may call to mind old-fashioned character-based interfaces, but it's common on other platforms such as kiosks, DVDs, automated tellers, mobile phones, and MP3 players. The Palm OS for handhelds, as shown in Figure 15.7, is a classic example. Most telephone-based customer service interfaces also employ this structure, with a recorded voice offering a list of numbered options such as account balance, transfer, and so forth.

This is an effective pattern for interfaces that tend to get used for single transactions; walking up to an ATM and picking a couple of menu options isn't all that painful because you're probably doing just one thing and not returning to the menu. It's also a good option for devices with small screens that can't support persistently available navigation options. However, this pattern becomes inefficient and annoying when users constantly switch tasks or content; the continual back and forth (which Jared Spool aptly calls "pogo-sticking") is like having to go outside of your house to get from the kitchen to the dining room. Although a hierarchical menu is the obvious choice for most customer-service phone interfaces, listening to so many options makes for very slow interaction, so many companies are moving toward voice command systems.

Combining the hub-and-spoke pattern with "previous" and "next" buttons, such as in a photo gallery or music playlist, minimizes pogo-sticking if users will spend time paging through items at the same level in the hierarchy.

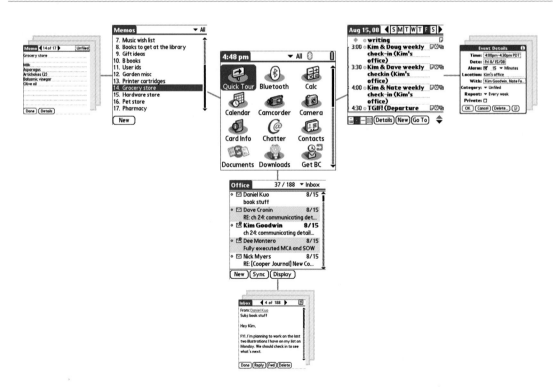

Figure 15.7. Palm's Treo interface is a classic hub-and-spoke that requires users to return to a main screen to choose a different application.

416

PARALLEL WORKSPACES AND MODES

Parallel workspaces are a bit like parallel universes in science fiction: They exist side by side, and a person exists in only one of them at a time. An interface with parallel workspaces lets users switch views to reach distinct sets of tools and information. Parallel workspaces differ from a hub-and-spoke arrangement in that the navigation mechanism is persistently available from anywhere in the interface, so there's no pogo-sticking up and down the hierarchy (unless there are submenus, as on a Web site). This pattern is sometimes called a **context switch**, though this term may be better to avoid because it means something different in software engineering. Some people also call it a **tabbed interface**, even though links, drop-down lists, or physical buttons can be used for the same effect. Figure 15.8 illustrates the basic pattern.

Some device interfaces use this pattern, as well. A car stereo, for example, might have individual buttons labeled AM, FM, CD, and MP3, each of which is a separate mode that affects not only the source of the sound, but also the exact behavior of some controls.

Utility applications such as operating system preferences use this pattern to group related settings.

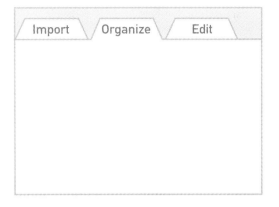

Figure 15.8. The parallel-workspace pattern usually employs tabs to let users switch contexts.

Web browsers such as Safari and Firefox use it to manage multiple pages. In multifunction information managers such as Microsoft Outlook and Entourage, each workspace is a different set of tools and information, such as an e-mail view, a calendar view, and a contact view. Many complex enterprise applications such as analytical tools, purchasing applications, and IT administration applications tools rely on this idiom, as well. Google uses it to provide very different search results and appropriate tools depending on whether you're looking for a Web site, map, or image (see Figure 15.9).

Figure 15.9. Google provides different workspaces with different tools depending on whether you're looking for an image, a map, or another sort of information.

Framework

Parallel workspaces are useful whenever users perform distinct sets of tasks within a single product.

Parallel workspaces are useful whenever users perform distinct sets of tasks within a single product; in essence, switching context creates separate "rooms" dedicated to particular uses. They're inappropriate for tightly intertwined tasks, such as writing and formatting text in a document. Although it's possible to implement tabs on small devices, it's often difficult to spare real estate for dedicated navigation.

Parallel workspaces can also be used for sequential activities, as in some tax-preparation programs; typically, the sequence is suggested but not strictly enforced, allowing users to return to previous steps at any time.

WIZARDS AND TUNNELS

A **wizard** (often called a **tunnel** when it's used on a device) is an enforced sequence of actions; users may not make a change at each step, but must at least pass through it. Unlike the parallel-workspace pattern, a wizard doesn't allow skipping around from step to step; at most, it offers the ability to page forward and back. Figure 15.10 illustrates the tunnel concept.

Installation programs on desktop computers, such as the one shown in Figure 15.11, are probably the best known wizard example.

Figure 15.10. A wizard or tunnel is an enforced sequence of steps.

Figure 15.11. Installation programs are some of the most familiar wizards.

Framework

The typical digital alarm clock or watch interface shown in Figure 15.12 is also a tunnel: You can adjust or skip past the hour as it blinks, then the minutes, then perhaps AM and PM or the date. Glucose meters, stereo systems, and other devices with inexpensive segment-based displays often employ tunnels, as well.

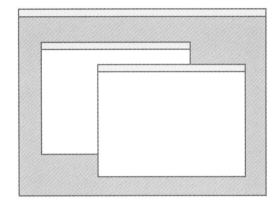

Figure 15.12. Digital watches and alarm clocks are familiar examples of tunnels.

Figure 15.13. MDI generally involves a parent window containing one or more child windows.

The tunnel pattern is also common in audible interfaces in which a system asks the user several questions in a row, such as, "Please enter the amount you'd like to transfer ... please enter the account number you'd like to transfer money from ... enter the account number you'd like to transfer money to." In an audible interface, this pattern is sometimes referred to as a **directed dialogue.**

Word processing applications and spreadsheets are the best-known MDI examples, but the pattern is common to many other authoring and editing tools, such as Photoshop, shown in Figure 15.14. Instant messaging applications may allow multiple windows for tracking different conversations.

Tunnels are clear and simple; they make it hard to get lost. They're often the only viable option for changing settings on devices with segment-based displays. However, they're a poor choice for anything users need to do often, and they quickly become tedious if changing one commonly used setting requires stepping through a dozen others.

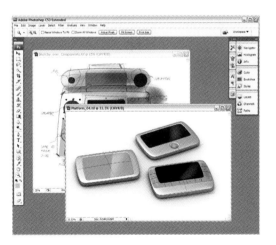

MULTIPLE DOCUMENT INTERFACE

A **multiple document interface (MDI)** has a single parent window that allows multiple child windows to be open at a time, as shown in Figure 15.13. The windows are typically free-floating and resizable.

Figure 15.14. Adobe Photoshop is a familiar example of an MDI.

The MDI pattern is useful for comparing content between two documents or for copying and pasting content between one document and another.

However, it can require excessive window management.

Some applications employ a sort of "managed MDI," such as that used in tabbed Web browsers, though this is really more like a parallel workspace than true MDI. It's also possible to manage MDI with a variety of mechanisms for tiling different windows so they don't overlap on the desktop.

FIRST-PERSON ENVIRONMENT

A **first-person environment** is an immersive artificial environment (usually in three dimensions) in which the world is shown through the user's eyes, such as in Figure 15.15.

The vast majority of first-person environments are video games, including many combat games and some adventure or role-playing games. Solitaire, chess, and other common PC desktop games not usually considered video games are also first person. The Google Maps "street level" view is a sort of first-person environment embedded within a more typical desktop interface.

A three-dimensional, first-person environment is useful for teaching skills that may be dangerous

Figure 15.15. This image from Microsoft Flight Simulator X is an example of a first-person environment.

or expensive to practice in the real world, such as flying or driving, and it adds realism to games. It can take a fair bit of processing power, though, and may also require a specialized input device, such as a joystick, game pad, or steering wheel. Some users have difficulty deciphering three-dimensional spatial relationships on a two dimensional screen.

THIRD-PERSON ENVIRONMENT

In a third-person environment, the user watches the action from the perspective of an off-screen viewer, much like watching a movie, and controls the actions of some sort of character or object in the environment. The game in Figure 15.16 is a typical example.

Many video games are third-person environments, from Pong to Wii Sports. Most maze games (such as Pac-Man), platformers (such as Sonic the Hedgehog or Super Mario), and side-scrolling games (such as Space Invaders) are viewed from a third-person perspective. Educational software for children often makes use of this pattern, too.

A third-person point of view often works better than first person in two-dimensional games, and may allow for greater variability in game play.

Figure 15.16. Lego Star Wars II from LucasArts is played from a third-person point of view.

Framework

Combinations of patterns

While these individual patterns provide limited options, combining them allows for considerable flexibility. For example, you could use tabs in an organizer to switch among different types of data objects; Microsoft Outlook (shown in Figure 15.17) works this way, though the controls are not represented as tabs. Many Web sites combine a tabbed structure for top-level navigation with a hub-and-spoke arrangement at lower levels. World-building games often use a third-person camera view combined with an organizer or parallel workspaces. Audible interfaces are increasingly employing a **mixed initiative** approach, which combines command-line-style open-ended prompts with menus or directed dialogue (tunnels).

Nearly any combination of these patterns can work, so long as it's appropriate to the context of use.

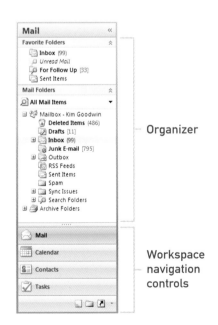

Figure 15.17. Microsoft Outlook's left pane acts as both an organizer and a set of tab equivalents for switching workspaces among the e-mail, calendar, and other views.

Patterns work partly because they provide predictable behavior, so it's important to apply the pattern consistently; for example, if you use a row of tabs across the top of the screen to indicate what context users are in, it may be confusing if a screen exists outside that structure.

Organizing by nouns or verbs

Regardless of what patterns you use to structure the interaction, it's usually best to organize it consistently using either objects (nouns) or actions (verbs). For example, a digital media management application with parallel workspaces could be organized primarily around media types, with tabs for music, video, and audiobooks. Within each tab or on a global toolbar, you'd then have controls for importing, finding, and playing the content. You could also arrange things by activity, with tabs for the import, find, and play functions. (This is an oversimplification, but you get the idea.) If you had a tab called music and a tab called play, on the other hand, it could get very confusing: If someone wants to play music, which tab should she use? The mixture of nouns and verbs makes your scheme unclear.

Additional ways to manage real estate

Even on a generously sized monitor, you may need to make more information or tools available than you have room for. You might also find that there are some things that get used often enough to keep close at hand, but not so often they should always be visible.

FLEXIBLE PALETTES AND DRAWERS

Most of the patterns described here can coexist with either persistent or somewhat transient collections of tools and supplemental information, such as floating or dockable palettes (sometimes called "inspectors") or collapsible drawers that can be opened or closed with a click. Figure 15.18 illustrates these two patterns.

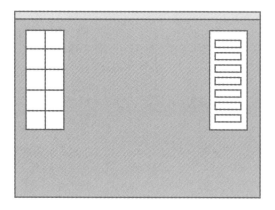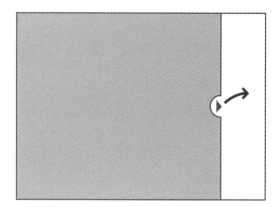

Figure 15.18. Floating palettes allow space-constrained users to keep tools visible but out of the way. Drawers that open and close with a click provide similar benefits, often with less effort.

Photoshop and many drawing tools make use of floating palettes; some allow palettes to be docked along one side of the screen. Some photo management programs, such as Aperture, provide collapsible drawers that show details about an image.

Palettes and drawers can be a good option when there's a combination of complex tools and information not suited to a toolbar, that users only want now and then, or that is likely to get in the way of work that takes a lot of screen space, such as image editing. Floating palettes are impractical in most mobile applications due to space constraints, but drawers can sometimes work.

Be wary of adding unnecessary window-management chores. Although they keep tools persistently available, palettes that don't dock can get in the way. A drawer that snaps open or shut with a single click can sometimes be a better solution than a palette, particularly if users don't need something in it every minute or two. Clicking to open or close it is work, but in some situations it's less work than constantly repositioning a palette.

PROGRESSIVE DISCLOSURE

Another strategy for managing space is progressive disclosure, in which a control expands the

pane (or dialog box) to reveal additional details and controls. This can be useful when the additional controls are rarely used or when space is at a premium, but irritating if it's done just to make things look simpler. Photoshop makes good use of progressive disclosure with its collapsible tools, shown in Figure 15.19.

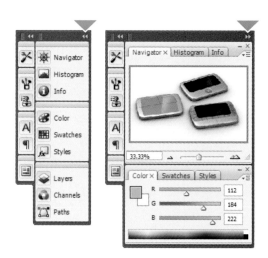

Figure 15.19. Photoshop makes use of progressive disclosure in its floating palettes.

Summary

Being effective as a designer requires more knowledge of principles and patterns than you'll find in these pages, but these should get you off to a good start. As you apply these and other patterns, remember two things:

— What principles and patterns apply depends on the context of use, including the goals and skills of your personas.

— Mix and match patterns all you like, but when you use a pattern, apply it consistently so users know what to expect.

Framework

CHAPTER 16

Designing the Form Factor and Interaction Framework

Any effective approach to design starts with defining the big ideas, iterating until you get them right, then adding more detail and iterating until the product or service is ready for people to use. The fundamentals of this process look very similar whether you're designing hardware, software, services, or environments: Start with the best idea you can think of based on your understanding of users, examine it in various ways to find problems, then throw it out if it's hopeless or refine it if it's close to working.

However, unlike other design problems, interactive products and services change state over time and engage in a type of conversation with their users. These factors are what make personas and scenarios so useful as design tools—personas help you predict user behavior and desires in any circumstance, while scenarios help you see how the product should change state over time. Of course, this early part of the design work also takes considerable visualization skill, an ability to think in systematic terms, and a deep knowledge of design principles and patterns to come up with a solution that's not just workable, but *desirable*.

The approach outlined in this chapter focuses on how to visualize form and behavior: what the product or service is, what it does, and how it looks and works from a user's point of view. Design processes are never as neat and linear as they look in diagrams—there's always some variation due to the design problem and the working styles of individual team members. However, there are certain thought processes that need to happen (whether explicitly or in a designer's head) for good design to emerge. Some of them are usually best done earlier than others, as shown in Figure 16.1; the process is recursive but has an overall flow. The process for designing behavior is much the same regardless of whether there is hardware design involved; simply ignore any boxes in the diagram that don't apply. Sections in this chapter describe how the process applies to specialized design problems.

If you're designing a service, the first step is to figure out what "products," environments, or modes of interaction comprise the service, then design each as you would an individual product. The same is true for designing product lines.

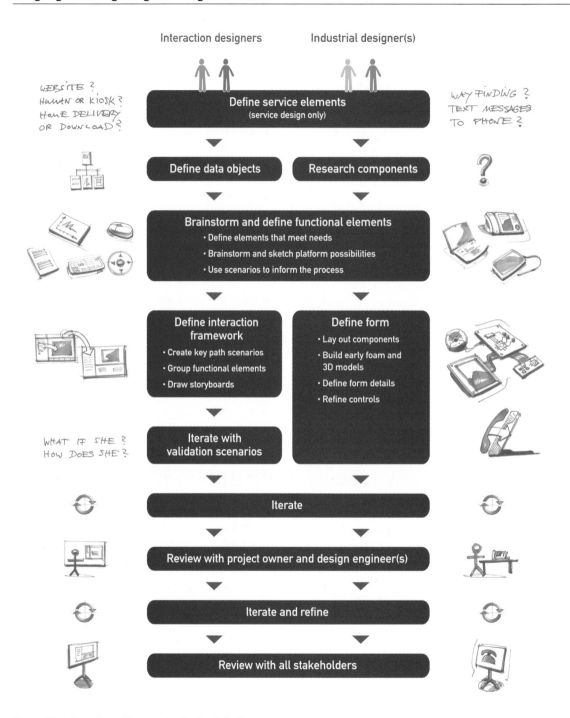

Figure 16.1. Overview of form and behavior definition process.

For each product (or service component), first focus on the puzzle pieces appropriate to each discipline. Interaction designers (IxDG and IxDS) must clearly define the data objects, their attributes, and their relationships. At the same time, industrial designers must understand the various components (such as batteries and circuit boards) that are likely to be required, as well as any physical or engineering constraints on their layout; these factors will influence the volume and shape of the device to some extent. Industrial designers generally collaborate early on with mechanical engineers to determine what flexibility there is. Once the members of each subteam are satisfied that they understand the issues, they should come together (along with the visual designer) to begin developing solutions.

Early solution development is both analytical and generative. Some teams find it useful to begin with the analytical by translating functional needs into specific solution components, while others prefer to begin in a more generative fashion, brainstorming a wide array of solutions and then using an analytical approach to determine which possibilities will be most fruitful. The analytical starting point is helpful when time or constraints are tight, since it helps eliminate possibilities very quickly, or when the system is very complex. It can also be useful if the team is having difficulty being generative, though this is not usually a problem with experienced designers in the room. In reality, although I've explained them as separate tasks, most teams bounce back and forth between the generative and the analytical, exploring possibilities and ruling them out as they go.

Whichever starting point you choose, both activities need to happen. The whole design team needs to begin making some decisions about how to address functional needs; many are purely design decisions with little business impact, while a few require input from other product team members or stakeholders. The whole team also needs to spend some time (whether it's an hour in a tightly constrained project or a week for a more ambitious one) doing broad exploration.

When designing a device or a service that involves a physical environment, the whole design team sketches possible solutions together, then narrows these to the best candidates. Members of each discipline iterate these concepts for a day or two, with interaction designers using scenarios to evolve the behavior while the industrial designer(s) evolve the form based on ergonomics, engineering considerations, and other factors. The visual designer(s), in the meantime, begin working on visual language studies (as discussed in Chapter 18). How early the industrial designer(s) incorporate the design language is largely a matter of personal preference, though it's usually not worth focusing on this until the basic form is settled.

What one subteam learns during this independent iteration affects the work of the others, so the whole design team checks in anywhere from daily to twice a week, depending on how interdependent the software and hardware are and how much each team member tends to stray during exploration. Members of each discipline may have somewhat differing points of view about the design approach. This tension is usually productive as long as each sees the value in the other's concerns. Personas can help resolve most differences; the team lead may need to do so if there is an impasse, but this should be a rare event in an effective team.

It's important to review work in progress with the project owner and design engineer(s) as soon as one or more good directions emerge, usually about four or five days into the design. This helps avoid wasting time on solutions that aren't feasible or viable from a business perspective. Good design engineers can often help improve the design, as well.

The remainder of this chapter outlines each aspect of this process in more detail. Because the

The kinds of "objects" users think about help shape the design.

fundamental ways that industrial designers work are well understood in that profession, I won't go into great detail on the industrial designer's tasks, but will focus primarily on how the interaction design develops, how form and behavior drive one another to achieve a coherent solution, and how personas and scenarios affect form.

IxDG and IxDS: Define Data Object Types and Relationships

Just as it's important to know what sorts of things will be stored in a kitchen or carried in a vehicle, you need to determine what kinds of objects the personas would use in your product. Although what constitutes an "object" in a user's mind isn't always an "object" in a programmer's mind, what you define at this point is the foundation of the **data model**; engineers may make a few adjustments to your version so it fits their needs, but they'll find it tremendously helpful.

A **data object type**[1] is a species of thing a user can create, manipulate, or look for, such as a file on a hard drive, a person in a contact list, or a store in a shopping mall directory. A data object is usually something on a screen, but could also be something physical (such as an airplane boarding pass) or aural (such as a telephone call). In almost all cases, an object type is something there can be multiple instances of.

Not all of the information needs you identified as requirements (see Chapter 12) will become data objects. For example, consider the data needs of Katie, our photographer persona, which are outlined in Table 12.1. She needs to understand how many shots will fit on her camera's memory card, whether she has enough battery power remaining to take those shots, and what the exposure settings are. These are things she has to see in some kind of information display, but they're not object types because she can't create them or move them around. The only data object type in her camera interface is a photo. In the photo management application on her computer, though, there are multiple object types, including photos, groups of photos, and perhaps master photos with adjusted copies.

In an ideal world, the data object types would come directly from your personas' mental models. This is possible in some simple applications, though in more complex cases it's often necessary to introduce new object types that don't exist in the mental model. Profiles are a

---

1. It would be more precise to call it an "interface data object type" to distinguish it from a programming object, but the term is cumbersome.

good example of an introduced object type. They don't exist in most users' mental models, but clustering a complex group of network or data analysis settings into a single profile (such as "work" or "home") can help users make time-consuming changes with a single click. You may also find that there's a mental model analogue that needs to be translated; before the advent of digital music management, for instance, you wouldn't have found a mental model object called a playlist, but anyone who was a teenager in the era of cassette tapes probably had some awareness of individual songs collected into "mix tapes." It's perfectly acceptable to introduce new types of data objects if you have a good reason for doing so, provided you're building on the mental model rather than breaking it.

Figure 16.2. Apple's iPhoto arranges photos in albums, which makes sense, but who stores albums in folders?

Physical-world metaphor is both useful and limiting in this respect. Apple's iPhoto, for example, relies on albums as the data object representing groups of photos. This is consistent with most users' mental models. However, Apple then introduced another type of data object called a folder, which exists solely to organize albums (see Figure 16.2). In the real world, though, albums don't fit in folders. Also, unlike folders in the operating system, iPhoto folders cannot contain individual photos; they can only contain albums. Both of these points are contrary to expectation, which makes the data model less easy to grasp than it could be. It's relatively easy to overcome in a simple application like iPhoto even if it's a bit like a door hinge that squeaks every time you use it. In more complex applications, though, this kind of dissonance can create significant usability problems.

Avoid getting overly abstract in your definition of object types, though. It might seem elegant to say that both patients and doctors should be tracked in a hospital system as "people," but users need different information for each and definitely don't think about them in the same terms.

Object types alone don't paint a complete picture, however. Your initial draft of the data model should include the following for each type of object:

— What it's called

— What it is

— How it can be related to other object types

— What users can do with it

— What states it can be in

— What attributes it has that your personas care about

Framework

Don't be concerned if you can't articulate all the attributes, states, and actions yet. The objects, their definitions, and their relationships are most critical at this point, but you might still uncover some as you design; document templates or e-mail filters, for example, might not occur to you as data objects until you work through less-common scenarios. Include any future objects you anticipate, even if they won't be part of the first release. Table 16.1 shows an example of a preliminary data model.

Table 16.1. **Preliminary data model for a veterinary practice management application.**

Object	Definition	Relationships	States	Actions	Attributes
Client	A human or organization whose pet has been seen (or has an appointment to be seen) by a veterinarian or technician	— Always contains one or more pets — Usually contains one or more bills	— Incomplete (record started but missing information) — Active (current client) — Archived (manually archived or has not visited in some number of years)	— Create — Edit — Read — Archive — Find	— Name — Address — Phone numbers — E-mail — Account standing — Billing history
Pet or patient	An animal who has been seen (or has an appointment to be seen) by a veterinarian or technician	— Always part of a client file — May contain one or more visits	— Incomplete (record started but missing information) — Active (current client) — In need of follow-up — Archived (manually archived or has not visited in some number of years) — Deceased	— Create — Edit — Read — Find	— Name — Species — Breed — Age — Sex — Color — Temperament — Health history — Medications — Allergies

Framework

Object	Definition	Relationships	States	Actions	Attributes
Visit	An instance of a pet being seen	— Always part of a client file — Usually associated with a bill	— Incomplete (record started but missing information) — Complete	— Create — Edit — Read	— Notes — Vital signs — Procedures performed — Tests ordered — Diagnoses — Prescriptions — Supplies used — Amount billed — Follow-up required
Appointment	A time scheduled for a visit with one or more pets and a veterinarian or technician	Always associated with a client, one or more pets, and a veterinarian or technician	— Incomplete (record started but missing information) — Complete	— Create — Edit — Read — Delete	— Client — Pet(s) — Veterinarian or technician — Date — Time — Room — Equipment — Procedure or appointment type
Bill	A statement of the amount due for one or more visits	Always part of a client file	— Incomplete (record started but missing information) — Unsent — Awaiting payment — Overdue — Paid	— Create — Edit — Read — Mark paid	— Client — Pet(s) — Veterinarian or technician — Date — Time — Procedure or appointment type — Supplies used — Amount owed

Continued

Object	Definition	Relationships	States	Actions	Attributes
Veterinarian	A doctor of veterinary medicine who treats pets at this facility	Associated with multiple clients, pets, visits, bills, and appointments	— Active — Inactive (no longer seeing patients at this hospital) — Available — Unavailable	— Create — Edit — Make inactive	— Name — Availability — Procedures and appointment types they do or don't do
Technician	A non-veterinarian who assists veterinarians, gathers information, and performs some routine treatments	Associated with multiple clients, pets, visits, bills, and appointments	— Active — Inactive (no longer seeing patients at this hospital)	— Create — Edit — Make inactive	— Name — Availability — Procedures and appointment types they do or don't do
Room	A location that can be reserved for a visit	Associated with certain procedures and appointments	— Available — Unavailable — Inactive (permanently unavailable)	— Create — Edit — Make inactive	— Name — Availability — Equipment — Associated procedures
Cage	A pet holding area that can be reserved for boarding or ongoing care	Associated with certain appointments	— Available — Unavailable — Inactive (permanently unavailable)	— Create — Edit — Make inactive	— Name — Availability — Size or appropriateness for certain animals
Piece of equipment	An in-demand medical device that can be reserved for a visit	— Associated with certain appointments — May be part of a room	— Available — Unavailable — Assigned to a room — Inactive (permanently unavailable)	— Create — Edit — Assign — Revoke assignment — Make inactive	— Name — Availability — Room — Associated procedures

Explicit **nomenclature** and object type **definitions** are important even for seemingly obvious terms; if one person thinks of a "photo album" as a simple collection of images with no explicit organization while another thinks it has a user-specified page layout, miscommunication will bog down your design meetings until you straighten it out.

Framework

Relationships are also important to articulate. Like mental model objects, data objects may be related in several ways, such as:

— **Many to many:** many people may send many messages

— **Many to one:** many documents may reside in one folder

— **One to many:** one folder may contain multiple documents

— **One to one:** one company has one tax identification number

— **Hierarchical:** albums contain photos

— **Temporal:** a law is generated from, and replaces, a bill

It may not be critical at first, but sooner or later you will also need to define what **actions** (such as creating, moving, editing, and deleting) users can and can't perform upon each type of object, as well as what **states** each object can be in. Your scenarios are good guides for this. Don't worry if you can't write down a lot of detail yet, since some necessary actions and states will only become clear as you work through the design.

Finally, you need to develop some understanding of what object **attributes** your personas care about, such as the sender and subject of an e-mail message or the vendor and terms in a purchase order. These attributes usually map to database fields later on. As with actions and states, don't be too concerned about filling out every possible detail at this point; what you most need to understand is whether the personas need a lot of information about each object or only a little; this determines how much screen space you'll need to display that information. You'll continue refining the attributes as you do detailed design.

To develop the contents and structure of your data model, start with the mental models you gleaned from your interviews. As you add any new object types, check them against your personas and

scenarios. First, ask yourself if the new object type is really necessary or if you're making a fine distinction that never matters to the personas. Scenarios are also critical to generating data objects. Look for the nouns in your scenarios: lists, documents, images, or whatever else is being used, viewed, or manipulated. Not all will be data objects, so compare them to the criteria above. Finally, consider whether the object type as you've defined it will make sense to your personas.

Most data objects are easy enough to figure out, but complex software such as analytics or IT administration tools can require more careful thought. Some additional data objects might emerge as you design, but for now, ask yourself whether there are dependencies between any of the object types on your list and any others, whether any of the objects need to grouped into higher-level objects, or whether business constraints will result in any specific objects (such as a log that provides an audit trail). This may help you define some of the trickier object types.

> **Exercise**
>
> Define the data object types, relationships, attributes, and valid actions and states for the LocalGuide or RoomFinder.

Full Design Team: Define Possible Functional Elements

Once you have a good idea of what the data model looks like (and a good grasp of the product's likely internal components, if hardware is involved), you're ready to start translating the functional needs identified during requirements definition into a set of possible functional elements. If you are designing a multi-environment service or a dedicated device rather than software for an existing platform, it's essential that industrial designers be involved in these initial discussions.

Framework

Functional elements are solution components that are visible to users.

Functional elements are solution components that are visible to users; they take up space on the screen or have some physical representation (such as a button or knob) on a device. In a way, making decisions about functional elements is like listing the rooms, storage areas, and staircases you'll need in a building before determining how they'll be laid out. As with every part of the design process, this is iterative: Start with a list of major elements, begin using those to draw screens or hardware configurations, and then gradually add more detail to your list as you draw. Don't get too attached to solutions until you begin sketching and trying them out, especially when you're doing broad exploration for a novel platform.

Each functional need in the requirements list (see Chapter 12) leads to a functional element that addresses the need. In many cases, these are pretty obvious; a need to play video implies a video display and either physical or virtual playback controls. Tedious as this kind of translation may seem, it's still worthwhile for a couple of reasons. One is that any designer can benefit from having an explicit list of all the puzzle pieces that have to fit on the screen or device. This is especially useful for less-experienced designers (who might otherwise miss an important element and have to start over) or those who aren't natural visual thinkers (who might otherwise be uncertain where to start on a blank whiteboard).

The other is that on nearly every project, there are one or two items in the list of needs that have major business implications, such as whether to use an inexpensive segment-based screen, which allows for very limited flexibility in what can be displayed, or a more expensive, pixel-based LCD.

Many experienced designers almost unconsciously develop a mental list of functional elements rather than an explicit one. This can work, particularly if you're stuck designing alone, but has a couple of drawbacks. The most important is that an unconscious list of elements doesn't get examined explicitly. Mental lists are also difficult for others to engage with. It's not just that your teammates won't have access to what's in your head—you're also likely to find collaboration difficult if everyone on the team is working from a slightly different mental list of functional elements.

It's not necessary at this point to identify every possible functional element in the product; all you need to do is figure out the major ones. What these are varies depending on the nature of the design problem.

Functional elements in product design

Whether you're designing a Web site, a desktop application, or a device with some sort of information display, there are generally three basic types of functional elements critical to accomplishing the scenarios:

— Display areas for data or content, such as a video or a list of email messages

— Tools or controls, such as on-screen widgets or hardware buttons that interact with screen contents

— Places to put tools and controls, such as toolbars or palettes on a screen, or control surfaces on a device

Display areas, physical navigation or input controls, and areas to put software tools are important at this point, but individual software controls (such as buttons and list boxes) are not. Trying to identify every widget would be a waste of time because you'd unmake many of those decisions later on. Just focus on things that will require significant amounts of physical or screen space; you'll figure out the rest when you get to detailed design.

Although interaction designers are inclined to think about the parts of the hardware that are directly involved in the visual and tactile interaction, such as knobs, buttons, and displays, industrial designers must also think of functional elements that address sound, power, storage, ergonomic needs, physical connectivity with other devices, and so forth.

Table 16.2 shows a partial list of needs translated into functional elements for an office telephone, including both interactive elements and other important hardware components. Table 16.3 shows a similar partial list for an e-commerce Web site. Some people find it helpful to portray the scenario in the same table to show how they relate (see Table 16.7 later in this chapter).

Table 16.2. **Functional elements for an office telephone.**

Functional need	Functional element
Place calls to known contacts and colleagues	Contacts list/directory displayed on screen
Place calls to numbers not in contacts list	Keypad (physical or virtual)
Review messages	On-screen display; audio playback for remote access
Manage calls (hold, transfer)	Hold button, transfer button (physical or virtual)
Adjust tilt of keypad and display	Adjustable stand to tilt entire device
Use headset	Standard wired headset port in addition to wireless
Capture and play sound as a speakerphone	Microphone along front of device; speaker
Store handset	Cradle

Framework

Table 16.3. Functional elements for a shopping Web site.

Functional need	Functional element
Find a specific product	Search field
See what's available	Category listing
Learn about a product	Product information display area
Store items under consideration	Shopping cart

Service design usually entails interaction with multiple channels and environments—in other words, multiple "products."

Functional elements in service design

Service design is unique in that it often entails interaction with multiple channels and environments, so it may involve the design of multiple "products." On the simple end of the service design scale, a movie rental service includes selecting the movies you want, getting them, watching them, and then returning them. This might all occur on your computer: Pick a movie from a Web site, download it, watch it on your computer, then have your rental privilege expire. It might also involve multiple devices and channels: a Web site to select movies, a delivery service that brings you the discs, your home DVD player to watch them, and some sort of packaging and service to return them. At a minimum, you can design the Web site and the packaging; ideally, you could design the whole service from end to end.

Service design is mostly about making sure you understand every point at which you can affect a user's experience, then finding some way to make it better. Your context scenarios should have covered each of these points; the tricky bit is in identifying where you need to design new products, where you can take advantage of existing third-party solutions, and how to work around aspects of the service you can't change. In a sense, this is defining what "products" you need to design, then following the design process described here for each.

For example, if you were to redesign airline travel, you might start by translating your list of needs into service elements. Table 16.4 shows a partial list of example elements. Once you had identified the solution components of the service, you could then use more detailed scenarios to define the functional elements of the Web site, the cell-phone-boarding-pass interaction, and so on.

Table 16.4. **Service elements for airline travel.**

Functional need	Service element
Find a flight that fits time and budget needs	Web site that acts like a really good travel agent ("Did you know you could save $200 by flying on Sunday?")
Find the best place to stay on a business trip and the best way to get there	Web site that offers hotel and transportation options based on preferences and meeting location
Know when to leave for airport	Web site that estimates time based on route to airport, typical traffic, and typical security wait times; airline sends notice to mobile phone if anything changes
Avoid boarding pass hassle	Send electronic boarding pass to passenger's mobile phone; allow those without phones to print from Web site
Quickly deal with unexpected situations such as a cancelled flight	Easy access to a live human in the airport or on the phone without a long wait time
Avoid checked luggage hassle	Offer unique RFID luggage tags that automatically associate the bag with passenger and flight that day; just put the bag on a conveyor belt

Making decisions

As Tables 16.2 through 16.4 imply, defining functional elements involves making both business and design decisions, which are largely about trade-offs. If there are multiple solutions that might address a need, which is the best fit for the personas, scenarios, and goals? Which requires the least effort (both mental and physical) on the part of users? Which is easier to build? Which might generate additional revenue? Which solution is more economically, socially, and environmentally sustainable?

Consider voicemail for an office telephone as an example. When someone checks messages, you could provide an audible list of new messages or you could display a list of calls on a screen. First,

consider which is better from a design perspective by thinking through scenarios using each possible solution. If your persona has several messages when she returns to her desk, a visual display has the benefit of letting her quickly choose whichever message is likely to be most important to her at the moment. When she has to check voicemail while out of the office, audio playback may be the only option if you don't also control her mobile-phone interface. This probably means you have to have audio playback, but there's a good design argument for also providing a visual solution. The visual solution will require more than the two-line display that's common to office telephones, though, as well as additional coding time, so you'd need to involve the appropriate stakeholders to decide whether the gain in revenue potential is worth the cost.

Ideally, there is time to explore multiple platforms and architectures for physical products.

If a design choice mostly affects usability and desirability without major business implications, then it's generally best to make that decision within the design team. Of course, you won't always be entirely correct about which issues do or don't have a business impact; this is one good reason for frequent check-ins. Some of your decisions may be subject to change as you iterate the design, but it's usually most effective to make the best decision you can and move on, rather than researching every possible implication of every choice.

Exercise

1. For the LocalGuide: Define functional elements for the end-to-end service, then for the device itself.
2. For the RoomFinder: Determine whether it's a single interface on a single platform or a multiplatform system and then define functional elements accordingly.

Full Design Team: Define Possible Platforms

For some design projects, such as constrained redesigns, the range of possible solutions is narrow—there is no doubt about whether you're designing a Web app, a handheld device with a touch screen, or an inexpensive kiosk with membrane buttons and a segment-based display. In other cases, the possibilities are much broader, so the design team's job is to help the product team think creatively and explore multiple **platforms**. A platform is defined by its:

— **Form factor:** If it's a device, is it a semiportable tablet, a tiny handheld that fits in a pocket, or a massive console with a dedicated room in a hospital? What size and orientation is the screen, if any, and what technology does it use (such as segments, pixels, or electronic paper)?

— **Input and output methods:** By what mechanisms does a user navigate, select, consume, and enter data? Is it a touch screen, a physical keyboard, voice input, or some technology no one has ever seen before?

Ideally, the design team has time to explore several platforms, since each will have different advantages and disadvantages regarding usability, cost, revenue potential, and future flexibility. However, the differences among platforms can have a tremendous impact on the behavior of a device, so the interaction designers usually need to walk through a set of scenarios for each one. This makes multiplatform exploration more time-consuming than, say, developing multiple physical appearance concepts for the same basic phone or looking at several different structures for a Web site. For this reason, it's usually necessary to narrow the platform options to two or three in fairly short order, develop some sketches and quick foam models, and focus on one platform as soon as stakeholders are confident. It's a rare organization that will fund more than one platform possibility through detailed interaction design.

However, the industrial and interaction designers may still explore multiple **architectures**—arrangements of essentially the same components—for each platform. Figure 16.3 illustrates three different platforms: a touch screen, a version with a four-way controller, and an option with soft buttons (physical controls around the edge of the screen that have varying functions identified by on-screen labels). It also shows a rendering of two different architectures for the platform with the four-way controller; the control's physical placement (and hence the overall shape of the device) differs, but the input method and the orientation of the screen are the same, so the interaction with either device will be essentially the same. As a result of this approach, industrial designers may show stakeholders a handful of different architecture sketches for each platform, such as those in Figure 16.4.

Interaction designers, on the other hand, generate plenty of ideas at the whiteboard, but they exercise each possibility using scenarios, resulting in fewer options (often only one option per platform) being visible to stakeholders. It's not that interaction designers are less generative or open to exploration, but that interaction design simply cannot be evaluated with a single sketch. A recent client is a useful example; the company was working with us on interaction design for a

> Interaction design cannot be evaluated with a single sketch, so exploring multiple concepts takes a fair amount of time.

Framework

Three different platforms

Two architectures for one platform

Figure 16.3. Platforms versus architectures.

Figure 16.4. A range of architecture and platform sketches.

new platform, but had hired a separate firm to do visual design, hoping to generate some goodness through using firms with two different approaches. Naturally, that firm's visual designers were interested in interaction just as our interaction designers were interested in the visual expression of the behavior, so their team threw out a few interaction design concepts. Stakeholders thought one of the ideas looked pretty slick, fell in love with it, and asked the interaction designers to incorporate it. Unfortunately, the concept had never been vetted with a scenario, so it really didn't work very well, leaving the stakeholders frustrated.

Input and output methods

For devices, input and output methods play a large part in determining form factor. The most important considerations usually involve how much text your personas will enter, how direct the manipulation must be, and what your COGS (cost of goods sold) budget is. The usage environment and scenarios should help you decide whether visual or audible output is best and whether input should be optimized for voice, one hand, two hands, or even feet.

Most interactive products use visual output, which is appropriate in most circumstances (at least for sighted users) because it's a richer communication medium and because it's quiet and private. Audible output is common in customer service systems, which makes sense because it shouldn't require a computer to tell your utility company that your power is out. Audible output is also useful when users really need to look somewhere other than at a screen, such as when they're driving.

The input options are more complex. Table 16.5 describes advantages and disadvantages of some common input methods.

Table 16.5. **Advantages and disadvantages of various input methods.**

Method	Advantages	Disadvantages
Touch screens	— Allow direct manipulation — Flexible display of most appropriate options in any context — Gestures offer useful shortcuts for common tasks	— Expensive — Can get smeared — Not so good for text input — Add weight and thickness — Require large controls unless you use a stylus
Soft buttons (on-screen labels used to indicate what a nearby physical control will do)	— Usually cheaper and lighter than touch screen — Allow fairly direct manipulation; little cognitive effort if button and label are clearly associated — Somewhat flexible display of most appropriate options in any context	— Less flexible than touch screen — Gets very clumsy if you have more options than buttons

Continued

441

Method	Advantages	Disadvantages
Cursor-based selection with up-down and/or left-right buttons plus a selection button (as in a television remote control or on many phones)	— Can be relatively fast, especially if you accelerate scrolling speed when the button is held down — Less expensive than touch screens — Familiar idiom for most users	— Slower than touch screen or soft buttons if you're trying to choose among just a few options — Less direct than touch screen or soft buttons; requires more cognitive effort — Repetitive-motion strain if you require individual button presses instead of accelerating
Cursor-based selection with a mouse, scroll wheel, or trackball	— Faster than 2-way or 4-way controller for selecting among a few options — Generally less expensive than touch screens — Familiar idiom for computer users	— Requires fine motor control — Slower than touch screen or soft buttons if you're trying to choose among just a few options — Less direct than touch screen or soft buttons; requires more cognitive effort
Gyroscopes and accelerometers	— Allow gesture-based input to control orientation, speed, etc.	— Imprecise — Unfamiliar idiom for many users
Knobs and dials	— Can allow very precise control depending on engineering — Allow quick access if dedicated to a single function — Jog dials (which return to a fixed position) can allow for fast scrolling	— Protrude more than other controls — Cost varies depending on characteristics — Mapping of clockwise and counterclockwise rotation to vertical or horizontal movement may have to be learned
Stylus on touch screen or separate input pad	— Great for drawing and handwriting input — Minimize fingerprints and smearing on touch screens	— Easily lost; people may use pens and pencils instead — Writing can be slower than typing — Handwriting recognition is usually imperfect
Voice	— Hands-free input is safer in some circumstances — No repetitive-motion injuries	— Imprecise except for a limited set of commands — Inappropriate in noisy or open work areas or for confidential information

Framework

Method	Advantages	Disadvantages
Keyboards, number pads, and other physical buttons	— Fast text entry — Familiar idiom	— Large — Repetitive-motion injuries are common with keyboards — Buttons covered in membrane can be too stiff and membranes can puncture
Foot pedals	— Appropriate for some applications when both hands are occupied, such as performing surgery or playing a guitar	— Awkward in most situations

Input methods for desktop applications or any other software running on an existing platform are largely predetermined, though you don't always have to stick with a keyboard and mouse; voice, pen, or other input options may be feasible for specialized activities.

Other form factor considerations

Context plays a major role in determining form factor. The more portable the device needs to be, for example, the smaller users will generally want it. Internal components also have a great deal of influence—if there's no cost-effective way to make them smaller, then the device must be at least a certain size or shape.

The other big driver of form factor is the size and orientation of the screen, which should be guided by the type of content you need to display. Any device that largely involves lists of selectable items, such as songs on a music player or medications on a hospital infusion pump, usually benefits from a portrait orientation that allows for display of more list items; extra horizontal space is usually wasted. Landscape screens are usually better for columns of data, graphs of events over time, or video. With multifunction mobile devices,

you can allow for viewing either way depending on the type of content or even the device's physical orientation.

Full Team: Brainstorm with Sketches

It's best to begin discussing functional elements and platform considerations even before you begin sketching. However, don't feel like you have to make firm decisions about everything before you draw, because what you learn through sketching will inform your thinking about all of these issues. An efficient design team is unlikely to spend much more than an hour on discussion before they start putting sketches on the whiteboard.

As discussed in Chapter 12, brainstorming encourages creative thinking and can result in some great ideas; it can also clear flawed ideas out of your head to make room for better ones. Unlike requirements brainstorming, early solution brainstorming is usually most effective with just the design team, though I've encountered a few design engineers who have a lot to offer. The key is to keep the group small so it doesn't get bogged down by a lot of people wanting air time, and to

Framework

Dip into detail to see if the solution works; then quickly return to a higher level.

include only people who are good at thinking in unconstrained ways, comfortable with sometimes-messy exploration, and able to interpret high-level sketches.

Begin with broad exploration at first—even the obviously flawed ideas might spark better ones. Many designers are facile at proposing one idea after another and don't need much help with this stage, but even the most prolific designers have slow days. It's helpful to revisit your context scenarios even during brainstorming; storytelling stimulates the imagination and can help you get started. Changing the rules, such as by pretending the product is magic or is a helpful human, can also help spark new ideas.

Give yourself permission to propose partial solutions based on other designs. For example, if you're thinking about a medical device, perhaps there's something about the way a game controller or mobile phone is designed that's partly applicable. Some designers deliberately use a list of specific product types to stimulate thinking, such as, "What's good about [cars, mobile phones, toys, video games, etc.] that would apply in this situation?" This is where the variety inherent in consulting comes in handy; something about the golf course irrigation system you designed last month might stimulate an interesting idea for a video game design or assisted-surgery system. This is one reason to treat an internal design group as a consulting organization in which designers aren't dedicated to a single product for years at a time.

Regardless of the range of design problems you get to work on, having a brain full of design patterns (and knowing how to apply them) makes a tremendous difference when you're developing initial solutions. Experience is one effective way to build your vocabulary, but it's possible to do so through examining multiple products and reading books on the topic (see Chapter 15 for several important patterns).

The design meeting techniques discussed in Chapter 14 are critical in this early ideation, though because this is brainstorming, it's best to elicit and clarify ideas without going on to critique them just yet; instead, elicit and clarify, then build on the idea or propose another idea of your own. Unlike most design meetings, it's common in this one for multiple people to stand at the board with markers in hand. However, it's still advisable to have someone (typically the IxD synthesizer) ensuring effective work process. Use the biggest whiteboard available so your ideas aren't constrained by space.

As you propose and evolve your ideas, you'll likely find yourself revisiting the list of functional elements and other characteristics, either explicitly or unconsciously. It may or may not be useful for you to keep track of a list in writing; since these functional elements are represented in the sketches, many designers don't feel a need to update a written list. This is fine, since the list of functional elements is not meant to be an administrative task, but merely a way to make an important thought process explicit.

Once you have a number of possible solutions on the whiteboard, you can start evaluating them. Personas, goals, and scenarios are typically the most useful tools for this (see the discussion of validation scenarios in the "Evaluate, iterate, and refine the framework" section). Dip into detail just long enough to figure out if you can make something work. Quickly return to the high level. Although you shouldn't be overly obsessed with cost or other constraints at this point, you should be able to throw out any solutions that are simply too far out there to be viable; before you throw them out, though, consider whether there's anything about them that might be worth incorporating into another solution. Capture rejected ideas before you erase them, however; such notes can serve as a reminder (for the design team and stakeholders) of why you didn't go down a particular path.

Brainstorming for software on a fixed platform

For software on a known platform, this initial brainstorming is generally brief since there are only so many patterns and idioms to use. An hour is usually more than enough to get some crazy ideas up on the board, evaluate them, and clear your head for a more scenario-oriented approach. If this brainstorming goes on too long, you may get attached to ideas that are unsuitable.

Brainstorming for services and new platforms

The initial brainstorming session is more critical for designing services and new hardware/software platforms, since the range of possibilities (and their effect on associated costs) is much greater.

Your sketches should identify major product or service components and approximate interaction among them. Focus on questions like how users will enter data and make selections, rather than on exact screen contents or control types. It's fine to note great ideas about these details if they come to you, but move on once you've done so to avoid getting bogged down.

How many ideas you select to pursue in more detail depends on how much time you have. Ideally, you'll be able to choose at least two to iterate for a few days: one that you think represents the best interaction (which often involves pricier components) and one that will allow for a decent experience at lower cost. If you have the luxury of pursuing more than two directions, you might use other criteria to select them, such as what will look most different from the competition, what will be the smallest or sturdiest, or what will best emphasize some other desirable quality.

Table 16.6 shows a condensed version of how a design team narrows and refines a set of office telephone ideas. Note how the IxDS keeps the discussion moving and continually brings the persona into the evaluation. You can also see that the designers are relying on their knowledge of design principles and patterns as they go. Each team member acknowledges where there are problems to be solved, ensures that someone is responsible for exploring each issue further, and moves on.

Framework

Table 16.6. Brainstorming and narrowing office telephone concepts.

Sketches	Discussion among team members
	**IxDS:** We've brainstormed a bunch of ideas now; let's try to narrow things down and refine them a bit. This idea of docking a cell phone on a speaker-phone base is great, since the average cell phone is much smarter than desk phones already. It seems pretty far out from our mandate, though. **IxDG:** Yes, you're right. It doesn't fit the business model at all. We should offer it up as an idea and see if they want to pursue it, but not spend a lot of time on this.
	**VisD:** I think we should also rule out this one with the separately hinged screen; there's nothing inherently wrong with it, but it looks like every other desk phone out there.
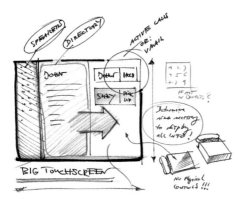	**IxDG:** Agreed. What about the big touch screen idea? It would allow for very direct interaction—no figuring out which line you're putting on hold—and good integration with the directory. **ID:** Yes, there's a lot to be said for that direction. It would have to be big to get all that on the screen at once, though. Also, I'm concerned about having no physical controls at all, though I'm not sure why that bugs me. **IxDS:** What happens when Scott needs to dial a number that's not in his directory?

Framework

Sketches	Discussion among team members
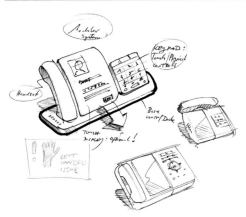	**ID:** There you go ... I knew there was a reason it seemed bad. That argues for a physical keypad. Maybe we can make it modular, like this, to allow for selling the phone with or without a touch screen. **IxDG:** I think that could work. Isn't that going to pose a challenge to anyone left-handed, though?
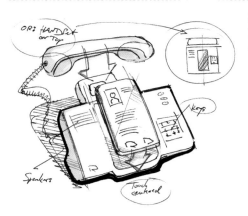	**ID:** Not necessarily, but we could put the handset on top. It would certainly be nice for visual balance. I can try it out both ways.
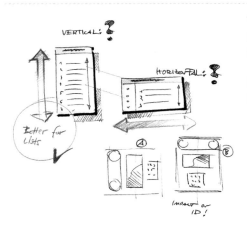	**VisD:** We should aim for a portrait screen in either case. It will be better for scrolling through a directory of contacts. **ID:** That makes sense. Portrait screens are a little harder to source, but not a big deal.

Framework

Continued

Sketches	Discussion among team members

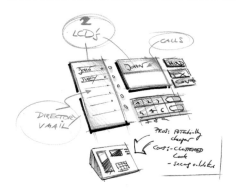

IxDS: So, that seems like one good direction to pursue. It's on the expensive side, though. Which of the cheaper possibilities seems like a good alternative? Soft buttons, maybe?

IxDG: Yes, we could use plain old LCDs with soft buttons, like this ... maybe one screen for the directory and voicemail and one for calls.

ID: By the time you deal with two separate screens, I'm not sure it's cheaper. I understand that the interaction is pretty clear that way, but it also leaves an impression of being complicated.

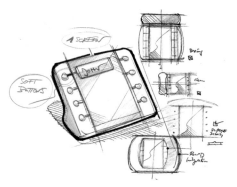

IxDS: [The IxDG] and I will see if we can find a way to do it in one screen.

IxDG: Yeah, we can figure that out. If we could put soft buttons all around it, the interaction could be almost as direct as a touch screen.

ID: Hmm ... that could look pretty crazy with that many buttons. Let me think about how to keep it from getting too busy.

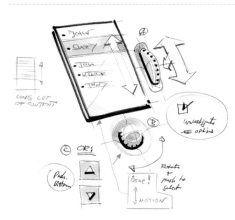

IxDS: So, it sounds like we should spend some more time on this direction. How would Scott scroll through a long list, though?

ID: If it's just in two directions, the best option is probably a jog dial. The scrolling can accelerate depending on how far you turn it.

IxDG: Nice. I wonder about the mapping of scrolling up or down to turning a dial clockwise or counterclockwise, though.

ID: I see what you mean. We can do pretty much the same thing by basically putting the dial edge-on, so Scott just pushes it up or down. There are other controls that do similar things. I can work with the mechanical engineer to see what our options are.

Spend a little more time refining each of your chosen ideas as a group before splitting up to refine the various aspects of the design. The interaction designers should focus on defining an interaction framework for each platform, including interactions with any physical controls, while the industrial designers explore ways that each platform would allow for comfortable use, necessary hardware components, and so on. Visual and industrial designers also begin work on the design language at this time; see Chapters 17 and 18 for more on this.

ID: Refine the Form Factor

While the interaction designers are working through scenarios, the industrial designer continues exploring the form, ideally in collaboration with a second industrial designer to encourage broader exploration. This may involve some sketching, but typically moves quickly to crude physical prototypes built out of malleable materials, such as foamcore, cardboard, string, paperclips, and whatever else is at hand. Some industrial designers like to "sketch" in three dimensions with tools and blocks of foam. If the design includes components or mechanical issues the designer isn't familiar with, he may consult a design engineer. Figure 16.5, for example, shows how the ID begins thinking about the volume required for internal components using both hand sketches and quick 3D renderings.

The industrial designer's first objective during this day or two is to see if anything about each form factor (such as its size, cost, or fragility) is unlikely to work, so the entire design team can change direction as quickly as possible. At the same time, the industrial designer works toward

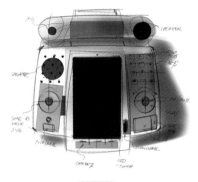

Figure 16.5. Industrial designers must consider internal components early on.

refining the candidate form(s) to feel good in the hand, accommodate the necessary components, and so forth, consulting with mechanical and electrical engineers as necessary.[2]

---

2. Note that the sort of process described here is focused on interactive products, which have a minimum of moving parts and a relatively predictable set of internal components (boards, fans, screens, batteries, buttons, storage, dials, etc.). This means form can be driven by design; in more mechanically complex products, the mechanical and electrical engineers need closer involvement from day one and may even be driving the nature of the solution. In any case, the industrial designer usually needs to consult closely with the engineers on any product that needs to be small, since compactness usually introduces plenty of engineering challenges.

Framework

IxDG and IxDS: Define the Interaction Framework

Key path scenarios will help you group functional elements and lay out your sketches.

As soon as you have either a known or potential platform and input method, such as a desktop computer with keyboard and mouse or a mobile phone with a three-inch touch screen, you can begin working out the interaction framework. For most applications, this is a definition of the major screens or other functional divisions (such as pages for a Web site or menus for an IVR system), the approximate structure and contents of those divisions, and the means for navigating among them, including any relevant hardware controls and how they interact with on-screen content.

Develop a first draft of the framework

Developing the framework is, for many people, the "magic" part of interaction design. It can be a daunting task for any team without strong visualization skills and is the hardest part of the design for even skilled and experienced designers to get right. The techniques described here help with both generating concrete ideas and with ensuring that they're reasonable.

There are three thought processes that tend to lead to reliably good design in a short period of time. They may occur in sequence, but are more likely to occur somewhat simultaneously. One is the iteration of your context scenarios into **key path scenarios,** which begin to describe the functional elements that help accomplish the activities. Another is the **grouping of functional elements** into sets of tools and display spaces that are commonly used together. The third is the development of **sketches** that represent how the different screens and major components will look.

Many generative interaction designers begin with a few sketches, then use the scenarios to adjust them. If visualization is not your strong suit—or if you're good at visualization but feeling at a loss about where to start—try starting with the scenarios, then using them to dictate a first cut at the screen layout. Most people get better results this way. The grouping of functional elements usually happens implicitly in either case, though some people are most comfortable with *explicitly* grouping the functional elements based on the scenario before they sketch. This also has the advantage of making it easy for others to understand your reasoning. I'll describe the process using this explicit approach, then discuss what it looks like with a different starting point.

Framework

DEVELOP KEY PATH SCENARIOS

The **key path scenarios** are revised context scenarios that describe flow using the major functional elements. Key path scenarios are still at a fairly high level for all but the simplest of interfaces; they're focused on the most critical (or "key") paths through the interface rather than on exact controls, on-screen text, or the variations on the key paths.

Example—a veterinary hospital management application

Imagine that you're designing a practice management application for veterinary hospitals (this example is considerably simplified for the sake of illustration). Say you've determined that you need two distinct interfaces, a business interface and a clinical one. Laura, the receptionist, is the primary persona for the business interface. Her goals are to:

— Stay calm amidst the chaos

— Keep clients and clinical staff from getting cranky

— Keep all the details straight

Her key activities include the following, which can be expressed in individual context scenarios or, more likely, in a few longer scenarios that reflect her constant interruptions:

— Review the day's appointments

— Create records for a new client

— Check someone in

— Check someone out

— Send bills

— Follow up on a billing question

— Follow up on overdue bills

— Make an appointment

— Change an appointment

— Take a message for a vet

For the sake of illustration, though, let's consider these as separate scenarios; otherwise, the example will get too complex. Let's focus on making an appointment; the progression from context scenario to requirements to functional elements is shown in Table 16.7.

Table 16.7. **Example context scenario translated into needs and elements.**

Context scenario	Functional needs	Functional elements
Laura takes a call from Mr. Cowell, who needs to make an appointment for his cat to have a tumor removed. Laura looks him up and sees that he has two cats.	— Look up callers among existing clients — See overview information about each client and pet	— Area to view client list — Display of overview information for client — Display of overview information for multiple pets
Xena is flagged for follow-up, so she confirms with Mr. Cowell that the procedure is for Xena. She selects that pet's name and chooses the procedure type.	— See what pets need follow-up of some kind without delving into detail	— Visual feedback on pet name for follow-up — Area to set appointment parameters

Continued

Context scenario	Functional needs	Functional elements
The system shows the next several non-urgent appointments for Dr. Harvey, Xena's usual vet, when the surgery and hospital space required for the procedure are also available.	— System should know how much staff time and what facilities or equipment are required for typical procedures — System should suggest suitable appointment times when all required resources are available, excluding some appointments that may be reserved for more urgent procedures	— Editable default settings that allocate staff time and resources to procedures (admin interface) — Display of best appointment times
She suggests the first couple of dates to Mr. Cowell, who says he was hoping to take care of it sooner. Dr. Bailey also has an opening sooner, but Mr. Cowell prefers Dr. Harvey. She can also see that Dr. Harvey has two slots that are close to the required parameters but don't quite fit them. She looks at the calendar to see what's on either side. One is just Dr. Harvey's administrative time. She moves that to later in the day and offers the new alternative to Mr. Cowell, who accepts.	— See other times that almost work to allow for human judgment	— Display of appointment times that might work if calendar is modified — Calendar display for all appointments by veterinarian
Laura tells him he'll get a confirmation in the mail. The postcard immediately gets sent to the printer on Laura's desk. Laura hangs up the phone and greets the client at the desk, who's ready to check out.	— For clients without e-mail, automatically print reminders	— Practice-wide preferences for default printing and e-mail reminders (admin interface)

To turn this context scenario into a key path scenario, add the functional elements, like this:

Laura takes a call from Mr. Cowell, who needs to make an appointment for his cat to have a tumor removed. Laura finds him in the **client list** and opens his record to see detail in the **client overview display area**, which shows that Mr. Cowell has two cats, one of whom is flagged for follow up. She looks at the **pet overview display area**, sees that Xena needs surgery, and confirms with Mr. Cowell that the procedure is for Xena. She clicks to create a new appointment and chooses the procedure type in the **appointment parameters area**.

In the **best appointment display**, the system shows the next several non-urgent appointments for Dr. Harvey, Xena's usual vet, when the surgery and hospital space required for the procedure are also available. She suggests the first couple of dates to Mr. Cowell, who says he was hoping to take care of it sooner. Dr. Bailey also has an opening sooner, but Mr. Cowell prefers Dr. Harvey. She can also see two time slots in the **alternate appointment display area** that are close to the required parameters but don't quite fit them. She looks at the **calendar** to see what's on either side of these. One is just Dr. Harvey's administrative time. She moves that to later in the day and offers the new alternative to Mr. Cowell, who accepts. Laura tells him he'll get a confirmation in the mail. The postcard immediately gets sent to the printer on Laura's desk. Laura hangs up the phone and greets the client at the desk, who's ready to check out.

Notice that the level of detail doesn't change much—the focus is on chunks of screen real estate, not on widgets and detailed data. You'll want to translate each of your context scenarios into a key path scenario. You can tackle one scenario, sketch the framework for it, and then do a second scenario, or you can iterate all of your scenarios and do some explicit groupings first. Visually oriented people may be most comfortable with one scenario at a time, since this gets to sketching faster.

Whether you write down each scenario in detail depends on how much time you have and how much your stakeholders want traceability in the process. An experienced design team in a hurry can often do this kind of thing live in a meeting, without writing everything down. I recommend taking the more thorough approach until you've mastered it, though.

GROUP FUNCTIONAL ELEMENTS

The next step is to look for evidence of which functional elements should be used together and which don't belong in the same screen. This grouping of elements into screens is based on the fundamental design principle that things people use for a particular task should be within easy reach, while things they don't use for that task should be out of the way. A **screen** (or a page on the Web, or a menu in a voice interface) is a distinct collection of tools and content that your personas will think of as a "place" to go. The contents of a "place," and sometimes their arrangement, can change to some extent without users feeling like they've left one room and gone to another; changing a calendar from week view to day view, for example, doesn't feel like going to an entirely different place, but switching from a calendar to a list of e-mail messages does. At this point, you should mostly be concerned with screens or places rather than the individual states they can be in.

Because good grouping is based on natural flow, scenarios are indispensable tools for determining how elements relate: If several elements are used together, they may belong on the same screen, while an element that doesn't get used alongside them probably belongs on another screen. Microsoft PowerPoint and Apple Keynote are clear examples: You need text and drawing tools at your fingertips when you're creating slides, but they'd only get in the way when you're delivering a presentation.

Some people find it easy enough to look at a scenario and see which elements are used together, but others find it helpful to list major functional elements on the whiteboard, then diagram the flow among them for each scenario.

Figure 16.6 illustrates this for the veterinary appointment scenario above. In this case, a single diagram is not terribly informative, but you can

Framework

see that Laura will return to the client list after this fairly brief transaction. Diagramming the other scenarios would show a similar tendency to return to the client list every couple of minutes. This implies that an organizer/workspace pattern (see Chapter 15), with the client list persistently available, might be a good place to start sketching if you want to avoid pogo-stick navigation.

Figure 16.7 illustrates a more subtle case using the following scenario, in which a persona named Ray organizes his images:

After a day of hiking on his New Zealand vacation, Ray has two memory cards full of landscape and wildlife images. He hooks the card reader up to his laptop and turns it on. PhotoMaster opens as soon as the laptop detects the card. It automatically begins importing the images into a default "new imports" category, which appears in the category organizer, quickly loading image previews into the multi-image preview area so he can start organizing images while the large files from his 12-megapixel camera slowly load. An indicator tells him

this card will take about 10 minutes to load. He has a little time before dinner, so he begins to do so.

Ray starts by applying several keywords to the entire batch of photos using the keyword pane. He then looks at each image in the single-image viewer and decides whether to keep it, sometimes comparing a few side by side in the comparison area to determine which ones are best. Nearly half the photos are rejected; they disappear from the screen but stay in temporary storage for a while in case he changes his mind. He then adds keywords to each image using the keyword pane.

When the card has finished loading, PhotoMaster notifies Ray that it's finished. He inserts a new card, and PhotoMaster automatically starts loading these images into the same group as Ray continues working. As soon as all the images are loaded and the rejects deleted, Ray tells the application to back the images up to his PhotoMaster online archive and heads to dinner.

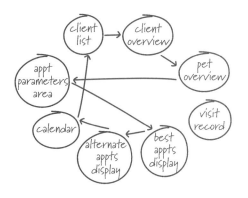

Figure 16.6. Flow among functional elements—a diagram of how major functional elements are used in the veterinary appointment scenario.

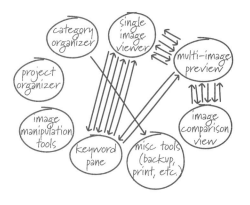

Figure 16.7. A flow diagram example for organizing photos.

Ray is constantly moving between the single-image view and multi-image view. He's also moving back and forth between the multi-image preview and the image-comparison view, but he does not move directly between single images and comparison. This implies that the multi-image preview needs to appear persistently during this activity, but that the single-image view and comparison view don't need to be visible at the same time. You can also see that the image manipulation tools, which are required for another scenario, are not used in this one, so they may not need to be accessible at the same time as the keyword pane. Other scenarios may disprove this hypothesis, but it provides a reasonable starting point for sketching some tentative screen layouts.

START TO STORYBOARD SCREENS AND NAVIGATION

The point of all this thinking is to visualize good, concrete solutions on a deadline—to help you jump across the chasm between understanding users and solving their problems, and to bring others across that gap with you. This requires drawing an approximation of each major screen or other "place," being able to describe how it works in combination with others (and perhaps hardware controls), and having confidence that the details you haven't addressed yet will be straightforward to work out later on.

Start by storyboarding one scenario for the primary persona using simple thumbnails. These usually consist of empty rectangles describing what major elements go on each screen and how they relate to one another. These rectangles might contain the name of the functional element or some kind of rough conceptual representation of the element's contents, but should not contain specific widgets or detailed text. As discussed in Chapter 14, staying at a high level at first helps you move faster and develop a cleaner, more consistent design approach.

The scenario's flow usually suggests how to position the screen elements: For readers of Western languages, whatever the persona uses first probably belongs at the top or left side of the screen. Whatever she uses next belongs to the right of or below that first element. The nature of each element's contents often suggests its size and shape: tall, narrow rectangles for long lists, most of the screen for photos or other rich content, and so forth. You'll have to take your best guess at how much space is needed based on your understanding of the objects and attributes. Of course, these elements may change size, shape, or location as you evolve the sketches, but everything gets easier once you have something on the whiteboard to work with. Table 16.8 shows an initial set of storyboards for the veterinary appointment scenario.

The point is to visualize good, concrete solutions on a deadline— and to help others get there with you.

Framework

Table 16.8. Sketching from a scenario.

Scenario step	Sketch	Comments
1. Laura takes a call from Mr. Cowell, who needs to make an appointment for his cat to have a tumor removed. Laura finds him in the **client list** and opens his record to see detail in the **client overview display area**, which shows that Mr. Cowell has three cats, one of whom is flagged for follow-up.	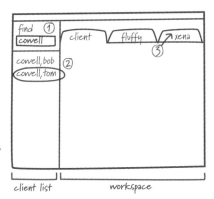 client list workspace	This first sketch draws upon the organizer/workspace pattern and the data model, which indicates that pets are parts of the client record. The "find" field is understood as a placeholder for some way or ways to locate clients.
2. She looks at the **pet overview display area**, sees that Xena needs surgery, and confirms with Mr. Cowell that the procedure is for Xena. She clicks to create a new appointment.	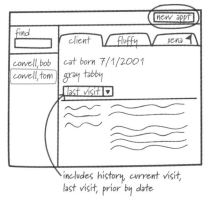 includes history, current visit, last visit, prior by date	Whoops, better add a toolbar for that "new appointment" button. Notice there's a little bit of detail about what may be on the screen. The interaction designer captures an idea for navigating visits, but quickly moves on.
3. She chooses the procedure type in the **appointment parameters area**. In the **best appointment display**, the system shows the next several non-urgent appointments for Dr. Harvey, Xena's usual vet, when the surgery and hospital space required for the procedure are also available. She suggests the first couple of dates to Mr. Cowell,	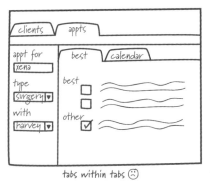 tabs within tabs ☺	Uh-oh ... what should happen when that button is clicked? Does it make sense for a calendar to live as a tab inside the client record? It seems more like a global tool, so the team decides to have a client screen and calendar screen, with top-level tabs to switch between them. Tabs within tabs are unfortunate, but the team recognizes this as an issue they can solve later and keeps going. Perhaps the client

Scenario step	Sketch	Comments

who says he was hoping to take care of it sooner. Dr. Bailey also has an opening sooner, but Mr. Cowell prefers Dr. Harvey. Laura can also see two time slots in the **alternate appointment display area** that are close to the required parameters but don't quite fit them.

list doesn't need to be visible in appointment view, so they use that space for appointment parameters. The content shown is understood as a placeholder for more complex controls. Appointment possibilities appear on the right. The screen shows the best and alternate appointments on the same screen for comparison; the best options should be at the top.

4. She looks at the **calendar** to see what's on either side of these. One is just Dr. Harvey's administrative time.

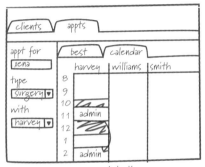

moves admin time

Clicking on one of the alternatives brings Laura to a calendar view, again shown with tabs. The team acknowledges that this jumping from tab to tab might seem awkward, but it's probably not worth worrying about until they've storyboarded the other scenarios. The calendar view shows other veterinarians (who might be alternatives if the first choice vet doesn't work out) and highlights the open appointment time and potentially adjustable administrative time.

5. She moves that to later in the day and offers the new alternative to Mr. Cowell, who accepts. Laura tells him he'll get a confirmation in the mail. The postcard immediately gets sent to the printer on Laura's desk.

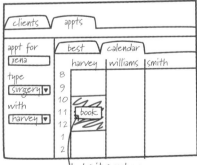

books it somehow...

Laura grabs the administrative time and moves it, and then somehow books the appointment. The "book" button is understood as a placeholder for some more refined mechanism.

Continued

Framework

Scenario step	Sketch	Comments
6. Laura hangs up the phone and greets the client at the desk, who's ready to check out.		Laura goes back to client view. Hmmm … perhaps making the client list available only in the client view is a bad idea after all, since most of the scenarios indicate she'll go back to it often. The team decides to back up and see what would happen if the client list were persistent, as the diagram in Figure 16.6 indicated.

Relying on your scenario will yield better design decisions than using abstract reasoning.

If you pause and consider the persona, the scenario, and the data model from Table 16.1, you might recognize a few problems with the storyboards in Table 16.8. One is that the sketch in step two is showing a lot of information about each pet, which a receptionist like Laura has no need to see. Another is that there's most of a screen dedicated to general client information, but the data model tells you that other than bills—which may be complex enough to warrant their own tab—there's not much to track about each client beyond a name and contact information. You may also see that where the design goes a little astray is where the team forgets the scenario and decides, based on some abstract reasoning, that appointments should be a global tool. What the team *should* be asking is whether they can think of any scenarios in which a view of appointments is not linked to a client.

What the previous paragraph describes is just the sort of conversation that should happen in a design meeting once there's a design on the board. Getting this kind of storyboard developed doesn't take long, so a little patience doesn't cost much even if the solution seems off base at first.

When you get to a point like this where the design isn't quite working, sometimes the right thing to do is to backtrack and try again. So, imagine that the design team has realized they're dedicating a lot of space to things Laura doesn't need in her role as a receptionist, so they take another crack at the storyboards using a persistent client list, as the flow in Figure 16.6 suggested. Table 16.9 shows how the design might evolve.

Table 16.9. **Revising the design.**

Scenario step	Sketch	Comments
1. Laura takes a call from Mr. Cowell, who needs to make an appointment for his cat to have a tumor removed. Laura finds him in the **client list** and opens his record to see detail in the **client overview display area**, which shows that one of his cats, Xena, is flagged for follow-up because she needs a surgery appointment. She confirms with Mr. Cowell that the procedure is for Xena. She clicks to create a new appointment.	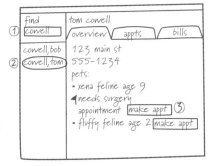	This first sketch again supposes that appointments are part of the client record, rather than a top-level tool. It also eliminates the tabs for each pet, since Laura doesn't need all the clinical information, and just puts a summary on an overview tab.
2. She chooses the procedure type in the **appointment parameters area**. In the **best appointment display**, the system shows the next several non-urgent appointments for Dr. Harvey, Xena's usual vet, when the surgery and hospital space required for the procedure are also available. She suggests the first couple of dates to Mr. Cowell, who says he was hoping to take care of it sooner. Dr. Bailey also has an opening sooner, but Mr. Cowell prefers Dr. Harvey. She can also see two time slots in the **alternate appointment display area** that are close to the required parameters but don't quite fit them.	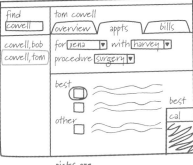	Laura can go straight to the appointment tab without an intermediate screen, so this is better. The IxD generator-sketches two sub-tabs for a calendar view and the two sets of appointment options, though this seems overly complex.

Continued

Framework

Scenario step	Sketch	Comments

3. She looks at the **calendar** to see what's on either side of these. One is just Dr. Harvey's administrative time.

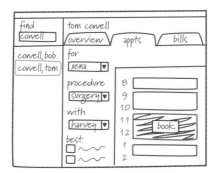

moves admin time

In this view, the IxDG tries a slightly different layout, since using a pane that's wider than it is tall, as in the previous step, is less effective for displaying a list of appointments. This version is a better use of space, but still has the unfortunate sub-tabs.

4. She moves that to later in the day and offers the new alternative to Mr. Cowell, who accepts. Laura tells him he'll get a confirmation in the mail. The postcard immediately gets sent to the printer on Laura's desk. Laura hangs up the phone and greets the client at the desk, who's ready to check out.

In this step, the IxDG tries a version without tabs, reasoning that a list of potential appointments doesn't take that much screen space and can be used to drive the calendar. The calendar view may not have room to show the other veterinarians (who might be alternatives if the first choice vet doesn't work out), but this seems a reasonable compromise. The scenario is accomplished with less extraneous navigation, so this looks like a better direction.

ADD TO THE DESIGN AND ADJUST IT FOR ADDITIONAL SCENARIOS

Although you could start with fresh "rectangles" for each scenario and try to combine them later, it generally works better to start with the structure you roughed out in the first scenario—even if it seems like it's a little bit wrong—and use what you learn from subsequent scenarios to add onto it and adjust it. In other words, rough out scenario number one, change that structure based on scenario two, make sure it still works for scenario number one before moving on to do the same

for scenario three, and so on. A structure should start to coalesce after two or three scenarios.

For our veterinary application, let's say that scenario number two involves Mr. Cowell calling up to change his appointment. Figure 16.8 shows how a relatively small adjustment to the design (from Table 16.9) accommodates the additional scenario; existing appointments are listed above the tools for new appointments and can be selected to appear in the calendar. There are some niceties of the interaction that will need to be ironed out, and it may not be quite the right answer yet,

Framework

but the fact that this design concept mostly works after a second scenario is a good sign that the team is headed in a productive direction.

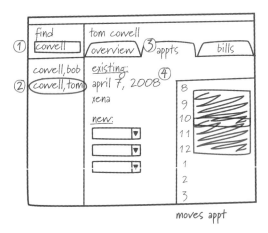

Figure 16.8. A minor adjustment to the design accommodates an additional scenario.

As you can see from the examples, what actually happens at the whiteboard is a combination of the scenarios, the data model, design judgment, and a good vocabulary of design patterns. Other ideas and considerations will affect what you draw, sometimes with good results and sometimes not. If you always return to the scenarios and goals as your touchstone, though, more abstract considerations are less likely to get you into trouble. When teammates make assertions not based in the current scenario, ask them to describe a scenario in which their assertion makes sense.

This kind of iteration is very fast; with an effective design team, the entire progression from key path scenario to this point would likely take less than half an hour. Even though the design team is not developing multiple directions to show stakeholders, they're quickly trying and eliminating many directions at the whiteboard.

As you proceed through each of your context scenarios, consider whether you can consolidate any of the screens you've drawn. Are two screens showing slightly different views of the same content? If so, perhaps they can be combined. Do you have two screens that use the same functional elements in different places? Maybe you can find a way to use just one layout for both, as long as it doesn't introduce major problems; the gain in simplicity is usually worth the minor trade-off of moving a pane to a different spot. Are there any other ways you can apply design patterns to simplify the overall structure?

Your context scenarios probably include either a scenario for a task unique to a secondary persona or a scenario describing how the primary and secondary approach the same tasks differently. You can either do all of the scenarios for the primary and then adjust for the secondary, or do the secondary persona's version of the similar scenario before moving on to a different set of tasks. Try both approaches to see which works better for you. If what you've drawn for the primary persona works, that's great. If not, adjust the drawing to accommodate the secondary persona's needs, then revisit the primary persona's scenario to make sure your change doesn't introduce problems. If you need to introduce additional elements to address a secondary's needs, make sure you do so without getting in the primary persona's way; otherwise, it's possible you really have two primaries who need separate interfaces.

Develop rough thumbnail storyboards for *all* of your key path scenarios before you delve into more detail on any one screen; otherwise, you're likely to waste a lot of time refining a screen that you'll wind up throwing away. (Worse yet, you might get attached to it and not *want* to throw it away.) It's easier to stay at a high level if you plow through thumbnail storyboards for the entire set of scenarios in a short time, such as an afternoon if you have a handful of scenarios, or perhaps a day if you have a dozen. If you were working on a device, the level

Framework

of detail shown here would be sufficient for the interaction designers to share with the rest of the design team and confirm whether the selected platform is likely to work out. However, it usually takes another couple of days before things are solid enough and articulated enough to be worth sharing with the project owner and design engineer(s).

HOW THE SKETCH-FIRST APPROACH DIFFERS

Most generative interaction designers are inclined to sketch screens before working through functional groupings and turning context scenarios into key path scenarios, often because they've done some of this thinking in their heads, but sometimes because they think much better in sketches than they do in words. If you want to use this approach, go ahead and get your ideas on the board, then immediately turn to your context scenarios and walk through what you've just drawn. If the flow makes sense and your sketches adhere to good design principles, then the context scenarios with your functional elements plugged in become the key path scenarios. Chances are, however, that your first round of sketches doesn't quite work. If there's not an easy fix you can see from walking through the scenarios, then it's usually best to start over using the scenario-first approach.

EVALUATE, ITERATE, AND REFINE THE FRAMEWORK

Next, you'll want to sketch each screen with slightly greater resolution, though without worrying about exact widgets, text, and similar details. Plan your time so you can spend about half a day for a straightforward scenario or about a day for a more complex one. You can also carve up your time by screen rather than by scenario; this is more manageable, but can sometimes be less coherent since a scenario may require more than one screen to complete. In either case, limiting the amount of time you spend on each design topic helps ensure that you're evolving the entire design to the same degree.

Try iterating your key path scenarios and your list of functional elements (whether it's in your head or written down) to a slightly greater level of detail. Draw a rough draft of each screen on the whiteboard, indicating approximately what sort of tools and content appear in each pane or region. Adjust each screen as needed for any secondary personas, just as you'd adjust for a second scenario (as shown in Figure 16.8). Indicate specifics only where necessary to accomplish the key path scenarios; don't obsess over whether a widget is the best choice or what its label should be. These are only placeholders, since you might realize later that your first guess doesn't work very well.

It feels good to get the design articulated this far, but don't get attached to it yet. You need to start throwing more scenarios at it to determine whether it will hold up to a realistic range of circumstances. There's usually no need to write up detailed scenarios or formal use cases to evaluate and refine the design. **Validation scenarios** are informal "what ifs" posed by a member of the team (usually the IxD synthesizer) once there's a design on the board. The person who proposed the solution (usually the IxD generator) then shows how the situation would be handled by the existing proposal or, if the design doesn't address the need, modifies the design to address the issue. For example, using Figure 16.8 as a starting point, the conversation might go something like this:

> **IxDS:** What would happen if Mr. Cowell wanted to make an appointment for both cats at the same time?

> **IxDG:** That does seem like a pretty common case. I suppose Laura could use a multi-pet appointment control on the overview tab, but I think those controls are really shortcuts and Laura would understand that you do more complex appointment setup by going to the appointments tab. Once she's there, we could either add "multiple pets" as an option in a pet selector list box

or maybe use some kind of multi-select control. We'd have to offer an appointment type for each pet, and then the system would suggest open times that are long enough to account for all of them. The screen might get a little dense, but I think we can work it out.

IxDS: OK, that doesn't seem like it will break the framework. We can save the details for later. What about ...

This example is typical of how loose and informal validation scenarios usually are. Notice how the IxDG offers just enough detail to ensure that something can be worked out. Once both designers are satisfied, they move on. (If you have any non-designers in the room, they may be uncomfortable with this because they don't have the pattern and principle vocabulary to see how the problem could be solved. Plan to spend more time on this activity than you otherwise would.)

Early validation scenarios should be variations on the key paths that are either relatively common or, if they occur infrequently, are somehow essential to the product's success. It's still much too early to throw obscure edge cases at the design. If your key path scenario involves the persona ordering a routine prescription refill from a pharmacy, it's reasonable to explore how the proposed design would handle a prescription that's not covered by insurance or is too old to be refilled. What happens if someone has to have a prescription delivered while she's traveling out of the country is probably something to save for later. You'll need to solve this problem eventually, but it's obscure enough that it shouldn't be driving the design.

If a teammate proposes a validation scenario that seems too far out there for this stage of the design, make sure you understand where the concern is coming from; it's possible he just isn't being very articulate. If you feel he's hung up on an inappropriate detail, use the 15-minute rule or, if you can't get someone else in the room right away, put the issue in the "parking lot" until you can. (See Chapter 14 for a description of both techniques.)

You'll know you have a workable direction when the design you've sketched seems to handle multiple validation scenarios without breaking. Once you reach this point with any part of your framework, make sure you've got a clean set of whiteboard drawings with all the necessary parts in the right states. Assign explicit, straightforward names to each screen, pane, and important widget. Pause for a few minutes to capture your sketches, label elements, and take notes about behaviors you discussed. The design may not be ready to show to the

Early validation scenarios should be common or important variants of the key paths.

Framework

entire set of stakeholders yet, but it's probably ready to share with your project owner and design engineer(s). If you're developing multiple design directions, this is a good time to move on to your next one.

How to approach specific design situations

The process described above works very well for single-interface desktop applications. It's equally effective for almost any design problem, but some circumstances require slight modifications to the approach.

TIGHT CONSTRAINTS

If you're doing a relatively minor update of a legacy product or facing some other tight constraints, inventing new functional elements and navigation structures would be a waste of time because nothing close to your solution would get built. However, a less ambitious version of the same process can yield great results. (It also helps if you view constraints as just another part of the design problem, rather than as frustrating limitations.)

Start by making a list of the existing functional elements. Develop your key path scenarios to describe the ideal flow among them. It may not be that difficult to put components on different screens if the scenarios suggest a different grouping for the elements; it all depends on how they're built. If there are needs in the scenario that can't be met with existing functional elements, you have a starting point for a discussion about feasibility. If it turns out that you can't add or make significant changes to elements and can't change what appears on which screen, then you're really working at the level of detailed design; see Chapters 20 and 22.

MULTIPLE INTERFACES

When you have multiple roles and therefore multiple primary personas, as in many enterprise applications, each primary persona will need a unique interface with tools and information focused on his specific needs. Unique logins ensure that each user sees the appropriate interface. This adds another layer of complexity to the framework definition puzzle because each primary's framework usually has at least a partial overlap with the others. Maximizing that overlap without compromising the needs of any primary is tricky, but it's desirable for a couple of reasons. The one most development teams focus on is cost: The greater the overlap in the design, the more efficient coding, testing, and ongoing maintenance can be. However, some overlap in interface components also helps users in different roles teach one another, troubleshoot problems, or discuss issues related to a shared file.

When you have multiple interfaces to address, start by doing rough storyboards for each primary persona's interface (to about the level shown in Table 16.9) before you get into detail on any one of them. Once you have basic structures in mind for each, step back and look for opportunities to share components. If it won't cause problems to modify two similar functional elements to make them identical, collapse them into a single element shared across the two interfaces. Once you've made the components as modular as you can without hampering any of the personas, you can work through the scenarios for each primary and associated secondaries in more detail. Just leave yourself a little time to revisit each primary's framework after you've done this to see if any elements you were hoping to share aren't working out and whether any more opportunities for consolidation have emerged.

Framework

WEB SITES

Information-focused Web sites involve two unique considerations not addressed by the generalized version of this scenario-to-framework process. One is that informational sites seldom have complex interaction; the primary design challenge is to get users to the right piece of information. The other is that users with entirely different needs are all coming to the same place; it's not practical to separate people into unique interfaces the first time they visit, and sometimes not worth bringing people to different home pages based on cookies.

Getting users to the right information

The interaction framework of an informational site (and of many e-commerce sites) is seldom about managing distinct sets of tools and data for distinct tasks. Other than the occasional bit of account management, there's usually just one task: find the right piece of information or the right product. The field of information architecture, which I would argue is a specialized subset of interaction design, is focused on addressing this need in various contexts.

Solving this problem starts with understanding whether your personas are looking for a uniquely identifiable product or piece of information, such as a copy of a particular book or the date of the first lunar landing, or for something they can't specifically identify, such as a new outfit to wear to a friend's wedding. Search works well in the first case, but categories usually work better in the second; the hard part is figuring out what structure of categories will lead your personas to the right sort of information or product.

Scenarios help you envision the sequence in which your personas will look for information; when combined with the taxonomies in mental models (see Chapter 7), they can help you get users to their desired items with very little effort. When your persona is looking for a new outfit, what information does she know when she starts,

and what criteria does she use first to filter out the information or products she doesn't want? What criteria does she use after that? Shoe-shopping Web sites such as Zappos.com or Endless.com are good examples of this: Most women looking for shoes think first about what style and color of shoe they need, so the categories start there, allowing users to identify potentially interesting shoes before filtering by size, width, and other criteria.

Focusing on differing persona needs

Although there is generally one primary persona for a Web site, you can use other personas as primary for certain sections or types of content. An emotional buyer, for example, makes a good primary for a luxury car Web site because the site will lose him if *any* part of it doesn't appeal to his self-image. However, it makes more sense to direct detailed specifications at other sorts of prospective buyers who are more likely to care about them.

Use the **site primary** to develop your first take on the framework, with the others serving the same purpose as any other secondary persona. Once you get into areas of the site for which the site primary isn't the main focus, use the most relevant persona as the **section primary** for that part of the design.

DEVICES

Handhelds, telematics, medical instruments, and other devices clearly present unique interaction design challenges due to their physical forms. One of those challenges is squeezing the necessary software controls and information into a small display (as on a handheld) or relatively low resolution (as on most televisions, though this is improving with HD). A parallel workspace or hub-and-spoke pattern (see Chapter 15) usually works to manage information on a small screen. Before you spend a lot of time at the whiteboard, though, mock up a screen of the appropriate physical size and resolution on your computer to see how much text or other information you can realistically display.

The other challenge involves assessing and refining the form factor for a new platform or figuring out how to work within the hardware specifications of an existing device.

New devices

When designing a new device, you're probably either working with a single candidate platform or comparing a couple of possibilities. In either case, the first priority is to carry the interaction framework far enough to assess the proposed form factor and input methods, so you can work with the industrial designer to change directions if necessary. This begins much like desktop software design, with a quick run-through of each scenario (for each possible direction, if applicable).

The trickiest problem with hardware/software interaction design is determining what sort of hardware controls you need and how they'll interact with the on-screen content. With desktop software and Web sites, interaction designers are accustomed to having dedicated screen space and buttons for just about everything, so no widget has to serve multiple functions. This makes the interaction more clear; no one has to wonder why that button sometimes prints and sometimes closes the application. For this reason, if the device does not involve a touch screen or movable cursor, an interaction designer's first instinct may be to have dedicated physical controls (and sometimes even dedicated displays) for just about everything; the multiscreen sketch in Table 16.6 illustrates this tendency. It's fine to start here, but a device with a button for everything starts to look like the inside of a 747 cockpit and may add too much size or cost.

If a device has a touch screen, on the other hand, interaction designers may be inclined to do just about everything on-screen, since they can make specific controls available only in the context where they're needed. This may be great from a cognitive perspective, but it may be the wrong answer for

some interactions due to ergonomic or safety considerations, or the need for immediate access to a function at all times. There are also some interactions that just feel better with physical controls.

Go ahead and start your initial storyboards with whatever combination of software and hardware controls you think you'll need. As with software-only design, step back when you're done and consider the possibilities for consolidation, as well as which controls need to be physical. Collaboration with an industrial designer adds valuable perspective. In general, the following are good candidates for dedicated physical controls:

— Anything people need to use without looking, such as the volume control on a car stereo

— Controls that have to be instantly available at all times, such as a mute button on an office telephone

— Functions that are divorced from the on-screen interaction, such as power buttons or "lock" controls that prevent accidental input on pocket devices

— Anything that needs to be very responsive and able to take a beating, such as direction and firing buttons for a game controller

— Things that must be accessible to the visually impaired with no adjustments required, such as elevator buttons

— Functions that need to be found in the dark, such as the pause button on a remote control

— Interactions that require manipulating multiple controls at a time, such as mixing audio (though multitouch screens can also accommodate this)

However, transient choices or functions that are only sometimes available should rarely employ physical controls, partly because they're not worth the real estate, and partly because it's difficult to convey that a hardware control is unavailable under certain circumstances (though it can be done with LED backlighting, for instance). Touch screen controls, a movable cursor, or soft keys are usually better options.

When deciding whether a single button can serve more than one purpose without a soft label, consider how closely related the actions are. Play and pause, for example, make sense as a single control because they're opposite states; this idiom is familiar from light switches and power buttons. (Mind you, it's easy for users to get confused about button state if you change the label and there's no clear audio or video playback, as in a Web conferencing application; does the right arrow mean that "play" is the current state, or that clicking the button will cause the system to play?) Holding down a menu button to turn on a backlight, though, is obscure because there's little relationship between the two functions. Also explore how different types of information can take over the screen temporarily as needed, rather than trying to show everything at once. Consider the following conversation and the resulting sketch, shown in Figure 16.9.

> **IxDS:** Scott arrives at his desk, sees that he's got messages, and looks at a visual list to pick the top priority. He gets a call while he's listening, so we have to have space for an active call to show up without totally losing his context. The same is true for the directory; he could be looking something up when a call comes in. For that matter, he could be on a call and need the directory to add someone to a conference call.

> **IxDG:** Right. So, it seems like each of these tools takes over the screen, but has some flexible behavior to allow screen sharing when a call comes in. There's no reason he'd need the directory and voicemail at the same time, though, so those don't need to coexist, right?

> **IxDS:** Probably, yes.

> **IxDG:** OK. That implies that the directory and voicemail should essentially be tabs, but that the tabbed area shrinks as needed when a call comes in, something like this (draws on board). Each tab slides open like a drawer and slides partially closed as needed. He'd reasonably need the directory information while he was on a call, though I don't think he'd ever open up the voicemail while on a call. Still, I don't see a reason for the two to behave totally differently. This seems pretty clean.

> **IxDS:** Sounds like it will work. Let's try some scenarios to see if it breaks.

When designing for several possible hardware platforms, carry each interaction framework design far enough to evaluate how well each form factor and input method works.

Framework

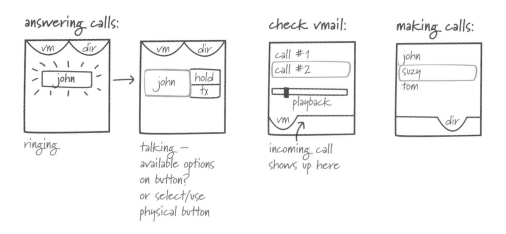

Figure 16.9. Making the office phone work with one screen.

As with any other design problem, consider what will or won't make sense to your personas and adjust your design accordingly. Run through your key path scenarios, then use validation scenarios to continue assessing and iterating the design. You'll know you're headed in a good direction when the design is handling every scenario you throw at it.

Existing platforms

Designing for an existing device can be frustrating if the hardware design wasn't done with the software in mind. I had a client once who wanted interaction design for a multifunction device with exactly one hardware button; they wanted the device to be dead simple, so they apparently thought nothing could be simpler than a single button. Unfortunately, the visual simplicity added a lot of cognitive complexity; two more buttons for separate navigation and selection would have been much more clear. However, not all devices can be redesigned, either because of time and money constraints, or because you're designing an application to run on third-party hardware.

If the hardware is reasonably flexible, such as a smart phone with keyboard and touch screen or cursor-based navigation, you can proceed much

as you would for a desktop application. When the input is limited to a few soft buttons, you'll probably need to use a hub-and-spoke pattern, with the number of spokes determined by the number of soft buttons; structuring the information in this case is a lot like structuring a Web site's information architecture. Even more constrained devices may require a tunnel (see Chapter 15 for explanations of both patterns). If the hardware has an unusual configuration, take stock of what you have and brainstorm about how you can use each of the existing controls.

VEHICLE INTERFACES

Automobile interfaces (such as dashboard controls, navigation systems, and entertainment systems) are much like other device interfaces, but they involve one unique and critical factor: The person operating them is probably driving a two-ton missile down the highway at high speed, so designers must consider safety of paramount importance—first, do no harm.

Use physical controls that can be distinguished by position and feel to help keep the driver's eyes on the road. (You should see the stares I got shopping for a car stereo once, as I closed my eyes and felt my way around the different faceplates to find one I could use without looking!) Minimize reliance on text and images; make them large and high contrast if they're unavoidable. Make typical interactions, such as switching between a radio station and CD, easy to accomplish with a single physical control. Consider putting a couple of commonly used controls, such as the stereo skip/seek and mute buttons, within thumb reach on the steering wheel to limit one-handed driving. Use audible feedback and simple voice commands when possible.

In addition to keeping eyes and hands free for driving, you also need to help keep the driver's *mind* on the road. Numerous studies indicate that cognitive distraction, not just visual distraction or fumbling with controls, is a major factor in safety. Even hands-free cell phone conversations decrease response time and substantially increase the risk of accidents. Redelmeier and Tibshirani[3] found that accidents quadrupled when drivers were talking on the phone. McKnight and McKnight[4] found that simple, quick calls (such as "I'm stuck in traffic and running late") made by younger drivers were slightly less distracting than tuning the radio, but that more involved conversations such as business or intense personal calls had far greater effects on reaction time and other driving safety factors. Older drivers were distracted by even brief calls. Research into other in-vehicle distractions (such as listening to e-mail using a voice interface)[5] indicates similar problems due to the cognitive load.

First, consider whether a particular interaction really needs to happen in a moving vehicle. If it's unavoidable, be sure you not only follow good design principles, but allow time for extensive usability testing and iteration. Whatever you do, though, don't force a driver to scroll through and accept two pages of legal disclaimers before she can use the navigation system; it might keep you from getting sued, but is even more likely to cause an accident.

AUDIBLE INTERFACES

Most audible interfaces have something in common with informational Web sites: The challenge is to get users to the right information or transaction as quickly as possible, and there are a limited number of ways to do so. The safe route is a hub-and-spoke, menu-driven approach: "To access your existing accounts, press one. To create a new account, press two." Even if you're planning to use random-access voice input, it's still worth drawing a menu structure of all the options (and listing every way you can think of to phrase them) so the system can recognize a wide range of requests and offer them as a list when users can't think of a command.

As in information architecture, use the scenarios and mental model to determine what questions or identifiable tasks the persona is starting with, what words she uses to describe it, and what her decision-making process looks like from that point on. Rough out a menu structure based on your first scenario for the primary persona, add to it using other scenarios, then assess and refine it using secondary personas and validation scenarios.

Framework

3. Redelmeier, D.A. and Tibshirani, R.J. "Association between cellular-telephone calls and motor vehicle collisions." *New England Journal of Medicine*, February 13, 1997.

4. McKnight, J. and McKnight, A.S. "The effect of cellular phone use on driver attention." National Public Services Research Institute/ AAA Foundation for Traffic Safety. http://www.aaafoundation.org/resources/index. cfm?button=cellphone#a23.

5. Joanne Harbluk in "Interview with Joanne Harbluk on safety and usability in vehicles." http://www.carleton.ca/ hotlab/hottopics/Articles/May2003-InterviewwithJoan.html.

Game design is partly about the world you've envisioned and partly about what the users bring to that world.

You may find that your set of scenarios essentially defines the top-level menu. For example, imagine that your primary persona for a bank's automated phone system typically does the following things:

— Checks her balance before paying bills or planning a big expenditure (often)

— Transfers money between accounts (often)

— Orders checks when she's running low (sometimes)

— Investigates discrepancies on her statements (infrequently)

If you also have a secondary persona who is a new customer, he likely has a scenario involving opening a new account; this plus your primary persona's four activities are a logical place to start for your top-level menu, and their frequency implies where they belong in the sequence.

Next, focus on one scenario, such as checking the account balance. Once your primary persona says she wants to check her balance, she needs to select one account or listen to the balance for all accounts; which approach is more likely to work for her? If her balance is low, what next step will she take, and what additional information will she want? After you've run through each scenario, you'll have a partial menu structure. You can then throw validation scenarios at your tentative framework and adjust it as necessary.

GAMES

I'll confess that I've never personally designed a game, though I've had multiple game designers ask me how personas and scenarios apply. So, here are a few thoughts on the subject, for what they're worth.

Game design is partly about the story and the world you've envisioned and partly about what the users (who play the main characters) bring to that world: Just imagine how *The Matrix* movie would have differed if Woody Allen had played Neo. For this reason, I believe personas and scenarios offer useful ways to engage a broad range of users. Suppose you were designing an action/adventure game for these personas:

— Jason, a methodical person who reads magazines from front to back and bought the animated Star Trek on DVD just so he'd have every series.

— Tony, who thinks of blowing up monsters as stress relief and is easily bored by action that's too slow.

— Lisa, who competes with her brother in everything from school grades to how fast she can brush her teeth.

You'd want to offer plenty of chases, explosions, and high-speed action for Tony, but you could hide weapons, supplies, or clues to a mystery in various levels for Jason. If Jason weren't among your personas, it might not be worthwhile to develop these details. You could make Lisa happy by showing when she's approaching or passing her brother's top score.

Scenarios seem applicable in predicting possible user behavior so you can decide what's possible within the confines of the game and how the game responds to various actions. If Tony encounters a monster, he'll attack it with guns blazing. What happens if Jason decides to dodge the monster in favor of going after a clue? Does it give chase or continue to guard the basement door? Answers to these and similar questions seem like they would be helpful in creating a rich experience.

Full Design Team: Iterate Form and Behavior Together

Once you've spent a day or two exploring a device design from both the hardware and interaction design perspectives, get the whole design team together to share what you've learned and decide where to go from here. Ideally the next steps

involve detailing and improving on the existing directions(s), but if something you've learned makes a platform not viable, you'll need to pick up another direction from your earlier brainstorming or come up with something else. In Figures 16.10 and 16.11, for example, designers use a range of sketches as well as rough foam models to review and refine the hardware architecture.

Interaction designers and industrial designers may have different biases when it comes to the number, location, and types of input controls. Interaction designers are often most concerned with cognitive issues, such as how self-evident the device's behavior will be, while industrial designers may lean more toward visual simplicity and minimal physical effort. These differences should decrease the longer the two disciplines collaborate, but can be noticeable when each works with the other for the first time. Talking through the issues using the personas and goals for perspective resolves most disagreements. Generally, interaction design considerations should drive the number, type, behavior, and locations of controls while ergonomic and engineering considerations should guide their exact form. However, if skilled, reasonable people from all disciplines can't agree on a solution, chances are you need to keep looking for alternatives.

Figure 16.10. Reviewing work in progress.

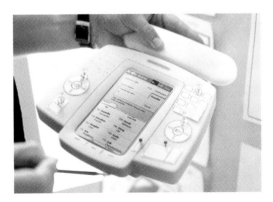

Figure 16.11. Using a foam model to refine control placement.

Framework

A great design that seems elegant and obvious is not necessarily obvious before it exists.

Once the essential form factor and input mechanisms are settled, each discipline can work slightly more independently if necessary; daily check-ins are still a great idea, but every few days can be workable.

> **Exercise**
>
> Design the interaction framework (and any hardware platform) for the LocalGuide or RoomFinder.

Typical Challenges in Designing the Framework

A great design that seems elegant and obvious is not necessarily obvious before it exists; simplicity is difficult to achieve. Although they strive for simplicity, most interaction designers are fascinated by complex systems, subtle distinctions in human behavior, and obscure details that seem irrelevant to other people. These traits are helpful to a point, but can get in the way when you're creating solutions.

Many first attempts at interaction frameworks—by designers of all skill levels—are more complex than they need to be. This is not surprising, given that designers who have just filled their brains with many research details must set them aside and focus on the largest issues. It's also a natural part of any design process; simple, elegant designs of any kind, from posters and packaging to complex machinery, are almost always the result of many iterations and the work of multiple people. If someone looks at your framework and says it's too complex, listen closely, because they're probably right.

Most often, this complexity is due to insufficient distillation, such as failing to recognize that two similar elements could be combined into one. Attempting to over-distill the design to reduce navigation can create excessive visual and cognitive work, though, so this is always a matter of balance. Complexity can also result from a designer's insistence on making some distinction most users don't care about, such as separating songs released on albums from songs released as singles in a list of music. Designing for edge cases too early in the process is another common culprit.

Broken or incomplete data models may not seem to cause trouble right away, but can lead to gaps in the design that are hard to fill later. Over-abstraction of the data object types can also make it hard for users to find their way around, and can make it hard to structure the interface.

Although a designers' mind-set during early concept development should be optimistic, it's also possible to overshoot reality by too much. A slightly ambitious design entices stakeholders to consider where they can stretch, but an overly ambitious one either causes despair (since they'll never be able to ship it) or makes them wonder why they hired you. Over time, you'll learn to read situations and determine how much to push, but checking in with your project owner just a few days into design should help you avoid going over a cliff.

Of course, any designer can obsess over a specific idea he thinks is cool, to the detriment of the rest of the design. Personas and scenarios help minimize this problem, but just about every designer has an occasional case of stubbornness. Sometimes it takes a whole design team weighing in to help deflect a designer from a problematic course. If that doesn't work, a room full of stakeholders can do the trick. Failing that, you have to fall back on a usability test (or worse, market feedback). The earlier the problem is caught, the cheaper it is to fix, both in terms of time and money and in terms of designer credibility; this is another reason frequent check-ins are worthwhile.

> The essential project management challenge in framework definition is getting the right sort of feedback at the right time.

Project Management for Defining Platforms and Frameworks

Other than time management (which is discussed in Chapter 14) the essential project management challenge in framework definition is getting the right sort of feedback at the right time. On one hand, it's important to uncover major problems as early as possible. On the other, a design concept at this stage has a fragile existence; it's far too easy for stakeholders who are not accustomed to ambiguity to lose faith in the proposed design (or worse, in the design team) for the wrong reasons.

It's best to start by getting feedback from the most understanding audience (the rest of the design team), followed by the most knowledgeable external audience (such as the project owner, design engineer, and perhaps a subject matter expert), and finally the rest of the stakeholders (see Chapter 19 for more on that meeting). You might also be considering direct user feedback or usability testing.

Internal design team check-ins

Even though each design discipline can and should work separately on different aspects of the problem, frequent team check-ins are important because each team member may be able to improve on the work

Framework

of others, and because each needs to understand where the others are headed. The team lead needs to ensure that everyone is going in the same direction, that the direction is going to meet the expectations of the stakeholders, and that the work is at the right level of detail and quality.

One form of team check-in is centered on an internal milestone, such as reviewing a first draft of the framework or design language studies (covered in Chapter 18), developing an outline for a presentation, or some other activity that needs to be done by a certain date. For example, I know from leading a lot of projects that if a team doesn't have some coherent platform sketches and interaction design rectangles emerging by day two or three of the phase, they may need a little help.

Another is a more generic, "What's everyone up to?" affair that ideally happens on a daily basis, generally at the beginning or end of the day. These are often gatherings at someone's desk to see what she accomplished the previous day, or in a conference room to look at what's on the whiteboard. If anyone is falling behind or needs help with anything, this is a good opportunity to discuss it. Unscheduled check-ins may occur as needed if someone on the team needs help with a sticky problem and calls in one or more of the others.

Although someone is responsible for leading each aspect of the design and the accompanying narrative, the entire team should share responsibility for the entire design. If one person sees a design or communication solution that seems broken, he should ask the rest of the team to explain it, ask why the proposed solution is good, and offer a critique if the explanation doesn't address the concern. Visual designers should look in particular for opportunities to simplify the on-screen grid (the structure for laying out screens; see Chapter 21). Industrial designers should look for ergonomic and other issues with the type and placement of controls, as well as where there might be opportunities to improve interaction using physical

controls. Interaction designers should use personas and scenarios to assess visual and industrial design. Everyone should look for framework and narrative coherence, simplicity, and adherence to persona goals and behaviors.

Once one or more concepts start to emerge, start thinking about how stakeholders will react and what questions they'll have when they see sketches. If you know someone will ask a particular question, object that a pet idea isn't represented in the design, or raise some other concern, discuss how you'll respond. It's also likely that you'll have a few questions for stakeholders as you work through the design; make sure someone on the team is following up on these. E-mail is a great tool for tracking this sort of conversation; consider using a team e-mail alias so each designer sees the discussion with the client team and can judge what parts of it affect her work.

Project owner, SME, and design engineer review

Before you spend too much time on any direction, it's important to get business and technical perspectives on your work. This means scheduling an hour or two with your project owner, design engineer(s), and perhaps a subject matter expert or two if necessary; some design engineers (especially mechanical engineers) might have been involved already. This informal meeting usually happens after three to five days of design, depending on the complexity of the problem. A short framework phase may have just one such meeting before you share the work with other stakeholders; a longer phase might involve two. Whether you have one meeting or two, there are several things that are important to accomplish: You need to get a sanity check on the design, make sure the project owner and design engineer(s) are prepared to support the design direction in the larger stakeholder meeting, and prepare for any bombshells you expect other stakeholders to drop in that meeting.

Framework

DETERMINING WHOM TO INVITE

With just a few days to do design, what you can show at this point is bound to be incomplete and probably a bit wrong, so unless you're working within a product team that understands how to look at early design and has a lot of faith both in you and the design process, it's important to have a small and reasonably friendly audience for this first review. In most cases, it will only be a week or so more before you're ready to show something to a larger (and more skeptical) group.

The one person who absolutely has to see the work in progress before other stakeholders is the project owner; it would be disastrous for him to be surprised by your work in a public meeting. If he knows what the likely sticking points are going to be ahead of time, he can work to prepare individual stakeholders as necessary.

It's also a good idea to include the design engineer(s), provided you have someone who can play that role. A good DE is adept at assessing sketchy ideas and can not only give you helpful feedback about how difficult various parts of the design will be to engineer, but may also offer up some possibilities you weren't aware of that can improve the design. However, I have worked with some clients whose engineers were obstructionists, usually due to insufficient skills or to managers who did not allow them reasonable amounts of time for their work. It would be a bad idea to exclude engineers from your process for very long, but it can be helpful to get executive buy-in (and perhaps bring in additional engineers) to keep the design from "dying in committee." No matter what the culture is, though, the project will fail unless you find productive ways to collaborate with the engineering team.

Some subject matter experts can provide invaluable insights early in the process. The majority I have worked with, however, are uncomfortable with very ambiguous early sketches and are convinced the design team can't possibly understand what they're doing; SMEs of this sort can do more harm than good. Consider the aptitudes and inclinations of any subject matter experts before showing them anything particularly rough. Some SMEs are best involved only when you share the design direction with the other stakeholders.

SETTING EXPECTATIONS

Regardless of who is attending the meeting, you need to make sure they know what to expect. Emphasize that the meeting is an informal walk-through of work in progress at the whiteboard. If you have any handouts, they'll just be copies of sketches. Tell your meeting participants that sketches are ambiguous, you've only considered a couple of high-level scenarios so far, and your answers to many questions might be, "We don't know yet." Make sure they understand what you need from them: expertise, a gut reaction about how it fits user and business needs, and a general sense of what about the design may pose challenges (political, technical, or otherwise).

PREPARING YOUR AGENDA AND MATERIALS

An informal check-in of this sort shouldn't take a lot of special effort to prepare for, but you need to spend a few minutes considering what you're going to show and in what sequence, as well as what questions you need answers to. If possible, put some drawings on the board before everyone arrives; this saves time and reduces the pressure you're under during the meeting (though some designers like to wow stakeholders with their on-the-spot whiteboard skills).

Make sure each team member has a set of meeting notes handy and everyone knows what he or she is responsible for in the meeting. Most often, the IxDG or IxDS talks through the scenarios as the IxDG draws on the whiteboard. The industrial designer typically talks through the hardware design progress, either with a sketch or a crude

Framework

physical prototype. The IxDS is responsible for capturing action items and responses to questions, though the need for this is often minimal. The visual designer, who may be mostly observing at this meeting, supports the design arguments from a visual design and brand perspective.

There are generally two narrative approaches to this sort of meeting. One is to start by describing the anatomy of the design in conceptual terms, then walk through scenarios. The other is to start with scenarios, then discuss anatomy in more detail. Which approach works better depends on the nature of the design problem, how different your solution is for the status quo, the tendencies of the audience, and your comfort with either approach. See Chapter 19 for more on this topic.

CONDUCTING THE MEETING

Before you get started, recap the expectations about what participants will and won't see and what you need from them. Ask them to tell you whether the design makes sense and seems likely to solve the business problems.

If there's a design engineer in the room, ask for an assessment of implementation difficulties. I usually start by saying something like, "First, tell us if you see anything that makes you want to scream." This acknowledges that you know you're pushing on constraints. Some engineers (who aren't temperamentally inclined to be design engineers, or whose skills aren't up to the job) might say, "We can't do that." What this really means is that they can't do that within the timeframe or other constraints they've been given (or it can mean they don't know how). Don't ask, "Is this technically feasible?" Almost anything is, given sufficient time and money. Instead, ask, "What would it take to build this?" Say that you're not looking for specific commitments about what's feasible in the allotted time, since you understand it will take some work to figure out just how hard certain things are. The business project owner,

who is also in the room, can then say whether he wants to rule anything out right away.

If this is your last (or only) meeting before the larger stakeholder review, talk about what you're planning for that meeting. Ask the project owner what questions and concerns she expects people to raise and discuss how you should handle them. If the project owner hasn't hosted a similar meeting before, describe what she can do to prepare certain stakeholders.

You might also want to review the section on conducting the more formal design vision meeting in Chapter 19; many of the questions asked at that meeting will also crop up during informal check-ins.

User feedback

I've had a number of clients over the years who wanted to conduct usability testing as soon as there was an approximate concept. The underlying motivation is usually a good one: "We all think it's good, but we should see if users agree." Although testing is a good idea for most products—and a must for some—the framework is almost always too early to conduct a test because there just isn't enough design detail for users to perform tasks using a sketch of the interface. Although you don't need to wait until design is completely finished to test some kinds of products, you do need more than squiggles or *lorem ipsum* fake text.

What you can sometimes do to get user feedback is present the design much as you would to stakeholders (see Chapter 19) and ask for reactions. This may or may not be worth your time, depending on how engaged and thoughtful your users tend to be. Consumers are unlikely to be helpful at this point, but demanding users of very specialized professional tools (who are essentially subject matter experts) may provide useful insights.

However, regardless of how sophisticated the users are, be prepared for some amount of negative response based on the low fidelity of the sketches. This is no problem if the response doesn't get back to stakeholders (don't count on it!) or if they know how take such feedback. Perfectly normal comments that are probably due to ambiguity rather than design flaws can cause uneducated stakeholders to panic and want to abandon a good direction prematurely. Always prepare stakeholders for this issue before seeking any user feedback.

It's easier and more effective to get user feedback on a visual direction or approximate hardware form factor at this point, though either has limited value since users and customers will eventually respond to the entire product rather than isolated parts of the design; an iPod without its software is a pointless block of metal and plastic. Rather than spending time and money on focus groups, most designers just figure out who in the office is most like the target users and ask them for a 30-second impression, such as how comfortably a foam prototype fits their hands.

Summary

The image of the designer who magically brings forth brilliant ideas like Athena springing from the head of Zeus is as iconic—and as unrealistic—as the image of the programmer/inventor tinkering in his garage and coming up with an overnight success. Does it happen? Maybe, but not to most designers, and never on a deadline. Design absolutely takes creativity and a dash of inspiration, but it also takes teamwork, iteration, and a lot of thought. Good process makes that easier. Any process that reliably and quickly gets you good results (i.e., good design that stakeholders can understand, believe in, and build) is a fine process; the one presented here is probably not the only one, but has been proven to work for numerous designers in a wide range of situations.

Whether or not the nuances described here work for you, I've yet to work with any designer who didn't benefit from implementing some core concepts:

— Treat the user experience as one design problem, whether it includes software, hardware, or services; you can break the problem into parts, but only if you keep bringing those parts back together to make sure they still fit.

— Define your data model early, since a user's data helps define her tools and the structure of her environment.

— Take some time to translate your functional needs into functional elements before you start to draw; don't worry about the tiny details, but use the exercise to help identify good design opportunities and important business trade-offs early on.

— Regardless of what you're designing, use scenarios to guide ideation, iteration, and assessment. Don't be afraid to judge a design by other criteria, but always go back to the scenarios.

— Get early feedback from the sources who are most likely to have the right information and know how to respond to work in progress.

Framework

CHAPTER 17

Principles and Patterns in Design Language

The focus in defining a product's form factor and interaction framework is largely on utility: identifying what solution will best accomplish the job in the simplest way. However, good design balances utility and usability with desirability or other appropriate emotions—a consumer entertainment product may evoke feelings of desire, a medical product should simultaneously look precise and reassuring, and a business product should convey no-nonsense professionalism. Design should also express a product's brand and make it identifiable as coming from a certain company, whether with unique signature elements or a more understated style that is nonetheless consistent.

Experience attributes, discussed in Chapter 12, describe this intersection of user emotions and expectations with brand qualities. The **design language** expresses those attributes, along with the practical information the design must communicate, in visual and physical form. This chapter briefly describes some of the most important building blocks you need to express various qualities. If you studied graphic design or industrial design in school, you can probably skip ahead to Chapter 18, which describes how to develop design language directions in a way that helps

stakeholders see your reasoning. This chapter is intended to help jack-of-all-trades designers make better visual decisions and to help those without a classic design education be more effective reviewers of design language.

General Principles

Like all aspects of design, the design language should adhere to the design values discussed in Chapter 15: It should be ethical, purposeful, pragmatic, and elegant. An ethical design language may involve minimizing eyestrain or choosing materials and processes that are less damaging to the environment. It minimizes work by making it clear what elements do and making it easy to find the most important information and controls. In a purposeful design language, there is a reason for every decision about color, shape, and other elements. A pragmatic design language considers whether a form or material will be difficult to clean, or whether semitransparent interface elements will be unreasonably difficult to code. An elegant language is unified across hardware, software, and service elements, and uses the smallest effective difference to communicate.

Many design principles become more critical during detailed design, but a handful are important to consider as you begin exploring the design language. These are outlined in the following pages.

Visual information + context = meaning

Although you may think of the visual aspects of design as being pretty far removed from science, an understanding of human perception—how our brains interpret what we see—is essential to any visual communication, whether of data or of brand. Simply put, our eyes pass visual information to the brain, which latches onto only the essential part of that information. We're quick to focus on movement and recognize basic shapes at first glance. This makes biological sense, since responding to the movement and silhouette of a predator was a good skill for survival in a primitive world. Color is another attention getter; no doubt the ability to spot a red fruit in a tree once meant not going hungry. We are slower to respond to more detailed information such as texture, perhaps because it is not so closely linked to survival.

Visual information only assumes meaning with our context and experience, however. Consider the "+" shape in Figure 17.1. In one context, it means the viewer should add numbers together, but in others it might indicate that there's an intersection ahead or that disaster relief has arrived. To a small child, perhaps none of these symbols has any meaning. To someone in Istanbul, a red crescent would be more meaningful than a red cross.

For this reason, context is essential to every visual design decision. Yellow as a dominant color might be seen as bright and warm, but yellow used as a highlight on certain controls or data might indicate a warning. An icon of a cylinder might say "database" to a technical user and "mysterious cylinder icon" to another. A style that seems friendly and approachable to someone intimidated by technology might feel childish or simplistic to a more knowledgeable user.

Figure 17.1. Meaning depends on context.

Visually communicate what elements do

The design language is a form of communication. It sets a user's expectations about her experience of the brand and the product. It also implies what various parts of the product do: A protruding handle says it should be pulled, a three-dimensional look hints that a button made of pixels is clickable, and a scroll bar implies that there's more content below what you can see on the screen. This visual hinting at function is called an **affordance** (after James Gibson's 1977 work, "The Theory of Affordances"). Figure 17.2 shows some typical software UI affordances: Textures on the corner of a window and the edge of a pane indicate that they're movable, and a three dimensional treatment on the scroll bar controls hints that they can be clicked.

Avoid setting false expectations with your affordances; Figure 17.3 illustrates the classic example. I once saw a medical device that consistently suffered cracking at one edge of an access panel because a concavity there implied

Framework

"grab here to open," when users actually had to unlatch the panel along the other side. An affordance can be so strong that it's difficult to overcome, even with time; you probably find yourself pulling on the protruding handle of a door you've gone through dozens of times even though you know you need to push it.

The illusion of dimensionality on a screen won't cause breakage but will cause frustration if you

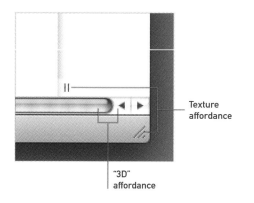

Figure 17.2. Textures and dimensionality indicate the on-screen items can be manipulated.

Figure 17.3. Whatever the text says, the protruding handle yells, "Pull me!"

use it on visual interface elements that can't be manipulated. However, complete lack of appropriate affordance implies that something cannot be manipulated. This problem is common to many Web sites, though experienced Web users have learned that a row of labels across the top or down the left of the screen is clickable, even with no other visual indication.

Have a purpose for every element and a reason for every decision

Every visual element, like every functional element, should have a reason to exist. Those reasons can be functional in themselves; a slight gradient, for example, can be used to give a button a clickable affordance. Even decorative elements can exist for a reason, though. The subtle gleam and reflection Apple uses on its Web site (in Figure 17.6) and in its software (such as the iTunes image in Figure 17.4) hints that their products are shiny, new, and perfect. The boxes and borders within borders in Figure 17.5, on the other hand, have no evident purpose and are therefore distracting.

In addition to having a rationale for every element to exist, you should also have a reason for why you

Figure 17.4. The subtle reflections in Apple products and marketing materials exist for a reason.

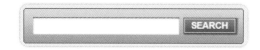

Figure 17.5. This search tool includes unnecessary visual elements, such as the multilayered border on the search entry field.

Framework

You'll make better design decisions—and be better at explaining them to stakeholders— if you and your teammates have a reason for every choice.

shaped, colored, or textured it a certain way, either based on usability considerations or on reinforcement of the experience attributes. I once had an industrial designer say to me that the hardware buttons on a glucose meter should be arranged in a certain way to look like a paw print. He couldn't say why this was good; it detracted from the usability and had nothing whatever to do with supporting the brand. This is an extreme example, but you'll make better design decisions—and be better at explaining them to stakeholders—if you and your teammates have a reason for every choice.

Repeat elements for unity

Repetition of a shape, a color, a material, or a texture can bring unity to a single design or even an entire product line. (Conversely, varying elements for no particular reason makes visual communication less clear.) Just take a look at the Apple products pictured in Figure 17.6. Nearly every product you see uses the same curvature on the corners or, in the case of the iPod Shuffle, on the vertical edges. This shape softens Apple's "shiny and high-tech" image to make it more approachable. Most of their products also employ white plastic or brushed metal. Now look at the visual language of the Web site itself, and you'll see the same curved corners and metallic accents. This subtle repetition helps keep a fairly busy page from being overwhelming. It also tells you everything you're looking at is from the same company.

Figure 17.6. Repetition of the same elements in the physical and visual design language.

Framework

Of course, heavy-handed repetition can wind up looking clumsy, especially if it uses elements that don't exist for a clear reason. Look at the fictitious (but not unrealistic) Web site in Figure 17.7. Slices off the upper corners of several elements echo the navigation buttons. The texture on some headers is also repeated, as are the arrows on some buttons and links. These elements are not at all subtle, though, and they appear to be applied somewhat randomly, so the overall impression is clumsy rather than unifying.

Be decisive, but use the smallest effective difference.

Figure 17.7. The repeated elements in this Web site seem arbitrary and heavy-handed.

Be decisive, but use the smallest effective difference

If you're using a contrast in color, size, or some other characteristic to convey meaning, that contrast only works if it's decisive. An excessively subtle distinction also adds cognitive work as a viewer tries to decipher whether it is meaningful. However, overly sharp distinctions can look amateurish. In Figure 17.8, for example, you can barely tell that the text on the top is rendered in two different point sizes. The text on the bottom looks awkward because the difference is too great. The text in the middle shows a clear distinction that isn't overdone. Figure 17.9 shows a real example of an exaggerated difference.

Framework

10 point	11 point
10 point	12 point
10 point	**16 point**

Figure 17.8. Use the smallest effective difference.

Figure 17.9. An example of too exaggerated a difference in an antivirus application.

Patterns and Principles for Specific Elements

In order to represent qualities in visual and physical terms, you need a vocabulary of patterns. In the realm of design language, patterns are primarily centered on how to manipulate visual elements such as color, shape, and size to evoke certain associations and emotional responses. I've also included a few element-specific principles that are worth considering at this stage of design; you'll find more in Chapter 21. Many of these concepts are worth whole books in themselves, so my intention here is just to highlight a few key points.

Color

You can use color for many purposes, most commonly to draw attention to important information or controls, show relationships, evoke particular emotions, or reinforce a brand identity. Your use of color to evoke emotion or enhance usability will be more effective if you understand certain properties, principles, and patterns.

Every unique color can be described in terms of three different properties. **Hue** is what we normally think of as color; red, yellow, and blue are all hues. The intensity of the color is described as its **saturation**. Green is a saturated color; khaki, which is green plus gray, is desaturated. The lightness or darkness of the color is its **value**; white is a high-value or bright color, while black is a low-value or dark color. Figure 17.10 illustrates these three properties of color. A **tint,** such as pink, is the pure hue with white mixed in, while a **shade,** such as maroon, is the pure hue with black mixed in. Some hues are naturally higher value or brighter than others; yellow, for example, has a higher or lighter value than purple. People who are entirely colorblind cannot really distinguish one hue from another if all hues are of the same value, but may be able to distinguish yellow from purple because of the difference in value. You may also hear about color **temperature**—red, orange, and yellow are seen as warm in most situations, while green, blue, and purple are seen as cool.

Our perception of color is not absolute; a color that seems very green in one context may seem blue in another. A bright blue paired with saturated red is anything but cool. Unfortunately for digital design, color also varies widely depending on the display type; even a single screen's color rendition can shift over time. Unless you control the hardware and its settings, you'll need to try colors on many displays to see how they look under various conditions.

Hue

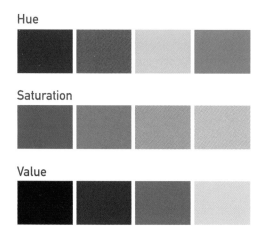

Saturation

Value

Figure 17.10. Every color can be described in terms of its hue, saturation, and value.

USING COLOR TO ENHANCE USABILITY

Although many usability decisions regarding color come later in the process, your choice of color palette now can have quite an impact later on. Consider the following principles in determining what palettes may work.

A little color goes a long way

Using one or two contrasting colors can reduce visual work by emphasizing important elements and improving scan speed, but overly complex color coding of data and controls increases cognitive load and memory work. Avoid using more than half a dozen or so hues in any color coding scheme, though you can use multiple values of the same hue to indicate gradation, such as water depth on a map. As you can see in Figure 17.11, it's much easier to spot the orange circle when it's the only one that's colored.

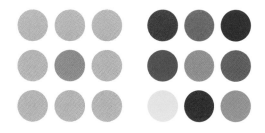

Figure 17.11. Too many colors obscure differences.

Use warm, bright, saturated colors for emphasis

Warm, high-value, saturated colors emphasize information and make it pop (see Figure 17.12). Dark, desaturated, cool colors cause information to recede. Any color contrast will draw attention, but reds, yellows, and oranges will generally do so more effectively than purples, blues, and greens. However, avoid using one saturated color on top of another because it causes eyestrain. This is especially true with blue and red, which seem to vibrate, causing a condition known as **chromostereopsis** (or in simpler terms, a guaranteed headache), illustrated in Figure 17.13. In hardware, you can use illumination of labels or of entire controls to achieve additional emphasis, or to provide the function of color in a low-light environment.

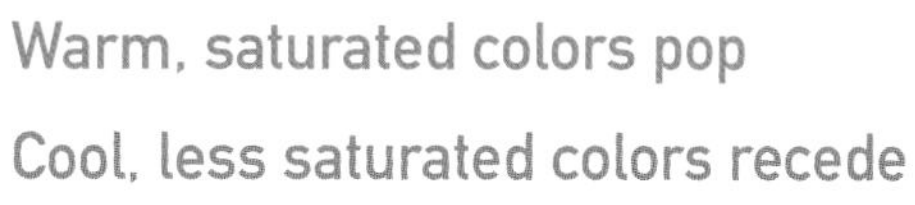

Warm, saturated colors pop

Cool, less saturated colors recede

Figure 17.12. Use warm, saturated colors for emphasis.

Chromostereopsis

Figure 17.13. Chromostereopsis—dreadful, isn't it?

Figure 17.14. Contrasting part colors can change the visual impression of mass made by hardware.

Dominant brand identity colors may make poor dominant interface colors

If the dominant color in your company's identity is something assertive like bright red, it probably makes a lousy dominant color for your interface because it drowns everything out. It's a bit like having someone write a letter in all caps; it shouts at the viewer and makes it impossible to see subtle distinctions. Instead, use very bold colors only for accents in the interface; use more subdued colors in most cases for backgrounds and large areas of screen real estate.

Use different values to minimize perceived device size

Contrasting values on physical parts can help make a product appear lighter and smaller. For example, if you use a light color for the upper bezel of a product and a darker value for the bottom part, the lighter-colored part may leave the impression that it's the entire product at first glance. Strong contrast can also make users focus on a specific part and tune out the rest. Compare the two phone renderings in Figure 17.14. The one with the silver screen bezel draws attention to the display, while the one with a body-color bezel leaves a more massive impression.

Don't rely solely on hue to communicate

Approximately 8 percent of men and 0.5 percent of women[1] are at least partially colorblind, so you should never rely solely on hue to communicate. Always use some additional communication vector, such as texture, size, or contrast in value. This will also prove useful when users send information from a screen to a black-and-white printer. In Figure 17.15, the image on the right has been completely desaturated to simulate the effects of color blindness; the result is that the most important control on this defibrillator now looks like the least important.

Figure 17.15. Effects of color blindness.

---

1. National Institutes of Health. http://ghr.nlm.nih.gov/condition=colorvisiondeficiency.

PATTERNS FOR COMMUNICATING EMOTION WITH COLOR

Along with physiological responses that are independent of culture, colors elicit associations, memories, and other more context-dependent reactions; white is the color of weddings to some and of funerals to others. In general, tints of nearly any color are seen as softer. Shades, the darker variants on any color, are usually seen as more mature and powerful. A shiny, metallic version of any hue is richer, colder, and more high-tech. Sharp contrasts in color are always more bold and decisive; using closely related colors makes less of a statement.

Red stimulates excitement and energy. The color of blood and stop signs, it is often associated with danger. Warm tomato red also conveys outspoken prosperity and power (doubtless one reason red sports cars are so popular). It's the color of good fortune in China. Cooler, darker reds, such as burgundy, are seen as more mature and refined and are a good choice for conveying understated wealth and luxury.

Pink, a tint of red, elicits a wide range of responses. Bright, shocking pinks convey the same high energy as red, but without the same associations of class and power; if anything, pink is seen as trendy, feminine, and possibly cheap. Reddish-purple pinks are more grown up. Bubblegum pink can be sweet; in the wrong context, it may be cloying. A rose pink implies health and warmth.

Orange is vibrant, playful, youthful, and friendly. It's a bold, modern color that's hard to ignore. It is seldom associated with sophistication or wealth. Lighter peach tones seem soothing and approachable.

Yellow is the color of sunshine, cheerfulness, and bright ideas, which makes it suitable for the simple, friendly tone of the application in Figure 17.16. Bright yellow is highly noticeable. Used as an accent color, particularly in combination with

red and green, yellow may communicate caution or slowness; combined with black, yellow always attracts attention and may signify danger. Greenish yellows may be associated with acidity and may not be well received in Western cultures except by children and teenagers. Pastel yellows are seen as soft. Golden, brownish yellows are warm, welcoming, and homey.

Figure 17.16. Goldmail, a simple application for assembling and mailing voice-over slide shows, uses plenty of bright yellow to emphasize its simplicity.

There's a reason so many health-care environments are blue; light and mid-range blues are restful and soothing. Blue and pure tints imply cleanliness, especially when used with white, but may be seen as cold. Darker blues such as navy are reliable, mature, and authoritative without being as ominous as black. Used with a bit of gloss or sparkle, blue can be electric and lively. Teal, a greenish blue, says your product is unique, but these in-between hues often go in and out of style.

Greens are usually associated with nature. They seem cool, clean, and calm. Light greens are fresh, while darker greens are seen as more conservative and prestigious. Bright, yellowish greens can be bold, modern, and high-tech. Mint greens are refreshing and cool.

Purple can be bright, electric, and futuristic, with darker shades and desaturated hues seeming more quiet and sophisticated. Light purples, such as lilac, are sweet, soothing, and unobtrusive. However, associations with purple may be less predictable than associations with other colors, so although it's an appropriate color for SciFi.com, it's a risky choice for many applications. If nothing else, purple says your product is unique.

Nearly any hue of brown says your product is reliable, durable, and approachable. Brown is the color of the earth and is therefore substantial and stable. Chocolate brown has come to be associated with a certain understated luxury, particularly if it has a sheen. Of course, brown can also be associated with dirt, which makes it difficult to use in health care applications. Brown is not the color to use if you want to say that your product is cutting edge and dynamic (which makes Microsoft's choice of brown for its first-generation Zune media player a peculiar one).

White says clean, bright, and pure like no other color. White is modern and minimalist, but can be seen as stark if not relieved by some other hue. It can be warm and sophisticated with the slightest hint of yellow or brown added to it, or it can be cool and nearly invisible with just a touch of blue or gray.

Black is dramatic, powerful, and often elegant. A glossy black is high-tech. A matte black may be rich and sophisticated. Black is massive; it implies solidity and durability. All these qualities make black a suitable dominant color for Autodesk.com, shown in Figure 17.17, since the company makes powerful software used by designers, architects, and engineers. Black accents are sharp and decisive. Too much black can be ominous.

Gray is unobtrusive, which can make it a worthwhile choice as a backdrop. It can also be seen as indecisive; it lacks the purity of either black or white, so it's never going to make a very bold statement.

Figure 17.17. Autodesk's black Web site background implies that they have seriously powerful technology.

Silver is gray's wealthier sibling; a matte silver finish is precise yet unassuming, while large quantities of chrome can be flashy and outspoken.

Size

No doubt you know that controls and data should always be large enough to find, read, and use under typical conditions, but size can be manipulated for other purposes. Varying the size of elements and information can enhance usability by creating a clear hierarchy and drawing attention to the most important items. The overall size of controls and text also creates an aesthetic impression. In general, large controls and text appear friendly, simple, approachable, or playful. This makes large controls a good choice for children's toys or some consumer products, but usually a poor choice for tools that are meant to appear professional, sophisticated, or powerful. Compare the elements from iPhoto, Apple's consumer-oriented photo manager, with those from Aperture, its professional cousin, both shown in Figure 17.18. This association of simplicity with larger controls can be challenging when you want a professional or sophisticated-looking touch screen application or automotive interior, in which large type and controls may be necessary for usability.

Figure 17.18. The presence of text labels and a difference in text and icon size distinguish a consumer application from a professional one.

Shape

An object's shape, particularly from the most common viewpoint, is one of the first things people recognize about it. Although the average Web site or desktop application tends toward rectangles for efficiency's sake, the other shapes used in any application or device can make it seem precise or approachable, luxurious or practical, sophisticated or down-to-earth. Rounded corners are soft, human, friendly, or simple—even childlike. Eggs, pebbles, and most living creatures are made up of curved surfaces, so shapes with curves are seen as more organic and natural. Complex shapes imply a certain attention to detail and the resources not to be strictly practical; they're also less recognizable at a glance. Compare the cell phones in Figure 17.19. One is rounded and foreshortened, which makes it seem friendly and young, while the other's more elongated, generally rectangular form makes it look more like a grown-up business tool.

However, there's a pragmatic side to the shape of a device. Shapes provide affordances that tell users what an object does and how to pick it up and hold it. An object's shape also affects how easy it is to drop, how well it withstands damage, and how easy it is to clean. Ridges and sharply angled indentations, for example, tend to retain grime, which can make a kitchen appliance or hospital device look anything but pristine after a while.

In software, sharp corners and an ordered layout grid appear clean, modern, and precise. Taken too

Figure 17.19. Different shapes give otherwise similar phones a very different feel.

Figure 17.20. The image of the chair keeps the grid from being too static.

far, rectangles can be dull. Notice how the Crate and Barrel Web site pictured in Figure 17.20 uses an irregularly shaped product, shot at an angle, to break up what might otherwise be a static grid, without losing its overall clean and modern look.

Line weight and style

Thin, sharp lines look precise and sophisticated, while thick, bold ones are simple, friendly, and perhaps childish. Compare the thin, low-contrast lines used on the Volvo Web site in Figure 17.21 with the thick, high-contrast lines used on the

Figure 17.21. The line styles used in the Volvo, Lego, and Cost Plus World Market Web sites all imply very different brand attributes.

Lego site. Irregular or patterned lines can have many characters; they can be casual, sophisticated, or playful depending on the exact treatment, but are probably not going to look precise or clean. Cost Plus World Market, for example, uses a variety of decorative line styles on its Web site to imply that its wares are exotic.

Type

Due to the low resolution of a screen in comparison to print, many typefaces are inappropriate for screen use except at large sizes used for decoration or headings. In general, a good screen font has a wide punch width, wide letter spacing, tall x-height, and simple strokes (see Figure 17.22). Sans-serif faces such as Verdana and Tahoma are usually more legible than serif fonts, especially at small sizes. Most visual designers try to avoid Arial because it's an overused and poorly-executed imitation of Helvetica. A few serif fonts, such as Georgia, have been specifically designed for the screen and are legible at reasonable sizes.

Wide
letter spacing

Wide
punch width

Tall x-height
Simple strokes

Figure 17.22. Characteristics of a good screen font.

When it comes to emotion and branding, the corporate identity system is usually the best place to start. However, the identity fonts are often best applied to headers and other large elements rather than to the majority of a screen's content, since they are often selected without low-resolution displays in mind. Although typefaces vary widely in personality, in general, serif faces

are classic, sophisticated, and sometimes a bit conservative. Sans serif faces provide a clean, modern look. Use script or very eclectic faces sparingly and with good reason.

Texture

Technically speaking, texture is a physical attribute we experience through the sense of touch. In industrial design, texture is partly a matter of material choice and process and partly a matter of deliberate application. A texture can be inherent in an authentic material, such as a leather or wood, or it can be designed in a mold to add aesthetic richness, clarify an affordance, or perhaps make a grip more secure. However, we also perceive texture visually; something with bright highlights and a clean gradient looks hard and smooth, like a polished stone or the product of a high-tech process. An image with a subtle mottling seems like it might be soft to the touch. An interface control depicted with subtle ridges provides an affordance that says you can grip and move it. All of the visual textures take on the emotional qualities of the materials they mimic.

Because texture is one of the last visual properties we notice, it's not a good choice for calling out important information; if you use contrast in texture to communicate about anything other than emotion, reserve it for low-priority distinctions.

Images

Aside from icons, imagery is seldom used in applications, but is a critical component of most Web sites. Effective use of imagery is worth a graphic design course in itself, so I'll limit discussion here to a few key points.

The first question is whether to use photography or illustration. Photography is often the best choice; it imparts a polish that's difficult

Framework

Figure 17.23. If you were designing a Web site for a taxi service, what would each of these image styles imply?

to achieve with illustration. However, illustration can be informal and friendly. Both photography and illustration can look amateurish if poorly done. In either case, the image style should be consistent with the brand and experience attributes. Illustrations take their style from the elements described above: color, line, shape, and so forth. Photos take their style from the camera angle, depth of field, lighting, and other attributes; objects and people on clean white backgrounds look simple and precise. People in realistic environments are more human. Objects and people in motion are more exciting and dynamic. Compare the images in Figure 17.23.

Materials and manufacturing

Although many of the visual elements described in the previous pages are shared across hardware and software, hardware is unique in that it is made of materials by means of manufacturing processes. Material qualities such as weight, density, flexibility, porosity, and thermal properties affect choice of manufacturing technology, resistance to damage, ability to disperse heat, and many other properties of concern to engineers and industrial designers. However, a complete course in materials science is well beyond the scope of this book; let us instead focus on how materials and manufacturing methods elicit emotional responses. For example, compare the images in Figure 17.24. Which looks more precise? Durable? Cold? Expensive? Approachable?

Figure 17.24. These materials and finishes leave different impressions.

AUTHENTICITY

It's relatively common to find imitation materials in physical products, usually due to cost or sometimes functional necessity (an all-metal cell phone, for example, might have problems with the material blocking the cellular signal). Material imitation effects usually involve applying a secondary finish process—such as painting or applying a thin film with an image on it—to an ordinary plastic part. No doubt you've seen this kind of thing on the "wood" panels in a car. Another option is to engineer special plastics that have other compounds, such as metal flakes, mixed in. Although these processes can add visual richness to a product, it's difficult to imitate the tactile qualities of real materials, so the end result can often seem cheap. These finishing methods can also introduce problems with durability and recyclability.

"TEMPERATURE"

Some materials seem warm while others appear cold. This is not due to actual temperature, but to the conducting or insulating properties of the material; metal feels cold because it conducts heat away from the skin, while wood feels warm because it is a poor conductor of heat. Materials we don't inherently associate with temperature, such as plastic, are likely to take on the "temperature" qualities of their colors and finishes instead; plastic painted to mimic metal looks nearly as cold, though it seldom fools the sense of touch.

"SOFTNESS"

We associate softness with materials that are smooth and not stiff. A baby's skin and hair are soft because of their fine texture; a smoothly finished piece of wood furniture can likewise feel soft to the touch, though we know it is actually fairly hard. Rubber, because it is flexible, leaves an impression of greater softness than plastic or metal. However, even a smooth and flexible material is unlikely to be perceived as soft if it has a glossy finish and sharp edges. An area that looks soft, such as the rubber handle on a hammer, tends to imply that users should grip there.

"DURABILITY" AND SUITABILITY

To an engineer, durability is about tensile strength and resistance to impact and wear. To a user, these qualities often have more to do with weight, density, stiffness, and proportion. Something that is heavy and inflexible seems more likely to endure; metal hinges and casings leave an impression of higher quality than the same components made of plastic. Things that simply look heavier and chunkier are assumed to be more robust. A heavy car door that closes with a satisfying thump implies that you're driving a well-made, safe piece of machinery.

Of course, there are pragmatic considerations; materials should certainly be able to withstand typical conditions. A mobile device that gets thrown in a purse or carried everywhere will be subject to scratching. The plastics in a hospital device should withstand frequent cleaning with harsh chemicals. A glossy finish won't look so precise and special when covered in smudges. Any material that's more suited to the showroom than the usage environment will eventually cause some dissatisfaction.

MANUFACTURING AND PART ASSEMBLY METHODS

The average end user can't define the difference between injection molding and thermoforming, but will tell you that the product with precise joints looks better made. However, highly visible part lines, exposed bolts, and welded seams provide an appearance of industrial strength and robustness in certain product categories, whereas hidden fasteners and sharp contrasts in materials that emphasize precise part breaks imply precision and quality in consumer electronics.

Exercise

Look at a couple of different Web sites you don't normally frequent. Look at your cell phone and at the dashboard of a particular car. What attributes would you ascribe to these products based solely on the design language? Deconstruct the design: How do specific choices of shape, color, line, type, size, texture, images, and materials contribute to that impression? What design language choices, if any, seem at odds with the rest?

Signature elements

Combinations of various visual and/or physical properties can be used as **signature elements**:

Framework

unique treatments of a brand identity or functional elements that are highlighted in some special way, usually across multiple products. Cars are well known for signature elements, such as BMW's distinctive front grilles or Volvo's flared tail lights (which you can see in Figure 17.21).

Some signature elements involve special treatment of a company or product identity. Dell computers all have the company's logo represented on top of a round, convex silver "badge" that contrasts with the surrounding material; this makes the products recognizable from a distance and, on close inspection, celebrates the logo as a mark of quality. The Microsoft Office button (see Figure 17.25) aims to accomplish something similar in software, though one might argue that it's less effective than many physical signature elements.

Figure 17.25. The Office button is a sort of software signature element.

Other signature elements are functional, such as Apple's use of the click wheel on most of its iPods or Oxo's black rubber handles on kitchen gadgets.

Summary

Although there will always be an element of subjectivity to what makes a "good" design language, by understanding how different visual properties are perceived, you can learn to make better decisions and communicate about why they're good. As Chapter 18 will show, you can use this knowledge to encourage stakeholders to discuss design language decisions in terms of relatively objective attributes rather than entirely subjective personal preferences.

Of course, design language is always some combination of emotion and usability; while you're figuring out how to convey the right attributes, step back and consider how colors, typefaces, materials, and other aspects of the design language will affect the practical aspects of the experience; putting your own brand imperatives before user needs will *always* undermine your message.

Framework

CHAPTER 18

Developing the Design Language

The appearance of any product or environment will always say *something* to the people who look at it; a designer's job is to ensure that it says what it should by establishing an appropriate **design language**. To most people outside the design team— and even to some design team members who are not responsible for it—this design language development is often a mysterious process. Many designers make it seem even more mysterious because they can't explain how they arrived at the design language they're showing. In the absence of clear rationale and assessment criteria, stakeholders tend to evaluate the design language based on personal preference or to rely on the inexpert opinions of a focus group to choose the appropriate expression of their product's brand.

Although developing a design language is largely a matter of experience and skill in manipulating visual (and sometimes physical) properties, the process described here will help you focus your skills and educate stakeholders. The point of design language exploration is *not* to provide untutored stakeholders with an a la carte menu from which they can pick and choose colors, type, and materials; rather, it is to help them select a clear visual communication strategy based on sound reasoning.

You may be able to skip this chapter if you're working on a product that has an established design language, though even in this case it's important to understand and communicate the effect of specific design decisions on the visual messaging.

The Process of Developing the Design Language

Much of what's described in this chapter happens invisibly inside the head of an experienced designer, but is worth discussing with a colleague nonetheless, especially if you're new to this activity. As usual, the process is most easily explained in linear fashion, though in reality the thought process is more iterative.

Informed by your research and personas, you might begin by looking at other product categories, environments, or elements of the natural world for inspiration to help inform your use of visual and material properties. It's best to discuss certain characteristics of your studies with the rest of the design team before you begin to render them, though.

Unless stakeholders are unusually sophisticated consumers of design, most have great difficulty separating the interaction from its visual representation.

As with developing the interaction framework and physical platforms or architecture(s), you'll need to determine right away how many directions to share with stakeholders. These directions are embodied in **design language studies**, which are the equivalent of fabric swatches and paint chips that show elements of the design language working together, though not necessarily in the context of the interaction framework or hardware architecture.

A visual language study for on-screen elements is usually best divorced from the interaction design sketches except when the project is simply a visual upgrade of existing interaction design. Unless stakeholders are unusually sophisticated consumers of design, most have great difficulty separating the interaction from its visual representation, even if you have already discussed the interaction design with sketches. If you show visual design applied to an interaction design they don't understand or don't agree with, many stakeholders won't be able to get past that. Likewise, if you describe rough interaction with images that include detail about color, type, and texture, stakeholders tend to focus on these visual elements rather than on structure and flow. However, there are exceptions to this general rule; a friend of mine who works at Apple says the emphasis on the visual is so strong there that stakeholders would be unwilling to accept rough interaction sketches divorced from visual design, even though this adds considerable time to the design schedule.

An industrial design language is possible to illustrate with sketches of hardware details, but this more abstract approach can be difficult for stakeholders to interpret, so an industrial design (ID) study is usually a rendering of surfacing, colors, materials, and finishes applied to an entire device. However, the same problem with conflating functional design and design language applies, so if you haven't focused on a single architecture yet, this is usually a generic device sketch (like the one in Figure 16.3) that's similar to, but doesn't quite look like, any of the candidate architectures. The final architecture is an appropriate basis for studies if you've settled on a single direction or are simply restyling an existing architecture. It often does not include every control or final placement of elements, since these depend on a variety of issues yet to be explored. It would be nice to show each design language direction applied to each physical architecture if you haven't settled on one, but this is seldom possible within a typical design budget.

Studies for environments, wayfinding, or other experiences that aren't simply about hardware and software may take other forms. A study for a retail environment would include sketches of the interior space, images of commercially available furnishings and fabrics, and so forth. A study for wayfinding in an airport might include a few example

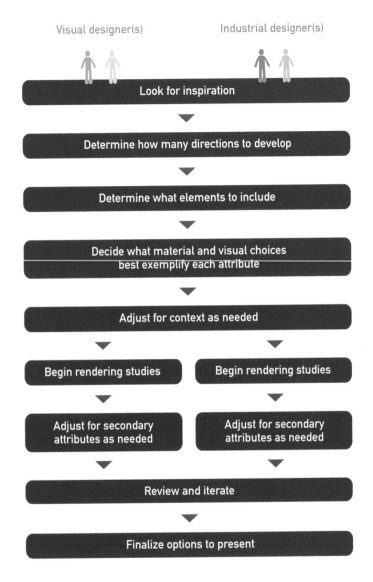

Visual designer(s)   Industrial designer(s)

Look for inspiration

Determine how many directions to develop

Determine what elements to include

Decide what material and visual choices best exemplify each attribute

Adjust for context as needed

Begin rendering studies | Begin rendering studies

Adjust for secondary attributes as needed | Adjust for secondary attributes as needed

Review and iterate

Finalize options to present

Figure 18.1. Overview of design language development.

renderings of signage using various colors and typefaces, along with a simulated image or two of those signs in context.

Once you develop a range of potential directions, you should review them with the entire design team, select which options to present to stakeholders, and iterate them as needed. Figure 18.1 provides an overview of the process.

Look for inspiration

Experienced designers rely on a large vocabulary of design language patterns like those described in Chapter 17, but many still find it helpful to look for inspiration in other products—especially in other genres—and perhaps even in nature. A kitchen appliance could inspire the form or control panel of a scientific instrument. The luster of a

Framework

 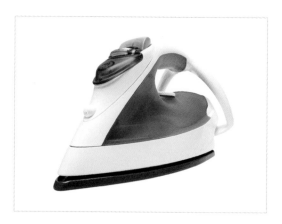

Figure 18.2. When the original iMac was a hit, even irons started using white and translucent teal.

seashell could inspire the finish on a cell phone. A sports car might provide an idea for a repeated element in an application's visual language.

You probably started looking for inspiration during requirements definition (see Chapter 12) when you assembled images that conveyed appropriate attributes, so it's seldom worth spending much more time on this. Studying any particular product too closely may yield a "me, too" design language; when the original iMac was released in 1998, for instance, even vacuum cleaners and clothes irons were suddenly sporting shiny, white finishes and translucent, blue-green plastic accents (as in Figure 18.2).

Determine how many directions to share

Even one visual choice, such as color, can have a tremendous effect on how a product is perceived. This makes it worthwhile to explore multiple directions for the design language as long as you can afford a week or two (depending on whether the ID studies are hand sketches or loose 3D renderings). If you can't, you might need to develop a single reasonable direction that will be "good enough." This may not be faster in the end, though, if stakeholders are unhappy with the direction.

The experience attributes (Chapter 12) guide the design language exploration much as persona goals and scenarios guide interaction and form factor design (Chapter 16). There is a natural tension among the experience attributes; your product may be meant to convey both simplicity and power, but the visual and material properties that say *simplicity* are not the same ones that express *power*. Trying to depict three or four attributes with equal emphasis on each would be like trying to make yourself understood in a crowded, noisy restaurant—your message would be lost entirely.

For this reason, each study focuses on just one primary attribute. If you have four experience attributes, this means developing a minimum of four design language studies, though you may develop additional studies per attribute as you have time, then eliminate the less-effective ones. (It's sometimes possible to skip an attribute if it is largely hygienic—i.e., a must-have to be on par with the competition, such as *sturdy* with respect to industrial machinery or *friendly* for preschool educational software—but this is not common.) This is not to say that any of the studies should completely ignore any of the attributes, but that each study should lean in one direction or another. The other attributes are treated much like secondary personas: Tweak the design to accommodate them, but not to the extent that you overwhelm the primary attribute.

It's entirely possible that the final design won't look quite like any of the studies; in fact, this is usually the case. However, the studies are an effective tool for helping stakeholders say, "This direction seems almost right; that one is definitely not right." The idea is to explore a broad range in these small, inexpensive studies to help stakeholders agree on a strategy; this also lets you get most of the design language settled before applying it to increasingly expensive physical models or multiple screen states.

Some designers are able to generate many options with incredible breadth, each looking entirely different from the last. Most designers have a somewhat narrower range, which makes it advisable to assign two or more visual designers and two or more industrial designers to this effort if you can afford to do so—the less overlap in their stylistic tendencies, the better. One designer can do a fine job on a tight budget, however, and a visual designer and an industrial designer working together will each stretch the other's thinking.

Studies for visual and industrial design are closely related in that they should use related shapes and textures; the on-screen elements, for example, might repeat a signature element of the hardware language to unify the overall look. However, it isn't always necessary to have one visual language study matched to one industrial design language study; it's possible to have just one industrial design study and multiple visual design directions, for example, particularly if most of the interaction with the device is based on the screen. However, industrial and visual designers should always develop these directions in concert, as in Figure 18.3, since software and hardware that don't share a language will never quite feel like a unified experience.

Figure 18.3. Visual and industrial designers need to collaborate on design language development.

Determine what elements to represent

ID studies usually include most of the important visible elements of the physical product (expressed using a somewhat generic form); visual language studies typically consist of a few example elements rather than an entire screen. Using only a few or generic elements saves design time and allows broad exploration, just as temporarily ignoring constraints helps interaction designers ideate at first. The constrained representation also makes it clear to stakeholders that the focus is not on the interaction or form factor.

The elements shown in the visual design study should reflect the type of content the screen will eventually show; a study for a Web site might include a photo or two, whereas a study for an analytics application would show part of a graph or table. Visual language studies almost always include treatments of typography and common interface controls such as buttons. They might also include an icon or two, though these can be time-consuming to develop. Each study should treat exactly the same visual or physical elements, so that designers and stakeholders alike are comparing apples to apples.

Framework

501

Decide what choices best represent primary attributes

Using your knowledge of principles and patterns, such as those outlined in Chapter 17, think about what colors, shapes, materials, finishes, and other elements will best represent each attribute. As shown in Figure 18.4, the more elements you use to portray a quality, the more strongly it will be emphasized. Slightly rounded corners on a software button hint at simplicity and approachability. Very rounded corners, thick outlines, and bright colors portray a degree of friendliness and simplicity appropriate only to interfaces for children. Type is seldom a big emphasis for productivity applications since so few faces hold up well in complex system designs.

The visual and industrial designers should discuss these choices together, sketching forms, surfaces, and shapes, then looking at colors, materials, and finishes. If both have the same starting point in mind, there is a greater likelihood that their initial explorations will be complementary.

Adjust for context as needed

Next, consider whether any of these choices is inappropriate to the context of use. Thin, sharp lines incised in the handle of a plastic medical device might look precise and imply where to grip it, but are also likely to trap grime. Bright red controls could be consistent with the brand and the experience attributes, but might need to be reserved for communicating status along with yellow and green.

Begin to render the studies

Depending on the amount of time available and the comfort level of stakeholders, an industrial design study might be a neat pencil sketch, an Illustrator or Photoshop drawing, or even a loosely rendered, three-dimensional model. A quick 3D render with a few details hand sketched on top, as in Figures 18.12 through 18.14, is a nice compromise because it shows the qualities of the materials and finishes, which are essential to the physical aspect of the design language, without requiring a tremendous investment of time. Hand sketches like the one in Figure 18.5 are the best choice for an initial review within the design team, since they take little effort, but they don't work as well with stakeholders, who are usually unaccustomed to reading sketches.

Visual design language studies are most effective rendered in pixels as a color palette and a swatch or two representing likely interface elements. A palette of typefaces is worth including if type plays a big role, such as on some Web sites. A medium to dark gray background provides a neutral backdrop for evaluating each study.

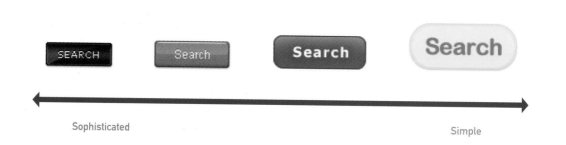

Figure 18.4. The more properties you vary, the stronger the visual message.

Figure 18.5. Hand sketches work well as first-draft ID studies within the design team; this one is a precursor to Figure 18.14.

The visual and industrial designers are working in such different materials that, although it's important to begin sketching and discussing color and material choices in tandem to ensure a cohesive language, it's much easier to draw the studies separately at first. However, for a device in which the screen is a significant visual presence, it's difficult to make a fair assessment of the direction until stakeholders see both together, so in most cases you'll also want to apply the screen treatment to the physical product rendering using Photoshop or a similar tool.

If there's time, try to develop more than one study per attribute. You can do this by having each designer do one study for each attribute, thereby giving you at least two studies to choose from for each, or you can have each designer develop a range of options for a subset of the attributes.

Adjust for secondary attributes as needed

Once you have a first draft of a study, pause and examine it to see if it clearly emphasizes one

attribute without completely losing the others. If another attribute seems to be missing entirely, try varying just one or two visual properties— such as shape, texture, or line style—to bring in just a hint of the missing attribute, as described for Figures 18.6 through 18.9.

Review, iterate, and finalize options to present

Once you are satisfied with your set of first-draft studies, show them to the rest of the design team to see if they agree that each attribute is well represented and to determine whether they foresee any usability or other issues with any of your choices. Iterate each study as needed. Never show stakeholders a study that anyone on the team believes is problematic unless you are explicitly using it as a negative example; Murphy's Law makes it almost inevitable that stakeholders will like it! This doesn't mean each study has to be perfect, though. As with the interaction design framework or form factor, it's fine if the design has a few problems as long as you're confident you can work them out later.

Exercise

Create hardware and software visual language studies for the LocalGuide.

Example: NetApp

NetApp is a leading provider of network storage and data management solutions. As the inventors of the first networked storage appliance,[1] NetApp has a reputation in the industry for providing both innovation and simplicity, which is a key competitive differentiator. A team of Cooper visual designers, led by Nate Fortin and Nick Myers, has been

1. http://www.netapp.com/us/company/leadership/strategic-direction.html.

Framework

working with NetApp to define a visual language for its applications that conveys the following experience attributes:

— **Complexity, simplified:** Two-word experience attributes of this sort are unusual, but this tension is an essential part of the NetApp brand platform. Simplicity alone might imply *simplistic*, which would be problematic in a powerful tool.

— **Brilliant:** NetApp provides intuitive, innovative solutions. *Innovative* is not a great experience attribute because it has no particular visual qualities associated with it; *brilliant* evokes sharp contrasts and a bit of sparkle.

— **Mature:** At the same time, NetApp makes stable, high-quality products, not untested technology that's likely to fail. *Mature* exists in

tension with *brilliant*; it implies a certain quiet orderliness and perhaps a bit of conservatism in visual style.

— **Empowering:** This is another slightly unusual experience attribute; how does one depict a product as empowering? The obvious choice here would have been *powerful*, but this can be intimidating. Although they drew on visual patterns that embody power, the team chose *empowering* as a reminder that all of this power must serve the persona; ultimately, it must make *him* feel powerful.

Figure 18.6 represents *complexity, simplified*. The somber, graduated blues, which relate to the dominant identity color, are reminiscent of looking into increasingly deep water. Coupled with the small, sans-serif type and crisp, graph-paper-like

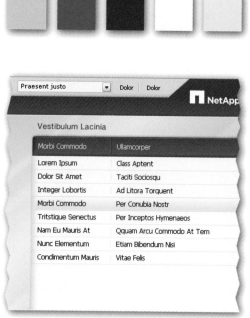

Figure 18.6. Complexity, simplified.

Framework

background of the chart, they visually imply the depth and precision one would expect from a powerful, complex IT tool. These qualities are balanced by the neat, plain rectangles, which are unornamented except for the slight softening of the corners, and by the touch of bright color that helps imply simplicity. The sharp, white line on the graph and the slight highlights on the colored bars add just a touch of brilliant sparkle, without being so bright as to seem immature.

Figure 18.7 emphasizes *brilliant*, which is associated with clarity, bright light, and sparkling highlights and reflections. The palette in this study uses plenty of white. Notice how the amount of white in the gradients makes some elements, such as the blue selection highlight on the right, almost luminous. The colored stripe on the selected tab at the top left has a strong highlight, making it look nearly metallic. The basically rectangular elements are softened further with greater rounding on the corners. The line on the graph is done in bright yellow to add a bit of liveliness. The graph-paper background is still there, but downplayed; along with the small type and substantial amounts of gray, it still indicates that for all its bright sparkle, this application is no simple toy.

Each study emphasizes a single experience attribute.

Framework

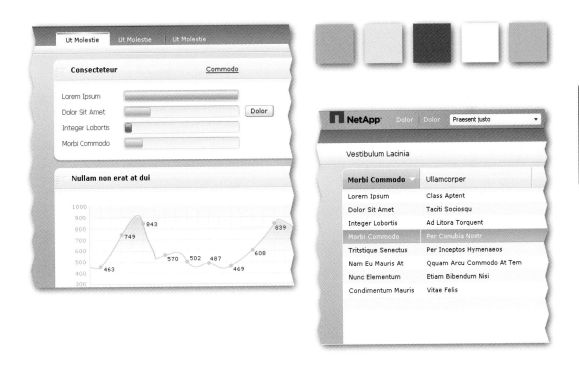

Figure 18.7. Brilliant.

The secondary attributes should not be entirely absent from any study.

Figure 18.8 represents *mature*, which is associated with dark, sober, desaturated colors such as gray or navy blue. One would expect a mature professional to be crisp and decisive, hence the sharp, square corners on the elements of this study. However, maturity taken to extremes could be seen as static or rigid—one reason the designer added the angle on the tab at the upper left, which is repeated in the colored bars below it. Lest the palette become too drab, he also added a bit of bright color on the bars and in the narrow, cyan stripe near the top of the tab. After showing it to another designer, however, he realized that the bright color and was a bit much to seem entirely mature and that the color was too flat to be brilliant. The strong, purely decorative elements, such as the cyan line, also seemed at odds with simplification.

Figure 18.9 is a second, more successful take on *mature*. This version uses a slightly darker gray background. It retains the sharp corners as well as the angled elements to avoid becoming too static. Instead of the flat, saturated colors, the bars are rendered in softer, almost translucent tints with sparkling white highlights on the edges. The heavy, navy blue selection highlight is brightened so it does not conflict with the softer colors.

Figure 18.8. Mature, version 1.

Figure 18.10 is focused on *empowering*, and nothing says *power* like black and dark gray, which are plentiful in this study. It's possible to have a touch of brilliance even with all these dark shades; the subtle gradients on many elements stop just short of making them look metallic. Similarly, the tan used in the selection highlight and some text is almost (but not quite) golden. At the upper left, a set of angled black "vents" echoes the industrial design language of NetApp's powerful hardware.

The study in Figure 18.11 tries to do a little bit of each. The dark gray bar along the top implies power. The almost-sharp corners and simple rectangular elements, along with much of the color palette, imply maturity and simplicity. The highlights on the colored bars still add a touch of brilliant sparkle. However, this study expresses none of these particularly clearly. Of the set, it is the least successful at communicating the strategy—a logical choice for the team to eliminate before presenting to the client, unless they wanted to illustrate what not having an emphasis looks like.

Studies that don't emphasize one attribute are usually less successful.

Framework

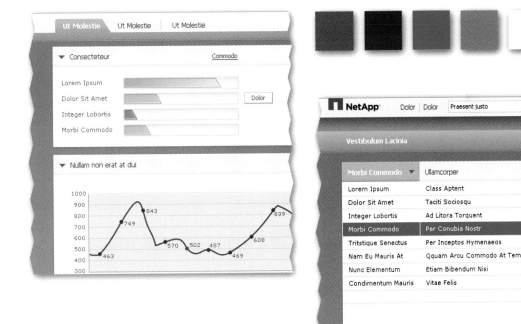

Figure 18.9. Mature, version 2.

507

Figure 18.10. Empowering.

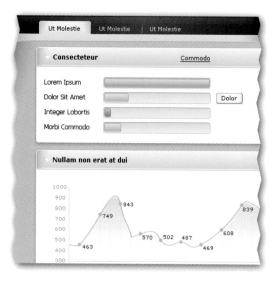

Figure 18.11. A little bit of each.

Example: Executive Telephone

The following studies by visual designer Daniel Kuo and industrial designers Michael Voege and Chris Weeldreyer are focused on a single architecture for an executive telephone that incorporates touch-screen interaction with a directory, voicemail, and call management. You saw some of the early ideation for this device in Table 16.6. These experience attributes guide the studies:

— **Exceptional:** Although it must be reasonable to build with existing technology, everything about the design has to say it's a quality product. It needs to be the sort of thing an executive would want to show off and anyone would want to use—professional, but an object of desire all the same. Related words include unique, elite, advanced, sleek, and inspired.

— **Trustworthy:** Companies expect their phone systems to be more like furniture than computers: long-lasting and reliable. Our primary persona, a project manager named Scott, would be impatient with a telephone that crashed or made him look stupid. This implies a sense of solidity and quality in fit and finish, along with straightforward visual communication. Related words include professional, efficient, and competent.

— **Approachable:** A telephone must be a simple appliance that anyone can walk up to and use the first time. Some executive phones look complex enough to control a nuclear power plant. Although this phone will rely heavily on a touch screen, it still has to look familiar, helpful, and inviting.

Let's take a look at how the hardware and software studies depict these qualities. Although stakeholders would initially see the hardware and software studies separately before seeing them integrated, they're shown together here to illustrate how the on-screen visual design relates to the hardware design.

Figure 18.12 leans toward the *exceptional* attribute. The visual designer and industrial designer both used crisp, angular lines and a strong geometric layout grid that imply a certain precision and attention to detail. The black and dark gray of the hardware and visual design are solid, businesslike colors, but with a more modern edge than reliable navy blue would have. The black implies depth and power. The on-screen gradients give certain elements a sleek, glossy finish that mirrors the smooth black surface of the phone. The bright yellowish-green selection highlights on the screen seem futuristic and high-tech; the dark, neutral palette allows the color to shine in an almost jewel-like manner.

Stakeholders need to see how the physical and visual expressions of the design language relate to one another.

Framework

Figure 18.12. Exceptional.

The aluminum parts on the body of the phone and the handset frame the product almost as if it were a work of art. A visible groove between the front surface and the aluminum edge makes the body of the phone seem to float within its frame.

The overall effect leans a little toward being cold; if this phone were an executive assistant, it would wear a fashionably tailored suit and have every hair in place. The two rounded hardware controls and the slightly rounded corners on the tabs and action button on the screen soften the look just a little and keep it from being entirely unapproachable.

Figure 18.13 is more *approachable*. The form is more familiar and solid. Due to its sharp contrast with the material of the phone's body, the substantial metal bezel surrounding the touch screen calls attention to the most unusual aspect of the product. The brushed aluminum material choice implies both quality and solidity through its appearance and tactile properties. The scale of this element also adds a sense of mass, reinforcing

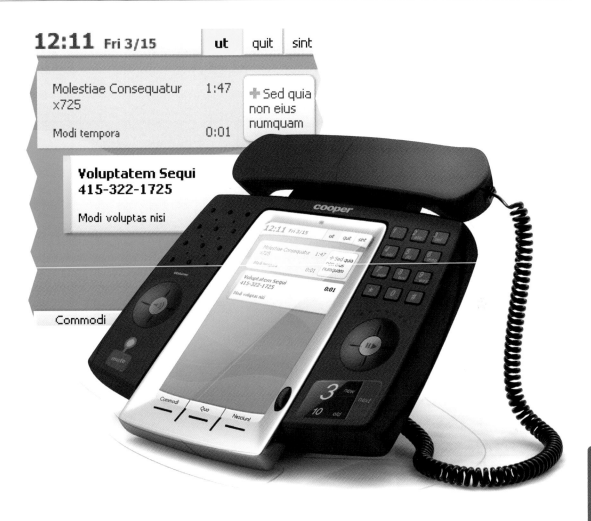

Figure 18.13. Approachable.

that this is a reliable device, though the slight curvature to the bezel and body of the phone, as well as the material contrast, add a dynamic quality and keep it from seeming overwhelmingly massive. The rest of the body is rendered in a dark gray matte finish on its face, which is both professional and familiar; glossy black in combination with the aluminum bezel would be too cold to promote the approachable nature of the phone.

You might imagine an approachable executive assistant as organized but cheerful, with personal touches like trinkets and photos of the kids on her desk. The rounded corners and yellow highlights in the visual design study (echoed in the voicemail indicator on the phone's body) embody that cheery friendliness. The subtly patterned green background is distinctive; it draws the eye and tempts the viewer to touch it. It's easy to imagine enhancing this effect by making the waves undulate in a barely noticeable way when the device is not in use. The controls at top and bottom unify the design language by echoing the curvature and color of the hardware bezel.

Figure 18.14 focuses on being *trustworthy*, but is also more *approachable* than the first study. The overall form of the device looks heavier than in the other two studies, both due to its form and the absence of the strongly contrasted aluminum parts, though the dark base still makes the face of the device appear to float. The lighter material and the uplifted screen promote a sense of openness. The form is simple; the integrated

cradle for the handset creates a less-complex outline at the top of the phone. The overall effect says there's no hidden complexity here. The volume and voicemail-playback controls are implemented as chunky yet precise-looking knobs, which provides a greater sense of both solidity and control than the more delicate, dished controls in the other studies.

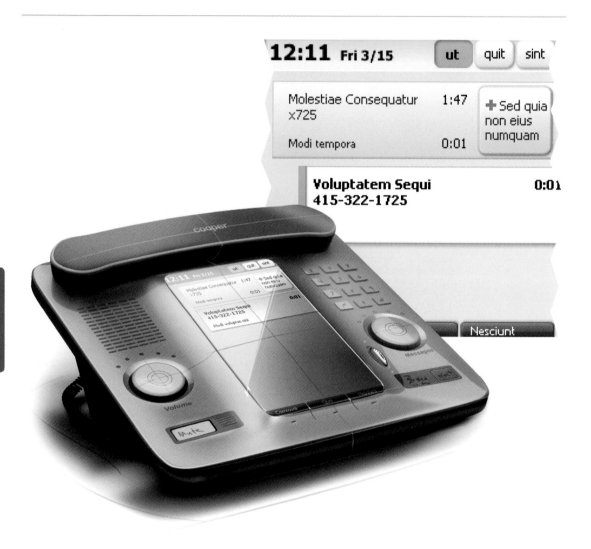

Figure 18.14. Trustworthy.

The lighter visual design palette and matte texture are businesslike yet open, likewise creating a sense that what you see is what you get. While the first study is a bit of a show-off, this one says, "I'm just sitting here waiting to do my job." The additional rounded buttons and bright yellow highlights add an air of approachability. *Exceptional* is downplayed this study; as an executive assistant, this phone would wear practical clothes and be quiet, competent, and helpful.

Project Management for Design Language Exploration

The activities described in this chapter generally take anywhere from a few days to two weeks, though it is certainly possible to spend more time, especially for consumer products for which style is an essential selling point. One or two visual designers usually spend a couple of days on the first round of studies, with an internal review on the second day and a day or two of refinement after that. A single industrial design study can take a few days or even more, depending on the level of detail.

Interaction between the visual and industrial designers—and with the rest of the design team—is essential both before studies begin and once a first round of studies has been created, especially since the two sets of studies need to converge. Once the entire team is satisfied with the studies, they can be presented to the appropriate stakeholders, as discussed in Chapter 19.

If you are designing new hardware and have easy access to your stakeholders, you can either develop the design language using a generic volume, or have a formal meeting about the platform/architecture and interaction framework possibilities first to narrow the directions before you delve into the design language. If you must travel to present your framework and design language, though, you will probably find it more efficient to present everything at once.

Summary

An effective design language cannot simply be a matter of taste. To ensure that the product ultimately emphasizes the qualities that are most important to the brand, you must help stakeholders assess aesthetic choices in light of how effectively they express those attributes. Rather than shooting in the dark by coming up with a range of random styles, focus your efforts on studies that emphasize one attribute at a time. Even though the final design probably won't be exactly like any of the studies, the conversation the studies stimulate will help ensure that the final design language speaks clearly and appropriately.

Framework

CHAPTER 19

Communicating the Framework and Design Language

As soon as you're confident in the design direction(s) you've developed, it's time to share them with the entire product team. There are two primary objectives for communication at this point. One is to see whether stakeholders identify any problems or opportunities you may have missed, so you (and they) know you're working on a viable direction. The other is to achieve consensus about one direction and build enthusiasm for it—this meeting is your best chance to be a cheerleader for the design. This is no easy task; many organizations get stuck in analysis paralysis or try idea after idea because they fail to make a real commitment to one direction.

Getting that commitment nearly always requires presenting the design at a single meeting of all stakeholders, so they can all see the design together and discuss its implications. At Cooper, we call this the "design vision" meeting, but you could call it a concept review or whatever other term serves your purpose. This kind of formal communication is critical because it facilitates shared understanding, expectations, and commitment among product team members as no other method can (see Chapter 13).

However, sharing early concepts is tricky. Stakeholders are anxious to see design, but they're not necessarily practiced at consuming design work in progress or assessing the appropriateness of a solution that isn't entirely concrete. There are many questions you can't answer yet. If stakeholders don't understand the design or its value, you may be forced to dump a worthwhile direction and start over. Worse, stakeholders could lose faith in you or in the design process. However, these things are unlikely to happen if you're well prepared and thoughtful in your communication.

Although a formal presentation is usually important, there are only a couple of circumstances that make more extensive documentation worthwhile. Many large organizations use an incremental funding model for projects; budget is approved up to a certain point, but progress and plans are subject to review by an executive committee before further funding is released. If you can't get committee members to attend a meeting because your project doesn't have sufficient visibility, you'll need to give them documentation that can be persuasive on its own. A document may also be a good idea if you have a large or geographically distributed product team whose members won't all be attending the meeting or watching remotely.

Preparing Stakeholders for the Meeting

Don't rely on stakeholders understanding the design without explanation; help them connect the dots.

Anyone who participated in stakeholder interviews probably needs to attend the design vision meeting. Work with your project owner to determine whether there are any new stakeholders who also need to be involved. Get this meeting on everyone's calendar well in advance, since it can take several weeks before a busy executive has a large enough time slot—typically two to three hours. It's often better to postpone the meeting than to have it without all parties present or able to teleconference in, since lack of consensus will likely cause an even bigger delay. Whenever possible, avoid presenting to managers who then brief the executives separately; no one else will be able to answer questions or sell the design as effectively as the design team can. Instead, show the managers the design first so they're comfortable before you have a second meeting where you present to the executives and managers together.

Send stakeholders a note a day or two before the meeting reminding them of the time commitment, what to expect, and what you need from them. This kind of note is sometimes more effective coming from the project owner. Here's an example:

> The design team is excited to show you our work in progress for PurchasePro on Wednesday. We'll be starting in the main conference room at 9:00 Pacific. Come early to make sure you get a bagel! Teleconference information is attached at the end of the message for those dialing in.
>
> We'll be reviewing work in progress for both interaction and visual design. We'll outline the main screens and navigation, and then walk through a couple of high-level scenario storyboards to illustrate the flow. We'll also present a few approaches to the visual design emphasizing different aspects of the experience strategy. The ideas are far from complete, and it's not unusual if they need some adjustment at this stage.
>
> What we'll be asking from you is:
>
> 1. **Your attendance for the entire meeting.** We'll be discussing the future of our product and trying to reach consensus on our direction at the end of the meeting, so it's important that everyone be present.
>
> 2. **Your honest feedback.** Does the design accomplish what's necessary in a way that appeals to our audience and that we can build in a reasonable amount of time? We won't be asking the engineering team for any specific commitments—we

just need to know if anything looks like a problem *so far.* We also need people to voice questions and concerns in the meeting where others can hear them.

3. **Your patience.** This is very much a work in progress. We wouldn't be showing you the design if we weren't confident in it, but there will be many questions we can't answer yet.

4. **Your agreement** about how to move forward from this point.

If you anticipate needing to make specific trade-off decisions, forecast that in your e-mail, too. Ask the design engineer(s) to investigate any unusual components or complex behaviors ahead of time so they're prepared to discuss the ramifications.

Catch up with any new stakeholders in advance. Ask them to review your user and domain analysis document or presentation—better yet, offer a brief encore presentation of that material. The design vision meeting will go more smoothly if everyone is up to speed on the personas and the problems you're trying to solve.

Enlist your project owner in preparing stakeholders privately for any politically difficult issues, such as an executive's pet idea that's not incorporated in the solution or a concept that deviates significantly from what you think the product team is expecting to see. Executives hate to be surprised in public.

Crafting the Story

The design vision meeting could be based on a set of whiteboard sketches if you have an informal culture and stakeholders who are accustomed to design reviews, but a formal presentation is usually most effective both because it lends weight to what you're saying, and because a slide show makes it easier to walk through scenarios and the

design language studies. In either case, spend some time crafting the narrative. Like an attorney making a case to a jury, you don't want to rely on people seeing the evidence and drawing the right conclusions; for your argument to be compelling, you have to help them connect the dots. As you may have learned once upon a time in a writing class: Tell stakeholders what they're going to see, show it to them, and then explain what they just saw (and why it's good). Also revisit the tips for creating effective presentations in Chapter 13.

Decide on your narrative structure as a team. A typical agenda (and document structure, if applicable) for a **single-interface product** goes something like this; numbers are provided as examples only.

— Briefly summarize project tasks and timeline to date (two to three slides)

— Set expectations for the presentation (one or two slides)

— Review key personas and requirements (three to six slides)

— Introduce the big ideas and major anatomy for your first platform/interaction framework (three or four slides each for hardware, software, and other big ideas)

— Show how it works using scenario storyboards (one slide per major state)

— Revisit anatomy (including data object models, information architecture, process models, or any other underlying organizational concepts) in more detail (a few slides per topic)

— Summarize how the design serves each persona's needs (one slide per persona)

— Repeat major anatomy, storyboards, details, and benefits for each platform/interaction framework

— Have a discussion about form and behavior (including pros and cons of each direction, if you have several) now or after the design language

Framework

Explain the big ideas, tell a story, and then review any details.

— Review the experience attributes (four to ten slides)

— Introduce the design language studies and rationale (a slide introducing what studies are, one slide per study, one slide showing all studies together for comparison and discussion)

— Discuss and get agreement on direction and next steps (not focused on slides)

Though this outline is described in terms of a product, the structure of a presentation for a **service design** is much the same—explain the big idea(s), tell a story, and then review whatever details you've worked out so far.

When you're describing **multiple interfaces** for multiple primary personas, such as for a complex enterprise application, it generally works best to cover common interface components in brief, then reintroduce each persona followed by the functional explanation and scenarios specific to her interface. The resulting outline looks more like this:

— Briefly summarize project tasks and timeline to date

— Set expectations for the presentation

— Review persona set in brief

— Review *shared* requirements

— Introduce the big ideas and major anatomy of *shared* components

— *Review primary persona #1 and key secondaries*

— Describe any *unique data objects and product anatomy* for this persona

— Show how the design works using scenario storyboards

— Revisit anatomy and other key concepts in more detail

— Summarize how the design serves this persona's needs

— *Repeat persona overview, unique data objects and anatomy, scenarios, details, and benefits for additional primary personas*

— Have a discussion about form and behavior now or after the design language

— Review the experience attributes

— Introduce the design language studies and rationale

— Discuss and get agreement on direction and next steps

518

If you're showing multiple architectures and/or interaction frameworks, introduce each one briefly; present more detail and a scenario or two for each, much as you would for each primary persona. If time during this phase permits, you might also show a more advanced rendering of the design language, such as a visual-design-archetype screen or somewhat-detailed foam model of the hardware (see Chapter 22).

Each of these steps is broken down in the following sections.

Project summary and expectations

The main points of your project summary should include:

- Agenda and meeting logistics (break times, etc.)
- Project mandate, timeline, and overall approach
- Review of decisions made in the user and domain analysis meeting
- What the framework is and isn't
- What you need from stakeholders in this meeting

As discussed in Chapter 13, a brief review of your mandate, your timeline, and your approach to the project serves as a useful reminder for continuing stakeholders and a brief but important introduction for any new ones. This content isn't usually worth more than half-a-dozen slides. It's also useful to review decisions made by the stakeholder group in the previous meeting. This won't forestall someone truly determined to revisit past decisions, but does at least remind most people why you designed for a particular platform or chose not to focus on a particular persona. Follow this summary with a slide or two explaining what to expect from the meeting; this is probably much like what you put in your pre-meeting e-mail.

Review key personas and requirements

The essential points to cover about personas and requirements include:

- What personas are and why they're useful
- Overview of the set
- Review of detail about key personas
- Review of key requirements agreed upon for each persona

> Reminding stakeholders of past decisions helps prevent unnecessary rehashing.

Framework

Personas are the basis for your argument that this design is good. Unless all of the stakeholders were present at the user and domain analysis discussion, add a couple of slides about what personas are, how they're derived from behavior patterns in the research, and why they're useful. Consider inserting these slides anyway and skipping them in the meeting if they're not necessary; leaving them in allows for surprise guests and helps future readers understand what they're seeing.

Reuse the persona set overview slide from your last presentation, but don't go into detail about every persona—stakeholders are itching to see design. Instead, just recap the key details for each primary and any important secondaries. For a multi-interface tool, review which interfaces are associated with which personas, but save the detail about each important persona for the introduction to the appropriate interface. See Table 19.1 for an example of how you can quickly cover the key points.

Table 19.1. **Reviewing the essentials about personas.**

What the slide shows	What the presenter says
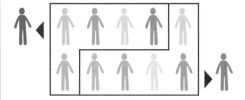	For those who have recently joined the product team, personas are user archetypes that represent the user behavior patterns we saw in our field research. Focusing the design on the personas helps keep us true to the data and avoid basing decisions on personal opinion. That's why you'll hear us referring to the personas throughout this discussion.
	As you know, we introduced six personas in our last meeting, including Maureen Keller and Amanda Lee, a vet and a technician in a large practice, and Pete Harvey, a vet in a small practice. Tina Lopez and Carol Martin are the office manager and the receptionist in Maureen's practice, and Laura Brown plays both roles in Pete's practice.

What the slide shows	What the presenter says

They need two distinct interfaces

Clinical

Maureen Keller
DVM

Amanda Lee
Vet Tech

Pete Harvey
DVM

Administrative

Laura Brown
Office mgr & receptionist

Tina Lopez
Office manager

Carol Martin
Receptionist

The clinicians and office staff have distinct enough needs to require two different interfaces. Maureen is the primary persona for the clinical interface, which Pete and Amanda also use. Laura is primary for the administrative UI, and Carol and Tina are secondary.

[A few slides introducing shared components] — [description of shared components]

Laura Brown, administrative primary

Goals:
- Stay calm
- Keep clients and clinical staff happy
- Keep track of all details

Needs:
- Appointments and billing
- Instant access to client info
- A way to stay oriented and avoid half-done tasks

You might recall that Laura's goals are to stay calm in a chaotic environment, keep clients and clinical staff from getting upset, and keep track of all the details. Her interface has to help her handle appointments, client records, and bills. She needs the right data immediately when a client calls. She's constantly getting interrupted, so it has to help her stay oriented and not leave tasks half finished. So, let's look at how we can help with that.

Framework

There's no need to review every single requirement for each persona; just spend a slide or so on the key issues, especially any that were controversial in the previous meeting. You might review the experience attributes at this point if they played a big role in defining the architecture(s) or interaction framework(s), but it's usually better to revisit these immediately before showing the design language studies later on.

Introduce the big ideas and major anatomy

For each distinct platform and/or interaction framework, your main points should include:

- Any "Aha!" ideas that challenge the status quo
- Overview of the platform, if applicable (relate to personas as needed)

— Brief discussion of any data objects requiring explanation (limit to shared objects if you have multiple primary personas)

— Overview of key screens, idioms, and interaction flow (limit to shared components if you have multiple primary personas)

Not every design solution involves a big "Aha!" but if yours does, you'll want to explain it early on to get people used to the idea of a totally new data structure, input method, or other big change. Explain how you came to the new solution and what it enables. Note that you might want to describe any necessary data objects before you get into a discussion of multiple potential platforms, since data objects are consistent across platforms. For an example, see Table 19.2, which shows how a design team might introduce the big idea for a gardening Web site.

Table 19.2. **Introducing the big idea.**

What the slide shows	What the presenter says
Ella Frasier  **Goals:** — Be creative — Make her garden beautiful — Enjoy a relaxing hobby **Needs to:** — Select plants that work in her climate — Know how to take care of her plants — Control when plants arrive	As you may recall from the user and domain analysis, one of the biggest frustrations for Ella, our average gardener persona, wasn't about the online store at all. She has only a vague idea of how to care for her plants and doesn't have much time to learn more, so she gets frustrated when her plants get diseases and pests, or just don't thrive.
What Ella values Her local garden center provides easy access to expert advice (but not quite enough of it) 	So, in addition to thinking about improvements to navigation and such, we thought about what Ella values most in her local garden center: the advice of the master gardener who works there. So, without having her talk to a person, how can we provide advice that goes beyond what she can get at her local nursery?

What the slide shows	What the presenter says

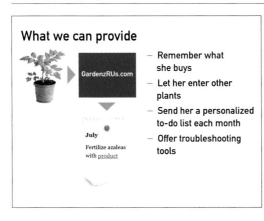

The design we're about to show you includes a new service that aims to fill this need: proactive gardening advice. If we remember every plant Ella buys from the Web site and let her enter information about her existing garden, we can send her timely information about when to prune and fertilize, or even whether she's choosing plants that are all appropriate to her climate conditions.

EXPLAIN FORM FACTOR(S) AND RATIONALE

If you're showing both hardware and behavior, introduce the hardware and its key controls and components (independent of design language) first, then explain the interaction framework and scenarios appropriate to that platform. If you are presenting several platforms and/or architectures, make a clear recommendation as to which you believe is the best choice (and why). Use it as a comparison point for the others, discussing what is gained and lost with each. If you are presenting a single platform or architecture, be honest about its challenges but focus on selling its virtues. Briefly mention other possibilities you explored and why you discarded them so stakeholders understand that you don't have a one-track mind. For example, see the introduction of the executive phone design in Table 19.3.

Table 19.3. **Form factor rationale.**

What the slide shows	What the presenter says

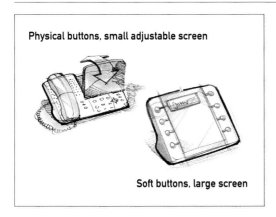

We considered several options for the office phone platform. A small screen with multiple hardware buttons would not be much of an improvement over current units, so we didn't spend any time on it. A larger LCD with soft keys would be an improvement, but offers limited flexibility and a cluttered look.

Continued

What the slide shows	What the presenter says
	The platform we're designing for includes a large touch screen because it offers very direct manipulation of calls. We think you'll see why this is good when we walk you through the scenarios. It also offers Scott a way to make calls right from a directory, since most of his calls are to known numbers. We're using a portrait orientation because that's better for displaying lists, such as a directory or list of messages.
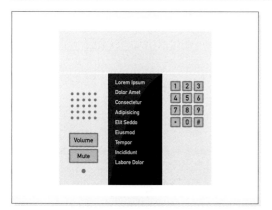	We've included a physical keypad because not all of Scott's calls are initiated from the directory, and the tactile nature of physical buttons makes them less error prone and more satisfying. We've included physical controls for volume and mute for the same reason. These are grouped with the speaker and microphone so that all sound manipulation lives together.
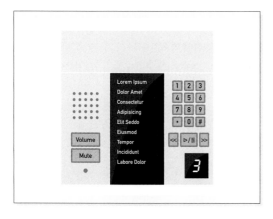	We've also included a small display that shows the number of voicemail messages. We could use the large screen for this, but it would consume a lot of electricity to keep that on at all times, and it's useful for Scott to walk into the office and see at a glance how much voicemail is waiting. We've added physical controls for message playback partly because these are easier from an ergonomic standpoint. Also, we can reuse these controls and the small voicemail display on lower-end phones without the large screen, which provides a repeated element to help unify the product family.

What the slide shows	What the presenter says
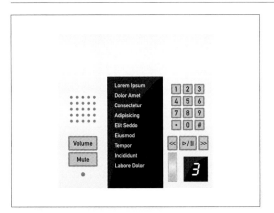	A scroll wheel next to the screen helps navigate long lists, prevents Scott's hand from blocking the screen as he scrolls, and can also be repeated on units without touch screens.
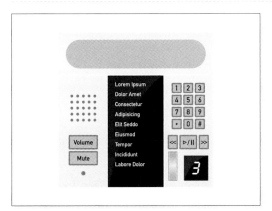	The handset is located at the top of the phone because this creates a smaller foot-print on Scott's desk. A handset along the side would likely block his view of or access to the screen at some point, and this arrangement is equally good for left-handed and right-handed people. It also serves to distinguish the phone from anyone else in the market.

INTRODUCE BASIC INTERACTION DESIGN ANATOMY

When you introduce the interaction framework, briefly list any data objects that require definition, and then introduce your key screens. Describe how users navigate from screen to screen, as well as any distinct states or major divisions of real estate within each view. Focus on explaining rectangles and relationships, not widgets. Stakeholders will have more patience for detail after they've seen a couple of storyboards and understood the gestalt of the design. For an example, see Figure 19.1, which explains part of the interaction framework that designers Tim McCoy, Lane Halley, Daniel Kuo, and David Fore developed for Cross Country TravCorps, a Web application for traveling nurses and other temporary health care professionals. For this first look, the presenter doesn't need to say much more than is shown on the slides.

Framework

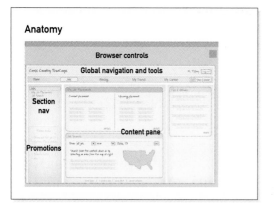

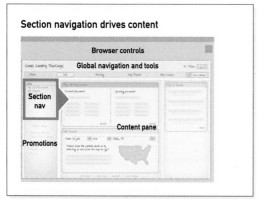

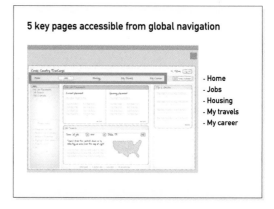

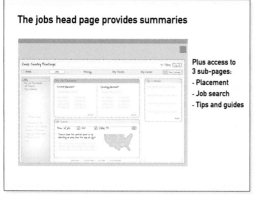

Figure 19.1. Introducing the interaction design anatomy.

Illustrating the interaction framework

One of the more challenging aspects of communicating your interaction framework is getting your

sketches at the right level of detail. Stakeholders need to see some amount of example screen content to understand what they're looking at, but can be distracted by excessive detail that isn't well thought out. Also, if you represent the interaction design in a way that looks too polished, your audience will assume that the thinking behind the design is as complete as its visual rendition, or will focus on the fact that they don't like how your buttons look. Sketches that look "sketchy" keep the focus on structure and flow, while silently reminding stakeholders that this is only a work in progress. As a general rule, portray only the elements necessary to communicate your key path scenarios—gloss over the rest. These guidelines can help you develop sketches at the right level:

— **Use colors and typefaces that are clearly unrealistic.** Stakeholders are unlikely to view pencil lines and a script font as anything but a placeholder. Don't make it look hideous, though, or stakeholders will react negatively to that.

— **Use scribbles, gray bars, or nonsense text** in most places. Scribbles are fast to render and look more sketchy than fake Latin text.

— **Use empty squares to indicate "some buttons or fields go here."**

— **Avoid using realistic-looking objects**, such as actual photos in an interface sketch for a photo manager.

— **Work at realistic resolution, but avoid working in pixels.** Photoshop seems to encourage a focus on rendering. Instead, consider using hand sketches or vector-based tools such as Illustrator or PowerPoint.

At Cooper, we use a "pencil sketch" style template that designers John Dunning, Berm Lee, and Nate Fortin created for Adobe Fireworks, which is our usual drawing tool. Unlike PowerPoint or Illustrator, which many designers use for initial sketches, Fireworks combines the capabilities of both vector and raster-based image creation. This means the template gives us a realistic idea of what we can fit on the screen because it is based on pixel dimensions, yet it allows us to create images with the speed of a vector application and without obsessing over pixels. Having a style template also ensures a sketchy-but-neat look and keeps visually inclined interaction designers from getting sidetracked into detailed rendering. Figure 19.2 illustrates this using interaction designer Tim McCoy's sketch for Cross Country's job search page.

Of course, if you're doing a fairly simple revision of an interface with an established visual style, it can be a waste of time to step backward into sketch renderings rather than just using the components you already have. In that case, though, your thinking is probably more solid because you're working on more narrowly defined problems, so the more concrete representation isn't as problematic.

The visual representation of your design should be no more polished than the thinking behind it.

Framework

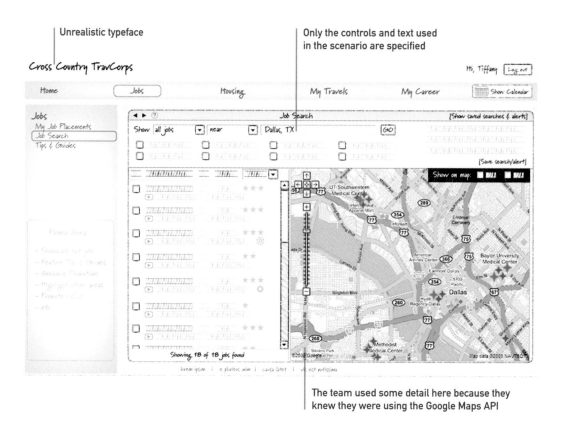

Figure 19.2. Example of an appropriate framework sketch.

Why to separate functional explanation from scenarios

Although the scenarios are essential to explaining the design, it's generally best to separate them from functional explanation; combining the two is problematic because it clutters up the scenario and interferes with telling a simple, compelling story about the persona using the product. Functional explanation is also less clear when sprinkled throughout a story. Separating the two requires a few more words but makes for far more effective communication. Compare these two approaches, for example:

Less effective: Scenario and explanation combined

Carrie turns on her mobile phone and presses this hardware button, which is for the contacts list. There are three other buttons: one for the calendar, one for the to-do list, and one for the main menu. The contacts list contains everything she's loaded from her PC's contacts, plus manual entries. She scrolls through it to "Brad Smith," which is filed under B. She could also type in the name using the keypad to search. She selects Brad and the phone dials his mobile number. She can set a default number for each contact, or she can she can scroll down to select the number she wants.

Framework

More effective: Scenario and explanation separated

There are four hardware buttons: contacts, calendar, to-do list, and main menu. The contact list contains everything she's loaded from her PC's contacts, plus manual entries. It's possible to access names by scrolling through the list, which is sorted alphabetically by first or last name, or by typing in a couple of letters, which presents a shorter list of possible matches. There's a default number for each contact, which is what the phone dials when the name is selected; Carrie can also pick another number by scrolling down and selecting it.

Here's how it works: Carrie turns on her phone and presses the contact button. She sees the list, which she's sorted alphabetically by first name. She scrolls through to Brad Smith and selects his name. The phone dials his mobile number.

> Provide a basic functional explanation first; this helps keep people oriented during the scenarios.

For most products, it works best to provide at least a bit of basic functional explanation first, particularly where you're introducing novel structures or idioms; this helps keep people oriented during the scenarios. Show a sketch or two and point out important components and their functions; *then* tell the story. Don't get bogged down in details before the story, though, or you'll lose your audience.

It can work to present scenarios before functional explanation if the interface structure is very simple or familiar, but this is seldom effective for complex applications. If you go this route, consider revisiting your scenarios after the functional explanation so people understand what they're seeing.

Show how it works using scenario storyboards

Your description of the scenarios should include:

— A reminder of what scenarios are and why they're useful
— Individual key path scenarios illustrated with storyboards

As in the user and domain analysis (see Chapter 13), the scenarios are your opportunity to get stakeholders out of the analytical frame of mind and into the heads of users. Scenarios demonstrate the simplicity and power of your design in a way that more-abstract discussions of structure and behavior cannot. Start with a reminder that scenarios are high-level, idealized descriptions of typical interactions from the personas' points of view, and that you have deliberately avoided focusing on edge cases. See Table 19.4 for an example using the Cross Country framework.

Framework

Table 19.4. Illustrated key path scenario example.

What the slide shows	What the presenter says
 **Christine looks for her next assignment** ICU Nurse 8 years experience, 3 traveling Christine's goals — Balance job, money, and location — Get the best package — Visit her boyfriend when possible **She has a few minutes free, so she logs in to see if there's a good assignment near her boyfriend in Dallas.**	To show you how job search works, let's look at how Christine finds her next assignment. She has a few minutes free, so she logs in.
Christine looks for "all jobs near Dallas, TX" 	On the home page, she starts by looking for jobs near Dallas, where her boyfriend lives.
She refines her search on the job search page 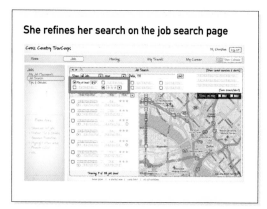	The job search page opens up with a big set of results. Christine refines the results by looking for at least $30 an hour at a highly rated facility.

What the slide shows	What the presenter says
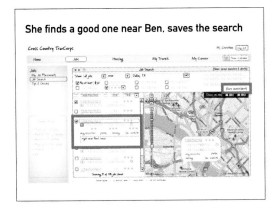	She looks through the positions. She looks at the position details and the map, then marks a couple of interesting positions, including one that's really close to Ben's house. Christine decides to save this search in case anything else crops up later.
	She names the search "near Ben" and sets an alert so she'll get e-mail if any new jobs match her criteria.
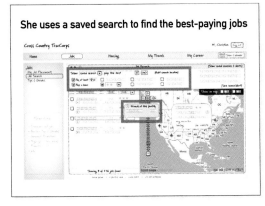	The job near Ben is interesting, but she also needs to pay off a hefty credit card balance, so Christine uses a previously saved search to see where the best-paying jobs are. She sees four around the country that meet her criteria. An icon on the Arizona listing shows she has a friend on assignment at the facility. She hovers over it and sees that's Lara. It would be fun to work with Lara again, and the job looks interesting.

Continued

What the slide shows	What the presenter says

She wonders if the dates will work for her, so she opens up the calendar widget. Yes, the dates look good.

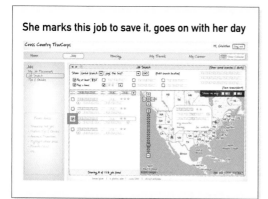

Christine marks the job for later reference, then goes on with her day. She has to think about this. She'll call Lara later on.

After talking with Lara, Christine decides she's probably most interested in the Arizona job, so she logs in again and searches for previously marked jobs.

What the slide shows	What the presenter says
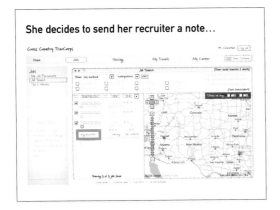	She looks over the details again and decides the Arizona job is definitely the one, so she decides to send her recruiter a note.
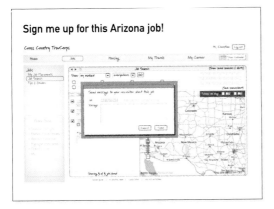	She tells her recruiter that as long as she can get the housing allowance she wants, she's interested.

Putting at least a title on each slide—such as "Christine logs in"—can help you remember where you are when you're presenting the scenario. Adding a callout or circling the relevant parts of the screen is useful for any remote participants who can't see where you're pointing, as well as for anyone who reads the slides later. Including the full scenario text on every slide is distracting, makes the screen image harder to see, and can make your presentation seem stilted if you read it word-for-word. However, since presentations usually have a surprisingly long life, it's useful to paste the scenario steps into the notes area of the presentation so people looking at this a year from now will know what your screen sketches mean.

There's usually no need to come up with brand-new communication scenarios—stick with the key path scenarios that evolved from the context scenarios unless these are somewhat long and convoluted. Break up lengthy scenarios into more digestible chunks as long as the resulting scenarios are still realistic. If you're working in a complex domain, have a subject matter expert review your scenarios before you present them; you don't want stakeholders looking at your screen and saying, "The patient would be dead if she took those two medications together! Isn't the application going to be smarter than that?"

Framework

Focus your detailed discussion on novel or critical interactions.

Be careful to paste each screen image in the same spot on the slide at exactly the same size; otherwise, the screen will appear to jump around in a distracting way as you flip through the scenario slides.

When to go beyond storyboards

Animated demos can be expensive to produce and are unnecessary for describing most common interactions. However, for any interaction that relies on motion to communicate behavior, you may need to show a short animation. Unless you have plenty of time and budget, though, focus the animation just on the part of the interaction that needs it; you will probably find that producing an animation of the entire scenario requires more behavioral detail than you've had time to think through.

It's often sufficient to do a "poor designer's animation" using your presentation software. Just draw a picture of the screen without the elements that move to use as your "stage," then paste in the moving elements as separate images and use the PowerPoint or Keynote animation features to move them around. Fireworks can also create simple animations.

Revisit anatomy in more detail

Your coverage of more detailed anatomy should include:

— Any additional detail on navigation structure

— Contents of each screen

— Any novel or especially important behaviors

— Hardware architecture and functional elements

— Any technical or other challenges you anticipate

— Discussion of data objects and any additional process models if necessary

After you've shown stakeholders how things work, they're likely to have detailed questions about the design. Describe each physical control and other important component. Dive into each interaction in as much detail as you can. Describe the major divisions of real estate on each screen and the relationships between them. Don't spend time on every field and widget, especially since you haven't designed most of them yet, but do review any interactions that are novel, are critical to the design, or have major implications for implementation. These issues aren't always about UI—introducing new data objects can be a major issue if you're redesigning a legacy system. Crop and scale images as necessary to ensure that everyone looking at slides from across the room can see important details, as shown in Table 19.5.

Table 19.5. **Describing interaction detail.**

What the slide shows	What the presenter says
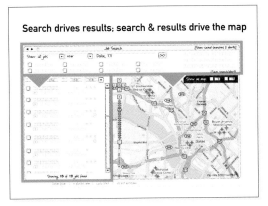	The job search page is a Google Maps mash-up that lets Christine find jobs that match certain criteria and see details about them. It has three functional areas: a set of filter controls, a results list, and a map.
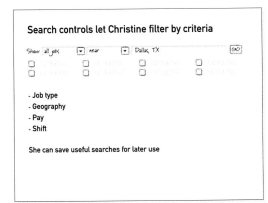	The filters drive the contents of the results list and map. Christine can select a specific result to see it displayed on the map.
 Search controls let Christine filter by criteria - Job type - Geography - Pay - Shift She can save useful searches for later use	The filter controls let Christine build queries in plain English. We need to spend some time on exactly how the controls work, but they should let her search based on where the jobs are, how they're rated, what kind of experience they'll give her, and how good the pay is. A series of checkboxes or other controls lets her narrow a search even more. Once she's built a search she finds useful, she can save it to use later.

Continued

What the slide shows	What the presenter says
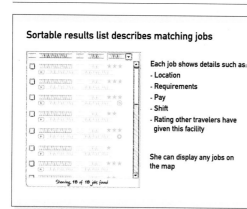 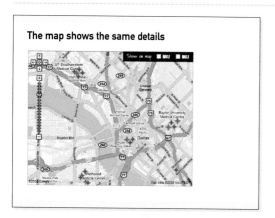	The results list shows the most critical information about each job, such as where it is, how much it pays, how other travelers have rated the facility, and whether she knows anyone working there. She can expand any job listing to see more about it, show it on the map, or select it to remember later. The map shows all of the results as pins, then shows the detail for a selected result in the map info window, which is what Google calls that little balloon.

If you're not confident in some part of the design, consider showing it with a disclaimer. Use phrases like "contents *include* …" or "options *such as* …" to reinforce that you have a lot of work yet to do.

Describe how the design serves persona needs

Main points for this portion of the presentation include:

— How the design accomplishes persona goals

— How the design serves other needs

Connect the dots for your stakeholders: Conclude either your scenarios or your description of the design with a slide or two highlighting how the design serves the personas' needs. How will it delight them? How does it address their goals? See Figure 19.3 for an example.

Also be sure to acknowledge any ways in which the design falls short of expectations or does not include a stakeholder's favorite idea, and provide an explanation for this before the question is asked (because it will be).

How we serve Ella's needs

— Help her select plants that work in her climate

— Let her find plants by size, color, bloom season, etc.

— Offer proactive advice specific to her plants and climate

— Help her diagnose and solve problems

— Give her control over shipping schedule

Figure 19.3. Describe how the design serves each persona.

Introduce the design language(s)

The main points for introducing the possible design language directions are:

— Revisit experience attributes

— Show hardware and software design language options

— Explain the rationale for each direction

— Guide stakeholders in focusing the strategy

As noted in Chapter 18, the design language is usually best discussed independent of form and function, because most stakeholders have a hard time focusing on one or the other when presented with both. The design language works best later in the presentation (unless it's the sole focus of the project) because stakeholders are typically most anxious about the product's basic form and behavior, so many would be impatient if you started with the more "touchy-feely" discussion of how to represent the desired experience attributes. Also, introducing the interaction design and platform/architecture directions first helps stakeholders keep this important context in mind as they assess the design language. Finally, because a well-executed design language operates on a more

emotional level, this can be a great opportunity to build enthusiasm about the overall design direction before you attempt to build consensus in the last part of the meeting.

Just as it's a good idea to remind stakeholders of the personas as the basis for your design of form and behavior, it's critical to start off with a summary of the experience attributes that drive the design language. Be sure to remind stakeholders of how these attributes relate to the brand and differentiate the product from the rest of the market. You can recycle the slides from the user and domain analysis presentation here, though you can usually cover these points more briefly. It's sometimes useful to include any early visualizations, such as the collage in Figure 12.15 or the is/is-not visualization in Figure 12.16.

Next, explain what design language studies are: exploration based on snippets of possible design language elements such as color, texture, type, line, and shape for software, and color, material, finish, overall shape, and surfacing for hardware. Describe how the experience attributes drive the different directions. Explain that this discussion is about communication strategy.

Show each study alone on the screen with little or no text, since the focus is on the visual impression it leaves. Instead, describe the rationale verbally during the presentation (and perhaps jot down a few thoughts in the presentation notes field) or create a second slide explaining each study's rationale. Whether you start with hardware or software studies (or the two combined) depends on the story you have to tell, but it works best in most cases to separate the two at first and then show them together. If you have a single industrial design study and several software (i.e., screen-based) studies, starting with the ID makes it easy to show the visual design in context, but pairs of explicitly related hardware and software studies will work best together. End with a slide showing the whole set of studies; you'll use this

Framework

537

one to drive discussion and come to consensus. Table 19.6 shows a set of slides for the office phone studies, which were introduced in Figures 18.13, 18.14, and 18.15.

Table 19.6. **Presenting the design language.**

What the slide shows	What the presenter says
 **Design language studies are:** — Quick explorations of how to represent experience attributes — Each attribute represents a different strategy — Each study emphasizes a different attribute — Not actual screens or finished hardware — Focused on the first 5 second reaction	**ID or VisD:** Now that you've seen the direction we're headed with the physical form architecture and behavior of the product, we'd like to show you some explorations of how it might look. We'll do this using design language studies, which are kind of like fabric swatches and paint chips—they're explorations of color, shape, texture, and so forth.
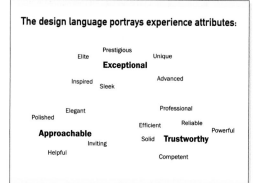	**ID or VisD:** The design language uses form, color, materials, type, and other visual properties to do several things. Of course, it has to appeal to the audience, but it also has to communicate the experience attributes we discussed last time so the design says the right things about the brand. It also serves to differentiate the brand and the product from the rest of the market. An effective design language also unifies the hardware and software for a seamless experience. As you may recall from last time, this product needs to be exceptional, something an executive really wants seen on his desk. It also has to be approachable and familiar, an appliance rather than a mission control console. Finally, it has to seem trustworthy—businesslike, capable, and not full of nasty surprises. Each of the studies you're about to see emphasizes a different attribute because if we try to give every aspect equal weight, we won't be saying anything clearly enough to be understood.

Framework

What the slide shows	What the presenter says

What we need from you is a gut reaction to how well these studies portray the attributes, and which strategy will best appeal to the audience and differentiate us from the competition.

ID: The first study focuses on the *exceptional* attribute. What you saw of the architecture and scenarios earlier tells you that the touch screen is going to dominate the face of the phone as well as the interaction. This approach would really let the software interface stand out but without explicitly calling a lot of attention to it.

ID: The overall form here is more like a slim tablet than a bulky, wedge-shaped enclosure. The surface is largely flat and the layout of components is very geometric, with a beautiful symmetry to the functional elements, giving it a simplicity that's both modern and elegant. The glossy, black finish tells you the device is sophisticated and powerful.

ID: This polished aluminum part frames the face of the phone like a piece of art; you can see this groove here lets the face float within the frame. Real metal shows that we didn't just make the cheapest phone possible; it says there's both quality and precision here. We've repeated that metal on the handset, so the part of the phone Scott touches every day is equally special.

Framework

Continued

What the slide shows

What the presenter says

ID: The overall look could be just a little bit cold, so we've made it a little more approachable by making the voicemail playback and volume controls slightly concave, with a soft curvature that's tempting to touch.

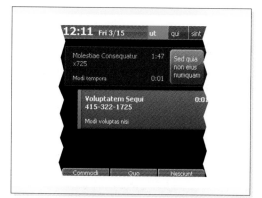

VisD: The visual design makes use of a similar palette, with a black background that matches the surface of the phone. The active elements stand out from the surface in dark gray, which is still sophisticated but a bit more touchable; slightly rounded corners and a 3D affordance add to that touchable effect. As you can see, the gray elements use a gloss that says everything about the device is polished to perfection. The selection highlights use a bright, yellowish green that's high tech and a bit futuristic in feel; that says this is the latest technology sitting on Scott's desk.

VisD: The sharp rectangles and clean grid look right at home on the face of the phone.

[Additional slides showing "approachable" and "trustworthy" studies]

[Additional discussion of "approachable" and "trustworthy" studies]

What the slide shows

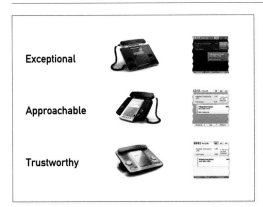

Exceptional

Approachable

Trustworthy

What the presenter says

VisD or ID: So, we'd like to hear your first-five-second reaction to each of these, and then let's talk about which of these strategies makes the most sense.

As with the discussion of which persona is primary in the user and domain analysis (see Chapter 13), the design team may leave the design language presentation neutral or may encourage stakeholders to choose the direction they believe is the strongest.

Discuss and get agreement on direction and next steps

The whole point of the meeting is to build consensus around a direction, or at least a clear sense that you'll go mostly in direction A, but with some aspects of direction B. This means you'll need to encourage frank discussion. A slide that lists important questions, trade-offs, or other sticky issues that need to get resolved helps you remember these points. Projecting them on a screen for all to see also tends to help stakeholders face these issues, too; if everyone seems to be avoiding a topic, a stakeholder may help you out by chiming in, "Well, what *about* that second question up there?"

Listing your questions or open issues also reinforces that this is work in progress, and tells stakeholders that *you* don't think your work is done. This helps focus stakeholders on the big

issues, rather than nitpicky things you can address later on. With software, these issues often center on how much to take on in an upcoming release—what's essential to address for users right away? What can be incorporated as a value add in an upgrade? It's also common to start by developing the interfaces for just one or two personas in a multi-interface system. With different hardware platforms, the discussion is more likely to focus on the pros and cons of using a fairly expensive component. The design language discussion will probably be about what direction best reinforces the brand and differentiates the product from competitors; with hardware, there may also be some debate about whether a more-expensive, authentic material is worthwhile.

Stakeholders are more likely to view the design team as leaders if you have recommendations for most of the issues you're raising—they may be business or technical decisions, but chances are that one approach or another is better from a user-satisfaction point of view.

Exercise

Develop a presentation for your LocalGuide or RoomFinder design.

Managing Your Time and Preparing for the Meeting

When preparing your presentation, focus on communicating the essentials, not perfecting the design.

Depending on the complexity and breadth of the design, allow anywhere from one to three days to prepare for the presentation. Plan your narrative as a team and discuss who will present which portions of the material; those people need not be responsible for roughing out the slides, but should take the last pass at the content and structure of their sections to ensure that they'll be comfortable presenting the material. In a common division of labor, the generative interaction designer (IxDG) describes the anatomy and behavior detail, the synthesis-oriented interaction designer (IxDS) reviews the personas and/or walks through the scenarios, the industrial designer explains the hardware architecture (perhaps with the lead mechanical engineer's involvement), and the visual designer (with the industrial designer, when appropriate) presents the design language.

In most cases, the IxDS assembles the first version of most of the slides while the IxDG and any industrial designer(s) develop final form and behavior sketches. The lead visual designer often assembles her own slides because the studies are already done.

Assuming you've had sufficient design team whiteboard reviews of scenarios and sketches, there should be little if any change to the design as you develop the presentation; there's always more detail to add, but it's important to focus on communicating the essentials rather than trying to perfect your rough draft of the design. Images should generally be finalized and a rough draft of all slides complete about a day before the presentation so presenters have a chance to tweak their slides. Also be sure to do a careful review of scenario slides; it's easy to introduce an incorrect screen state in one slide that will confuse your audience and make the story ineffective.

The entire design team should review the presentation the day before it's to be delivered to adjust the narrative, identify missing assumptions or bits of explanation, QA the images, and make sure any text is clear (yet diplomatic where necessary). This is a good opportunity for the presenter(s)—no matter how experienced they are—to practice their delivery and responses to likely questions, concerns, or objections; I often play this "stakeholder" role in presentation reviews with my teams. Consider inviting your project owner to this review to help anticipate likely issues and ensure that your explanation is clear to a non-designer.

Spend a little time as a team discussing how you'll respond to sticky points, whether a particular person will be responding to questions of a certain type, and so forth. Make sure you have a rationale for every design decision—"because I'm the designer" and "because it looks cool" won't get you very far. The personas and experience attributes are the best foundation for most decisions because even the most self-referential CEO cares about what customers are like and has a hard time arguing with user data. Justification based on obscure usability principles may make you sound educated, but is likely to lose stakeholders (and may even annoy them). If you must use technical rationale, think about how you can explain the principle briefly and in lay terms.

Time-saving tips for assembling screen drawings and slides

Drawing is time-consuming, so the fewer screens you can draw the more time you'll save. Make a list of the drawings you need to convey the action based on your key path scenarios. If the list seems long, consider whether your scenarios are more complex than they really need to be: you don't need to illustrate multiple examples of the same task, for instance. See Chapter 14 for tips on what aspects of a scenario require illustration. Try to avoid creating separate drawings for scenarios and for anatomy explanation; you can usually use a scenario image to describe form and function.

Drawing scenario storyboards electronically is faster than drawing by hand if you recycle as many drawing elements as possible. Using frames or layers in your drawing application, such as Fireworks or Photoshop, you can create a single "backdrop" containing the window title, toolbar, or device image, and then use a separate layer or frame for each scenario step to reflect state changes.

To create a consistent look for buttons and other elements, you can create a style as we've done with Fireworks at Cooper. Another option is to create a layer that's a repository of templates for typical elements, such as buttons and fake text that aren't shared across every screen, and then copy and paste common elements from your repository layer into the other layers as needed to create unique screens. This way, you'll only have to draw one button or list box, copy and paste it as needed for consistent sizing, and change the label or contents as needed. If you're using Illustrator or PowerPoint, you can use a blank page or slide as this sort of repository.

Passing files back and forth (and sharing the work of getting images into slides) is easier if you have a naming convention for image exports and the layers you're using to assemble the images. A useful convention for storyboard images is "persona name_scenario name_step number_description," such as "kate_registration_02_enter address.jpg." You might name any unique anatomy images as "persona name_screen name," with detailed crops named something like "persona name_screen name_element name" unless you're cropping the images in the presentation software.

Depending on how your presentation is set up and how you manage your files, you may be able to import images into your slides by reference, rather than pasting and manually re-pasting images as they're updated. This requires saving each image in the same folder and saving any updated images with the same file name. If you're pasting images manually, consider noting the file name in small text at the bottom of each slide; this makes it easier to replace image number 12 of 30 when you realize there's a mistake in the sketch.

> Make sure you have a rationale for every design decision— "Because it looks cool" isn't good enough.

Framework

Conducting the Meeting

Many of the suggestions for managing the U&DA meeting (see "Delivering the presentation and leading the discussion" in Chapter 13) also apply to this presentation, so they're worth a review. All team members need to be on their toes because this is probably the most challenging meeting you'll have. If you're not currently speaking, be ready to clarify a point, get the conversation unstuck, and take notes about items to follow up on, while allowing the current presenter to lead the discussion; although these tasks are usually a specific responsibility of the IxDS, all team members should pitch in.

Start the meeting by reviewing expectations about what stakeholders will and won't see and what you need from them. Ask them to tell you whether the design makes sense and seems likely to solve the business problems. Encourage participants to ask questions if something isn't clear, but hold discussion for later; you need a chance to make your case before people start to critique the design. Thank any of the product team members who have provided informal review or expertise during this phase; this both gives credit where credit is due and makes it clear (in a subtle way) that the design team isn't showing crazy ideas without vetting them. Reinforce that what stakeholders are about to see is incomplete work in progress, that it deliberately pushes at the constraints a bit, and that it's perfectly normal if it's a little bit wrong.

Presenting the material

Move quickly through the agenda, project timeline and mandate, personas, and requirements, but do expand on these points as necessary if there are new stakeholders in the room. If anyone wants to revisit decisions made in the last meeting, suggest tabling the topic until later; if necessary, look to your project owner to reinforce that the decision has been made and it's time to move on.

Show some excitement as you introduce any big ideas as well as the basic concept(s). Stakeholders usually respond well to an interesting anecdote about how you arrived at a novel idea, whether it was inspired by some aspect of the research or by something else. Briefly explain that you arrived at the design through a combination of the context scenarios and good design principles. Don't dwell on detail yet—share just enough that people can understand what they're seeing in the scenarios.

Remind stakeholders what scenarios are and why you're focusing on the most critical and common cases for now. Then, just as in the U&DA meeting (see Chapter 13), focus on the storytelling. Use the persona's name and describe what she thinks and feels as she uses the new design. Avoid functional explanation during the scenarios.

Later, as you describe what detail you can about hardware, software, or service components, describe the idea and the rationale while acknowledging any unknowns. Describe behaviors in terms of familiar products, Web sites, or human interactions where that's helpful, such as, "The service is like a human assistant—it knows when Rob is in a meeting, but it gives certain privileged callers the ability to interrupt him if it's important."

Don't dwell on the experience attributes since these are review, but do explain how they inform the studies you're about to show. Tell stakeholders that although there is a subjective aspect to assessing a design language, the point is not to select something they personally like. You need them to decide on what attributes they want to emphasize in their visual communication and to provide feedback on how successfully the studies portray those attributes, especially in light of the competition. Explain what about each study communicates the primary attribute. Invoke other products that use similar colors, materials, or other elements to communicate the same things.

Point out where you're deliberately contrasting with a key competitor.

Facilitating discussion and handling concerns

As with the U&DA, once you've concluded your presentation, be prepared to facilitate the discussion and walk the fine line between defending your design and being defensive. Ask stakeholders what questions and concerns they have. Once they've covered the issues that seem most important to them, return to your list of open issues. Encourage quiet stakeholders to chime in; revisit Chapter 13 for some hints on managing difficult stakeholders. Watch and listen for what people aren't saying: "Tom, you seem unhappy. Is there a concern you haven't expressed?" Those concerns will get expressed at some point, so it's best to air them now in a public forum.

It's often possible to achieve consensus about form and behavior during the meeting, but people may need a few days to research or consider the implications of the design. Make sure that you leave the meeting with a list of those open questions, people assigned to dig up more information, and a deadline for meeting again to make decisions. In the meantime, you need to move forward, so get agreement about what working assumptions you should use. Plan to focus on some part of the design that isn't dependent on the open issues, if that's possible. Tell stakeholders you'll get back to them with a plan tomorrow if you need a little time to think about it.

There's hardly ever a reason *not* to reach agreement about the design language strategy during the meeting, since it seldom depends much on unknowns. It may be difficult to reach agreement if the design team has done studies that are simply too extreme or if the appropriate brand stakeholders are not in the room, but both of these situations are avoidable.

Remember that this is the most terrifying part of the process for stakeholders because they can start to see the design, but they may still have more unanswered questions than answers. It's not only inevitable that people will ask questions and bring up concerns—it's desirable. You can't move forward (without moving backward later) if you don't get consensus now. If no one raises a concern during this meeting, it doesn't necessarily indicate that you've done a great job; it might just mean some issue is lurking in the shadows to ambush you later.

SOME GENERAL PRINCIPLES

When you're explaining design, never say (or even think) that people should believe you because you're "the expert." They're experts, too, in their own way. Always have a specific reason for every design decision. Turn to the personas and the research they're based on as your primary tools for justifying form and behavior decisions. The experience attributes (and the research, persona experience goals, and brand attributes from which they're derived) should be the foundation of your case for the design language. Also, a few points from Chapter 13 bear repeating here:

— Make your case firmly, but focus on hearing people and gaining agreement, not on trying to be "right."

— Make sure you understand each question or concern before responding.

— Ask if you've answered the question before moving on.

— Be willing to defer to a teammate who is better equipped to respond, especially if you're feeling uncertain or defensive.

— Be willing to say you don't know (followed by how and when you *will* be able to answer the question).

— Acknowledge what's good about someone else's idea before explaining why you went in a different direction.

Framework

545

COMMON QUESTIONS AND CONCERNS

There are issues unique to every design vision meeting, but there are a handful of questions and concerns that crop up fairly often. Here are some suggestions for handling them.

"How does _____ work?"

For every scenario you're able to describe, there are probably a dozen or more cases you haven't been able to cover. Some stakeholders are anxious about these unanswered questions, perhaps because they relate to an issue they've heard about from users, or perhaps just because they're struggling with the idea that this is work in progress. Engineers often ask these questions because those details really do matter when it comes to implementation. Sometimes stakeholders ask this kind of question because they see a real flaw in your design, so listen carefully.

The best way to respond depends partly on your level of confidence. If the question is about something you touched on during a design meeting or have spent some time thinking about, you might say something like, "We haven't looked at that in detail yet, but we can probably handle it with another field or two on this screen," or "It will probably either be detents or a friction hinge, but we have to look at it more closely." If you really have no idea, though, don't just make something up—say you'll have to spend some time considering it, but you're confident you can solve it within the design framework you're presenting.

The other thing to consider before answering is what's motivating the question. Is it idle curiosity or a general anxiety about incomplete design? This is the usual reason, and it's nothing to worry about. However, a stakeholder with some thwarted ambition might keep throwing edge cases at you or—much worse—tell others outside the meeting that the design doesn't address all the needs. It's important to address this kind of thing right away, ideally during the meeting.

Sometimes it's enough to answer a couple of these questions in a row with a specific idea of how the design could address each issue, perhaps even with a sketch at the board. If this person is just being obstructionist and continuing to list trivial issues, other stakeholders will usually see that the problem is not with the design and ask this person to let it go. Just be *very* careful not to seem flip as you respond to these points. If the issue persists after you've demonstrated at the whiteboard a couple of times, you might say something like, "You seem to have a lot of concerns about situations the design might not be able to handle. Why don't we make a list of these at the end of the meeting, and we'll see how soon we can work through them." This lets you move on and prevents this person from dominating the discussion. Check in with the project owner after the meeting and see if he wants you to deal with those questions right away, or if he's willing to help wrangle the difficult stakeholder.

"This is a big change. Won't users be confused?"

Companies, like individuals, get comfortable with things that seem to work "well enough." If they're making money with an existing installed base for a legacy product, there can be hesitation about alienating current users by asking them to learn something new. I usually respond that if you're suddenly targeting novices when most of your users are intermediates, or you're rearranging things for no good reason, of course it will alienate people—just look at the uproar over Microsoft Office 2007 or Apple's 2008 version of iMovie. However, if the change provides a significant benefit (as your design will, of course), users are perfectly happy to adopt it; air travelers weren't used to checking in for flights online from home, but were quick to embrace it when they understood the time savings. That being said, enterprise customers will certainly be unhappy if constant change means retraining their workforce every couple of months; they'll be far happier if you introduce a few big changes at once instead of releasing them piecemeal every few months.

Framework

"How do you know this is right? Will you do a usability test?"

This doesn't necessarily mean the stakeholder disagrees with the design. It's common for some stakeholders to be risk averse, especially in companies with cultures and compensation structures that reward taking the safe route. These stakeholders are looking for certainty, which is all but impossible to guarantee in any new product venture or significant redesign. Some stakeholders either find usability tests and focus groups genuinely reassuring, or want to be able to point to them in case of failure and say, "See? The market told us it was right, so how could we have known?"

If you're a skilled, experienced designer with decent research behind you, you've got a pretty good chance of being right. If you're a responsible designer, you also want to do what you can to ensure success; getting some user reaction to your design is a good way to help do that. However, as explained in Chapter 16, design that's just barely ready to share with stakeholders is almost never ready to test or to put in front of a focus group—there's not enough detail for a realistic user reaction, and stakeholders are usually overly sensitive to negative feedback at this point.

The best response to this kind of question usually makes three points. First, remind stakeholders of how you got here: You (ideally) did thorough research and used it to inform your design in multiple ways, which gives you confidence that your solution is at least pretty close. Second, point out to stakeholders that if all the experts in this room think the design is right, that's a good sign that you're on the right track. Finally, explain why it's a little early to test (as discussed in Chapter 16), but talk about when and how you *do* plan to vet the design.

"I don't like it" or "I wouldn't use it that way."

I once had the head of a huge software company, who had absolutely nothing in common with the end users, tell me that he didn't like the design because it didn't reflect how he would use the product. It can be excruciating not to respond to this sort of comment with a snotty remark! Fortunately, it doesn't happen that often, especially if you've done a good job of explaining the design based on the personas and experience attributes.

One way to help retain your calm as you ponder your response is to ask for more information: "Could you tell me more about what you don't like?" It's possible the comment is based on misunderstanding or is mere bluster. Usually, though, the best response turns out to be a discussion of how the person who doesn't like it differs from the personas, and why designing for the stakeholder would be counterproductive. If you really want to be diplomatic about it, you can say something like, "You know, I can see why you'd say that—I'd probably use it the same way. Carla's not like us, though, so she wouldn't be satisfied with a product that worked the way you and I would expect."

"Why didn't you design it [like this]?"

Once in a while, the person asking this question has a better design idea than what you're showing. Often the question is simple curiosity—the design differs what from the stakeholder is accustomed to or was expecting, and although he assumes you have a good reason, he'd like to know what it is. Now and then, though, the person asking the question either has delusions of being a design expert or is pushing some competing (and usually inappropriate) idea.

In any case, listen to the idea with the assumption that it might just be a great one. Get excited about it if it is. If it doesn't quite make sense, say something like, "That's an interesting idea. Can

Ask stakeholders to frame their critiques and ideas in terms of persona needs.

you tell me what need of Carla's or Ray's that would address?" This phrasing allows for the possibility that you just don't understand why the stakeholder's suggestion is important, but requires the stakeholder to justify the idea just as you've been doing; often, the person with the idea has no particular rationale for it and you can move on to the next comment. If the idea is one you've considered and discarded, or that's clearly misguided, an appropriate response is something like, "That's an interesting idea. We considered it, but didn't go in that direction because it adds a lot of complexity to account for a situation Debbie and our other personas aren't likely to be in."

"Why didn't you give us multiple ideas to choose from?"

You might get this question if you're only showing one direction due to time and budget constraints, which is fairly common for interaction design and not that unusual for industrial design. The stakeholder could be asking the question out of dissatisfaction with the work you've shown or annoyance that you apparently haven't explored her favorite idea, in which case it's important to deal with the underlying issue. Most often, though, the questioner just wants to make sure she's getting the "best" design. If you're not sure of the stakeholder's motivation, ask.

Briefly remind stakeholders of the time and budget trade-offs you and the project owner made—perhaps even with this stakeholder's input—but don't dwell on this because it will sound like you're making excuses. Instead, focus on what you *have* done to explore multiple concepts. Here's an example:

> That's a great question. As you might recall from our initial kickoff meeting, we all agreed that we'd need to focus on one direction within the first few days of design in order to hit our target ship date. When we started designing, though, we came up with quite a few ideas. It would have taken a lot of time to flesh all of those out to this level of detail, but the beauty of personas and scenarios is that they let us eliminate a lot of directions very quickly and inexpensively.

If this explanation isn't sufficient, offer to schedule some time to walk through some of the ideas you threw out and why—hopefully you took some whiteboard photos or good notes. You can always work with your project owner to change the schedule and spend time on other ideas, but there were probably good reasons for the decision in the first place.

"We can't build this. It's not technically feasible."

Most designers are inclined to push boundaries, so if the engineers are running screaming from the room, perhaps you've given them reason to do so. However, many engineers are inclined to sandbag a little. It's understandable, considering how often they're given mind-bending problems to solve with insufficient resources—many have learned to under-promise and over-deliver. Engineers who aren't up to the task may sandbag more than a little. Your past experience with engineers in general (and hopefully these engineers in particular) can help you assess how much of this response is a real concern with your design, how much is routine sandbagging, and how much is a lack of skill.

The best response to this assertion is not a response, but prevention. Get the design engineer(s) involved in at least one informal review before this meeting so you and they are prepared to discuss the implications. If you trust the engineers and they're telling you you're nuts, adjust the design before bringing it to the whole group of stakeholders. Most likely, though, the engineers' discomfort is a matter of degree, and the design is feasible if the stakeholders believe the design is worth a change in the project's parameters.

The best way to elicit a constructive assessment of the engineering challenges is to ask, "Let's assume anything is possible given enough time and money. Roughly what do you think it would it take to build this? I realize this depends on a lot of details we can't give you yet, so feel free to tell us what assumptions you're making." It's only fair to give the engineers some warning so they can prepare to answer this question intelligently.

Summary

No matter how you choose to communicate your design language and framework, remember that the idea is to build consensus around the right direction. That requires persuasive arguments and leadership on the part of the design team. You have to put some thought into how you'll help stakeholders understand the design and your rationale for the decisions you've made. It also requires that you recognize when it's time to stop defending your design and accept that business reasons may justify some design compromises; the best design has to be not only usable, useful, and desirable—it also has to be feasible within a timeline and budget that will make it viable in the marketplace.

Framework

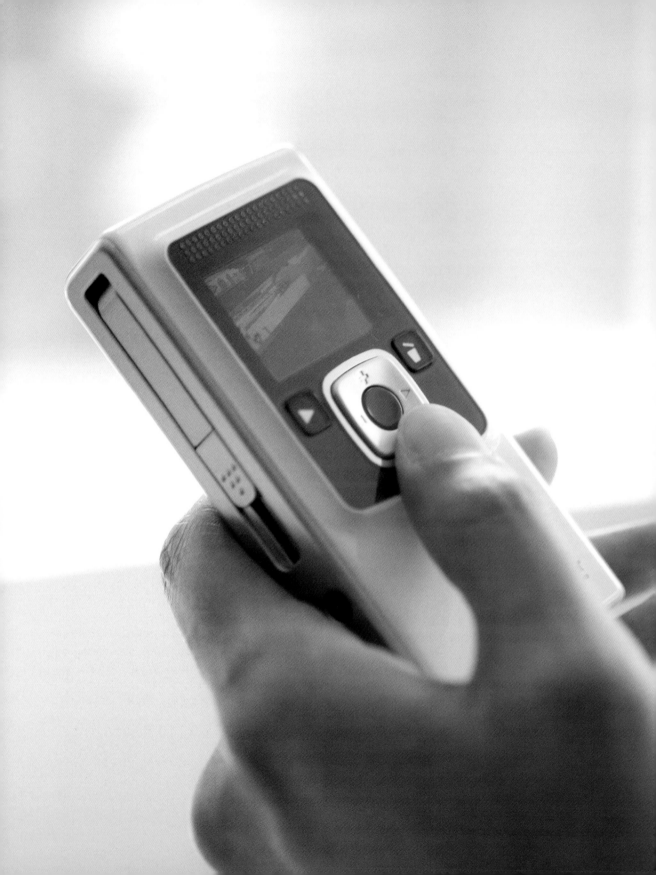

CHAPTER 20

Detailed Design: Making Your Ideas Real

Congratulations—you've survived the most nerve-racking part of any project, the delivery of your design framework. By this time, you've hopefully got everyone excited about the design direction, and much of the uncertainty is behind you. Now, though, you have a big pile of hard work ahead. Fleshing out the detailed design means resolving numerous difficult questions: How much is essential to accomplish by a reasonable ship date? How will the engineers implement the functionality you've imagined? How will the design handle all those details and edge cases you've been able to ignore until now? How will that complex data visualization tool you've glossed over really look? It's not surprising that the detailed design work often takes more time than the rest of the process combined.

Aside from creating the best possible design within your business constraints, the objective of detailed design is to give the product team—especially the engineers—as clear and comprehensive a blueprint for the product's form and behavior as you can manage within the time you have. Good specifications help engineering managers develop more accurate estimates of effort and cost, while letting engineers focus on how to build the product instead of spending time on how

it behaves and looks. Specs also help the quality assurance team plan their testing, let technical writers begin documentation early, and even allow the sales and marketing teams to start generating excitement before anything is built.

Equally important, detailed design specs help ensure clear communication and accountability on all parts of the team. Rather than arguing over whether a half-baked implementation meets a fuzzy requirement, a product manager can point to a spec and say, "It doesn't work or look like this, so it isn't done." In turn, engineers can say to management, "That's not what's in the spec we based our estimate on. It's going to take more time." You can get away with minimal specification and some missing details if you're doing a simple product with a small team of talented engineers, but detail and clarity are essential when you're building complex products with large teams or outsourcing any engineering or manufacturing.

This chapter outlines a handful of general principles to use in approaching detailed design of any sort, provides an overview of process and roles, and describes a couple of options for structuring your time depending on the engineering process and schedule.

Essential Principles of Detailed Design

Detailed design doesn't usually entail flashy feats of design acrobatics, as framework definition sometimes does; rather, it requires good balance and excellent juggling skills. On a daily basis, you must weigh pragmatism about implementation against optimistic advocacy for the most desirable solution. You must keep implications for the entire system in mind while you focus on the design of a single screen or component. You'll need to collaborate more frequently with more people than ever before, juggling their concerns and involvement with your own need for quiet design time. Like previous phases, detailed design requires a specific mind-set; integrating the following principles into your practice will help you succeed.

Collaborate, collaborate, collaborate

Although a *brief* period of relative design team isolation is useful for focus during modeling and framework definition, if it goes on for long, your design is unlikely to see the light of day. As you begin detailed design, frequent collaboration with multiple people becomes critical to success. You need design engineers to help you understand what's expensive to do and what's within reason. You may need subject matter experts to ensure that your design follows industry best practices and regulations. You'll probably work closely with a copywriter for a large corporate Web site. If you're designing an enterprise application, especially in a legacy environment, you'll most likely need business analysts to help you understand business rules and system capabilities; business analysts also help engineers know what aspects of which systems to tweak. Usability testers and perhaps human factors experts can help minimize the possibility for error and confusion in most products, and are especially critical for medical devices or any other application with potential

safety issues. In any case, you're certain to need business decision-makers involved at critical points. External consultants with limited-length engagements should also make sure the project owner or someone else inside the client organization joins enough design meetings to understand the design intent inside and out.

Within the design team, collaboration happens in informal meetings and check-ins throughout each day. Outside the design team, collaboration is usually a combination of brief, informal communication and more-structured meetings. It's fine to drop by someone's desk or send an e-mail to ask a question or get an opinion, but decision making and detailed review of design in progress should happen with all of the necessary experts present, preferably at least once a week. Otherwise, you risk poor communication and uninformed decisions; even though extensive collaboration can feel like a drag on your schedule, it saves doubt, process thrash, and rework in the long run.

Drive to complete detail, but maintain a systems view

One of the most common mistakes in detailed design—especially interaction and visual interface design—is not being thorough enough. It's easy to plop a field or widget on the screen and think you're done, but interaction designers need to consider what kinds of data can and cannot be entered in that field, how to minimize errors, and whether the field is available or unavailable in certain circumstances.

With a complete spec in hand, engineers should not have to make a single guess about the appearance or behavior of the product. If you're designing a service with human "components," you might need to create scripts, guidelines, training materials, collateral, or other non-electronic tools. This kind of detail takes a fair bit of time or, if the details aren't terribly interdependent, a large team.

As in framework definition, you also need to consider the entire system, even when you're focused on details. What else in the system is aware of or affected by the contents of that field? How does the system get that bit of data to display it in a graph? Will moving that hardware control half an inch affect the screen layout? Can you use any red for common interface elements, or do you need to reserve it for visual feedback? If someone chooses "ship my items as they become available," how does that affect the shipping cost and the back-end fulfillment process? Every decision has the potential to affect some other aspect of the design.

Touch everything a second time after it's documented

Design consultants have a reputation for chucking a document over the wall to the engineers and running for the hills. There's some truth to this—most don't do it as a matter of practice, but even the best consultancies may be forced to do it as a matter of budget. Unless they are building the product as well as designing it, external consultants are often asked to provide only limited support once there's a detailed first draft of the design. After all, the design is done, right?

Any engineer or in-house designer knows this is not the case; even the best designer in the world isn't going to produce perfect solutions that are perfectly implementable the first time through. Fast whiteboard iteration and informal design reviews can catch a lot of issues and get that first draft of the spec pretty close, but subject matter experts, business analysts, and engineers usually need to spend some time reviewing the design's finer points to spot more subtle issues, such as a workflow detail that isn't quite in line with best practices, some aspect of the visual system that's going to be difficult to build, or a physical-surface detail that will be tricky to mold in manufacturing. Also, the point at which you have a complete or nearly complete first draft is usually the right time to do a thorough usability test to make sure you haven't made little design mistakes that only users can help you identify.

For these reasons, it's best to document the completed design once you've gone through a round of whiteboard or physical prototype iteration with the necessary experts, then give the draft spec to the whole project team for an intensive review while you either work on another chunk of the design or prepare for a round of usability testing. Once you've got useful feedback, you can clean up any problems—which are typically minor if you've used good process so far—and revise the spec to make it "final." (Always keep in mind that unexpected issues could

> **Even the best designer in the world won't produce perfect solutions that are perfectly implementable on the first try.**

Detailed Design

still arise during implementation.) In other words, budget your time to touch every part of the design twice; the second iteration should go much faster than the first.

For interaction and visual design, this document-then-iterate cycle involves not only piles of screen drawings, but also a fair bit of text. Industrial design documentation consists primarily of CAD files, renderings, physical test models, and color/material/finish (CMF) specs, which are then reviewed and iterated—usually a few times—with the mechanical engineering team. In either case, expressing the design intent in concrete and detailed terms is necessary to ensure thorough review.

Some designers advocate multiple rounds of iteration and testing, but this approach provides diminishing returns for a couple of reasons. One is that multiple rounds of very fast iteration are already happening at the whiteboard or in CAD files, then being assessed using personas and scenarios. Another is that the methods and practices described in this book, when applied by skilled designers, tend to yield design that has only minor usability issues; advocates of multiple rounds of testing are often assuming that design is based on inadequate research, done by unqualified individuals, or done using poor process. (Of course, if your first test is a disaster, that tells you that something about your research, process, or skills needs some work! If you get a poor test result, you'll want to do another round of iteration once you identify and address that larger issue.)

Design for the appropriate time horizon

As part of your post-framework discussion with stakeholders, you'll need to establish how far ahead your design should look. It's usually important in a deadline-driven project to focus the design on only what can be built in that immediate release. This may seem obvious, but it's a

challenge for many designers to dial down their natural idealism. Don't let go of it entirely, though. Advocate for the better design solution—just pick your battles carefully.

Sometimes, however, it's useful to develop detailed software design in a slightly more ambitious way, including functionality or more challenging design approaches you anticipate might not make it into the near-term release. As a more complete design emerges, everyone on the product team can make a better assessment of what is or isn't worth stretching the schedule, then you can pare down the detailed design as needed for final implementation.

If you haven't reached consensus on your focus in the design vision meeting (see Chapter 19), hopefully your project owner is making sure the appropriate people are researching the open issues. Within a few days, you should be able to sit down with the necessary stakeholders to agree on what probably will or won't be in the upcoming release and how far out you should design.

Settle the big issues quickly

For devices, it's best to settle on the basic physical requirements—such as approximate size and shape, key moving parts, input methods, and component architecture, including screen size and type—before investing too much in evolving and detailing the physical product design. For interaction design and visual design on any platform, you need to know the input mechanisms as well as the physical size, resolution, and bit depth of the target screen. Screen requirements can be tricky with desktop and Web applications, since end users typically have a range of display setups; the best solution is usually to aim for what most of your target market is likely to have by the time you ship. It's also helpful to know what tools the programmers will use to develop code, so you can take advantage of existing libraries.

You may find it surprising how often stakeholders don't understand the time and cost impact of changing their minds about any of these topics. On a project for a handheld consumer device, I once had stakeholders insist that a segment-based display—which has very little flexibility from an interaction design perspective—was necessary for cost reasons. A few months later, before the rather complex engineering was anywhere near done, pixel-based displays had dropped enough in price to be feasible. The interaction and visual design had to be done over. On another occasion, the project owner insisted on a device with a 12-inch touch screen, only to ask for a screen half the size once she saw a near-final appearance model. She expected that the on-screen elements could just be shrunk to fit, though of course this would lead to illegible type and unreasonably small touch targets. In both cases, various members of the design team had done their best to educate stakeholders about the implications of their choices; clearly, communication about this is something you can't overdo.

Consider the cost-benefit equation

Every design decision has a cost and a benefit in terms of time, money, usability, desirability, sustainability, and competitiveness. Some of these decisions are up to designers while others can be worked out between designers and engineers, but the most critical trade-offs have to be made by the product owner or a larger group of stakeholders. Most often, your job as a designer is not to decide what trade-offs to make, but simply to decide what's worth advocating for from the perspective of desirability and perhaps sustainability—other stakeholders typically have time, money, and competitive considerations covered.

The cost-benefit equation is well understood by most teams delivering physical products. It's clearly worth adding a few gigabytes of storage that cost you 10 percent more if it lets you charge 30 percent more, but probably not worth using an expensive color LCD just to display one line of text on an office phone. The environmental cost-benefit is becoming increasingly clear to product companies and manufacturers, as well; even when the more sustainable option adds a little bit of up-front cost, there are often savings elsewhere in the process from reclaiming used products, not having to clean up toxic waste, and not having to combat negative publicity. Moreover, being seen as "green" can be a useful differentiator with environmentally conscious consumers.

These trade-offs can be less clear in software since there's not a manufacturing cost to consider, but even so, "reduce, reuse, recycle" still applies. In the environmental sense, *reducing* means considering whether

> Every design decision has a cost and a benefit in terms of time, money, usability, sustainability, and competitiveness.

you really need that processor-intensive capability (which will cause people to dump their old hardware and buy new) just because it's cool. In the economic sense, it also means considering whether a custom control that takes three weeks to code is really that much better than something "off the shelf." Reusing and recycling involve looking for opportunities to leverage a bit of code written for one function in another. Rather than using two slightly different controls or screen layouts, see if the same design can serve both purposes. This saves expensive coding time and usually leads to a cleaner, simpler, and more desirable design.

Reinforce the experience attributes

Many detailed design decisions involve conveying the appropriate experience attributes. Many of these considerations are related to the design language, which is covered in Chapters 17 and 18, but the design language is not the only communication vector. Consider how your on-screen text, the product's surfacing details, and overall behavior either contribute to or detract from the desired attributes.

This is especially important with consumer products, where your ability to delight users can make the difference between a ho-hum device and an enormously successful one. What delights people is usually an extra touch that's novel, playful, and somehow unexpected. Apple excels at this—the nearly physical "inertia" effects used in scrolling on the iPhone, for example, add a bit of life to an otherwise tedious task. Keep these touches subtle so they won't become annoying when the novelty wears off, though; the genie-returning-to-the-bottle animation used to minimize windows in Apple's OS X doesn't get in the way, but the ripple effect for adding new widgets to the desktop would be a bit over the top for a frequently used function. Mind you, if you don't have usefulness and usability taken care of, the extra goodies won't overcome user frustration.

Process and Project Management for Detailed Design

Process and project management are closely intertwined during detailed design; the design team must coordinate a multitude of varied, interdependent tasks and still generate a huge volume of work in a short time. The overall process builds on the same techniques used during framework definition, but requires steady output at a greater level of detail.

Expanding the team

The core design team of design team lead, interaction designers, visual interface designer, and sometimes an industrial designer should remain intact through this phase for most medium and larger projects; very small or narrowly focused projects may only have one or two of these roles from the outset. However, there are times when it's useful to expand this team (or keep any additional visual and industrial designers involved) after the design vision meeting. Whether to do so depends on which is more important: finishing the design sooner or doing it at lower cost?

It's sometimes possible to increase the number of people working on a project to finish a design in less calendar time. The feasibility of this depends on the nature of the design problem. It's difficult to divide and conquer when you're designing a simple product with tightly integrated functions, such as a basic e-mail application, because the inefficiency introduced by the larger team is likely to erase most of the gain in calendar time. However, larger teams can work well with multi-interface enterprise systems, service design with multiple components, or anything else with distinct aspects that aren't too interdependent. For example, a museum information system that involves a kiosk and a handheld device could make use of two interaction design pairs, with one pair focused on each platform, as well as a couple of junior designers to assist the lead visual and industrial designers with details and production.

This larger-team approach is a bit less efficient than having one smaller team design the complete system; it requires more time from the team lead and more intrateam meetings to ensure the consistency and coherence of the solution. Unless they were involved in the framework definition phase, the additional team members also require a bit of ramp-up time, but you can minimize this problem by distributing the original team members (e.g., one of the original IxD pair works on problem A with a new team member while the other works on problem B with another new team member) and having the ID and VisD maintain lead roles. This is shown in Figure 20.1. It's effective to develop two or three significant parts of the design in parallel as long as you have an experienced team and a full-time project lead, but simultaneous design on four or more complex problems is likely to result in some design incoherence, because one team lead may no longer be able to keep the whole design in her head.

Integration with engineering methods

Historically, product designers of various types have often been called into the engineering process at the end to put a pretty face on an already-engineered product or to spackle some usability over the cracks in the walls while the house is falling over. In reaction, many designers of various disciplines have been insistent that design needs to come before engineering; in software, some have said that design must be finished before coding begins. Some people incorrectly interpret Goal-Directed Design in this way; the *framework* should ideally be designed before major technology decisions are made, but it's essential that design engineering happen in parallel with detailed design.

We all see the world through the eyes of our own professions, so of course everyone involved in product development thinks his discipline is the horse that has to go before the cart; this has been the genesis of many product development methods. People tend to forget that a horse with a cart but no human to drive it might be happy for a while,

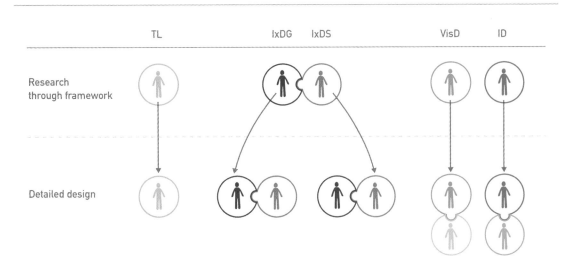

Figure 20.1. When expanding a team to handle multiple interfaces or system components, keep one person from the original team involved in each aspect of the project.

Detailed Design

Anyone designing software has to contend with a whole minefield of strongly held beliefs, particularly of the waterfall-versus-agile sort.

but he'll eventually wander around, irritated by dragging the cart and not accomplishing much. Engineers without designers and designers without engineers will do the same. It takes more effort, but engineering and design must function less like a horse and cart and more like a constant feedback loop: The designer says, "I'd like to have it work like this," the engineer responds that "this" is going to be very difficult, and the designer either convinces a business stakeholder that the difficulty is worth it, or the designer and engineer together come up with an alternative.

Perhaps because they are less mature than other forms of product development, the design and engineering of software seem to create a great deal of angst about who's driving and how the whole effort gets from point A to point B. That's not to say there's no design versus engineering tension in hardware development—simply that anyone designing software has to contend with a whole minefield of strongly held beliefs, particularly of the waterfall-versus-agile sort.

WATERFALL METHODS

Product managers (PMs) and other non-engineers have long struggled to gain visibility into and control over the engineering process. When it comes to software engineering, in particular, the work product remains invisible for a long time, so it's hard for an outsider to understand or respond to it until construction is nearly complete. Combine that with poor or absent design and you get a product that's not what the PM expected. The PM then says the product doesn't satisfy the requirements, the scope changes, and suddenly the engineers are in trouble for slipping the deadline.

Waterfall methods attempt to address the problem by getting maximum clarity on requirements before coding begins: Each phase of the work is theoretically complete and correct before the people downstream begin work on the next phase. Many designers slip comfortably into this sort of process. However, some engineers understandably resist these methods when they're handed a *fait accompli* (often in the form of poorly articulated requirements) and told to go make it work. Overly narrow interpretation of waterfall principles leads to isolated silos, uninformed decisions, and a lot of inefficient rework.

There are cases in which a waterfall-like approach is advisable, though, such as with less-skilled engineers and on large, complex, or mission-critical projects that require structure and predictability. Design can effectively bridge the gap between requirements and technical specifications in the Rational Unified Process (RUP) and other waterfall processes, which helps alleviate many engineering concerns. However, strict waterfall is pretty much never a good idea—at a minimum, there should be informal design engineering reviews throughout the detailed design work, so that information flows in both directions.

AGILE METHODS

In software development, frustration with waterfall approaches has led to the emergence of various **agile** methods. These differ in details but have a handful of assumptions in common:

— Ever-changing requirements are developed by business stakeholders and given to engineers

— Coding should be time-boxed in short periods (called "iterations" or "sprints") to allow for continual value generation and learning

— Small engineering teams should succeed or fail as a group

— Communication should be frequent and face-to-face

— Working code should be the primary measure of progress

From what design teams have seen at Cooper and heard from our clients, agile methods are most successful with small teams of skilled engineers who are working on fairly simple products. We routinely see these methods fail on large-scale IT projects, however, and for every client we encounter who has enthusiastically adopted agile methods, we encounter one who has abandoned them for being ineffective.

Agile methods and Goal-Directed Design are similar in that both involve iterative approaches, small teams, and an emphasis on frequent communication and visible work product. The most fundamental difference between the two—and the source of some "religious" wars—is in the assumption about whether requirements and design are really engineering problems. GDD, as you've no doubt seen throughout this book, is based on the premise that design should be done by designers. Also, rather than giving up and assuming that requirements are unknowable (which is an understandable view given the experience of many software engineers), GDD is all about nailing down requirements by making them concrete in the fastest, cheapest form possible: sketches.

For the two approaches to work together, engineers need to agree that designers have something important to add, and that it's best for the design team to do their own "iterations" in sketches to reduce the amount of time wasted on badly articulated requirements before the first coding sprint begins. The design team, in turn, should ideally deliver design in small (but not arbitrarily defined) chunks. Figure 20.2 shows how this approach differs from the others.

Design works well with both waterfall and agile engineering methods, and can address weaknesses in each.

Detailed Design

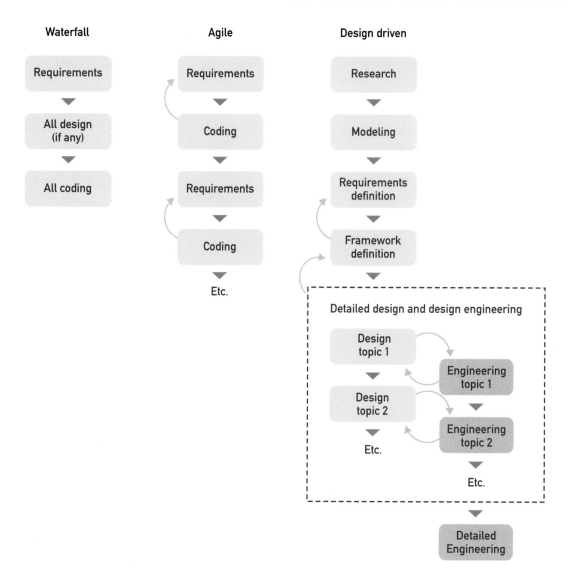

Figure 20.2. A comparison of waterfall, agile, and design-driven product development approaches.

Typical detailed design tasks by role

Design team members continue to have some overlapping responsibilities during this phase, but they also spend more time working alone at their desks on role-specific tasks. Frequent design team check-ins are still essential, as is planning a detailed project calendar together. In contrast to the framework phase, though, there are quite a few meetings that can happen without the entire design team involved.

Note that the following tasks and the subsequent few chapters focus on software and convergent software/hardware devices; the artifacts involved in service design—which may include anything from building architecture to printed collateral to employee training materials—are too varied to describe in any great detail, though the general process of collaborative refinement is similar.

INTERACTION DESIGNERS

In particularly complex domains, the interaction designers (generator and synthesizer, IxDG and IxDS) may begin the phase (or the work on a specific part of the design) with a bit of supplemental research. Aside from this, most of their days are spent generating additional scenarios—starting with common variations on the key path scenarios (see Chapter 16) and ending with edge cases—then filling out and adjusting the design to address them. This work still happens largely in design meetings, but as the design work progresses, the two spend an increasing amount of time each day at their desks.

The IxDG, working with a set of widgets and styles defined by the visual interface designer, does the initial layout for each screen. Much of this work is just capturing decisions made at the whiteboard, but there is nearly always a little bit of adjustment that happens as things get translated from sketches to pixels.

At the same time, the IxDS uses his notes from each meeting to begin drafting the specification, typically using whiteboard photos as image placeholders until more-finished renderings are available. Just as drawing the design tends to reveal flaws in structure and layout that seemed to work on the board, documenting the design helps reveal incomplete thoughts and problematic workflow.

Throughout the process, the interaction designers meet with software design engineers, subject matter experts, business analysts, or copywriters as needed. The IxDG and visual designer work closely together on the visual system, while the IxDS works closely with the VisD on making sure the visual style guide and the form and behavior documentation work together in a coherent whole.

Interaction between the industrial designers and the rest of the team may decrease as the design language and the control types and locations are firmed up, though any contemplated changes require ongoing discussion.

VISUAL INTERFACE DESIGNER(S)

The visual designer uses the feedback on the design language studies to create one or two archetype screens. These show the visual language applied to a real screen design, which allows for a more detailed assessment of how well it's working. Depending on the time available and the level of detail achieved in the framework phase, this might happen late in framework definition or at the beginning of detailed design.

After this, the VisD develops a first draft of the visual system based on the archetypes and his understanding of what other screens are likely to contain. This system contains a specific grid for the layout, a set of fonts of specific size, color, and style for various purposes, and detailed treatments for controls and data. As the interaction designers develop more-detailed designs for the content and structure of each screen, the VisD adds to and evolves the visual system. He also improves upon the IxDG's first take on each screen, optimizing layout and hierarchy, and adjusting the system if needed. He reviews these with engineers to ensure that the way controls are drawn will work with how the code is being written.

As the major functional elements of the visual system start to settle down, the VisD can begin working on icons or other visual elements that aren't on the critical path for the rest of the design; such tasks might also be assigned to a second designer. These, too, must form a coherent system. When there is hardware involved, the visual designer generally collaborates with the industrial designer to ensure that any graphics or labels on the device are both usable and appropriate to the brand.

Detailed Design

Like the IxD synthesizer, the VisD documents the system as it takes shape, partly as a way to avoid a time crunch at the end and partly to aid in identifying holes. As a last step, the visual designer (or perhaps a junior production designer) slices up any assets the programmers need for construction; this may occur as part of a separate development support phase (see Chapter 25). In the case of physical products, he also supplies any text-labeling specs and image files to the mechanical engineer for either print application or emboss/deboss specifications, so the mechanical engineer (ME) can fully document all aspects of the product for manufacturing.

INDUSTRIAL DESIGNER

The industrial designer's work combines aesthetic, brand, and practical considerations in a tight iteration loop. He works with interaction designers to fine-tune physical control input behaviors, such as how a rotary knob communicates one step, how much friction there is, whether there should be a tactile or audible click, or how quickly the screen scrolls in response to the dial. Based on this collaboration, the ID works with the ME to identify and test a range of controls.

ID collaboration with engineering is, if anything, even closer than the collaboration of interaction designers and visual designers with programmers. Along with refining the overall form, proportion, surfacing, colors, and finishes, the ID works closely with mechanical and electrical engineers to finalize materials, prototype potential mechanisms and parts to ensure good fit and function, optimize the fit of components inside the device, and finalize the part count and assembly method to make manufacturing efficient and reliable. The ME team generally takes responsibility for the final CAD database delivered to manufacturing.

This process is pretty straightforward if there aren't a lot of moving parts, a need to house many components in a tiny space, or a requirement for waterproofing or heat and electrical shielding. The average DVD player, for instance, is primarily an aesthetic redesign exercise because it is an established architecture without novel engineering challenges, whereas a tiny cell phone employing unique interaction or technology takes more back and forth, since it may require extensive testing with electrical engineers for thermal management and other issues; the need for airflow and cooling of internal components can drastically affect the industrial design. A device that must withstand considerable physical abuse or wet conditions can also require more time, and perhaps even research and development in materials science.

This phase typically involves some hand sketching to communicate design intent, but relies more heavily on 3D modeling over the final component layout in a CAD application, with files passed back and forth between the ID and ME. Photorealistic renderings based on the CAD file are critical communication tools within and outside of the design team. Inexpensive foam or resin models focused on size, shape, and major mechanical functions have generally been developed in the previous phase to aid in narrowing the design direction, but might still be used in the early stages of detailed design. As confidence in the design increases, the hardware team develops more elaborate (and expensive) working prototypes and appearance models as learning tools before committing to final tooling and manufacturing.

DESIGN TEAM LEAD

The team lead's role remains the same: ensuring that the design is good, that the whole design team is on schedule, and that internal and external collaboration are going well. She also clears obstacles, gets the team additional resources when needed, and sometimes pitches in on design or documentation if a schedule crunch is unavoidable. No project lead is equally proficient at all aspects of design during this phase, so she

Detailed Design

ideally involves other senior designers as needed to review work and support various members of the team.

Drafting a work list and detailed project plan

Either immediately before or immediately after the design vision meeting (see Chapter 19), you'll need to develop a list of design topics that require further work. You'll then estimate the amount of effort they will entail, suggest priorities and get agreement from stakeholders, work with the engineers to decide how you'll deliver them, and finally develop a day-by-day project plan as a team.

DEVELOP A TOPIC LIST AND TIME ESTIMATES

Using your framework and key path scenarios (plus a list of less common scenarios you already know you have to cover), you should be able to generate a list of design topics to use as a discussion tool. Although each team member might prefer to start a list individually, it's best to generate or at least review the topic list together, since one person's list might remind others of topics they haven't considered.

The list need not include every widget—you'd drive yourself crazy. Instead, focus on tasks and elements that will take you half a day or more to draft. For an e-mail and calendaring application, for example, the interaction design topic list might look something like this:

— Main e-mail list view

— Alternate e-mail list views (conversation view, detail list view)

— Managing folders and conversations

— Composing and formatting messages

— Mailbox filtering rules

— Spam handling

— Mail error handling

— Main address book screen (alphabetical list)

— Alternate address book views (by company, detailed view)

— Creating and managing contact groups

— Creating and managing contacts

— Address book error handling

— Main calendar screen (week)

— Alternate views (daily, monthly)

> **Develop a detailed topic list with time estimates in half-days or days. This will help you develop a day-by-day plan and keep everyone on schedule.**

- Creating and managing one-time appointments and meetings
- Recurring appointments
- Integration of meeting invitations with messages
- Calendar error handling
- Main toolbar and menus
- Help behavior (not content)

The visual designer's list would mirror this, but also contain key visual design tasks related to establishing the visual system, such as the layout grid, icons, and typography. When there is hardware involved, such as on a phone, the industrial designer's topic list would include things like angle adjustment and the handset, as well as the keypad and various controls.

Next, estimate how long a first pass at each of these design topics will take. Estimating in half-day chunks works well. There's no specific formula for doing this; it depends on the complexity of each bit of design. However, if you're estimating design topics at more than a couple of days each, break them down into smaller bits; larger chunks make it difficult to see whether you're running behind. In complex domains, you might want to allow for a day or so of detailed questions with a subject matter expert before you start each design topic.

Collaboration, essential though it is, eats a lot of time. For interaction design and visual design, one day of collaboration for every four days of design is usually an effective metric if your collaborators are accustomed to working with designers; I've sometimes allowed a bit more than this when the lead engineer or project owner tends to revisit old decisions and get pulled into edge cases too early. Effective collaboration usually yields a list of things to adjust, so allow another day or so per collaboration day to modify the design. (Note that this doesn't necessarily mean collaboration will occur only on specified days.)

For industrial designers, collaboration is more likely to be ongoing throughout the day, especially early in the phase when the mechanical engineer is essentially a design partner; unlike interaction designers and programmers, the ME and ID are working in much the same medium, even though their CAD applications may differ slightly in focus. The amount of ID time required depends on the complexity of the product, the skill of the engineering team, and the need for further exploration, but the ID might spend as little as a week or two of effort in this phase for a simple product architecture.

Documentation should be occurring as design progresses, but you will also need some dedicated time to draw and write as the design settles down. For interaction and visual design, documentation typically requires about one dedicated day per three design days, plus one to three days for team-member review, proofreading, and cleanup. These estimates don't include any sort of interactive prototype or animation.

Industrial design documentation is generally lighter; the ME is responsible for turning the CAD files into final specs for manufacturing. The ID does typically document his intent for color, material, texture, finish, and any application of graphical elements.

If you're able to make a second pass at the design, such as after a round of usability testing or extensive review by subject matter experts and engineers, plan on spending about 30 to 50 percent of the original design time estimate on revising the design and its documentation, depending on how complex it is.

Most project managers add 10 to 15 percent to their time estimates to allow for forgotten details, unexpected problems, communication delays, and other potential frustrations. Whether you should do this depends on what you think will be more effective with your stakeholders in the long run: Is it better to hit them with the bad news first and

Detailed Design

avoid setting high expectations, or to state that your numbers assume no delays and deal with the additional time only if they're a problem? I usually find that stakeholders hate surprises, so it's better to plan on the contingency time if you can. Your project owner may have a different preference. At a minimum, though, allow for a couple of days to address topics that were more challenging than you expected.

Figure 20.3 provides a summary of these metrics for estimating your design time. Note that these estimates assume each team member has a consistent amount of time per day to spend and that each is experienced and comfortable with her tools and tasks. Note that the amount of time spent on a topic (and therefore the amount of overall time spent) varies widely depending on the team's experience and skill level; experienced designers can move 25 to 50 percent faster than less-experienced designers and easily twice as fast as non-designers (such as subject matter experts or product managers) doing the same tasks.

Once you have your list and estimates, recommend what you think the priorities are, especially if there is a limited time in which to design and build a product. I've generally found that three levels of priority offer enough distinctions:

— **Essential:** You won't have a product or a coherent design without it.

— **Important:** There may be a noticeable lack in the product or design without it.

— **Optional:** The world won't end if it gets postponed to a subsequent version.

When you're done, you should have something like Table 20.1, which will serve as the basis for a critical discussion with stakeholders.

> The amount of time spent on each topic varies widely depending on the team's experience and skill level; experienced designers can move 25 to 50 percent faster than less-experienced designers.

| Supplemental research days per topic, if needed | Design days (divided into topics of 2 days or less) | Collaboration and revision days | Days of documentation time | Second pass, if possible |

$$\left(\frac{1}{2} \text{ to } 1\right) \quad + \quad N \quad + \quad \frac{N}{2} \quad + \quad \left(\frac{N}{3} + 1 \text{ to } 3\right) \quad + \quad \left(\frac{N}{3} + \frac{N}{2}\right)$$

Add 10–15% for contingency, if possible

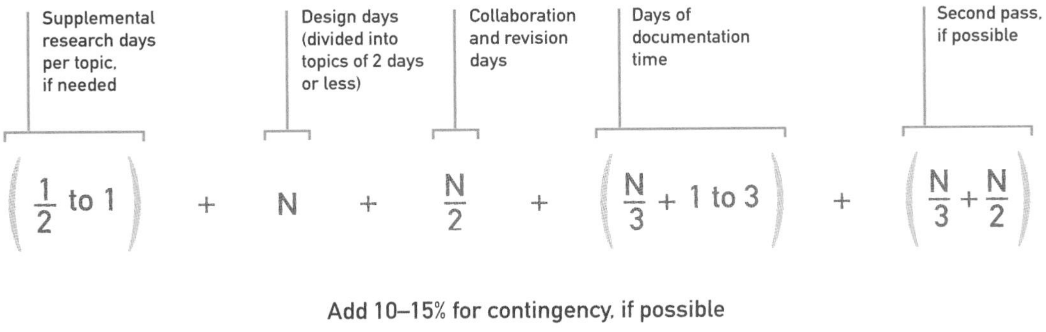

Figure 20.3. A summary of useful metrics for estimating interaction design time.

Detailed Design

Table 20.1. An example list of design topics and time estimates with tentative priorities for stakeholder discussion.

Topic	Detailed research	Initial design days	Collaboration and first iteration (design days x 0.5)	Drawing and documentation (design days x .33)	Second iteration (design days x .5)	Contingency (all days x .15)	Total topic days
Recommended essential topics							
Main email list view	0	1.5	0.8	0.5	0.8	0.5	4.0
Managing folders and conversations	0	1.0	0.5	0.3	0.5	0.3	2.7
Composing and formatting messages	0	0.5	0.3	0.2	0.3	0.2	1.3
Mail error handling	0	0.5	0.3	0.2	0.3	0.2	1.3
Main calendar screen	0	2.0	1.0	0.7	1.0	0.7	5.4
Creating and managing one-time appointments and meetings	0	1.5	0.8	0.5	0.8	0.5	4.0
Recurring appointments	0	0.5	0.3	0.2	0.3	0.2	1.3
Integration of meeting invitations with messages	0	0.5	0.3	0.2	0.3	0.2	1.3
Subtotal	0	9.0	4.5	3.0	4.5	3.1	24.1
Recommended important topics							
Spam handling	1	0.5	0.3	0.2	0.3	0.3	2.5
Main address book screen	0	1.5	0.8	0.5	0.8	0.5	4.0
Alternate address book views	0	1.0	0.5	0.3	0.5	0.3	2.7
Creating and managing contacts	0	2.0	1.0	0.7	1.0	0.7	5.4
Address book error handling	0	0.5	0.3	0.2	0.3	0.2	1.3
Alternate calendar views	0	1.0	0.5	0.3	0.5	0.3	2.7
Help behavior (not content)	0	1.0	0.5	0.3	0.5	0.3	2.7
Subtotal	1	7.5	3.8	2.5	3.8	2.8	21.2
Recommended optional topics							
Alternate email list views	0	1.5	0.8	0.5	0.8	0.5	4.0
Mailbox filtering rules	0.5	2.0	1.0	0.7	1.0	0.8	5.9
Creating and managing contact groups	0	1.0	0.5	0.3	0.5	0.3	2.7
Subtotal	0.5	4.5	2.3	1.5	2.3	1.6	12.6
Additional documentation time					2.0		
Final stakeholder presentation					1.0		
Totals	1	21.0	10.5	9.9	10.5	7.6	**58.0**

OTHER ISSUES THAT WILL AFFECT YOUR TIME ESTIMATES

There are a couple of other decisions that will affect how much time the detailed design takes. One is how you'll deliver your work. The other is whether or not you need to do any usability testing. You should plan on discussing both with stakeholders.

Delivery approach

Whether you deliver design in a single, meal-sized document or serve it up in smaller, snack-sized pieces isn't entirely about how the engineering team structures their time. It's possible for an agile team to work from a completed first-draft spec if they're starting behind the design team, as long as design engineering has occurred along the way. It can also be useful for a more waterfall-oriented team to get chunks of specification ahead of time, so they can start building some of the more complex pieces of code, working out tricky mechanical problems, and the like.

Many software or service design problems lend themselves to a chunked approach in which the design team delivers part A and goes on to work on part B, while the engineers review and perhaps begin to work on part A. However, as with splitting the design effort across a larger team, the overall gain in calendar time results in some loss of efficiency for both designers and engineers. For example, if you were designing an e-mail, calendaring, and task management application, you could presumably deliver the calendar part of the design, then turn your attention to the to-do list. When you suddenly realized that it would be useful to display to-do items for each date on the calendar, you'd need to let the engineers know right away that the design was going to shift, then go back and revise the calendar design.

This need to adjust design after the first draft has been documented leads to a certain amount of inefficiency, so you'll want to add a little bit of design adjustment and documentation time, such as a day or two for each two weeks of design.

Usability testing

The role and timing of usability testing are discussed in Chapter 23, but it's a good idea to determine whether you'll be doing any before you lay out your detailed schedule. If a third party is conducting the test(s), each test need not add more than a day or two to the design team's schedule, as long as testing happens in parallel. If the design team is conducting the tests, each test could add as much as ten days or more, depending on the degree of fidelity and formality, the size of the sample, and the location of your tests.

DISCUSS SCOPE AND PRIORITIES WITH STAKEHOLDERS

Once you have a list of your design tasks and some idea of how long they will take, sit down with your key stakeholders to review and prioritize the list. This should happen as soon as possible after the design vision meeting. The engineering leads should take part in the discussion as well; although engineers probably cannot provide an accurate estimate of engineering effort until the design is a bit more crystallized, stakeholders need to understand their best guess as to how much time and cost will be involved in executing various parts of the design.

When time and budget are limited, less-critical features and functions are usually the first things to go. If you must, consider trimming your contingency time, usability testing, and second pass at the design. Reducing the collaboration time is a last resort; you may produce a larger volume of design in a short time, but there is a greater risk that you will spend time polishing something that is too difficult to build.

If you're asked to leave some parts of the design to engineers—an unfortunately common occurrence in software—explain that this does not actually save time and generally delivers worse results. If you are still forced to do so, at least make sure you build in plenty of collaboration to ensure that the engineers understand not only the design, but the principles and rationale that guide it, and make sure the parts you leave undone are limited to routine forms and other straightforward components.

CREATING THE PROJECT PLAN

Finally, you'll need to lay your tasks out on a calendar. Start by drawing (or projecting) an actual calendar on the board and filling in the design team's vacation dates and any conflicts for key stakeholders, and then lay out your tasks.

Know what everyone is working on every day

If you've done a good job on the framework, you should know what most of your tasks are at this point, barring any feasibility issues that come up along the way. The best way to avoid a crunch at the end (or worse, a missed deadline) is to plan your work day by day. Lots of small deadlines will help you see if you're falling behind so you can catch up right away. They're also essential in coordinating the work of multiple designers and engineers. In a team environment, hitting the one big deadline at the end isn't good enough, because last-minute work on your part means last-minute work for everyone else, too.

Put the big rocks in first

As the saying goes, if you put the little rocks into the jar first, you might not be able to get the big rocks in at all. What this means for design is that you should start with the design problems that are either foundational or big and sticky. This can usually be driven by your design instincts, but there may be some aspect of the design the engineers need first; it's fine to be guided by this as long as the engineers' priority topics don't depend on you designing something else first. Follow these issues with those of medium difficulty, and leave straightforward things until the end. For interaction design, this means handling navigation issues and big, complex tools first, with routine forms and dialog boxes at the end. For visual design, the layout grid, common controls, and other aspects of the visual language should come first; it causes little difficulty to save icons until last. Industrial designers must address overall shape, assembly, and moving parts before focusing on purely cosmetic details.

There are several reasons to handle the big issues early. One is that more aspects of the design depend on them, so you'll save rework later. Another is that if you're stuck with a fixed (and inadequate) budget, especially for software, it's better to leave the engineers with the routine bits than with the trickiest parts of the design problem.

Insert check-ins where they make sense

It's always handy for you and your collaborators alike if your check-in schedule can be routine, such as every Thursday at 2:00. However, it's usually more important that check-ins occur when you need them; if that means one on Monday and another on Thursday, your collaborators will probably be happy to oblige as long as you're making good use of their valuable time.

If you have a fixed deadline, work backward from it

Depending on how your design time is accounted for, you may be asked to deliver whatever design you can fit in by a certain date. If this is the case, you'll need to work backward from that date. Note your delivery date and put in a day or two for documentation review right before it. Divide the remaining time by four, then allocate the last quarter to documentation. Add a day or two of contingency time just before the documentation days. Finally, drop your design topics and collaboration time into the remaining days.

Exercise

Draft a topic list and develop time estimates for your RoomFinder or LocalGuide design. Turn them into a first draft project plan, first assuming that you don't have a firm deadline, then assuming you have a maximum of five weeks to deliver as much design value as you can.

Summary

While detailed design is usually less dramatic than earlier phases, it remains critical to success. Your ability to collaborate with others outside the design team to translate your vision into a buildable product is what determines whether that vision gathers dust on a shelf or makes it into the hands of users. Detailed design demands not only a solid understanding of design principles, patterns, and process, but also excellent time management, collaboration, and communication skills. In some ways, your collaboration during framework definition is merely a warm-up for the actual design performance, in which every part of the symphony must play in tune and in perfect time.

Chapter 21 outlines some useful principles and patterns for detailed design. Chapter 22 describes how to evolve the form and behavior and develop a visual system. Chapter 23 will help you determine how and when to integrate assessment techniques, such as usability testing, into your process. Finally, Chapter 24 offers guidance on effectively communicating the details of your design to engineers and other constituents.

Detailed Design

CHAPTER 21

Detailed Design Principles and Patterns

Although your personas' goals and mental models should still guide your decisions during detailed design, personas aren't the most useful tools for deciding whether to use a list box or radio buttons, how large a click target should be, or whether physical controls should be convex or concave. For this reason, principles and patterns play an increasingly large role in detailed design.

As discussed in Chapter 15, design principles are guidelines that help you choose the best way to organize and portray information and tools so users can take action with minimal time and effort. Patterns are types of solutions that tend to be useful for certain kinds of problems. The principles and patterns discussed in Chapters 15 and 17 still apply, but detailed design requires a larger vocabulary of both. As in those earlier chapters, I won't attempt to describe every useful tidbit, but will cover some highlights and offer additional resources. Experienced designers may wish to skip or skim this chapter; that said, it never hurts to revisit fundamentals.

Principles and patterns are not necessarily unique to one design discipline or another; Lidwell et al. illustrate this nicely in *Universal Principles of Design*.[1] This is particularly true of detailed design, where it becomes difficult to separate where one discipline stops and another begins. For example, information design—the presentation of data in the most understandable way—involves considerable overlap between interaction and visual interface design. For this reason, I have not attempted to describe principles and patterns for each discipline, but have instead focused on the issues they address.

Principles: a Bit of Science, a Bit of Common Sense

Some principles are rooted in the scientific study of human cognition, vision, motor skills, and other capabilities, or are backed by a good bit of experimental data. It is useful for designers to understand the scientific underpinnings of our

---

1. Lidwell, W., Holden, K., and Butler, J. *Universal principles of design: 100 ways to enhance usability, influence perception, increase appeal, make better design decisions, and teach through design.* Rockport Publishers, 2003.

Products should be like good waiters: unassuming and unobtrusive, but always anticipating needs and learning preferences.

work in order to make use of their implications, though most of us will never have reason to employ the actual Fitts's Law[2] equation or worry overmuch about microsecond differences in mouse target acquisition. All we really need to know is that larger mouse or touch targets are easier to acquire, and that targets on the edges of the screen are "infinitely large" by virtue of having edges that stop the mouse cursor.

Deborah Mayhew's *Principles and Guidelines in Software User Interface Design,*[3] though dated, cites experimental data to provide a more science-based introduction to interface design principles than most. For those with more extensive curiosity or more esoteric needs, the academic literature is an excellent resource; along with texts on Gestalt and cognitive psychology, the ACM Digital Library[4] is a good starting point.

However, there are other useful principles that may not be based in science, but are simply about good manners and common sense. Many of these can essentially be summarized in a sentence: If the behavior would be rude or unhelpful from a human, it's at least as bad coming from a computer. Products should be like good waiters: unassuming and unobtrusive, but always anticipating needs and learning preferences. They should never interrupt or waste time with silly questions like whether your food is good or if you'd like to save that document you've been working on for the past hour.

For interaction design, being helpful could mean remembering and learning from previous user behavior or displaying related accessories on a shopping site. Mannerly visual design assumes the content is more important than its packaging; an operating system, for example, shouldn't call undue attention to window frames and such. Thoughtful industrial design might offer a place to wind a power cord for storage, a shelf for holding a purse or backpack at an automatic teller, or a stereo volume control in a convenient spot on a car steering wheel. Helpful service design might include home grocery delivery or a prepaid product return label with every order. See Figures 21.1 and 21.2 for examples.

Detailed Design

2. Fitts, P.M. "The information capacity of the human motor system in controlling the amplitude of movement." *Journal of Experimental Psychology*, June 1954.

3. Mayhew, D.J. *Principles and guidelines in software user interface design.* Prentice Hall, 1991.

4. Association for Computing Machinery, http://portal.acm.org/dl.cfm

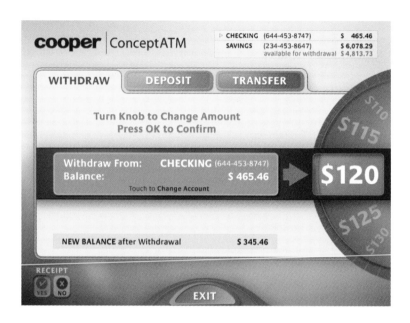

Figure 21.1. This design for an automated teller remembers each user's most common transaction and presents that as the first option.

Figure 21.2. This laptop power adapter includes brackets for winding the power cord, as well as a small clasp for securing the cord's end.

You can find many specific principles of this sort in *About Face 3*.[5] However, you can derive many of these for yourself if you routinely consider what your personas would find helpful, and if you remember these key principles from Chapter 15:

— Good design is ethical, purposeful, pragmatic, and elegant.

— Good design nearly always minimizes unnecessary memory, motor, mental, and visual work.

— The best solution is always appropriate to the user's context.

Communicating Flow, Priority, and Relationships

Much of the work in detailed design is focused on communication: what's important, what the personas want or need to know at various points in their tasks, and what input the system needs. Principles focused on effective visual communication are largely drawn from the

5. Cooper, A., Reimann, R., and Cronin, D. *About face 3: The essentials of interaction design*. John Wiley and Sons, 2007.

Detailed Design

fields of graphic design, semiotics, and cognitive and Gestalt psychology. These overlap the work of interaction designers, visual interface designers, and industrial designers alike. These principles outlined in Chapter 17 form a good basis for clear communication:

— Visually communicate what elements do.

— Use visual hierarchy to emphasize important information and controls.

— Have a purpose for every element and a reason for every decision.

— Repeat elements for unity.

— Be decisive, but use the smallest effective difference.

Detailed design continues to rely on these ideas, as well as others that will help you reduce, prioritize, and organize tools and information to communicate in limited time and space. In addition to the key principles and patterns highlighted here, I recommend *Designing Visual Interfaces: Communication Oriented Techniques* by Kevin Mullet and Darrell Sano.[6]

Map visual flow to workflow

Whether someone is cooking dinner, processing photographs, or doing brain surgery, it's possible to optimize workflow by making sure the right tools are available nearby and in the right sequence, so it seems like common sense that visual flow in a product should be mapped to workflow. In Western cultures, this means the tools and information used at the beginning of the scenario belong at the top left, while those used later belong at the bottom or toward the right. Surprisingly, this basic concept is often ignored.

Consider the photo in Figure 21.3, which shows a ticket kiosk for BART, a regional transit system serving the San Francisco Bay Area. Although locals can buy an electronic pass that automatically charges a credit card, infrequent riders and the area's many tourists buying single-trip tickets must first look at the screen, then at the printed fare list at the upper right to see what the one-way fare is to their destination (and do the mental math if they're taking a round trip). If they aren't familiar with the station names, they have to walk several steps to a printed route map on the wall, which still doesn't offer good information about what's near each station. Once they've figured out the fare, they then have to look below or to the right of the screen to insert cash or a card, then back to the screen to adjust the amount up or down. A better approach would be to integrate the route and fare information with the electronic tools, and to adjust the layout so there's a clean flow from top left to bottom right.

Figure 21.3. This ticket kiosk is an example of poor visual flow.

6. Mullet, K., and Sano, D. *Designing visual interfaces: Communication oriented techniques.* Prentice Hall, 1994.

Detailed Design

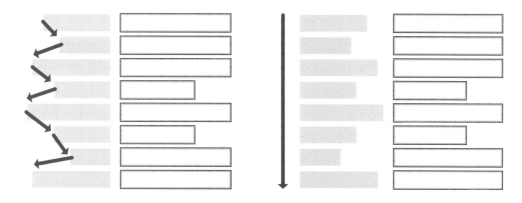

Figure 21.4. Scanning a complex form is much easier with left-aligned labels and fields than with right-aligned labels.

You may find that this basic application of visual flow breaks down somewhat as you apply multiple scenarios to a first draft of your design, but it's always a good starting point for laying out on-screen widgets and information as well as physical controls.

Exercise

Redesign the kiosk in Figure 21.3 so the visual flow maps to the workflow.

Align elements for readability and simplicity

The alignment of elements contributes to readability and to an overall impression of order and simplicity. There are a couple of basic things anyone can do to maximize readability.

From a simple usability standpoint, you should right align currency and integers, but left align most labels and widgets, with the longest label ending within one or two characters of the widget. Although many graphic designers like the clean gutter formed between right-aligned text and left-aligned widgets, this makes text more difficult to scan, as shown in Figure 21.4.[7] It doesn't particularly matter for, say, a login screen, where there's little data entry and people won't refer back to it, but right-aligned text would slow down someone looking up information in a customer record. People generally do not have trouble associating labels and widgets unless there is an extreme difference in label lengths, as shown in Figure 21.5. If pressed for horizontal space, consider placing text labels directly above the input fields and aligned along the left edge.

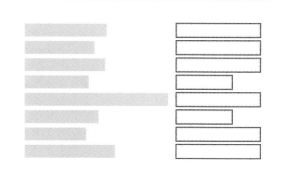

Figure 21.5. Extreme differences in label length can make left-aligned text awkward; ideally, adjust the length of the label rather than right aligning.

7. Mayhew, D.J. *Op. cit.*

Detailed Design

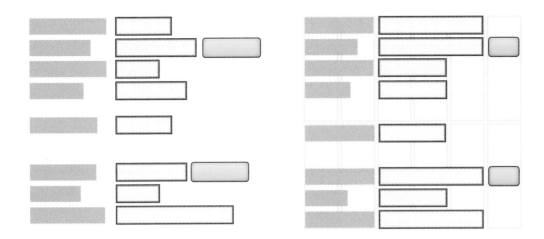

Figure 21.6. See how much neater and simpler the screen looks when elements are aligned in a grid.

Beyond simple usability, you should look for opportunities to align elements along shared axes. Even without a good visual system, you can reduce the impression of clutter by, for example, making fields the same length or aligning a row of physical controls with the edges of a display bezel. Better yet, a deliberately designed grid system offers an invisible set of columns and rows to guide the placement of each element. Compare the layouts in Figure 21.6 to see what a difference the grid makes. Devices likewise benefit from a simple grid, as shown in Figure 21.7. Chapter 22 outlines how to develop an effective grid.

Use visual properties to establish a clear hierarchy

Good design makes it easy to find the most important information and controls by drawing attention to them and by downplaying less important items. Take the remote controls in Figure 21.8, for example. The one on the left has buttons that are all the same color and mostly the same shape, making it difficult to locate frequently used controls. Even though the color choices on the playback buttons are unfortunate (green means stop and yellow means play), the remote on the right is at least successful in drawing attention to frequently used controls.

Figure 21.7. Many devices benefit from a simple grid, as well.

Figure 21.8. The remote control on the left does not have a clear visual hierarchy. The remote on the right at least highlights important functions with color, though the choice of green for a stop button is unfortunate.

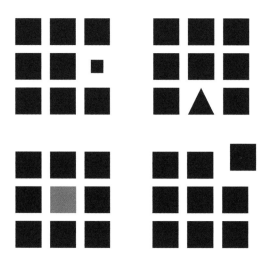

Figure 21.9. Manipulate visual properties such as size, position, shape, and color to create visual contrast.

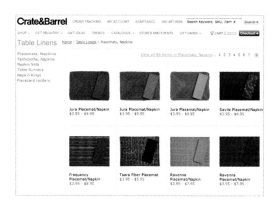

Figure 21.10. Good use of hierarchy.

As shown in Figure 21.9, you can establish a clear visual **hierarchy** through contrast in visual properties such as size, shape, color, and position. Many e-mail applications, for example, use bold type to draw attention to unread messages, along with icons to indicate urgency. The stronger the contrast, the more clear the hierarchy; you can strengthen contrast by varying multiple properties. However, varying every property is likely to be overkill; remember to use the smallest effective difference to achieve your aims. Also be sure that any brand signature elements fit appropriately within the hierarchy. The Crate and Barrel Web site shown in Figure 21.10 makes good use of type size and weight, position, and color to keep users oriented. The products have the most visual weight—as they should—followed by the name of the store. The checkout button and the "Table Linens" category header are at about the same level, while the subcategory header is a notch lower in the hierarchy.

Although visual hierarchy is important to keep users oriented, a strong hierarchy can also help draw attention to exceptions without using offensive beeps and obnoxious pop-up messages. Modeless visual feedback such as highlights, icons, changes in color or weight, and illuminated physical parts are all visible but polite ways to indicate that something could use attention. Figure 21.11 shows several examples. Bold text and an icon or number on a tab or file can indicate that new items need attention. Red and yellow backgrounds or borders can indicate missing or problematic data.

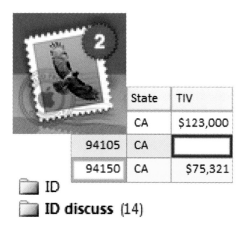

Figure 21.11. Examples of modeless visual feedback.

Detailed Design

577

Use visual properties to establish association

It's often important for users to understand associations within their data or among their tools.

It's often important for users to understand associations within their data or among their tools. For example, it's helpful to know what other e-mail messages are related to the selected message, which files will open what applications, or which knob on the stovetop affects which burner. The two most effective ways to establish relationships are proximity and similarity.

Whether we see two people walking side by side, a stack of documents on a desk, or several hardware or software controls in close proximity to one another, humans tend to assume that proximity equals relationship—imagine your surprise if the switch near the kitchen sink were for the lights and the one near the door were for the garbage disposal. In contrast, items with a fair amount of space between them tend not to be associated, as in Figure 21.12. You can also group items by putting them in some sort of container together, such as an inset with a different material for a physical product or a bounding box on the screen. However, this brute-force approach can be overdone; physical space is often the better option.

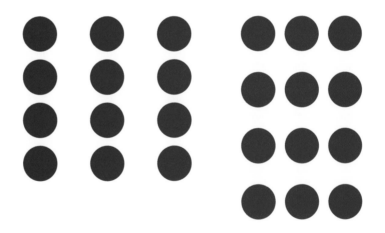

Figure 21.12. Whether you see three columns or four rows depends on how the objects are spaced.

Items that look similar or have similar relationships are also seen as related; dissimilar things are harder to associate. The classic bad example is a stovetop: If the knobs and burners were arranged in the same pattern, it would be easy to figure out which knob affected which burner. Instead, many manufacturers attempt to convey this with a schematic next to each knob, as in Figure 21.13. Highway signage offers a better example: Within one country, navigation signs are generally one color (usually blue or green), caution signs are a different color (usually yellow or orange), and points of interest (such as rest stops or historical sites) are still other colors. On a remote control, playback buttons might be one shape while navigation controls, such as numbers and menu buttons, are another.

Exercise

Redesign the dialog box and remote control below to map visual flow to workflow, associate related items, and develop a clear visual hierarchy.

Figure 21.13. The burners and knobs on this stovetop are difficult to associate because their positions are poorly mapped.

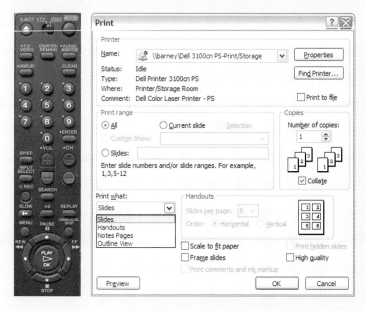

Communicating Data: Information Design

Nearly every desktop application, Web site, and interactive device communicates some amount of data. Even the simplest cell phone says what time it is, whether the signal is weak or strong, and how much juice (or better yet, time) is left in the battery. Complex analytical applications help users identify trends and relationships in enormous data sets.

Plain textual information is often not the most effective way to communicate data. Using numbers and equations, most of us would take a couple of minutes to predict where a thrown ball will land, if we could do it at all. In contrast, it takes less than a second for us to look at the ball, determine its speed and trajectory, and then reach out a hand to catch it. The human brain is an amazingly adept visual information processor, so designers should not be afraid to use it. Presenting data in visual terms often makes it more immediate and compelling. It usually takes up less space, too.

The effective visual presentation of data (also called **information design**) puts data integrity before all other considerations: Your representation of data should never be visually misleading, and cutesy or overly complex representations can obscure the data. As Edward Tufte puts it, keep your data-to-ink ratio high; see Figure 21.14.

Of course, good information design starts with your personas and scenarios: What information do your personas need immediately and at a glance? What do they need next? What do they need to see only when there's a problem? These priorities tell you what to emphasize and what to minimize in the visual hierarchy.

Though some information designers lament the relatively low density of digital displays versus paper, the one advantage of the digital display is the

ability to do progressive disclosure: Make the critical information prominent, make the less=critical information visible, and show minor details only when someone hovers a mouse or clicks on something. Ben Shneiderman[8] refers to this as "details on demand." See Figure 21.15 for an example.

The best information design goes well beyond clear hierarchy, however. You should also help viewers put information in context. Show a meaningful comparison with something else, such as an industry average, a target, or the same data for a previous time period. Use multiple variables together to help viewers understand causality, especially for expert users who spend a lot of time with their data. Figure 21.16, for example, shows how a graph representing automobile accidents becomes increasingly useful as more variables are compared.

In interactive systems, a simple variety of information design is effective for communicating state and providing useful feedback in a modeless way.

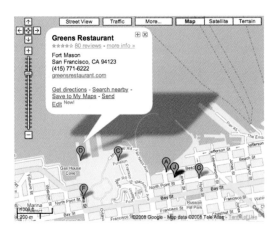

Figure 21.15. Google Maps offers several types of details on demand, and even offers multiple levels of drilldown.

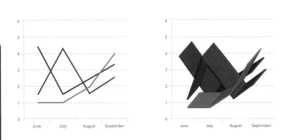

Figure 21.14. Note how the 3D graph is harder to read than the simple 2D version.

8. Shneiderman, B. *Designing the user interface: Strategies for effective human-computer interaction.* Addison Wesley, 3rd edition, 1998.

Detailed Design

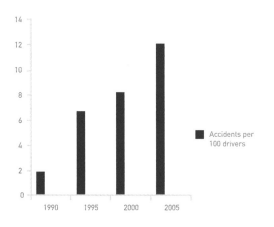
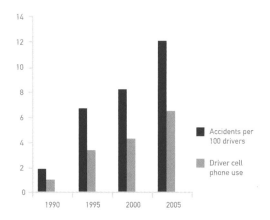

Figure 21.16. The chart on the left shows only an increase in automobile accidents, which might lead a viewer to conclude that driver safety programs were not working, but the second chart explains the trend.

On-screen indicators can hint that, for example, a user's instruction about a medication dosage exceeds a safety parameter, or that an entry is outside of certain preferred guidelines; Figure 21.11 shows several good examples of this. A physical switch could indicate by its position or LED color state that it's turned on. Figure 21.17 shows the problem with switches that don't indicate state, while Figure 21.18 shows a better example.

For more information design principles, *The Visual Display of Quantitative Information* and

Figure 21.17. These switches in my MINI Cooper S look slick but don't show state very well because they return to the same position regardless of whether they are activated. There's a tiny LED at the end of the switch for traction control, but it's so invisible it might as well not be there.

other books by Edward Tufte are informative and full of interesting examples. Though they emphasize print applications, many of the ideas can be adapted for on-screen display. Richard Saul Wurman's *Information Anxiety*[9] and Robert Jacobsen's *Information Design*[10] are also worth a look.

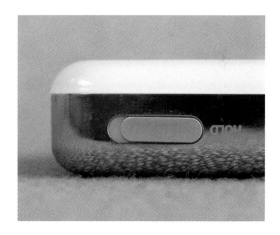

Figure 21.18. This iPod's "hold" button, which prevents accidental activation of other controls, uses a bright orange color to indicate that it is on.

9.   Wurman, R.S. *Information anxiety 2*. Que, 2001.

10. Jacobson, R. (Ed.) *Information design*. The MIT Press, 2000.

Detailed Design

Using Icons to Communicate about Objects and Tools

Although icons are seldom ideal for first-time use, they are helpful in file systems and lists for indicating object type and status. They're usually good choices for controls in productivity applications because they occupy less space than text labels. Sometimes, they're useful for communicating simple ideas to an international audience without a common language. They're almost always poor choices for any tool that should be instantly usable, such as a kiosk or Web site; good text labels are better because they're unambiguous. The exception is in applications that must be language independent, such as wayfinding in an airport full of international travelers.

There's seldom a good reason to combine both text and icons in a toolbar; this punishes intermediate users by eating up precious screen space, and if you're catering to novices, the icons don't gain you much. Microsoft's execution of the "Ribbon" in Office 2007 (shown in Figure 21.19) is puzzling in this respect; although novices may have an easier time finding functions, the vast majority of users lose considerable screen space and immediate access to controls because the tools combine large and small icons with text.

Icon style is an important part of the design language that communicates emotional qualities and reinforces brand attributes (see Chapter 17); the icons within an application should all have a family resemblance that reinforces the desired experience attributes. However, the way your icons are designed also has a significant impact on their usability. In addition to style considerations, effective icons are immediately recognizable, understandable within their context, and part of a coherent system. Figure 21.20 is an example of what not to do with icon design. As symbols, these icons from an online calendaring system

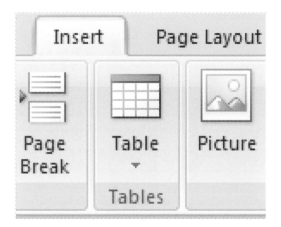

Figure 21.19 Microsoft's "Ribbon" doesn't seem optimized for intermediates.

are difficult to decipher; even the ones that seem predictable actually mean something different from what you'd expect. The low contrast and level of detail in some makes the images difficult to understand. They also lack a family resemblance, and the muddy yellow and purple—which are totally unrelated to the company's brand—don't make this application a place where users want to spend time.

Figure 21.20. What not to do with icon design.

Making icons recognizable

If you'll recall the discussion of human perception from Chapter 17, we recognize shapes most quickly, followed by color and only much later by texture and other surface details. The implications of this are clear, and are borne out by experimental data:[11] simple, schematic icons

11. Mayhew, D.J. *Op. cit.*

Detailed Design

with distinct shapes are more immediately recognizable than highly detailed, photorealistic ones. The more visual information there is in an icon, the longer it takes to decipher. Icons that have borders or are all the same shape require even more time to figure out. This is why road signs, which must be recognizable at 65 miles an hour, use simple schematic symbols. In Figure 21.21, you can compare these with Apple's nearly photographic application icons. Safari, iTunes, and iDVD all have very similar shapes and colors, as do iPhoto and iWeb; if I'm only half paying attention, I still sometimes click the wrong icon on the dock even after years of using these applications. Certainly there is a brand aesthetic value for Apple in these glossy illustrations, but there is also a significant usability trade-off. Particularly when speed and accuracy matter, keep your icons visually simple and use shapes that are distinct from one another. When representing an object, choose the most familiar outline of its shape; showing a telephone from above, for example, would be an unusual perspective that would make the object less familiar.

Also consider that icons usually have to be rendered at different sizes, often as little as 16×16 pixels, which doesn't allow for much visual information. The simpler your image, the easier it will be to render at low resolution or incised into a physical surface. Anti-aliasing doesn't always work well for icons that must look good on multiple backgrounds. Icons may also have to be legible printed in a black-and-white user manual, though this is becoming the exception rather than the norm.

Making icons understandable

As discussed in Chapter 17, humans derive meaning from both content and context. Much like an unfamiliar word used in a sentence, an

Figure 21.21. The human brain is quick to process simple, distinct shapes. Similar shapes and colors and excessive visual detail make icons harder to recognize.

icon that may not be clear by itself takes on meaning from other icons around it. The text-formatting controls shown in Figure 21.22 are classic examples of this. Of course, culture and experience provide their own sort of context, as well; the average teenager, for example, has never used a floppy disk or a roll of film, and a German driver flashing you the American "OK" sign on the autobahn is calling you something rude, not telling you how cool you are.

Figure 21.22. Icons take meaning from the context of other icons around them.

Icons may also take meaning from similar icons that aren't nearby. Repeating the same icon with slight differences, such as adding a plus or a star to a folder icon, can indicate actions or properties related to whatever the original icon represents. This is called **inheritance**. You can use the same concept to convey status, such as an e-mail icon that changes when you've replied to or forwarded the message. Figure 21.23 shows an example of inheritance.

Detailed Design

Figure 21.23. Icons inherit meaning from another icon that forms the basis of a series.

Successful icons generally represent familiar **objects**, **actions**, or desired **end results**. Most data objects (see Chapter 16) can be represented by simple object images, such as a document, a folder, a person, or a computer. Tools and actions are often best represented by an image of an object plus an action, such as an arrow indicating an open folder, or by the desired end result, such as text shown in bold. Once in a while, it's possible to illustrate only an action without an object, generally because there is only one type of object to which the action could apply. Abstract symbols, such as a radiation hazard symbol or a cylinder to represent a database, are more difficult to learn unless they're already part of your personas' context. Figure 21.24 illustrates each of these icon types.

Figure 21.24. Objects, actions, objects plus actions, and abstract symbols can all make effective icons provided they are appropriate to the context of use.

Because icons take meaning from their context, it's preferable to use a consistent type of icon (such as combining object and action) when possible. Don't be too dismayed if it's not possible to be consistent, however; it's more important that each icon be recognizable and understandable on its own.

   Metonymy

 Litotes

 Synechdoche

 Metaphor

Figure 21.25. Icons as figures of speech.

However, many actions can be tricky to represent with an object and indication of movement, and not all end results can be represented visually. In these cases, understanding how icon design patterns relate to literary figures of speech—which I bet you never thought you'd use outside of a classroom—can help you select images that are more likely to be successful. Figure 21.25 shows icons representing each of the following figures of speech.

Metonymy is the use of one thing to represent a closely related thing, such as saying "the White House policy on immigration" to mean "the President's policy on immigration." In icons, metonymy generally involves either using a container to represent the thing it contains, as an envelope represents an e-mail message, or using a tool to represent the end result, such as a pair of scissors to mean "cut."

In **synechdoche**, a part is used to represent the whole. For example, if you say in a design meeting that you need to get another brain or another pair of hands, you're talking about another person. Highway signs that show a knife and fork to represent a restaurant are using synechdoche. This literary device can be a bit indirect, so use it with care. The icon for Mac Mail in Figure 21.25, for example, is a poor use of synechdoche, especially since a small version of the icon looks more like a photo than a stamp.

Litotes is used to convey an idea by negating an accomplishment, as in, "Winning an Olympic medal is *no small feat*." In icon design, this usually involves negating something represented through metonymy, such as by showing an X or circle and slash on top of an object icon to indicate deletion, or the use of a minus symbol inside a magnifying glass to indicate zooming out.

Metaphor is the use of one unrelated object to represent another, as in "all the world's a stage." The relationship is distant enough that the connection can be difficult to make. The icon representing Apple's backup utility, for example, is an umbrella, presumably so you're pre-pared for a figurative rainy day. It's memorable enough for a frequent user once the mental connection is made, but difficult to decipher at first. It's usually best to minimize the use of metaphor.

A summary of useful icon guidelines

Here's a summary of useful icon design guidelines to keep in mind:

— Use icons only when users will have an opportunity to learn them and at least one of the following applies: space requires it, users need to differentiate objects in a list, or you need to communicate status.

— Combine objects and actions when possible.

— Avoid obscure metaphors and visual puns.

— Use objects and symbols that are recognizable to your personas, and that will work internationally.

— Avoid unnecessary realism, borders, colors, 3D treatment, or other visual complexity.

— Make sure icons work with all possible resolutions, color depths, and backgrounds applicable to your application.

— Make sure the icon can be rendered clearly at all applicable sizes.

— Portray objects from the most recognizable point of view; avoid un-usual angles.

— Be consistent about perspective, lighting, style, and color palette for all icons within the application (and often the platform).

— Relate the visual style of the icons to the style of the overall inter-face and to the experience attributes.

> Use icons when space requires it, users need to differentiate objects in a list, or you need to communicate status.

Detailed Design

Make icons visually distinct, especially with respect to shape and color.

— Make icons visually distinct (especially with respect to shape and color). Try the squint test—if you can't easily tell them apart with your eyes mostly shut, they're not distinct enough.

— Reflect the appropriate hierarchy in your set of icons; make the most important icons more visually prominent than less-used icons, and make status indicators smaller than icons used as controls.

Exercises

1. Sketch icons for the following actions:
   — Bookmark a Web page
   — Delete a customer's record from a database
   — Geocode a set of data (i.e., verify that each address in a data set corresponds to a real location on a map)
   — Resize an image in a document
   — Put a car navigation system into voice input mode
   — Take an x-ray image of a patient

2. Render one of the above icons:
   — In full color at 32×32 pixels, with the ability to display on either a gray or white background
   — In full color at 16×16 pixels, with the ability to display on either a gray or white background, in a style suited to a child's device with the following experience attributes: playful, approachable, warm
   — In full color at 16×16 pixels, with the ability to display on either a gray or white background, in a style suited to a medical device with the following experience attributes: precise, professional, clean
   — In black and white (not grayscale) at 16 ×16 pixels in one of the above styles

Text and Type

Text is an essential element of many systems, from wayfinding to controls, navigation, and content. Although Chapter 17 offers some advice on selecting appropriate screen fonts, you must also consider readability—how quickly someone can grasp your meaning—and legibility.

Type size

There are all sorts of guidelines for how large your type should be. The only truly reliable one is based on how many degrees of an arc the type fills in a reader's vision; this accounts for resolution and distance from the screen. Most designers rely on simple guidelines instead of painful calculation; unfortunately, such guidelines generally fail to consider several important factors:

— **Hierarchy.** Critical information should be large; supplemental information can and should be smaller.

— **Typeface.** Good screen fonts are legible at small sizes, whereas others must be large even on paper.

— **Context.** Older populations, beginning readers, poorly lit environments, screens with protective coverings, large blocks of text, people working far from the display, and hazardous situations (such as driving) all call for larger type. Three-millimeter text may be tolerable on a portable music player if you have good eyesight, but would be dreadful for reading any amount of content.

— **Resolution.** Pixels on the same screen are smaller at, say, 1024×768 than at 800×600, so it's entirely possible for text to become too small. Specifying type size in pixels provides greater control of the design, but specifying it in points allows an operating system to adjust the type based on resolution. For the sake of accessibility, users should be able to increase type size, so consider how your screen layout will degrade gracefully with large type.

— **Screen size.** A resolution of 1024×768 on a 12-inch laptop screen will still render 10-point type much smaller than 1024×768 on a 20-inch desktop monitor.

— **Contrast.** Type that doesn't contrast strongly with its background is harder to read.

All that being said, for most applications on most platforms, the right sizes for type are generally between about 9 and 24 points. Your best bet is to choose a size (or a range of sizes, in a hierarchy) that feels about right, then try it out on a range of screens of various sizes and resolutions. It's easy to simulate screen sizes and resolutions on paper by manipulating your print settings.

Additional principles

A few other guidelines will help you maximize legibility and readability:

— Keep instructions and labels short and simple. Avoid unnecessarily repeating words in sets of multiple controls (such as checkboxes and radio buttons).

— Use active voice in content and instructions.

— Skip any jargon that isn't part of your personas' daily vocabulary.

— Use enough words to make it clear what sort of content is behind a Web site link; single words are often insufficient.

— For interfaces that will be translated into multiple languages, leave extra space between labels and controls—German and French, for example, take up more space than English—or find an intelligent way to adjust the screen layout for translated text.

— Run translated text by at least one native speaker of each language. Poor translation can make an interface incomprehensible. At best, it erodes any impression of quality.

— Avoid serif faces at small sizes.

— Avoid traditional anti-aliasing; modern operating systems handle this automatically. Turn off even this at small sizes.

— If using large blocks of content, as on a Web site, stick to an average line length of 10 to 12 words (65 to 70 characters).

Detailed Design

587

— Use single spaces after periods.

— Separate headings or subheadings from other text by a full line space or more.

Widgets and Data Entry

Widget selection—sometimes even widget design—is a key part of detailed interaction design. A good widget choice minimizes errors and balances clarity and efficiency with effective use of screen space.

Use widgets appropriate to the task and input method

Whatever widgets you use should be suited to the primary input method, if not for the product, at least for the task at hand. Perhaps the most common problematic example is address entry on many e-commerce Web sites: Users must enter name, street, and city information using the keyboard, but are often forced to select a state or province from a drop-down list with a mouse. This interrupts flow and is inefficient. While there's nothing wrong with bounded input, such a list box should allow keyboard-based selection because the rest of the task involves the keyboard by necessity. Text fields, combo boxes, and radio buttons generally work fine with keyboard primary input; list boxes and spin buttons can work if implemented to accept typed input. Checkboxes tend to be difficult in keyboard-primary situations.

Also select widgets that are appropriate to the type of data your personas will be entering. Bounded input widgets prevent errors by allowing only certain values or types of data to be entered; this is better than letting someone enter invalid data and popping up an error dialog. Table 21.1 outlines effective uses for common widgets.

Table 21.1. **Common interface widgets and their uses.**

Widget	Appropriate use	Comments and cautions
Buttons with text	Used for taking immediate action on mouse-up (or finger-up on touch screens). Default buttons (which will be activated by the ENTER or RETURN key) should be highlighted. Ellipses after the text on a button indicate that it will launch a dialog.	Not ideal for applications with limited space; use icons instead if users have a chance to learn them over time.
Buttons with icons	Used for taking immediate action on mouse-up (or finger-up on touch screens). Best where space is tight and users will have a chance to learn and remember the icon's meaning.	Avoid icons if users won't spend much time with the application (or if you can't come up with a good icon).

Detailed Design

Widget	Appropriate use	Comments and cautions
Calendar controls 	Used for mouse-driven date entry.	Useful for reference even in keyboard-primary applications as long as you also allow text entry.
Check boxes 	Used for yes/no answers and making multiple selections in a list. Put labels to the right of the control. When using multiple check boxes, stack them vertically for easier scanning.	Not ideal for keyboard-primary applications.
Combo boxes 	Used for choosing among multiple mutually exclusive values, but allow flexibility to enter a new value. Put labels either above or to the left of the control. Use auto-complete to minimize typing.	Don't confuse combo boxes with menus by including commands. These break the widget's normal behavior.
Links 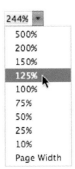	Used for navigating to other places or viewing secondary information. Unused links are typically blue and followed links are purple.	If you break the color and underline conventions for aesthetic reasons, at least differentiate link words by color and type style, and make the underline available on mouse-over. Also, users expect links to be for navigation, not initiating other actions.

Continued

Detailed Design

Widget	Appropriate use	Comments and cautions
List boxes and drop-down list boxes 	Used for choosing among multiple (usually mutually exclusive) values where new entries are not desirable. The drop-down version is typical when space is limited; otherwise, showing all options is more efficient. Multiselection is sometimes possible using CTRL and SHIFT keys or embedded check boxes. Put labels above or to the left of the control. For explicit targets (such as the name of a state) consider an alphabetical or other predictable sort order. For targets that are not explicit (such as "I want to find a new mystery novel") categorization often works better.	Don't confuse drop-down list boxes with menus by including commands. These break the widget's normal behavior.
List buttons 	An alternate version of a command button used to fit more options in a compact space. Clicking the icon or text area activates the default command. Clicking the arrow portion of the control reveals the list of other options.	Make sure the hidden options are closely related to the default command; otherwise, users will struggle with finding what you've hidden.
Menus and cascading menus 	Used to access less-frequently-used commands not available in a toolbar. As with buttons, commands activate immediately unless followed by ellipses. Use predictable sort order for explicit targets and categorization for others. Consider duplicating frequently or recently used items at the top of the menu.	Menus are excellent teaching tools. By repeating a toolbar icon and showing keyboard shortcuts in the menu, you can teach people to find options the faster way next time. When you must use cascading or "flyout" menus, leave wide latitude for mouse imprecision. Avoid forcing users to click "more options" just to see another few commands.
Progressive disclosure controls	Used when a list item or control includes additional detail that shouldn't always be visible. Icons on most progressive disclosure controls reveal future state (what can be expected once the control is activated), such as in the common + and - controls.	Rotating arrows are becoming more common, but because they reveal current state rater than future state, their function is less evident to inexperienced users.

Widget	Appropriate use	Comments and cautions
Radio buttons ⊙ All ○ Current page	Used for choosing among a small number of mutually exclusive values. If you have more than three to five values, use a list box instead. When possible, stack radio buttons vertically rather than laying them out horizontally. Place the label to the right of the control.	Avoid using a single radio button for a yes/no answer; a check box is the correct choice for this.
Spin buttons Top: 1.6" Bottom: 1.49"	Used for precise control of quantitative increments in mouse-driven or touch screen applications.	These typically allow direct number entry; for input, a list box is usually a better choice.
Sliders	Used for less precise control of quantitative increments (such as sound volume) in mouse-driven or touch screen applications.	Awkward in keyboard-primary interactions.
Table (a.k.a. grid) controls ▲ Name 57 Home, Pt. 2 58 Flight of the Phoenix 59 He That Believeth In Me 60 Kobol's Last Gleaming, ... 61 Six Degrees of Separation 62 Tigh Me Up, Tigh Me D...	Used for making multiple data entries or for sets of data that must be sortable. Use an up or down arrow and visual emphasis to indicate which is the primary sort column and which way it's sorted.	3D button affordances on column headers lead users to expect they can sort by the columns; avoid this affordance if columns cannot be sorted.
Tabs Themes Desktop	Used for switching context without losing orientation.	If possible, avoid using large numbers of tabs together or using tabs within tabs. Definitely avoid stacking tabs, which rearrange themselves in a disorienting fashion.
Text fields Save As: ch 21 DD principles_AR.doc	Used for free text entry. The length of field should roughly indicate how many characters are permitted or expected, though you can tweak this a bit to align with a layout grid.	Avoid displaying noneditable text with field affordance and a gray background; these conflicting affordances confuse users. Just remove the box and don't display the text as a field.

Continued

Detailed Design

Widget	Appropriate use	Comments and cautions
Toggles 	Used singly for on/off options or as a set for choosing from a small number of mutually exclusive options when space is limited.	Toggles are less standard than radio buttons or checkboxes, so use those instead if you have space.
Tool tips	Used to provide supplemental information when a user hovers the cursor over something (such as a toolbar icon). Disappears when the mouse is moved.	Avoid using tool tips for large amounts of text.
Trees	Used for user-defined filing systems or for items with predictable categories.	Unfortunately, tree controls are overused because they are easy to build. Humans are lousy at remembering the locations of things, though, so this isn't always the best way to go; various types of search are sometimes more useful.

Allow flexible input even in bounded widgets

If a customer support agent on the phone asks for your name, you probably find it obnoxious if he insists on getting your last name first (at least if you're from a Western culture). It's equally obnoxious for applications to insist on having dates, phone numbers, and other common types of data formatted in rigid ways. It's not that hard to figure out that 415.267.3500 is the same as (415) 267-3500, or that 7/4/09 is July 4, 2009, in the U.S. and April 7, 2009, in Europe. It's not even particularly difficult to figure out that if I type "Kim Goodwin" into a name field, chances are good that "Kim" is my first name and "Goodwin" my last name.

Use custom controls only with good reason

Designers are inventive people, so we can be tempted to create new solutions just for the sake of doing so. However, novel controls require custom code or expensive hardware engineering and are generally more expensive to implement, so think long and hard about whether you really need to go beyond what standard libraries offer. Custom widgets are sometimes worthwhile for visual feedback, such as in the table shown in Figure 21.11, or for situations where some direct visualization of results makes actions more understandable. See the examples in Figures 21.26 and 21.27.

Detailed Design

EXERCISE

Either choose an appropriate standard widget or, if it's more appropriate, design a custom widget for each of the following in a PC environment:

— Entering a credit card expiration date when checking out of an online store

— Adjusting volume on a video player

— Adjusting the position and intensity of the light source illuminating a 3D model

— Ordering a small, medium, or large pizza online

— Telling your design instructor which of the following best describe her: brilliant, charming, gorgeous, kind, witty

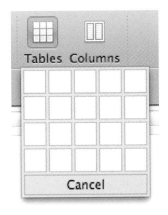

Figure 21.26. This "insert table" widget from Microsoft Word is a good use of a custom widget because it allows for easy visualization of results.

Considerations for touch screens

As with text size, you may read multiple guidelines for the size of widgets or other targets on a touch screen, ranging from about 9 mm to 20 mm or more. As with type, the right size depends on context:

— A stylus is more precise than fingers and thumbs, so it makes small targets more manageable.

— People with short fingernails tend to use the tips of their fingers, but people with long nails need to use the pads of the fingers (which are larger and less precise) unless the particular touch screen technology accepts fingernail input.

— As with mouse target acquisition, people who are farther from the screen or trying to work quickly need larger targets to be accurate.

— Sequential targets are slightly easier to hit.

— Different ways of interpreting finger position allow for more or less accuracy; reading the center of the average finger position cuts down on errors.

Unless you have the luxury of doing a detailed study, you may want to try a quick and dirty method (literally) of figuring out how large your touch targets need to be. Draw your screens with a reasonable guess at target size and print them out at the correct size. Put them on a hard surface at the right height, distance, and angle. Swipe your finger across an ink pad (of the sort used with rubber stamps) and walk

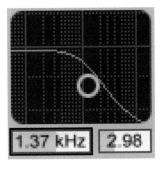

Figure 21.27. This reverb input processing widget from Ableton's Live sound editing application allows for direct manipulation of filter frequency using the yellow circle. A logarithmic scale in the background and colored bars on the numeric indicators provide feedback.

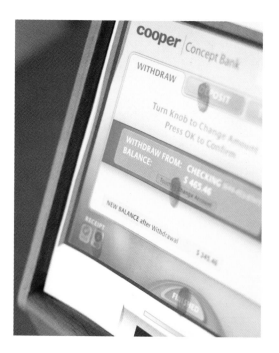

Figure 21.28. A paper prototype and ink pad provide a quick and dirty way to assess the size and spacing of your touch screen targets.

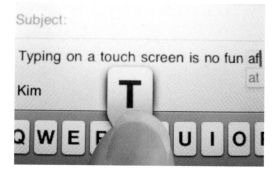

Figure 21.29. When a fingertip covers a very small target that's close to other targets, provide additional visual feedback about which target is selected.

through several tasks at a realistic speed. Ask colleagues with large hands or long fingernails to do the same, and you'll get something like Figure 21.28. If there's ink slopped over onto adjacent targets, you'll either need to make your targets bigger or farther apart, or get the programmers to do some very smart interpretation.

A few additional guidelines will help you minimize input errors:

— Act on finger-up, not finger-down. As with a mouse, this provides the opportunity to cancel an action by moving off the target. It also makes target acquisition a bit more accurate. If targets must be small and close together, use a balloon or other indicator not covered by the fingertip to show which target is acquired, as in Figure 21.29.

— Make the size of the touch target a little bigger than the visible target.

— Replicate the experience of pressing a physical button to the extent possible. The experience is comprised of both sound and movement. A subtle, audible click for each button press can go a long way toward providing the illusion of movement. **Haptic** technology, which provides physical feedback, is starting to appear even in small devices. A display surface that moves even a fraction of a millimeter or provides a short, minute vibration can feel almost like the real thing.

Managing Large Data Sets

Many applications—from CRM tools to digital music managers to e-commerce Web sites—involve finding one or several files among many thousands. The usual ways to handle this are with "simple" keyword search, more complex or detailed queries, and categories, which are each useful in different situations.

Search versus categories

Search fields have become nearly ubiquitous on Web sites and in operating systems, but they're applied with varying degrees of success. Many search utilities simply look at document titles or don't make any effort to interpret users' imperfectly phrased or imperfectly spelled queries, but with smart technology to back them up, plain keyword searches can turn up surprisingly useful results (as any Google user will tell you).

Whether to employ search or categories as the primary mechanism for helping users find their way around isn't just about how much you can invest in technology, however. Search is very effective for people retrieving specific objects that are likely to have unique identifiers. For example, if you know you want to buy a copy of *Designing for the Digital Age*, you can type the title into the search field of your favorite online bookstore and get exactly the result you're looking for. On the other hand, if you're looking for a pair of shoes to wear to your sister's wedding, search is going to be much less successful; you'll have much better luck drilling through a series of categories, such as shoes > women > pumps > 2-3" heels.

Detailed queries

Database administrators, financial analysts, and other technical types who need very specific things from their data learn how to write complex queries in SQL. For most users, though, merely mastering the correct use of Boolean and/or/not terminology is too much effort. To give ordinary mortals the power of very specific searches without the hard work, you can use a constrained query builder to assemble flexible, complex searches from more or less plain English. The pattern described below is also useful for constructing e-mail filtering rules, smart playlists, or any similar operation.

Though you can do all sorts of things with this pattern, a straightforward version typically contains an object type, a query type, and a specific value for the query, as shown in Figure 21.30.

Together, the three widgets form something close to a coherent sentence, such as: "Show [movies] [that won awards for] [set design]."

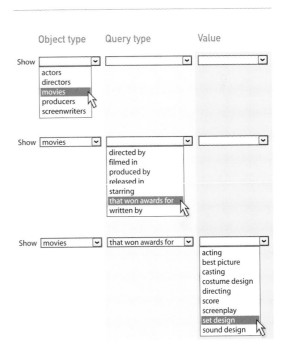

Figure 21.30. A constrained query builder.

The object type is selected from a list box containing all of the available object types, such as actors, directors, movies, producers, and screenwriters. The types of queries available in the query type selector are based on the first selection; if the selection in the first box is "screenwriters," then "filmed in…" wouldn't make much sense. The third control is then driven by the second control; available values for "filmed in…" would include every applicable value available in the data set, such as Africa, Asia, Australia, Europe, North America, and South America.

Although the first two controls are usually list boxes, the third control (and perhaps subsequent controls) could be almost anything: a text field,

Detailed Design

a list or combo box, a set of two date controls, or even a color picker. The type of control can change depending on the selected query type. Here are some examples of queries that can be built with standard widgets:

— Show [customers] [who have spent more than] [$10,000]

— Show [claims] [filed between] [January 1, 2009] and [March 31, 2009]

— Show [songs] [written by] <text entry field>

— Show [photos] [with any of these tags:] [bird] [beach]

There are various ways to make setting up the search more efficient. You can offer an option to save a few commonly used queries as favorites, offer one-click shortcuts to the most common queries, or let users step through a history, as in a Web browser. Sometimes, it's even worth offering a series of checkboxes to narrow the results.

Audible and Speech Interfaces

As discussed in Chapter 16, audible output may be combined with visual output and with input from on-screen interaction, physical controls such as a number pad, and speech input. Systems based on number pad input usually include some combination of **directed dialogue** (in which the system prompts users to enter specific bits of information in a sequence) and hub-and-spoke, hierarchical menu selection. Voice-activated systems may use these patterns, but may also use a **mixed initiative** approach, in which users provide information or a request and the system prompts for any missing pieces. Chapter 15 addresses when to use each of these.

Once you have identified your approach and overall structure, the details of voice interface design involve a complex combination of emotion and usability, along with a number of strategies for handling the shortcomings of both voice output and voice input technology.

Personality, emotion, and anthropomorphism

If humans interact with computers as if they were also human, as discussed by Byron Reeves and Clifford Nass in *The Media Equation*,[12] then this seems even more true for computers and other software-powered devices with voice input and output; after all, if it talks, it must be able to think, right? Hearing a "smart" but stupid voice interface say, "I'm sorry, I didn't understand that" three or four times in a row is enough to inspire violent impulses in the most dedicated pacifist. In their very readable 2005 book, *Wired for Speech*, Nass and another colleague, Scott Brave, assert that, "People draw conclusions about technology-based voices and determine appropriate behavior by applying the same rules and shortcuts that they use when interacting with people."[13] In particular, they've studied how the linguistic and paralinguistic characteristics of both recorded and synthesized voices affect perception, attention, judgment, and performance.

GENDER, PERSONALITY, AND THE SIMILAR-TO-ME EFFECT

The psychology and sociology literature is full of examples of how people tend to prefer others who are like them in gender, ethnicity, appearance, personality, and a wide range of other characteristics. Nass and Brave describe how this carries

12. Reeves, B., & Nass, C. *The media equation: How people treat computers, television, and new media like real people and places.* Cambridge University Press, 1996.

13. Nass, C., and Brave, S. *Wired for speech: How the human voice activates and advances the human-computer relationship.* The MIT Press, 2005.

over to interaction with voice systems: Their experiments showed that people tend to perceive both real and synthesized voices that seem to share their gender, regional accent, age, and personality as more likeable, persuasive, and trustworthy.

Gender

People assign gender to voices based on their pitch, range of modulation (or "expressiveness"), and to some extent on word choice and inflection. According to Nass and Brave, both men and women tended to react more positively to voices perceived as their own gender, though women responded better to male voices than men did to female voices. Male voices were seen as more credible when discussing stereotypically masculine topics, such as technology and sports, while female voices got a better response when discussing stereotypically feminine topics, from relationships to sewing. Voices with ambiguous gender characteristics were widely viewed as unlikable and untrustworthy. If you're designing educational software, you might consider having a female voice teaching math and science and a male voice discussing literature to help children break away from these harmful stereotypes. If you're designing a voice system for investors, you might need to accept current reality and use a masculine voice.

Regional accents

Most people likewise appreciate a voice with an accent similar to their own (which you might be able to guess based on an address or a caller's area code). However, if you're using a single voice for everyone, consider what people associate with the accent you choose. Americans, for example, tend to attribute sophistication to certain accents from European countries and former colonies, and may be more likely to see accents from Australia and the southeastern U.S. as warm and approachable. Accents from some regions may also have negative stereotypes associated with them; in the U.S., for example, the elocution of people from the southeast and certain areas of the northeast can be viewed as uneducated. Again, as with gender, there is a difficult choice between not reinforcing a stereotype and dealing with the effects of its reality.

Personality

People ascribe personality partly based on volume, pitch, range, and speed; loud, fast, high-pitched, and highly modulated voices are seen as more extroverted. Quantity and content of speech also tend to indicate personality, as extroverts tend to talk at greater length, use more

> **Humans interact with computers as if they were also human; this seems even more true for systems with voice input and output.**

Detailed Design

adjectives and adverbs, and use more first and second person pronouns ("I" and "you"). According to Nass and Brave, people generally responded best to voices that reflected their own personalities, but the best default would be no surprise to anyone in sales or advertising: Extroversion gets a better response from a mixed group.

Emotion

Finally, any voice conveys some sort of emotion; even the lack of any particular intonation is viewed in an emotional light. Higher pitch, rising inflections, and a wide range of pitch and volume tend to come across as happy. Mild happiness is better received in most circumstances. An unhappy machine is noticeable; for several days after we installed a new phone system at Cooper's office in San Francisco, people commented on the doleful female voice that responded to deleted phone messages by saying "duuh-leted," dragging out the first syllable and drooping at the end, kind of like a mopey teenager asked to take out the garbage.

Nass et al.[14] found that in a simulated driving situation, drivers who got feedback from a voice matching their emotional state (either happy or subdued) had fewer than half the "accidents" of drivers whose feedback was delivered in a mismatched voice. While it's impractical to assess mood in the average human-technology interaction, this finding highlights just how distracting inappropriate affect can be; users can't help but find it puzzling because another human would sense what tone was appropriate to use. When it comes to identifying appropriate emotion to convey, your best bet is to consider your experience attributes and your personas and scenarios, then adopt a tone that seems most likely to fit. Also, remember that tone can vary: A voice that's otherwise cheery can adopt an apologetic tone when delivering bad news.

BEING MORE HUMAN (BUT NOT TOO HUMAN)

How human your system should sound might seem like purely a branding issue: If your brand is friendly or high-end, the more human the better, right? Yes and no. Bits of speech recorded or synthesized out of context inevitably sound not quite right due to odd pauses, emphasis on the wrong syllable, or lack of a rising inflection at the end of a question. More human speech patterns do seem warmer and more polished. One good strategy for accomplishing this is to use the context of the conversation to determine appropriate inflection.

However, a machine that claims humanity by referring to itself in the first person is potentially treading on a nerve. I know I want to smack my bank's voice system for its presumption when it says something like, "If you'd like to speak to an agent, say 'Agent please.'" I believe in saying "please" to other humans, but I don't politely ask the cat to move off the couch, and I'm certainly not going to extend the courtesy to a computer (though I think it ought to apologize to *me* when it can't help). According to Nass and Brave, I'm not alone. Most people in their experiments had no problem with an obvious recording of a human saying "I," but were irritated by synthesized voices using the first person. Even the recorded voices didn't get a warm reception when using the first person to deliver bad news; it only increased the listener's perception of the system's incompetence.

Minimizing frustration

Personality only goes so far in driving user satisfaction with voice systems. The errors and inconsistencies (as well as the poor navigation) in many voice systems drive users to sites like dialahuman.com, which offer tips for working around the voice sys-

14. Nass, C., Jonsson, I-M., Reaves, B., Harris, H., Brave, S., and Takayama, L. "Increasing safety in cars by matching driver emotion and car voice emotion." Proceedings of the Portland CHI Conference, Portland, Oregon, 2005.

Detailed Design

tems to get to a human—not at all the outcome companies that install voice systems have in mind.

MINIMIZE SHORTCOMINGS BY MINIMIZING CONTRAST

Perhaps the most interesting point Nass and Brave demonstrate is how contrast of any kind draws attention to system shortcomings. This makes intuitive sense from everyday life; you might be content driving your five-year-old economy car until you ride in a colleague's brand new sports car, or think Madonna sings well until you hear Ella Fitzgerald in her prime. In audible interfaces, the unfortunate contrasts underscore the ways in which the technology simply can't replace a human. Typical problematic contrasts include:

— **Inconsistency in personality and content.** There's a reporter on one of my local TV news shows who has an irksome tendency to report on the death toll from the latest global catastrophe with a smile on her face, which always makes me wonder what kind of strange things are going on in her head. Similarly, people are less likely to enjoy or trust their interactions with a system that cheerfully reports an inability to help or that seems terse or unfriendly in the course of ordinary transactions.

— **Combining high-quality output with low-fidelity input.** If a system talks in complete sentences using a recorded human voice but can't parse a simple request or recognize common words, it comes across not only as a technologically limited system, but as a deliberately obtuse and infuriating person. Clear but obviously synthesized speech leads to lower expectations of "intelligence."

— **Mixing recorded human voices with synthesized output.** Dynamic content—such as e-mail, news, and Web site content—is difficult or impossible to construct from prerecorded bits of human voices, so synthesized output is sometimes necessary. Having a human voice

speak part of the content while a synthesized voice speaks the rest is distracting.

PLAN FOR ERRORS

Voice input systems can be tripped up by unexpected vocabulary, unclear or unfamiliar pronunciation, and ambient noise, so error prevention is a significant part of detailed design. Here are a few things that can help:

— **Encourage mimicry.** Write prompts in a way that encourages people to use the system's vocabulary, such as, "Would you like to place an order, check order status, or return something?" Open-ended prompts such as "How can I help you?" elicit a wider range of responses and increase failure rates.

— **Prevent random input.** In noisy environments, such as automobiles, where random input is likely to be a problem, use a button for intercom-style voice input. For a hands-free version of this, use a word that's unlikely to crop up in normal conversation to tell the system to listen to the next bit of input.

— **Escalate detail in prompts.** It's fine to start with simple questions if the system can parse a wide range of answers, but subsequent prompts should ask for specific detail if the system doesn't understand the first response.

— **Confirm important transactional input.** Although confirmations are usually a bad idea in GUIs, they're often a good idea in VUIs. However, don't confirm every bit of input—just repeat back what the system understood before you commit that flight reservation or bank transaction—and don't confirm non-transactional information.

— **Place blame appropriately when necessary.** Anything that even implies blame to a user won't be well received. It's better for the system to accept responsibility and apologize for its failures, though this can lead to an impression of system incompetence according to Nass and Brave—they suggest blaming a third party, such as ambient noise. However, this does not always seem practical and could soon become tiresome.

OTHER USEFUL SOLUTIONS

A few other behaviors will help your system seem more like a reasonable human being or allow for some fudgeability, thereby preventing a good deal of user frustration:

— Let users "barge in" on the computer. Repeat users learn menu options and other prompts over time, so the system should stop talking and act on user input whenever it happens.

— Use progressively shorter prompts for multiple entries, like this:

1. What's the first e-mail address?

2. What's the next address? If you're finished, say, "Done."

3. What's the next one? Or, say, "Done."

4. Next?

— Use nonverbal audio such as music to deal with system latency. Users confronted with long silences may assume the system has become nonresponsive and either start repeating themselves or pressing random buttons; worse, they may disengage entirely. However, pausing for a second or so to indicate that the system is "thinking" about a complex request seems less abrupt and more human.

If you're designing your first VUI, *Voice User Interface Design*[15] contains a good technical overview of how voice systems interpret input, as well as some useful tips on designing good prompts and working with voice actors on the right stress and inflections.

Products Involving Safety Concerns

One 1999 report[16] estimated that in the United States alone, some 98,000 people die each year from hospital errors. It's difficult to estimate the role of design problems, but consider this: As many as half of FDA medical device recalls in the late 1980s were due to poor product design.[17] In 2005, the U.S. Department of Transportation estimated that motor vehicle crashes were the leading cause of death for adults under the age of 34.[18] How many deaths could design prevent? It's hard to say, but a 2006 study[19] by the Virginia Tech Transportation Institute found that drivers engaged in secondary tasks were two to three times more likely to have accidents or near misses; dialing a phone, for example, made an incident 2.8 times more likely.

15. Cohen, M., Giangola, J., and Balogh, J. *Voice user interface design.* Addison-Wesley, 2004.

16. Kohn, L., and Corrigan, J., (eds.), "Building a safer health system." Institute of Medicine (IOM) Committee on Quality of Health Care in America. National Academy Press, 1999.

17. United States Food and Drug Administration. "Human factors implications of the new GMP rule overall requirements of the new quality system regulation." http://www.fda.gov/cdrh/humfac/hufacimp.html

18. Traffic Safety Facts Research Note, April 2008. "Motor vehicle traffic crashes as a leading cause of death in the United States, 2005." http://www-nrd.nhtsa.dot.gov/Pubs/810936.PDF

19. Klauer, S.G., Dingus, T. A., Neale, V. L., Sudweeks, J.D., and Ramsey, D.J. "The impact of driver inattention on near-crash/crash risk: An analysis using the 100-car naturalistic driving study data." National Highway Traffic Safety Administration/ Virginia Tech Transportation Institute, April 2006.

Individual responsibility certainly plays a role, but clearly, safety is a critical factor in the design of medical devices, manufacturing systems, systems used in moving vehicles, and any other product that could increase the likelihood of injury or death. The challenges are exacerbated by the fact that medical residents work long shifts and drivers get behind the wheel under the influence of anything from a bad day to a controlled substance. It's also common to find nurses or other professionals who are working at a given facility temporarily and haven't received training in using every device on hand. Detailed design for any of these situations should absolutely include close scrutiny from experts in human factors and safety analysis, as well as extensive usability testing. However, it helps if you carefully consider these common possibilities for error when users are in a hurry, fatigued, or unfamiliar with equipment:

— **Unsafe defaults.** Defaults are useful in most applications, but defaults in medical devices can cause tremendous problems. If a medical record includes a default number for a patient's weight, for example, it could lead to a medication dosing error. A dosing pump or radiation therapy device with a default setting for adults could severely overdose a child. A glucose meter that defaults to European measurements could cause a harmful misunderstanding for an American patient or physician.

— **Misread data.** Similar words and small or illegible fonts are a problem in any design, but are even more likely to be misread by a driver or health care professional who's just glancing at them. Numbers can be misread if digits or parts of digits are obscured by a screen bezel when observed at an angle.

— **Invisible or misleading status.** A life support system, factory power readout, or other critical system should make it glaringly obvious if it's turned on but not working.

— **Sticky keys.** I once used a new office phone system that was overly sensitive to the slightest key jiggle. Dialing 9 (for an outside line) followed by 1 (for a long distance number) led the system to dial 911 (for an emergency) if a user faltered slightly in pressing the buttons. Now imagine that applied to a medication delivery device: pressing 5 delivers 55 units of medication, overdosing the patient by a factor of 11.

— **Improper component installation.** If you have a few electronic devices, you probably have a whole collection of USB and other cables that are all similar but slightly different. Now imagine a setting in which you have to find the right cable among 20 or more, and someone's health or life depends on your speed and ability to plug it in correctly. Hazardous or life-saving devices should have distinctive components that can be installed in only one way.

— **Lack of protection on critical controls.** There's a great *Far Side* comic by Gary Larson that shows someone sitting in an airplane seat with two identical controls on the arm: one says "recline" and the other says "eject." An emergency shutdown switch next to a routine control or a medication dosage button that's easily bumped by visiting family members is a recipe for disaster.

— **Inappropriate alarms.** Constant beeping eventually gets ignored. In a health care setting, a dozen devices might all emit a similar alarm sound, so it's also difficult to identify the source of the alarm. Use alarms only when you really mean it, and make them distinct and loud enough to be identifiable.

— **Requiring unnecessary attention.** Keeping a user's eyes, hands, and mind on the road (or the scalpel or whatever) is critical. Consider what you can do to require minimal attention and input, such as using the fewest possible words, using audible cues, and so forth.

Detailed Design

Accessibility

Ability and disability are not binary states; each exists along a spectrum, from the person who has a more acute ability than most to the person for whom a particular ability is entirely absent. The U.S. Census Bureau[20] estimated in 2002 that more than one in five people in the United States had some degree of impairment, and nearly 14 percent had a severe disability of some sort. Some people are born with disabilities, but any of us can become temporarily or permanently disabled through accident or illness. As the population ages, the percentage of people with disabilities only increases; more than half of census respondents over 65 had a disability. Clearly, accessibility is an important consideration for design.

Most designers would agree that the ideal is universal design: a solution that can be used by anyone without the need for adaptation or compromise. Many of the keys to accessible design, such as legibility and simplicity, are good for everyone. There are, however, a few considerations that may not be obvious. Accessible systems should be:

— **Flexible.** Allow for multiple input and output methods. Make devices and environments usable for people who are standing or sitting.

— **Patient.** Allow plenty of time for someone who has difficulty with input before timing out a session or beeping for attention (mind you, this is often rude for *any* user).

— **Compatible.** Make it possible to use typical assistive technologies, such as screen readers.

— **Forgiving.** Although users shouldn't have to exert much force to operate controls, it shouldn't be too easy for unintentional movement to activate them, either.

Unfortunately, designers may face dilemmas when the universal design ideal is not achievable. For instance, what if you can make financial analysts more effective by providing interactive data visualization that would be difficult for a screen reader to interpret? Does this mean no financial analyst should have this tool? Few people would make that argument; it's not possible for every part of every product to be 100 percent usable for every person. However, every design decision of this sort has the potential to close a door for someone, and designers should endeavor to keep as many doors open as possible, especially when it comes to products and services used by the general public.

Here are a few useful resources with more detailed information on accessibility:

— The W3C Web Accessibility Initiative: http://www.w3.org/WAI/

— The Center for Universal Design at North Carolina State University: http://www.design.ncsu.edu/cud/index.htm

— The University of Wisconsin-Madison Trace Center: http://trace.wisc.edu/

— Adaptive Environments universal design resource list: http://www.adaptenv.org/index.php?option=Content&Itemid=294

"That Little Extra Something"

A couple of weeks ago, I was talking with a senior executive who was trying to put his finger on what makes people loyal to products. He rightly identified that what makes people want to "date" a product isn't what makes them want to "marry" it, and that both impulses include pragmatic as well as emotional components. His conclusion was that products people love have "that little extra something," but he couldn't quite figure out what that was.

---

20. United States Census Bureau publication P70-107. "Americans with disabilities: 2002." http://www.census.gov/hhes/www/disability/sipp/disab02/ds02t2.html

"That little extra something" is really a combination of many things, not all of which are little. People don't tend to love products unless they get the big stuff right: accomplishing goals. Many of the "little" touches, like getting a peel and stick return label in the box with your online purchase, are really operating at that goal level: Who wants to buy online if returns are a hassle?

However, there are subtle touches that make a product more appealing and encourage ongoing interaction. Some of these contribute mostly to first impressions and are ignored thereafter, but others can provide pleasure for some time, much as beautifully designed furnishings and artwork do. In software design, many of these tiny delights come from graceful animation or from some aspect of behavior that provides a nearly physical sensation, such as a faint but satisfying sound that acknowledges input or task completion, or a touch screen interface that imitates physical inertia in scroll or drag operations. In physical product design, the design language, shape and texture can make something seem eminently touchable. Quality materials and precise engineering continue to make an impression, too; every time I close the hefty door of my MINI, for example, I'm reassured that there's plenty of solid metal between me and all those SUVs.

If you want your products to have "that little extra something," address the goals first, then look for ways to add pure delight in some subtle way that doesn't run counter to those goals.

> **Address goals first; then look for ways to add pure delight.**

Summary

If you get things right at the goal level, users will often forgive a multitude of tiny sins; many of today's most popular consumer products and Web sites are filled with low-level usability problems. However, too many minor issues—including poor performance due to an overly ambitious design—can become a major issue when they turn a solid design concept into a product only a mother could love. Products that users love generally show attention to detail along with good choices about the big issues.

Though principles and patterns play a large role in detailed design, context is, as always, critical to their application. Chapter 22 explains how personas and scenarios—along with extensive collaboration to ensure feasible and appropriate solutions—continue to guide design decisions down to the last detail.

Detailed Design

Detailed Design Process and Practices

Although there's a great deal of work to do during detailed design, the good news is that, with the exception of visual system development, it largely builds on the techniques used during framework definition. However, this is also the work that makes the difference between your design getting into the hands of users or gathering dust on a shelf, so your collaboration and time management skills and your ability to juggle a thousand details are just as important as your knowledge of detailed design principles and patterns.

This chapter describes techniques for evolving each aspect of the design, ways the disciplines can work together to ensure coherence and completeness, and some ideas for handling common difficulties.

Evolving the Interaction Design: Round One

The interaction designers may begin the phase (or the work on a specific design topic) with a day or two of supplemental research, especially if the domain is complex. As shown in Figure 22.1, the ideal process then involves taking a first crack at the nearly complete behavioral design (whether for a whole interface or a discrete topic) at the whiteboard level, then reviewing it informally with design engineers and subject matter experts to get their initial feedback. By "nearly complete design," I mean that every widget, word on the screen, and likely scenario are all accounted for, but that you haven't spent time on the very finest details such as tool tips, detailed error handling, keyboard accelerators, or the number of characters each field takes.

After that first informal review, you'll ideally have a bit of time to adjust the design as needed, then develop a first draft of your documentation. That draft should provide most of what's needed for a typical paper-prototype test, if you're doing one, though some interactions benefit from higher fidelity. (See Chapter 23 for more on this.)

While subject matter experts, design engineers, and hopefully users are poring over the first draft of the design in detail, you can either move on to the next design topic or work on the very fine details for this topic, such as accelerators and (if you haven't addressed it yet) how the design works with assistive technologies.

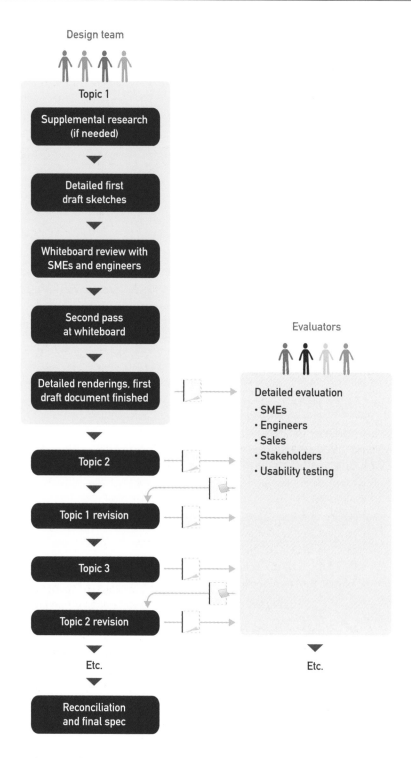

Figure 22.1. Process for expanding upon and evolving the interaction design.

Once you've gotten detailed feedback, you're ready to make a "last" set of tweaks to the design and documentation. I say "last" because it's only the last in theory; there should be minimal change between spec and final product if you've worked with effective design engineers, but some little issues inevitably crop up along the way.

Supplemental research

Your initial research should give you enough information to figure out the essential flow, but don't be too dismayed if you're not 100 percent certain what goes in every list box or how fast to accelerate a scrolling display using a jog dial. In a truly complex domain, such as financial portfolio management, radiology, or network administration, it's impossible to gather every tiny detail you'll need for design during up-front research. In these cases, you should build in a little supplemental research time with subject matter experts (SMEs).

This usually involves a couple of days at the beginning of detailed design or perhaps a half day at the beginning of each discrete design topic, depending on how you've structured your design time and how available your SMEs are. Two or even three SMEs are better than one; one expert may be idiosyncratic about something or even just plain wrong. More than two or three can get a bit hard to manage, however. Consider inviting your design engineer(s) to these meetings, as they may have related questions for the SMEs and might think of potential pitfalls that don't occur to non-engineers.

To prep for your meetings with SMEs, review the key path scenarios related to your design topics. Make a list of scenario variants you know you need to cover as well as any other questions you have. Send these to your SMEs ahead of time if you can to reduce the need for them to do further research after the meeting.

Lay out your agenda at the beginning of the meeting. Start by listing the key path variants and less common scenarios you know you'll need to cover; then ask the SMEs what you're forgetting. Once you've got a list, walk through each scenario in detail to fill in gaps and ensure that you understand the possible choices and bits of information necessary at each step. Here's an example of this sort of conversation:

> **Designer:** So, after Rhonda specifies the medication name and form, she has to fill in the other details. Is there anything other than dosage and frequency?
>
> **SME #1:** Yes, she also has to specify how the medication is to be administered.
>
> **Designer:** Oh, right, like orally or intravenously. Could we review all of the forms a medication might come in and all of the relevant ways it can be administered? I know some of them are medication specific, but we need to know the range of what's possible.
>
> **SME #1:** Sure. There are some that are only ever administered one way. OK, so medications can come in liquids, gels and creams, pills, capsules … um …
>
> **SME #2:** There's also powder, spray, aerosol …

You might also have questions about specific parts of the design or scenarios. For example, you may have envisioned a trend spotting and analysis tool that would show a handful of key indicators. You probably have a clear idea of what some of those are from your earlier research, but now is also a good time to ask, "Do we have the right trends shown in this preliminary sketch? What are we missing?" Detailed sequence is another common question: Does A have to be known before B can happen?

Avoid saving a lot of decisions for solo drawing and writing time.

Don't be surprised if your SMEs sometimes disagree with each other; that's one reason to have two or three. If necessary, facilitate some discussion between them. Often, they don't actually disagree—they've just made different unspoken assumptions, so they wind up agreeing once these are surfaced. Other disagreements are usually differences in work style—which your personas have hopefully accommodated—or flawed recollection. In the rare case that your SMEs simply can't agree on something, get them to agree on what additional information they need to resolve their differences and when they'll get you an answer, and then move on.

Detailed design meetings

Once you've got the information you need, you can start filling in more detail. Most design teams tackle the work screen by screen, focusing on the parts of scenarios that take place on a given screen, rather than trying to detail every screen for one scenario. However, you could certainly approach it that way.

At the beginning of detailed design, the interaction designers spend most of each day in meetings. These are much like design meetings during framework definition (see Chapter 16), but with a greater emphasis on keeping track of details. As the phase progresses, the proportion of time spent in meetings versus working at a computer shifts; late in the phase, meetings may only occupy a couple of hours a day. This is because drawing and documentation become an increasingly important part of the design process, with detailed pixel-level renderings and behavioral descriptions providing insight into the design's effectiveness.

However, you should avoid saving a lot of decisions for solo drawing and writing time. You'll make faster progress and better design decisions if the IxD synthesizer still has the opportunity to poke at the ideas and help improve them. Likewise, both the IxD generator (IxDG) and synthesizer (IxDS) will be more effective during solo work time if you're not trying to figure things out independently. Draw every widget on the whiteboard and figure out its behavior, contents, and states. Get as close to a realistic screen layout on the whiteboard as you can, then pause to capture detailed notes. However, don't spend too much time fussing over a detailed layout problem; these are usually best dealt with in pixels.

The detailed interaction design process looks much like the framework definition process described in Chapter 16, except that it happens at a greater level of detail. For each topic:

1. Develop more detailed scenarios if you haven't already done so with your SMEs; then focus on the scenarios and partial scenarios relevant to the current topic.

2. Extract the data and functional needs from your more detailed scenarios. In reality, you might also anticipate other needs from scenarios you haven't articulated yet; this is fine as long as they make sense in reasonable scenarios later on.

3. Determine what data and functional elements (such as widgets) will best meet the needs.

4. Use the primary persona's scenario to help you lay out the elements in a way that matches visual flow to workflow, at least in the more common cases.

5. Throw secondary persona scenarios and additional validation scenarios at the design to assess and adjust it as needed, just as in framework-level design.

6. Immediately after the meeting, the IxDG should draw the screens in pixels and the IxDS should document them, so issues are revealed as soon as possible.

To illustrate this, let's take a look at the first step of the veterinary application scenario from Chapter 16. Figure 22.2 shows the corresponding framework sketch.

> Laura takes a call from Mr. Cowell, who needs to make an appointment for his cat to have a tumor removed. Laura finds him in the **client list** and opens his record to see detail in the **client overview display area**, which shows that one of his three cats, Xena, is flagged for follow-up because she needs a surgery appointment. She confirms with Mr. Cowell that the procedure is for Xena. She clicks to create a new appointment.

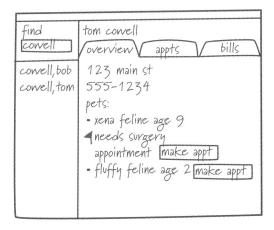

Figure 22.2. This framework sketch shows the first step in the appointment scenario.

The functional needs listed in Chapter 16 were:

— Look up callers among existing clients

— See overview information about each client and pet

The functional elements were:

— Area to view client list

— Display of overview information for client

— Display of overview information for multiple pets

A more detailed version of this scenario step might look like this:

> Laura answers the phone. The caller says, "Hi, this is Tom Cowell. I need to make a surgery appointment for my cat." Laura says, "Sure thing, Mr. Cowell, let me just find your record." She types his last name into the client list and sees the list narrow as she types. By the time she enters the first three letters, she can see his name. She clicks on it to bring up his record in the client overview display area, and sees a follow-up flag on the client tab. She asks,

Challenge teammates to use suspect ideas in a scenario or justify them from the research.

"Is this for Xena to have a tumor removed from her left hind foot?" He says yes, and she clicks the flagged item to create a new appointment.

As you can see, this isn't a *lot* more detail than the original scenario, and it's not going to be enough to design everything on the client overview tab. You'll need at least another scenario or two, such as:

Laura has a little time on her hands, so she decides to catch up on calling some clients with seriously overdue bills. In the client list, she selects "Show clients with bills outstanding for 60 days." She sees a list of a dozen people sorted by how long their bills are overdue. She clicks on Tom Cowell, who is at the top. The alert at the top of his client overview tab shows that he owes $32.60 for a medication that was mailed to him. She clicks on the alert to see detail. So far, he's received two automated e-mail notices. She looks at the list of next actions and selects "Call daytime phone number." The application automatically logs the phone call. When Mr. Cowell answers, she politely reminds him of the overdue bill. He apologizes and says he'll send a check the next day. Laura makes a note and asks if he received the notices sent to tomcowell@abcdefg.com. He says did not receive the notices because his e-mail address has changed. Laura enters the new one, says thanks and goodbye, and moves on to the next person on the list.

This adds a couple of useful data and functional needs, such as the ability to:

— Use the client list to see clients matching various criteria, such as those with overdue bills

— See overdue bills as soon as a client is selected

— Get more detail about how much is owed and for what, what attempts at collection have been made via what avenues, and what next steps can be taken

— Contact the client directly from the entry and have that action noted in the record

— Annotate the entry

— Edit contact information

You could take the time to detail every possible scenario in order to derive all of the screen's contents, but as you can see, this could take a very long time. You'll probably find yourself listing some data and functional needs without explicitly using a scenario. There's nothing wrong with this, since your brain is certainly capable of coming up with reasonable needs based on what you know from research. However, teammates should challenge one another to use suspect ideas in a scenario or justify them from the research. For example:

> **IxDG:** I think it's safe to assume that Laura needs the usual contact information: name, mailing address, multiple phone numbers, and e-mail.

> **IxDS:** Yes, and she'll need more than one client name in a lot of cases. And pet sitter information, too.

> **IxDG:** Really? When would she use that?

> **IxDS:** If someone comes in with a sick animal and says it belongs to so-and-so, Laura can immediately see whether that person is authorized to get care. Do you remember our interview with Marie the pet sitter? She talked about what a hassle it was for the vets to find that information.

> **IxDG:** Oh, right! Yeah, Laura probably should be able to see that right away, though I wouldn't want to put the detail in her face all the time.

> **IxDS:** That makes sense.

As with framework definition, it's very useful to list needs explicitly on the whiteboard (or in a spreadsheet if you have a lot to keep track of), then translate them into functional and data elements. Any physical controls are usually defined by now, so for the most part, this involves deciding what kind of widget would be best: Bounded or unbounded input? A list box or a set of radio buttons? (See Table 21.1 for an overview of common widget uses.) Experienced designers generally do this in their heads without articulating it explicitly, so teammates should keep their eyes

open for bad widget choices. Once you've got a detailed list, you'll then use scenarios again to lay out the elements, assess the design, and tweak as necessary.

For the veterinary client overview, for example, the detailed list of elements would be something like this:

— Client name field × 2

— E-mail address × 2

— Address field

— Phone numbers × 3

— Other authorized parties (probably collapsed by default)

— Alerts with ability to expand detail and take action directly from the alert

— Visit and billing history table (filter/sort controls, date, pet, total, details on demand, paid/unpaid status)

Figure 22.3 shows how an initial sketch might look. As you worked through additional scenarios, you would likely be adding more controls to the toolbar, client list, and other areas.

As in framework definition, the sketches evolve as you throw additional scenarios at them or simply have ideas for improving or enhancing your first take. Much of the discussion involves widget-level interactions, like what's outlined in Table 22.1.

Along with your various scenarios, the experience attributes are a useful check on your design. Imagine that you're designing an automated teller for a bank, and one of your experience attributes is "friendly." Take a look at your interaction and on-screen text. Does, "Transaction complete, remove card," sound friendly? Something more along the lines of, "Thanks for banking with us! Please take your card," would be a better fit.

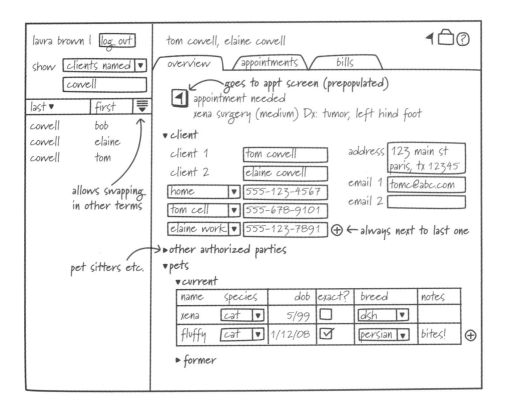

Figure 22.3. A first-draft detailed design sketch.

Table 22.1. **Example detailed interaction design meeting discussion.**

Sketch	Discussion
client 1 — tom cowell client 2 — elaine cowell home phone — 555-123-4567 work phone — 555-678-9101 cell phone — 555-123-7891	**IxDS:** So you've got three phone number fields up there for home, work, and cell phone, but you've got two pet owners in the record. How do you know whose work or cell phone is whose?

Sketch   **Discussion**

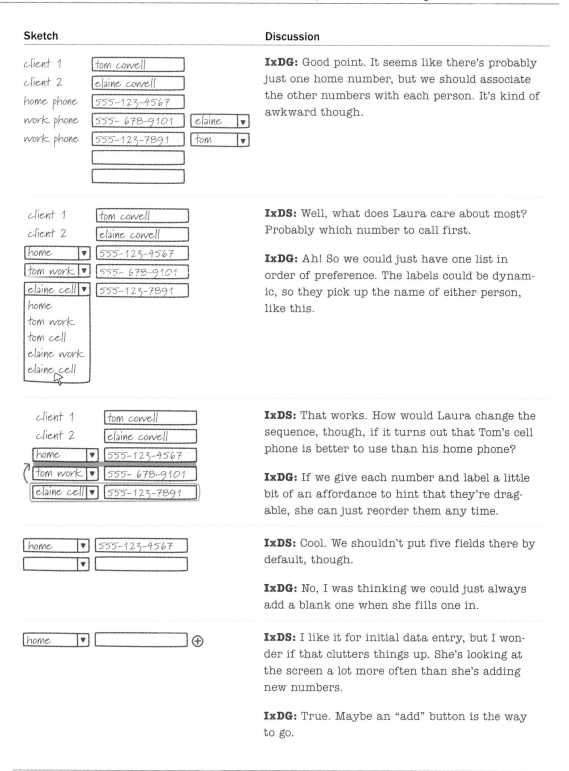

IxDG: Good point. It seems like there's probably just one home number, but we should associate the other numbers with each person. It's kind of awkward though.

IxDS: Well, what does Laura care about most? Probably which number to call first.

IxDG: Ah! So we could just have one list in order of preference. The labels could be dynamic, so they pick up the name of either person, like this.

IxDS: That works. How would Laura change the sequence, though, if it turns out that Tom's cell phone is better to use than his home phone?

IxDG: If we give each number and label a little bit of an affordance to hint that they're dragable, she can just reorder them any time.

IxDS: Cool. We shouldn't put five fields there by default, though.

IxDG: No, I was thinking we could just always add a blank one when she fills one in.

IxDS: I like it for initial data entry, but I wonder if that clutters things up. She's looking at the screen a lot more often than she's adding new numbers.

IxDG: True. Maybe an "add" button is the way to go.

Detailed Design

Once things appear to be working for a wide range of scenarios, your last, purely pragmatic step before a design review is to fill out what you know of each bounded-input widget's possible values (e.g., what the exact contents of each list box are) and states. In the veterinary application example, it might be fine to put off the alerts discussion if this is a separate topic on your project calendar, but otherwise, both the alerts and the table filtering and sorting should be addressed in more depth. The idea is to get to as much detail as possible in your design meetings, then go back to your desk and make sure it all works as it's explained in words and drawn in pixels.

Exercise

Refine one scenario or screen from your RoomFinder or LocalGuide framework.

PROCESS DIFFERENCES FOR SPECIFIC DESIGN PROBLEMS

I've described the process using a typical desktop application as an example. The approach works equally well for other kinds of design problems, but it's worth discussing the ways in which those are (or aren't) different.

Web sites

Many Web sites these days are a lot like desktop applications: a small number of pages or screens with a lot of interactivity. Others such as news sites and many e-commerce sites have thousands of pages based on content slurped from a database, which makes it impossible to design every page a user sees.

In these cases, detailed design is really about identifying all the different types and attributes of content you expect, then designing page templates that will allow for automated production of most pages, perhaps with the flexibility to develop

more customized layouts for special features. In that sense, you're designing for both the end-user personas and for a production designer who will be frustrated if your templates aren't flexible enough.

However, there are a limited number of templates to design, and once you understand the range of parameters in the data, you just have to account for the variability. This is similar to designing a report template for a productivity application; the designers may not develop every report, but need to explore the options enough to provide a basic structure with some rules for variation. The process is pretty much the same.

Devices in general

For any interaction design involving a novel hardware platform, you will likely have a meeting or two with the industrial designer about the exact behavior and hierarchy of physical controls. For example:

— Is a function activated when the button is pressed or when it's released?

— Are there circumstances in which physical controls are inactive? If so, how will you communicate about state?

— What other states do physical controls need to communicate, and how will you express them?

— Does a knob increase a value (such as stereo volume) in a continuous, smooth curve, or does it use detents? How many detents are there?

— How quickly does a jog dial or a continuously pressed button accelerate scrolling? How long is a "continuous" button press?

— Which physical controls need to be most visually prominent or easily accessible? Which need to be protected from accidental activation?

— Do controls communicate with tactile clicks, audible electronic feedback, or using some other means?

Detailed Design

Mobile devices and in-vehicle applications

When it comes to products that must function in ever-changing contexts, such as mobile devices and in-vehicle applications, the process isn't much different. However, be sure to consider environment changes in your scenarios. For example, what happens when your personas need to:

— Use a Web-based mobile phone application in an area where there's no service?

— Manage car dashboard controls wearing thick gloves due to cold weather?

— Drive using a displayed map and directions both in the dark and in bright sun?

Consider these cases early enough that's it's not too difficult to adapt your design.

Telephones

Interaction design for telephones—and especially for complex multi-line business systems—is in part an exercise in imagining all of the possible call states and figuring out what to do with potential collisions. More than most applications, call handling requires an exhaustive and detailed set of scenarios. For example, what happens if a user:

— Has set calls to go to voicemail but sees an incoming call he wants to pick up?

— Wants to merge two lines into one conference call?

— Wants to pass control of a conference call to someone else?

— Needs to barge into the boss's call in progress for something urgent?

These are mostly behavioral rather than visual problems in a typical phone UI; you have to figure out at what point the first call is on hold, whether the boss has to accept the barge-in or whether it just happens, and a dozen other nuances for the whole range of possible call states. Even on a touch screen, the details of sequence and timing are critical, so scenarios (at least in the informal, undocumented sense) are essential to figuring out desirable flow.

Audible and speech interfaces

Audible and speech interfaces likewise require a heavy emphasis on scenarios. A first round of scenarios should help you detail out the contents of every menu or the set of possible actions from every prompt.

After that, you'll need to spend time fine-tuning the sequence of the dialogue. For example, here's how you might evolve part of a menu for a bank:

> **IxDG:** So, let's talk through the flow for money transfer. Joan needs to specify an account to transfer money from, an account to transfer money to, and an amount. Anything else?

> **IxDS:** She's trying to save money, remember, so she'd probably also want to do an automatic recurring transfer, like putting $500 a month in her savings account.

> **IxDG:** Right, good thought. Well, it would be easy to say, "Would you like to make that recurring?" after she set up a transfer, but is that too hidden?

> **IxDS:** I think Joan might be confused if she couldn't tell how to do that right away, so maybe we should ask that first.

> **IxDG:** OK, so when Joan says she wants to transfer, our first question is whether it's one time or recurring. Should our second question be the account number or the amount?

> **IxDS:** If she were talking to a human, she'd say, "I want to transfer $500 from checking to savings," so that seems like the right sequence.

Detailed Design

IxDG: Yeah, and she wouldn't have to tell a human the account number. We can't just say "checking" or "savings," though, since she has multiple accounts. You know, it would be cool if we could pick up the account nicknames she's assigned on the Web site so the voice interface can just ask her if she wants to transfer to and from checking, college savings, or house savings.

IxDS: Great idea. I'll send [the design engineer and business analyst] a note and ask how painful that is to do. So, we'll ask for an amount, the account to transfer from, and the account to transfer to, right? And then repeat it back?

IxDG: That sounds right.

Next, develop and fine-tune the language of every prompt to ensure that each option is clear and concise. For voice input, you'll also need to provide options that sound distinct (to minimize errors in interpretation) and determine how to structure follow-up questions, such as, "You want to transfer $300 from checking to savings. Did you mean house savings or college savings?" Ultimately, you'll need to work with a voice actor (or with whoever is responsible for speech synthesis) to ensure that the words in each prompt and response have emphasis and inflections appropriate to natural human speech.

Services

The approach to service design is still scenario driven, though you may not be drawing screens to go with the scenarios. Instead, you might be designing a merchandise return procedure, an envelope for receiving and returning DVDs, an airport check-in process from home to departure gate, or a hospital admissions procedure.

Start by identifying all of the details that must be designed. What will your personas see, hear, touch, smell, and taste in the course of the

interaction? Determine whether there is an artifact to be designed, a policy or procedure to be developed, or a skill in which employees need to be trained. From there, you can use scenarios and goals to drive the design of each system component, or determine which components to outsource to experts in a particular area.

Additional iteration through individual work

Although most decisions should be made in design meetings, both the IxDG and IxDS need to spend at least a couple of hours a day—and eventually more—on individual work. This work is not done in isolation, however; it needs to be reviewed by teammates on a regular basis, as discussed later in this chapter. It's meant both to capture what was discussed in the previous design meeting and to inform the next.

THE IXD GENERATOR'S DESK WORK: DRAWING

After each design meeting, the generative interaction designer's primary task is to translate whiteboard sketches into pixels, working within a visual system developed by the visual interface designer. In some organizations, interaction designers and information architects never touch pixels; they just hand the visual designers a series of wireframes drawn in a vector application like Illustrator or Visio. Unfortunately, this can lead to some things getting lost in translation, and it doesn't give IxDGs a chance to learn from working at the pixel level. Although experienced designers eventually get pretty good at estimating what can fit on a screen at a given resolution, sometimes things just don't turn out quite the same once they're rendered in a realistic way. Also, a "waterfall" approach to the relationship between interaction and visual design doesn't take full advantage of the visual designer's problem-solving skills and expertise, so your solution may suffer. The end result of this collaboration should look like the drawing in Figure 22.4, which is an iteration of Figure 19.2.

Figure 22.4. A typical end result of detailed design drawing.

As the IxDG learns through this even finer level of sketching, he should keep a list of things to discuss with the IxDS or other teammates in the next meeting or, if seating arrangements and preferred work styles permit, just turn around and say, "Hey, you know that table on the client overview screen? It's not working in pixels the way I sketched it, so here's what I'm thinking …"

THE IXD SYNTHESIZER'S DESK WORK: DOCUMENTATION

The IxD synthesizer's work is likewise a learning process. Although it's beneficial to begin documentation early to ensure that details are captured and avoid a crunch at the end, documenting right away also provides another mechanism for reviewing the design. A missing decision or peculiar flow that isn't evident in the casual back-and-forth of a design meeting can become glaringly obvious in the documentation.

For this reason, as well as for the sake of efficiency, it's best to translate scribbled meeting notes and whiteboard photos directly into a rough draft of the final document, rather than spending a lot of time writing up detailed notes in some other format. Use whiteboard photos as placeholders for final art to help you plan your page layouts as well as to be thorough in your explanation. See Chapter 24 for more on developing documentation.

BEHAVIORAL PROTOTYPES

Although an experienced designer doesn't need a working prototype to visualize the behavior of standard forms and widgets, it's worthwhile to develop a behavioral prototype if you're designing custom widgets, interactive data visualizations, animated behaviors, and some hardware/software interactions. Such a prototype doesn't need to be complete—all it has to do is demonstrate the specific behavior you have questions about.

Detailed Design

617

Some interaction designers who are technically inclined may prefer to develop prototype code of their own, but this is not an essential interaction design skill. A large enough design group may be able to employ a full-time prototype developer (with expertise in a tool such as Flash, HTML, or Expressions) to develop animations and clickable prototypes. Some visual designers have strong skills in this area. In other cases, the ID and design engineers may be your best resource, especially for working device prototypes.

Defining the Visual System: Round One

The visual designer's work in this phase (or in the later part of framework definition, depending on how long that phase is) begins with settling on a single visual style and applying it to an **archetype screen** or two. After a review with stakeholders, she then begins turning the archetype(s) into a **visual system** that reduces complexity by minimizing arbitrariness, limiting the number of unique elements, and simplifying the relationships among elements. Ultimately, the visual system includes specifications for:

— An overarching grid system

— Images of every unique screen with layout specifications

— Pixel-level specifications for controls and spacing

— A library of illustrated states for every type of control or other dynamic element on the screen

— A library of icons used on the screen and physical surfaces

— Specifications for every color used on the screen

— Type specifications including font, size, weight, color, and spacing

— Photo treatment guidelines, if any

— Use of the corporate identity (and product branding if applicable)

The first draft of the system is initially articulated in a drawing file to be shared with the IxDG. It might be accompanied by some very rough documentation describing intent, such as a screen printout with some notes scribbled on it. The visual system continues to evolve as the interaction design evolves. When not working on the major structural and layout elements, the visual designer works on icons, visual feedback, or other problems that aren't on the critical path for screen layout and begins documenting the on-screen visual system. Figure 22.5 summarizes this process. As with other aspects of design, this activity isn't strictly linear.

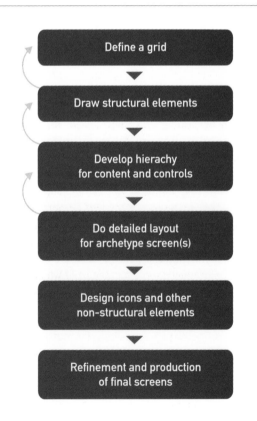

Figure 22.5. Detailed visual design process.

Detailed Design

Although most of a visual designer's detailed design work is in front of a computer, he is also collaborating closely with others on the design team and outside it. He works with the:

— Interaction designers to refine layout, hierarchy, information design, and widget-level interaction

— Industrial designer to ensure the consistency and unity of the on-screen visual system and the hardware design language

— IxDS to mesh visual style guidelines with behavioral description in the form and behavior specification

— Design engineers to ensure that things are drawn in a way that's feasible to build and will result in a responsive UI

Incorporating early stakeholder feedback

The design language studies are each meant to emphasize one strategy, usually represented by an emphasis on one of the experience attributes, so it's rare that subsequent work looks exactly like one of the studies. Stakeholders usually wind up saying that study number two is almost perfect, but the glossy highlights from study number one and the typeface in study number three are awfully nice. Handling this feedback can be one of the trickier parts of the visual and industrial design process. Taking it literally would mean treating the studies as an a la carte menu, but a peanut butter sandwich and a glass of sauvignon blanc together would be peculiar at best, and perhaps indigestible.

The visual designer's (and sometimes the industrial designer's) job is to figure out whether stakeholders are drawn to particular things due to personal taste or for other reasons, and what they're trying to accomplish by saying, "If you could just use this color scheme on that one

over there …" What is lacking in one study or the other? Does the comment about making things glossier mean the study is too plain, doesn't imply quality and specialness, or what? Once the intent behind the comment is clear, you can decide on the best way to address it.

For work done by experienced designers, the necessary tweaks are usually minor enough that you can proceed directly to developing one or two archetype screens. If the feedback was that all of the studies were way off, you'll need to figure out whether the problem is the quality and appropriateness of the studies, the effectiveness of your communication about them, or stakeholders who are determined to stick to their personal likes and dislikes. Get an opinion from another designer who can help you be objective about the problem, and then start over. If you're not accustomed to doing studies, you should probably plan on a second round as a matter of course.

The visual system first draft: archetype screens

Although design language studies are a great way to make visual concepts concrete enough for most people to discuss, they're not quite real enough to make a final assessment about how well a direction expresses the experience attributes or communicates the behavior. If you've ever had someone agree with you in conversation but react differently to the same thing in writing, you've had a similar experience. Seeing the visual choices applied to a complete, detailed screen or near-final form factor can highlight implications that weren't previously visible to the audience (and sometimes the designer). This is why industrial designers use more-realistic appearance models and visual designers use archetype screens.

Detailed Design

SELECTING SCREENS FOR ARCHETYPE DEVELOPMENT

The first step in translating a study into a system is selecting one or more **archetype** screens based on emblematic quality and interaction design completeness. By "emblematic quality," I mean the screen's contents should be fairly typical of the application, but should also include a wide range of the kinds of data and widgets you expect to represent. If your application includes a

fair number of tables and charts, choose a screen with a table and chart on it, if at all possible. Sometimes it takes a couple of archetypes to cover a sufficient range of screen contents. This is analogous to selecting the right scenarios in interaction design.

Consider Microsoft Outlook (shown in Figure 22.6) as an example. E-mail is the core function of the application, so it would be a logical archetype candidate if you were designing the application.

e-mail

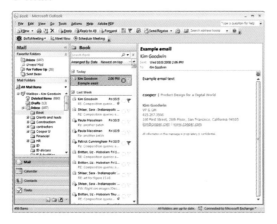

contacts

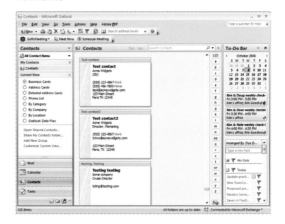

tasks

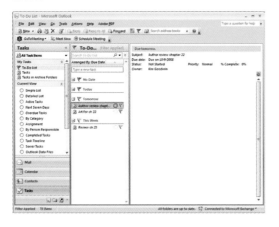

calendar

Figure 22.6. If you were designing Outlook, the e-mail and calendar views would make better archetypes than the contacts or to-do list views.

Detailed Design

It doesn't seem tremendously complex from a visual standpoint, but there's a lot of visual hierarchy to work out with the text and other elements. The contacts and task views offer fairly similar visual problems, so they're not going to be that educational as archetypes. The calendar view, on the other hand, is visually rather different from the other screens, which means it would be ideal to develop that as an archetype, as well.

It's also important for the interaction design to be reasonably complete, at least as far as text, widgets, and anything else persistently visible on the screen; that said, it's fine if these things are close but not quite right—the essential thing is that the interaction design be at a realistic level of detail. There may be some tension between getting the best archetype candidate and working with fairly complete interaction design, since the archetype needs to happen as early as possible in detailed design. Along with interaction design and engineering dependencies, the whole team should consider the visual designer's need for a useful archetype when deciding which interaction design topics to schedule first.

For data-oriented applications, some amount of realistic data is also essential in order for the visual designer to judge field size, column spacing, and so forth; *lorem ipsum* and similar fake text don't help with detailed visual decisions such as field length or information hierarchy. It's also preferable to have rough-draft copy for Web sites with relatively fixed content.

Even with the best sketch, the visual designer and interaction designer need to have a conversation about the contents of the screen, including what each item is, why it's there, how it works, and what states it can be in. This usually looks something like an interview, such as:

VisD: Tell me about this graph.

IxDG: That's meant to help Claire understand her household water usage. She needs to see what her current usage is and how it compares to her target and her usage last year. She also needs to see where she's using the most water.

VisD: So, I'm guessing the difference between actual and target is the most important thing, right?

IxDG: Right. Although if she's using a lot more water on, say, laundry than comparable households, that should be prominent enough to make her think about it.

VisD: OK, so what we really need to communicate there is the exception.

> For visual design to be effective, it's important for the interaction design to be reasonably complete.

Detailed Design

This discussion is also an opportunity for the visual designer to contribute to the interaction design, either by identifying potential issues or offering ideas for improvement. As with documentation, visual design can also force clarity where, for example, the interaction designer's sketch is ambiguous about hierarchy, or the interaction designer has an inexplicable aversion to making things that act like tabs look like tabs. For example:

> **VisD:** So, why does Claire need to see usage compared to last year? If the utility has set a conservation target of 10 percent versus the prior year, doesn't that tell her everything she needs to know? It would really help simplify the graph if we could drop that comparison and just focus on the target.

> **IxDG:** Huh ... that's true. Yeah, I think we can drop that.

Clearly, these discussions can lead to minor changes in the design, so the IxDG should catch up with the IxDS if he's not present.

DEFINING A GRID

In the late 1940s and 1950s, a number of graphic designers began to use a rational, Constructivist layout approach based on a grid. Since the 1961 publication of *Grid Systems in Graphic Design*[1] by Swiss designer Josef Müller-Brockmann, the use of a flexible **grid system** as the basis for page layout has become a standard component of graphic design education. By providing an invisible but coherent structure, an effective grid improves the readability of content and makes the work of detailed layout easier. Grids have their uses in three dimensions, as well (see Figure 22.7). In the design of interactive systems, a grid allows other designers or even programmers to make good layout decisions as the design evolves.

Figure 22.7. The LEGO System is an example of grid-based design in three dimensions. The base unit is a single-stud plate; everything is built up from there. Bricks are three plates tall and some number of studs long and wide. This ensures that everything fits together.

A layout grid is not simply a sheet of graph paper; it's a system of proportional spacing meant to guide the placement of type and other elements. There are very simple grids and very complex ones. Some are based on traditionally pleasing ratios such as phi—the classical "golden ratio" of 1:1.618—or the international paper standard's square-root-of-two ratio (1:1.414), which ensures that two halves retain the same proportions as the original. Others simply use whole number proportions (such as the 4:3 ratio of most older monitors, or the 1:3 composition ratio taught to most illustrators and photographers). Autodesk.com, shown in Figure 22.8, is a good example.

In interface layout, a grid consists of atomic **base units** and larger **macro grid** units that are divisible by the base unit. For many applications, this base unit is as small as three or four pixels square. Designers at Cooper usually refer to grids as "base-n," a shorthand that tells someone drawing widgets for a "base-four" grid, for example, that both height and width should be divisible by four pixels. Of course, the horizontal and vertical dimensions of the base unit can differ, but square

---

1. Müller-Brockmann, J. *Grid systems in graphic design*. Arthur Niggli, 2001.

units are often easiest to work with. Horizontal and vertical macro units usually do differ, for reasons you'll see below.

In applications and Web sites, the layout of major components on every screen or page should be a variation on the same macro grid. Five to seven variations are plenty for most applications and sites; if you use too many variants, you start to lose the cohesiveness that consistency provides. The Autodesk page layouts in Figure 22.8 provide a good example of a simple yet flexible grid.

To develop a grid, you first need to determine the size of your available display area, or **canvas**. After that, you can work from what I think of as the "outside in"—meaning the size of your canvas drives the grid—or the "inside out," using your text or widget dimensions (your base unit) to build up your grid. In reality, you'll probably experiment a bit and wind up using some combination of both. Note that the following approach is a starting point, but won't always get you to exactly the "right" answer; some tweaking may still be necessary.

Determine your canvas size

Resolution is a critical factor in determining your canvas size, of course. If the end user's screen resolution isn't something you can control, you need to work with stakeholders to determine the minimum resolution. Use the personas and market data to drive this. Although 800 × 600 may be the safest choice for most Web pages, highly paid stock market analysts, radiologists, and other information-dependent professionals aren't reluctant to use large, high-resolution monitors to run their critical, information-dense applications.

The canvas is often the entire screen on a handheld device. On a PC, operating system components such as the Windows task bar or Mac OS X dock-limit window size. Standard window title bars and borders—and in the case of Web sites, the

Figure 22.8. Autodesk.com uses a simple grid with pleasing proportions. Even the lines the eye follows down the sides of the building in the illustration are related to the grid.

Detailed Design

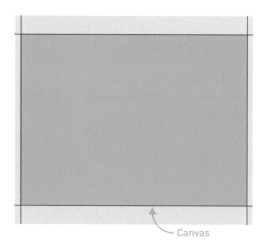

Figure 22.9 The dimensions of the usable area depend on what's left after the usual window dressing.

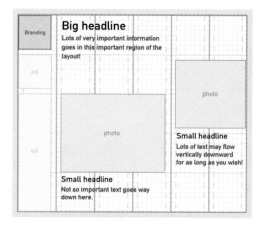

Figure 22.10. Visible columns and screen elements usually span multiple macro units.

usual browser controls—further limit the size of the canvas, as shown in Figure 22.9. The remaining dimensions are what you have left to work with for your grid. The canvas could extend beyond the bottom of the window on a Web site and in some applications, but don't worry about that for now.

Determine horizontal spacing

Look at the interaction framework sketches and the detailed interaction design for your archetype screens, paying particular attention to the densest, most visually complex screen. How many panes appear across the width of the screen? What's the maximum number of widgets or text elements that appear in a row? This should give you an idea of how many horizontal macro units you need. Note that these aren't necessarily the same as visible columns, which can span multiple macro units as shown in Figure 22.10.

In Figure 22.11, you can see in the detailed sketch that there are up to seven elements laid out across the screen, which implies that you need at least seven horizontal units. Now look at the framework sketches for the rest of the screens, shown in Figure 22.12. Will that number of units

work for these screens? If not, adjust the number and see if you can make it work. Most PC applications and Web sites require five to seven horizontal units; some require as many as 12 to 15. Much more than that will likely be too granular.

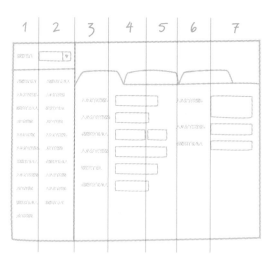

Figure 22.11. This screen has seven elements laid out across it, so chances are you'll need at least seven horizontal units.

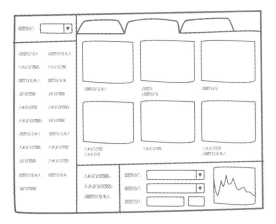 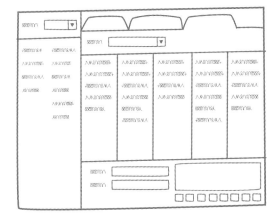

Figure 22.12. Look at the framework sketches for other screens to see how they'd translate into your potential number of columns.

On a technical note, all this is easier if the interaction design sketches already exist in your drawing tool. At Cooper, we use a sketchy house style template to develop interaction framework sketches, which we can then use to guide detailed design drawings right in the same file.

Before you commit yourself to a number of columns, though, consider the proportional relationships among any major divisions of the screen, such as an organizer and workspace or a Web site's left navigation and text. Look for a unit that allows these to occupy exactly some simple fraction of the canvas width, or to be related in one of the classical pleasing ratios. You can use quarters or sixths, but thirds, fifths, and even sevenths are generally more interesting to look at. If this isn't complicated enough, your macro unit should also allow columns of text (if applicable) to be 40 to 50 characters wide if you're using multiple columns or 45 to 75 characters for single columns.

Finally, make sure the pixel measurement of each unit is divisible by a small number you can use as your base unit, such as three to five pixels. Add an empty space the width of the base unit inside the edges of each column, as shown in Figure 22.13; this results in a gutter between columns that's twice your base unit, which is usually about right.

You can, of course, add another unit to widen the gutter if that seems necessary. These gutters guide the placement of elements within the columns.

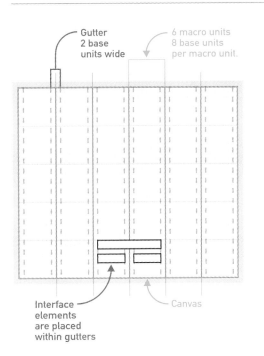

Figure 22.13 Gutters are empty space except when an element spans multiple units.

Determine vertical spacing

Vertical spacing should be in pleasing proportion to the horizontal spacing; widgets that are ten pixels high with a minimum horizontal unit of 100 pixels would look a little strange. Your vertical units, like the horizontal units, are determined partly by the need to divide the screen vertically and partly by the base units.

Let's assume, for example, that your base unit is four pixels square, and your predominant font is eight pixels tall as measured from the baseline (the invisible line upon which letters without descenders rest) to the top of the ascender. Within a text box, you'd want to leave perhaps four pixels above and five below, as shown in Figure 22.14; an optical illusion always makes the bottom edge look a bit smaller than it is, so it's usual to leave a bit of extra padding there. By the time you add a single-pixel border with a subtle, single-pixel drop shadow under the bottom edge, you've got 20 pixels. Add four pixels of padding either above or below for spacing with other widgets, and you've got a vertical macro unit of 24 pixels to use in creating rows of widgets.

Figure 22.14. Developing a vertical unit for a base-four grid.

As with horizontal units, you'll want to make sure your vertical units fit within your canvas (if it has a fixed vertical dimension) and allow for pleasing division of real estate. If you've got a couple extra pixels left over, you can put them in the margin at the bottom of the screen, which can always use a little extra. Don't worry if your

vertical unit runs off the bottom of the page on a Web site or other application with scrolling content; the fact that something is split in half provides a visual clue that there's more stuff available.

Lay out the first screen using guides

Either using guides or in an empty layer of your drawing application—Fireworks or Photoshop—draw your grid, starting with the horizontal macro units; then add the gutters in another color or another layer. You'll mostly work with the gutters, so being able to turn off the original measurements unless you need them can clean up the view. Use colors that will contrast strongly with your design; hot pink, cyan, or lime green often work well. Add horizontal lines spaced according to your vertical units in the same color as the gutters. Now you're ready to lay out your visual elements according to the guides.

Tweak if necessary, break by rare exception

Your first take on a grid might not quite work as you begin laying out elements. Rather than ignoring the grid at whim, tweak the grid until you get it right, always ensuring that your adjustments come together in a coherent structure. A sufficiently flexible grid generally doesn't need to be broken, particularly in application design. In Web page design or playful applications, such as games for children, breaking the grid is sometimes necessary to provide a livelier or more brand-appropriate feel. Wise designers usually do this in a very judicious way, though; breaking the grid repeatedly simply creates a disorderly layout that's hard to read and use.

Dynamic versus fixed grids

You may well be wondering what happens when a user resizes the type or adjusts the size of a window. Most interface elements shouldn't rearrange themselves based on window size, though there are times when scaling text columns up or down (to a minimum width) makes sense.

However, it should generally be possible for accessibility reasons to increase the size of text. Assuming your engineers are willing and able, you can create dynamic grids based on percentages and proportional units, such as ems or dialog units, rather than pixels. If area A is set to be 33 percent of the width of area B, it doesn't matter what size each area is. If your base unit is one em (a distance equal to the type size as measured in points) for your predominant font, then everything can scale up in proportion to it as the type scales. This sounds easier than it is in reality; most implementations end up degrading in some way when text is scaled.

EXERCISE

Design a grid that will work for your RoomFinder or LocalGuide screens.

DEFINING THE BACKDROP: FRAMES, SURFACES, AND DIMENSIONALITY

Theatrical set designers know that in order to showcase the action on stage, an effective backdrop must support the story without stealing the show. The same is true for interfaces: The actors (widgets and data) must exist on a background that makes them appropriately visible, helps make their relationships clear, gives them room to do their thing, and supports the overall visual language in an unobtrusive way. That backdrop is generally rendered in the form of surfaces and framing elements, such as those shown in Figure 22.15.

Look at the interaction framework sketches and any more-detailed interaction design sketches. Identify which elements are both static and shared across each screen. For applications, this often includes some sort of title area, a menu and/or toolbar, some sort of frame around the edges of the window, and possibly a persistent organizer pane or something similar. This is where you want to start.

Most visual interfaces include some sense of dimensionality: the illusion that widgets protrude from or are pressed into a surface, and that some surfaces are either above or below one another. Highlights and shading provide this illusion. When it comes to window frames and dividers, dimensionality either provides an affordance that something is dragable or establishes some layering relationship between the framing elements and the rest of the screen content.

Theatrical set designers know that in order to showcase the action on stage, an effective backdrop must support the story without stealing the show.

Detailed Design

627

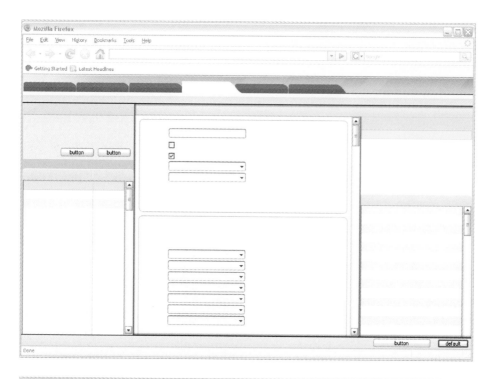

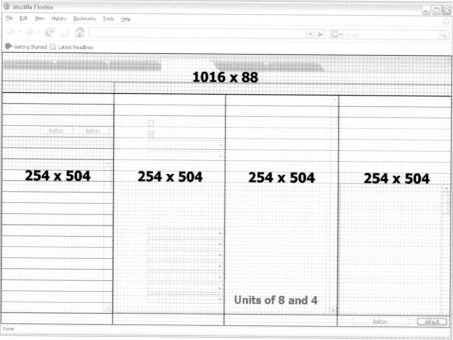

Figure 22.15. The "backdrop" elements of the visual system, related to the grid and ready for widgets and content.

Detailed Design

Figure 22.16 Sloppy use of dimensionality creates puzzling layers and unproductive visual tension.

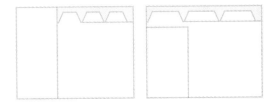

Figure 22.17 A simple visual choice implies entirely different things about the relationship between the organizer and workspace.

In both Windows and Mac operating systems, the imaginary light source that illuminates widgets and icons is above and to the left of the screen. This means users will find icons shaded differently subtly uncomfortable. It also means they're accustomed to interpreting anything highlighted along the top and left, and shaded along the bottom and right sides, as protruding from the surface, while anything with reversed shading is viewed as indented. Abrupt shading implies angularity, while gradients imply curvature. This convention is pretty straightforward, and most designers follow it without even thinking.

Where people sometimes run into trouble is in using dimensionality in the structural elements of an application. The two most common errors are inconsistency and complexity. Inconsistent or thoughtless use of dimensionality can hint that a layer is simultaneously on top and underneath, an impossibility in anything but an M.C. Escher drawing.[2] In Figure 22.16, you can see that along the top pane, A appears to be on top of B, which is on the same level as C, yet there is no layering implied between A and C.

Early on, you need to make a decision about whether the panes of each screen are sitting on top of the background like pieces of paper on a

desk, or whether they're recessed in a frame or bezel, like a painting or LCD. Likewise, you'll need to decide whether any window dividers and scrollbars exist on the same plane as the content or are part of the interface structure.

Relatively subtle visual choices can make a significant difference in how relationships are interpreted. Consider the seemingly minor difference between the two screens in Figure 22.17. In the first one, the organizer appears to be part of the overall interface structure, implying that it will be persistent and that selection in the organizer might even result in different tabs appearing in the workspace. In the second, the organizer seems to be a peer with the workspace, hinting that other tabs might or might not have organizers within them.

DEVELOPING A HIERARCHICAL LANGUAGE OF CONTENT AND CONTROLS

As discussed in Chapter 21, a clear visual hierarchy clarifies and establishes relationships and helps users process the most important information first. The first draft of your visual system should include appropriate visual hierarchy. Because an effective visual system reduces arbitrariness and unnecessary variation, you should

2. Escher was best known for his drawings of impossible perspectives, such as a staircase that is a continuous loop. See particularly *Convex and concave*, 1955, *Ascending and descending*, 1960, and *Waterfall*, 1961. Images are available at www.mcescher.com.

Detailed Design

try to limit your hierarchy to a small number of levels. Four are sufficient for most design problems:

1. **Urgent.** Examples include the single most important item featured on a Web site or an urgent exception in a business system or medical device. Strong visual contrast (including illumination of physical controls) is appropriate for these situations; motion is occasionally warranted.

2. **Important.** There are usually several important things on a given display, including the information your personas are most interested in and any items (such as headers) used to organize other information or keep users oriented. Default actions (such as an OK button) are often appropriate at this level, as well. Larger or bolder type, brighter colors, heavier outlines, and imagery such as large icons are all common at this level.

3. **Ordinary.** Most content on a screen should be at this level, including most widgets, labels, and text. Regular type and limited contrast are appropriate. Small icons indicating object type are also common.

4. **Less important.** This content isn't entirely *un*important, or it wouldn't be on the screen; however, it's generally secondary information that's viewed only after someone has decided to look more closely. Relatively low contrast and small (but still readable) type are suited to this sort of content.

The sketches developed by the IxDG should include a clear indication of which information is at what level of importance, though a visual designer who has been closely involved in the project can probably figure this out. Some interaction designers tend to introduce too much nuance to the hierarchy; the visual system (and some vigilance on the part of the visual designer) helps keep this in check.

Type is usually a good starting point for establishing a hierarchy. A good type system for an application has one very readable, sans serif screen font, such as Tahoma, as the primary typeface for content. Headers can sometimes be rendered in a second face, such as a serif or humanist sans serif font, or one of the faces from the brand identity system. Some content-rich Web sites might make effective use of slightly more complex type systems, but most content still relies on just one or two faces. As you might expect from the general discussion of hierarchy above, most systems require three or four type sizes to provide a clear hierarchy. Three sizes can provide four levels of hierarchy through manipulation of weight and color. Make the sizes clearly distinct: at least two points or pixels should separate each size.

Expand on and refine the color palette used in the relevant design language study. Define colors for urgent, important, ordinary, and less important text and visual feedback. Define a set of highlight and shading colors. No doubt you'll end up evolving this, but taking a first crack at it in a systematic way will help ensure you're making deliberate choices that all fit together later on.

If your engineering team needs to use a standard widget library, the widgets and states may already be defined, and their dimensions may define your grid's base unit by default. For more novel designs or re-skinning of standard libraries, however, you may need to define everything from button size and shape to the exact colors used in every pixel in every widget state: when a control is unavailable, available, selected, and used as the default action (such as when the enter/return key is pressed). As noted above in the discussion of grids, use the base unit to define the scale of your widgets.

As you begin to develop the rest of the visual language of widgets, icons, and the like, use the squint test to assess where they stand in relation to the hierarchy established by your type. Things at an equal level of importance should stand out to about the same degree when you squint your eyes to blur the image.

DESIGNING A COHERENT SYSTEM OF VISUAL FEEDBACK

Controls, interface objects, and data may all need to communicate a range of information, such as:

— Selection state

— Object type (documents, images, folders, etc.)

— Actions taken (such as links that have been followed or messages that have been read, forwarded, or replied to)

— Other types of status (available, unavailable, protected, offline, in need of attention, etc.)

— Affordances for manipulation

— Relationships to other objects

You can use color, line weight, size, texture, shape, type style, and icons to relay this information. It's best to follow existing conventions such as graying out text and controls to make them unavailable, or using a colored background behind text or objects to indicate selection. For any visual feedback not covered by convention, you'll need to develop a language that uses visual properties consistently. Use each specific visual property to mean only one thing. Certain colors in your system should be reserved for certain things; if you use red, yellow, and green in some places to indicate status, don't use them elsewhere (other than as incidental details in an icon) without attaching that same meaning. Likewise, use dimensional affordance, shape, and other properties in consistent ways. Using multiple properties will let you provide a great deal of information about each object.

REFINING AS YOU GO

As your archetype comes together, you'll find yourself refining various aspects of the visual system. However, the system doesn't need to be perfect yet, particularly since this activity generally takes only a couple of days. Just get things as close as you reasonably can, with particular attention to structural issues (such as the grid and standard widgets). New screens will inevitably "break" some part of the earlier design just as new scenarios can break interaction design. Tweaking widget styles and such isn't too difficult later on if you set up your files correctly (see the "Shared Image Files" section later in this chapter).

Use the "squint test" to assess the effectiveness of your hierarchy.

Detailed Design

Figure 22.18. These icons are part of a system developed for NetApp. Note how the different icons incorporate the same elements for similar actions and status indications.

Continued expansion and evolution

Once you've reviewed your archetypes with teammates and clients and set up a file to share with the generative interaction designer, you'll be dividing your time among several activities:

— Working on icons and any other visual elements that aren't critical to initial screen layout

— Designing any new widgets or information displays that weren't included in the archetype(s)

— Beginning the first draft of the style guide documentation (see Chapter 24)

— Tweaking screens rendered by the IxDG and adjusting the visual system as necessary

— Reviewing interaction design work in progress and collaborating on solutions as needed

— Working with engineers to determine exactly how elements will be rendered in code (such as how widgets are built, whether you'll have subpixel rendering available for text, and so forth)

The icon system

Not every visual designer excels at icon design, which is partly about choosing appropriate symbols and partly about being able to render clear and appropriate images with a limited number of pixels and colors. Fortunately, icons are the easiest part of the visual design to outsource to a second designer in your group or even to a contractor who specializes in them.

Good icons start with appropriate choices of symbols and images. Spend some time deciding what images will best represent each concept and reviewing them with your teammates and subject matter experts before you begin the time-consuming process of rendering. Icons for objects often need modifiers for various actions (such as creating a new object of that type, copying, forwarding, replying, and so on) or status indications (online, offline, or in need of attention, for example). For this reason, it can be easier to do most icons in the latter half of the phase, once you know what most of them are and can anticipate what elements will be shared across the system. See Figure 22.18 for examples of icons that relate well in a system.

Personas, scenarios, and experience attributes

You may notice that so far, the discussion of detailed visual design hasn't made much reference to personas and experience attributes. That's because work at this level is mostly about principles, clear communication, and consistency—the essence of the visual language, which is driven by the personas and experience attributes, has already been established. However, these tools remain essential in certain ways.

The personas play a role in icon design as the visual designer attempts to come up with imagery that will be familiar and understandable. Will a teenage persona understand an icon of a vinyl record, floppy disk, or roll of film? Will a non-technical user know that a cylinder represents a database?

To the extent that the desired hierarchy isn't supplied by the interaction designer's initial rendering, the visual designer must think through personas and scenarios to determine it if his teammates aren't readily available. He also relies on personas and scenarios to enhance the interaction design with modeless visual communication and to review and contribute to the interaction design work.

The experience attributes (and the related patterns discussed in Chapter 17) continue to drive the design and critique of individual widgets and icons. They even influence the grid; an open and spacious feel with plenty of padding between elements, for example, is usually essential in communicating simplicity or luxury. A clearly evident grid structure creates a sense of order, modernity, and rationality, whereas a playful Web site for children may need a grid that's less obvious.

Experience attributes are also indispensable for thinking about the way objects move. Should a window close with a businesslike snap or a more fanciful slurp? Should a movable element on a touch screen jiggle playfully, light up, or pulse when touched? Should any pop-ups fade in, unfurl, or simply appear? Due to the solo nature of most detailed visual design work, the personas and experience attributes are mostly things the designer keeps in mind, rather than tools used in an explicit

process. However, they are a constant reference in discussion with other designers, such as:

Designer 1: What do you think of this icon for video?

Designer 2: Has Amanda ever even seen a film projector? Something like a photo with a play button might be better.

Or:

Designer 2: I think the concept works. If you're trying to convey playfulness, though, it's a little drab. Maybe it would help if you gave it a bit of a tilt or made the lines a little less precise.

Shared Image Files

Close collaboration between the generative interaction designer and visual designer is tricky but essential in this phase, since a product's behavior and how that behavior is communicated are often inseparable. This is why I find it surprising that so many interaction designers and information architects develop wireframes and hand them off to visual designers; in my experience, interaction designers who understand pixels and visual designers who can influence control selection and layout not only find the work more satisfying, but also achieve better results.

The tricky bit is that these two roles need to work in the same file—perhaps this is enough of a hassle to explain the wireframe handoff phenomenon. However, developing some shared conventions and good version control can make it work smoothly. At Cooper, we've found that using the same tools and work practices is essential, particularly since team membership is likely to change from one project to another, and teams can't afford to develop whole new ways of working on every project.

Detailed Design

The same file gets handed back and forth as often as two or three times a day. The interaction designer generally sets up the first version of the file during framework definition. The visual designer then builds the archetype(s) and drafts a system, defining the grid and replacing sketchy elements with more polished styles. Common components are set up in a predefined place (such as an element library in Fireworks).

The interaction designer does the first draft layout of most screens using the structure and styles defined by the visual designer, inserting any new controls and elements. The idea is for the IxDG to get all of the necessary elements, including realistic data, into the file because the visual designer doesn't have the time to decipher meeting notes and fill in missing or ambiguous details. The visual designer then adjusts layouts, designs new elements as necessary, and fine-tunes the visual system as needed, reviewing each final image with his teammates. The visual designer generally works in the file when the interaction designer is in meetings, which is most of the day at the beginning of the phase. Individual elements (such as controls and icons) can be developed outside the primary file, which minimizes conflicts as the interaction designer works in the file.

In the early days at Cooper, most of us used Adobe Photoshop to do our screen renderings. We switched to Fireworks around 2001 because it had more sophisticated layering and allowed for faster production; even the couple of holdouts on our staff soon realized that even though it was geared toward designing for the Web, it was the better tool for most of what we do. Our visual designers still rely on Photoshop for a few things, such as sophisticated image editing and

some kinds of icon work that are more difficult in Fireworks due to its blend of vector-based and raster-based drawing. While some of the following tips are specific to Fireworks,[3] many of them can be adapted to Photoshop if that's your preferred tool.

— **Use the same tool from framework through detail.** Rendering your framework sketches in the same tool you'll use for detailed design makes it easy to refer to the original sketches in developing the grid and visual system.

— **Keep everything in as few files as possible.** Splitting your images across multiple files might keep your computer from bogging down due to lack of memory, but it can make updates more difficult and makes errors more likely if, for example, you need to change the colors of an element you have treated as a symbol. Trust me; the hardware upgrade will more than pay for itself by increasing your productivity. That said, for truly massive projects, splitting files is sometimes worth the hassle. It's best to split the files along the lines of platforms (such as a kiosk and handheld) or by personas or scenarios.

— **Define repeated elements as symbols.** Few things are more annoying than manually pasting over every instance of an icon or other element that you've used in 20 different places. Defining these elements as symbols allows you to update every instance at once and can make updates easier if you must split your work into multiple files.

— **Use states and layers to group elements.** Put your various elements, such as an image of a button drawn as "available" and separately as "unavailable," into separate layers.

---

3. For additional Fireworks-specific tips, see "Designing interactive products with fireworks," an article Nick Myers wrote for the *Adobe developer connection* in June, 2008. http://www.adobe.com/devnet/fireworks/articles/cooper_interactive.html

Set up a state for each scenario step and share the necessary layers across the relevant states, then just turn them on and off as needed for each state. This also makes exporting images for documentation easy later on.

— **Keep unique elements separate from common elements.** Put common elements in one layer so they're easy to track; then put varied elements in their own layers so they're easy to turn on and off. Keep related layers next to one another, with the varied layers on top of the shared layer. Items that appear in only one state need not be shared.

— **Use a consistent naming convention.** If you follow the approach to states and layers above, it works well to label states by persona name and scenario step (e.g., kate_registration_02_enter address) and layers by element with any necessary status information (e.g., countrylist_expanded).

— **Use some form of version control.** At its most basic, version control can consist of saving the file on a shared server location with the date, time, and the initials of whoever touched it last as part of the file name. Cooper teams have found that Adobe Bridge and Version Cue offer a somewhat better approach.

Even with all of these practices, working in the same file takes constant communication between the visual and interaction designers. However, I think you'll find the effort is worthwhile.

> Working in the same file takes constant communication between the visual and interaction designers.

Evolving the Industrial Design

As with the visual system, there is variability in the degree of industrial design fidelity at the beginning of detailed design. If the industrial design problem is a simple restyling of an existing platform, it's entirely possible that the industrial design will be closer to completion than the interaction design will be. In many cases, however, and especially when there is a novel platform involved, the industrial design will be at the foam model stage when detailed design begins.

The platform—i.e., one of the basic form factor and input method combinations presented at the design vision meeting—should be agreed upon during or immediately following the design vision meeting with stakeholders. The input method(s), screen size, resolution, orientation, and color depth are essential to detailed interaction and visual design, so these need to be resolved immediately even if other aspects of the form are in flux.

Detailed Design

635

The ID essentially has multiple detailed design partners depending on the activity. The ID and visual designer refine the design language based on stakeholder feedback, typically based primarily on one concept. The ID and mechanical engineer (ME) collaborate closely to make the form appropriately durable, sustainable, and cost effective to manufacture; in some cases, the design ME is largely focused on external surface engineering, part breaks, and assembly method, while a contracted manufacturer provides most of the internal engineering and final part design for tooling. The ID collaborates with the interaction designers on control placement, behavior and hierarchy. The ID also reviews and contributes to the work of the other design team members on a regular basis.

Refining the form and materials

For the first one to three weeks of the phase, the ID is primarily focused on refining the form factor, assuming the components and the type and placement of physical controls are fairly well defined. This always involves work in a CAD application, such as the one in Figure 22.19; if there is much change to the form, it might also involve

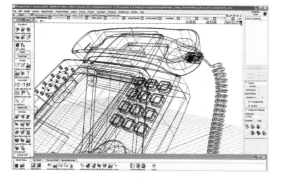

Figure 22.19. The mechanical engineer or a 3D-modeling expert builds a detailed 3D database.

a round of physical models using machined foam or a 3D printer, which builds a prototype directly

from a CAD file using layers of plastic. Even for IDs—who are accustomed to working in three dimensions—physical prototypes are necessary visualization and learning tools.

There are many considerations in optimizing a form, some of which may exist in tension with others:

— **Internal component fit.** Although the initial concept should have had the internal components in mind, the ME probably still needs to finalize the layout of circuit boards and other internal parts. This may require some adjustment of the device's interior volume or overall size.

— **Ergonomics.** A number of people with different physical characteristics should handle foam models to assess what fits comfortably in the hand, works well for seated or standing use, and so forth.

— **Context appropriateness.** The design may need to be adjusted to enhance durability, reliability, or other necessary qualities.

— **Manufacturing cost.** A large number of parts can increase the cost of assembly, but large, complex parts may be more difficult to mold without flaws. The ID must work with the ME and manufacturing expert to accomplish the design intent in the most economical and reliable way.

— **Sustainability.** The way parts are assembled or painted can make them more or less difficult to recycle.

— **Design language effectiveness and consistency.** The design language is an integral part of the form's evolution and no longer a separate consideration.

— **Integration with the interaction design.** Scroll wheels, buttons used to activate soft keys, and other controls must relate appropriately to the screen.

Internal components and parts such as those shown in Figure 22.20 need to be finalized as early

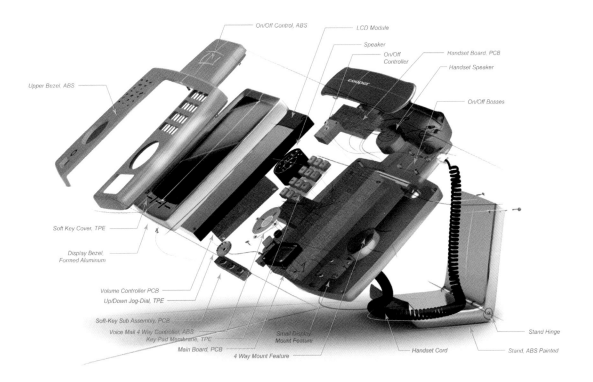

On/Off Control, ABS

LCD Module

Speaker

On/Off Controller

Handset Board, PCB

Handset Speaker

Upper Bezel, ABS

On/Off Bosses

Soft Key Cover, TPE

Display Bezel, Formed Aluminum

Volume Controller PCB

Up/Down Jog-Dial, TPE

Soft-Key Sub Assembly, PCB

Voice Mail 4 Way Controller, ABS

Key Pad Membrane, TPE

Main Board, PCB

Small Display Mount Feature

4 Way Mount Feature

Handset Cord

Stand Hinge

Stand, ABS Painted

Figure 22.20. Part lines and component layout must be finalized.

as possible. The mechanical and electrical engineers drive most of this, though the design team expresses what's needed from the hardware in terms of weight, screen resolution and bit depth, battery life, and so forth. The ID and ME may purchase a number of off-the-shelf parts, such as hinges, to assess their function, look, and feel.

Decisions about materials are not simply cosmetic; they are critical to how the product will be manufactured. Material choices are driven by cost, functional suitability, and brand or aesthetic considerations. The ID typically starts with some idea of materials, color, and texture, which may be very specific or might be as general as "dark gray rubber" or "polished metal." The ME weighs in with specific materials based on engineering and manufacturing considerations; a completely metal enclosure, for example, can interfere with the function of a wireless antenna.

The ME imports the ID's database into his own application, such as Pro/ENGINEER, and creates a more precise 3D model using the ID file as a template. The ID and ME pass the file back and forth to ensure that it captures the design intent. The ID does not modify the ME's file, but may in essence draw on top of it to indicate, for instance, that a curve should be a little sharper, or a button profile should be a little different, as shown in Figure 22.21. Together, the ID and ME refine transitions and part breaks—the seams that indicate where two parts are joined. They then produce quick models to assess the impact of their changes. In the meantime, the ME works with other engineers and the manufacturer to develop thermal simulations as well as any necessary electrical shielding, moisture seals, and so forth.

Detailed Design

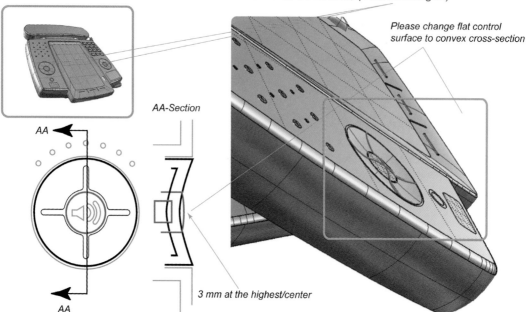

Figure 22.21. The ID requests various adjustments to the model.

Refining color and surface details

The ID works with the visual designer to ensure that the grid used on-screen and the grid used on the device relate to one another, and that the alignment of physical controls and soft keys on the screen is just right. Also, it's often desirable for the visual style of soft keys to create a nearly seamless look with adjacent physical controls.

The ID also works with the VisD and IxDG to relate the visual hierarchy of physical controls to the visual hierarchy on the screen; an unimportant physical control should not, for example, stand out more than an important piece of information on the screen. With hardware as with on-screen elements, hierarchy is mostly determined by size, position, and color. Illumination can emphasize important physical elements; blinking illumination should be reserved only for critical failure indicators, such as a battery that will be running out in a few minutes.

Although the ID takes the lead on defining colors and surface textures, close involvement with the VisD is essential to ensuring a seamless look for the entire product. The visual designer typically develops the type and icons to be used on physical surfaces and provides these to the ID as vector images rendered in Adobe Illustrator. The ID or a model maker then applies these assets to the appearance model and adjusts them as necessary, since an icon or label designed for a 2D surface seldom looks quite right when applied to a curved surface. This treatment is generally sufficient if the icons or text are simply to be pad printed on the surface of the device. If the images or text are to be embossed or debossed, the ME must painstakingly model a 3D version of the asset so it will appear in the final mold. Similarly, the ME must model any custom surface textures or work with a texture vendor who can create custom-textured production mold parts.

Appearance models as design and communication tools

Once the detailed industrial design is in good shape, the ID provides an in-house or external model shop with the ME's database and a set of color and material specifications in order to create an **appearance model**. This is a high-fidelity physical model that mimics the look and feel of the final product as closely as possible within the budget. Some appearance models may also provide a limited mock-up of a critical mechanical function, such as a hinge that opens and closes. An appearance model generally does not involve working electronics. If time and budget permit, the model can incorporate realistic materials, but it may simply be plastic that's painted to mimic some other material. Representative screen contents are typically printed and applied, and icons and text are applied to physical surfaces as decals. The model may also be weighted to simulate the correct materials and internal components.

Appearance models are important communication tools because they help stakeholders (and perhaps end users) envision the final product in a way that machined foam and 2D renderings simply cannot accomplish. A high-fidelity appearance model can also be used for product photography, which helps the marketing department get started on materials for the product release long before manufacturing has any functional products available.

However, an appearance model—like interaction and visual design documentation—is also an important design tool. Its physical nature and level of detail highlight shortcomings that aren't visible in 2D renderings or lower-fidelity foam models. A color that worked as a subtle accent on a computer screen might be too bright on the physical object, or a polished surface might feel too slippery. For this reason, it's wise to assemble the model's parts using some temporary technique, such as double-sided tape, that allows parts to be switched out for repainting or other adjustments. Appearance models are expensive—ranging from a few thousand dollars for a simple device with no moving parts and few part breaks, to perhaps $20,000 for a more complex model such as a laptop—and time-consuming to build, so it's far cheaper to replace one part than to redo the entire model.

For more on presenting an appearance model to stakeholders, see Chapter 24.

> Appearance models help stakeholders envision the final product in a way that machined foam and 2D renderings simply cannot accomplish.

Design Reviews and Collaboration

Regular reviews are an important practice during detailed design. Design team check-ins help ensure design quality and smooth collaboration. Reviews with design engineers—and sometimes with business analysts—are necessary to ensure feasibility and clear understanding for implementation. Scrutiny from subject matter experts (and anyone else, for that matter) helps find holes and flaws in the design.

Within the design team

Brief check-ins within the design team should be routine events. As during framework definition, these serve two purposes: keeping everyone on track and ensuring the quality and completeness of the design. A regular appointment with the full team, such as 20 minutes at the beginning or end of the day, gives everyone a chance to get immediate feedback on tough design problems, stay in sync as the design evolves, and exchange timely information, such as:

— Requests, comments, or news from the project owner, engineers, or other stakeholders

— Design changes that may affect anyone else's work, such as a physical button that needs to be moved slightly, an adjustment to the interaction framework that will affect the visual system, or a grid change that eliminates an unnecessary variation

— Updates to the visual system that the interaction designer should use in rendering screens

— Things you need to review with the design engineers, project owner, or subject matter experts

Often, these reviews are peripatetic, moving from one individual's desk to another's to look at the latest screen and hardware renderings or document draft. To allow for more detailed review, you can either extend these meetings to a half hour or build in an hour-long review session every few days. Which works better depends on individual team preferences and skills. Of course, this is not to say that designers don't talk to one another as the need arises—just that most people are more productive when not interrupted a dozen times a day for routine details.

The divide-and-conquer approach that's most effective for detailed design means that team members are making more individual decisions about how best to express the team's collective vision in pixels, words, and physical materials. This requires each team member to find a difficult balance between being a diligent reviewer of her teammates' efforts (since you succeed or fail as a team) and letting colleagues do what they do best. This takes practice!

WHAT TO LOOK FOR

Whether you're reviewing bitmap screens, animation, industrial design surface details, or documentation, keep your eyes open for:

— **Divergence from design intent.** Does the artifact clearly communicate the necessary behavior, hierarchy, or information?

— **Oversights and bad assumptions.** Does it seem like the solution fails to address part of the problem?

— **Inelegant solutions.** Is the solution more awkward, complex, or inefficient than it could be?

— **Arbitrariness.** Does it seem that some decision was made without good reason?

— **Inconsistency.** Was a similar interaction or visual design situation in two places handled in two different ways when it could have been addressed with only one solution?

— **Unnecessary distinctions.** Are there more levels of visual hierarchy than are really useful?

- **Divergence from principles and goals.** Does the solution interfere with a persona or business goal, undermine the experience attributes, or violate some known principle of good design?
- **Unnecessary implementation difficulty.** Does some decision make coding or manufacturing difficult without good reason?
- **Just plain great ideas.** Not every comment should be constructive criticism; praise any great ideas you see, and don't hesitate to offer a brilliant solution if you see an opportunity to do something even better.

HOW TO GIVE FEEDBACK

Although it's sometimes appropriate for a project lead or senior team member to provide specific direction, design reviews—like all design meetings—work best when people test one another's ideas with the intent of helping to improve them, rather than trying to "win" in some fashion. Your teammates are on the same side; you're trying to give them an assist, not score against them.

Here are some helpful hints for reviewing specific types of work in ways your teammates will appreciate.

- **Don't forget to say what's great.** It will help teammates receive the rest of what you have to say in a better mood.
- **Ask first.** Point out what you see and ask for more information about it before expressing your concern. There might be a good reason for the decision that you just don't know yet.
- **Explain what's wrong before offering solutions.** This will allow the person receiving your feedback to decide whether they have a better answer than your suggestion.
- **Be specific.** Don't just say it's no good; explain exactly what about the solution doesn't work.

- **Base your critique in something objective.** Don't just pit your opinion against your colleague's; relate your critique to the personas, goals, scenarios, experience attributes, intended hierarchy, or accepted principles.
- **Remember that your suggestions are just that.** Don't tell your colleague what to do about the concern; offer your suggestions as nothing more than ideas: "Maybe it would help if you did it this way ..."
- **Offer suggestions if asked.** If someone asks how you would do it differently, at least make the attempt to help them solve the problem.
- **Involve the rest of the team.** Don't turn it into a back-and-forth between two people; get the rest of the team to weigh in and see if you can reach a consensus.

HOW TO TAKE FEEDBACK

The ability to accept and deliver constructive criticism is essential not only to the success of a particular project, but also to your development as a designer. None of us is perfect, no matter our seniority or experience. In my view, no designer is truly senior until he actively seeks feedback on his own—not because he lacks confidence in his skills, but because he knows collaboration makes his work better. Regardless of its source or style of delivery, you should learn to accept feedback as a gift and make the most of it.

- **Assume competence and good intent.** None of us delivers feedback in a perfectly gracious manner every time, and not every piece of poorly articulated feedback is worthless. Look for what you can learn from it anyway.
- **Ask for the problem behind the suggestion.** Maybe the suggestion is trying to solve a problem, and not just an instance of, "That's not how *I* would do it."

Detailed Design

— **Ask for something constructive.** If someone is just being negative, ask for specificity and constructive suggestions.

— **Ponder before defending.** Understand the comment and sit with it for a minute before pushing back.

— **Write it down.** Make a note of the comment so you don't forget it. This also tells your teammates you're taking them seriously.

— **Do something about it.** Unless you can reach agreement as a team that the feedback was off base, try to address it. If it doesn't work, follow up and explain why. Don't just nod and ignore it.

— **Thank people for good feedback.** Offering critical feedback is just as hard for some people as accepting it is for others. Appreciation now will get you more help later.

You'll find these skills useful in collaborating with the rest of the product team as well. Don't underestimate the importance of collaboration; most design leads I know would far rather have a team of solid but not brilliant designers who collaborate effectively (thereby elevating each other's skills) than individually brilliant designers who don't work well with others.

With design engineers, SMEs, and business analysts

Close collaboration with engineers is critical to ensure the feasibility and thoroughness of your design, as well as a faithful translation from spec to finished product. For highly technical products or enterprise software, subject matter experts and business analysts may also be essential. It's often convenient if your project owner can attend these sessions, but not critical unless a significantly more desirable design solution will affect engineering or manufacturing costs or timelines. This kind of issue only arises

a few times on each project, so it's usually possible to move on to some other topic while you find a time to talk with the project owner.

Meeting with these experts less than once a week is a sure way to waste time fumbling through incorrect or impractical solutions. Meeting for an hour every day or two gives you and the engineers chance to ask questions and review work in progress. Collaborating all day, every day would not be an effective use of anyone's time.

Although these collaborative meetings are informal working sessions, they'll be far more productive if you lay some groundwork. First, make sure you get the right people there—generally the design engineers, possibly a couple of SMEs and a business analyst. Avoid huge crowds; people with nothing to contribute belong in a more general stakeholder review rather than a working meeting.

Go to each meeting with an agenda in mind and a list in hand:

1. **What do you need to ask about?** Keep a running list of questions during design meetings so you don't forget any.

2. **What do you need to show and get feedback on?** Bring a set of the sketches, scenarios, CAD files, or other design details you need to review. Drawing on the whiteboard or bringing physical models sets an appropriate "work in progress" tone and invites others to engage with the design artifacts. Projecting pre-drawn sketches saves time, but can be less inviting unless you project them on a whiteboard where others can interact with them.

3. **What do the engineers need from you?** Give the engineers a chance to review what they're working on and ask questions of their own.

As you begin working through detailed design with this group, you'll probably need to be specific about the sort of feedback that's helpful. Most of what your design teammates are looking for is also good for this group to think about, but they should place special emphasis on oversights, bad assumptions, and implementation challenges. Some of this might happen via e-mail, especially if it's very detailed. For instance, a visual designer might get an e-mail like this from an engineer:

> The latest table images look great. Unfortunately, thanks to how Swing draws tables, I don't think we'll be able to achieve the look you're going for using these files. Swing assumes that all cells have single-pixel grid lines except headers, which don't have grid lines between the columns. We should be able to make it work or at least get pretty close if you can give us a separate file to use as a table header background that has the lines built into the image.

With other stakeholders

Periodic reviews with other stakeholders help ensure that they see the progress you're making, particularly on large projects for which the detailed design phase lasts several months. If you're delivering documentation for a few design topics at a time, use the first draft documentation of each design chunk as an opportunity to share your work with stakeholders who might be outside the day-to-day work of the project, such as the heads of marketing and sales. There shouldn't be any glaring holes in the design by that point if it's been reviewed at the whiteboard by engineers and SMEs, and the design is expressed in sufficiently concrete terms to be satisfying for stakeholders who are uncomfortable with sketches.

Remote collaboration

Remote collaboration is becoming increasingly common in today's world of teams distributed across continents as well as time zones. In my experience, remote collaboration is no problem at all for design *reviews*, but isn't entirely satisfactory for design *creation*. For one thing, designers in two different time zones may have difficulty finding enough meeting time together, and informal over-the-shoulder reviews at someone's desk are difficult to manage. For another, although remote-meeting technologies have come a long way, the need to deal with a system between you and your design partner can interfere with flow (see Chapter 14). I suspect it's possible to overcome this in time.

> **Remote collaboration is no problem at all for design *reviews*, but isn't entirely satisfactory for design *creation*.**

Design review meetings are less about creative flow because the acts of design creation are brief and intermittent. As long as you can see an idea in concrete form, converse about it, and ideally scribble on it together, you can be effective. Videoconferencing is getting more reasonable; you can install a basic system with HD video at both ends for around $15,000, and Skype (which is free) is tolerable for short chats. However, even the priciest videoconferencing system can't replace face-to-face contact. Spend the first few days of detailed design in the same location with your engineers and SMEs to build up rapport. After that, it generally doesn't matter if you don't even have video.

Perhaps the most annoying thing about remote collaboration is the inability to work at a whiteboard together. A tablet PC at either end connected with a desktop-sharing application will allow people in either room to "pick up the whiteboard marker." Attached to a projector, it still lets everyone see what's going on.

Even without these technology solutions, it's possible to review design by sending images or document pages electronically, then reviewing them over the phone. To make this work, you'll need to number the images or give them simple, distinctive names, and spend some time clearly labeling the components in the image.

Iteration After Feedback

Whether it's from an internal review or a usability test (discussed in Chapter 23), you will inevitably have to adjust your design to respond to feedback. Start by compiling a list of the issues and any good ideas you've heard. Spend a few minutes assessing each issue identified to determine whether you think it really needs to be addressed. Would your personas find it a problem, or is a stakeholder just making a comment based on

personal tastes? Does the result of the usability test make sense, or do you suspect some problem with the test design or facilitation? I don't mean to imply that you should be dismissive of feedback—quite the opposite. Rather, you should examine it closely and figure out whether to take it at face value, or whether there's really something else underlying it.

Tackle the biggest, most difficult issues first. If you've used good process so far, a "difficult" issue might cause you to rearrange some screen components or adjust the design of a widget. Larger issues should be rare.

An iteration meeting is just like any other design meeting except that you probably have a list of small issues to work through rather than a couple of big topics. As always, rely on scenarios to help make sure your adjustments make sense.

Common Challenges During Detailed Design

Like every part of the process, detailed design has its potential pitfalls, some of which are within the design team's control and some of which are not. Most stem from a shortfall in skills or discipline on the part of one or more project participants or from insufficient time or diligence in earlier phases of the project. At least one of these things is likely to happen when key project participants are inexperienced either working as designers or working with designers. By watching out for these situations, you can catch them early and minimize problems.

Framework flaws

Most framework-level design by experienced designers holds together surprisingly well. Sometimes, though, you'll learn that something about your hardware architecture, interaction framework, or design language simply doesn't work when it's translated into detail. This means you failed to anticipate something at the framework level. Framework adjustments don't usually involve starting over entirely; something like adding a screen or rearranging a couple of panes usually does the trick. It's unlikely to cost you more than a day, if that. It's worth examining your process and learning how you might have prevented it, but this is why design is iterative. You might find yourself needing to remind stakeholders of this, but most won't be too concerned if you treat it as a natural part of the process.

Unavailable or unhelpful SMEs or engineers

The success of detailed design is very much dependent on the level of cooperation you get from subject matter experts (if you have them) and engineers. If they're too busy with other priorities, they might not be available enough. It's also possible you've got the wrong people for the job if they can't answer most of your questions or aren't giving your work a thorough review. Start by having an honest conversation about what you need that you're not getting. Ask if the SME or engineer feels that he can provide it. Treat this as a partnership, however, and ask if there's something *you* could be doing differently. Be sure to establish specific deadlines for the information you need.

If this doesn't produce a satisfactory result, the best option is usually to continue designing based on your best guess and discuss the situation with your project owner, who might be able to get you better support. Whatever you do, don't stay silent about the issue; otherwise, any lack of progress or thoroughness in the design will be laid at your feet, regardless of its cause.

Shifting assumptions and constraints

Few things are more frustrating to designers and engineers than constraints and assumptions that keep shifting. Good process prevents a fair amount of change by providing clarity and rationale, but even the best process can't account for changes in business conditions or (let's be honest) the occasional capricious executive. Changes in scope sometimes have a reasonable basis: a shift in a company's financial position requires a tighter scope or allows a larger investment, a new regulation requires some adjustment, or perhaps a desirable hardware component that looked too expensive has suddenly dropped in price. They may also occur because of a change in leadership; new executives often have different priorities.

Aside from these situations, people changing their minds about the target audience, feature set, or other project parameters are usually falling back on bad old habits. If possible, have a discussion with the relevant stakeholders about the decision-making process. If they're adamant about the change, your job is to help them understand its implications: how much additional design time it will take and how much cost it will add. Sometimes, helping people see that a change won't really save them money can keep things on track.

Team member time management

The members of the design team are always interdependent, but during detailed design, the dependencies are so numerous (especially among the visual designer and interaction designers) that any slippage on the part of one team member can have a cascading effect on the others. This makes day-by-day calendaring essential; each team member needs to know right away if she's running behind so she can catch up and not delay her teammates. Daily design team check-ins and

Detailed Design

Budget constraints often force designers to choose between breadth and depth.

regular internal milestones make progress (or lack of it) visible to everyone, so any team members who aren't successfully managing their time get immediate support.

Consistency within a brand or product family

Most companies make more than one product. Unfortunately, few companies do a good job of creating a consistent design language and predictable behavior across an entire product family; one company might have, for example, 20 different renderings of the icon for a power button, or two applications in the same software suite that handle cutting and pasting in different ways. It's impossible to tackle this kind of problem on a project-by-project basis; the best you can do is follow an existing style guide (if there is one) and avoid unnecessary differences between your design and closely related products. However, it's a good idea for each company or major division to establish a style guide (for use by designers, not engineers) and a shared repository of icons and other design language elements as well as interaction design patterns.

Uneven depth

One challenge that's especially common for anyone designing software is a budget that's too small for complete design. This always results in some trade-offs between depth and breadth: Do you provide rough design for most of the screens, or do you provide deep design for the most important parts? On one hand, I've seen more companies successfully build upon the latter approach. On the other, the often complex relationships among parts of a system may lead to problems if you design screen A without considering what's going on in screen B.

Perhaps the most common example of this is related to system configuration. Because this is an infrequent task, it's often the first thing on the chopping block when a project plan has to be trimmed. However, the rest of your design might be dependent on the system having certain information, such as in a medical device that intelligently displays different things depending on whether it's in an oncology unit, operating room, or pediatric intensive care. Users won't take advantage of this helpful functionality if the configuration of this information is too difficult.

There's no easy solution to this problem, other than to explain how more design won't actually increase costs because without it, engineers will waste time struggling with undefined behaviors. If that's not an option, do your best to consider dependencies in prioritizing your topic list.

Using later work to improve earlier work

By the end of a detailed design phase, you will have made a multitude of small and large design decisions. Chances are that some of your later decisions were better than earlier ones because they were better informed—you learned from your earlier work. If you don't allow at least a couple of days at the end of a typical project to revise earlier visual and interaction design, your work may suffer from inconsistencies and may not give users the full advantage of what you've learned throughout the iterative design process.

Summary

A successful detailed design phase requires thoroughness, good time management, and close collaboration both within and outside of the design team. Day-by-day scheduling helps ensure smooth collaboration and makes all the detail seem manageable. Although months of detailed design may be less dramatic and exciting than earlier phases, there's something very satisfying about solving the hundreds of little (and sometimes big) intellectual puzzles involved in turning ideas into reality. Seeing your initial vision taking concrete, polished form is a reminder that the joy of design lies in creating beautiful, functional things that improve people's lives.

Detailed Design

CHAPTER 23

Evaluating Your Design

In my experience, the methods described in this book yield consistently good results when applied by skilled practitioners. However, it's unlikely for even the best designer to be exactly right about everything. Collaboration with other designers, design reviews with a team lead, and reviews with engineers, subject matter experts, and stakeholders provide a form of ongoing design evaluation throughout any project. However, it's a good idea to do a more formal type of evaluation at least once before you send your product out into the world. Think of this as the designer's equivalent of QA.

One chapter isn't enough to do any evaluation method justice; my intentions here are merely to introduce the topic, to demonstrate how design evaluation and common evaluation methods fit within the context of Goal-Directed Design, and to help you avoid a few of the most common pitfalls.

Why, When, and What to Evaluate

When and how you evaluate your design depends on why you're evaluating it. Design evaluation can serve several purposes:

— **Persuading people there's a problem.** If you're the only one who's convinced the existing product or design direction needs work, an evaluation can be an effective tool for changing minds.

— **Improving design.** Some types of design evaluation can help you see if you've designed the right product, while others can help you see if you've designed the product right.

— **Helping designers choose between two approaches.** Personas, scenarios, and a collaborative approach usually point clearly in one direction. If that's not working, you can use an evaluation to help you decide which approach is better.

— **Demonstrating design's effectiveness.** If you're convinced your design is right, an evaluation can help show stakeholders what a great job you're doing—and if the evaluation isn't so good after all, you'll learn something useful.

— **Gathering kudos for marketing.** Taste tests aren't just for soft drinks. This one isn't usually a designer's concern, however.

The one thing design evaluation of any kind doesn't do is *generate* good design. Some people expect usability testing, in particular, to be a complete solution: Prototype your best guess, test it, then keep tweaking and testing until you get it right. This is a bit like living on ice cream and potato chips and expecting your doctor to fix you with a pill; if I can repurpose the cliché, an ounce of good design is worth a pound of evaluation. This is why I always advise clients with tight budgets to forgo testing in favor of more up-front research and design time. However, I would never advise skipping evaluation for any product or service where a usability problem could be disastrous, such as for a medical device or vehicle interface.

When to evaluate your design depends on what you want to accomplish. A **formative** evaluation helps you know whether you're on the right path. It may only focus on a single interaction, so you can do this kind of evaluation anywhere along the way. Although many designers find formative evaluations helpful, I've found that research-based personas, scenarios, and experience attributes, along with good collaboration, have never left me in doubt about how to proceed. A **summative** evaluation is meant to help you polish odds and ends or persuade people about the design (one way or the other). This is most effective when you have a complete or nearly complete design, usually once you've finished documenting the first draft of your interaction design or, for hardware, when you have an appearance model. A **comparative** evaluation that pits two or more products or concepts against one another could be either formative or summative.

What to evaluate depends on the product or service as well as your own confidence in the design. If you're uncertain as a team about a particular design decision, you'll want to evaluate that specific decision. For hardware, it's worth assessing whether the product and its controls work ergonomically for the target audience. For most products, you'll want to evaluate whether you made any mistakes in general, especially in the most important areas of the product; tiny flaws in obscure corners aren't always worth looking for.

Types of Evaluation

There are several useful ways to evaluate design. Which approach works best depends on your timeline, budget, and—most important—your objective. For identifying usability issues and evaluating functional design directions, usability testing, expert reviews, and discussions with individual users are the methods of choice. Focus groups and individual user discussions are common approaches to assessing aesthetic impact.

Focus groups

I've worked with clients who believe strongly in focus groups (or individual interviews along the same lines) for predicting how well a design concept or design language will be accepted. Let me be blunt: Focus groups are pretty much useless for assessing interaction design because until someone interacts with the product instead of just looking at it, their opinions are uninformed at best. Even for assessing design language, I must say I'm not a fan of the approach.

Why not? Focus groups are easy to do badly (see Chapter 9). Far too many people take focus group results as gospel rather than as one of many data points to consider; I'm always concerned by the idea of letting users decide how a brand should be represented. Also, what people are drawn to in a focus group can't really predict what they'll be drawn to in a store jammed with products; self-reported behavior often has little to do with reality.

Detailed Design

If you are working with people who insist on doing a focus group, you should at least argue for not asking people what they *like*. Instead, consider using the experience attributes to drive the discussion. Which of these words best describes the design: powerful, simple, smart, or friendly? Which design is the most elegant? Take these as input about whether you've accomplished your design intent, not as guidance on what decision you should make.

Expert reviews

In an expert review, an experienced design or usability professional steps through the product or design looking for likely problems and evaluating their severity. Expert reviews are generally quick and inexpensive. They have fallen somewhat out of fashion because they're based on the opinions of an individual, and are therefore seen as less scientific than other approaches. Although it's certainly true that expert reviews only work when done by someone who actually is an expert, there's nothing wrong with relying on expert opinion: People do it in law, engineering, and many other fields.

However, unless the reviewer has considerable experience in your product's particular domain, an expert reviewer can usually identify only the issues that violate broadly applicable design principles, not those based on flaws in domain-specific workflow. For this reason, an expert review is most effective when combined with a day or so of field research, or at least a couple of hours discussing users and typical scenarios with subject matter experts. In my experience, an expert review does a better job of identifying and prioritizing issues when it involves some consideration of user goals and workflow in addition to design principles.

If you're hiring an expert to review your work, she will typically offer anything from a day of live discussion to a few days with a written report and possibly recommendations for adjustments. Take a look at an example report and see if the expert describes the basis for his assessment (i.e., ties each critique to design principles or experience with relevant users) and distinguishes disasters from nits. A helpful expert review may also point out things that *might* be issues, even if the reviewer is uncertain—for example, "The sequence of fields here seems odd because it differs from the mental model I would expect these users to have. However, since I haven't interviewed any users, this assessment may be incorrect. Consider having some users look at it."

> What people are drawn to in a focus group can't really predict what they'll be drawn to in a store jammed with products.

Usability testing

Rigorous though good usability testing methods are, various studies show they're not the foolproof science many people believe them to be.

In a usability test, individual users work through a series of fairly realistic tasks. Some tasks may be timed, but most often, each participant talks out loud to describe his thought process as he uses an actual product or prototype. Many people believe this approach is both more objective and more effective at identifying issues than an expert review, so testing has become a sort of gold standard in design evaluation. It's also tremendously persuasive; if five out of ten users couldn't accomplish a task, few people would doubt that there's a problem.

Rigorous though good testing methods are, however, various studies show they're not the foolproof science many people believe them to be. For example, since 1998, Rolf Molich and a number of his colleagues have conducted a series of seven studies called CUE: comparative usability evaluations. In each, they've asked a set of experienced teams to evaluate the same product either employing testing or expert review techniques. While each study had a slightly different focus, the results have consistently shown that a usability test doesn't find every problem, and that tests conducted by different people find different results. In the CUE-1, CUE-2, and CUE-4[1] studies, for example, anywhere from 60 percent to 91 percent of the usability issues were reported by only one team, and many of these were severe issues that resulted in failure to complete tasks. Of the 340 usability issues reported in the CUE-4 study, only nine issues were common to more than half the teams. Jacobsen, Hertzum, and John[2] found a similar phenomenon in a 1998 study in which four HCI experts reviewed a video of exactly the same test. The experts again offered divergent analyses, with only one evaluator reporting 46 percent of the issues. In other words, the effect of the evaluator is substantial in anything but a purely quantitative study.

High tech methods, such as eye tracking and usability labs full of equipment, promise a more objective approach, but the results are questionable. Objective comparisons of task time with one design versus another are hardly the only measure of effective design. In the as-yet-unpublished CUE 7 study[3], Molich found that eye tracking did not identify any issues that weren't already identified using less expensive

1. Molich, R., and Dumas, J.S. "Comparative usability evaluation (CUE-4)." *Behaviour & information technology*, Vol. 27, issue 3, 2008.

2. Jacobsen, N.E., Hertzum, M., and John, B.E. "The evaluator effect in usability studies: Problem detection and severity judgments." Proceedings of the Human Factors and Ergonomics Society 42nd Annual Meeting, October 1998.

3. Molich, R. Personal communication, August 6, 2008.

Detailed Design

methods. While his small sample makes the results inconclusive, they make sense—eye tracking can tell you, for example, whether a participant is reading or scanning, but it can't tell you whether she's actually absorbing what she sees. Expensive labs and tools are useful for fundamental HCI research, but for evaluating products, you're probably better off using less expensive techniques like those shown in Figure 23.1.

Figure 23.1. An inexpensive usability test using a paper prototype and basic camcorder.

So, what should you take from all this? There's no foolproof way to evaluate a design's effectiveness; the people evaluating designs are no more perfect than the people creating them, and even the world's best design could fail in the marketplace if it's priced incorrectly or marketed poorly. That doesn't mean you shouldn't evaluate your design, but it does mean that the more important it is to get the design right, the more evaluation techniques and evaluators you should use.

PLANNING A TEST

Planning a test consists of identifying what you want to learn and from whom, coming up with some tasks that will help you learn it, deciding how to describe those tasks to users, and determining what level of prototype fidelity you'll need.

Deciding what you need to learn

Do you need a quick answer to a self-contained problem or two, or do you need a comprehensive hunt for problems in your design? Your answer (and, yes, your budget) will determine how thoroughly you'll need to test. Quick answers are easy enough to find in a couple of days. A thorough test of multiple tasks can require a month or more to plan, execute, and evaluate. The first sort is usually easy enough for a design team to squeeze in unless there's no flex in the schedule; the second probably calls for a dedicated usability tester to handle the bulk of the work.

Identifying participants

Determining the number and type of test participants you need is a lot like planning your user interviews (see Chapter 6). Unless you have questions involving a specific user population—such as whether your design is as accessible as you think it is—it's usually fine to use the same recruiting criteria. As in field research, small samples of four or five people are fairly effective for narrowly defined roles, whereas you'll want a larger group of 15 to 20 for applications and Web sites with diverse audiences.

Of course, there's also the truly low-budget, informal version of recruiting participants: Waylay your colleagues in the hall or tell them to stop by for a snack and walk through a task. This only works well if your colleagues are reasonably similar to end users, however.

Detailed Design

For systems used by experts, it's not particularly important—and may be counterproductive— to test ease of learning; efficiency over time is more important.

Determining your focus

One of the most important decisions you need to make is whether you're interested in ease of learning or efficiency of use over time. It's reasonable to assess whether a passenger can walk up to an airport kiosk and use it right away, but it's not particularly important—and may even be counterproductive—to test whether an air traffic controller can immediately understand how to use his complex system without training.

When efficiency of use for intermediate or expert users is the more important metric, you need to include some form of pre-test training before you jump into test tasks. At minimum, this can consist of a quick walkthrough of the prototype and perhaps a handout that identifies controls by function. For greater realism, you would need to assess how users did after working with a functional system for a while, such as in a limited beta release.

Designing tasks

As Carolyn Snyder says in her very useful book, *Paper Prototyping*,[4] an effective task:

— Is based on user goals
— Is related to issues of importance for product success
— Has an appropriate scope (not tiny, but finite and manageable)
— Has a limited and predictable set of possible solutions

As it turns out, the tasks that form the basis of your key path scenarios (see Chapter 16) generally meet all of these criteria and are a perfect starting point for most tests. Better yet, if you're at the point where you've got a first draft document, you already have most of what you need for a simple paper prototype study.

Deciding what kind of prototype to use

A prototype can be either high or low **fidelity**: either faithfully rendering the eventual user experience or only approximating it. A high-fidelity appearance model is very similar to the mass, finish, and (rarely) some of the mechanical functionality of the final product. A high-fidelity software prototype is most likely clickable, with realistic

4. Snyder, C. *Paper prototyping: The fast and easy way to design and refine user interfaces.* Morgan Kaufmann Publishers, 2003.

Detailed Design

data entry and renderings of animated behavior, such as button clicks. Good fidelity is important for testing complex or subtle interactions, such as a dense information display with a lot of direct manipulation. High-fidelity prototypes can frustrate users if their fidelity isn't quite high enough, however; if it looks like a real system, users tend to expect that every button works and is as responsive as production code.

Low-fidelity prototypes, such as the sketches on paper shown in Figure 23.2, are quick and inexpensive to produce, and they don't set unrealistic user expectations. Unfortunately, they can introduce a certain type of error simply by being so unrefined. For example, a prototype without thoughtful visual design is probably missing essential clues about hierarchy, which would make it more difficult for a participant to pick out what's important on the page. Typical wireframe conventions, such as using a box with an X to represent an image, often don't make sense to users, either. This may not be critical with a simple, form-based screen but is essential for many rich data displays.

The happy medium for most software is a paper prototype based on your detailed screen drawings, like the touch screen prototype shown in Figure 21.28. This allows fast production, especially since you probably have most of the screen states you need drawn for scenarios, but still gives users the benefit of clear hierarchy, clean layout, and any rich visual feedback.

Although you can get feedback on future product concepts even with sketches, many systems involving hardware are best tested with higher-fidelity prototypes. For assessing interaction, these don't need to have realistic surfaces. However, they should use the correct controls in a realistic relationship to a display of appropriate size and resolution, and should be positioned in the way they'll eventually be used. For example,

Figure 23.2. A low-fidelity paper prototype.

you could mount a touch screen and number pad for an automatic teller on a piece of acrylic, then mount the acrylic to a wooden frame at the correct height and angle.

Whatever you do, don't assume the low fidelity of a prototype means the design can be half-baked; even if you're using the lowest degree of fidelity, the text and widgets on the screen or the function of hardware controls should still be thoroughly considered and expressed.

WHO SHOULD FACILITATE A TEST AND INTERPRET DATA?

While the design team should always be closely involved in planning a test, it's not ideal to facilitate your own tests. It's difficult to maintain objectivity; you may find yourself leading the witness or providing excessive coaching. However, it's better for the design team to conduct the test than for someone like a product manager—who is probably less knowledgeable about testing and equally likely to have biases—to do it. Bring in an outside tester if you can, even if it's another member of your design group who hasn't worked on this particular project.

Detailed Design

The test facilitator and design team should interpret the test results together.

The test facilitator and design team should interpret the test results together. An expert facilitator knows how to read user responses during a test, but the design team's field-research experience may provide explanations for some responses. For this reason, I don't recommend having a third party test your design and hand the report to management without your involvement; some unfortunate misunderstandings might happen.

USABILITY TESTING RESOURCES

Clearly, I can't do usability testing justice as part of a brief chapter; it deserves a book all its own. Fortunately, there are some good ones out there. While you'll need to do some interpretation to see how the methods fit within the design process described in these pages, you'll find a wealth of information on planning, moderating, and interpreting tests in Carolyn Snyder's book, as well as in *The Handbook of Usability Testing*,[5] Jeff Rubin's popular book, which he and Dana Chisnell recently updated.

Comparative evaluations

For a comparative evaluation of any sort—whether usability test, focus group, or expert review—the biggest potential pitfall lies in the fidelity of the things being compared. Comparing an incomplete design to a finished product introduces bias in both directions. A finished product may fare better simply because it is more polished. On the other hand, a low-fidelity prototype might not get as much critique simply because there's not that much to comment on. Expert reviews are less prone to this sort of problem than direct user feedback, but even experts may succumb.

The best approach is usually to dumb down the real product to the same level of fidelity as your design. If you're using a paper software prototype, create similar sketches of the real product as your basis for comparison. If you're comparing a foam or appearance model to an existing physical product, you might have to disable controls, weight the foam model so one doesn't feel more "real," or paint the real product a flat gray to match your model.

5. Rubin, J., and Chisnell, D. *The handbook of usability testing: How to plan, design, and conduct effective tests.* John Wiley and Sons, 2008.

Detailed Design

Summary

Just as every author needs an editor, every designer can benefit from having someone evaluate the effectiveness of her design. Usability testing and expert review are no more a science than design is, but both offer a rigorous approach and some tried-and-true techniques. Focus groups, on the other hand, yield inconsistently reliable data at best. If it's at all possible, you should build a test or expert review into your project plan. That said, if you would have to shortchange design or initial research to do it, focus on the activities that prevent problems, rather than trying to make up for a rushed effort with some last-minute QA.

Search

5

18

ter

80

15

10

r review

CHAPTER 24

Communicating Detailed Design

The fate of your design is determined in part by how effectively you communicate about it with both stakeholders and engineers. As discussed in Chapter 22, frequent collaboration is essential to communicating and evolving detailed design. However, more formal communication is nearly always required. A detailed representation of the final product helps stakeholders be patient during the long implementation process. A clear and detailed blueprint for construction—manufacturing in the case of physical products and production coding in the case of software—helps ensure effective translation from design to finished product. Your communication must be particularly thorough and unambiguous in the event that you're not around during implementation, which may happen if you're a consultant or using outsourced engineering.

A form and behavior specification—abbreviated as the "F&BS" at Cooper, tongue firmly in cheek—describes every visible aspect of the product's form and behavior. This isn't limited to physical controls and pixels; it also includes everything from workflow to evident business rules, such as how long messages stay in a phone's inbox or how much battery time remains when a device asks to be plugged in.

What the specification does not include is any calculation or structure affecting the back end: how server loads are balanced, how the device assembly line will work, or what database tables are involved in a transaction. These important issues are usually beyond a designer's expertise; design engineers and business analysts fill in these last gaps between design and construction.

For most software-only products, the F&BS tells a skilled engineer nearly everything he needs to know. The F&BS doesn't necessarily stand alone, however. It should ideally be supplemented with production-ready digital assets. In some cases, animations of any subtle behaviors help engineers understand the behavior you envision. Software engineers and business analysts might also follow the F&BS with a technical or "functional" specification that describes how an application needs to be constructed.

For physical products, you will of course need a CAD database for manufacturing. An appearance model—a close physical approximation of the product's finished look—will help designers and stakeholders alike to visualize the end result.

Don't forget that your spec also has an invisible audience: people who will need to understand your project in the future.

A prototype that simulates the function, fit, and assembly of components can provide a final sanity check before manufacturing.

By the time you develop the text, drawings, and models that make up the specification, the cost/benefit trade-offs have (hopefully) been made. However, it's still important to do a live presentation—or several, if you've chunked your design delivery—for the entire group of stakeholders. This ensures that they at least see the detailed design (even if they never crack open the spec) and publicly agree that the design is ready to go. Moreover, a presentation serves as a public celebration of what might have been a lengthy process. It's difficult to build momentum for design in many companies, so don't pass up an opportunity to show off your work in its best light.

The Form and Behavior Specification

With the current popularity of agile software engineering approaches, many designers are being asked to provide "light" documentation, such as sketches with a few notes. This can work well if you have an established visual system, a relatively uncomplicated product, and a small engineering team working closely with you. However, large or distributed engineering teams can't all collaborate closely with you, and the more engineers there are on a project, the greater the likelihood of inconsistency in skills, judgment, and interpretation of loosely defined specs. Less-skilled engineers are likely to take shortcuts based on what's easier to code if there's any ambiguity in the spec. Any time you don't have a very close relationship with the engineers, such as when your company is outsourcing development, specificity is essential.

Documentation is also an important design tool for ensuring the correctness and thoroughness of your design; skipping it simply means you'll discover design flaws after writing code, which is far more expensive than writing a few pages of documentation. Detailed specs are also indispensable for QA and user documentation. Instead of skipping the detail, designers working with agile teams should provide thorough documentation in an incremental fashion.

Effective documentation combines text and images to describe the anatomy and physiology of a product. If you supply only drawings with minimal text, engineers have to guess at behavior. If you supply only an animated or clickable prototype, they have to deconstruct its form and behavior for themselves. If you supply only text, wireframes, or UML diagrams, the potential for ambiguity is enormous.

You can develop the F&BS as a static document using a tool such as Adobe FrameMaker or InDesign, or you can assemble it in interactive form as an intranet site, which will let you build in clickable cross-references and links to asset files such as icons. Electronic documents also ensure that everyone is looking at the latest version. However, many people seem to prefer more traditional printed documents such as the one in Figure 24.1. Perhaps this is partly because large documents are still easier to read in print than on a screen. Engineers can annotate printed documents and leave them open on a desk without having to switch windows. Also, there's something about the *thud* of a big document on a table that makes people feel it's authoritative. Whether you decide it's more important to save trees or to save your engineers' eyes, the following discussion is equally relevant.

Figure 24.1. A thorough form and behavior spec can be a massive document.

The primary target audiences for the specification are the engineers, quality assurance team, and any business analysts responsible for helping translate design into technical reality. Most other stakeholders, aside from perhaps a product manager or subject matter expert, don't need to know the design quite so thoroughly. A formal presentation and a casual flip through the document may be sufficient. However, don't forget that your spec also has an invisible audience: people who will need to understand your project in the future, such as new designers, engineers, or managers who may join the team a year after you're gone. I've also had clients tell me the F&BS is an excellent recruiting tool for programmers, since it not only shows they'll get to work on interesting things, but also conveys that this is a company that has its act together.

As with formal communication on the earlier stages of your project, decide on your narrative structure as a team. However, the same contents and structure work well for most situations. A typical F&BS starts with sections covering:

— Background

— Executive summary

— Personas

— A product or service overview

Sometimes the majority of the user and domain analysis document is included as an appendix. Next, the document covers these topics for each primary persona's unique interface:

— An interaction framework overview, including any hardware interaction

— A small set of scenarios representing the key paths

— Form and behavior details for each screen and physical control

It would be tedious and inefficient to document the behavior of every control on every screen; instead, document any widgets or larger components that are shared across multiple screens (or between the screen and physical surfaces) all in one place:

This document may be the only one a reader ever sees, so you can't assume familiarity with the project and your work product to date.

— Common components and interactions

— Visual system overview

— Color palette and CMF specifications for hardware

— Type specifications

— Icons

— The grid

— Screen specs with measurements (may also go in behavior section)

If you have time, document some key principles and rules for expanding upon the design; hopefully the engineers aren't doing this on their own design, but you or another designer may find these useful later.

Background

The main background points to cover are:

— Project mandate, timeline, and overall approach

— Any conventions used in the document

This document may be the only one a reader ever sees, so you can't assume familiarity with the project and your work product to date. Briefly review your mandate, timeline, and approach to the project. Explicitly call out the engineering timeline and any aspect of the product or service that wasn't in scope—this helps readers who are late to the party understand the project context, without which they might judge your work by the wrong standards. Happily, you've probably written most of this already if you did a user and domain analysis document (see Chapter 13). You'll just need to update the timeline and add any conventions used for documenting design, such as, "**Bold text** represents the name of a button or other on-screen control."

Executive summary

Executive summary main points include:

— Quick product overview

— Highlights of big ideas and unusual design components

— Explanation of the design's value

An executive summary is not a must, but is a good idea if you have time because it gives busy executives (and anyone reading the document a few years down the road) a sense of what it contains and whether it's worth reading further. Keep the summary short; explaining the design's key points and benefits in a page is good rhetorical practice anyway.

Personas and critical requirements

Main points for the personas and critical requirements are:

— What personas are and why they're useful

— Overview of the set

— Review of details about key personas

— Review of key requirements agreed upon for each persona

Yes, that's right—you're not done with the personas yet. An effective spec weaves the personas throughout and uses them to explain design rationale, so it's helpful for readers if you reintroduce them. Also, chances are that not everyone reading the document was involved with the design team during the user and domain analysis discussion. Briefly describe what personas are, how they're derived from behavior patterns in the research, and why they're useful. You can probably borrow this section from your user and domain analysis, too. Rather than describing a large set of personas all at once, you could simply show a matrix summarizing the whole set, then introduce details for only the relevant personas as you begin describing each interface.

Product or service overview

The main points of the product or service overview include:

— Any unusual ideas that are the basis for the design

— Experience attributes

— Overview of the form factor(s), if applicable

— For a multi-interface product, overview of who gets what tools and why

It may seem odd to describe the big idea behind the product or service in a spec, since presumably everyone knows this by now. However, new people get hired, project funding gets postponed for three months, and people need to be grounded in the project's fundamentals all over again.

Readers will better understand the design language and some of the more subtle aspects of behavior if you remind them of the experience attributes (see Chapter 12). Those little animated touches or other nuances may be a pain to code, but they exist for a reason.

If there's a single hardware form factor shared by multiple interfaces, review it here; otherwise, do so in the framework overview for each interface. Outline the number of distinct interfaces and the personas associated with each. You should be able to borrow the basic outline of this content from your framework presentation.

Interaction framework overview

The interaction framework overview consists of:

— An introduction of relevant persona descriptions, if not already covered

— Overview of the form factor and physical behaviors, if applicable

— Number and functions of key screens

— Any major elements (such as an organizer pane and toolbar) common to key screens

— Navigation and relationships among common elements

— Data objects relevant to the interface

This section is combined with the product overview for a single-interface product. You'll have multiple interface overviews for a multi-interface product. The chapter on each interface should outline what screens exist in the interface and what common structures (such as those in Figure 24.2) are shared across multiple screens. If your

663

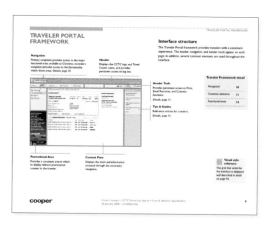

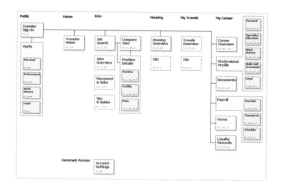

Figure 24.3. A navigation map for an application with many screens.

Figure 24.2. A typical framework overview describes the number of screens and the key components.

product follows a hub-and-spoke pattern or has a large number of screens, such as on many Web sites, this is a good place for a navigation map (see Figure 24.3).

The overview provides context for the design details, introduces any new vocabulary, and helps readers stay oriented. Engineers also find it helpful to understand the overall intent of the product design even if they're only focused on a subset of functionality. When there's hardware involved,

provide a description of each hardware control, its functions, and its relationship to screen contents, as in Figure 24.4.

If you think this sounds like a recapitulation of your framework presentation, you're right. This is important both because your framework may have shifted since the earlier presentation and because people tend to look at the most recent piece of documentation, forgetting that others exist. For example, a couple of years ago, my team did an abbreviated detailed design phase for just one of several interfaces in our frame-

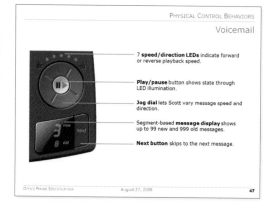

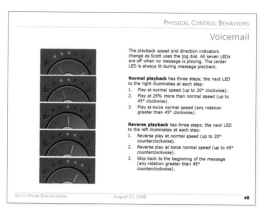

Figure 24.4. A description of hardware controls and how they work within the interaction framework.

work design. Due to the tight timeframe, we didn't spend any documentation time on the framework. A year or so later, the client's team was trying to use that form and behavior spec as a basis for the other interfaces, but they kept feeling the need to invent new things that deviated from the framework and added a lot of complexity. When they called me in to help them get back on track, it turned out that the information they needed was all in the framework presentation, but they had stopped using that as a reference tool once they had the F&BS.

Scenarios for each interface

The scenarios section of your document should include:

— An introduction of scenarios and their role in the design process

— A list of the scenarios covered

— The individual storyboarded scenarios

As discussed in Chapter 19, scenarios demonstrate the value and intent of the design in a way that no amount of functional description can. The fact that your design is essentially finished doesn't mean you can stop selling it; on the contrary, you must continue to promote its value even throughout implementation, when some unfortunate shortcuts can happen if stakeholders and engineers forget why they agreed to build something difficult.

Briefly introduce the concept of scenarios (since you may have new readers) and explain that they focus on key elements of the interaction, so they're not meant to be exhaustive. Don't try to illustrate every possible interaction. Instead, turn your key path scenarios into communication scenarios that show the product at its best. The scenarios aren't there as much to provide specific construction guidance as they are to help readers understand and value the design. For a typical desktop platform, a layout with two screens to a page, as shown in Figure 24.5, allows for details to be visible.

Important as the scenarios are, if you're truly pressed for time, err on the side of documenting behavior detail rather than doing a lot of scenarios; the necessary screen state changes are time-consuming to draw. Don't feel like you have to illustrate every behavior with a scenario. Keep the scenarios simple to make the story more effective.

> The fact that your design is essentially finished doesn't mean you can stop selling it; you must continue to promote its value even throughout implementation.

Detailed Design

665

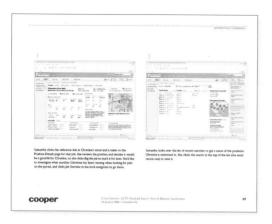

Figure 24.5. An example of scenario documentation.

Overview and details for each screen or function

The overview and details section for each screen or function should address:

- An overview of the screen's or function's purpose
- Screen anatomy
- Contents of individual widgets and data displays
- Behavioral details for any widgets or data displays unique to the screen
- Exact measurements for screen layout (if not in visual style guide section)

These elements are detailed in the following sections.

OVERVIEW

Give each screen within the interface a name, such as Calendar, Contact List, and Mail. Again, keep readers oriented by providing some context about what each screen is and why it exists. Using the personas in the overview serves as a reminder that everything you've designed has a rationale behind it. If there are distinct views or states within that

screen, such as a day, week, or month view in a calendar, identify what they are and why they exist.

FULL SCREEN ANATOMY AND RELATIONSHIPS

Next, introduce the screen's contents. A nearly full-page image with callouts is usually an effective way to do this. On the side of the interface closest to each unique element, list the element's name and a very brief description of what it does, such as:

View control. Switches the calendar among daily, weekly, and monthly views.

Use a line to point to each element. Callout lines look neater if they are exactly vertical or horizontal, with perhaps a few at 45° angles if necessary. Callout lines that overlap each other or at random angles can be confusing, especially with a dense screen.

For particularly dense screens, you may not be able to call out every control or data display. Instead, focus on naming the areas of the screen, such as an organizer and workspace, along with the most important elements within each area. You can then zoom in on each screen area in subsequent pages with callouts identifying every component of a dense area, as shown in Figure 24.6.

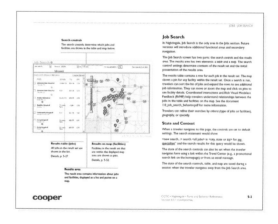

Figure 24.6. The Cross Country job search anatomy page with callouts.

Detailed Design

If there are any unique relationships among areas of the screen—such as one pane that drives another—describe those here if you haven't already done so in the framework overview.

INDIVIDUAL COMPONENT OR FUNCTION DESCRIPTIONS

Imagine your document as a map that's zooming in from 30,000 feet to 20,000, 10,000, and eventually ground level. If your screen is divided into, say, three major areas (such as an organizer, workspace, and toolbar), you'll want to zoom in on these, then break them down into discussions of every widget and piece of data they contain.

Again, use an image with callouts followed by detailed description, as shown in Figure 24.7. You'll want to do the same for functions and idioms shared across screens. You may also want to describe all of the valid states, possible values, field-level validation, measurements, icon file names, and so forth. See the description of selection behavior and the error state diagram in Figure 24.8 for examples of important details.

However, global controls (or idioms) shared by every screen, such as a toolbar, are usually best explained at the end of the interaction overview, before you dive into individual screens. You may not need to describe fundamental behaviors for

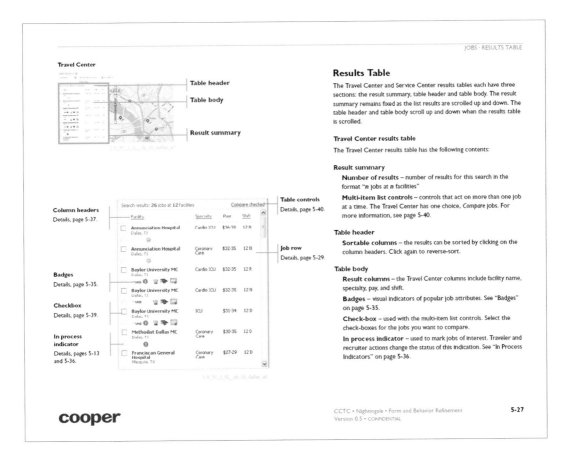

Figure 24.7. An overview of the results list for Cross Country's job search function. Note how the callouts refer to subsequent pages for details.

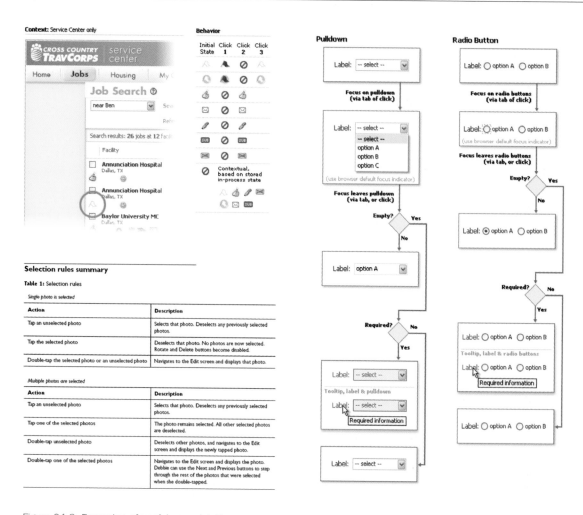

Figure 24.8. Examples of useful spec details.

common widgets—such as how autocomplete works in a combo box—if you're using a standardized widget library. However, you should certainly describe any novel widgets or deviations from standard widget behavior. You could document the details about each widget in each place it appears, but this is inefficient and may lead to inconsistencies in your specification. Instead, use a cross-reference or link to point to the widget section of the style guide (discussed later in this chapter). This will let you limit your screen-specific documentation only to the widget's values and parameters for that context.

EXACT MEASUREMENTS AND COLORS

You need to provide exact pixel measurements and color specifications for each element (see Figure 24.15). Ideally, you should also list the file names and locations of any production-ready assets such as icons or photos. You can provide this information either in the context of the individual screen or in a separate visual system section with links or cross-references from the behavior description. Putting these specs in the individual screen section lets the programmer building that tool see most or all of the necessary information without flipping back and forth. However, on most engineering teams, the people building the screens are not coding the behavior at the same time, or even at all. Integrating these details into the body of the F&BS also requires more coordination between the visual designer and IxD synthesizer, and time is often in short supply at the end of a project. For both of these reasons, leaving detailed visual specs in the visual style guide section is usually more successful, but ask your engineering team how they work before you make the decision.

Visual system or style guide

The contents of the visual style guide section include:

— What a visual system is

— Use of the corporate identity for hardware and software

— On-screen color palette and hardware color, materials, and finishes

— Type specifications for hardware and software

— Photography guidelines

— Icons for hardware and software

— Widgets

— Layout

— Individual screen specifications, if not provided in context earlier

The term "style guide" is somewhat overburdened because many companies use style guides instead of form and behavior specifications (and therefore instead of interaction design). The theory seems to be that as long as the engineers all line up their field labels and draw their buttons the same way, usable systems will follow. If you've gotten this far in this book, I don't need to tell you this is a false hope.

However, a visual style guide is still a useful tool for exposing shortcomings in the visual system, just as the rest of the F&BS helps ensure the completeness and coherence of interaction design. It also helps ensure consistency in screen rendering within a single design team, across multiple design teams working on related products, or when a new designer continues work started by another.

Although the sequence of the style guide subsections is not critical, it's a good idea to put the corporate identity information first, both to acknowledge the importance of the brand and to explain why some aspects of the visual system may deviate from print identity guidelines. Individual screen layout specs, if included in this section, generally come last simply because there are so many of them. The color palette and type are incorporated into widgets and text, so these are generally placed right after the identity discussion.

USE OF THE CORPORATE IDENTITY

Print and even Web guidelines for the use of the corporate identity sometimes have to be modified for use in applications, in which a mark might be reduced to a tiny icon in a window title bar. The specification needs to show how the identity can degrade gracefully at lower resolutions without becoming debased entirely. For example, if the image and word mark that make up the identity are never separated in any other materials, the corporate brand stewards would have good reason to feel uncomfortable with you using the image alone as an icon. However, since most companies don't have brand manuals that consider software or hardware, a translation (in close cooperation with the corporate branding team) is nearly always required.

Document the fundamental aspects of using the mark in an application or applied to hardware. These include:

- Ensuring that it is represented using the closest digital approximation of your identity colors

- Maintaining its aspect ratio and the spacing between image and word mark

- Ensuring a certain amount of breathing room so the mark is accorded a special status, not crowded in amongst a bunch of controls

COLOR PALETTE

The color palette for an application or Web site generally begins with the primary and accent brand colors (or the closest digital approximation), supplementary colors for interface elements, and any colors reserved for color coding and visual feedback (such as red, yellow, and green). If a primary identity color is not particularly visible in the interface, explain why heavier use of that color wouldn't have been a good idea from a usability point of view. Explain the intent and any usage guidelines for color coding, such as, "Use red only for problems so severe they will prevent the analysis from running," or, "Use 'selection blue' only for selected items and default actions." Specify colors using RGB or hexadecimal numbers, depending on the development platform and engineer preferences, as shown in Figure 24.9.

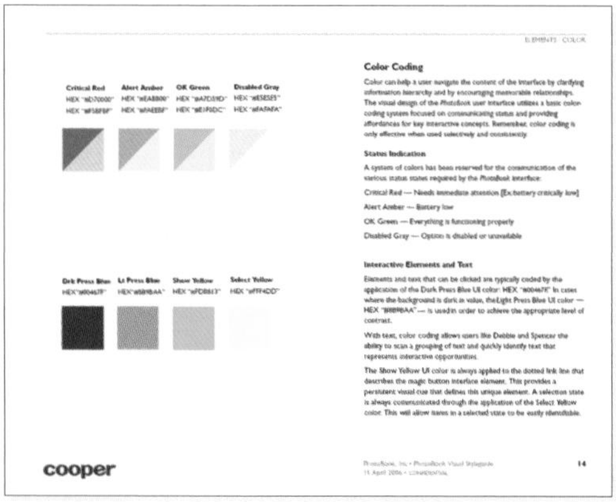

CMF (color, material, and finish) specifications for hardware are generally delivered to manufacturing separately from the rest of the F&BS—for which manufacturing has no use—but are useful to repeat in the spec just so everything is in one place. Most often, these specs consist of hardware renderings with callouts specifying material, color, and intended finish (see Figure 24.10) using a system such as Pantone's plastic color system or an automotive paint system for metallics. If the designer and manufacturer don't use the same proprietary color system, the color "spec" may consist of a set of physical samples the manufacturer needs to match. A model making vendor usually develops these under the industrial designer's supervision.

TYPE SPECIFICATIONS

Specify which fonts, sizes, and styles should be used for various purposes. As with color, explain why any deviations from the brand manual are necessary, such as why the primary corporate face(s) would be a poor choice for most content and why your choices are appropriate. Explain the type sizes and treatments for each level in the hierarchy, when it is appropriate to use each level, and which sizes should or should not be anti-aliased.

Figure 24.9. A typical page specifying part of an application's color palette.

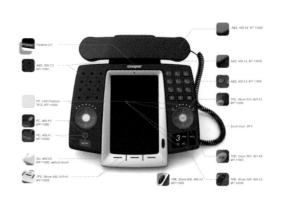

Figure 24.10. Color and material specifications for hardware.

Specify how type is aligned (generally along the left side and on the baseline). Explain any conventions you've established regarding capitalization (such as sentence caps or title caps) and punctuation. For content, specify line spacing (leading), paragraph spacing, and any special spacing for headers. Figure 24.11 shows excerpts from typical type specifications.

Include text for hardware labels and such in this section, as well. The manufacturer will need this information delivered separately, but it's useful to see how text used on the surface of a device relates to the rest of the system.

Explain why any deviations from the brand manual are necessary.

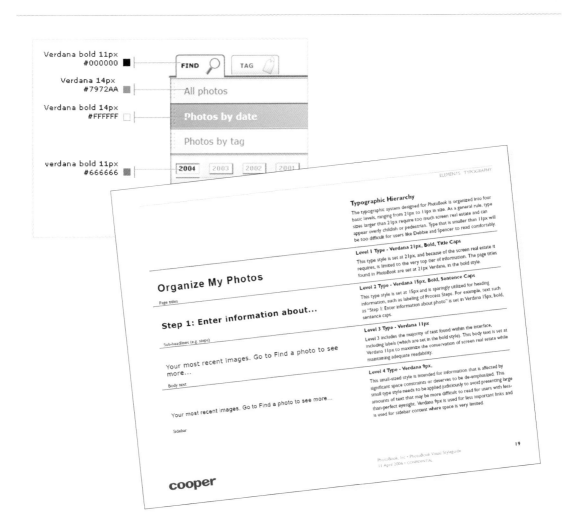

Figure 24.11. Typical type specifications.

PHOTOGRAPHY GUIDELINES

Where photographs are part of a Web site or other product, they are critical to establishing a cohesive style; for example, soft-focus color images photographed at oblique angles don't usually mix well with sharp, head-on, black-and-white images. Unlike icons and other interface components, Web site photos may be added to or updated frequently. Use the experience attributes to explain what the images are supposed to express. Refer to a corporate style guide as appropriate. Be specific about any photographic style issues such as angle, lighting, and depth of field. When appropriate, also specify content, such as:

— Whether images always have people or other specific content in them

— Who the models are (e.g., what range of diversity they should represent, whether they should look average or beautiful, etc.)

— What models are wearing (e.g., solid colors, conservative business clothes, or rumpled casual clothes)

— What the models are doing (e.g., looking at the camera or involved in some natural-looking behavior)

— What emotions the models should convey (e.g., pleased but not grinning)

— What the background is like (e.g., neat, cluttered, indoors, in nature)

— Any signature color palette (e.g., earth tones, bright colors, etc.)

Beyond this, specify any instructions for image processing to achieve a specific, consistent look, such as applying a specific Photoshop filter. It's useful to provide a template file, as well.

ICONS

Describe any general principles and conventions you've adopted, such as using one color scheme for most applications and another for utilities, always using object-plus-action, or always using two-dimensional schematics rather than photorealism. Explain the rationale for the icon style both in terms of usability and the experience attributes.

Categorize the icons by function, such as object icons versus action button icons, as shown in Figure 24.12. Show each icon in every necessary state and size. Include any hardware icons as a category, as well. These are delivered separately to manufacturing, but are useful to relate to the rest of the visual system.

Assuming you're providing digital assets, note the file name of each and, in any online documentation, provide a link to its location.

WIDGETS

Any common controls—widgets that aren't unique to a single screen—should be explained here. Engineers don't rebuild widgets for every screen, so it's unnecessary to put these specs in the individual screen documentation. Show all possible widget states (such as selected, unselected, unavailable, rollover, or default). Specify any detailed behavior such as the maximum number of lines in a drop-down before it scrolls, whether and how a combo box autocompletes text, and so forth. Describe screen-specific behavior in that context rather than here. Figure 24.13 shows an example.

LAYOUT

The layout section explains the purpose of the grid and provides an overview of the horizontal and vertical divisions at the macro level. Often, you can export interface images with your guides superimposed, so much of the drawing work is already done. This section also describes what happens when a window is resized or someone has a lower- or higher-than-expected resolution, if applicable. See Figure 24.14.

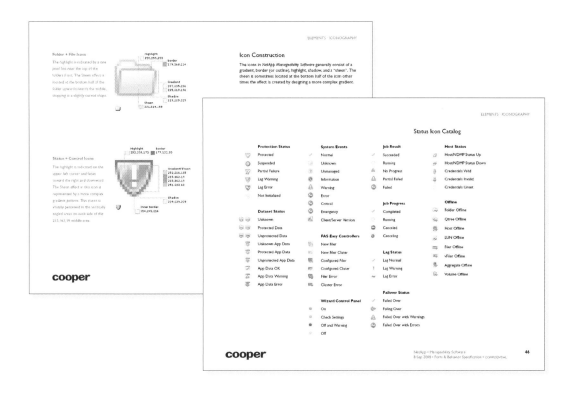

Figure 24.12. Pages from a typical icon catalog.

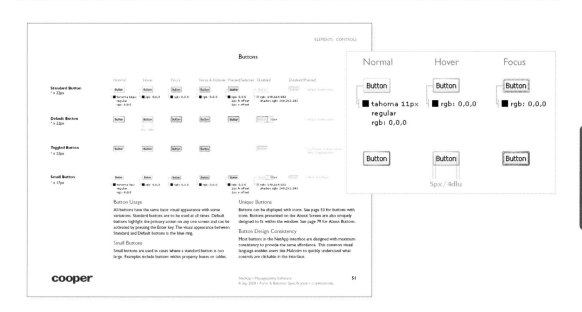

Figure 24.13. Part of a typical widget specification.

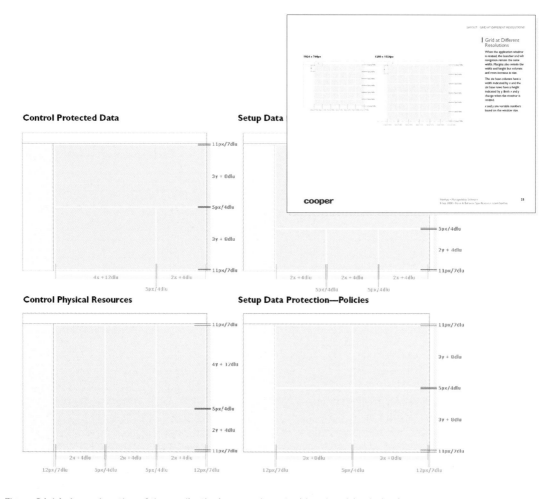

Figure 24.14. An explanation of the application's macro layout grid and resizing behavior.

SCREEN AND ELEMENT SPECIFICATIONS

Once engineers understand the macro grid, they may be able to use guides in their development tools to lay out elements. However, detailed layout and color specs take the guesswork out of building elements and laying them out. There may also be good reasons to deviate from the grid here and there, so call these out and explain them. For each screen (or pane or smaller area for complex screens), use callouts and measurement lines to specify spacing, color, and file names for any incorporated images, such as

icons or gradients. Figure 24.15 shows a typical spacing and color spec.

Ways to expand or cut back: the F&BS as a product roadmap

Most often, the form and behavior specification documents the next release of the product: whatever is getting built in the near term. Every now and then, though, the F&BS is used for release planning: what fits in the next version and what comes after that. If you're a consultant, the implementation of this version or the next might

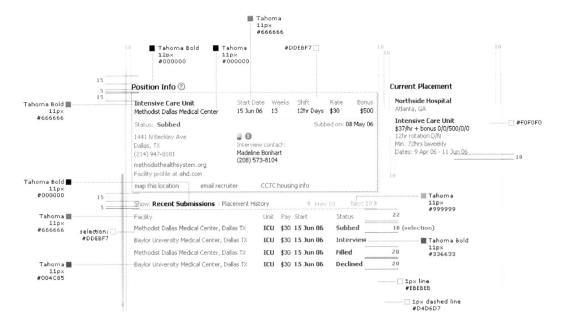

Figure 24.15. Example spacing and color specifications.

happen without you, so you may want to throw in a few longer-term ideas or ways to step back from the current design in case it proves harder to build than expected.

If you expect the product will grow without you, it may be useful to include a section on how to extend the design, such as what kinds of additional data and functions should (and should not) be added to various parts of the interface. You can also include specific ideas for fancier functionality throughout the text, designating these ideas with a light bulb icon or other special treatment to indicate that they're not a near-term specification.

If you think the engineers may have a harder time building the application than they expect to, you can also add some thoughts—either in a single section or woven throughout the document—about how to scale back. Indicate the aspects of the design that you believe are most critical to meeting the personas' needs and the components that could be temporarily replaced by a more economical option.

Qualities of an Effective Spec

The effectiveness of your specification is not determined only by its content and structure, but also by how you express the content. A good spec is prescriptive, clear, explanatory, efficient to read, and appropriately formatted. It also stands alone, with no need for readers to be familiar with earlier documents.

Prescriptive, not suggestive

Many product managers write requirements documents using the terms "must" and "should"—anything with the word "must" in front of it is presumably nonnegotiable, and anything with the word "should" in front of it can fall by the wayside if the engineers run out of time.

However, everything in the form and behavior specification is a prescription that's meant to be implemented, not a collection of suggestions. The contents are not open to interpretation, so your

Most people aren't that fond of surprises. Nothing in your spec should be news to the engineering team.

language should not imply that they are. Write with confidence and conviction about the product and the people who will use it. Avoid saying what the product should, could, or might do; say what it *will* do.

Clear and professional, not pretentious

The form and behavior spec is a professional business document, so appropriateness, organization, grammar, and spelling all count. If you're sloppy about these, some readers will wonder if you were similarly sloppy in your design thinking. As discussed in Chapter 13, use active voice and simple sentences, and don't feel compelled to show off your prodigious vocabulary. Have a good copy editor take a look at it. Likewise, ask your teammates to give the document an editing pass; see the "Technical review and document QA" section later in this chapter for guidance on this topic.

Unsurprising

Aside from, say, getting a fabulous gift or a bigger tax refund than expected, most people aren't that fond of surprises. Engineers who have to build impossible things on tight deadlines are less fond of surprises than most. Nothing in your spec should be news to the engineering team—they should have seen it all before, at least in the form of a whiteboard sketch. Of course, some things are more alarming in a final spec than in a whiteboard meeting because they're more detailed. This sort of thing may be impossible to avoid entirely, but constant communication and incremental delivery of specification chunks can keep it to a minimum.

Persona-focused

People who understand why difficult or unpleasant things are important are more likely to do those things. Engineers and product managers are no exception. Even though there should be no surprises in the spec, the engineer coding it three months down the road (and two days before his deadline) may not recall the rationale for that custom widget. It's best to make sure that rationale is clearly documented, especially if you're not always sitting right across the room to provide it on a moment's notice.

Throughout the document, refer to your personas by name to keep them present in everyone's mind. In the product, interface, and screen overviews—and as needed for custom widgets or other tricky bits of the design—describe how the solution benefits the persona(s). Sidebars are a useful way to do this within the detailed parts of the specification.

Standardized

A template used by your whole organization helps streamline document creation. If you know what sections belong where and you have page templates for typical layouts, you can focus on communicating the content instead of on how large your margins should be or how a level two header should look.

A standard template also gets engineers accustomed to looking for certain things in certain places. Although some engineers may have idiosyncratic preferences in documentation, it's not productive to vary your documentation for every engineer. However, some aspects of document structure and style, such as whether page layout specs are separate from behavioral specs, absolutely should flex depending on how a particular engineering team works.

Arriving at a spec template that makes sense for most people on most projects will take some collaboration among members of the design group and the engineering group. Once you've arrived at a workable template, try it out on a few projects and then check in with everyone about how it's working. Revisit the template every couple of years to see if it's falling behind the times.

Effectively formatted

Most specifications are, to put it kindly, not something people want to pick up and read. This is understandable; a giant wall of text occasionally broken up by headers or wireframes is certainly unappealing. An effective spec design, like an effective product design, finds the right balance between what users (mostly engineers)

need and what can be put together in a reasonable time. It also encourages people to pick up the document and peruse it.

SIZE AND ORIENTATION

Many design firms have a fondness for printing large-format documents, but I've found these are sort of like the proverbial greased pig: slippery and hard to handle. They tend to slide off desks and are too big to fit in typical bookshelves or file drawers. The engineers will thank you if you stick to standard A4 or 8½ x11" paper, as will anyone who tries to print the file later without access to a large-format printer. Spiral binding is ideal if the document is small enough, since pages can be folded over completely and the document will still lie flat on a desk. Three-ring binders are usually the best option for large documents and for large teams, where individual engineers only care about certain sections.

The most common objection to standard size paper is that you can't print large images on it. However, if the orientation of the page matches the orientation of most of your images, you can make good use of the real estate you have. This means that if you're doing mobile phone applications, a portrait orientation is fine, but if you're doing desktop apps, a landscape document will let you use much larger screen shots.

LAYOUT AND WAYFINDING

Like a good screen layout, an effective document page layout relies on a grid that guides the placement of text columns, images, headers, and footers. Four page formats cover most of what you'll need in a desktop application spec: a full-page image with room for callouts, a single column of text with one or more images, two columns of text, and a set of two or three screens side by side for a scenario. All four are shown in Figure 24.16.

Detailed Design

Figure 24.16. Three or four page layouts cover most application spec needs.

Also keep readers oriented by:

— Using consistent section headers at the top of each page

— Using thumbnails of the whole screen if you're zoomed in on a single component

— Repeating the same image on each relevant page if text spans multiple pages

— Making liberal use of cross-references

TEXT FORMATTING

Remember to format content for flippers as well as readers (see Chapter 13); tabs or colored section breaks can help with this in a large document. This is especially important considering that most readers will use the spec as a reference document rather than reading through it from start to finish. A quick skim should acquaint readers with the purpose and scale of the product. A casual read—by a busy executive, for example—should provide a sense of the product's scope, complexity, and benefits. A detailed review should answer nearly every question necessary to produce a technical specification for the product; I say "nearly" because there's often some remaining work for a business analyst to do.

You can make the document easier to scan if you format content according to its purpose:

— For sequences, use numbered lists

— For lists of related items or ideas, use bullets

— For comparisons or tabular information, use tables

— For narrative, use paragraphs of text

If you can convey ideas without making people read complete sentences, do so.

Documentation Process and Practices

Creating a detailed form and behavior specification is time-consuming; it requires about one day of writing and drawing time per three days of detailed design meetings, plus a couple of days at the end for editing and proofreading. However, this doesn't mean documentation happens only at the end—it needs to be an ongoing process for multiple reasons. Documenting design as you go helps:

— Ensure its completeness and effectiveness

— Ensure that everyone on the team has a shared understanding as the design evolves

— Avoid a big time crunch at the end of the project

— Avoid forgotten or incorrect details

— Deliver incremental specs to engineers and SMEs for detailed review

The interaction designers generally spend five or six hours a day in detailed design meetings, with two or three hours of solo work time. While the IxDG renders screens and works through issues with the visual designer, the IxDS translates meeting notes and sketches into draft documentation. Even if the design evolves later—and it often does—it's easier to adjust the documentation than to write the whole document at the end of the design time.

Documenting as you go

Start by outlining your document; either do this as a team or review your outline with your team before investing too much writing time. You should be able to do a fairly thorough outline on the first or second day of the phase based on the topics in your work list and calendar.

Page templates make it easy to start dropping in content, even if it's rough. Copy any reusable sections from your user and domain analysis document. If you find yourself staring at blank pages, start laying out at least the overview pages by dropping in your framework sketches and notes.

As you begin to have design meetings, add your meeting notes to the document each day. It's better to leave things as bullet points for now than to write sloppy paragraphs, which have a way of sneaking into the final document. Add empty headers where you don't have information; these may also serve as reminders for topics you still need to cover in the next design meeting.

It's useful to paste in digital photos of whiteboard sketches as place-holders for screen drawings. This lets you start thinking about page layout and makes it easier to visualize and explain the design. Some people find it easiest to do the anatomy callouts for the sketch, then use those to generate a set of content headers for subsequent descriptions. However, don't add lines pointing from the callout text to the image yet; you'll save yourself a lot of tweaking if you add these after the visual design is finalized.

It's likely you will find unresolved issues in the design as you write. If the answer seems straightforward, go ahead and write down the behavior that seems most appropriate, but highlight this text in another color so you'll remember to discuss this with your design partners. Format open issues in some color that stands out, as well. Circulate drafts to your teammates to make sure everyone has a shared understanding of the design.

Whether you're delivering the design topic by topic (which is ideal) or all at once, you'll need a bit of time to turn your bullet lists and sentence fragments into a coherent document. For most people, the first pass is about making sure the content is complete and readable. A second pass allows for polishing, adding lines between callout text and components, and inserting any missing cross-references.

> **Documentation should be an ongoing process, not something that happens at the end.**

Managing images

Drawing screens can be even more time-consuming than writing about them, particularly if you try to illustrate every screen in every state. Instead, identify what drawings will give you the most leverage; for example, if you need to show what a list box looks like in the open state, can you reuse an image you drew for a scenario rather than drawing a separate image for that purpose? A detailed picture list makes it easier to minimize the number of unique images you'll need.

As you finish each design topic at the whiteboard, identify what screens and components you need to depict for the anatomy and behavior to be clear. After that, develop a detailed version of your key path scenario, including selection states and any specific data to illustrate; this will help the IxDG put the right contents in the screens. Determine how few images you can use to tell the story; what can you describe clearly enough with just text? Finally, see how many of the images from your story can be recycled in the anatomy section.

As the IxDG and visual designer update screens, they should be dropping exported images into a consistent folder. As long as the new images are saved with the same names and in the same location, you can import them by reference, which saves a lot of cutting and pasting time and minimizes versioning errors.

Technical review and document QA

It's essential to make sure teammates agree with what the documentation says, but you'll also benefit from having someone edit your documentation to ensure that:

— The design is correctly described.
— Engineers will have all the information they need.

— The organization makes sense.
— The document is clearly written.
— You haven't unintentionally stepped on anyone's toes.
— You've explained the reasoning behind design decisions, especially any that deviate from conventions or are difficult to build.
— You've used the personas throughout the document.
— Every state illustrated in the screens is correct.
— Components are correctly and consistently labeled.
— Callouts point to the right things.
— Cross-references are correct.
— Data in screen shots is free from potentially distracting errors in spelling, calculation, etc.

However, reviewers shouldn't try to rewrite the document in their own voices; as long as the way you've written it is clear and unlikely to offend stakeholders, that's what's important.

Circulate drafts early. If you can, have your teammates sequentially mark up the same copy of the document; this keeps them from spending time on the same edits, surfaces any disagreements, and gives you a chance to make updates from one place rather than trying to work through two or three separate sets of comments. Let reviewers know if you're not ready for detailed proofing and only want comments on content. As you get comments back, use a highlighter to mark off edits as you go (or note that you're ignoring them) so you're sure you've got them all. If you disagree with a significant comment or edit, discuss it with your teammates rather than disregarding it.

Documentation tools

Microsoft Word is unsuitable for large specs because it doesn't allow terribly precise control of page layout, and it may not be quick or stable with very large documents. Cooper started using Adobe FrameMaker, which is geared toward large, complex technical documents, around 1999. It allows for cross-referencing, better control of images, and a number of other useful behaviors. However, the learning curve is steep, and there are some ways in which the application is inflexible because it's aimed more at documenting finished systems than at documenting a design as it evolves. It's always been a love-hate relationship at best.

Now that there's finally a stable cross-referencing plug-in for Adobe InDesign, we've begun using that for most documents. No doubt we'll find it involves some trade-offs of its own, but it seems to be working well so far.

Regardless of what tool you choose, look for something that:

— Allows you to import images by reference instead of pasting

— Provides automated cross-referencing

— Lets teammates and reviewers mark up soft copies without mastering an obscure tool

— Handles multiple page-layout styles in the same document

— Allows precise control of image and text position

— Is stable and not too slow when the file gets large

Presenting Detailed Design

Formally presenting the detailed design provides stakeholders with an overview of the design, gives you an opportunity to show off what you've accomplished, and gives everyone yet another chance to ask questions. This can happen in a single, large presentation near the end of the project or, if possible, in several smaller presentations as you work your way through various design chunks.

Detailed hardware design often involves more than one formal milestone. A discussion of the appearance model(s) may still result in some evolution, especially if you've done two or more models to help finalize the design language or some other aspect of the form. The final delivery of a prototype (which could take place during the support phase rather than detailed design) lets stakeholders assess every detail, though this is primarily targeted at the engineering and manufacturing audience.

For nearly any product, it's useful to split your presentation into two sessions: an hour or two for a general audience of all stakeholders, followed by a detailed review with the engineers, any SMEs, business analysts, or manufacturing reps, and perhaps the QA lead. This lets you cover the high points with the general audience while giving the people who need it a chance to examine the minutiae.

Structuring and delivering a stakeholder presentation

An effective presentation for a mixed audience is a lot like the framework presentation (see Chapter 19), except with bitmap screens, no separation of visual and interaction design, and fewer supporting arguments for the overall structure (since most decisions have already been made). If you present the scenarios plus what's in the product, framework, screen-level overviews, and a hardware overview with an appearance model (if applicable), you'll be at about the right level. A typical outline looks like this:

— Project background

— Quick persona recap (more detailed if new stakeholders are present)

Detailed Design

— Product and interface overview, including hardware and design language

— Scenarios

— Benefits (how the design serves the personas)

— Hardware detail and interface anatomy slides (for those who care to stay and discuss)

The product and interface overview helps remind stakeholders of major decisions made to date. A quick overview of the interface anatomy and a review of the hardware design set the stage for the scenarios.

Although the appearance model serves as the main focal point for discussion of the hardware function and physical design language, photos of the appearance model are useful references, especially for any remote stakeholders who cannot see the model. The ID typically passes the appearance model around the room toward the end of the hardware discussion (with an appropriate caution about its fragility).

Notice that details such as screen-level anatomy and hardware assembly details are at the end. This allows stakeholders to step out of the meeting if they don't need to understand the details. It's usually effective just to show a full-screen slide of each major view as a visual aid for discussion of whatever the audience cares about. You might also want to include zoomed-in views of any complex elements that are especially important.

In most ways, delivering a detailed design presentation differs very little from delivering more conceptual work. You might get a few more comments that someone doesn't like this or that icon, but overall, the guidance in Chapter 19 should serve you well in explaining and defending your decisions.

Comprehensive walkthroughs

Hardware and software engineering teams are certain to have different questions and interests,

so you may want to split the comprehensive discussions into separate groups for convergent products. The detailed software discussion requires the interaction designers and visual designer. The ID may be the only team member required at the hardware discussion.

SOFTWARE REVIEW

For the detailed software review—which can take anywhere from a couple of hours to a couple of days, depending on how big a chunk of design you're delivering—a slide deck is often not the best tool. It's typically more useful to hand out the documentation (if it exists in hard copy) and to project the document pages up on the screen as you discuss them. Engineers may fail to read even the best-designed documentation, so a thorough introduction will help everyone see that the answers to nearly all of their questions are easy to find.

This meeting is usually more of a facilitated question-and-answer session than a presentation, though it's a good idea to start out with an overview of the document and its contents. The questions and discussion are likely to require the expertise of every design team member. However, the meeting could get chaotic, so one person should still be the team's primary facilitator, asking participants to hold a question for later, writing down open issues, and referring questions to teammates as needed. An experienced IxDS is often best suited to this role, both due to a natural inclination toward facilitation and to a deep familiarity with the documentation.

HARDWARE REVIEW

During an appearance model review, the ID's goals are to make sure the engineers and manufacturer understand the design intent and to minimize engineering decisions that will unnecessarily compromise that intent. This is the first opportunity for the entire hardware team to review a detailed physical representation of the design and determine whether adjustments are needed.

The ID and ME tend to share the stage during this discussion. The ID focuses on the aesthetic and usability issues, including color choice, material selection, finish strategy, visible part breaks, and the behavior of physical controls or mechanisms. The ME may project a CAD file on the screen to discuss internal components, part count, and overall manufacturing strategy.

A prototype review (which could happen during the support phase, also) is similar. The mechanical, electrical, and manufacturing-focused engineers can disassemble the prototype to examine every tiny detail of how components fit and attach. This discussion is focused primarily on tooling and manufacturing issues; the design intent is presumably understood by this point, so this meeting is primarily the ME's show.

Summary

Communication about detailed design, although it may result in a single, massive specification, should never be a single event. Informal communication needs to happen with engineers, business analysts, and subject matter experts on a regular basis. Multiple instances of formal communication are ideal if you can document your design in chunks, since this gives the appropriate collaborators a chance to review the finer nuances of your work.

Regardless of the frequency of formal communication, be sure to include plenty of detailed images and explanatory text. Be prescriptive: What goes in the spec needs to be exactly what gets built, except to the extent that the design and engineering teams need to modify the spec together for cost or timing reasons. However, never surprise the engineering team with anything new in the spec; it might make your delivery a bit anticlimactic, but a product that gets built is far more rewarding than having an audience surprised by your brilliance at a final presentation.

Detailed Design

CHAPTER 25

Supporting Implementation and Launch

Although it must seem that a designer's work is surely done when the final specifications are in the hands of the engineers, there are a multitude of potholes in the road between handing over a spec and seeing your product released as designed. Questions and problems are inevitable even with complete stakeholder commitment and the best engineering collaboration in the world. A competitor launches a similar product and the project manager doesn't want to be seen falling too far behind. The venture capitalists are pushing for an earlier return on their investment. A huge company buys up the next year's supply of a vital part. Something the engineers thought they could do is simply harder than it looked. In any of these cases, someone is going to make a decision that affects the design, and it's best if that decision is in the hands of the design team.

Unfortunately, many designers limit—or are required to limit—their involvement once the spec is "done." Saying, "Here's the spec—call if you need me," doesn't look like help to many engineers; instead, it can look like the designers are running away while there are still real problems to be solved. Of course, most designers are eager to

be involved, but find some engineers want to take the spec and run, or the budget holders don't see the need for more design time.

It's often difficult to get both engineers and budget holders to recognize that design involvement in implementation is every bit as critical as engineering involvement in design. Some engineers, especially in software, don't appreciate construction analogies, since the work they do is often far more complex than any high-rise building. However, I've often found the analogy helpful in explaining the need for ongoing design to stakeholders. Even the most detailed building blueprints don't solve every problem—the electricians, carpenters, and other expert craftspeople still have a host of decisions to make to ensure that the heating, air conditioning, and other building systems are reliable and efficient. Many of these have nothing to do with the building's architecture, while others have the potential to affect the architect's design intent. An architect routinely walks through her construction sites both to make herself available for consultation on such issues and to ensure that what's getting built is a correct interpretation of her intent.

It's not that the architect doesn't trust the construction team—quite the opposite—but simply an acknowledgement that blueprints are neither perfect nor perfectly understood.

Mind you, not all of a designer's support tasks are necessarily engineering focused. The design team may be asked to create a demo to introduce the product at a trade show or secure another round of startup funding. An industrial designer and visual designer might work on packaging design or supervise a round of product photography for collateral. Any member of the design team might present to customers or talk about the product design process in a promotional video. If you're asked to do any of these things, take it as a tremendous compliment to the importance and effectiveness of your work. If you're not asked, offer: Some people just haven't learned to see design as a selling point yet.

Supporting Software Construction

The interaction designers and visual designer focus mostly on supporting software construction. This usually involves slicing up image files to deliver production-ready assets, being available on a regular basis to answer questions, and reviewing engineers' work in progress to ensure that it's true to the design intent.

Asset production

There is inevitably a need for translation between how assets are drawn in an application like Fireworks and how they are built in code. At the beginning of the support phase—or ideally even earlier, during detailed design—the visual designer and GUI engineer(s) need to walk through the interface elements in detail and determine how they will be built, what file formats the engineers need, and what file-naming convention you'll follow as you export sliced assets.

One key decision is which controls and text elements will be built using static images and which will rendered computationally. In other words, will the programmer be telling the computer to display image file X, or will he be telling the computer to draw a rectangle of a certain size using a one-pixel black line? The capabilities of the development platform have a lot to do with the approach. Java, for example, supports a technique called nine-slicing, in which the middle of a control (both horizontally and vertically) can be rendered separately from the edges. In Figure 25.1, for example, you can see how a visual designer would slice the image of a button with rounded corners to ensure a consistent look as the button is scaled for text labels of different lengths. The four corners of the image remain static while the middle sections—the edges of the button between the corners—are stretched by the application. If the entire button scaled, instead, the corners would be distorted.

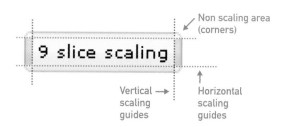

Before

After

Figure 25.1. An example of how nine-slicing works in Java.

Another decision you must make in conjunction with the engineers is how transparency will be handled. For example, if an icon appears on top of a gradient that scales with the screen's resolution, it would look odd if the icon's background didn't match the gradient. Designating certain pixels in the icon as transparent allows this to happen, but platforms handle the issue in different ways.

Initial asset production usually happens after the style guide is finished. A first pass at slicing and exporting all of the assets will generally take a chunk of time equivalent to 15 to 25 percent of the detailed visual design time. The more unique icons, controls, text snippets rendered as images, and states there are, the more time is required for production. This work typically goes a bit faster over time as you find a rhythm for it, so there are slight economies of scale on larger projects. Good file management can save time; it takes a while to learn when you're better off keeping everything in one file for the sake of consistency or splitting the file into several smaller ones. In any case, it's best to make edits in your drawing file and export the sliced assets using a batch approach.

As implementation continues, the engineers will often determine that some initial assumption or other isn't working, and the assets will need to be sliced differently. Some amount of as-needed production may continue to happen for several months, though a skilled GUI engineer can often handle small tweaks himself.

Questions and reviews

To an engineer on a deadline, the slightest delay can be unacceptable. If you're not immediately available to answer a question, he's apt to make a decision—right or wrong—and move on. This isn't usually through any intent to shut designers out of the process. It's at least partly the "out of sight, out of mind" phenomenon—if you're not

close at hand, it simply might not occur to an engineer to ask you a question instead of making the call himself.

Engineers who know they'll see you on a regular basis are less likely to stray from the specification, both because your availability is predictable and because your presence is a continual reminder of that availability. Engineers in highly functional teams appreciate regular design "office hours" when they can drop by to ask questions or show you the latest work. However, drop-in hours may not be enough with some teams who aren't accustomed to working with designers; a regular meeting at which attendance is expected is sometimes the only way to go. Designers can't enforce this expectation, but can work with an engineering lead or project owner to do so.

At first, you might find yourself responding to many of the engineers' questions with, "Did you look at the description of that on page 43?" Engineers who aren't used to working from detailed specs may not have learned to rely on your form and behavior specification yet, but they'll lean on it more as they become accustomed to finding their answers in it.

Of course, there will always be some questions that are new. Answer these at the whiteboard when you can. Take good notes and update the spec as soon as possible. Once in a while, you might get a topic complex enough to require that you have a design meeting before you can respond.

The other purpose of a regular meeting or scheduled office hours is to review what the engineers are doing. Like the architect with the construction team, you're not telling them how to do their jobs, but only whether what they've built achieves the design intent. This is particularly important with fine behavioral details that are difficult to express in a specification, such as how scrolling behavior or button presses should look and feel. Sometimes, it turns out that the engineers followed

Ensuring Success

687

Blueprints are neither perfect nor perfectly understood.

the design intent exactly, but this has introduced other issues, such as an unacceptably slow response. In such cases, you'll work with the engineers to find alternate designs solutions or, if the original design is critical to maintain, work with the project owner and engineers to determine whether the technical problem can be overcome within a reasonable budget and timeline.

Supporting Hardware Manufacturing

The vast majority of hardware design issues are of course resolved before tooling begins, so the need for industrial design support is limited. Even so, issues can arise as the manufacturer begins tooling molds and gearing up for production. The mechanical engineer handles most of these problems, but the ID needs to be involved if the manufacturer requests any changes that might affect aesthetics or usability.

The only scheduled ID involvement in manufacturing support is usually an inspection of the first set of production parts. Along with the ME, the ID looks for defects and issues with fit and function. The ID might ask the manufacturer to fine-tune a plastic color that isn't turning out quite as expected. If there are visible flow lines that show where plastic was injected into the mold, the ID and ME work with the manufacturer to adjust the plastic type for smoother flow or perhaps apply a texture to hide what otherwise looks like an imperfection.

Common Challenges

From a designer's point of view, implementation can be virtually stress free if you've done your job effectively, you're working with a great engineering team, and no external factors pull the effort off course. However, market shifts and changes in direction do still happen; see Chapter 22 for more discussion of these. The two issues that tend to crop up most in detailed design have everything to do with the composition and culture of the engineering team.

Specification as suggestion

Few things drive a designer crazy more than having engineers cherry-pick a design, incorporating some parts of it while ignoring others entirely. Sometimes this happens because the communication between design and engineering is poor—either the engineers are using a standard widget library or have some other constraints the design team didn't take into account, or the design was poorly communicated.

Heavy collaboration throughout the design process can generally prevent the former, and detailed specs can usually help avoid the latter.

In some organizations, however, there's simply no accountability as long as the engineers ship the feature list on time. In this sort of environment, the engineers and everyone around them see the creation of products as an engineering endeavor, and any input other than some key requirements is simply a suggestion.

As an individual designer, there are a couple of things you can do about this situation. One is to work closely with the engineers throughout the process to gain their trust and respect. Most engineering cultures are meritocracies to some extent; only a demonstration of skill earns you a place at the table. Diffidence won't serve you well, though—if you present your ideas as suggestions and act as if the engineers have a choice about implementing what you design, you'll lose any chance at moral authority.

The other is to work through the business project owner, who hopefully has complete authority with respect to the product. If this person is diffident with the engineers, that's part of the problem. The project owner needs to establish the expectation that a spec is not a suggestion and instruct the QA team to kick back spec deviations as bugs. If the engineers don't understand part of the spec or believe it's problematic, they need to work through this explicitly with you.

Of course, this is not to say that engineers should blindly build everything you design. It's desirable for engineers to think deeply about the specs and challenge them where solutions don't quite make sense or seem unnecessarily difficult to build. However, in a healthy process, most of this back-and-forth takes place through collaboration, so that what goes in the spec is both solid and implementable to the best of the design engineer's knowledge.

Insufficient engineering skills or resources

Perhaps the greatest challenge in designing implementable solutions is calibrating the design difficulty to the size and capabilities of the engineering team. It's usually possible to do some assessment in framework definition or at least during detailed design; if engineers are balking at fairly routine solutions, it's either a sign that the engineering schedule is far too tight or the skills of the engineers aren't up to the task.

While I always start a project with the assumption that the engineering team is as good at their jobs as the design team is at ours, the

> Implementation goes better if you've worked closely with the engineers throughout the process to gain their trust and respect.

Ensuring Success

When an engineer starts to code something that was specified months earlier, deviations are more likely because the discussion isn't as fresh in his mind.

unfortunate truth in any profession (including design) is that skill levels vary widely. Not all programmers or CAD experts are trained engineers, and not even all trained engineers are up to the same skill level. This is especially true when there is a shortage of skilled people, as was the case during the dot-com bubble. Ideally from a designer's perspective, companies would hire engineers at the necessary skill level to implement whatever the design is, but this is simply not going to happen in many cases.

There's also the tendency of managers to underestimate the effort involved in engineering, especially when it comes to building software. In my experience, the majority of software engineering teams are understaffed for the timeline they're expected to hit and the complexity of the work they're being asked to do.

This can lead to a couple of problems. One is that parts of the design start to fall by the wayside as the deadline looms, and some of the decisions made under pressure may not be good ones. The other is that, even if the deadline is extended, the design has far outpaced the engineering. Ideally, the engineering team is big enough not to fall too far behind the incremental delivery of the F&BS. Some lag is to be expected, but when an engineer starts to build something that was specified four months earlier, deviations are more likely because the discussion isn't as fresh in his mind. The fact that's it's also not as fresh in *your* mind can make it harder to make those little design adjustments for feasibility.

The worst-case scenario with understaffed or underpowered engineering teams is that implementation fails to hit the deadline or just plain fails, and the finger of blame is pointed at overly ambitious designers. There's no easy solution. As always, prevention is better than treatment, so keep your eyes open for issues early in the process. If the problem is a lack of engineering skills, discuss your observations with the project owner if at all possible, and adjust your design ambitions as necessary. If the problem is a lack of engineering resources, the engineering manager probably shares your concern and will be thrilled to have an ally in arguing for more staff.

If you don't identify the problem until you're in the middle of supporting implementation, it becomes a matter of damage control. Look for the first point at which someone in management sees that the engineering team is starting to miss milestones. They see the problem but may not be sure of the cause, so they may be more open to your observations. If it becomes necessary to cut back on what's getting built, make sure the design team is closely involved in the triage, if not leading it.

Summary

There's a nursery tale that begins, "For want of a nail, the shoe was lost. For want of a shoe, the horse was lost." It goes on to say that the rider, the message, the battle, the war, and the kingdom were all lost … all because someone didn't make sure the shoes on the messenger's horse were securely fastened. Thousands of product development projects go astray for want of similar attention to detail during implementation. Make an effort to educate stakeholders about the value you can provide during implementation—the results are more than worth it.

CHAPTER 26

Improving Design Capabilities in Individuals and Organizations

The techniques and work practices in this book assume that you have both a certain amount of design skill and some ability to determine how you work with engineers and stakeholders. One or both may not be the case for you. So, how can you attain that skill or move your organization toward embracing design? The latter is worth a hefty book in itself, but hopefully this chapter will leave you with a few useful ideas about both topics.

Most designers have more ability to control and influence their own careers than to influence the entire organization; as you try to influence your organization, consider how to build your own skills—the better you are at your job, the more compelling your argument for design as an organizational priority will be.

Realizing Your Own Design Potential

Designing products in the digital age comes with plenty of frustrations. It's easy for designers—most of whom start out as idealists—to become disheartened and cynical when products don't ship or when others don't recognize the value of

what we do. Some move from company to company, hoping to find one that will let them do design "right." Some leave the field when they realize that the world doesn't often live up to their ideals. Others stay in one place but give up, assuming they'll always be helpless to affect how their companies or clients develop products. However, many designers are able to find enough success to remain happy and productive throughout their careers. In my experience, these designers have learned a few key things:

— **Idealism and pragmatism are both essential.** Effective designers never stop helping their colleagues see the possibilities, but realize that the best design isn't just the most usable or most novel solution: It's also the one that can be built, distributed, and maintained within the capabilities and constraints of the sponsoring organization.

— **The design is only half of the problem.** I don't know any designers who got into the profession because they enjoy organizational politics; many would be perfectly happy doing a bit of research, then hiding in the studio and coming up with clever solutions. However, communication, collaboration, and consensus building with non-designers are essential to all but the most junior design production roles. You'll be happiest if you learn to get as much satisfaction from a great meeting as from a great solution, rather than viewing these parts of the job as necessary evils.

- **Control what you can, influence what you can't, and let go of the rest.** Designers don't—and shouldn't—control every aspect of product development, much as you may sometimes wish you did. What you *can* control is your own behavior: You can make opportunities instead of waiting for them to be handed to you, and you can make the most of the opportunities you have. You can't control how others see you and your work or how they approach project budgets and timelines, but you can have a great deal of influence on these things.

- **Do what you do (and love) best.** Most designers are not equally good at (or equally fond of) every aspect of the work. While I strongly believe that focusing on only one part of the process (e.g., just research or just conceptual work) leads to missed opportunities, focusing on one specialty within that process doesn't necessarily do so. To the extent you can, focus on what you do best—whether that's form or behavior, visualization or explanation, idea generation or facilitation—and surround yourself with other people who are good at the rest.

Making the most of your particular aptitudes starts with identifying a role that plays to your strengths. You might find the descriptions in Chapter 2 a useful starting point. If you're not sure quite what your strengths are, try a generalist role for a while and see what activities you gravitate toward.

Regardless of role, though, every member of a design team needs to:

- Be well versed in design principles
- Empathize with end users
- Understand and value business objectives
- Possess an active imagination
- Be curious about the world, from technology to human behavior
- Have good listening skills
- Be able to conduct field research
- Quickly grasp new concepts
- Identify patterns and extract meaning from field data
- Express ideas in an appropriate medium (speech, text, 2D or 3D rendering)
- Express a rationale for ideas
- Be comfortable with ambiguity and high-level exploration
- Be able to eliminate ambiguity when it's time for detail
- Accept and value appropriate critique
- Provide constructive critique
- Manage their own time
- Collaborate with designers, engineers, SMEs, and stakeholders
- Understand enough about technology to have an idea of what's easy and what's feasible with effort

In addition, people playing the generative interaction design, visual design, and industrial design roles must excel at generating ideas in concrete, visual terms. People playing the interaction design synthesis role must excel at narrative and facilitation.

In my experience, some of these skills are teachable, while others are not. People who don't empathize with users, don't have an aptitude for synthesis or visualization, and aren't inclined to be curious about the world around them may be better off in other parts of the product development process. However, I've always found that people with the right fundamental aptitudes can learn design principles, research skills, tools, and technology basics within a few years. Strong "consulting" or "soft" skills generally come a bit later, though professionals switching to design from other fields may have a strong grounding in these skills already.

An academic environment is an ideal starting place, particularly for visual and industrial design. Interaction design programs are harder to find, but some good ones do exist. Design programs are most useful for the IxDG role; a background in design research, HCI, or any design field will serve you well in the IxDS role.

All that being said, since interaction design is a relatively young discipline, you'll find that the most experienced interaction designers in the industry either moved into the field from another design discipline, an evaluation-oriented role, or more distantly related professions such as product management, technical writing, or engineering. Many of these folks have demonstrated that self-education is a viable option, though the percentage of formally trained people in the field will continue to increase as more colleges and universities develop programs.

Academic programs

There are always exceptions to any generalization, but in many years of hiring designers, I have consistently found that graduates of industrial design, graphic or communication design, and interaction design programs are more comfortable with generating ideas on a tight timeline than people with degrees in HCI, ergonomics, human factors, or cognitive psychology. Although large design groups and companies that design certain types of products certainly need the analytical expertise these programs provide, people with strong design backgrounds are very much in demand in consultancies and fast-moving corporate environments.

However, not all design programs—including those with the biggest reputations—are equivalent. Each has an explicit or implicit emphasis that graduates tend to carry with them, so be sure you understand what that is before choosing a program. Based on what I see in their graduates, I would loosely classify the emphasis of various design programs as follows:

— **Design as creative expression.** Some programs strongly encourage designers to express their inner vision. This kind of program may be ideal if you want to design products that emphasize expressive form over practical function, such as interactive advertising and simple consumer products.

Making the most of your particular aptitudes starts with identifying a role that plays to your strengths.

Ensuring Success

695

- **Design as social/political act.** An emphasis on participatory design, extensive research, and community involvement tends to give graduates of some programs an analytical and philosophical approach to design. Some of these programs emphasize design strategy (i.e., big ideas) over design execution. This kind of education is well suited to designers working in nonprofits and the public sector, design research, service design, and some design leadership positions.

- **Design thinking as a business tool.** Akin to the design strategy emphasis, some programs developed in conjunction with business schools are more about "design thinking"—i.e., using design techniques to inform business thinking—than about creating designed artifacts. This is a useful approach for executives who want to think more like designers, but in my view, such programs are unsuitable for those who wish to practice hands-on design.

- **Design as problem solving.** Some programs focus on design as a tool for solving human problems, which include both practical and aesthetic considerations. These schools generally encourage designers to trust their own judgment but to inform it with field data whenever possible. If you've read much of this book, no doubt you can tell this is my bias; I find graduates of these programs are well prepared for a variety of design problems and project situations.

- **Design as technical trade.** Some schools offer design programs that emphasize tools (such as PhotoShop, Illustrator, and 3D rendering tools) over classic design skills. Although I believe each of the other approaches has its place, I find that graduates of these programs are usually ill prepared in the fundamentals, and may have difficulty progressing beyond production roles.

Looking at the course list and asking the program's faculty what they view as important in a design curriculum will help you figure out what the program's emphasis is. You may also want to talk with experienced designers (and especially design managers) to get a sense for how they view a particular program.

Self-education

The beauty of self-education is that you can do it on your own timeline and at a fairly low cost; anyone can read the same books used in an academic curriculum and get a great deal out of them. The various publications referenced in this book are a great start at a design education. Conferences and in-depth workshops are another. You can also hone your skills daily in small ways:

- Practice visualization by building things with your hands

- Build your imagination by watching and reading science fiction

- Practice ideation by forcing yourself to sketch a dozen different solutions to a problem over the course of five or ten minutes

- Feed your curiosity (and remind yourself what curiosity looks like) by spending time with children and seeing how eager they are to know things

- Practice active listening skills in every conversation, not just in interviews

- Ask a colleague to give you feedback on your interviewing technique

- Videotape yourself during an interview or presentation and review what you're doing well or not so well

- Every time you make a design decision, have someone ask you, "Why is that good?"

- Seek out critique from people whose opinions you respect

- Subject your designs to a usability test or other form of feedback

The problem with self-education is that it seldom involves collaboration, critique, and learning by doing. Without studio work and an experienced eye to review it, you may think you grasp certain aspects of design that you understand only poorly. In other words, as a self-educated designer, you may not know what you don't know.

Experience and mentoring

Regardless of whether you've attended the best design schools or just read a bunch of good design books, there's no substitute for experience. You may understand your craft in theory, but you have to fail a number of times in various ways before you learn how to get it right without a lot of trial and error.

However, experience as a lone designer in a startup won't necessarily do the trick. In that environment, it's easy to fail and not even know you've failed. The best way to make significant progress as a designer is to work with people who are better and more experienced than you are. This is one reason that employers value design applicants from reputable consultancies or product companies known for good design—it's usually a safe assumption that working with a bunch of good designers has taught them something.

Of course, not everyone moves into a design role right out of school, and starting as a junior designer in a studio isn't an option for everyone. You can get the mentoring you need right where you are if your company has an experienced design manager or senior designers on staff. If not, look for resources outside your organization. Take some design courses at a local university. Find a consultant who will periodically review your work and offer coaching. You might also be able to find mentoring through a local professional organization; some local chapters of the IxDA,[1] for example, have begun offering informal workshops where experienced design mentors coach participants through hands-on exercises.

Expanding Design's Role in an Organization

Improving an organization's design capabilities is far more challenging than working on your own skills, whether you're starting as a staff designer or an executive. However, designers have a unique set of skills well suited to organizational change: human-centered problem solving.

> # The best way to progress as a designer is to work with people who are better and more experienced than you are.

---

1. The Interaction Design Association, www.ixda.org.

Becoming an organization that truly values design requires changes in structures, processes, and the attitudes and behavioral norms that constitute corporate culture.

Designing an organization's structure and processes is a lot like designing a product, and bringing people along in that process is a lot like collaborating with engineers and building consensus with stakeholders. Mind you, organizational change is more challenging and more personally frustrating than any other sort of design problem—the solution is inherently design-by-committee, and you probably have a tremendous personal stake in the outcome.

How difficult it will be to attain greater integration of design depends on where your organization is today. Generally toxic work environments that discourage creativity are not at all conducive to design, but most companies are starting from a less challenging place. In an organization where most people view design as cosmetic, optional, or something that gets slathered on at the end, you have a steep (but not impossible) hill to climb. If senior executives realize they need design but aren't sure how to get there, you're in a better position than most.

Characteristics of successful change efforts

Even some experienced executives approach integrating design as if they were leasing a new phone system: Make a decision, delegate the details, and move on to the next thing. It's not that easy. Turning a marketing-driven or engineering-driven organization into one that truly values design requires changes in structures, processes, and the attitudes and behavioral norms that constitute corporate culture.

INTEGRATING DESIGN IS A PROCESS, NOT AN EVENT

Opening a usability lab, declaring that this is the year when people will start to enjoy using your products, or having a consultant in to talk about the value of design won't do the trick. Integrating design generally takes at least three years, and that's in a small company with strong executive commitment. In larger companies where leaders have mixed feelings, efforts to integrate design could take five or ten years and may still fail along the way if there is insufficient commitment or vigilance regarding cultural change.

ORGANIZATIONAL CHANGE DEPENDS ON INDIVIDUAL CHANGE

Major change is a time-consuming process because a company doesn't really have a mind of its own; it's driven by the beliefs and behaviors of the dozens, hundreds, or thousands of individual people within it. Think about how hard it is just to change your own habits, then multiply that difficulty by the number of people in your company, and you'll see why integrating design into an organization is a complex, multi-year undertaking. Lasting change requires commitment from nearly all of the executives as well as most of an organization's middle management and staff. That takes time, along with involvement from people at all levels. As with designing a product, redesigning an organization requires a focus on the goals of its constituents, including employees, customers, and stockholders.

REAL CHANGE TAKES EFFECTIVE (AND SENIOR) LEADERSHIP

Because they set policy as well as provide visible examples of appropriate behaviors and attitudes, executives are the most critical individuals to affect; eventually, they need to lead the charge to embrace design. They must alter any business structures that are in the way of doing design, and must be vigilant to ensure that real change is taking place. That's not to say that you shouldn't attempt change without the executives on board; often, you need to begin the process and show them that it can work first.

INDIVIDUALS MUST BELIEVE THEY'LL GAIN MORE THAN THEY LOSE

People inevitably see loss in almost any change. When it comes to integrating design, other project participants may believe they're losing authority, status, independence, or other things that seem precious to them. An effective change process helps people see what they'll gain as individuals. Better products and more loyal customers make sense at an intellectual level, but they won't outweigh an engineer's perceived loss of autonomy or a product manager's belief that you're stepping on his toes. Instead, focus on gains that will have more personal benefits, such as how design can offer engineers fewer changes in direction or give product managers increased visibility and control.

Overcoming the sense of loss

Education isn't enough to change behavior; if it were, the world would be filled with people who eat only healthy foods, exercise daily, and always wear their seat belts. This is because any change involves some perceived loss, which creates a barrier people have to overcome. It doesn't do any good to belittle this reaction or tell people to get over it; an effective approach acknowledges the loss and deals with it instead.

I find it helpful to think of organizational change in terms of the grieving model proposed by Elisabeth Kübler-Ross[2] in her work on death and dying. In that model, people faced with a loss begin with denial, followed by anger, bargaining, depression, and finally acceptance. Let's consider how this applies to integrating design in an organization; understanding where your organization and the individuals within it are in their process can help you determine what kind of action will be most effective.

DENIAL

If your organization is even remotely successful with how things are being done now, you're likely to face considerable skepticism about the need for more investment in design. People may discount your argument as empire building on your part or as ignorance about how the organization works. Even if they begin to see the point of your argument, many people will shrug and say that this is just how things are at [insert your company's name here]. They'll tell you there's no way you'll change the attitudes of the engineers, marketers, or executives. Denial is normal; if you don't see any signs of denial, you may very well wonder if people are really listening to you.

The best way to help people through denial is usually to present them with compelling evidence

2. Kübler-Ross, Elisabeth. *On death and dying.* Simon & Schuster/Touchstone, 1969.

Keep in mind that you're bringing a bit of specialized expertise to a group of otherwise skilled professionals, not introducing ignorant cavemen to fire.

(and lots of it). Demonstrate how lack of good design led to a product failure or slipped schedule. Show that customers are more loyal to well-designed products and services. Assemble an estimate of how much poor usability is increasing your customer support costs. If there is any sort of crisis in which everyone sees a visible failure, take advantage of that—it's what educators call a "teachable moment."

ANGER

As people start to acknowledge (to themselves, if not to anyone else) that you may be right, it's likely they'll be somewhat angry. Product managers, engineers, and SMEs may all feel like their competence is being questioned. One newly hired design manager I know had a SME ask if he was there to take her job. Difficult as it is to handle, anger is understandable: Admitting the need to do more design means admitting that the current approach is flawed, and no one likes to admit failure. This is one reason change often doesn't happen until there's new leadership in an organization: The new boss isn't attached to how things have been done in the past.

Try not to take anger personally. Be very clear about how everyone's skills and experience are still critical. Keep in mind that you're bringing a bit of specialized expertise to a group of otherwise skilled professionals, not introducing ignorant cavemen to fire.

BARGAINING

As people begin to admit that something needs to change, they're usually inclined to start by taking easy, superficial steps that don't really challenge the status quo, kind of like hoping that you can eat a candy bar if you have it with the sugar-free soda. Having the engineers or SMEs take a class on design principles, hiring a lone designer to "skin" a product or give it a quick swipe of the usability polishing cloth, or retrofitting personas and scenarios to what the executives have already decided they want to do are all ways in which organizations try to bargain.

On one hand, most of these are at least steps in the right direction. On the other, it's all too easy for people to look at such minimal progress, pat themselves on the back, and declare victory. People who are opposed to a bigger change are especially quick to do this. Everybody feels good about things getting better, but the organization can get stuck in a situation where engineers are still squeezing some design in among their other responsibilities, requirements are still determined by some mysterious process (and subject to change), and whatever passes for design is having no real effect.

You may need to demonstrate all over again that the deeper issues are still not being addressed. This can make integrating design feel like a Sisyphean task: rolling a boulder uphill only to see it roll right back down again. Lest you become too discouraged, take note of where the boulder stops rolling; chances are, it's not going quite as far back down the hill as it used to. Take yourself to a conference or local professional gathering for a bit of moral support, take pride even in minor victories, and remind yourself of what fabulous products and services you'll ultimately be able to design.

DEPRESSION

As stakeholders and others begin to see that the easy way out isn't working, they can become disheartened; the need for change is evident, yet that change seems impossible. How can an organization that's "always" done things a certain way make real change? Surely, you still need to get products to market quickly and at low cost. Surely, you can't afford to have expensive engineers sitting around and waiting for design to be done. How is it possible to overcome these seemingly insurmountable obstacles?

This is where you need to help people see solutions. Yes, design needs to get ahead of engineering, but it doesn't mean the engineers sit on their hands and wait for you; just focus on the release after next while the engineers work on this one. Yes, design looks like a cost at first, but it saves engineering time, cuts support costs, and increases the likelihood of long-term market success. Case studies of companies that have succeeded with design can help people get through their doubts. It's even more powerful if you can point to small successes you've achieved in-house, since these demonstrate that not only is design possible, but it's also possible in your organization.

ACCEPTANCE (AND ACTION)

People are very capable of change when they see the need, view the potential benefits as greater than their sense of loss, and understand the specific actions required of them. It just may take a while to get there. You'll also find that different people get there at different speeds.

Instigating change from the bottom (or the middle)

Harvard business professor John Kotter[3] has observed that a successful approach to organizational change invariably looks something like this:

1. Establish a sense of urgency

2. Build a guiding coalition

3. Develop a vision and high-level plan

4. Communicate the vision

5. Enable action

6. Get short-term wins

7. Celebrate success; then expand and revise the plan

8. Solidify those changes; then lather, rinse, repeat

Although the change efforts he focuses on are largely driven from the top—and aren't specific to integrating design—there are some useful applications to the average designer's situation.

ESTABLISHING A SENSE OF URGENCY

Establishing a sense of urgency is the only way to overcome denial and inertia. Within the daily

---

3. Kotter, John. *Leading change.* Harvard Business School Press, 1996.

Ensuring Success

responsibilities of the typical designer, there are several possibilities for highlighting problems:

— Show carefully selected video of frustrated users in interviews or usability tests

— Circulate negative product reviews (or glowing reviews of your competitors' products and services)

— Share case studies and stories of how design has helped other companies, especially in your industry

With a bit of cooperation from people in marketing, customer support, and engineering, you may also be able to:

— Introduce project retrospectives that identify what made particular projects more or less successful

— Conduct and broadcast the results of customer satisfaction surveys

— Discuss the support costs involved in dealing with usability problems

If you can gain strong allies in marketing and sales, you might even be able to encourage them to measure (and communicate about) their activities differently. This is a tall order, though, since it requires risk taking on their part; often, only an executive can make this sort of thing happen:

— Measure lost sales and the reasons for them

— Raise the bar on customer satisfaction, communicating as if nothing less than a five out of five is acceptable

All of these activities will serve to raise the anxiety level. Inertia is one of the most powerful forces in life, so you have to make the place where your company is today seem less cozy; otherwise, there's no reason for people to start looking around for better options.

BUILD A GUIDING COALITION

Not even a powerful CEO can make change happen singlehandedly. The average designer has far less clout and must rely on influence rather than authority. What this means is that you need to assemble a group of allies who can provide useful perspectives, help advocate for change, and (eventually) have the authority necessary to remove barriers to doing effective design. John Kotter suggests four requirements for this "guiding coalition":

— Position power

— Expertise

— Credibility

— Leadership ability

By "position power," Kotter means that eventually your coalition must involve the people who are empowered to change the way business is done. Considering that the parameters driving product development usually come all the way from the top, you will probably need the CEO and the heads of marketing and engineering to decide that design is essential to their business.

Most designers need to start a bit lower down the corporate ladder, though. Consultants often have access to VPs and even C-level executives, but an in-house designer's initial coalition need only involve the product manager and engineering lead on a project. With the support of those two people, you'll have an opportunity to work the way you believe you need to work, at least within their power to affect project timelines and budgets. A product manager and engineering lead can become your champions with others in similar positions or with people higher up the org chart. If you can't even get the attention of these two project leaders, find a senior engineer whose opinions are respected by management and make him your best friend.

In addition to finding allies, you need to know which people are actively opposed to a larger role for design. You can't afford to ignore them. Instead, as you begin to build momentum with a handful of leaders, invite the naysayers among their reports to public check-ins. This will often make their unhelpful attitudes evident without you having to say a word and may bring peer pressure to bear in encouraging them to change.

DEVELOP A VISION AND HIGH-LEVEL PLAN

In an ideal change process, the guiding coalition develops the vision of what you want to achieve. When you're pushing for design from a staff or middle-management position, though, you may need to begin painting a specific picture of a more desirable future even for your allies.

Your vision needs to center on a goal: What do you want to accomplish? Describe the benefits that goal will provide to the organization and to the individuals involved. Articulate specifically what you think has to change in order to get you

there, as well as any structure or process you envision (and why it's good). What work should you do in-house, and what will you outsource? How large should the design organization be? Should it be centralized or a set of smaller groups within product teams? Where should design report? (See Tables 26.1 and 26.2 for pros and cons of some specific structures.) How many designers of what sorts do you need? How should the product development process change, and why?

Begin discussing these things with your allies. Eventually—and ideally with the support of your manager and others—you may want to write up your vision as a proposal and submit it to the head of your product group or another senior manager. Executives are often impressed by initiative, and are far more receptive to well-considered proposals than to complaints. In any case, think of your initial vision as a first design sketch at the whiteboard. Ask others to help you refine it and make it feasible.

Table 26.1. **In-house versus outsourced design.**

Benefits of in-house design	Benefits of outsourced design	A combined approach
— Essential if you ship a lot of new products or conduct your business online	— It's hard to be a prophet in your own land	— Use in-house teams for efficiency on known products
— No need to find a firm and deal with contracts and purchasing	— Outside perspective sometimes sees more clearly	— Use consultants for fresh perspective or when you need help persuading stakeholders
— Can be cheaper if there's enough work to do	— Designers aren't stale from working on the same problems for too long	— Use consultants for types of design your team isn't good at or doesn't always need
— Designers develop expertise over time (saves on ramp-up time)	— Good firms know how to hire, train, and manage good designers	
— Designers can educate people opportunistically	— Can be more cost-effective for some companies	
— Less tempting to stop design work too early	— Gets executive attention and moves things along	

Ensuring Success

Table 26.2. **Centralized versus distributed.**

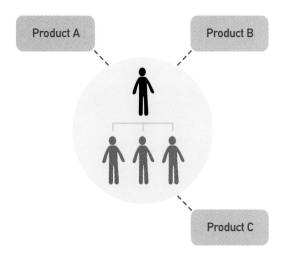

Centralized/internal consultancy

— Helps ensure consistency of practice and results across the company

— Allows effective coaching of junior designers

— Can maintain some degree of outside perspective if designers are rotated among products

— When spread too thin, may become "the design police"

— Can be seen as vendors instead of partners

— May get cut out of processes as external consultants do, especially if design isn't funded by its own budget

Distributed among product teams

— Designers develop specialized product expertise

— Proximity provides opportunities to build trust and partnership

— May have the wrong people doing hiring, training, and evaluation

— Designers have no advocate except a non-designer manager

— Designers can develop tunnel vision and get stale from working on the same product

— Designer skills and morale can suffer from lack of interaction with other designers

— Design is inconsistent across products and may duplicate efforts

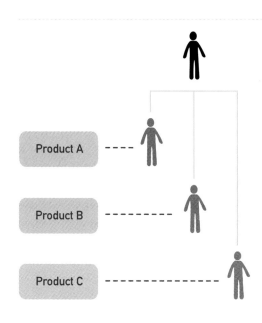

A matrixed approach

— Designers are hired, trained, and managed as part of a central team led by an experienced design manager, but distributed by product or business function (e.g., product, IT/internal, and Web)

— Assigned to projects for substantial amounts of time, but rotated regularly

— Priorities on a project are managed by project owner, with design manager providing regular coaching and design QA

COMMUNICATE THE VISION

Start communicating your vision to a narrow audience, especially as you're refining it. Continue reinforcing why the change is important. Tell stories from customer site visits. Use analogies to relate your challenges to some other industry or situation that will resonate with people. Use visual communication to describe time and cost savings and expected revenue gains.

Communication needs to go both ways. Don't just talk about how you envision integrating design; listen to the problems and concerns of the engineers, SMEs, and others you work with. Give them a chance to challenge you, offer feedback on your vision, and get reassurance about their fears. You (and design in general) have a lot to offer, but you don't have a complete solution.

However, you can't be the only one championing design. To reach the whole organization, the same message needs to come from higher up.

It needs to be constant and consistent, too; it won't work, for example, if the CEO says, "Hooray for design!" at a single company meeting but continues to reward engineering teams based solely on deadlines.

ENABLE ACTION

As people become convinced of the need for more and better design, they need the freedom to act. Executives are the only ones who can remove the barriers, require changes to structures and processes, and build in the accountability that makes a real focus on design possible. Without those changes, it will be clear to everyone that the organization's leaders aren't really serious about design.

GET SHORT-TERM WINS

Any significant organizational change is a long and painful process, and integrating design is no exception. Short-term wins are necessary to keep

Ensuring Success

A visible failure can set the change process back several years, so select your projects carefully if you can.

people from losing faith; even designers can become disheartened if there's no visible progress. The managers who are your strongest change allies will be willing to take only so much risk until they have results to show for it. Often, some short-term wins are necessary even to start the process of gathering allies.

For designers, the typical short-term win is a demonstration of positive effect on a project: decreased engineering time, better sales, or even anecdotal evidence that the new design is getting a good customer response. However, a failure—especially a highly visible one—can set the change process back by several years, so it's important to select your opportunities carefully if you have any control over what you work on. A good demonstration project:

— **Is small but very visible.** Small projects show results quickly, and it's easier to convince managers to take risks on a small scale.

— **Is familiar.** You only want one experiment going on in your Petri dish, and that experiment is design. New engineering teams or methods, new markets, and new technologies all introduce risks and increase the likelihood of a failure that reflects badly on design or on you. A project that's typical and familiar also offers better opportunities for comparison of results.

— **Is a reasonable concept.** Avoid underwater toasters, car-steering-wheel keyboards, or any other ill-conceived product that can't possibly make you look good, no matter how well you deign it.

— **Allows for clear measurement of results.** You should be able to compare project metrics (such as time and cost) as well as some measure of design effectiveness, such as abandoned shopping carts on an e-commerce site or customer support calls for an enterprise software issue.

— **Has an effective and committed project owner.** A project owner has more influence on a design project's success than just about any other factor. A reluctant project lead is more likely to abandon design halfway through and cause you to fail. If you must work with someone who doesn't really believe in design, make the risk very small indeed to keep him from getting queasy. Once you succeed, he'll let you gradually take bigger risks.

CELEBRATE SUCCESS AND THEN BUILD ON IT

Celebrate your short-term wins! The more visibility you get, the more momentum you'll build toward bigger and better projects. Don't declare victory, though, as this will kill the momentum; work with other partici-

Ensuring Success

pants to evaluate each project to learn what you can do better next time.

As you have more and more visible successes, demand for design involvement on projects will increase. One risk is that other people will lose faith in design as a solution if you can't scale to meet demand. On the other hand, they'll lose faith if you hire people who aren't good at what they do. In an effort to meet the demand, designers can become spread too thin, to the point where they're not actually driving design, but are simply advising engineers or being the "design police." There's not an easy solution to this dilemma, especially since good designers (of any type) are difficult to find. However, you can minimize the problem by:

— Limiting the scope of your communication (and ambition) to a single unit or division at first

— Allowing design leaders time to recruit, hire, train, and build infrastructure (such as templates and other shared tools) in addition to leading projects

— Assigning part of the group to provide brief consultations to engineers as a stopgap, while the rest are dedicated to single projects (Rotate this role so no one gets demoralized.)

LATHER, RINSE, REPEAT: DRIVE THE CHANGE INTO THE CULTURE

It will generally take repeated successes and multiple iterations of process and structure to achieve good integration of design. However, it's critical that you not stop at defining process, deliverables, and reporting lines; you have to drive change into the culture for it to stick.

The culture you're trying to change is like the stump of an old tree, shown in Figure 26.1—the roots are deep and well established, so even if you chop it down, it's likely to send up new shoots and take over again if you're not vigilant. The nascent design-oriented culture, in comparison,

is a shallow-rooted sapling that could be toppled by any storm, even if it looks green and leafy above ground. Until attitudes and behavioral norms are well established throughout the organization, people may revert to old habits at the first sign of difficulty or wavering commitment from the executives.

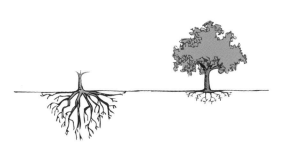

Figure 26.1. An organization's old culture has deep roots and may sprout again at any time. A newer culture that embraces design is fragile for a number of years due to its shallower roots.

One reason culture change takes so long is that there are always some people whose attitudes simply won't change. Over time, those people leave, and there's an opportunity to hire or promote new people whose skills and attitudes support the new behavioral norms you're trying to establish. Again, there's only so much you can do in this respect as a designer; at most, you may be able to encourage colleagues to consider how they hire and train people and what behavior they reward.

Still, even entire societies change over time, so have patience. Good ideas, competence, and common sense usually prevail in the end; I've seen even the most Paleozoic product companies make substantial progress when a strong internal design champion gains executive support. Even if you haven't won over an entire company, you've made a difference for large numbers of people by getting even one improved product out the door.

Ensuring Success

Concluding Thoughts

Many individuals and organizations have yet to master designing for the digital age we live in. However, I believe progress is inevitable. In the last five years, I've seen more and more senior executives who truly believe design needs to become a core capability in their businesses. Business-oriented publications like the *Wall Street Journal* and *BusinessWeek* have begun to feature more articles on design and innovation. I've spoken with many executives for whom the 2007 launch of Apple's iPhone was an epiphany: They've been forced to recognize that millions of people are delighted to pay more for a well-designed product, even if it isn't the first to market and doesn't include significant technical innovation. More executives are realizing that since the design of a digital product or service comprises most of what users and customers experience, their business *is* design. Ergo, design is becoming a must-have for interactive products and services just as it is for physical products, buildings, and corporate identities.

Unlike engineering, design looks easy to most people because its results are tangible and because good solutions seem obvious after the fact. Many companies have stumbled—and will continue to stumble—because they believe design is simple and superficial. They'll learn through experience that effective design is difficult, but that skilled people, rigorous methods, and a culture that promotes creative, sustainable, and user-centered thinking make it possible to deliver successful products and services again and again.

Designing a compelling product or service—and making sure it gets to market—*isn't* easy, but as the saying goes, worthwhile things never are. You can look forward to the satisfaction of holding a product you designed in your hand, of seeing a first-time user delight in a clever interaction, or of having a nurse burst into tears because she can see how the product you designed will help her save lives.

I hope the methods in this book have given you a strong foundation from which to build your own and your organization's practice of design. Over time, you'll make these methods your own, stretching and bending them to suit your needs but hopefully coming to rely on the fundamental principle: A shared understanding of human goals and behaviors leads to products that improve peoples' daily lives and make the world a better place.

INDEX

A

About Face 3 (Cooper, Reimann, and Cronin), 8

academic programs, 695–696

accelerometers, 442

accents in voice systems, 597

acceptance of change, 701

access issues in interviews, 148

accessibility
    considerations, 602
    as interviewee selection factor, 95
    requirements, 330

ACM Digital Library, 572

Acrobat Reader, 414

actions
    for change, 705
    customer questions about, 134–139
    icons for, 584
    on objects, 433
    pattern organization by, 421

active listening
    guidelines for, 59–61
    in meeting facilitation, 374

activities
    in form and behavior patterns, 413–420
    research, 354–356

activity diagrams, 212–213

Adams, Scott, 113

Adobe Acrobat Reader, 414

Adobe Fireworks, 527, 634

Adobe FrameMaker, 681

advertising in interview recruitment, 108

affinity diagrams, 215–217

affordances, 480–481

agendas for interaction framework reviews, 475–476

aggregate data, 221

agile methods, 310, 559–560

airline travel service elements, 437

alarms, inappropriate, 601

Alexander, Christopher, 9

alignment of elements, 575–576

analogies for company attributes, 75

analysis
    customer and user data. See customer and user data analysis
    user and domain. See user and domain analysis

anger and change, 700

anomalies in observations, 142

anonymity in interviews, 70

anonymous observations, 185–187

anthropomorphism in voice systems, 596–597

cooper

Innovation

Design

Research

Training

Consulting

DESIGN FOR A DIGITAL WORLD